THE HISTORY
OF THE
INDIAN NATIONAL
CONGRESS

THE HISTORY
OF THE
INDIAN NATIONAL CONGRESS

(1885-1935)

BHOGARAJU PATTABHI SITARAMAYYA, RAJENDRA PRASAD

IN TWO VOLUME
VOLUME 1

GYAN

Published by

Gyan Publishing House
5, Ansari Road
Daryaganj, New Delhi-110002
Phone: 011-47034999, 9811692060
E-mail: books@gyanbooks.com

Distribution Network
gyanbooks.com
India, USA, Canada, UK, Australia

ISBN: 978-93-7097-936-9 (Set)
978-93-7014-003-5 (HB)

First Published, 1935

2nd Impression 2025

Printed at: Gyan Press, Delhi.

THE HISTORY OF THE INDIAN NATIONAL CONGRESS (VOL - 1)
Author: BHOGARAJU PATTABHI SITARAMAYYA, RAJENDRA PRASAD

THE HISTORY

OF THE

Indian National Congress

(1885—1935)

BY

B. PATTABHI SITARAMAYYA

WITH AN INTRODUCTION

BY

RAJENDRA PRASAD

1935

PUBLISHED BY
THE WORKING COMMITTEE OF THE CONGRESS
ON THE OCCASION OF THE 50TH ANNIVERSARY

To

Truth and Non-violence

whose embodied spirit

hath

guided the destinies

of

The Congress

and

in whose service,

Innumerable sons and daughters

of

Hindusthan

have cheerfully made

heavy sacrifices

for

The Emancipation

of

Their Motherland.

FOREWORD

The preparation of the book was not undertaken by the author as of set purpose. It was the unwitting result of the scribbling of idle hours during the hot summer of the year and the notes of lessons given by him to the students of the Andhra Jatheeya Kalasala, Masulipatam, on the History of the Congress. A casual enquiry addressed to him on an allied matter by the Secretary of the A. I. C. C. from Allahabad happened to bring this little venture, through him, to the notice of the President who placed the matter before the Working Committee. The author expresses his sense of profound gratitude to the Working Committee for undertaking its publication on the occasion of the fiftieth anniversary of the great national organisation.

The plan of the book will be evident from a cursory glance at the synopsis that precedes each part. There was not much of plot to unravel in the story of the first thirty years, the happenings in which are dealt with subject by subject and character by character. The past twenty years have been treated year by year. The resolutions of the different sessions have not been categorically quoted. That alone would cover half the size of the volume in hand, which has already run into unexpected proportions.

The book is abounding in defects of which the author is only too well aware, and which the readers are requested to bear with. These are defects of plan as well as penmanship which might have been partly, at any rate, avoided by greater leisure and better attention. But the work had to be put through in a hurry. And hurry never conduces to perfection. Yet, during the all-too-short period of time available, the book has been gone through by the President, twice over, and the thanks of the public, no less than of the author, are due to him for the hard work which the task of revision and correction entailed upon him. Equally exacting was the strain imposed upon Syt. J. B. Kirpalani, the General Secretary of the Congress, and Syt. Krishnadas, Secretary, on whom fell the onerous duty of priming up the whole matter for the Press, and to whom the country's thanks are due.

The author acknowledges his obligations to the printers—The Law Printing House, Madras,—who have put their whole capacity and good cheer into the task and raced against time in printing a volume which has run up to one and a half times the anticipated size. Besides the printers, several others have rendered considerable help. The Proprietors

RAJENDRA PRASAD
1934 : BOMBAY

CONTENTS

Part III

THE ERA OF SWARAJ, 1921--1928

Part IV

THE ERA OF COMPLETE INDEPENDENCE, 1929--1935

Part V

THE ERA OF FIGHT

Part VI

The Era of Re-organisation

INTRODUCTION

Fifty years ago the Indian National Congress met for the first time in Bombay with a small number of delegates who could hardly be called elected representatives, but who were nevertheless true servants of the people. Ever since then it has been striving for winning freedom for the people of India. In the beginning its aim was indefinite but it has always insisted on a democratic form of Government responsible to the people of India and representative of all communities and classes inhabiting this vast country. It started with the hope and confidence that British statesmanship and the British Government would rise equal to the occasion and establish truly representative institutions giving the right to the people of India to govern India in the interest of India. The early history of the Congress is full of resolutions and speeches giving expression to this faith and confidence. The very demands of the Congress took the form of resolutions suggesting reforms and removal of objectionable measures—all having as their basis a hope that, if the British public and Parliament could be fully informed of this position in India and of the desire of Indians, they would set things right and ultimately confer on them the inestimable boon of Self-Government.

That hope and confidence have been gradually but none-the-less completely shattered by the action of the British Government in India and in England. The attitude of the British Government has become more and more stiff as the national consciousness has become more and more expressive. This initial confidence in the intentions of the British Rule received a shock during the administration of Lord Curzon who partitioned Bengal, and the great agitation that followed against that ill-fated measure was an index of the rising tide of popular national consciousness which had not a little been influenced by world events, such as the victory of Japan over Russia in the beginning of the 20th century. But India had not yet lost faith and during the great war, partly as a result of this faith resuscitated by the annulment of the partition of Bengal and partly on account of want of proper appreciation of the situation as a whole, the country responded to the call of the British Government to help the British Empire in its time of need. India's splendid help was acknowledged by all British statesmen and hope was engendered that the war, which was being ostensibly fought for the principle of self-determination of nations and for making democracy safe, would result in the establishment of Responsible Government in India. The announcement made by the Secretary of State for India on behalf of the British

Government in 1917 promising Self-Government by stages occasioned difference of opinion amongst Indians, which became more and more acute as the result of investigations undertaken by the Secretary of State and the Viceroy became known and the Bill, which ultimately became the Government of India Act in 1920, took shape and form. During this time of incubation of the Bill the war had ended in a victory for the British, and the feeling grew in India that as the pressure in Europe had relaxed on account of the successful termination of the war for Britain, the British attitude had changed for the worse towards India. This feeling was confirmed and strengthened by what was regarded as breach of faith with the Mussalmans in the matter of the Khilaphat and by the passing, in spite of the unanimous protest of the country at large, of what were known as the Rowlatt Bills, whereby the stringent provisions of the Defence of India Act which had been tolerated during the war were sought to be perpetuated, depriving the people of the elementary rights of free citizenship.

These naturally created an intensive agitation in the whole country, and Satyagraha, which had been tried in South Africa, and in a small way in Champaran and in Khaira in India, was put forward by Mahatma Gandhi for the first time as a method to be adopted by the country whereby to secure redress of these and other grievances. There were unfortunate popular disturbances in the Punjab and Ahmedabad resulting in loss of life and property which were followed by the Jallianwala-bagh massacre and the horrors of the Martial Law regime in the Punjab. There was naturally great indignation throughout the country which was not assuaged by the Report of the Hunter Committee appointed to investigate into these happenings and was considerably intensified by the debate on the Report in Parliament. The Non-co-operation movement was inaugurated with its programme of resignation of titles of honour granted by the Government, boycott of Legislative bodies, Government-recognised educational institutions and Law Courts and of foreign cloth on the one hand, and on the other the establishment of Congress Committees, enrolment of Congress members, collection of Tilak Swaraj Fund, opening of national educational institutions, establishment of Panchayats for decision of village disputes and the revival of hand-spinning and hand-weaving,—all to culminate by stages in a campaign of Civil Disobedience and non-payment of taxes. The Congress Constitution was changed and its object was defined as the attainment of Swaraj by peaceful and legitimate means. There was country-wide awakening followed by repression by Government, when thousands of men and women including some of the most reputed leaders were imprisoned towards the end of 1921. Efforts at bringing about a settlement with the Government did not fructify and the programme of non-payment of taxes in Bardoli had to be suspended on account of serious disturbances at Chauri Chaura in the United Provinces. Subsequently the other items of the Non-co-operation programme were one after another suspended or withdrawn, and Congress members entered the Legislatures.

The appointment by the British Parliament of what is known as the Simon Commission, from which Indians were excluded, for the purpose of investigating the working of the Constitution of 1920, led to another serious upheaval in the country, and the Congress in association with other public bodies framed a Constitution with Dominion Status as the objective for India for the acceptance of the Government. In the absence of any adequate response by the Government, the Congress at its session at Lahore in December, 1929, changed its objective as the attainment of Purna Swaraj (Complete Independence) by legitimate and peaceful means, and organised a campaign of Civil Disobedience of non-moral laws and non-payment of taxes, in the beginning of 1930. The Government of England on the one hand called a Conference in London to which it nominated certain Indians to advise it about a Constitution for India, and on the other adopted repressive measures, including the promulgation of a number of most drastic Ordinances for suppressing the Civil Disobedience movement in India. In March, 1931, there was a Pact entered into by Lord Irwin the Viceroy representing the Government, and Mahatma Gandhi representing the Congress, as a result of which Civil Disobedience was suspended and Mahatma Gandhi attended the Round Table Conference in London towards the end of 1931. As was to be expected, nothing came out of the Conference and the Congress was forced to revive the movement early in 1932 and carried it on till 1934, when it was suspended again. In the two movements of 1930 and 1932 hundreds of thousands of men and women and even children courted imprisonment, received *lathi* blows and other kinds of torture and suffered loss of property. Many were killed as a result of firing by the Government forces on crowds. The Satyagrahis showed remarkable power of organisation and suffering and were, on the whole, completely non-violent in the face of the greatest provocation. Congress organisation showed great vitality and powers of adaptability and survived the great attack made on it by the Government. The country has come out of the fiery ordeal with credit but without achieving its great objective of Purna Swaraj.

By a resolution passed at Karachi the Congress has assured to all Indians certain fundamental rights and has drawn up an economic and social programme. It has made it clear that, in order to end the exploitation of the masses, political freedom must include real economic freedom of the starving millions and has laid down fundamental rights of citizenship, such as freedom of speech and association, of person and property, of religion and conscience. It has also laid down that the interests of industrial labour shall be safeguarded, by securing for them healthy conditions of work, limited hours of labour, suitable machinery for settlement of disputes and protection against economic consequences of old age, sickness and unemployment and the right to form unions. It has assured the peasants to secure equitable adjustments of the burden on agricultural land by reduction of rent and revenue and exemption from rent or revenue for uneconomic holdings, with such relief as may be just and necessary to holders of small estates affected by such exemption or reduction in rent. It has also provided for a graded tax on net incomes from land above a reasonable minimum, death duties on a graduated scale on property above a fixed income, and drastic reduction of expenditure on military and defence and civil administration, fixing the salary of State servants at a maximum of Rs. 500/- per month. It has also laid down an economic and social programme of excluding foreign cloth, protecting indigenous industries, prohibition of intoxicating drugs and drinks,

State control of key industries, relief to agricultural indebtedness, regulation of currency and exchange in the interest of the country and provision for the military training of citizens for national defence.

The last session of the Congress at Bombay in October, 1934, endorsed the policy of entering the Legislatures and laid down a constructive programme including revival of and encouragement to hand-spinning and hand-weaving, promotion of useful village and small industries, re-construction of village life in its economic, educational, social and hygienic aspects, removal of untouchability, promotion of inter-communal unity, total abstinence, national education, spread of useful knowledge among the adult population, organisation of industrial labour and peasants and strengthening of the Congress organisation. Under a revised Constitution it reduced the number of delegates and made it proportionate to the number of primary members on the Congress roll and insisted on manual labour and habitual wearing of Khadi on all elected members and office-bearers of Congress Committees.

The Congress has thus marched on from stage to stage and covers practically every sphere of national activity. It is at present engaged in constructive work which is calculated not only to improve the economic condition of the masses but also to create that self-confidence among them which can be born of work accomplished and which can enable them to win Purna Swaraj. Starting as a small organisation it now covers the entire country with a net-work of branches and enjoys the confidence of the masses of the country. It has called forth sacrifice on an extensive scale for the attainment of Swaraj from people of all classes and has a remarkable record of work and achievement. The organisation itself is a great national asset which it should be the duty of every Indian to increase and preserve. It is bound to play an ever-increasing part in the struggle for freedom that still lies ahead. This is no time for resting on our oars. The work yet to be accomplished is great and needs much patient toil, endless sacrifice and unflinching determination. It is nothing less than the attainment of Purna Swaraj. Let us bow down our heads to all those men, women, and children, known and unknown, who have laid down their lives, who have suffered woes and privations, and who are still paying the penalty for loving their Motherland.

Let us also in grateful reverence recall the services of those who sowed the seeds of this mighty organisation, who nurtured it with their unremitting labour and sacrifice. The small seedling that was planted fifty years ago has now grown into a mighty tree with branches spreading over this vast country and has now blossomed in the sacrifice of countless men and women. It is for those that are now left behind to nourish the tree by their further services and sacrifice, so that it may bear fruit and make India the free and prosperous country that Nature intended her to be.

The pages that follow relate the story of the growth of the Indian National Congress. The author's knowledge and experience of the men and affairs of the Congress is wide. He himself has played no inconsiderable part in the later phases of its development. He is not a detached historian writing after the events and basing his conclusions on cold recorded facts. He has seen things with his own eyes and has himself acted and re-acted on them. He is writing not only with knowledge but also with faith. His conclusions and opinions are therefore his own, and need not be treated as in every case representing the official view of the Working Committee of the Indian National Congress which publishes the book and sends it out to the world. It is hoped, however, that it contains a faithful record of facts and will be found helpful to students of contemporary history.

Camp—Wardha,
12th December, 1935 } RAJENDRA PRASAD

W. C. Bonnerjee
1885 : Bombay
1892 : Allahabad

Dadabai Naoroji
1886 : Calcutta
1893 : Lahore
1906 : Calcutta

Budruddin Tyabji
1887 : Madras

George Yule
1888 : Allahabad

THE

HISTORY OF THE CONGRESS

Part I

SYNOPSIS

CHAPTER I

The Birth of the Congress

I

India under Subjection—The East India Company—Periodical scrutinies by Parliament—Acquisition of territory by the Company—Parliament's control—Charter Act of 1833—The spread of English Education—Vicissitudes of the Press—Acquisition of the Punjab and Sindh—The Rising of 1857—The Queen's Proclamation—The Arms Act—Famine and War—'Notorious political grievances' —Hume and Wedderburn's intervention—A seething revolt in incubation—Hume conceives the idea of the National Gathering—His letter to the Graduates of the Calcutta University—Pre-Congress Elders—British Indian Association in Bengal, 1851—Bombay Association—Mahajana Sabha in South India—Poona Sarvajanik Sabha—The Indian Association, Bengal, 1876—Lord Lytton's reactionary rule—Political Conference in Albert Hall, Calcutta, 1883—Need for an All-India Organisation —Hume takes the initiative, 1885.

II

Congress, a movement of National Renaissance—Rammohan Roy and his times—His great work in

England and India—The repercussions of Western Civilisation—The Brahmo Samaj and schisms in it—The Arya Samaj and the Theosophical movement as correctives to the denationalisation of the day—The Ramakrishna Mission—The Congress, a synthesis of all these movements.

III

Hume's original plans to eschew politics—Lord Dufferin's advice in favour of a political organisation—The first circular—Hume organises the Indian Parliamentary Committee in England—The first Session of the Congress, 1885.

IV

The real character of the Congress—Gandhi's description of the Congress at the 2nd Round Table Conference(1931).

CHAPTER II

A RAPID REVIEW OF THE RESOLUTIONS OF THE CONGRESS (1885—1915)

The India Council—Constitutional Changes—Public Services—Military Problems—Legal and Judicial Problems—Permanent Settlement, Water-cess, Poverty and Famines—Forest Laws—Commerce and Industry—Swadeshi, Boycott and Swaraj—Communal Representation—Indians Abroad—Salt—Drink and Prostitution—Women and the Depressed Classes—Miscellaneous—The Congress Constitution.

CHAPTER III

THE EARLY PHASE OF THE CONGRESS

The strategy of the earlier Congressmen—Loyalty, the key-note—Faith in the English Nation—Recognition of services by Government.

CHAPTER IV

Britain's Reaction to the Congress Movement and rise of New Forces and Parties

Dufferin's Hostility—Colvin v. Hume—Administrative restrictions—Sec. 124 (A), 153 (A), I.P.C.—Curzon's strenuous rule—Retrogression in Public Services—Partition of Bengal, Fuller's threats—India takes up the cause of Bengal—National Education—Boycott—Bepin Babu—Aurobindo—The Nine Deportees—The First Bomb—'Yugantar'—Violence in London—Partition of Bengal disowned—Partition annulled—But repression extant—Reactionary Press Laws—Mahomed Ali's case—Sir Lawrence Jenkins' condemnation of the Press Law—'New India' case—Press deputation—The outbreak of the Great War—Mrs. Besant on the scene.

CHAPTER V

Our British Friends

John Bright—Henry Fawcett—A. O. Hume—Sir William Wedderburn—Charles Bradlaugh—W. E. Gladstone—Lord Northbrook—The Duke of Argyll—Lord Stanley of Alderley—Eardley Norton—General Booth.

CHAPTER VI

Our Indian Patriarchs

Dadabhai Naoroji—Ananda Charlu—Wacha—Gokhale—G. Subrahmania Aiyar—Budruddin Tyabji—K. T. Telang—W. C. Bonnerjee—Tilak—Pandit Ayodhyanath—Surendra Nath Banerjea—Malaviya—Lajpat Rai—Pherozeshah Mehta—Ananda Mohan Bose—Man Mohan Ghose—Lal Mohan Ghose—Vijiaraghavachariar—Raja Rampal Singh—Kali Charan Banerjee—Nawab Syed Mahomed Bahadur—D. A. Khare—Ganga Prasad Varma

—R. N. Mudholkar—Sankaran Nair—Kesava Pillai—Bepin Chandra Pal—Ambika Charan Mazumdar—Bhupendra Nath Basu —Mazar-ul-Haq—M. G. Ranade—Bishan Narayan Dhar—Ramesh Chandra Dutt—Subba Rau Pantulu—Lala Murlidhar—Sachchidananda Sinha.

THE HISTORY OF THE CONGRESS

Part I

CHAPTER I

The Birth of the Congress

The History of the Congress is really the history of India's struggle for freedom. For centuries the Indian Nation has been under foreign supremacy and the Congress has striven for half a century to free the country from this subjection, the beginnings of which in its latest phase may be traced to the advent to India of a trading concern.

The East India Company had during nearly a hundred years of commercial and political activity acquired large tracts of the country in India and had begun to enjoy the rights of a ruling power. After 1772 its activities were subject to scrutiny from time to time by the British Parliament and every renewal of its Charter was preceded by an inquiry on behalf of the British Government. As the commercial aspect of its activity had gone more and more into the background and the political aspect come more and more into the forefront, this scrutiny had become more and more searching. While it would not be right to imagine that anything like a close supervision was maintained, there were not men wanting among the British who studied the Indian problem in great detail, followed the action and programme of the East India Company with care and vigilance, and were not slow to bring them before Parliament for consideration and redress. The great interest which Edmund Burke, Sheridan and Fox exhibited in the last quarter of the 18th century served to focus public opinion on the misdeeds of the Company's agents. Although the impeachment of Warren Hastings failed in its objective, it exposed the oppression and tyranny which used to be practised. Every periodical inquiry preceding renewal of the Charter resulted in the enunciation of some principles of far-reaching consequence, even though these principles were not followed in practice. More than once it was laid down as the policy to be followed that the agents of the Company should not attempt to extend its territorial acquisitions, but every time, an opportunity occurred or was created which enabled them to disregard the injunction, and the territories went on expanding. It is not necessary here to go into the history, full of black and treacherous deeds, full of the exhibition of low and rapacious human nature, full of the wreckages of broken engagements and treaties, of the acquisition of India by the East India Company. Nor is it necessary to go into an examination of the treachery and faithlessness of the Indians as amongst themselves, or of the ways and means employed by the agents of the Company to amass huge fortunes for themselves, apart from what they made available to the Company and its Directors. Suffice it to say that immense wealth was acquired, and formed in due course the nucleus, and perhaps the bulk, of that capital which enabled England on the advent of the steam engine and the machine to establish her industrial supremacy in the world in the nineteenth century.

When the Regulating Act was passed in 1774 and a Board of Control was appointed over the Court of Directors of the Company, and a Governor-General with a Council, the British Parliament for the first time took some responsibility for the administration of the territories already acquired. This control grew in course of time and another Act in 1785 followed. The Charter was renewed after investigations in 1793, 1813, 1833 and 1853. In 1833 it was enacted that "no native of the said territories, nor any natural born subject of His Majesty resident therein, shall, by reason only of his religion,place of birth, descent, colour or any of them be disabled from holding any place, office or employment under the said Company" and, the Court of Directors explained its import as follows:—

> "The Court conceive this section to mean that there shall be no governing caste in British India; that whatever other tests of qualification may be adopted, distinction of race or religion shall not be of the number; that no subject of the King, whether of Indian or British or mixed descent, shall be excluded from the posts usually conferred on uncovenanted servants in India, or from the covenanted service itself, provided he be otherwise eligible."

By the same Act the rights of the Company to trade in India were abolished and it became divested henceforth of its character as a trading concern and became entirely a ruling authority.

A controversy arose about this time regarding the introduction of English education into India. With the powerful support of Raja Rammohan Roy among Indians and Macaulay among the Britishers, it was set at rest n favour of English education as against education in Indian langugages and literature. Thus were laid the foundations of that system which continues to this day.

There was no Press in those days except such as was conducted by Englishmen, some of whom had to suffer even deportation from India. Lord William Bentinck's Governor-Generalship was remarkable for the aforesaid reforms and was also lenient towards the Press. His successor, Sir Charles Metcalfe, removed the restrictions against the Press which remained free till the Viceroyalty of Lord Lytton, with the exception of a brief period during the time of the Revolt of 1857.

Between 1833 and 1853 the Punjab and Sindh had been conquered, and the policy of Lord Dalhousie resulting in the annexation of the States of those rulers who died without issue, and of Oudh on the ground of maladministration by the then ruler, had added considerably to the territories of the Company, making the extent of British India what it has remained ever since. The economic drain resulting in the impoverishment of the people, the loss of territory and the establishment of a foreign rule had created resentment and discontent, and the Revolt of 1857 was the last armed attempt to throw off the foreign yoke. It was undoubtedly tinged with some religious motive, but the fact that the titular Emperor of Delhi, the descendant of Akbar and Aurangzeb, and the descendant of the Peshwa of Poona were the rallying points round whom the effort to estabish an Indian Raj revolved, shows that the Revolt represented not only the accumulated effect of all that had been perpetrated during a hundred years since the battle of Plassey in 1757,but also the natural desire in the human breast of every country and community to be ruled by its own people and no others. The Revolt failed but with it also disappeared the East India Company, and the Government of India directly passed into the hands of the British Crown, that is, the British Parliament The Queen's Proclamation issued on this occasion went a great way in creating an atmosphere of calm and faith which kept the country in a condition of peace. Whatever discontent there was became absolutely helpless. The nobility, particularly the Muslim nobility, was practically crushed.

out of existence and there was not even a titular person left to serve as a rallying point in any future adventure like that of 1857. The British Rule came to be recognised as a dispensation of Providence and India settled down with that resignation which is one of our national characteristics.

The Government of India, even after its assumption by the Crown, continued to carry on much in the same way as before except that there were no wars for twenty years to disturb the even tenor of its rule.

This does not mean that there was no trouble and no discontent. There were serious defects in British administration which were pointed out and sought to be remedied by sympathetic British officials like Mr. Hume.

As has been stated earlier the Act of 1833 had made Indians eligible for all posts for which they were qualified. When the Charter was under consideration in 1853 it was freely stated in Parliament that, although the Act of 1833 had theoretically made Indians eligible, they had not been in practice given any posts which they would not have occupied before that Act. When the system of competitive examination for the Civil Service was introduced in 1853, it was pointed out that that would put a great handicap on Indians, as they would find it practically impossible to come to England to compete with English boys in an examination in English language and literature on the off-chance of securing posts. In spite of the handicaps Indians, though few, crossed the seas and succeeded, and it was left to Lord Salisbury to reduce the age at which students could compete, thus enhancing the handicap on Indians who, with the support of Englishmen, had been crying for simultaneous examinations in India and England. Lord Lytton in India muzzled the Vernacular Press which, along with the English Press, had enjoyed freedom since the days of Metcalfe. He further passed an Arms Act which not only deprived Indians of the right of bearing arms but also introduced another galling distinction between Indians and Europeans.

Then there were famines which showed that it was not so much scarcity of food grains as the lack of the wherewithal to purchase them that resulted in the death of hundreds of thousands of people all over the country. There was also the expensive Afghan War. While famine and death were stalking the land it was considered fit to hold a Durbar at Delhi at which the Queen assumed the title of the Empress of India. "Economic, in addition to political, troubles were actively at work throughout the country. The physical suffering of the many, acted on by the apathy and selfishness of the few, was rapidly bringing popular unrest to the danger point."

The peasantry was oppressed by certain "notorious practical grievances" referred to by Mr. Hume in his celebrated letter to Sir Auckland Colvin. They led to complaints not loud but deep with regard to (a) the costly and unsuitable Civil Courts, (b) the corrupt and oppressive Police, (c) the rigid Revenue system, and (d) the galling administration of the Arms Act and the Forest Act. People prayed for but despaired of getting (a) justice cheap, sure and speedy, (b) a Police they could look up to as friends and protectors, (c) a Land Revenue system more elastic and sympathetic, and (d) a less harsh administration of the Arms and Forest Laws. That was, in fact, the situation towards the beginning of the eighties. Indeed it was such that Sir W. Wedderburn says that the bureaucracy had not only done their best to prevent new concessions; they had also, when opportunity offered, taken away the privileges inherited from a former generation of reformers,—the liberty of the Press, the right of public meeting, Municipal Self-Government and the independence of the Universities. "These ill-starred measures of reaction," writes Sir William, "combined with Russian methods of Police repression brought India under Lord Lytton within measurable distance of a Revolutionary outbreak and it was only in time that Mr. Hume was inspired to intervene." Something more: Mr. Hume had unimpeachable evidence that the political discontent was going underground. He came into possession of seven volumes containing reports of the seething revolt incubating in various districts, based upon the communications of the disciples of various *gurus* to their religious heads. This was towards the end of Lord Lytton's rule, the seventies of the last century. The reports were arranged according to districts, sub-districts, sub-divisions, and the cities, towns and villages included in these. Not that an organised mutiny was ahead, but that the people pervaded with a sense of hopelessness, wanted to do *something*, by which was merely meant, a sudden violent outbreak of sporadic crime, murders of obnoxious persons, robbery of bankers and looting of bazaars, acts really of lawlessness which by a due coalescence of forces might any day develop into a National Revolt." Such were the agrarian riots of the Deccan in Bombay. Hume thereupon resolved to open a safety valve for this unrest and the Congress was such an outlet. It was at this time that he conceived the idea of bringing into existence a national gathering of Indians and to that end addressed to the graduates of the Calcutta University, on the 1st of March 1883, a soul-stirring letter in which he asked for fifty men, good and true, men of unselfishness, moral courage, self-control and active spirit of benevolence. "If only fifty men, good and true, can be found to join as founders, the thing can be established and the further development will be comparatively easy." And what was the ideal placed before these men? A democratic constitution, freedom from personal ambitions and the dictum that "he that is greatest amongst you, let him be your servant." Hume did not mince matters at all but frankly told them that "if they cannot renounce personal ease and pleasure, then at present at any rate all hopes of progress are at an end; and India truly neither desires nor deserves any better Government than she enjoys."

The concluding portion of this memorable letter runs as follows:—

> "And if even the leaders of thought are all either such poor creatures, or so selfishly wedded to personal concerns that they dare not strike a blow for their country's sake, then justly and rightly are they kept down and trampled on, for they deserve nothing better. Every nation secures precisely as good a Government as it merits. If you the picked men, the most highly educated of the nation cannot, scorning personal ease and selfish objects, make a resolute struggle to secure greater freedom for yourselves and your country, a more impartial administration, a larger share in the management of your own affairs, then we, your friends, are wrong and our adversaries right, then are Lord Ripon's noble aspirations for your good fruitless and visionary, then, at present at any rate all hopes of progress are at an end and India truly neither desires nor deserves any better Government than she enjoys. Only, if this be so, let us hear no more factious, peevish complaints that you are kept in leading strings and treated like children, for you will have proved yourself such. *Men* know how to act. Let there be no more complaining of Englishmen being preferred to you in all important offices, for if you lack that public spirit, that highest form of altruistic devotion that leads men to subordinate private ease to the public weal, that patriotism that has made Englishmen what they are,—then rightly are these preferred

to you, rightly and inevitably have they become your rulers. And rulers and task-masters they must continue, let the yoke gall your shoulders never so sorely, until you realise and stand prepared to act upon the eternal truth that self-sacrifice and unselfishness are the only unfailing guides to freedom and happiness."

Before we proceed to narrate the details relating to the birth of the Congress, it is but meet to recall the names of certain pre-Congress Elders whose labours in a way had laid the foundations of public life in this country.

The British Indian Association in Bengal was started in 1851 and was the institution in whose name men like Dr. Rajendra Lal Mitra and Ramgopal Ghose had carried on public work for decades. The Association itself was an active power in the land for nearly half a century. In Bombay the organ of public work was the Bombay Association which had a shorter career than its fellow in Bengal, but had an equally vigorous record of work to its credit under the leadership of men like Sir Mangaldoss Nathubhai and Mr. Naoroji Furdunji. The Association owed its origin to Dadabhai Naoroji and Mr. Juggannath Sanker Seth. The East India Association, however, superseded this body in the seventies of the last century. In the South, public life was really inaugurated by *The Hindu* amongst whose founders were the honoured names of Messrs. M. Veeraraghavachariar, the Hon'ble Rangiah Naidu, G. Subrahmania Aiyar and N. Subbarau Pantulu. In Maharashtra, the Poona Sarvajanik Sabha which sprang up about the same time as *The Hindu*, was the medium through which public work was carried on by men like Messrs. Rao Bahadur K. L. Nulkar and S. H. Chiplonkar.

In Bengal the Indian Association was founded in the year 1876, the moving spirit of the new body being Surendra Nath Banerjea and the first secretary being Ananda Mohan Bose. It must be noted that even in the seventies, public life was beginning to make itself felt by the authorities though it was not well-organised. The newspapers were already a powerful factor in it, for in 1875 there were as many as 475 newspapers, mostly in the provincial languages. Surendra Nath Banerjea, who by a fortunate chance for the country was relieved of his duties as a member of the Indian Civil Service, made his first political tour in Northern India covering the Punjab and the North-West Provinces (U.P.). He was present at the great Darbar held in Delhi, in 1877, and met the leading Princes and people of India at that assembly. It is believed that the idea of organising a vast political gathering was first conceived by Surendra Nath Banerjea under the inspiration furnished by that gathering of the Princes and people of India in 1877. In 1878 S. N. Banerjea visited the Bombay and Madras Presidencies in order to stimulate public opinion on the reactionary policy pursued by Lord Salisbury in reducing the age-limit for the Civil Service Examination to 19 years, and to prepare an All-India Memorial to be presented to the House of Commons on the Civil Service question.

It was at this time that Lord Lytton inaugurated his reactionary rule, which was characterised by the Vernacular Press Act of 1878, the Afghan War, the costly Indian Darbar (1877) and the sacrifice of cotton import duties (1877). Lord Lytton was succeeded by Lord Ripon, who inaugurated a new era by concluding a treaty with the Amir of Afghanistan, by repealing the Vernacular Press Act, by promoting Local Self-Government and by introducing the Ilbert Bill. The last was a Bill introduced in 1883 by Mr. Ilbert, the Law Member of the Government of India at the time, the object of which was to remove the bar against the Indian Magistracy trying European and likewise American offenders. This was greatly resented by the Anglo-Indians, some of whom entered into a conspiracy "to overpower the sentries of the Government House and to put the Viceroy on board a steamer at Chand Pal Ghat and send him to England *via* the Cape." This conspiracy had been formed by a number of men in Calcutta "who had bound themselves to carry out the aforesaid plan in the event of Government adhering to their projected legislation." The original Bill was almost abandoned in 1883 in favour of a bare recognition of the principle in the case of the District Magistrates and Sessions Judges only. When Lord Ripon retired he was given a farewell by Indians from one end of the country to the other, which was at once the envy of Englishmen and an eye-opener to many of them. Sir Auckland Colvin, says Sir Surendra Nath Banerjea in his 'A Nation in the Making', exclaimed, "If it be real, what does it mean?"

The success of the Anglo-Indians awakened the Indians who were not slow to realise that the inwardness of the opposition to the Bill was based on an assertion of racial superiority and its perpetuation. It taught the public men of India at the time the lessons of organisation; and immediately in the year 1883 there was held a political Conference at the Albert Hall in Calcutta, at which both S. N. Banerjea and A. M. Bose were present. It was at this meeting that S. N. Banerjea specifically referred, in his opening address, to the Delhi assemblage as furnishing the model for a like political organisation intended to espouse the country's cause. Mr. Ambika Charan Mazumdar writes in his book 'Indian National Evolution' that "it was an unique spectacle, of which the writer of these pages still retains a vivid impression, of immense enthusiasm and earnestness which throughout characterised the three days' session of the Conference, and at the end of which every one present seemed to have received a new light and a novel inspiration." It was in the following year that the International Exhibition was held in Calcutta to which the Rev. John Murdoch traces the original inspiration for the Indian National Congress. It was in 1881 that the Madras Mahajana Sabha was established and Madras held a Provincial Conference in its turn. In the west the Bombay Presidency Association was started on 31st Jan. 1885 by that famous group of Elders,—Mehta, Telang and Tyabji.

It is thus clear that India was feeling the need for some sort of an All-India organisation. It is shrouded in mystery as to who originated this idea of an All-India Congress. Apart from the great Darbar of 1877 or the International Exhibition in Calcutta, which, as stated above, are supposed to have furnished the model for the great national assemblage, it is also said that the idea was conceived in a private meeting of seventeen men after the Theosophical Convention held at Madras in December 1884. The Indian Union started by Mr. Hume after his retirement from the Civil Service is also supposed to have been instrumental in convening the Congress. Whatever the origin, and whoever the originator of the idea, we come to the conclusion, that the idea was in the air, that the need of such an organisation was being felt, that Mr.Allan Octavian Hume took the initiative, and that it was in March 1885, when the first notice was issued convening the first Indian National Union to meet at Poona in the following December, that what had been a vague idea floating generally in the air and influencing simultaneously the thought of thoughtful Indians in the north and the south, the east and the west, assumed a definite shape and became a practical programme of action.

II

It was not merely the political forces and the sense of political subjection that gave birth to the Congress. The Congress doubtless had its political objective, but it also was the organ and exponent of a movement of national renaissance. For fifty years and more before the birth of the Congress, the leaven of national rejuvenation had been at work. In fact national life in its protean aspects was in a state of ferment so early as in the times of Rammohan Roy, who may in one sense be regarded as the prophet of Indian Nationalism and the Father of modern India. He had a wide vision and a broad outlook. While it is true that the socio-religious condition of his day was the subject of his special attention in his reformist activities, he had nevertheless a keen sense of the grave political wrongs by which his country was afflicted at the time and made a strenuous effort to seek an early redress of those wrongs. Rammohan Roy was born in 1776 and passed away at Bristol in 1833. His name is associated with two great reforms in India, namely, the abolition of *Sati* or *Sahagamanam* and the introduction of Western learning into the country. In the acute controversy that raged in the thirties of the nineteenth century, Rammohan Roy took no small part, and the final decision of Lord William Bentinck in 1835 in favour of Western learning, even as against the recommendations of the Court of Directors in London, was largely due to Rammohan Roy's own bias towards the Occidentalists and the influence he exercised over the public opinion of the day. In the closing period of his life he chose to visit England and his passion for liberty was so great that when he reached the Cape of Good Hope he insisted on his being carried to a French vessel where he saw the flag of liberty flying, so that he might be able to do homage to that flag, and when he saw the flag he shouted, "Glory, Glory, Glory to the flag!" Although he had gone to England primarily as the ambassador of the Moghul Emperor to plead his cause in London, yet he took the opportunity to place some of the pressing Indian grievances before a Committee of the House Commons. He submitted three papers, on the Revenue system of India, the Judicial system of India, and the Material condition of India. He was honoured by the East India Company with a public dinner. When in 1832 the Charter Act was before Parliament, he vowed that if the Bill was not passed he would give up his residence in the British dominion and reside in America. During his time he had witnessed the worst repression of the Press in India. "The good days of Indian Journalism inaugurated by Lord Hastings, the Governor-General, by relaxing the severe Press restrictions of former times were soon clouded by the temporary accession to the post of Governor-General, in 1823, of Mr. John Adam, a member of the Civil Service." As a result one Mr. Buckingham, the Editor of *The Calcutta Journal,* was deported from India on two months' notice and Mr. Sanford Arnot, his assistant, was arrested in his office and put on board an England-going vessel,—all this for some criticisms of the administration made by them. A press Ordinance was passed on the 14th March 1823 which imposed the severest censorship upon the entire Press, both Anglo-Indian and Indian, and made it obligatory on the part of intending publishers and proprietors of newspapers to obtain a license from the Governor-General. The Ordinance was pushed through the Supreme Court according to the Law then existing after only 20 days' publication in that Court.

Rammohan Roy fought against it in the Court by engaging the services of two lawyers, and when he failed he got up a public petition to the King of England with no better result. But the seed that he sowed bore fruit in 1835 when Sir Charles Metcalfe liberated the Indian Press once again. While in England Rammohan Roy had the satisfaction of seeing the appeal of his adversaries against the abolition of *Sati* rejected by Parliament and also of seeing the Charter Act passed.

The story of the 'Indian Mutiny' so-called, arising primarily from the policy of Lord Dalhousie in denying the right of adoption to the widows of certain Princes and declaring their States escheat is well-known. The suppression of the rebellion was followed by the establishment of the Universities in 1858, and of the High Courts and the Legislative Councils in India between 1861 and 1863. Just before the 'mutiny' the 'Widow Re-marriage Act' was passed as also the Act relating to conversion into Christianity. In the sixties of the nineteenth century then, intimate contact was established with Western learning and literature. Western legal institutions and Parliamentary methods were inaugurated. to mark a new era in the field of law and legislation. The impact of Western civilization on the East could not but leave a deep impress upon the beliefs and sentiments of the Indian people who came directly under its influence. The germs of religious reform planted in the days of Rammohan Roy, became broadcast erelong. Keshab Chandra Sen, on whose shoulders fell the mantle of Rammohan Roy, spread the gospel of the Brahmo Samaj far and wide and gave a new social orientation to its tenets. He turned his attention to the temperance movement and made common cause with the temperance reformers in England. He was largely responsible for the passing of the Civil Marriage Act,—III of 1872—which allowed a form of civil marriage to non-Christians, provided they declared themselves as not belonging to any of the following communities—Hindu, Christian, Muslim, Parsee or Jew. This Act abolished early marriage, made polygamy penal and sanctioned widow marriages and inter-caste marriages. Keshab interested himself further in trying to raise the marriageable age of girls and prepared a Bill in 1872 on the subject which adopted 14 as the minimum age.

Erelong schisms arose in the Brahmo Samaj on account of the early marriage of Keshab Chandra Sen's daughter with the Maharaja of Cooch Bihar, which evoked protests amongst his fellow workers and led to the carving out of a protestant section under the name of 'Sadharan Brahmo Samaj' under the leadership of Ananda Mohan Bose. It is interesting to note that Ananda Mohan Bose later became the President of the Congress in 1898. The Brahmo Samaj of Bengal had its repercussions all over the country. In Poona, the movement assumed the name of Prarthana Samaj under the leadership of M. G. Ranade, who, it will be remembered, was the founder of the Social Reform movement which for long years continued to be an adjunct of the Congress. One feature however of this reformist movement was a certain disregard for the past and a spirit of revolt from the time-honoured and traditional beliefs of the country, which arose from an undue glamour presented by the Western institutions and heightened greatly by the political prestige associated with them. Naturally then, there was bound to be a reaction, at any rate a correction, to the denationalising tendencies engendered by the reformist movements. The Arya Samaj in the north-west, founded by the venerable Swami Dayananda Saraswati, and the Theosophical movement from the south, furnished the necessary corrective to the spirit of heterodoxy and even heresy which the Western learning brought with it. Both of them were intensely Nationalist movements; only, the Arya Samaj movement which owed its birth to the inspiration of the great Dayananda Saraswati was aggressive in its patriotic zeal, and while holding fast to the cult of the infallibility of the Vedas and the superiority of the Vedic culture, was at the same time not inimical to broad social reform. It thus developed a virile manhood in the Nation which was the synthesis of what was best in its heredity, with what is best in its environment. It fought some of the prevailing social evils and religious superstitions in Hinduism much as the Brahmo Samaj had battled against polytheism, idolatry and polygamy. Of course, as was to be expected, there arose two schools in the Arya Samaj itself, composed of those of the Gurukula cult who stood for the Vedic ideals of Brahmacharya and religious service, and those who sought to regenerate society imbibing in due measure modern Western culture through the modern type of educational institutions. Swami Shraddhananda, the Martyr, and Lala Lajpat Rai, the Hero, stand out to us as marked exponents of the respective cults. The Theosophical movement, while it extended its studies and sympathies to the wide world, laid special emphasis on a rediscovery, as well as a rehabilitation of all that was great and glorious in the Oriental culture. It was this passion that led Mrs. Besant to start a college in Benares, the holy city of India. The Theosophical activities, while developing a spirit of international brotherhood, helped to check that sense of rationalist superiority of the West and planted anew a cultural centre in India which attracted the savants and the scholars of the West once again to this ancient land.

The latest phase of national renaissance in India prior to the Congress was inaugurated in Bengal by that great sage, Ramakrishna Paramahamsa, who later found in Swami Vivekananda, his chief apostle carrying his gospel East and West. The Ramakrishna Mission is not merely an organisation wedded to occultism on the one hand or realism on the other, but to a profound transcendentalism which, however, does not ignore the supreme duty of 'Loka-Sangraha' or social service. It also supplied the key to the solution of the many socio-political problems that confront the nations of the world to-day. All these movements were really so many threads in the strand of Indian Nationalism and the Nation's duty was to evolve a synthesis so as to be able to dispel prejudice and superstition, to renovate and purify the old faith, the Vedantic idealism, and reconcile it with the Nationalism of the new age. The Indian National Congress was destined to fulfil this great mission. How far it has been able to do it during the past half a century, it is for us to study.

III

It was in the midst of these conditions that the establishment of the great Indian National Congress was conceived. Mr. Hume's idea was originally to allow provincial organisations like the Indian Association of Calcutta, the Presidency Association of Bombay, and the Mahajana Sabha of Madras to take up political questions, and the All-India National Union to concentrate more or less on social questions. He consulted Lord Dufferin who had recently come out as Viceroy, and the advice he gave cannot be better rendered than in the words of Mr. W. C. Bonnerjee who wrote in his 'Introduction to Indian Politics', published in 1898, as follows:—

"It will probably be news to many that the Indian National Congress, as it was originally started and as it has since been carried on, is in reality the work of the Marquis of Dufferin and Ava when that nobleman was the Governor-General of India. Mr. A. O. Hume, C. B., had in 1884, conceived the idea that it would be of great advantage to the country if leading Indian politicians could be brought together once a year to discuss social matters and be upon friendly footing with one another. He did not desire that politics should form part of their discussion, for, there were recognised political bodies in Calcutta, Bombay, Madras and other parts of India, and he thought that these bodies might suffer in importance if, when Indian politicians from different parts of the country came together, they discussed politics. His idea further was that the Governor of the Province where the politicians met should be asked to preside over their deliberations, and that thereby great cordiality should be established between the official classes and the non-official Indian politicians. Full of these ideas he saw the noble Marquis when he went to Simla early in 1885, after Lord Dufferin had in the December previous assumed the Viceroyalty of India. Lord Dufferin took great interest in the matter and after considering over it for some time he sent for Mr. Hume and told him that, in his opinion, Mr. Hume's project would not be of much use. He said there was no body of persons in this country who performed the functions which Her Majesty's Opposition did in England. The newspapers, even if they really represented the views of the people, were not reliable and as the English were necessarily ignorant of what was thought of them and their policy in Native circles, it would be very desirable in their interests as well as the interests of the ruled that Indian politicians should meet yearly and point out to the Government in what respects the administration was defective and how it could be improved, and he added that an assembly such as he proposed should not be presided over by the Local Governor, for in his presence the people might not like to speak out their minds. Mr. Hume was convinced by Lord Dufferin's arguments and when he placed the two schemes, his own and Lord Dufferin's, before leading politicians in Calcutta, Bombay, Madras and other parts of the country, the latter unanimously accepted Lord Dufferin's scheme and proceeded to give effect to it. Lord Dufferin had made it a condition with Mr. Hume that his name in connection with the scheme of the Congress should not be divulged so long as he remained in the country, and his condition was faithfully maintained and none but the men consulted by Mr. Hume knew anything about the matter."

In March 1885, it was decided to hold a meeting of representatives from all parts of India at the ensuing Christmas. Poona was considered the most central and the most suitable place. From this meeting was issued the following circular:—

A Conference of the Indian National Union will be held at Poona from the 25th to the 31st Dec. 1885.

The Conference will be composed of Delegates—leading politicians well acquainted with the English language—from all parts of the Bengal, Bombay and Madras Presidencies.

The direct objects of the Conference will be: (1) to enable all the most earnest labourers in the cause of national progress to become personally known to each other; (2) to discuss and decide upon the political operations to be undertaken during the ensuing year.

Indirectly, this Conference will form the germ of a Native Parliament, and, if properly conducted, will constitute in a few years an unanswerable reply to the assertion that India is still wholly unfit for any form of representative institutions. The first Conference will decide whether the next shall be again held at Poona, or whether, following the precedent of the British Association, the Conference shall be held year by year at different important centres.

This year the Conference being in Poona, Mr. Chiplonkar and others of the Sarvajanik Sabha have consented to form a Reception Committee, in whose hands will rest the whole of the local arrangements. The Peshwa's Garden near the Parbati Hill will be utilised both as a place of meeting (it contains a fine Hall, like the garden, the property of the Sabha) and as a residence for the delegates, each of whom will be there provided with suitable quarters. Much importance is attached to this, since, when all thus reside together for a week, far greater opportunities for friendly intercourse will be afforded than if the delegates were (as at the time of the late Bombay demonstrations) scattered about in dozens of private lodging houses all over the town.

Delegates are expected to find their own way to and from Poona, but from the time they reach the Poona Railway Station until they again leave it, everything that they can need, carriage, accommodation, food, etc., will be provided for them gratuitously.

The cost thus involved will be defrayed from the Reception Fund, which the Poona Association most liberally offers to provide in the first instance, but to which all delegates, whose means warrant their incurring this further expense, will be at liberty to contribute any sum they please. Any unutilised balance of such donations will be carried forward as a nucleus for next year's Reception Fund.

It is believed that, exclusive of our Poona friends, the Bombay Presidency, including Sindh and the Berars, will furnish about 20 delegates, Madras and Lower Bengal each about the same number, and the N. W. Province, Oudh, and the Punjab together about half this number.

Having already armed himself with the blessings of the Viceroy in India, Mr. Hume proceeded to England and consulted Lord Ripon, Lord Dalhousie, Sir James Caird, John Bright, Mr. Reid, Mr. Slagg and other eminent men before he started the Congress. Under their advice he organised what became the nucleus of the Indian Parliamentary Committee in England to act for India by obtaining pledges from candidates for Parliamentary election, not that they would help India but only that they would take interest in Indian affairs. He further arranged an Indian Telegraph Union to provide funds to send telegrams on important matters to leading Provincial papers in England, with which he arranged for their publication.

A graphic account of the 1st session of the Congress is given by Mrs. Besant in her publication, 'How India Wrought for Freedom', and we are indebted to her for the following extracts therefrom:—

> "The first meeting did not, however, take place at Poona, for, only a few days before Christmas, some sporadic cases of cholera occurred, possibly presaging an outbreak, and it was thought wiser to move the Conference, now called the Congress, to Bombay. The Managers of the Gokuldas Tejpal Sanskrit College and Boarding House placed the whole of their fine buildings at the disposal of the Congress, and all was ready by the morning of the 27th Dec. for the reception of the Representatives of the Indian Nation. As we glance over the lists of those who were present, how many we see who became famous in the annals of India's struggle for Freedom! Among those who could not act as Representatives we note the Reformer, Dewan Bahadur R. Raghunatha Rao, Deputy Collector of Madras; the Hon. Mr. Mahadev G. Ranade, then member of the Legislative Council and Small Cause Court Judge of Poona, later to be a Judge of the High Court of Bombay, and leader honoured and trusted; Lala Baijnath of Agra was there, to be known as scholar and writer later on; and Professors K. Sundararaman and R. G. Bhandarkar. Among the Representatives may be noted Editors of well-known Indian papers, of *The Dyan Prakash, The Quarterly Journal of the Poona Sarvajanik Sabha. The Maratha, The Kesari. The Nababibhakar, The Indian Mirror, The Nassim, The*

Hindusthani, The Tribune, The Indian Union. The Spectator, The Indu Prakash, The Hindu, The Crescent. How many names shine out, familiar and honoured: Mr. A. O. Hume is there from Simla; W. C. Bonnerjee and Norendranath Sen from Calcutta; W. S. Apte and G. G. Agarkar from Poona; Gangaprasad Varma from Lucknow: Dadabhai Naoroji, K. T. Telang, Pherozeshah M. Mehta—then, as now, leader of the Bombay Corporation, D. E. Wacha, B. M. Malabari, N. G. Chandavarkar, from Bombay; P. Rangiah Naidu, President of the Mahajana Sabha, S. Subrahmania Aiyar, P. Ananda Charlu, G. Subrahmania Aiyar, M. Viraraghavachariar, from Madras; P. Kesava Pillai from Anantapur. These are among the earliest who wrought for India's Freedom, and those yet on earth, are working for her still.

"At 12 noon, on Dec. 28th, 1885, in the Hall of the Gokhuldas Tejpal Sanskrit College, the First National Congress met. The first voices heard were those of Mr. A. O. Hume, the Hon. Mr. S. Subrahmania Aiyar and the Hon. Mr. K. T Telang, who proposed, seconded and supported the election of the first President, Mr. W. C. Bonnerjee. A solemn and historic moment was that in which the first of the long line of men thus honoured by the Motherland took his seat, to preside over her first National Assembly.

"After alluding to the representative and weighty character of the Congress, he laid down under four heads the objects of the Congress:

(a) The promotion of personal intimacy and friendship amongst all the more earnest workers in our country's cause in the various parts of the Empire.

(b) The eradication, by direct friendly personal intercourse of all possible race, creed, or provincial prejudices amongst all lovers of our country and the fuller development and consolidation of those sentiments of national unity that had their origin in our beloved Lord Ripon's ever memorable reign.

(c) The authoritative record, after this has been carefully elicited by the fullest discussion, of the matured opinions of the educated classes in India on some of the more important and pressing of the social questions of the day.

(d) The determination of the lines upon and methods by which during the next twelve months it is desirable for Native politicians to labour in the public interests.

"The nine resolutions of the first National Congress mark the beginning of the formulation of India's demands:

The first asked for a Royal Commission to enquire nto the working of Indian administration.

The second for the abolition of the India Council.

The third dealt with the defects of the Legislative Councils in which then all the members were nominated, and asked for the admission of elected members, for the right of interpellation, for the creation of Councils in the N. W. P. and Oudh, and in the Punjab, and for a Standing Committee in the House of Commons to consider formal protests from majorities in the Councils.

The fourth prayed for simultaneous examinations for the I. C. S. and the raising of the age of candidates.

The fifth and sixth dealt with Military expenditure.

The seventh protested against the annexation of Upper Burma and the proposed incorporation of it with India.

The eighth ordered the sending of the resolutions to political Associations, and they were discussed and passed all over the country by political bodies and public meetings, an admirable plan which has fallen into desuetude, they were carried with much enthusiasm, and here and there amended on minor points.

The final resolution fixed the next Congress at Calcutta, on 28th December, 1886.

IV

Great institutions have always had small beginnings, even as the great rivers of the world start as thin streams. At the commencement of their career and course, they progress rapidly, and, as they widen, become slower and steadier. By the confluence of their various tributaries, they are enriched as they flow on, both in volume and content. The evolution of the Indian National Congress presents the same phenomenon. It had to cut its way through mighty obstacles and therefore entertained modest ideals. As it gained a foothold on the affections of the people, it widened its course and absorbed into itself several collateral movements wedded to the solution of social, ethical and economic problems. Its activities were in the earlier stages naturally characterised by a sense of diffidence and doubt. As it attained man's estate it became more and more conscious of its strength and capacity, and its outlook was soon widened. From an attitude of prayerfulness and importunity, it developed self-consciousness and self-assertion. This was followed by an intensive campaign of education and propaganda, which rapidly resulted in extensive organisation of the country and campaigns of direct action. Starting with the humble object of seeking redress of grievances, the Congress erelong developed into the one accredited organ of the Nation that proudly put forth its demands. Limited as its range of vision was in the earlier decades to matters administrative, it soon became a powerful and authoritative exponent of the political ambitions of the people of India. Its doors were thrown open to every class of citizens and to every grade of society. Though in the beginning it fought shy of problems that were described as social, yet in the fulness of time, it recognised no such compartmentalism of life; and surviving the traditional and time-honoured demarcation of life's issues as social and political, it has developed a comprehensive ideal in which life is considered as one and indivisible. The Congress then is a National organisation that knows no difference between British India and Indian India, between one Province and another, between the classes and the masses, between towns and villages, between the rich and the poor, between agricultural and industrial interests, between castes and communities, or religions. This was the claim put forward by Gandhi at the second R. T. C. in his speech before the Federal Structure Committee, and we cannot do better than extract here below the relevant portion of that powerful speech:—

> "I am but a poor humble agent acting on behalf of the Indian National Congress; and it might be as well to remind ourselves of what the Congress stands for and what it is. You will then extend your sympathy to me, because I know that the burden that rests upon my shoulders is really very great. The Congress is, if I am not mistaken, the oldest political organisation we have in India. It has had nearly 50 years of life, during which period it has, without any interruption, held its annual session. It is what it means,—National. It represents no particular community, no particular class, no particular interest. It claims to represent all Indian interests and all classes. It is a matter of the greatest pleasure to me to state that it was first conceived in an English brain. Allan Octavian Hume we knew as the Father of the Congress. It was nursed by two great Parsees, Pherozeshah Mehta and Dadabhai Naoroji, whom all India delighted to recognise as its Grand Old Man. From the very commencement the Congress had Mussalmans, Christians, Anglo-Indians, I might say, all religions, sects, creeds, represented upon it more or less fully.

The late Budruddin Tyabji identified himself with the Congress. We have had Mussalmans as Presidents of the Congress, and Parsees too. I can recall at least one Indian Christian at the present moment. Kali Charan Banerjee (an Indian Christian), than whom I have not had the privilege of knowing a purer Indian, was also thoroughly identified with the Congress. I miss, as I have no doubt all of you miss, the presence in our midst of Mr. K. T. Paul. Although, I do not know, but so far as I know, he never officially belonged to the Congress, he was a Nationalist to the full.

"As you know, the late Maulana Mahomed Ali whose presence also we miss to-day, was a President of the Congress, and at present we have four Mussalmans as members of the Working Committee which consists of 15 members. We have had women as our Presidents; Dr. Annie Besant was the first, and Mrs. Sarojini Naidu followed. We have her as a member of the Working Committee also; and so, if we have no distinctions of class or creed, we have no distinctions of sex either.

"The Congress has from its very commencement taken up the cause of the so-called 'untouchables'. There was a time when the Congress had at every annual session, as its adjunct, the Social Conference, to which the late Ranade had dedicated his energies, among his many activities. Headed by him, you will find in the programme of the Social Conference, reform in connection with the untouchables taking a prominent place.. But in 1920, the Congress took a large step and brought the question of removal of untouchability as a plank on the political platform, made it an important item of the politcal programme. Just as the Congress considered Hindu-Muslim unity, thereby meaning unity amongst all the classes, to be indispensable for the attainment of Swaraj, so also did the Congress consider the removal of the curse of untouchability as an indispensable condition for the attainment of full freedom.

"The position the Congress took up in 1920 remains the same to-day, and so you will see that the Congress has attempted from its very beginning to be what it has described itself to be, namely, National in every sense of the term. If your Highnesses will permit me to say so, in the very early stages, the Congress took up your cause also. Let me remind this Committee that it was the G. O. M. of India who sponsored the cause of Kashmir and Mysore, and these two great Houses, I venture in all humility to submit, owe not a little to the efforts of Dadabhai Naoroji and the Congress.

"Even up to now the Congress has endeavoured to serve the Princes of India by refraining from any interference in their domestic and internal affairs. I hope, therefore, that his brief introduction that I thought fit to give will serve to enable the Sub-Committee and those who are at all interested in the claims of the Congress, to understand that it has endeavoured to deserve the claim that it has made. It has failed, I know, often to live up to the claim. But I venture to submit, that if you were to examine the history of the Congress you would find that it has more often succeeded, and progressively succeeded than failed.

"Above all the Congress represents, in its essence, the dumb semi-starved millions scattered over the length and breadth of the land in its 7,00,000 villages, no matter whether they come from what is called British India, or what is called Indian India. Every interest which, in the opinion of the Congress, is worthy of protection, has to subserve this interest, and if there is a genuine real clash I have no hesitation in saying on behalf of the Congress that the Congress will sacrifice every interest for the sake of the interest of these dumb millions. It is, therefore, essentially a peasant organisation, and it is becoming so progressively. You, and even the Indian members of the Sub-Committee, will perhaps be astonished to find that to-day the Congress, through its organisation, the All-India Spinners' Association, is finding work for nearly 50,000 women in nearly 2,000 villages, and these women are possibly 50 per cent. Mussalman women. Thousands of them belong to the so-called untouchable class. We have thus, in this constructive manner, penetrated these villages and the effort is being made to cover every one of the 7,00,000 villages. It is a superhuman task, but if human effort can do so, you will presently find the Congress covering all of these villages and bringing to them the message of the spinning wheel."

Here in a nutshell is the description by Gandhi of this great National organisation. If the Congress has achieved nothing else, it has done this, namely, it has discovered its own destiny, it has focussed the thoughts and activities of the Nation to a single point. It has developed a certain self-consciousness amongst the teeming millions of India and animated them with a sense of unity, hope and self-confidence. The Congress has further given a distinctly national turn to the thoughts and ambitions of the Indians and enabled them to rediscover their common language and literature, their common crafts and arts, and above all their common aspirations and ideals. It has not had a smooth course of progress during the past fifty years, and the graph of its career indicates its own rises and falls, synchronising with the hopes and fears of the people and the victories and reverses of their struggle. To describe the origin of such a virile organisation, to recount the services of the many patriarchs and progenitors that assisted at its birth, to trace the activities of the patriots that nurtured this institution in its formative period of life, to portray the vicissitudes through which the organisation has passed in its adolescence, to delineate the glories and greatness of its achievement in its manhood as well as the sorrows and shame that it has sustained, to review the phases through which its faith and philosophy have passed before the Congress became pledged to "the attainment of Swaraj by all peaceful and legitimate means," these are the objectives held in view in attempting to chronicle the history of the Congress over the past half-century of its existence.

CHAPTER II

A Rapid Review of the Resolutions of the Congress (1885—1915)

We do not propose in this Chapter to take the sessions of the Congress year by year. It would be better to take up the important matters which formed the subjects for discussion, and resolutions at successive Congresses, and thus show at a glance the course of the Congress policy and programme up to say 1915, after which a new orientation in policy and somewhat different methods of treatment came to be adopted. For this purpose the important subjects of discussion and resolution may be divided into separate main-heads and dealt with one after another

The India Council

At its very earliest session, the Congress urged the abolition of the Council of the Secretary of State as it was constituted, and the proposal was reiterated at two subsequent sessions, the tenth Congress proposing the constitution, in its place, of a Standing Committee of the House of Commons to advise the Secretary of State. But the mover of the resolution, Mr. Eardley Norton, was not free from doubt about this latter proposal. He said:

> "Personally I am not very much enamoured of the suggestion that in lieu of the Secretary of State's Council we should have a Standing Committee of Parliament at Home, because I feel that the Standing Committee may in course of years become the monopoly of the retired Anglo-Indian official who trickles into Parliament......But personally I would sooner

embark on any venture; sooner trust to any new tribunal; sooner pin my faith on any proposed combination than entrust anything in which I felt a personal interest to the clutches or the carelessness of the India Council. With me there is no mending that Council. It must be ending. The Standing Committee of the House of Commons will at any rate have this advantage; in the first place it will be very much less expensive, because it will sweep away the £ 1,200 a year of these gentlemen, and in the second place you will have the advantage of its members speaking in public, subject to public opinion, subject to debate, and subject to criticism. So far as I am concerned this part of the resolution is only tentative. I shall be open to discuss and consider any better substitute for the Council."

Specific proposals of reform were made by the Karachi Session held in 1913, which passed the following resolution:—

That this Congress is of opinion that the Council of the Secretary of State for India, as at present constituted, should be abolished, and makes the following suggestions for its reconstruction:

(a) that the salary of the Secretary of State for India should be placed on the English Estimates;

(b) that with a view to the efficiency and independence of the Council, it is expedient that it should be partly nominated and partly elected;

(c) that the total number of members of the Council should be not less than nine;

(d) that the elected portion of the Council should consist of not less than one-third of the total number of members, who should be non-official Indians chosen by a constituency consisting of the elected members of the Imperial and Provincial Legislative Councils;

(e) that the remaining portion of the nominated Councillors should consist of officials who have served in India for not less than ten years and who have not been away from India for more than two years;

(f) that the character of the Council should be advisory and not administrative;

(g) that the term of office of each member should be five years.

The reason for the modified resolutions passed at a few later sessions is not a weakening of conviction that the abolition of the Council is desirable, but the feeling that there was less probability of early abolition than of reform. That the conviction of the inutility of the Council is still there, is proved by the clause advocating its abolition in the scheme of Reforms adopted in 1917.

Constitutional Changes

Few people could lay the charge of immoderation against the Congress at its inception and for a long time thereafter. All that was prayed for at the first Congress was that "the Supreme and existing Local Legislative Councils should be expanded by the admission of a considerable proportion of elected members (and the creation of similar Councils for the N.W.P. and Oudh (U.P.) and also for the Punjab)," holding that all Budgets should be referred to the Councils, that the right of interpellation be granted, and that "a standing Committee of the House of Commons should be constituted to receive and consider any formal protests that may be recorded by majorities of such Councils against the exercise by the Executive of the power, which would be vested in it, of overruling the decision of such majorities." That is to say, in 1885, the Congress wanted a Parliamentary safeguard against bureaucratic actions, such as have been lately witnessed in profusion in the Assembly in respect of the rejection or vetoing of popular demands accepted by a majority, and the certification of Government demands rejected by the people's representatives. The second session of the Congress elaborated a scheme of Council Reform, and while asking for a 50 per cent. elected strength, conceded the principle of indirect election by Municipalities and Local Boards, by the Chambers of Commerce and the Universities, to the Local Councils, and by the Local Councils to the Supreme Council. It further conceded to Government the right of overruling the decisions of the Councils, but provided for appeals against Executive action to the Government of India and to the Standing Committee of the House Commons, to which bodies the respective Executives concerned should, within a month of overruling, duly explain their action. The same resolution was repeated in 1887, 1888. 1889. In 1890 the Congress supported the Bill to amend the Indian Councils Act introduced by Charles Bradlaugh as calculated to secure a substantial instalment of Reforms. The Bill, it may be noted in passing, was dropped. In 1891 the Congress reiterated its conviction that India could not be governed well until her people were allowed, through their elected representatives, a potential voice in the Legislatures. Lord Cross's Act of Council Reform was passed in 1892, and then the Congress concentrated upon an attack on the Rules of the Government of India and the practice of Local Governments which necessitated many alterations.

We must not omit to mention the fact that the Reforms of 1892 did not provide for the election of the representatives to the Legislative Councils. The so-called right of election to the Legislatures enjoyed by Local Bodies and by other Electorates amounted merely to nomination by those bodies, and it was up to Government to accept them or to reject them. In practice, however, Government invariably accepted the nominations. The fact was that Lord Lansdowne's Government uniformly resisted the principle of election even of an indirect character. The representation to the Supreme

Council was similarly arranged, only four seats being open to be filled up by the recommendation of the non-official members of the four Provincial Legislative Councils then in existence,—Madras, Bombay, Bengal and N.W.P.

In 1892 the Congress, while accepting in a loyal spirit the Indian Councils Act, regretted that the Act itself did not in terms concede to the people the right of electing their own representatives to the Councils. In 1893 it thanked the Government for its liberal spirit in giving effect to the Act but also pointed out material alterations considered necessary, if real effect was to be given to the Act. It also reiterated the demand for a Council for the Punjab. These requests were repeated in 1894 and 1897. The Reforms of 1892 however conceded the right of interpellation for the members of Councils in 1893, and the Congress asked in 1895 for the right to preface their questions by short explanations which is not permitted even to-day.

The Morley-Minto Reforms

It was not till 1904 that the Congress reverted to the subject. In that year a demand was also made in favour of direct representation to the House of Commons, at the rate of two members to each Province, and a further expansion of the Councils in the country, with the right to divide the House on financial matters, the right of veto to the Head of the Government being of course conceded. A plea was also put in for the appointment of Indians to the Council of the Secretary of State and to the Executive Councils in India. In 1905 the Congress again pressed for Reforms, and in 1906 expressed the opinion that the system of Government obtaining in the Self-Governing Dominions should be extended to India, and as steps leading thereto, there should be simultaneous examinations held in England and India, adequate representation of Indians in the Council of the Secretary of State, an expansion of the Supreme and Provincial Legislative Councils, allowing larger and truer representation of the people and larger control over the financial and executive administration of the country, and an increase in the powers of local bodies. In 1908 the Congress began to rejoice over the coming Reforms before time for it, gave a most hearty and unqualified welcome to the Reform proposals, and expressed the hope that the details would be worked out in the same liberal spirit in which the proposals were conceived. Disappointment, however, was in store for the country. Even apart from the measure of representation, there remained the fact that the Regulations passed under the Reforms Statute of 1909 were even less liberal than John Morley had indicated in his Despatch earlier. This reminds us of later events in which the pronouncements of Lord Irwin were toned down by the Round Table Conferences of 1930-33, and the plans of the Conferences were further diluted by the White Paper, which in turn was softened by the J.P.C. Report, while the Bill went lower down than the Report, and the Act finally has emerged as an attenuated form of the Bill.

It is necessary at this stage to review rapidly what the Reforms were, which were for a decade associated with the names of Minto and Morley. The Supreme Council consisted of 60 additional members, of whom only 27 were elected representatives. Of the remaining 33, not more than 28 might be officials. But the Governor-General also nominated three non-officials to represent certain specified Communities, and had at his disposal two other seats to be filled by nomination, more to represent interests than territories. The elected seats themselves were partly shared by certain special constituencies, such as the Landowners in seven Provinces, the Muslims in five Provinces, Muslim Landowners in one Province (at alternative elections only), and two Chambers of Commerce, while the residue of open seats was filled by election by the non-official members of the nine Provincial Legislative Councils. Lord Morley made no secret of the fact that the "Governor-General's Council, in its Legislative as well as its Executive capacity, should continue to be so constituted as to ensure its constant and uninterrupted power to fulfil the constitutional obligations that it owes, and must always owe, to His Majesty's Government and to the Imperial Parliament." Of the Reforms themselves Morley stated: "If it could be said that this chapter of Reforms led directly or indirectly to the establishment of a Parliamentary system in India, I for one would have nothing at all to do with it." But the verdict of Lord Chelmsford and Mr. Montagu as embodied in their (Montford) Report on these Reforms is doubtless even more authoritative: "They have ceased to satisfy Indian opinion, and their continuance can only lead to a further cleavage between the Indian members and the Government and a further cultivation of criticism unchecked by Responsibility."

Before dealing with Congress resolutions on the subject, we may here anticipate events and complete the picture.

The Morley-Minto Reforms opened the next stage of the question. Two Indians (since increased to three) were appointed in 1907 as members of the India Council, one was appointed to the. Governor-General's Executive Council in 1909, and one each to the Executive Councils of the Governors of Madras and Bombay in 1910. An Executive Council was constituted in Bengal in the same year and an Indian member was appointed to it. Subsequently the Province was raised to the status of a Presidency under a Governor-in-Council. The separate Province of Bihar and Orissa was formed in 1912 under a Lieutenant-Governor-in-Council with an Indian member in it.

In 1909 the Congress passed four resolutions dealing with the Reforms. In the first it recorded its sense of disapproval of the creation of separate electorates on the basis of religion; it expressed dissatisfaction at "(a) the excessive and unfairly preponderant share of representation given to the followers of one particular religion; (b) the unjust, invidious and humiliating distinctions made between Muslim and non-Muslim subjects of His Majesty in the matter of electorates, the franchise and the qualifications of candidates; (c) the wide, arbitrary and unreasonable disqualifications and restrictions for candidates seeking election to the Councils; (d) the general distrust of the educated classes running through the Regulations; and (e) the unsatisfactory composition of the non-official majorities in the Provincial Councils, rendering them ineffective and unreal." By the second resolution it urged the creation of Executive Councils to assist the Lt. Governors in the U. P., the Punjab, Eastern Bengal and Assam, and Burma. By the third resolution the Congress pointed out the unsatisfactory nature of the Reforms Regulations for the Punjab in (a) that the numerical strength of the Council was inadequate, (b) that the elected element was unduly small and altogether insufficient, (c) that the principle of protection of minorities applied in the case of Muslims in other Provinces was not applied to non-Muslim minorities in the Punjab, and (d) that the Regulations tended to practically keep out non-Muslims of the Punjab from the Imperial Council. By a fourth resolution the Congress expressed dissatisfaction at the non-establishment of a Council for the C.P. and Berars and at the exclusion of the Berars from participation in the election of two members of the Imperial Legislative Council by the land-holders and members of District and Municipal Boards of C. P.

In 1910 and 1911 the Congress practically reiterated the objections and suggestions of 1909 regarding the Reforms and further protested against the extension of the principle of separate electorates to District Boards and Municipalities.

In 1912 the Congress expressed disappointment at the non-removal of the defects mentioned in the previous resolutions, and prayed for an elected majority in the Imperial Legislative Council and in all the Provincial Councils, the system of voting by delegates to be done away with, the franchise to be widened, removal of the disqualifications of candidates on the ground of conviction not involving moral turpitude, the right of putting supplementary questions and similar other reforms. It reiterated the resolutions regarding the establishment of an Executive Council in the Punjab and condemning the extension of separate electorates to Local Bodies. Curiously enough, the Congress resolutions on the Reforms had a clause to the effect that "a person ignorant of English should be ineligible for membership." The Congress expressed satisfaction at the recognition by the Government of India of the necessity of introducing Provincial Autonomy and protested against an interpretation sought to be put upon the Despatch which was contrary to its letter and spirit. The same resolution was practically reiterated in 1913.

In 1915 the Congress was held in Bombay under the

presidency of Sir S. P. Sinha who was the first Law Member of the Government of India. Resolution XIX of the Bombay Congress (1915) instructed the All-India Congress Committee to confer with a committee of the All-India Muslim League. and as the result of the conference, a scheme was drafted embodying the aspirations of United India, and the Lucknow Congress of 1916 approved of this scheme. The Congress demanded a definite step to be taken towards Self-Government and that India should be raised in status "from the position of a Dependency to that of an equal partner in the Empire with the Self-Governing Dominions." The scheme that was then elaborated, strangely enough, provided for 4/5 elected and 1/5 nominated members in the Provincial Legislative Councils, for elections being direct and being based on as broad a franchise as possible, adequate provision being made for the Muslim minorities by Separate Electorates and the following quotas:—Punjab 50 per cent., of the elected members, U.P. 30 per cent., Bengal 40 per cent., Bihar 25 per cent., C.P. 15 per cent., Madras 15 per cent. and Bombay 1/3. They were not to contest in any other Election (Imperial or Provincial) than those representing special interests. It was also provided that "no Bill, nor any clause thereof, nor a resolution introduced by a non-official member affecting one or the other community, which question is to be determined by the members of that community in the Legislative Council concerned, shall be proceeded with, if three-fourths of the members of that community in the particular Council, Imperial or Provincial, oppose the Bill, or any clause thereof, or the resolution." In the Imperial Council there should be a four-fifths elected element, and a third of the Indian elected members should be Muslims elected by separate Muslim Electorates in the proportion, as nearly as possible, in which they are represented in the Provincial Councils by separate Muslim

Electorates. This is the Hindu-Muslim concordat passed at Lucknow and subsequently accepted by, and *en bloc* incorporated in, the Montford Reforms.

The scheme comprised various details which need not be gone into here. The Congress-League Scheme is extracted in full in the Appendix. The Congress did not rest content with the passing of the resolution. An Executive Committee was appointed to carry on educative and propagandistic work in this behalf. The General Secretaries referred the scheme to a lawyer of eminence, Mr. S. Varadachariar, who has recently become a Judge of the Madras High Court, for preparing an Amending Bill to carry out the changes proposed in the Government of India Act in accordance with the Congress-League Scheme. The Home Rule agitation led by Mrs. Besant, her internment, the scheme of Passive Resistance thought of jointly by the Congress and the Muslim League, the great speech of Mr. Montagu on the Mesopotamian muddle, the resignation of Mr. Austen Chamberlain, the then Secretary of State, and the appointment of Mr. Montagu as S. of S. for India, the famous Announcement of August 20th, 1917, adumbrating the future policy in India, Mr. Montagu's promised visit, Mrs. Besant's release and her election as President of the Congress are only enumerated here, though they are dealt with in detail elsewhere (in Part II), as they form the background for the picture of the Calcutta Congress of 1917.

In Calcutta (1917), the grateful satisfaction of the Congress was expressed over the pronouncement that the establishment of Responsible Government was Government's object, and the Congress asked that a time-limit be fixed in the Statute itself for its full realization, and that as a first step the Congress-League Scheme of

Reforms should be introduced. The reader may note how the Congress had in mind an elastic and self-expanding scheme of Reforms.

Mr. Montagu arrived in India in November 1917. The Montford Report itself was published in the month of June, 1918, and the scheme therein set forth was discussed at a Special Congress held in Bombay in September 1918, presided over by Mr. Hasan Imam. The Congress-League Scheme was eclipsed by the scheme elaborated in the Montford Report, and Dyarchy was its central factor. A Second Chamber in the Central Legislature—namely, the Council of State—was contemplated, and "grand committees" in the Provinces in order to help the Governor-General and Governors to have effective power in respect of measures not approved of by the popular Chambers. The Bombay (Special) Session resolved, "That there shall be no Council of State, but if a Council of State is to be constituted, a system of reserved and transferred subjects similar to that proposed for the Provinces, shall be adopted for the Central Government. At least half of its total strength shall consist of elected members and procedure by certification shall be confined to the Reserved subjects. Dyarchy was accepted and a Second Chamber in the Centre was agreed to in return for an extension of Dyarchy in the Centre, which was demanded by the Congress but which the Montford Scheme had not contemplated. The Congress-League Scheme was really much nearer to the Home Rule idea than the bicameral scheme which successfully puts down the popular voice of the Lower House without the odium of a veto by the Governor-General or the Governor.

Government took what was given, *viz.*, the Council of State, and did not give what was demanded as a *quid pro quo,* viz., Dyarchy at the Centre. The Bombay Special Congress was a complete triumph for Mr. Montagu. That it considered the Montford proposals, as a whole, disappointing and unsatisfactory, or that in reaffirming the demands of the two previous Congresses it added a section relating to fundamental rights, namely; equality of all subjects before the law, guarantees of liberty, life and property, freedom of speech or writing or of association, right to bear arms, freedom of Press, and the making of corporal punishment equally applicable to all, does not really disprove this statement. The Delhi Congress (1918) which was presided over by Pandit Malaviya also re-affirmed these conditions, but demanded full Responsible Government in all Provinces, not Dyarchy. At Delhi, Dyarchy was pleaded for in the Central Government, Foreign Affairs, the Army and the Navy being agreed to be left as Reserved subjects. On the question of the Second Chamber, the Bombay Special Congress resolution was repeated, a half of the total strength being required to be elected. The War ended by the declaration of armistice on 11-11-1918, and the Congress quoted the pronouncements of President Wilson, Lloyd George and other British statesmen, stressed that the principle of self-determination be applied to all progressive nations, and resolved that it be applied to India, and that all repressive laws be repealed. Strenuous times were ahead, however, for the Congress. Before the next session met at Amritsar, the Rowlatt Bills and the Satyagraha movement, the shootings at Viramgam and Delhi and the Jallianwalabagh tragedy, Martial Law in the Punjab and Sir C. Sankaran Nair's resignation from the Government of India, the Hunter Commission and its failure,—these were the chief occurrences that engaged and even perturbed the national mind.

PUBLIC SERVICES

The Congress has always attached great importance to the employment of Indians in the public services, and particularly in what are known as the covenanted services. It will be recalled that in 1833 the eligibility of Indians to all posts had been recognised by statute, and when in 1853 competitive examinations were introduced it was pointed out that Indians were under a great handicap. During the regime of Lord Salisbury the age of candidates for competitive examinations for the Civil Service was reduced, and this was regarded as adding to the handicap from which Indians suffered. Indians had always demanded simultaneous examinations to be held in England and India so that handicap might be at least partially removed. The very first Congress advocated simultaneous examinations.

Let us study the subject in greater detail. It may be mentioned here that the demand for simultaneous examinations has been made by the Congress ever since 1885 when its first session was held, and that it dates back to at least eighteen years earlier, apart from the important circumstance that, as early as 1861, a committee of the India Council recommended the same as essential if justice was to be done to India and if the promises of Parliament were to be fulfilled. The resolution in support of simultaneous examinations passed by the House of Commons in June 1893 was acclaimed by the Congress and throughout the country, and the decision of Government, announced in the following year, not to give effect to it was received with the deepest disappointment. The evidence of the Indian witnesses before the Royal Commission on the Public Services in India left no room for doubt as regards the persistence of the opinion that justice could never be done to the claims of Indians unless this reform was accomplished, and the principal reason for the emphatic disapproval of the Majority Report of the Commissioners was that they negatived this proposal.

At the second Congress a sub-committee appointed in this behalf formulated certain details and demanded that simultaneous competitive examinations be held in India and England open to all subjects of His Majesty, that a classified list of appointments be made in order of merit, than with the holding of these simultaneous examinations, the Statutory Civil Service be closed for first appointments which, however, should be left open to the members of the uncovenanted service and to professional men of proved merit, and that all other appointments be filled by competitive examinations held in the Provinces. The practice then prevalent was that certain young men were being chosen as Deputy Collectors straightway. By the time of the fourth session the agitation met with a measure of success. The Congress appreciated the concessions proposed in the Report of the Public Service Commission but complained of their inadequacy. No doubt the age-limit for the I. C. S. examination was raised from 19 to 23 as was desired by the Congress, but otherwise the position was made worse by the Government's orders on the Commission's recommendations, for the Indian officials were compelled either to remain in the position they then held in the Statutory Service or to enter the Provincial Service, the members of which were banned from all the higher Executive offices. Gokhale made an indignant speech at the 5th Congress in which he stated: "The terms of the enactment of 1833 and the Proclamation of 1858 are so explicit that those who now try to withhold the privileges then assured to us must be prepared to face the painful dilemma of hypocrisy or treachery, must be prepared to admit that

England was insincere when she made those promises or that she is prepared to break faith with us now." The position then was that first, there were competitive examinations for the All-India Services, secondly, there was the Statutory Covenanted Service in which 1|6 of the posts, by the enactment of 1861, were reserved for Indians, and thirdly there was the uncovenanted service which was wholly Indian. In 1892 the Congress regretted the resolution of the Government of India on the Report of the Public Service Commission and had a humble petition submitted to the House of Commons. Out of 941 posts under the second category, a sixth, i.e., 158 posts belonged to the Indians. But the Public Service Commission said 108 *should* be given, and the Secretary of State changed the word "should" and said they *may* be given. As a matter of fact even out of 108 posts left to the discretion of Government as against 158 which had formed the rightful claim of Indians, only 93 were given to them in 1892.

Matters soon grew worse. The Government of India Resolution on the subject was confirmed by a despatch from the S. of S. and a positive disability founded upon race was created against the Indians in 1894, for the despatch laid down that a minimum of European officials in the Covenanted Service was indispensable. It gave the go-bye to the Resolution passed by the House of Commons on 2-6-1893, that the question of holding simultaneous examinations should be speedily carried out as an act of justice to the Indian people. While India was demanding facilities through simultaneous examinations for entering the Indian Civil, Medical, Police, Engineering, Telegraph, Forest and Accounts Services, Government took a reactionary step in 1895, for, in reorganizing the Educational Service which Indians could enter in any grade and on equal pay with Europeans, Government published a Resolution stating that "in future Natives of India who are desirous of entering the Educational department will usually be appointed in India and to the Provincial Service." Thus in the field of Educational Service a new injustice was perpetrated in the scheme for its reorganization. Indians were excluded from the higher grades of that service. The scheme divided the superior Educational Service into two—the higher, the I.E.S., to be filled by persons appointed in England and the lower, the P.E.S. to be filled in India. Before 1880, in Bengal, both Indians and Europeans in the higher service received the same pay. Both began on Rs. 500. In 1880 the pay for Indians was reduced to Rs. 333 and in 1889 to Rs. 250, although the Indians had graduated in an English University. The highest pay for the Indian was to be, in 1896, Rs. 700 however long he might serve, while the Englishman had Rs. 1000 at the end of ten years. The new scheme further barred the Indians from the Principalship of certain Colleges reserved for Englishmen. The regret at these changes was all the greater, said Mr. A. M. Bose, as they were brought into force, in the year of Her Majesty's Diamond Jubilee (1897). It is thus that as the Congress movement became more real and more earnest, the bureaucratic reaction became more unabashed and more naked.

In 1896 and 1897, the Congress demanded a place for Indians in the Executive Councils of Bombay and Madras. The Civil Medical Service came in for some attention in these and subsequent years. In 1900, the Congress deplored the exclusion of Indians from the higher branches of the P.W.D., Railway, Opium, Customs and Telegraph Services and also the restriction of eligibility for appointment through the Cooper's Hill College of Engineering only to two. An additional invidious distinction was made in respect of guaranteed appointments in connection with the College at Roorki. The separation of the Indian Civil Medical from the Military Medical Service became another topic of agitation and the same old grievances continued to be reiterated at subsequent sessions.

MILITARY PROBLEM

The Congress of the period had dealt with nearly two hundred subjects during the thirty years covered by this period. Amongst these subjects, there was one of unfailing interest which became an annual theme for years but which obtained no redress or relief in spite of repeated protests and prayers from the Congress. The very first Congress protested against the proposed increase of military expenditure and suggested that if it was inevitable it should be met by retrenchment of other expenditure and by a reimposition of Customs duties and extension of the License tax on those officials and non-officials till then exempt therefrom, taking care however to maintain a sufficiently high taxable minimum. In the next year a plea was put forward for the admission of Indians as volunteers who would be of immense assistance to Government, in view of the unsettled state of public affairs in Europe. In the third year India's claims for admission into the higher grades of military service were pressed on the plea of India's loyalty and of the Queen's pledge in her Proclamation of 1858. To this end, Congress asked for the establishment of Military Colleges in this country. The fourth and fifth Congresses confirmed the earlier resolutions, the sixth ignored the subject. The seventh resumed discussion on the subject and while urging that "Government should conciliate Indian public opinion and encourage and qualify the Indians to defend their homes and Government," demanded a certain relaxation of the rules under the Arms Act, the organisation, throughout the more warlike races of the Empire of a system of Militia Service, and the establishment of Military Colleges and of a system of Volunteering. The abnormal increase of military expenditure in spite of these prayers and protests was made the ground by the eighth Congress for a demand that England should share a portion of this expenditure with India. The ninth Congress turned its attention to a social aspect of the question, namely prostitution and contagious disease in Indian Cantonments, and this was confirmed by the tenth session. In 1894, the Welby Commission was appointed and was to consider the question of apportionment of military expenditure between England and India. The eleventh and twelfth sessions passed over the subject but the thirteenth reverted to it on account of the Frontier policy adopted by Government and asked that the expenditure necessitated by it should be shared by England. The fourteenth session followed suit. The fifteenth Congress touched a new aspect of the matter and pointed out that inasmuch as it was thought prudent and safe to withdraw large bodies of troops outside India, the cost of 20,000 British troops be borne by the British Government. The Frontier emergency having passed, the Congress harked back to the question of a Military College at its 16th session. With this the 19th century closed, Queen Victoria passed away in 1901, a new sovereign (King Edward VII) ascended the throne, but India's military woes remained as ever before. In 1902 at its 17th session, the Congress demanded a division of expenditure between England and India on the ground urged at the 15th session. Things soon became more concrete. The Welby Commission of 1894 had reported and the small relief given to India was more than compensated by a fresh burden of £7,86,000 per annum imposed on the country by an increase in the pay of the British soldier. This was the subject of protest at the 18th session.

Moreover it appeared at the time that more British troops were to be saddled on India,—and this, after the Boer War and the operations in China which had drawn lots of troops from India had conclusively shown that it was quite safe and prudent to withdraw them outside the Statutory limits of British India. The 19th session took a comprehensive view of the situation and recalling how the Army Amalgamation Scheme of 1859 had worked hardship on India, attacked the Military policy of Britain in India as really an Imperial policy for which England must pay its quota, especially in view of the fact that the British troops in India, forming as they did an Imperial garrison, amounted to a third of the whole British Army. Lord Curzon's forward policy in Tibet was by this time in operation though he had described his Tibetan expedition as a "political mission" and incurred expenditure thereon without the express sanction of Parliament as was required by the Statute of 1858, under which Indian Revenues should not be spent without such sanction outside the Statutory limits of British India, except to repel foreign aggression. Now in the year 1935 we see the Indian Reform Act validating this deviation from an age-long law. The 20th Congress protested against this act of Lord Curzon's and also pointed out how the military expenditure was growing and becoming unbearable on account of Lord Kitchener's army reorganization scheme at an additional cost of £ 10 millions. Towards the end of Lord Curzon's renewed term of office—1905, acute differences arose between him and Lord Kitchener on the question of Civil Control over the Military, the former upholding it, the latter upsetting it.

The Congress at its 21st session held at Benares in 1905 protested against any change in the prevailing policy which ensured the supremacy of Civil Control over the Military authorities, and drew attention once again to the question of military policy in India being dictated by British policy in the East. It further emphasised the fact that such Civil Control could not be exercised except by representatives of the tax-payer. In 1906, in the midst of the new forces of National resurgence, this hardy annual was not given the go-bye and it was pointed out that within twenty years the military expenditure had nearly doubled from 17 crores to 32 crores a year and that during a period which synchronised with the most disastrous famines that ever raged in India causing no less than 11 million deaths for want of food.

In 1908 the Congress emphatically protested against a fresh burden of £300,000 which the British War Office had imposed on the Indian Exchequer on the recommendation of the Home Committee and urged upon the British Government the necessity of revising the Army Amalgamation Scheme of 1859 and the desirability of laying down a fair and reasonable principle which should free the Indian Exchequer from unjust exactions of this character. In 1909 and 1910 the annually growing military expenditure was commented upon. In 1912 and 1913 at the 27th and 28th sessions, resolutions on the injustice of keeping the higher ranks of the Army closed against Indians were again passed.

In 1914, the Congress repeated its demand that the higher ranks of the Army should be thrown open to Indians and that Military Schools and Colleges should be established and Indians should be allowed to volunteer. His Royal Highness the Duke of Connaught had urged the first two points. Lord Kitchener, it was said, was in favour of admitting Indians as far as Majors and it was fondly hoped that the King would announce this in 1911. Indians were in no way debarred from volunteering in those days and when the question was first raised in the earlier years of the Congress, Mr. S. B. Sankaram declared that he was a volunteer. It is of interest to note that Mr. B. N. Sarma who became in 1920 a member of the Viceroy's Executive Council was himself a volunteer. But in 1898, the Indian Volunteers' names were taken off and in 1914, only Indian Christians were allowed to volunteer. A partial reparation for the great damage done to Indian name and character in the military sphere was made in 1917 when the racial bar against the admission of Indians to the commissioned ranks of the Army was removed and nine Indians were appointed to such ranks. The Congress of 1917 (Calcutta) expressed its satisfaction over the matter and urged the formation of Cadet Corps for young men between 16 and 18 years of age.

Legal and Judicial Problems

The Congress, dominated as it doubtless was from its earliest days by men of high legal position and attainments in the country, was naturally punctilious about safeguarding the legal rights of the people. Neither popular experiences nor bureaucratic repression advanced far enough to compel the realization that all legal forms and procedure are only for normal times and for submissive subjects. When once the subjects of the State become conscious of the rights that legal forms are designed to secure to them, that is, when the spacious life incidental to a nascent nationalism begins to dawn upon a country or community, the hollowness of those forms and that procedure at once will become apparent. So did it when the Government having introduced the system of trial by Jury in all its fulness, thought fit to make an innovation in 1872 in the system of such trials, by depriving the verdicts of Juries of all finality and vesting in Sessions Judges and High Courts powers of setting aside verdicts of acquittal. The very second Congress (Calcutta, 1886) declared such an innovation injurious and asked for its immediate withdrawal and subsequently protested against further reactionary changes proposed in the system, and later Congresses repeated the request from time to time but without effect until even to-day.

Certainly more important than the curtailment of the powers of Juries, was the combination of the Judicial with the Executive functions which made the same authorities, prosecutor, judge and jury—all rolled up into one.

The movement for this reform in British India dates from the time of Raja Rammohan Roy, who died in England over eighty years ago after he had given evidence before a Parliamentary Committee, and who placed a memorandum, as we have already said, before the Parliament on this amongst other questions. It is interesting to recall that one of the reforms which he advocated was the separation of Judicial from Executive functions, for which the Indian National Congress and the All-India Muslim League have been pleading in vain. Incidentally, the history of this question illustrates, about as well as anything can do, how unfavourable are existing conditions for the introduction of even much needed reforms. Among others, the Marquis of Dufferin as Governor-General, Viscount Cross and the Earl of Kimberley as Secretaries of State, and Sir Harvey Adamson as Home Member of the Government of India acknowledged at different times the soundness of the Congress proposal, and the last-named officer promised on behalf of Government in 1908 that it would be tried as an experimental measure. But Judicial and Executive duties are still combined in one and the same officer. A band of devoted workers, of whom Mr. Dadabhai Naoroji was the most prominent, took up the cause of reform after Rammohan Roy, and associations were formed for the purpose in Bengal, Bombay and Madras. Of these, mention may be made in particular of the Bengal National League. With the spread of education the movement gained in volume and momentum, and the Indian National Congress took up the subject in 1885.

The second Congress opined that a complete separation of Executive from Judicial functions was an urgent necessity. The third called for this reform even though this should involve some extra expenditure. By the next year, this subject as well as the Jury question came to be bundled together and were perilously near finding a place in the omnibus resolution. The Congress repeated however this resolution year after year to the point of feeling, in 1893, that the combination of the two functions constituted "one of the gravest stigmas on British Rule in India, one fraught with incalculable oppression to all classes of the community throughout the country," and the Congress expressed its sense of "hopelessness of any other redress" and "humbly entreated the Secretary of State to order the immediate appointment in each Province of Committees to prepare suitable schemes in this behalf." How innocent the Congress was, rather how desperate it must have felt, to believe that a Government that would not initiate a reform, would appoint a Committee to work out all the necessary details for its initiation! This shows the void that was already beginning to appear in Congressmen's minds and before Congressmen's vision. Only a year later (1894) the Congress was able to quote the admission of its contentions by two former Secretaries of State (Lord Kimberley and Lord Cross). What matters really is admission by men in office and not those who are out of it. Agitation however continued in this behalf and the late Mr. Man Mohan Ghose made this question the subject of his special study. His death in 1896 was lamented by the 12th Congress which noted with satisfaction the support of public opinion both in England and in India which the question had received. Further support came in the year 1899 in the form of a petition presented to the Secretary of State-in-Council to effect the much-needed separation, by a body of eminent men like Lord Hobhouse, Sir Richard Garth, Sir Richard Couch, Sir Charles Sargent, Sir W. Markby, Sir John Budd Phear, Sir John Scott, Sir Roland K. Wilson. all Judges of eminence, Mr. Herebert. J. Reynolds and Sir William Wedderburn. In 1901, the Congress found matters had progressed further and that the question was under the consideration of the Government of India. But it was not till 1908 that any tangible progress was made, for in that year the Congress recorded its satisfaction that the proposal had received the sanction of the Government of Bengal in some definite shape for the Province of Bengal, but before 12 months elapsed, the Congress recognised its disappointment in that no effective steps had been taken in that direction and the same disappointment was repeated at two successive Congresses.

While the chronic sores of abridged Jury powers, and combined Judicial and Executive functions were still festering and showed no signs of improvement, new ulcers broke out in the body politic in 1897 which brought to light Regulation III of 1818 (Bengal) II of 1819 (Madras) and XXV of 1827 (Bombay) under which anybody could be deported without trial. This was applied to the Sirdars Natu who by the time the Congress of 1897 met had been imprisoned for over 5 months. Congress was aghast because a certain notification which even these Regulations required was not made before the imprisonment.

The year 1897 was a reactionary year in every sense. Lokamanya Tilak was convicted for sedition for publishing matter of which he was not the author. Punitive Police was quartered on Poona and the Law of Sedition 124 (a) and of spreading false alarms (505) was sought to be amended so as to make the sections even more stringent. The Congress duly protested against these invasions of popular rights and Surendra Nath Banerjea made one of his characteristic speeches which may be quoted for the eloquence of its expression:—

> "We regard the quartering of the Punitive Police at Poona as a mistake. We regard the imprisonment of Mr. Tilak and of the Poona Editors as a still greater mistake. For Mr. Tilak my heart is full of sympathy, my feelings go forth to him in his prison-house. A Nation is in tears. Englishmen have won for themselves the Magna Carta and the Habeas Corpus. The principles which underlie those concessions are embalmed in their glorious constitution. The constitution, I have no hesitation in saying, is ours by birthright. Born British subjects, we are entitled to the privileges of British subjects. Who will filch away these rights from us? We are resolved and this Congress will take the pledge, you and I will enter into a 'Solemn League and Covenant.' Let it go forth from this hall, let it impregnate the public mind of India. We are resolved, by every constitutional means that may be available to us, to assert under the Providence of God our rights as British subjects, not the least important of which is the inestimable right of personal liberty."

Permanent Settlement, Water-Cess, Poverty and Famines

India being predominantly an agricultural country, it is but to be expected that the Congress should have given its early if not first attention to the hardships caused to the ryots by the periodical revision of settlements, leading to ever increasing assessment. Accordingly the 4th session at Allahabad (1888) referred the matter to the standing committees and asked them to report to the Congress in 1889. Babu Baikunta Nath Sen dealt with the question in 1889 and pointed out that a famine in 1860 had led to a Commission which reported in favour of Permanent Settlement and this was approved of by the Secretary of State in a despatch in 1862. Sometimes the increase in assessment exceeded the total fresh produce of the village, as in one case dealt with by Mr. Colvin (later Sir Auckland Colvin). Dr. Besant gives the following interesting extract in her book, dealing with the allied subject:—

> "There is the same amount of water in the pot, but there are now six holes through which it runs out, when before there was but one."
>
> "We had our cattle in plenty, lots of grazing free and salt to keep them healthy; now the land is all taken up by the Forest Department and we have no grazing ground, and if the starving herds stray where there is food, they are run into the pound and we are fined."
>
> "We had plenty of wood for our houses, for our ploughs and for every agricultural purpose; now it is all under the lock and key of the Forest Department, and if we touch it without leave we are run in and if we want a stick we have a week's running about from one official to another before we get it, and we have to pay, pay, pay. We had arms, and we could shoot or destroy the wild beasts that ravage our crops, but now we have an Arms Act that allows a basketful of arms to every Negro rascal who lands on our shores, but takes good care that we poor cultivators, who need them to protect our subsistence from wild animals, are practically debarred from any."

In 1892 the Congress pleaded for fixity and permanence to the Land Revenue demand so as to permit "capital and labour to combine to develop the agriculture of the country" and urged the establishment of Agricultural Banks. Next year the Congress demanded the fulfilment of the pledges given by the Secretary of State in his despatches of 1862 and 1865 for a Permanent Settlement. In 1896 the Congress adopting the usual temporizing policy prayed for at least an interval of sixty years from one revision to another. On the 22nd December, 1900 the Government of India published a Resolution on the subject through its Revenue and Agricultural Department and the Congress demanded the publication of the Provincial Governments' views on paragraph 4 thereof. In 1903 the Congress went further and sought judicial and legislative restrictions on over-assessments. In 1906, the Congress contrasted the policy enunciated by Lord Canning in 1862 and by Lord Ripon in 1882, advocating a limitation of the State demand on land, with the policy of Lord Curzon announced in his Resolution of 1902, and protested against the view that Land Revenue is not a tax but is in the nature of rent; and with the repetition of a like resolution on another occasion in 1908, the Congress virtually gave up the subject in despair.

We may appropriately refer to the allied topics of water-cess, famine and its remedies. The Congress dealt with the question of water-cess but once, and that in 1894 in Madras, in which year the cess was raised by executive orders from Rs. 4 to 5 per acre. These ever increasing taxes and cesses were partly at the root of the ever recurring famines of recent times. The famine conditions of 1896 gave occasion to the Congress to review the economic policy of Government and charge them with extravagance in Military expenditure and put down the famines to excessive taxation and over-assessment. The neglect of indigenous and local arts and industries which had practically been extinguished was put down as another cause. The Government was called upon to redeem its pledges to constitute a Famine Insurance Fund. Permanent Settlement, Agricultural Banks and Technical Schools were advocated as the real remedies. Soon after, a Famine Commission was appointed. In the meantime generous help came in aid of famine from Britain and the U.S.A. and the Congress resolved to send a £1,000 to the Lord Mayor of London to put up a Memorial in some conspicuous part of London expressing India's gratitude for help rendered. This was in 1898. The Congress nevertheless did not lose sight of the real remedies all along advocated by it for famines and urged on Government once again in 1899 to stop the drain of wealth and curtail public expenditure, to moderate taxes and develop local and indigenous industries. A wider view of affairs was taken next year and a demand was made for an enquiry into the economic condition of the people of India. We no more hear of the subject, the outlook of the Congress having considerably changed in the later years of its career.

Forest Laws

The havoc done by the Forest Laws is not sufficiently appreciated. They vied only with Land Revenue assessments and the Salt Tax in burdening the people with fetters they could not bear. With a single stroke of the pen, as Mr. Paul Peter Pillai pointed out at Nagpur in 1891, Government had extinguished the immemorial communal rights of the ryot, and village society had thus been revolutionized. There is little doubt that these laws have served, as Dr. Besant said, to alienate the peasantry from British Rule more than any other thing. In one district, N. Arcot, 3,00,000 cattle perished in nine months in 1891. The best gifts of Nature to the ryot were denied to him. "Your land is on the hills but you cannot use the forest produce thereon, such as bush and scrub, and the very leaves of the trees grown by you, are not yours."

An earnest appeal was made in 1892-93 to the Government of India to investigate the hardships created by the Forest Laws, particularly in Peninsular India and the hilly tracts of the Punjab. The rules made by the Punjab Government were particularly cruel and unjust—"very arbitrary and unworthy of a civilized Government" as Pandit Meghan Ram pointed out at the ninth session. "An owner or occupant of land was made liable for an accidental fire caused by any one on his land and might, according to the rules, be treated as if he had been guilty of the infraction of the Rules." The hill men to whom the hill grass and wood was their very life and the life of their cattle were prevented from taking them. They could not warm themselves by kindling a forest fire. This agitation resulted in a Circular Resolution No. 2/F, dated 20th October, 1894 by the Government of India in which they had enunciated the generous principle of "subordinating fiscal interest to the needs and agricultural interests of the ryot population in the management of Forests."

The Congress urged that "in forests falling under classes 3 and 4, fuel grazing concession, fodder, small timber for building houses and making agricultural implements, edible forest products etc., may be granted free of charge in all cases under suitable restrictions and that, in any case, sufficient margin should be left in administering Forest Laws and fixing forest boundaries so as not to molest or annoy the agricultural population in the enjoyment of their communal rights." The 11th and 14th Congresses emphasised the view that Forest Laws were meant not as sources of revenue but only to conserve the forests and complained against the rules which worked a great hardship on the people. We no more hear of forests in the Congresses held after the year 1899 except as part of omnibus resolutions.

A new grievance added to existing ones diverted men's minds from the older ones to which they became accustomed and the dawn of the 20th century brought to the fore problems altogether of a different character. Moreover the Boer War and the Russo-Japanese War must have changed the outlook of Congressmen and shifted their attention from forests and water-courses, from Salt and Abkari to the larger questions of Nationalism and Self-Government.

Commerce and Industry

The salient points of the Indian problem under the British occurred to the minds of the earlier politicians like flashes of light which do not sustainedly brighten the path of the political traveller. That Indian interests were subordinated to those of Lancashire was recognised, that the village crafts and arts were neglected, if not positively ruined, was equally realized. R. P. Karandikar, who with Kelkar and Khaparde formed a trio of ardent and faithful followers of Lokamanya Tilak, speaking of the problem of Primary Education at the 20th Congress (Bombay, 1904), quoted Mr. Arthur Balfour's speech on Ireland, pointing out how,

> "One by one, each of her nascent industries was either strangled at its birth or handed over gagged and bound to the jealous custody of the rival interests in England, until at last every fountain of wealth was hermetically sealed so that the whole Nation was thrown on the land."

Even more interesting and thoughtful was the reply given by a politician comparing the English Rule with the Muslim Rule:—

"The English Rule is the better for security, Education and Railways, but for the wealth of India, the Muslim Rule was better, for the Muslims became Indians and the riches stayed in the country while the English carried the wealth of the country away." The same observation was made by Raja Rampal Singh in sporting language when he stated in 1893 at the ninth Congress that "the English Civilians made India their happy hunting ground."

In 1894 the Congress protested against the Excise duty on the cottons manufactured in British India and put on record its firm conviction that in proposing the Excise duty, "the interests of India have been sacrificed to those of Lancashire." Of course there was always the mentality of submission to a coming reactionary Law and an attempt to mitigate its hardships. In this case, the Congress added that,

> "In case the Excise Bill became law, this Congress earnestly prays that the Government of India will, without delay, seek the sanction of the Secretary of State to exercise the powers which the Bill confers on Government to exempt all cottons from twenties to twenty-fours from the operation of the Act."

At the 11th Congress it was declared that the objection taken by Lancashire to the exemption of Indian yarns below 'twenties' from Excise duty was not well founded. At the famous session of the Congress held in Calcutta under Dadabhai's presidentship in 1906, Pandit Madan Mohan Malaviya laid bare the secret of our failure in regard to our industries:

> "The raw material leaves the country and comes back as manufactured goods; if we were free we would adopt protection as all countries do when Industries are nascent."

Lokamanya Tilak deplored how it was the middle classes that were the greatest consumers of foreign goods. "Self-help, determination and sacrifice," and he, "are needed." With the birth of the Swadeshi spirit, supported by the Boycott Movement of 1906 and succeeding years, India's attention turned towards the resuscitation of Indian industries. In 1910 it fell to the lot of Mr. C. Y. Chintamani,—who was a young man as yet at the time but who gave ample proof of his future eminence,—to move the resolution on Swadeshi at Allahabad and he quoted Ranade, who said:—

> "India had come to be regarded as a plantation of England, growing raw products to be shipped by British agents in British ships, to be worked into fabrics by British skill and capital, and to be re-exported to India by British merchants in India through their British agents."

This Judge of the Bombay High Court who was a great Economist and a leading Social Reformer was the real power for years behind the Congress and was the one source of inspiration to Congressmen on matters economic and industrial.

The village and its perishing wealth of industries and agriculture were not neglected by the Indian politicians. So early as in 1898 Pandit Madan Mohan Malaviya proposed that "Government ought to foster Native industries and Native arts." People had recognized even earlier (1891) that the Forest Laws imposed severe hardships on the villages and revolutionized village society, leading to the destruction of village crafts, and the death of village cattle, 3 lacs of cattle having died in september 1891. Lala Murlidhar speaking in Urdu at the Nagpur Congress (1891) made a fervent appeal to the audience and said:—

"You, you, it seems are content to join with these accursed monsters in fattening on the heart's blood of your brethren (*cries of No. No.*). I say *Yes*: look round: what are all these chandeliers and lamps, and European-made chairs and tables, and smart clothes and hats, and English coats and bonnets and frocks, and silver-mounted canes, and all the luxurious fittings of your houses, but trophies of India's misery, mementoes of India's starvation! Every rupee you have spent on Europe-made articles is a rupee of which you have robbed your poorer brethren, honest handicraftsmen who can now no longer earn a living. Of course I know that it was pure philanthropy which flooded India with English-made goods, and surely, if slowly, killed out every indigenous industry,—pure philanthropy which, to facilitate this, repealed the import duties and flung away three crores a year of a revenue which the rich paid, and to balance this wicked sacrifice raised the Salt Tax, which the poor pay; which is now pressing factory regulations on us to kill, if possible, the one tiny new industrial departure India could boast of. Oh, yes, it is all philanthropy, but the result is that from this cause, amongst others, your brethren are starving. Not 30 years ago wheat sold for 1-½ maunds and gram for 2 maunds for the rupee, for our grain was not exported to foreign lands. Now it is six times as dear, and six times as hard for the poor to fill their bellies, because our philanthropists have conjured up the phantasm of free trade to drain our granaries. Free trade, fair play between nations, how I hate the sham! What fair play in trade can there be between impoverished India and the bloated capitalist England? As well talk of a fair fight between an infant and a srong man—a rabbit and a boa-constrictor. No doubt it is all in accordance with high economic science, but, my friends, remember this,—this, too is starving your brethren."

Pandit Malaviya made a characteristic speech in 1893 at the ninth Congress as follows:—

"Where are the weavers, where are those men who lived by different industries and manufactures, and where are the manufactures which were sent to England and other European countries in very large quantities year after year? All that has become a thing of the past. Every one sitting here is clothed in cloth of British-make—almost every one—and wherever you go, you find British manufactures and British goods staring you in the face. All that is left to the people is to drag out a miserable existence by agricultural operations and make infinitesimal profit out of the little trade left to them. In the matter of the Services, in the matter of trade, our people are not enjoying one-hundredth part of the profit and gain which they used to enjoy fifty years ago. How then is it possible for the country to be happy?"

The importance of the subject is evident from the emphasis that Sir S. Subrahmania Aiyar laid on Village Resuscitation, and the need for loan societies, in 1914, after his retirement from the Bench. The Congress was pressed by Lala Lajpat Rai in 1899 to devote a half-day for the consideration of educational and industrial subjects, and appoint a Committee in that behalf. This was done and as a direct result of their deliberations, we note that the first Industrial Exhibition in Calcutta was held in 1901 and this institution has gone on steadily improving until, in the latter-day developments, the Khaddar and Swadeshi Exhibitions have come to replace the old order of things. Attention was fixed on Industries by the Congress doubtless by the Excise duties on cotton goods levied in 1894 which had evoked a protest then and there against their imposition, and incidentally we learn that even the Governor-General's protest in this behalf was in vain. Not only was no relief granted but Lord Salisbury, it is said, "directed that steps should be taken to protect the British manufactures against the competition of the Indian manufactures." It was not merely an imaginary picture that was drawn of village poverty and the oft repeated theme of 40 millions of people going with a single meal a day, for, Wacha and Mudholkar took care to prove it by quotations from Anglo-Indian Satraps. Did not Sir Charles Elliot say, "half the agrarian population do not know from one year's end to another what it is to have a full meal"? The rise in the Revenue assessment in one sub-district was enhanced in 1891, 66 p.c., in another 99 p.c., and in a third 116 p.c., and in a few villages 300 to 1,500 p.c., while the military expenditure rose also by leaps and bounds.

The German soldier cost Rs. 145—the French Rs. 185 and the English in England Rs. 285, but in India Rs. 775 a year. This expenditure is contrasted with the income per head in England of £42—in France £23—in Germany £18 and in India £1. These were the figures given in 1891. Famines formed the subject of repeated resolutions, and so early as in 1887, a repeal was sought of the Pènal Labour Law.

SWADESHI, BOYCOTT AND 'SWARAJ'

The new spirit that pervaded the country from end to end in the latter half of the first decade of this century had its birth in the Partition of Bengal, although its gestation had been progressing for some years prior to that event under the warmth of Lord Curzon's reactionary rule. The 21st session of the Congress held in the sacred city of Kasi in 1905 lodged its formal protest against the Partition of Bengal and asked for its annulment or modification so as to keep the entire Bengali community under one administration. But the resolution that was passed by this Congress on the represssive measures then enforced was a somewhat circuitous one, for it recorded "its earnest and emphatic protest against the repressive measures which have been adopted in Bengal," and incidentally added an adverbial clause saying "after the people there had been compelled to resort to the boycott of foreign goods as a last protest, and perhaps the only constitutional and effective means left to them of drawing the attention of the British public to the action of the Government of India in persisting in their determination to partition Bengal in utter disregard of the universal prayers and protests of the people." Here it is not clear—nor perhaps was it meant to be clear—whether the Congress approved of the boycott of foreign goods. A kind of academic opinion was expressed to the effect that it was perhaps the only legitimate weapon left to the people. Apparently the Nationalist element had real difficulty in passing a less equivocal resolution, but Lala Lajpat Rai in seconding the one that was passed struck a high note when he said that we must show that we are "no longer beggars and that we are subjects of an Empire where people are struggling to achieve that position which is their right." The courage that appeared wanting in 1905 was soon recovered in 1906. While repeating the formal Resolution on the Partition, the Congress resolved that "having regard to the fact that the people of this country have little or no voice in its administration, and that their representations to the Government do not receive due consideration, this Congress is of opinion that the Boycott movement inaugurated in Bengal by way of protest against the Partition was, and is, legitimate." The Congress later urged the encouragement of indigenous industries even at some sacrifice. There it stopped. The conception of Self-Government did not travel farther than the formulation of certain Reforms comprising simultaneous examinations, expanded Legislative Councils with effective popular representation, and the appointment of Indians to the Council of the Secretary of State as well as the Executive Councils in India. This was all the national aspiration in 1906. The next year witnessed the Surat split, and the Moderate Congress of subsequent years eliminated the subject of Boycott, and adhered to Swadeshi, while the resolutions on Self-Government frankly reduced themselves to an examination of the Minto-Morley Scheme of Reforms. In 1910 there was a change of Viceroyalty and the Congress passed a resolution in 1910 appealing to Lord Hardinge, the new Viceroy, to release the political prisoners in the country. This was repeated in the succeeding year. But in 1914, the Congress that met in Madras made bold to demand that Government should redeem the pledges of Provincial Autonomy given in 1911 and recognize India "as a component part of a federated Empire, in the full and free enjoyment of the rights belonging to that status."

COMMUNAL REPRESENTATION

One is apt to think that communal representation is an idea of recent growth. From the days of Sir Auckland Colvin (1888) Lieutenant-Governor of the North-West Provinces (U.P.), there was an attempt to make out that the Muslims were opposed to the Congress and the position thus created was considered by Hume to be so important as to find a place in his long reply to Sir Auckland. There was no doubt that the success of the first two or three sessions of the Congress upset the mind of the bureaucracy which found its mouthpiece in this famous Lieutenant-Governor. The reaction of such a view on the Muslim community itself was sufficiently quick, and how they must have resented the partonizing attitude of the officials is shown by the fact that at the fourth Congress, held in Allahabad, in the face of the opposition offered by the European elements, Sheik Raza Hussein Khan, in supporting the election of Mr. Yule as President of the year's session, produced a Fatwa, supporting the Congress, from the spiritual leader of the Sunni community of Lucknow and declared that "it is not the Muslims but their official masters who were opposed to the Congress." Those acquainted with the recent Fatwas in 1921 onwards would welcome this fact doubtless.

It was really during the time of Lord Minto that the idea of communal representation took shape. Earlier of course had Curzon kindled deliberately this baneful communal consciousness in partitioning Bengal and carving out Eastern Bengal and Assam as a separate Province with a Muslim majority. Although Lord Minto was sent to ease the horse which Lord Curzon had ridden for seven long years almost to the point of death, still, the saddle of communal separateness on which Curzon had been riding was left intact on the animal's back. Minto's scheme of Reforms provided for separate electorates for Muslims and yet their rights to vote in the joint electorates were left intact. The narrow-minded politicians pointed out that the Hindu Minorties in East Bengal and Assam and the Punjab were not given a like privilege, but this was really going off the track. What was more egregious was the different franchises set up for the different communities. To become a voter, the Muslim had to pay Income-tax on Rs. 3,000 a year, while the non-Muslims had to pay on three lakhs a year. It was enough for the Muslim graduate to have a standing of three years to become a voter, while the non-Muslim was required to have a thirty years' standing. Three thousands against three lakhs of income, and three years against thirty years of standing! We hear occasionally echoes of a like demand when, in the absence of universal adult franchise, the Muslims demand varying standards of franchise for the two communities so as to maintain the proper ratios amongst the voters.

Now, the year 1910 found a critical state of affairs and Sir. W. Wedderburn presided over the Congress. The President intended holding a conference between Hindus and Muslims with a view to bringing about communal harmony. Separate electorates were just then proposed to be introduced in respect of Municipalities and Local Boards as well. In U.P. where there were none such, it was found that the joint electorates with the Muslims forming but a seventh of the population returned 189 Muslims and 445 Hindus to the District Boards, and 310 Muslims and 562 Hindus to the Municipalities and even a reactionary like Sir John Hewett, Lieutenant-Governor, U.P. was against disturbing the amicable relations of the two communities in the Province. Mr. Jinnah of course deprecated the extension of separate electorates to Local Bodies. The 'Burn' Circular in favour of Communal representation in Local Bodies advocated separate electorates for Muslims, while also allowing them to vote in mixed electorates as this would be helpful in maintaining friendly relations between the two great communities. "I will only say," added Bishan Narayan Dhar, presiding over the 26th Session, (Calcutta, 1911), "that this solicitude for promoting our unity is rather a heavy draft upon our credulity." He pointed out how "when, under the advice of Sir W. Wedderburn and H. H. the Aga Khan, the representatives of the two communities were about to meet at Allahabad a year ago, with the object of reconciling their differences, an Anglo-Indian paper which is believed to be an organ of the Civil Service, remarked: 'Why do these men want to unite the two communities, if it is not to unite them against the Government?' This one remark throws a ghastly light upon the political situation in India."

But shortly afterwards the world conditions underwent a certain change. The Balkans which had for over a century or two been the cockpit of Europe, once again furnished the arena for a fresh outbreak of hostilities and Nawab Syed Mahommed Bahadur, who presided over the Karachi Session of the Congress in 1913, drew attention to the "subversion of the Ottoman Empire in Europe and the strangling of Persia." He expressed the grief with which all the Muslims had felt the blow to the Turkish Empire. He concluded with an earnest plea that Hindus and Muslims should clasp hands and work for the Motherland. This reminds us of the Khilafat Movement of 1921 and its repercussions on the Hindu-Muslim relations in India. 'The Sick Man of Europe' (as Turkey was termed in the 19th century) has all along played a notable part in shaping the course of Indian politics. It was under these conditions that at the Karachi Congress (1913) the Hindus and the Muslims closed their ranks and the Congress "placed on record its appreciation of the adoption by the All-India Muslim League of the idea of Self-Government for India within the British Empire," and endorsed the plea of that body for harmonious co-operation between the two communities. The Congress further welcomed "the hope expressed by the League that the leaders of the different communities would make every endeavour to find a *modus operandi* for joint and concerted action on all questions of national good and earnestly appealed to all sections to help the object they had at heart."

The exaltation of spirit of Congressmen at the time was evident in the exuberant language employed by the speakers on the Resolution at Karachi in 1913, and we quote below from Bhupendra Nath Basu's speech:—"Hindus and Muslims must concentrate their attention on the one united ideal, for the India of to-day is not the India of the Hindu or the Muslim, nor of the Anglo-Indian, much less of the European, but the India in which all have a share. If there have been misunderstandings in the past, let us forget them. The India of the future will be a stronger, nobler, greater, higher, aye, and a brighter India than was realized by Asoka in the plenitude of his power, a better India than was revealed to Akbar in the wildest of his visions." Mr. Wacha said that the Congress had entered on a new Nativity and with the New Star they would achieve new success. Communal representation, however, came to stay.

Once the sore having started, it continued to be festering. If the Hindus had quietly and willingly conceded what the Muslims wanted, the problem would have been solved earlier. Doubtless it is true that appetite grows with eating, but equally true is it that eating and more eating leads to satiety. The Minto-Morley scheme of communal representation was forced on the country. People were not consulted on the matter. So when in 1916 a new dole of Reforms was being contemplated, India thought that a concordat should be brought into existence, and for this purpose the representatives of the Congress and the Muslim League met in the Indian Association rooms of Calcutta in November, 1916 to carry out the behests of the Congress in 1915 and to hammer out a scheme of representation based upon mutual understanding. Just then the Muslim League had adopted Self-Government as its object. The principle of self-determination was in the air. The War itself was being waged for its application to the smaller and the backward nationalities. The Calcutta deliberations were therefore undertaken and conducted in a suitable atmosphere. But the elders on the Congress side were slow to make an offer. It was therefore left to the younger men—perhaps the youngest man present there—to take the initiative. The Hindus and the Muslims were the two eyes of India, as Sir Syed Ahmed had said, and either without the other would deface the Mother's countenance. A spirit of give and take soon prevailed. A minimum of 15 per cent. representation in Councils was agreed to in all Provinces whose population fell short of the percentage. There remained only the Punjab and Bengal. As usual they were hard nuts to crack, but cracked they were at the Lucknow Congress of 1916, and the formula arrived at at Lucknow that December, was accepted by Mr. Montagu *en bloc* and incorporated in the Montagu-Chelmsford Scheme. The consciousness of a friendly concession made by a rival community is apt to be a greater power in bringing about amicable relations than the thought that any community owed its protection to the intervention of a third party. But it must be noted that separate communal electorates came to stay. The communal and the general electorates became exclusive, and equally exclusive was the right to stand as candidates.

Indians Abroad

While the fate of Indians in India was bad enough, that of Indians in South Africa was growing from bad to worse. In 1896, it was ruled that the Indentured emigrants in Natal, South Africa, should on the termination of the term of indenture, either renew their slavery, *i.e.*, renew their indenture for labour, or pay a poll tax amounting to half their annual earnings. It is interesting to recall a remark of Dr. Moonje in this connection, after his return from South Africa about 1903 where he had gone in connection with an Ambulance Corps in the Boer War, namely, "Our rulers do not believe that we are men." It was on the same question that Mr. B. N. Sarma warned England that there could not be, in the Empire, a permanent racial supremacy, one race dominating another. "If we are true to ourselves," said he at the 21st Congress, (Benares, 1905), "then the race that has produced the greatest philosophers, the greatest statesmen and the greatest warriors, shall not crouch for this or that favour at the hands of other people."

Mr. Madanjit was the man who for long years brought up the South African question before the Indian Congress. There were doubtless Indian friends who were visiting South Africa from time to time and bringing first hand information to the Indian people, but he was carrying on his mission from year to year. With his orange robes and short stature and tall stick, he was not to be missed in the Congress and his recent death at a ripe old age has removed a familiar figure from the National Assembly. The first protest against the South African disabilities really began in 1894 when the President moved a Resolution asking that the Bill of the Colonial Government disenfranchising Indians be vetoed. Thereafter at Congress after Congress, South Africa figured as an important subject and it was pointed out year after year "how we were not permitted there to travel without a pass, not allowed to walk about in the night after 9 P.M., how we were consigned to locations where refuse was shot in Transvaal, how we were denied admission to the first and 2nd classes on Railways, driven out of tramcars and pushed off footpaths, kept out of hotels, and refused the benefit of public parks, and how we were spat upon, hissed, cursed, abused and subjected to a variety of other indignities which no human being could patiently bear."

By 1898 three additional disabling Acts had been passed and by that time Gandhi had begun his famous agitation. The great pity was that Lord Elgin, the Viceroy, consented to the Natal Law being passed while the Secretary of State at the time, Lord George Hamilton, was content to characterize us as "nation of savages." "The incorporation of the former Boer Republics in the British

Dominions in 1900" was referred to by the 16th session (1900) as obviating the one difficulty Government had to contend against in dealing with the independent Boers, and the Congress urged that the Immigration Restrictions in Natal and the Dealer's Licences Acts of the Colony should be done away with. It was at the 17th Congress (Calcutta, 1901), that Gandhi moved a resolution on South Africa as "a petitioner on behalf of the hundred thousand British Indians in South Africa." A deputation was to wait in 1902 on the Secretary of State in regard to the subject but nothing came out of it and the Congress repeated its resolutions in 1903 and 1904. The Congress drew attention to the statement made in responsible quarters that "one of the declared causes of the recent Boer War was the treatment meted out to Indian Subjects of the King-Emperor by the Republic, and demanded that justice and equal treatment be secured to the Indian settlers." The position became worse by 1905 and the Congress protested that disabilities not enforced under the Boer Rule should have been enforced under the British Rule, and asked for the prohibition of Indentured Labour as well as for other retaliatory measures. It is gratifying to note that Government disallowed 'for the present' the ordinance in the Transvaal, but in 1906, a Constitution having been granted to South Africa, says the Resolution, there were clear apprehensions of its renewal. There was no relief even in 1908, and as the New South African Constitution was just then being implemented, the Congress urged that Indian interests should be simultaneously secured. At the 23rd Congress held in 1908 in Madras, Mr. Mushir Hasan Kidwai moved the resolution expressing the indignation of the Congress at "the harsh, humiliating and cruel treatment to which British Indians, even of the highest respectability and position, have been subjected by the British Colonies in South Africa," and giving a warning that such treatment was likely to result in "great injury to the best interests of the British Empire."

By 1909, it was found that the endless representations that had been made proved unavailing and Gokhale in moving the resolutions of the year described the breaches of faith of the authorities and the long patient struggle of the Indians led by Gandhi. The time had come for effective action and the great Passive Resistance struggle was inaugurated. "What is the passive resistance struggle?" asks Gokhale, and he gives the answer: "It is essentially defensive in its nature and it fights with moral and spiritual weapons. A passive resister resists tyranny by spiritual weapons. A passive resister resists tyranny by undergoing sufferings in his own person. He pits soul force against brute force; he pits the divine in man against the brute in man; he pits suffering against oppression; he pits conscience against might; he pits faith against injustice, right against wrong." A fund was called for and Rs. 18,000 was subscribed on the spot. Besides this, Ratan J. Tata, the second son of Sir Jamshedjee Tata gave a sum of Rs. 25,000 to relieve suffering in South Africa for which the 24th Congress 1909 (Lahore) thanked him publicly. By the next session of the Congress (Allahabad, 1910), the Passive Resistance struggle was at its height and the Congress expressed "its great admiration of the intense patriotism, courage and self-sacrifice of the Indians in the Transvaal, who, heroically suffering persecution in the interests of their countrymen, are carrying on their peaceful and selfless struggle for elementary civil rights against heavy and overwhelming odds." The 27th session (1911) of the Congress however met under more auspicious circumstances, for it could "cordially congratulate Mr. Gandhi and the Transvaal Indian Community upon the repeal of the Anti-Asiatic Legislation of the Province, regarding Registration and immigration." But the Congress had passed this resolution "anticipating the forthcoming legislation of the provisional settlement recently arrived at." It was discovered however next year (1913) that it had still to protest against the provisions of the Immigration Act in that they violated the promises made by the South Africa Union, and respectfully urged the Crown to veto the Act. Lord Hardinge was then the Viceroy and he took up a strong attitude in the matter and, to strengthen his hands, the Karachi Congress repeated its resolution in 1913 asking for the abolition of Indentured Labour. Soon after, it was abolished and the Congress placed on record its gratitude to Lord Hardinge for the partial settlement of the South African question, although it had to revert to the question in 1916 and 1917. The Karachi Session (1913) had also passed a vote of "admiration for the heroic endeavours of Mr. Gandhi and his followers, and their unparalleled sacrifice in their struggle for the maintenance of the self-respect of India and the redress of Indian grievances."

This was the real introduction of Mr. Gandhi to India, if one may say so, for he left South Africa soon after the Great War had broken out in August, 1914, and has been in India since 1915 carrying out his 'Experiments with Truth,' and his Satyagraha Campaign in Champaran, Kaira, Borsad, Bardoli and the whole of India, with results which are now well-known and on which we shall have occasion to dwell in the appropriate chapters.

An interesting problem was created for India by a particular clause of the Canadian Privy Council's order No. 920 known as the "Continuous Journey Clause," which formed the subject of a protest by the Congress at its 28th session (Karachi, 1913), on the ground that

"The order in question has practically the effect of preventing any Indian, not already settled there (in Canada), from going to Canada, inasmuch as there is no direct steamship service between the two countries and the steamship Companies refuse through booking, and further subjects the present Indian settlers in Canada to great hardship by precluding them from bringing over their wives and children. This Congress therefore urges upon the Imperial Government the necessity of securing the repeal of the said Continuous Journey Regulation."

When the Great War broke out soon after, an interesting incident which has become a romantic episode in modern Indian history, happened, which the coming generations should not fail to know. In order to challenge this clause, one Sikh gentleman, named Baba Gurudutt Singh hired a steamer called the *Komagatamaru* and took 600 Sikhs in it to Canada by making a continuous voyage, without the usual halts at Hongkong or Tokyo.

The steamship—*Komagatamaru*—was of course not allowed to land her passengers in Canada and had to return to India. On her return, the passengers were directed to go from Budge Budge, where they landed, to the Punjab and prohibited from going anywhere they liked. They were, however, unwilling to board the train for the Punjab, unless they were first allowed to make a representation to Government about the injustice of such an order and the loss that they would suffer thereby. They preferred to be arrested under a warrant. The subsequent story of the *Komagatamaru* men among whom was Prof. Mansukhani (now Swami Govindanand of Sindh), how a riot took place, how several were shot and imprisoned, how Gurudutt Singh was a fugitive for seven or eight years, wandering from place to place in Orissa, the Deccan, Gwalior State, Rajputana, Kathiawar and Sindh up to 1918, how after 1918 he went to Bombay and became the manager of a Ship-building Company at Mahal Bandar outside the Town, under the name of Valdraja, how in his exile he saw Gandhi (in November, 1921) who advised him to surrender himself, which he did, and how Government imprisoned him and he was released from the Lahore Jail on February 28, 1922 on the expiry of the term of the Ordinance under which he was imprisoned, do not really fall within the scope of this book.

Salt

The question of Salt Tax has, by virtue of the recent Salt Satyagraha movement of 1930, acquired a peculiar importance in Indian politics. Knowing as we do the genesis of the tax and the recommendations made by the Salt Commission of 1836, we cannot but feel a certain surprise that the grounds on which the tax was attacked in 1888 by the Congress were, not that it was iniquitous and meant to assist British Shipping industry and British export trade, but that it was recently enhanced and as such involved "a perceptible increase to the burthens of the poorer classes, as also the partial absorption, in a time of peace and plenty, of the only Financial Reserve of the Empire." In 1890 the Congress again demanded only the remission of the recent enhancement, not the abolition of the tax altogether. On eight other occasions did the Congress virtually repeat this prayer, only on one occasion it asked for the restoration of the rate of 1868 and on another the rate of 1888, and the last time it dealt with the question (1902), the Congress cited the causation of disease by insufficient salt consumption as an additional ground. Thereafter 'Salt' was promoted from the Congress to the Councils and became the special concern of Mr. Gokhale.

Drink and Prostitution

Purity claimed its own share of attention from the

Congress. The serious increase in the consumption of liquors led to a demand for a policy promoting sobriety and temperance. Messrs. Caine and Smith brought up the question before the House of Commons which passed a Resolution in this behalf in 1889 and the Congress urged that it be given effect to. In 1890 the Congress expressed its pleasure at "the increase in the import duty on spirits, the taxation imposed upon Indian-brewed malt liquors, the decision of the Bengal Government to abolish the out-still system and the closing of over 7,000 liquor shops by the Madras Government in 1889—90." But all the Provinces had not acted up to the instructions of the Despatch of the Government of India that 'efforts should be made to ascertain the existence of local public sentiment and that a reasonable amount of deference should be paid to such opinion when ascertained." For a decade the Congress did not revert to the question. It was only in 1900 that the Congress attributed the growing consumption of liquors to their cheap supply and appealed to Government "to pass measures like the Maine Liquor Law of America and Sir Wilfrid Lawson's Permissive Bill or the Local Option Act and impose an additional tax upon intoxicants not intended to be used as medicine." It is interesting to note Kumar M. N. Choudhuri quoting at this Congress, Keshab Chandra Sen's complaint that the British Government had brought Shakespeare and Milton to them, but also brandy bottles.

The Excise Commission of 1883 having shown great increase of drunkenness among the labouring classes, the Congress pointed out that the evil would defeat the benevolent intentions of Government to help the growth of Indian arts and industries.

An allied subject relating to Social Reform was the

eradication of State-regulated prostitution. It is well known that Government procured women for soldiers both when they were in camps as well as when they were on the move. These things when recognized for the first time looked horrible, but constant touch with them blunts the edge of resentment. The fourth session of the Congress (1888, Allahabad), under the presidency of Mr. Yule, offered co-operation with India's well-wishers in England who were putting forth exertions "for the total abrogation of laws and rules relating to the regulation of prostitution by the State in India." Captain Banon in a strong speech moved the resolution and Captain Hearsay, seconding, pointed out that over 2,000 Indian women were procured by Government "for the hideous purpose alluded to" and that this provision encouraged the boy-soldiers to loose living. The 8th Congress (1892, Allahabad) thanked the House of Commons for its vigilance "in regard to the recent purity legislation by the Government in India," and protested against "all State-regulated immorality in India."

Next year, the Parliamentary members of the India Office Committee submitted a Report on the subject of the Rules, Orders and Practices in Indian Cantonments with regard to prostitution and contagious diseases. The Congress declared that the practices and system in vogue "did not accord with the plain meaning and intention of the Resolution of the House of Commons on 5th June, 1888," and asked for "express legislation" to stop these malpractices.

WOMEN AND THE DEPRESSED CLASSES

The visit of Mr. Montagu to India brought to the fore the claims of women in respect of civic rights and it is astonishing to see how readily was conceded to the fair sex full equality of position with men in this country.

The Calcutta Congress of 1917 expressed "the opinion that the same tests be applied to women as to men in regard to the franchise and the eligibility to all elective bodies concerned with Local Government and Education." On the allied question of the Depressed Classes, which too claimed the nation's attention as forming an important factor in national reconstruction, the same Congress accepted a liberal proposition and urged

> "Upon the people of India the necessity, justice and righteousness of removing all disabilities imposed by custom upon the depressed classes, the disabilities being of a most vexatious and oppressive character, subjecting those classes to considerable hardship and inconvenience."

MISCELLANEOUS

Various miscellaneous subjects engaged the attention of the Congress from time to time during this period. The chief subject of interest was Education in its several aspects, Primary, University, Research and Technical. Provincial Finance as well as Imperial, Silver Duties, Income-tax, and Exchange Compensation Allowance form a separate and secondary group. "Local Self-Government in general and the Corporations of Calcutta and Madras in particular" roused much resentment by the reactionary legislation to which they had been subjected off and on. Sanitation, chiefly with reference to Plague and Quarantine, and Forced Labour were stray subjects. Loyalty to the Throne was avowed on many occasions. The passing away of Queen Victoria in 1901 and the demise of King Edward in 1910 were fresh occasions availed of by the Congress to proclaim its loyalty to the Sovereign. Due welcome was accorded to King Edward and to King George, to the latter as Prince of Wales in 1905 and as King in 1910.

Burma

To-day we find that a battle royal is taking place over the separation of Burma. Let us for one moment turn back to the year of the birth of the Congress and what the Congress had to say on its annexation. The first Congress (1885) "deprecated the annexation of Upper Burma," and said that "if annexation be considered inevitable, the entire country of Burma be separated from India and be constituted into a Crown Colony, as distinct in all matters from this country as is Ceylon."

The Congress Constitution

The question of the Congress Constitution has gained added interest in view of the wholesale innovations introduced into it in the 50th year of its age. It is well-known how the Congress did not start with Articles and Memorandum of Association duly registered beforehand like a Joint Stock Company, or the Rules and Regulations of a society registered under Act XXI of 1860, but that it was an informal gathering of certain well-known men, which gained, as time advanced, in volume and strength by virtue of the moral force on which it has all along relied for the achievement of its greater object. So early as in 1886, there was a "serious proposal to frame a constitution and rules for working the Congress" but the Resolution by which the Committee was appointed confined itself to rule making, deferring the constitution till the Congress had gained more experience and had visited other Provinces. Yet the need was apparent for continuing Congress work throughout the year as, at the time, little work was being done between two Congresses. By the year 1889, the number of Congress delegates began to swell in such a large measure that it was decided by the Congress of the year to limit the quota of the delegation to five per million of population. An Assistant Secretary was appointed in India and the Committee in England was given a paid Secretary in the person of the well-known Mr. W. Digby, C.I.E.

It was at the 4th Congress (1888) that it was decided that "no subject shall be passed for discussion by the Subjects Committee to the introduction of which the Hindu or Muslim delegates as a body object unanimously or nearly so." It may be recalled that the same rule, with the proportion of objectors fixed at 3/4, was adopted in the constitution later passed in 1908 after the Surat imbroglio.

The reduction of delegates to 1,000 was actually carried out in 1890 a year after it was passed (1899). The work in England was considered naturally important and one can gauge the emphasis laid on it by the fact that in 1892, a sum of Rs. 60,000 was voted for the expenses of the British Committee and of the publication of the Congress Journal, *India.* A like sum was voted at the 12th session (1896). There was a renewed effort made in 1898 to frame a constitution for the Congress. In fact a draft constitution was circulated by the Madras Congress (1898) and a Committee was appointed to consider it and submit a definite scheme at the next session. At Lucknow next year (1899) a full blown constitution was passed and it is interesting to compare the object of the Congress as then laid down with that accepted in 1908 and 1920 and 1929. At Lucknow it was laid down that,

> "The object of the Indian National Congress shall be to promote by constitutional means the interests and the well-being of the people of the Indian Empire."

To anticipate matters let us draw the reader's attention to the 'Colonial type of Self-Government,' accepted in 1908, 'Swaraj by all peaceful and legitimate means' approved of in 1920, and 'Complete Independence' demanded at Lahore in 1929. Under the Lucknow Constitution the affairs of the Congress were to be managed by a Committee styled the 'Indian Congress Committee,' consisting of 45 members elected by the Congress, of whom 40 were to be elected by the Congress on the recommendation of the different Provincial Congress Committees. The Committee was to have an Honorary Secretary and a paid Assistant Secretary. A sum of Rs. 5,000 was voted for the expenses, of which one-half was to be paid by the Reception Committee of the last Congress and the other half by the Reception Committee of the next Congress. Arrangements were made for continuous work throughout the year by organizing Standing Congress Committees and holding Provincial Conferences. The nomination of the President and the drafting of the Resolutions were to be done by the Indian Congress Committee.

A permanent fund was contemplated for the Congress, to be invested in the name of seven Trustees—one from each Province in India—to be appointed by the Congress. In 1900 the Indian Congress Committee of 45 was enlarged by the addition to it of certain ex-officio members, namely, the President of the Congress, the President-elect from the day of his nomination, the ex-Presidents of the Congress, the Secretary and Assistant Secretary of the Congress, the Chairman of the Reception Committee, and the Secretary of the Reception Committee nominated by the Reception Committee.

In 1901, work in London was organized, the newspaper *India* was placed on a firm basis by quotas of subscribers allocated to Provinces, aggregating to 4,000, and a special delegation fee of Rs. 10 was to be paid by the delegates as from 1902 onwards, in addition to the usual fee paid by them till then. It is obvious that the Congress had no narrow views regarding the extent of finances necessary to carry on Congress work in India or in England. At the 20th Congress (1904, Bombay), it was decided to send a deputation to England on the eve of the General Election to Parliament, and to raise a fund of Rs. 30,000 for the purpose. At Benares (1905), a Standing Committee of the Congress composed of 15 members was appointed to promote the objects of the Congress and implement its resolutions during the year. In 1906 Dadabhai put the object of the Congress in a nutshell when he said, "The whole matter can be comprised in one word, Self-Government or Swaraj, like that of the United Kingdom or the Colonies." Yet when it came to a question of a Resolution, the matter was softened, for the Congress demanded, in Resolution No. IX, "that the system of Government obtaining in the Self-Governing British Colonies should be extended to India," and "as steps leading to it" urged certain Reforms. The atmosphere of the Calcutta Congress being undoubtedly surcharged with the spirit of Nationalism, a further step in organizing the country was adopted and each Province was to organize at its capital a Provincial Congress Committee "in such manner as may be determined at a meeting of the Provincial Conference or at a special meeting, held for the purpose, of representatives of different districts in the Province." The Committee should "act for the Province in all Congress matters and it should be its special care to organize District Associations throughout the Province for sustained and continuous political work in the Province." The method of electing the Congress President was revised. The Reception Committee was to elect one from those nominated by the Provincial Congress Committees, by a 3/4 majority of its members, failing which the Central Standing Committee (a committee newly brought into existence composed of 49 members) was to make the final decision.

A new system of constituting the Subjects Committee was adopted. The Committee was to consist of 85 delegates, with ten extra from the Province where the Congress was being held, elected by the delegates from the respective Provinces. There were a number of ex-officio members including the President and ex-Presidents, ex-Reception Committee Chairmen, the General Secretaries, and the local Secretaries for the year.

The next phase of the development of the Congress Constitution was really epoch-making. The Surat split naturally led those who organized the Convention at Allahabad to frame a rigid constitution. So the first step taken was to declare that the election of the duly chosen President of the Congress could not be challenged, for the Surat dispute and the *causus belli* centred round Dr. Rash Behari Ghose's election. Next the real interest centred round the 'Creed' of the Congress. When the Surat Congress was split, the Convention that met a day after, i.e., on the 28th December, 1907, at Surat was composed only of those who subscribed to a view which afterwards materialized into Article 1 of the Congress Constitution. We quote the Article as finally passed:—

> "The objects of the Indian National Congress are the attainment by the people of India of a system of Government similar to that enjoyed by the Self-Governing members of the British Empire, and a participation by them in the rights and responsibilities of the Empire on equal terms with those members."

Under the Constitution of 1908, the All-India Congress Committee was to consist of:—

15	Representatives of	Madras
15	"	Bombay
20	"	United Bengal (including Assam)
15	"	United Provinces
13	"	The Punjab (including N. W. Frontier Province)
7	"	Central Provinces
15	"	Bihar and Orissa[1]
5	"	Berar
2	"	Burma

provided as far as possible that one-fifth of the total number of representatives shall be Muslims.

The Presidents of the Congress, residing or present in India, and the General Secretaries of the Congress who shall also be ex-officio General Secretaries of the All-India Congress Committe, shall be ex-officio members in addition.

The Subjects Committee was to be composed of the Members of the A.I.C.C. *plus* a small elected element, the electors being the delegates assembled at the Congress from each Province.

[1] It was under this constitution too that Bihar, which still continued to form part of Western Bengal, was carved out into a separate Congress Province and Bihar held its first Provincial Conference in 1908 under the presidentship of Mr. (later Sir) Syed Ali Imam.

[2] The strength of the A.I.C.C. was considerably raised later, until in 1917 it stood at 14 for Madras; 11 Andhra, 5 Sindh, 25 each for Bengal (including Assam) and U.P., 5 for Delhi Ajmere-Merwara and British Rajputana, 20 Punjab, 12 C.P., 20 Bihar and Orissa, 6 Berar and 5 Burma. The Subjects Committee was to be composed of the A.I.C.C. *plus* an equal number of elected members for each Province, the electors being the delegates of the Province assembled at the Congress.

The objects of the Congress "are to be achieved by constitutional means by bringing about a steady reform of the existing system of administration, and by promoting national unity, fostering public spirit and developing and organizing the intellectual, moral, economic and industrial resources of the Country." It was in the Constitution of 1908 that a clause appeared for the first time, under which 'any resolution that was repugnant to 3/4 of the Hindu or Muslim delegates was to be given up. On looking up old records we come across a curious application of this restrictive measure. A resolution was passed in 1899 at the 15th session of the Congress (Lucknow) condemning the Punjab Land Alienation Bill which was then before the Supreme Legislative Council with a view to restricting the alienation of land either by sale or by mortgage. We find however that at the succeeding session (16th Lahore, 1900) the Subjects Committee decided to postpone the discussion of the Punjab Land Alienation Act (apparently the Bill had been passed into Law) so as to watch its working for a year, since the Hindu and Muslim delegates disagreed on it.

Further amendments to the Constitution came in from the United Bengal Provincial Congress Committee and these were referred to a sub-committee in 1910 (Allahabad). The recommendations of this Committee were accepted at the 26th Congress (1911, Calcutta) and the A.I.C.C. was charged to send in further amendments. No material changes however took place for a time. From 1910 to 1915 the Congress was merely marking time. When the Great War broke out in 1914 and Mrs. Besant inaugurated her great political movement, it was done under the auspices of the All-India Home Rule League. It may be noted that by that time Lokamanya Tilak had organized a separate Home Rule

League in Maharashtra on the 23rd of April, 1916. It was not till the Congress of 1920 (Nagpur) after the Special Congress at Calcutta (September, 1920) had accepted Non-co-operation, that the Congress revised the Constitution, replacing the 'Creed' of 1908 by the simple statement in which it stands embodied to-day, and reorganized the whole plan of Congress work, includin the re-distribution of Congress Provinces on a linguistic basis. The question of a separate Andhra Congress Province was indeed mooted earlier in 1915 and 1916 and was accepted in 1917 by the Calcutta session, after vehement opposition from the President (Dr. Besant) and from some of the leading South Indian (Tamil) delegates from Madras. Even Gandhi thought in 1917 that the question might await the Reforms, but it was the foresight of Tilak that gave the Andhras a separate Congress Circle, and in consequence a sub-committee was appointed in December, 1917, to revise and settle the extent of representation of each Congress Circle on the A.I.C.C. This was followed by Sindh asking for and getting a separate Congress Circle for itself in 1918, but the demands of Karnataka and Kerala had to wait till the general re-distribution of Congress Provinces in India into twenty-one after the Nagpur session of 1920.

UNSATISFIED DEMANDS TILL THE YEAR 1918

To prove that India's national demand was not merely sentimental, that there were weighty and practical reasons which made it imperative, that under existing conditions reform had not much chance, it is enough to mention the repeated proposals and protests of the Indian National Congress, which after 32 years had not materialised on account of the attitude of the Government of India and the various Local Governments, and they were in 1918 as follows:—

(1) Abolition of the India Council (1885)
(2) Simultaneous examinations (1885)
(3) Equitable apportionment of military expenditure between India and England (1885)
(4) Extension of trial by Jury (1886)
(5) Finality to be given to the verdicts of Juries 1886.
(6) Enabling accused persons in warrant cases, to demand that instead of being tried by the Magistrate, they be committed to the Court of Sessions (1886)
(7) Separation of Judicial from Executive functions (1886)
(8) Volunteering among Indians (1887)
(9) Establishment of Military Colleges in India for the training of Indians as officers (1887)
(10) Amendment of the Arms Act and Rules (1887)
(11) An active policy of technical education and industrial development (1888).
(12) Reform of the Land Revenue Policy of Government (1889).
(13) Re. Currency Policy (1892).
(14) Constitution of an independent Civil Medical Service in India (1893)
(15) Abolition of Exchange Compensation Allowance (1893)
(16) Abolition of *Begar* (forced labour) and *Rasad* (forced contributions of supplies) (1893)
(17) Reduction of 'Home Charges.'
(18) Repeal of the Cotton Excise Duty (1893)
(19) Recruitment of the higher Judiciary from the Bar (1894)
(20) Condition of Indians in the Colonies (1894)
(21) Repeal of the Government of India's notification of 1891 relating to the Press in Indian States (1894)
(22) Measures for the relief of agricultural indebtedness (1895).
(23) Improvement in the conditions of third class railway travelling (1895)
(24) Financial independence to Provinces (1896)
(25) Reorganisation of the Educational Services so as to do justice to Indians (1896).
(26) Repeal of the Bengal, Madras and Bombay Regulations of 1818, 1819 and 1827, respectively (1897)
(27) Re. the Sedition Act of 1898 (1897)
(28) Re. the Criminal Procedure Code Amendment Act of 1898 (1897)
(29) Re. the Calcutta Municipal Act of 1899 (1898)
(30) Re. the Punjab Land Alienation Act of 1900. (1898)

(31) Inquiry into the economic condition of the people of India (1900)
(32) Larger employment of Indians in the minor Civil Services (1900).
(33) Restriction of the employment of Indians in the superior offices of the Public Works Department (1900).
(34) Admission of Indians to the Police competitive examination in England and their larger employment in the higher ranks of the Police (1901).
(35) Re. the increase of £ 786,000 per annum in the capitation charges borne by India on account of the British forces in this country (1902)
(36) Re. the recommendations of the Indian Universities Commission (1902)
(37) Re. the Indian Universities Act of 1904 (1903)
(38) Re. the Official Secrets Act of 1904 (1903)
(39) Cost of the India Office and the salary of the Secretary of State (1904)
(40) Revival of periodical Parliamentary inquiries into Indian affairs (1905)
(41) Advance in Local Self-Government (1905)
(42) Re. the Criminal Law Amendment Act of 1908 (1908)
(43) Re. the Newspapers (Incitement to Offences) Act of 1908 (1908)
(44) Free and compulsory primary education (1908)
(45) Reform of Legislative Councils Regulations (1909)
(46) Inquiry into the system of administration of the North-West Frontier Province (1909)
(47) To throw open the office of Law Member to advocates, vakils and attorneys (1910)
(48) Re. the Seditious Meetings Act (1910)
(49) Re. the Indian Press Act (1910)
(50) Inquiry into the growth of public expenditure (1910)
(51) Amnesty to political prisoners (1910)
(52) Mr. Gokhale's Elementary Education Bill (1910)
(53) Governor-in-Council for the United Provinces (1911)
(54) Constitution of an Executive Council in the Punjab (1911)
(55) Reform of the India Council (1913)
(56) Re. Indian students in England (1915)

CHAPTER III

THE EARLY PHASE OF THE CONGRESS

Fifty years have rolled by since the Indian National Congress was founded. During this long period it has covered several stages in the course of India's national evolution, and whatever differences may have come into being in its counsels in later years, the earlier ones—from 1885 to 1915 or even 1921, were years of programmes almost common to the different shades of opinion and schools of thought that were slowly developing in Indian politics. Nor were the differences of those earlier years of a very material type.

The greatest difficulty in choosing the fight or arranging the battle lies in selecting the scene of operations and the strategy that should guide them. The contending parties are tossed about between the aggressive and the defensive, between prayer and protest, between contending programmes as to whether we should invite the enemy to our parlour and, to that end, play a waiting game, or whether we should take time by the forelock and rush on him unawares and envelope him all round. These are the issues that rack the brains of Generals on the battlefields. These likewise are the issues in politics where the leaders should decide whether agitation should be in words or in conduct, and whether, if they should decide in favour of the latter, they should give fight by direct or indirect action. These issues are rapidly surveyed before our eyes and still more rapidly revolved in our brains. The progressive stages of a political fight take decades to evolve themselves and what appears to-day at the end of fifty years of strenuous struggle to be profoundly easy and simple would not have struck our forbears, who had started the Congress, as anything other than unthinkable. Imagine a proposal placed before men like W. C. Bonnerjee or Surendra Nath Banerjea, Sir Pherozeshah Mehta or Pandit Ayodhya Nath, Lal Mohan Ghose or Man Mohan Ghose, Subrahmania Aiyar or Ananda Charlu, A. O. Hume or W. Wedderburn, which pleaded for a boycott of foreign goods or of councils, courts and colleges, or a scheme of Civil Disobedience of select laws. It requires no imagination to see that they would have been scandalised by such ideas. Nor could such extreme programmes be evolved before the Partition of Bengal, the reactionary policies of Curzon and Minto, or the South African experiences of Gandhiji, or the Jallianwalla Bagh massacre. During the fifteen years of strife and struggle which the Congress had put in towards the end of the last century, the leaders of thought were mostly lawyers with a sprinkling of merchants and doctors who believed, and believed sincerely, that what India wanted was a lucid and balanced presentation of her case before Englishmen and their Parliament. For this purpose they wanted a political organisation and they found in the National Congress the required organ through which to voice forth the Nation's grievances and the National aspirations.

In recounting the personal forces that shaped as well as swayed the course of Indian politics and recalling the faith that lay behind them, we cannot lose sight of the several epochs into which the Indian political agitation during the past half a century divides itself. The circumstances under which the aspirations of the people and, prior to that, their grievances called for powerful expression, have been explained and the background of the Congress has been pictured in some detail. The times and conditions would not allow in the earlier years anything else than a reasoned appeal to the authorities for the redress of grievances and a moderate demand of new concessions and privileges. This frame of mind soon developed into an art. Forensic talent on the one hand and a richly imaginative and emotional eloquence on the other, were soon brought to bear on the task that lay before the Indian politicians. An irresistible statement of facts followed by irrebuttable arguments to prove the justice of the popular cause are to be met with everywhere in the speeches supporting the Congress resolutions and the addresses delivered by Congress Presidents. The burden of these utterances was that the English people are essentially just and fair, and that if properly informed they would never deviate from truth and the right, that the problem was the Anglo-Indian and not the Englishman, that what was wrong was the system and not the individual, that the Congress was essentially loyal to the British Throne and fell foul only of the Indian bureaucracy, that the English Constitution was the bulwark of popular liberties everywhere and the English Parliament was the Mother of Democracy all over, that the British Constitution was the best of all constitutions, that the Congress was not a seditious body, that the Indian politicians were the natural interpreters of Government to people and of people to Government, that Indians must be admitted into public services in larger measure, should be educated and made fit for high positions, that Universities, the Local Bodies and the public services should form the training ground for India, that the legislatures should be thrown open to election and the right of interpellation and discussion of budgets should be conceded, that the Press and the Forest Laws should be relaxed, the Police should become friendly to the people, that the taxes should be moderate, that the military expenditure should be curtailed by India's burdens being at least shared in part by England, that the Judicial and Executive must be separated, and Indians should be given a place in the executive Councils of Provincial and

Central Governments and in the Council of the Secretary of State, that India should have direct representation in the British Parliament at the rate of two members to each Province, that the non-Regulation Provinces should be brought into line with the Regulation ones, that eminent Englishmen in the public life of England should be sent over as Governors instead of members of the Civil Service, that simultaneous competitive examinations should be held in India for the Services, that the annual drain to England should be stemmed and indigenous industries fostered, that Land Revenue should be reduced and Permanent Settlement should be adopted. The Congress went the length of deprecating the Salt Tax as an iniquity, Excise Duties on cotton goods as unfair, and Exchange Compensation Allowance to civilians as an illegal gratification. So early as in 1893 Pandit Malaviya had the vision to sponsor a resolution on the resuscitation of the village industries of this ancient land.

From this rapid review of the themes that engaged the attention of the Indian politicians one can easily see how their minds should have been constituted. We cannot blame them for the attitude they adopted as pioneers of Indian political reform, any more than we can blame the brick and mortar that is buried six feet deep in the foundation and plinth of a modern edifice. They, it is, that have made possible the superstructure, storey by storey, of Colonial Self-Government, Home Rule within the Empire, Swaraj, and on the top of all, Complete Independence. Let us express our deep and abiding sense of gratitude to the great men that led the van of progress in the earlier generations of our public life. They had largely to quote English authorities in support of obvious propositions. They had laboured hard and made heavy sacrifices according to their lights and their capacities. If to-day, our course is plain and our goal is obvious, we owe it all to our forbears who did the spade work and cleared the forest.

Whatever periodical excitement and exacerbation of feelings there might have existed off and on amongst Congressmen, there is no doubt that the progress of the Congress from its inception in 1885 to 1905 was one even march based on a firm faith in constitutional agitation and in the unfailing regard for justice attributed to the Englishman. It was in that view that the Congress was represented in 1893 by Sardar Dyal Singh Majithia, Chairman, Reception Committee "as the greatest glory of British Rule in this country." For the obverse of the idea he added, "We happily live under a Constitution whose watchword is freedom and whose main pillar is toleration." Lord Ripon's view that "the Queen's Proclamation is not a treaty; it is not a diplomatic instrument; it is a declaration of principles of Government" was quoted by the official Representative of the fourth session of the Congress (1888, Allahabad). Lord Salisbury's dictum that "Government by representation does not suit Eastern traditions" was deeply resented and Sir Pherozeshah Mehta declared in 1890, "I have no fears but that British statesmanship will ultimately respond to the Call." Mahommed Rahimtulla Sayani's declaration as President of the 12th Congress in 1896 was unambiguous: "A more honest or sturdy nation does not exist under the sun than this English Nation." And when the nation met India's approaches and appeals with repression, Ananda Mohan Bose who presided over the Madras Congress in 1898 exhorted saying, "The Educated classes are the friends and not the foes of England,—her natural and necessary allies in the great work that lies before her." The faith placed in the Englishman and in England by those who have gone before us may sometimes appear pathetic and even abject, but it is our duty to recognize their limita-

Sir William Wedderburn
1889 ; Bombay
1910 ; Allahabad

Sir P. M. Mehta
1890 : Calcutta

P. Ananda Charlu
1891 ; Nagpur

Alfred Webb
1894 : Madras

tions and extend, to quote from Dr. Rash Behari Ghose's speech at the 23rd Congress in Madras, 1908, "some kindly thoughts for those who too, in their day, strove to do their duty, however imperfectly, through good report and through evil report with, it may be, somewhat chastened fervour, but I may say without boasting, a fervour as genuine as that which stirs and inspires younger hearts." The first serious agitation in the history of the Congress spread over five long years (1906—1911) and was attended with a measure of repression considered barbarous at the time, leading to a reaction in the outbreak of violence of a sporadic character, and was ultimately crowned with unqualified success in 1911 in the Royal Proclamation annulling the Partition. This led to a gushing praise of the British Government, a renewed faith in its sense of justice and a sense of profound gratitude expressing itself in unmeasured flights of oratory. "Every heart is beating in unison with reverence and devotion to the British Throne, overflowing with revived confidence in and gratitude towards British statesmanship," said Mr. Ambika Charan Mazumdar. "Some of us never faltered," he added, "no—not even in the darkest days of our trials and tribulations—in our hope, in our conviction and in our faith in the ultimate triumph and vindication of British Justice."[1] At the same time Congressmen did not lose sight of the galling laws still in operation in 1911 and in later

---

Congressmen loved to parade their loyalty in the earlier days. When in 1914 Lord Pentland, Governor of Madras, visited the Congress pandal, not only did the whole House rise and applaud the Governor, but Mr. A.P. Patro who was speaking on the despatch of the Indian Expeditionary Force was stopped abruptly and Surendra Nath Banerjea was asked to move the Resolution on the loyalty of the Congress to the Throne which he did with his usual exuberance of language.

A similar incident took place when, on the visit of Sir James Meston to the Lucknow Congress in 1916, the House rose to receive him.

years. The Patriarchs of the Congress had doubtless concentrated on reform of administration and the repeal of repressive laws, but it is wrong to suppose that they were thinking only of the parts and not of the whole of the Indian problem. "Self-Government is the ordering of Nature, the will of Divine Providence," said Surendra Nath in 1886 at the Calcutta session. "Every nation must be the arbiter of its own destinies,—such is the omnipotent fiat inscribed by Nature with her own hands and in her own book." Presiding over the 20th Congress, Sir Henry Cotton visualized the ideal of "a Federation of free and separate States, the United States of India." Dadabhai spoke of "Self-Government or Swaraj like that of the United Kingdom or the Colonies."

That the politicians of the earlier half of the Congress Jubilee Term were not the enemies of Government is amply proved, not only by their own unequivocal avowals made every now and then but from the marks of favour and preferment for which these sturdy patriots were singled out by Government from time to time. The Judiciary was naturally the field selected for such preferment. Sir S. Subrahmania Aiyar of Madras figured in the very first Congress; Mr. V. Krishnaswami Aiyar was solely responsible for the first Convention Congress held in Madras in 1908 under a cut and dry Constitution and Sir Arthur Lawley, then Governor of Madras, was good enough to lend his tents for the Congress session. It was Mr. Krishnaswami Aiyar that said, referring to the Nationalists and the Congress, that 'the gangrened limb' must be amputated. Sir Sankaran Nair presided over the Congress at Amraoti, 1897. Even Mr. Ramesam (Sir Vepa since) was a Congressman from the year 1898 in which he seconded the resolution on South African disabilities. Then there was Mr. T. V. Seshagiri Aiyar who appeared in the Congress in 1910 and Mr. P. R. Sundara Aiyar who was an ardent coadjutor of Mr. Krishnaswami Aiyar in 1908. All these six became Judges of the Madras High Court and two out of them became Members of the Executive Council, one of Madras and the other of Delhi. The first, who should have presided over the Congress in 1899 and was unable to do so as he was made a Judge of the High Court, reverted to the Congress in 1914 and, during the Home Rule agitation of Mrs. Besant, surrendered his Knighthood and provoked the ire of both Montagu and Chelmsford. It is said that there was a talk at the time of discontinuing his pension as a Judge, but, apparently, better counsels prevailed. Then again, both Sir P. S. Sivaswamy Aiyer and Sir C. P. Ramaswami Aiyar were Congressmen, the former figuring at the Congress of 1895, and the latter being a more recent recruit but ever more ardent than the former, for he actually signed the Passive Resistance pledge during the internment of Dr. Besant and her coadjutors. Between 1917 and 1919, Sir C. P. was the one star on the Congress firmament flooding the horizon of Indian politics with his radiance. Both these rose to the position of Members of the Executive Council. So did Sir Mahommed Habibulla who first appeared on the Congress platform in 1898 and gave a sample of his talents and eloquence. He became a Member later of the Madras and Delhi Governments. Sir M. Krishnan Nair, a Law Member of the Government of Madras, spoke at the Congress of 1904, and his successor—Sir K. V. Reddi—was, even on the eve of the birth of the Justice Party in 1917, an ardent and well-known Congressman. Sir M. Ramachandra Rao had for long been a devoted Congressman and was actually appointed Member of the Madras Executive Council in 1921, but was passed over at the last moment. Thus we had, from Madras alone, six Judges and six Executive Councillors. Mr. G. A. Natesan's recent elevation to the Tariff Board adds an example of preferment in some of the unusual lines, even as Sir R. K. Shanmukham's appointment as Dewan of Cochin furnishes still another deviation from the beaten track of the Judiciary and the Executive. Perhaps the earliest prizeman from the Congress ranks was Mr. C. Jambulingam Mudaliar, an elected member of the Madras Legislative Council in 1893, who was made a City Civil Court Judge. In Bombay, both Tyabji and Chandavarkar who presided over the Congress sessions of Madras (1887) and of Lahore (1900) respectively, and K. T. Telang, became Judges of the Bombay High Court. Mr. N. M. Samarth and B. N. Basu were made members of the Secretary of State's Council and Sir Chimanlal Setalvad was at a later stage made a Member of the Executive Council of Bombay.

In Calcutta, A. Chaudhuri who took a leading part in the anti-Partition (of Bengal) agitation became a High Court Judge, almost then and there. When Lord Morley wanted to select the Law Member of the Government of India in 1908, the choice, we learn from Lady Minto's biography of Lord Minto, lay between Messrs. Ashutosh Mukherjee "as the leading jurist of India, but as a sincerely orthodox man whose claims were carefully canvassed" and S. P. Sinha. It was stated by Lord Minto that Sinha was "a Congressman although a Moderate." S. P. Sinha spoke at the 12th Congress (Calcutta, 1896), on the deposition without trial of a native chief. And as we all know, the Congressman was preferred. Likewise, when a vacancy arose in the Executive Council of the Governor-General in 1920, Lord Chelmsford's choice fell on the Maharaja of Burdwan, but Mr. Montagu preferred an elected member of the Imperial Council and mentioned Mr. V. S. Srinivasa Sastri's name. Chelmsford would not have him, as he thought Sastri had failed him at the psychological moment and the choice fell on Mr. B. N. Sarma—a man that had not failed him at Amritsar, as we shall see later on. In Bengal, other names familiar to Congress circles, which have since been associated with high posts under Government, are those of Messrs. S. R. Das who spoke in 1905 on the question of Indians in Executive Councils, and who became the Law Member of the Government of India, and Sir Provash Chandra Mitter who became an Executive Councillor of Bengal . In U.P. Sir Tej Bahadur Sapru was the stalwart chosen for the Law Membership of the Government of India, and from Bihar Syed Hasan. Imam became, after inviting the Congress to Patna for 1912, a High Court Judge; Mr. Sachchidananda Sinha was raised to a place in the Executive Council of Bihar.

But let us add that the governmental recognition did not always take the form of posts. Pherozeshah Mehta was raised to Knighthood in 1905 by one of the most reactionary Viceroys—Lord Curzon. Gopal Krishna Gokhale would not accept a Knighthood, and would not have accepted even a Membership of the Government of India if it had been offered to him. He preferred to be the plain, unsophisticated Servant of India that he really was, and would have been happy not to have been made a C.I.E. Mr. V. S. Srinivasa Sastri was nominated a member of the Legislative Council by Lord Pentland during the Great War. Thereafter he was nominated to the Assembly under the Montford Reforms, and in 1921, was appointed India's representative at the Imperial Conference along with the Maharaja of Kutch, and shortly after made a Privy Councillor. Then he went to America and lectured on India and the Empire. The Dominions invited him, except South Africa which declined to invite him. The Government of India voted Rs. 60,000 for his expenses. But ample amends were made to him later when he was appointed in 1927 the first Agent-General in South Africa itself, to look after the interests of Indian settlers there. The very stone which was rejected became the corner-stone of the edifice of the Empire.

We have mentioned some instances of preferment of distinguished Congressmen. Let no one run away with the idea that these men were not fitted by their education, culture and high character to fill the posts to which they were appointed. These illustrations only show that the Government, too, if it wanted to have able Indians, had to look to Congress ranks for recruiting them, and that their politics were not regarded by the Government with such disfavour as to make them unfit for places of the greatest responsibility and trust.

CHAPTER IV

Britains' Reaction to the Congress Movement and Rise of New Forces and Parties.

The history of the British Rule in India is a continuous story of Reaction and Reform, the former always preceding the latter. Popular agitation gives birth to repression on the ground that, unless the people are thoroughly beaten, no concession should be made to popular demands. Lord Lytton's Press Act of 1870 which was however quickly withdrawn was the real forerunner of this policy. The Arms Act was another reply to the growing self-consciousness of the Nation and continued a festering sore. Later in 1886 came the Income-tax Act which was objected to seriously at the time. As the Congress grew from year to year, the officials began to eye it with suspicion. Lord Dufferin who had advised Hume to make the Congress undertake political organisation and not merely Social Reform, became an open enemy of the Congress and characterised it as seditious.

Although it was gratifying to Hume that in 1886 the Congress should have been duly received by Lord Dufferin, the Viceroy, in Calcutta, and in 1887 by Lord Connemara, the Governor, in Madras, yet in later years it evoked the hostility of Provincial Satraps like Sir Auckland Colvin of the North-Western Provinces (U.P.). This gentleman advised that the Congress had better turn its attention to Social Reform, not knowing that that was the original line of action chalked out by Hume for the Congress, and that it was later altered into a political organization at the instance of Lord Dufferin. Sir Auckland Colvin thought that the movement was premature, and in its aggressive phases—assumed since the 3rd session (1887, Madras)—was even dangerous. The denunciatory method would, he said, excite hatred and create a split between the Loyalists and the Nationalists. He added that Congress "unfairly claimed to represent the Indian population." Hume replied that "the hatred was already there and required to be assuaged, that any counter agitation would be taken up only by Anglo-Indians, uncultured men and time-servers." The "Muslims," he said, "were as intellingent as, and more democratic than, any one else and in their antipathy to Congress were only being used by a few ill-advised officials who clung to the pestilential doctrine of *Divide et Impera.*" "The wretched plea that they are inferior to Hindus," was, he added, "monstrous," and he quoted the names of Sir Salar Jung, Mr. Justice Budruddin Tyabji and Mr. Justice Syed Mahmud. On the question of Congress representing the people, he quoted the ten per cent. of the population that were polling at the English Parliamentary elections, as in those of constituencies like Aberdeen, and the two seats that Weymouth was selling, of which, by the way, it may be mentioned one was purchased by his father.

As for the Congress confining its attention to Social Reform, he pointed out how the Congress sought the regeneration of India on all lines—spiritual, moral, social, and political. Meeting the charge of the Congress propaganda being premature and mischievous, he warned officialdom as to how it was surrounded by self-seekers and flatterers and kept out of touch with real public opinion. "Indians of high character and public spirit," he said, "do not willingly present themselves in official quarters where they may be met with suspicion from the authorities and insult from underlings." He concluded by saying that the real question to be asked was not "Is it premature.?" but "Is it too late?" In narrating the story Sir W. Wedderburn appropriately winds up by quoting the parallel of the Bourbons at the close of the 18th century. "They had neither eyes to see, nor ears to hear, and sudden destruction was brought upon them by the hatred of the intellectuals energizing the dull despair of the peasant masses."

The fourth Congress held at Allahabad had untold difficulties in its way. It could not get grounds whereon to put up the tents. Mrs. Besant in her book on the Congress quotes the instance of a gentleman who had attended the Madras Congress in 1887 "in defiance of his district officer and was called on to give a security of Rs. 20,000 to keep the peace." Matters rapidly became worse and Government's hostility took the shape, in 1890, of a Circular issued by the Bengal Government to all Secretaries and Heads of Departments subordinate to it "pointing out that under the orders of the Government of India, the presence of Government officials, even as visitors, at such meetings is not advisable and that their taking part in the proceedings of any such meetings is also prohibited." The seven cards of admission sent by the Congress to the Private Secretary to the Governor were returned. A Government of India Notification was promulgated on 25th June 1891 (Foreign Department) restricting the rights of free Press in Native States which was protested against by the Congress in 1891. We extract below the Notification:—

"Whereas some misapprehension has hitherto existed as to the regulations in force in territory under the administration of the Governor-General in Council, but beyond the limits of British India, with reference to newspapers published within such territory, the Governor-General in Council has been pleased to make the following orders:—

1. "No newspaper or other printed work, whether periodical or other, containing public news or comments on public news, shall, without the written permission for the time being in force of the Political Agent, be edited, printed or published after 1—8—1891 in any local

> area administered by the Governor-General in Council but not forming part of British India.
>
> 2. If this is contravened, the Political Agent may by order in writing,
>
> (a) Require him to leave such local area within seven days from the date of such orders,
>
> (b) and prohibit him from re-entering such local area without the written permission of the Political Agent.
>
> 3. Disobedience of orders mentioned in the last foregoing paragraph shall make one liable to forcible expulsion."

The bogey of Muslim opposition to the Congress was set up quite in the early years of the Congress and it is curious to note that Sheik Raza Hussein Khan produced at the fourth session (1888, Allahabad) a *Fatwa* supporting the Congress from the Shams-ul-ulma, the leader of the Sunni Community of Lucknow, and declared that "it is not the Muslims, but their official masters who are opposed to the Congress." By 1893 the Legislative Councils were expanded and people's representatives—all too few, being seven in Madras, six in Bombay (including two for the Sirdars) and seven in Bengal—became vocal, with the result that Government thought it necessary to cut short certain privileges enjoyed by Indians in the Public Services (for further details see the Section on the summary of Resolutions on the Public Services). At first in the Educational Department Indians and Europeans were equally eligible for all offices; then, while the equality of eligibility was there, the grades were made unequal. Next the Indians were excluded from certain posts and their status was lowered while their pay suffered a still further cut. In the meantime the European officers began to receive what was called Exchange Compensation Allowance which was described by Lokamanya Tilak as "the crime of 26th June, 1893." And the drain of Home Charges increased from 7 to 16 millions of pounds in 30 years. Sections 124 (A) and 153 (A) were forged in the year 1897 and really created disaffection towards Government. It is interesting to note that sections 108 and 144 were first applied to politicals even in the last century. Secret Press Committees were established in 1898 which evoked a vehement protest from Mr. W. A. Chambers at the fourteenth Congress (Madras, 1898) and the Resolution was seconded by Mr. N. C. Kelkar, the able and cultured lieutenant of Lokamanya Tilak. Kelkar spoke against "the hateful institution of the Press Committees which are only a thinly veiled Press censorship and as such a distinct disgrace to British India." Even more obnoxious was the statement unearthed by Mr. Mudholkar who in 1897 referred to Sir James Fitz-James Stephen's standard of Loyalty as expressed in the following words of his: "Go to the English newspapers; whatever they say, you may say; that any body should want to be more offensive than they, is inconceivable." In 1899 the Natu brothers, who had been imprisoned without trial since 1897 in connection with the plague riots of Poona, were released. Bengal was hit and was clipped of its wings. The first five years of the 20th century witnessed the strenuous days of Lord Curzon's rule. His curtailment of the powers of the Calcutta Corporation, his Official Secrets Act, his officialization of the Universities which made education costly, his tirade against the untruthfulness of Indians, his budget of twelve Reforms, and his Tibetan Expedition euphemistically called the Tibetan Mission, and finally his Partition of Bengal, broke the back of loyal India and roused a new spirit in the Nation. Even more galling to our sense of self-respect than his speech in Calcutta regarding our untruthfulness, was his sweeping charge that we Indians were, by our environment, our heritage and our upbringing "unequal to the responsibilities of high office under British Rule." In fact, by his Resolution dated 24-5-1904, Lord Curzon made race the test of qualification not merit, so much so that the continuation of this policy made Lord Morley declare, as Secretary of State, that what India resented was racial domination, not so much political domination. Lord Curzon's term was characterized by activity, indeed breathless activity. He had a scheme of twelve Reforms and appointed several Commissions. "Commissions there are that shelve and Commissions there are that solve. But mine are of the latter category", said he. He did some lasting good, doubtless, to India. His Ancient Monuments Preservation Act is a blessing for which Indian Nationalism owes him a deep debt of gratitude. The manly way in which he punished a regiment in the Rangoon and O'Hara[1] cases remains as a tribute to his courage and sense of justice.

The period of time between 1900 and 1906 was one of a critical nature in the history of India. While the people were showing increasing signs of self-consciousness, the retrograde policy of Government could not but make itself more and more assertive and ever more naked. We shall show how one of the favourite themes of Surendra Nath Banerjea's was the Public Services. In 1893 there were only twenty Indians in the I.C.S., as against a thousand Europeans,—and this in 35 years after its introduction. The House of Commons had actually passed a Resolution on the need for simultaneous examinations in India about the year 1893, but ten years after, you have Lord Curzon's minute disparaging Indian talent. No wonder that Surendra Nath was forced to state that "the history of the Civil Services is one unbroken record

[1] The reference is to Lord Curzon's denunciation of a British battalion in Rangoon, some privates of which were believed to have outraged an Indian woman to death, but could not be detected, owing to a combination amongst the members. This took place in the year 1899. In 1900 the 9th Lancers at Sialkot were punished, because two privates were charged with having beaten an Indian cook to death for failing to procure an Indian woman for them and who too could not be detected.

of broken promises." Mr. N. M. Samarth bemoaned that Burke and Sheridan were not there to impeach Curzon and his policy. The result was a sense of helplessness which made the Congress pathetically ask for the periodical Parliamentary enquiries so late as in 1905, in a resolution at Benares moved by Ambalal Desai. While Lord Curzon's University Commission, followed by the Universities Act, "sealed up" in the words of Dr. Gour "the portals of knowledge with golden locks which would open only to golden keys," his Police Commission resulted in excluding the Indians from the special Police Services. On the top of these came Lord Curzon's speech to the merchants in which he stated that "administration and exploitation go hand in hand." All these led to what popularly was known as the National movement, intensified by the anti-Partition movement. The Partition of Bengal divided the Bengali speaking people into two Provinces against their wishes and was a signal for a most extensive and intensive agitation on the part of the people and an equally intensive repression on the part of the Government. Processions, meetings and demonstrations were organized, but erelong they were prohibited. *Hartals* came into existence and students and citizens alike were punished. Educational rules became strict and prohibited students from taking part in politics. Sir B. Fuller, Lt.-Governor of East Bengal, promulgated his threats; and his rudeness to respectable people whom he bullied saying, "Bloodshed may be necessary," was followed by the announcement of the arrival of Gurkha troops into East Bengal. All this, when there was not a trace of violence indulged in by the people, as pointed out by Pandit Madan Mohan Malaviya at the time. But like the ball that bounds the higher, the more it is hit, and the drum that sounds the louder, the more it is beaten, the newly awakened National spirit of 1905—1906 actually prospered under the oft-repeated blows of the ever growing repression which Government were compelled to adopt in all its nakedness. The events of the day in one part of the country became well-known throughout the rest of the land. Every act of reaction by Government had its repercussions all over the country. The cause of Bengal was made India's cause. Each local area forced to the front its own grievances which had long been pent up and made it an added cause of agitation. The Canal Colonization Bill of the Punjab gave occasion for a popular upheaval in that martial area, which led later to the deportation of Lala Lajpat Rai and Sardar Ajit Singh. The Calcutta Congress aptly chose the Grand Old Man of India to preside over its deliberations. And Dadabhai's introduction of the term 'Swaraj' only added incense to the flames of Anglo-Indian irritation.

The prohibitory orders against students participating in political meetings and demonstrations led to the boycott of schools and colleges, followed by the establishment of 24 National High Schools in East Bengal alone, and the organization of a Society for the Promotion of National Education in Bengal (Banga Jateeya Vidya Parishad) under the headship of ex-Justice Sir Gurudas Banerjee. Babu Satish Chandra Mukherjee was the Principal of this institution which was imparting education "on National lines and under National control and directed towards the realization of the National destiny," in accordance with the resolution of the Calcutta Congress on the subject in 1906. Babu Bepin Chandra Pal who had been, since 1903—1904, doing splendid work in the cause of National Renaissance through his weekly *New India,* became the avowed and authoritative exponent of the cult of Nationalism, National Education, and the New Spirit, throughout the country. His tour in the Andhradesa in the summer months of 1907 was a roaring success. His visit to Rajahmundry (Rajamahenvaram) led to a resolve by the townspeople to open a National High School there. An address presented to him by the students of the Government Training College led to the rustication of several students who became soldiers in the National cause. Thus did the unrestrained policy of repression manufacture our patriots and heroes. The seed of National Education sown by Pal in the year 1907 at Masulipatam (Machilipatnam) sprouted forthwith, was since watered and manured by the National movements of 1917 and 1921, and has grown into a tree and remains there to this day, bearing flower and fruit such as we can expect under the withering winds and the scorching heat of State displeasure. The year 1907 witnessed the implementing of the new slogans of Swadeshi, Boycott, and National Education in practical programmes. While National Schools and a National University were springing up here, there and elsewhere—in Bengal, Maharashtra, C.P., Punjab and Andhra—the Swadeshi movement spread far and wide. The handloom industry was once again revived but with the flyshuttle, and in order to give it an impetus a boycott of foreign goods was organized, the banner of boycott being first hoisted on the 7th August, 1905, a day which was observed for years with the same spirit of sacredness as was shown to the 16th of October—the day of the Partition of Bengal. The whole atmosphere was surcharged with a new enthusiasm and Governmental repression was keeping pace with the National upheaval. National Renaissance was thriving under State repression. In August, 1907, the situation in India was really acute, so much so that Lord Minto was thoroughly disappointed and happened to say of Gokhale, "I believe he is honest at heart, but the part he has played of late has disgusted me." That shows incidentally how some of the National leaders were caught between two stools.

Two characters emerged from Bengal at the time who played a notable part in making India's history. Bepin Bapu and his work has already been referred to. Aurobindo shone for years as the brightest star on the Indian firmament. His association with the National Education movement at its inception lent dignity and charm to the cause. He was during his early years brought up and educated in the English atmosphere and English schools and Universities. He came to India much as any European would come, to join the Educational Department of Baroda, he having failed to secure a place in the I.C.S. as he did not pass the Riding test. Aurobindo's genius shot up like a meteor. He was on the high skies only for a time. He flooded the land from Cape to Mount with the effulgence of his light.

Nine deportations took place in Bengal, namely of Krishna Kumar Mitra, Pulin Behari Das, Shyam Sunder Chakravarti, Aswini Kumar Dutt, Manoranjan Guha-Thakurta, Subodh Chandra Mullik, Sachindra Prasad Bose, Satish Chandra Chatterjee and Bupesh Chandra Nag. These leaders had been organizing Bengal—the youth of Bengal in particular. Physical prowess and courage were the ideal of the time. Sir B. Fuller's ideal, on the other side, was the Gurkha soldiery and "bloodshed if necessary." Things reached their acme in 1908. Press prosecutions were to be witnessed everywhere. The *Yugantar*, the *Sandhya* and the *Bandemataram* were the organs of the New Spirit and were all suppressed. Brahma Bandhav Upadhyaya, Editor of the *Sandhya* and a strenuous patriot, died in hospital. Aurobindo himself, after undergoing many hardships and three prosecutions, left the British Territory and started an Ashram in Pondicherry.

On the 30th April, 1908, fell two bombs at Muzafferpore on two ladies—the Kennedys—which were meant for Mr. Kingsford, the District Judge of the place. Khudiram Bose, a young man of 18, was executed for the crime. His photoes were circulated broadcast in the country. The cult of violence was openly preached in the columns of *Yugantar*, edited by a young man named Bhupendra Nath Datta, a brother of Swami Vivekananda. When the young man was given a long sentence, his mother expressed her joy at the service rendered by her son, and 500 Bengali women went to her to congratulate her. The son himself declared in Court that there were 300 million Editors behind the paper to take his place. That was the faith which sustained the movement. Sedition and its punishment therefore ceased to rouse any fears in the popular mind. People preached it far and wide, but when prosecuted employed all the resources of the Law to obtain a discharge or acquittal. Aurobindo's prosecution for sedition in the *Bandemataram*, was no exception to this plan of popular campaign. In Maharashtra, Bal Gangadhar Tilak was arrested on the 13th July, 1908, and on the same day were arrested in Andhra, Mr. Harisarvothama Rao and two others. After five days' trial, Tilak was given six years' transportation to which was added the half year remitted in his sentence of 1897. The nine months' punishment given to Harisarvothama Rao in Andhra was sought to be revised by Government and the High Court raised it to three years. Five years for sedition was quite a common affair. Soon, however, sedition disappeared from the land. It really went underground and the bomb and the revolver took its place. New measures, called the Seditious Meetings Act and the Press Act, were passed in the teeth of popular opposition in 1908, and two years later, the Criminal Law Amendment Act. Gokhale warned Government in the debate on the Seditious

Meetings Bill that the younger men were getting out of hand and that they, the elders, could not be blamed if they could not control the youth.

Sporadic murders of a political nature were taking place from time to time and the most daring of the kind was the murder of Sir Curzon Wyllie in London at a public meeting, in 1907, by a young man named Madan Lal Dhingra, who was hanged. In trying to rescue the victim, Dr. Lalkaka, a Parsee, also shared his fate. Pandit Madan Mohan Malaviya who presided over the 24th session of the Congress at Lahore (1909), deplored these incidents as well as the murder of Mr. Jackson, Collector of Nasik. The violence movement was rapidly spreading to different Provinces in India and had its support amongst a section of Indian students in London. The tension of feeling was not relieved either by the Minto-Morley Reforms or the admission of Indians into the Executive Councils of the Government of India, and of the Madras and Bombay Governments. As Gokhale repeatedly pointed out, Reforms delayed "lost half their value and all their grace." By this time Lord Morley began to see the mischief done by Lord Curzon's policy. He repudiated Lord Curzon's interpretation of the Queen's Proclamation of 1858 and the emphasis laid by him on the words "so far as may be" as the disqualifying factor in respect of obliterating "all distinctions of race." But there was no chance of any peace in the country until the 'settled fact' of the Partition of Bengal was unsettled. The prestige of the bureaucracy was at stake. It could not respond to agitation; for, once that was done, its rule would be at an end. A fine description of this "special creation of the Almighty—the Bureaucracy" was given by Pandit Bishan Narayan Dhar who presided over the 26th Congress session in Calcutta. The essence of bureaucracy is pithily expressed by Lord Minto in one of his speeches in which he said that Government would not yield either in response to agitation from below or in obedience to authority from above, but out of its own free will and on its own initiative. Therefore a device was found out to get out of the *impasse* created by the Partition, which, strangely enough, was disowned both by Lord Curzon who had conceived it, and by Lord Ampthill who signed it as the Acting Viceroy at the time. It was equally disowned by Lord Morley and by Viscount Middleton (Mr. Brodrick) who were the two Secretaries of State concerned. Anyway, when Lord Minto gave place to Lord Hardinge as Viceroy and Lord Crewe succeeded Viscount Middleton as the Secretary of State, advantage was taken of the King's Coronation celebrations in India to annul the Partition, and to shift the metropolis of India from Calcutta to Delhi. When the King was about to leave the pavilion at the close of the ceremony on the 12th December 1911, in Delhi, he stood and said:—

> "We are pleased to announce to our people that on the advice of our ministers and after consultation with our Governor-General-in-Council, we have decided upon the transfer of the seat of the Government of India, from Calcutta to the ancient Capital of Delhi, and simultaneously as a consequence of that transfer, the creation at as early a date as possible of a Governorship-in-Council for the Presidency of Bengal, of a new Lieutenant-Governorship-in-Council administering the areas of Bihar, Chota Nagpur and Orissa, and of a Chief Commissionership of Assam, with such administrative changes and redistribution of boundaries as our Governor-General-in-Council, with the approval of our Secretary of State for India-in-Council, may in due course determine. It is our earnest desire that these changes may conduce to the greater prosperity and happiness of our beloved people."

When it is said that the Partition was annulled, let it

not be understood that the *status quo ante* was restored. The partition of Bengal into West Bengal and East Bengal (with Assam) only underwent a change of form, Bihar which was, in the partition, included in West Bengal, being separated into a Province, along with Chota Nagpur and Orissa. So that in place of West Bengal and East Bengal (with Assam), we have Bengal as one Province, and Bihar, Chota Nagpur and Orissa as another Province, and Assam as a third Province. The one injustice left unredressed on the occasion of the Coronation celebrations in India has just now been repaired by Orissa being integrated into a distinctive Province. Lord Hardinge, they say, made his term memorable for the abolition of Indentured Labour in South Africa and the annulment of the Partition of Bengal, but what makes his administration memorable was that he worked for the Despatch of August 25th, 1911, which has formed the basis for all further Reforms in India and in which he unreservedly acknowledged the supreme claims of Provincial Autonomy in any scheme of National reconstruction.

With these achievements to the credit of the Congress, it is but to be expected that the highest jubilation should have prevailed over the country when the annual session met in Calcutta in 1911. Surendra Nath Banerjea made a handsome acknowledgment of the help rendered to Bengal by the whole of India and expressed the buoyant hope "that India would form part and parcel of the Self-Governing States of a Free and Federated Empire, rejoicing in our indissoluble connection with England and in the enjoyment of the inestimable blessing of new-born freedom." But there was a skeleton in the cupboard. In the midst of these wild rejoicings, people could not forget the Seditious Meetings Act (1908) and the Press Act (1908) and the Criminal Law Amendment Act (1910) which cut at the root of popular liberties. Above all, there were the century-old obsolete Regulation III of 1818 and allied Regulations in the different Provinces, under which the deportations of 1906-1908 were freely taking place. There were, too, the Excise duties on cotton goods manufactured in India. These directly jeopardised the security of person and property and national industrial interests. There were, above all, political prisoners in jail, notably Bal Gangadhar Tilak confined in the Fort of Mandalay, suffering from diabetes,—alone and unfriended, but full of fortitude. At this time, Gokhale's Elementary Education Bill was on the tapis, with poor chances of being passed, and there was the South African situation which called forth a nation-wide agitation.

That was the position in 1911. The political tension was somewhat relaxed in 1912. But a great tragedy was enacted in the year, when an attempt was made on the life of Lord Hardinge, who was perhaps the most popular Viceroy about the time. A bomb was thrown on him—and he narrowly escaped death—while he was riding an elephant in the procession organized on entering Delhi, the new Capital. The Congress deviated from its usual practice of dispersing at the close of the Presidential address at its Patna session (1912) and resolved to send a telegram to Lord Hardinge expressing its sorrow and indignation at the outrage. The Press began to be rigidly controlled, as was expected after such incidents, and this led in turn to an insistent demand for the repeal of the Press Act in 1913. Bhupendra Nath Basu gave the history of the vicissitudes of the Press in India, and described how in 1835 Sir Charles Metcalfe had liberated the Indian Press, but Lord Lytton gagged it in 1878-79 by his Vernacular Press Act, which was repealed later at the instance of Mr. Gladstone. In 1891, however, the Government of India published a Notification dated 25th June 1891 in the

Foreign Department, gagging the Press in territories under British administration in Native States, which evoked warm protests from the Congress in successive years. The latest reactionary measure was the Press Act of 1908—permanently placed on the Statute Book in 1910—which authorized Government to demand securities from new Printing Presses and newspapers up to Rs. 2,000, and from old ones up to Rs. 5,000. Sir Herbert Risley, the Home Member at the time, said that the Act would not affect existing papers and that the administration of the Law would not be in the hands of the Police, but both the assurances proved false. People lost sight of the fact—including Sir S. P. Sinha who, as the Law Member of the Government of India, was responsible for the final shape of the Bill,—that fresh declarations were necessary under the Printing Press and Newspapers Act of 1867 for various minor causes, such as change of premises, temporary absence of the printer or the publisher, death of the original owner, and change in the management. All these necessitated fresh declarations, and that meant security as for a new Press, especially under the inexorable reports of the secret Police. As soon as the Great War broke out, in 1914, a notorious instance of misuse of the Act occurred in respect of a pamphlet published by Mahomed Ali, entitled "Come over into Macedonia and help us," which was forfeited without the notification stating the grounds for Government's opinion as was required by the Press Act of 1910. The pamphlet was held to be not seditious and was outside the scope of the Penal Code. The Chief Justice of Calcutta (I.L.R. 41 Calcutta 466) stated that it would be the duty of the Court to hold, but for Section 22, that there had been no legal forfeiture. On the merits, His Lordship observed:

"The provisions of Section 4 are very comprehensive and its language is as wide as human ingenuity could make it. Indeed it appears to me to embrace the whole range of varying degrees of assurance, from certainty on the one side to the very limits of impossibility on the other. It is difficult to see to what lengths the operation of this Section might not plausibly be extended by an ingenious mind. They would certainly extend to writings that may even command approval. An attack on that degraded section of the public which lives on the misery and shame of others would come within this widespread net,—the praise of a class might not be free from risk. Much that is regarded as standard literature might undoubtedly be caught. The Advocate-General has contended, and rightly in my opinion, that the provisions of the Press Act extend far beyond the Criminal Law and he has argued that the burden of proof is cast on the applicant, so that, however meritorious the pamphlet may be, still if the applicant cannot establish the negative, the Act requires his application must fail. And what is this negative? It is not enough for the applicant to show that the words of the pamphlet are not likely to bring into hatred or contempt any class or section of His Majesty's subjects in British India, or that they have not a tendency in fact to bring about that result. But he must go further and show that it is impossible for them to have that tendency either directly or indirectly, and whether by way of inference, suggestion, allusion, metaphor or implication. Nor is that all. The legislature has added the all embracing phrase 'or otherwise'."

The C. J. added: "Mr. Mahomed Ali then has lost his book, but he retains his character and he is free from the stigma that he apprehended. And this doubtless will be some consolation to him when we dismiss, as we must, his present application." The colleague of Sir Lawrence Jenkins, the Chief Justice, was not less pronounced in his condemnation of the Press Act, for Mr. Justice Stephen observed: "So wide indeed are the powers which the Legislature has conferred on the Government, that they would be able to confiscate a newspaper containing words that might cause one man to hate or even to condemn a class, if such there should unhappily be, who sought to embarrass the Government of the country by murder and robbery." Speaking of the pamphlet he says: "I find myself in a position which is unfamiliar to me and in which, as far as I am aware, no Judge in the British Empire has been placed since the remote days of early English jurisprudence. I have to decide a question of fact on such evidence as is supplied by one document. The side on whom the onus of proving his case is cast, is not in a position to give evidence. As the other side has not called any witness, no cross-examination has taken place."

Regarding the case of *New India* edited by Mrs. Besant, the Officiating Chief Justice of Madras remarked: "Section 3 (1) imposes a serious disability on persons desiring to keep printing presses." Mrs. Besant forfeited Rs. 20,000 altogether, in 1917, under the Press Act. A deputation of the Press Association headed by Mr. B. G. Horniman and composed of Messrs. Malaviya, Chintamani, Sachchidananda Sinha and others waited on Lord Chelmsford on March 5th, 1917, and in reply the Viceroy rebuked the deputation in unmeasured terms. But that was not all; he rebuked the Judges already quoted, saying, "The function of a Judge is not to say what the Law ought to be, but what it is. Executive action is and must always be based upon information, experience, considerations of policy which find no place in the Courts of Law. Sir Lawrence Jenkins was not entirely consistent with himself. And I cannot but think that if he had any knowledge of the statistics I have given you, he would have hesitated before describing the keeping of printing presses and the publication of newspapers as an extremely hazardous undertaking."

It was only after the Montford Reforms were in operation that the Repressive Laws were repealed (except the Criminal Law Amendment Act) about the year 1922. We have digressed into the full story of the Press Law, in the course of describing the hardships it had worked on the public in 1913, even after the Partition of Bengal had been annulled and the violence movement had become quiescent. But the comparative lull and tranquillity in the political atmosphere were seen to give place to the commotion created by the Great War of 1914-1918, and one gratifying event took place on the eve of this world cataclysm. The Muslims who, ever since the Partition days, had remained aloof from National ideals and pinned their faith on the bureaucracy, saw better in 1913, and the Congress placed on record that year its "warm appreciation of the adoption by the All-India Muslim League of the ideal of Self-Government for India within the British Empire, and of the belief which the League had so emphatically declared at its last session 'that the political future of the country depends upon the harmonious working and co-operation of the two great communities'."

In July 1914, the Great War broke out and when towards November, that year, the Germans were knocking at the door of France, Lord Hardinge took courage in both hands and depleted India of her soldiery. England was in great peril. The soldiers in India were meant to save India for England, but if England herself was going to the bottom of the sea, why this Standing Army in India? So he packed off the Army to Flanders, marching it from Marseilles without a day's rest to the firing line. The Indian Army saved the Allies from a disaster which should have been theirs otherwise, before the close of the first winter in the War. In the Congress of 1914, therefore, the demand for Self-Government was revived. The Congress resolved that "in view of the profound and avowed loyalty the people of India have manifested in the present crisis, this Congress appeals to the Government to deepen and perpetuate it and make it an enduring and valuable asset of the Empire, by removing all invidious distinctions here and abroad between His Majesty's Indian and other subjects, by redeeming the pledges of Provincial Autonomy contained in the Despatch of the 25th August, 1911, and by taking such measures as may be necessary for the recognition of India as a component part of a Federated Empire, in the full and free enjoyment of the rights belonging to that status." We have quoted the Resolution *in extenso* because it represents the high water mark of National aspiration at the time. Mrs. Besant, however, did not place the Indian problem on the basis of a reward, but on the basis of a right. She boldly demanded the application of the principle of Reciprocity at the Madras Congress (1914), urging that India should exclude imports from countries from which her people were excluded. Mrs. Besant inaugurated her great Home Rule movement during the days of Lord Pentland. The same old programme was revived,—Swadeshi, Boycott, National Education and Home Rule. She disaffiliated her Theosophical Educational institutions at Madanapalle from the Madras University, established a National High School at Adyar, established other like institutions in Sindh and elsewhere, and organized a Society for the Promotion of National Education (S. P. N. E). under the headship of Dr. Arundale. The Home Rule League was being organized by Mr. B. P. Wadia. Mr. C. P. Ramaswami Aiyar, who had already begun to take part in the Congress, became an active participant in this movement. *New India* was the daily through the columns of which the Home Rule movement worked. The students became a great force in the agitation, and Lord Pentland promulgated the notorious G. O. 559 prohibiting them from taking part in politics. As usual, agitation led to repression and Mrs. Besant, Mr. Arundale and Mr. Wadia were interned in Ootacamund on June 16th, 1917. These events, from the year 1915 up to September, 1920, constitute really facts and factors of a thickly crowded era,—the era of the Home Rule movement—and are dealt with in a separate Chapter in Part II of the Book.

CHAPTER V

OUR BRITISH FRIENDS

Some members of the British Parliament and certain other eminent Englishmen played a notable part in the evolution of Indian politics.

Long before the Congress was organized by Mr. A. O. Hume, we had a number of members of Parliament who interested themselves in the Indian question and brought an altruistic spirit to bear upon the Parliamentary discussions relating to India. John Bright was the earliest of these, whose activities in the cause of India are traceable to the fifties and sixties of the last century. Mr. Bright entered Parliament in 1847, and from that time to 1880 he kept up his interest in India through all the vicissitudes to which this country was subjected. Next came Mr. Fawcett who entered Parliament in 1865 and moved the resolution in favour of simultaneous examinations in 1868. He condemned in 1875 the ball to the Sultan of Turkey given by Lord Salisbury in England at the expense of India, and from that time forward his career was one continued story of a warm espousal of India's cause. It was as a result of his protests that the cost of the Abyssinian War came to be divided between England and India. He condemned the cost of the Duke of Edinburgh's presents to the Indian Princes being debited to India's account and likewise saved India a debit of £ 30,000 spent on the visit of the Prince of Wales. Lord Lytton's sacrifice of cotton import duties, the Delhi Assemblage, and the Afghan War were all protested against by Fawcett. It is interesting to recall how, so early as in 1872, an address was voted in Calcutta expressing deep gratitude to Mr. Fawcett and how when in 1874 Fawcett lost his seat in Parliament, a purse of £ 750 was voted in this country to enable him to contest a seat.

The part which A. O. Hume played in organising an Indian Parliamentary Committee and the Congress has already been referred to. It is meet and proper that we know something more about this Scotchman who laboured for India's good, both as an official and as a non-official for over sixty years. He was a member of the Indian Civil Service and served India in various capacities. As a District Officer he laboured for "the cause of popular education, police reform, the liquor traffic, the vernacular press, the juvenile reformatories and other domestic requirements." His one interest was the village and its agriculture, his one care and concern was for the people. He had no doubt fought in the Mutiny in the district of Etawah and saved India for the British. The moment peace was restored, he began, however, to vindicate a policy of enlightenment declaring that, "Assert its supremacy as it may at the bayonet's point, a free and civilised Government must look for its stability and permanence to the enlightenment of the people and their moral and intellectual capacity to appreciate its blessings." This attitude evoked a Government circular dated 28th January 1859, in which objection was taken to the employment of native agency for the promotion of education, and the Collector was warned not to attempt to persuade the people to send their children to the schools or to contribute to their maintenance. Hume's protest against this is historic. "I cannot but found hopes of indulgence," he wrote, "on the intense interest I feel in the subject and the ceaseless attention that I have paid it. For years past, it has been the dream of my leisure moments, *the object* of my hopes, and although I have achieved little as yet, I cannot, as I watch the feeble beginnings, avoid recalling an Alpine scene of happy memories when I saw the first drops of a joyous stream trickling through the huge avalanche that had so long embayed, and feeling confidence from that augury that, day by day and month by month, that tiny rill gathering strength and size, will work out its resistless way and, at last, despite the whole chilling mass of ignorance, the accumulation of ages, pass on unobstructed to fertilise and enrich an empire." Hume's next favourite, "Police reform," was based upon a scheme which provided for the complete separation of Police and Judicial functions. Of Abkari he says, "while we debauch our subjects we do not even pecuniarily derive any profit from their ruin. All this revenue is the wages of sin; it may, in the words of the old adage, be truly said that 'ill-gotten wealth never thrives.' And for every rupee additional that the Abkari yields, two at least are lost to the public by crime and spent by the Government in suppressing it. I at this moment see no hopes of reform; yet I have no doubts whatsoever that if I be spared a few years longer, I shall live to see effaced, in a more Christian-like system, one of the greatest existing blots on our Government of India."

At the end of 1859 he helped in starting a vernacular paper called the *People's Friend,* 600 copies of which were taken by the North-West Provinces (U. P.) Government. The Viceroy appreciated it and copies of the paper were forwarded with translation to the Secretary of State for submission to Queen Victoria. So early as in 1863, Mr. Hume pressed for the establishment of a juvenile reformatory where the boys would be separated from adult criminals and given a chance of amendment by discipline, by instruction, and by training in useful industries. As Commissioner of Customs, his principal achievement was the gradual abolition of the vast Customs barrier, 2500 miles long, which had hitherto been kept up to protect the Government's salt monopoly by excluding the cheap salt produced in the Rajaputana States. "This grotesque fortification," it is said, "extended from West to East across India, from Attock on the Indus to near Cuttack on the Bay of Bengal." And Mr. Hume's success in bringing this about evoked praise from the Secretary of State.

In 1879, Mr. Hume prepared a scheme of agricultural reform and in spite of the sympathy Lord Mayo showed towards it his scheme came to nought. On the question of litigation he held the "Civil Courts in the rural districts directly responsible for the bondage of cultivators to the money-lender" and he recommended that "rural debt cases should be disposed of summarily and finally on the spot by selected Indians of known probity and intelligence" who should be "sent as judges from village to village to settle up, with the aid of village elders, every case of debt of the kind referred to in which any one of its inhabitants was concerned. These judges would be fettered by no codes and forms of procedure and they would hear both parties' stories *Coram Populo* on the village platform of the debtor's own village." "It is needless to tell any one who knows the country," said he, "that while, when you get him into court, no witness seems to be able to tell the truth, on his own village platform surrounded by his neighbours, no villager in personal questions like these seems able to tell an untruth. Everybody knows everybody else's affairs. Let the speaker deviate perceptibly from the facts, and immediately out go tongues all round, and hisses and cries of '*wah, wah*', remind him that he is not in court and that that kind of thing will not go down at home." In 1879, a detailed scheme on these lines was formulated for the benefit of the distressed Deccan ryot but it was disallowed by the Bombay Government. Mr. Hume was Secretary to the Government of India from 1870 to 1879 but he was ejected from that place for the offence that he was too honest and too independent. There was a chorus of condemnation in Indian papers, but in vain. Lord Lytton's proposal to give him a Lieutenant-Governorship was turned down by Hume himself, because he was not equal to the task of feting and feasting that it involved, and the alternative proposal to make him the Home Member was turned down by Lord Salisbury, on the ground that Mr. Hume was stiffening Lord Northbrook against the repeal of cotton duties. He retired in 1882 after spending £ 20,000 on a museum of ornithology, and £ 4,000 on the preparation of a great work on the "Game Birds of India."

The services of Sir William Wedderburn are too well-known to need recounting. He was the chief character for years together in running the British Congress Committee, for the expenses of which the Congress had been voting sums ranging from Rs. 10,000 to Rs. 50,000 annually. Sir William Wedderburn presided over the National Congress at two of its sessions,—in Bombay, (1889) and at Allahabad (1910). Mr. David Yule presided over the fourth session of the Congress at Allahabad in 1888 and was the author of the classical and oft-quoted statement which says: "The House of Commons regards India as a great and solemn trust committed to it by an all-wise and inscrutable Providence. The six hundred and fifty odd members have thrown the trust back upon the hands of Providence, to be looked after as Providence itself thinks best." In subsequent years the visit of members of Parliament to India and their presence at the Congress session became an annual event. We can recall such well-known names as those of Mr. W. S. Caine, the great Temperance Reformer, and Charles Bradlaugh, the protagonist of lost causes, Mr. Samuel

Smith, Dr. H. V. Rutherford and Dr. Clarke. In later years various other members of Parliament visited India. Ramsay MacDonald should have even presided over the Congress of 1911 but that his wife's death prevented this event, which would have been an interesting episode in the great tragedy of this Labour Leader's career in relation to India. Keir Hardie, Holford Knight, Maxton, Col. Wedgwood, Ben Spoor, Charles Roberts, Pethwick Lawrence, are a few more of the 'Commoners' that have visited India and attended different sessions of the Congress to study India's problems. But the ovation given to Charles Bradlaugh in 1889 was royal in its style and more than royal in its cordiality. His reply contains many noble sentiments, but his definition of loyalty is remarkable. "That is no real loyalty," he said, "which is only blind submission. Real loyalty means that the governed help the Governors, leaving little for the Government to do." The bureaucracy's definition, however, is quite the opposite, for they say that the people must leave every thing to be done by Government, themselves doing nothing.

Bradlaugh prepared in 1889 a draft Bill on the Reform of the Legislative Councils and circulated it. It embodied the views of the Congress as expressed till then, and the Congress in accordance with his wishes drafted certain proposals embodying the mature opinion of the Indian people on the subject. The Bill was dropped later. But Bradlaugh's position in Parliament was so strong that Lord Cross's first Bill itself had to be dropped in 1891 owing to Bradlaugh's opposition; and his second Bill was accepted, embodying the first instalment of Reforms, with the principle of election to the Legislatures indirectly given.

A name not less dear was that of William Ewart Gladstone. Pandit Bishan Narayan Dhar quoted the following declaration of the Grand Old Man of England, in Madras at the 3rd Congress (1887):—"I hold that the capital agent in determining finally the question whether our power in India is or is not to continue, will be the will of the 240 millions of people who inhabit India. The question who shall have supreme rule in India is, by the laws of right, an Indian question, and those laws of right are from day to day growing into laws of fact. Our title to be there depends on a first condition, that our being there is profitable to the Indian nation, and on a second condition, that we can make them see and understand it to be profitable." The repeal of the Vernacular Press Act relating to Lord Lytton's time was put down to Gladstone's abhorrence of it.

Gladstone's direct approval of the Congress movement was the real cause of his popularity in India. "It will not do for us to treat with contempt or even with indifference the rising aspirations of this great people," said he, in 1888. For years together his birthdays evoked congratulatory resolutions from the Congress. His 82nd birthday fell on 29th December, 1891 and was duly observed by the Congress. His advocacy of India's rights no less than Ireland's was the direct cause of such unparalleled devotion to a distant statesman. Gladstone was regarded as a friend of India and Eardley Norton quotes a statement of his at the tenth Congress (1894) regarding the Press Law, which was as follows:—"Suddenly in the dark, in the privacy of the Council chamber, I believe in answer to a telegram, without the knowledge of Parliament, without the knowledge of the country, a law was passed totally extinguishing the freedom of the Native Press. I think a law such as that is a disgrace to the British Empire." Gladstone's death was sincerely bemoaned by the Congress in 1898.

Lord Northbrook was thanked by the ninth Congress (1893) for pleading in Parliament for the reduction of 'Home' charges. In moving the proposition before the Congress, Gokhale quoted the Duke of Argyll's statement that the grievance should be remedied before the impression got abroad in India that there was such a grievance. The Duke was a great authority on public questions and Mr. Wacha quoted the following statement of the Duke at the 17th session of the Congress: "Of chronic poverty and permanent reduction to the lowest level of subsistence, such as prevail only too widely, amongst the vast population of rural India, we have no example in the Western world." The same Duke had said in 1888 that "they (the English) had not fulfilled the promises and engagements which we have made." The English friends were remembered with gratitude in their death, as they were for their services while alive. Lord Stanley of Alderley was another friend of the Nation and when he passed away in 1903, the Madras Congress recorded its grief over his death and over that of W. S. Caine. There were other Englishmen or Anglo-Indians who strove for the uplift of India year after year, who had spent their lives in this country, and whose services were memorable. At the very first Congress appeared Mr. D. S. White who wished to "stop the importation of these boys from England at great expense and to abolish the Civil Service, utilising, both from England and India, men of experience and reputation." Mr. Eardley Norton is a famous character. He was the son of John Bruce Norton who was a well-known public man in South India and whose portrait is hung in the Pachaiappa's Hall, Madras. The younger Norton spent the best part of his life in India and laboured like his father for India's uplift. In 1894, he moved the Resolution on the abolition of the India Council and formulated the conundrum: "If the Secretary of State is to be controlled by the Council, then abolish the Secretary of State. If the Council is to be controlled by the Secretary of State, then abolish the Council. The dual existence is useless, dangerous, expensive and obstructive." He gave instances of commercial incapacity of the Secretary of State and his Council, such as sanctioning the Calcutta and S. E. Railway, against Lord Canning's protest, guaranteeing interest at 5 per cent., and when it was practically bankrupt, buying it up at ½ a million sterling. Five per cent. interest was guaranteed on a million sterling for the Madras Irrigation Co., and as the work never paid its expenses it was purchased for India at par. The Council bought at Rs. 1,000 per share, the shares of the Elphinstone Land and Press Co., selling in the market at Rs. 339. The expenses of the India Council included, we are told, "the wages of 28 housemaids, a house-keeper and 3 charwomen." Amongst other English friends who stood by India was Mr. H. Morgan-Browne who, while seconding a resolution at the 10th Congress for an enquiry by the House of Commons into Indian Finance, pointed out how out of the Famine Insurance Fund of 24 crores of Rupees, only 16 crores had been spent as promised. The 'Stores,' he said, was one of the meanest and most corrupt departments and India was made to pay Rs. 1,20,000 for a ball in Constantinople. Another English friend was Mr. John Adam, a known Educationist of Madras who stood by the Congress in the earlier days.

There remains one great public character to whom we must make a reference. It is General Booth, who urged on the Nagpur Congress (1891) a scheme by which the poor, destitute multitudes could be settled on the waste lands of the country. A fitting reply was sent to him by telegram.

An account of the services of these European friends would not be complete without a reference to the names of Captain Banon and Captain Hearsay who respectively proposed and seconded a Resolution at the fourth Congress in 1888 (Allahabad) and pointed out how over 2,000 Indian women were procured by Government "for the hideous purpose alluded to (prostitution)," how the provision encouraged the boy-soldiers to loose living and how it would be better to encourage the soldiers to marry. Nor can Sir Henry Cotton and his abiding services to the Nation be forgotten in this brief narrative. The Cottons were a family long connected with India, and no sooner had the Chief Commissioner of Assam retired from the I. C. S. than he was called on by the Congress to guide its deliberations at the Bombay session in 1904. He it was that visualized the ideal of the Federated States of India for the first time.

CHAPTER VI

OUR INDIAN PATRIARCHS

Before we take up the further development in the Congress policy and programme, it is but meet and proper that we pay our tribute of praise and gratitude to the great leaders and founders of the movement for emancipation, who worked and toiled in the earlier days of the Congress. Looking at the Congress with its widespread organization and with its great National programme, we are apt to imagine that all this has come about in our time and as a result of our efforts. The programme and outlook of the progenitors of the Congress may not appeal to the Congressmen of to-day; and the programme and outlook of to-day may not have appealed to the progenitors of the Congress. But we must remember that what we are able to accomplish and aspire to-day would not have been possible without their hard pioneer efforts and great sacrifices. We would be therefore failing in a duty which we owe to the memory of those who have passed away, and to those who are still happily amongst us, if we did not devote a few pages to recording the great services and sacrifices of our patriarchs.

DADABHAI NAOROJI

The first name in the list of patriarchs is that of Dadabhai Naoroji who, beginning his connection with the Congress from its very outset, continued to serve it till the evening of his life, and took it through the whole gamut of evolution, from the humble position of being a people's organ seeking redress of administrative grievances, to that of a National Assembly working for the definite object of attaining Swaraj (Calcutta, 1906). He presided over the Congress thrice, in 1886, 1893 and 1906, and throughout his association with it, held aloft the Congress banner before India and England. Dadabhai's second selection to the Presidentship of the Congress was in appreciation of his election to the House of Commons as a member for Central Finsbury. At that time the idea of ventilating India's grievances in London was being seriously discussed. There was an earnest proposal in 1891, to suspend the Congress until a London session was held. But it was turned down. Just then A. O. Hume was about to depart for England, and about the same time there was a demand for direct Indian representation to the House of Commons. It was at this juncture that Dadabhai was elected Congress President for the second time, and he took the opportunity to exhort the British "not to drive this force (the educated Indians) into opposition instead of drawing it to your own side." "This Congress," said he, "represents the aristocracy of Intellect." Dadabhai hoped that "our faith in the instinctive love of justice and fair play of the United Kingdom is not misplaced." "The day, I hope," he said, "is not distant when the world will see the noblest spectacle of a great Nation like the British holding out the hand of true fellow citizenship and of justice." To the last day, Dadabhai's faith in the British remaind unimpaired. "Indians are British citizens," he said in 1906, "and are entitled to and claim all British citizens' rights." When Dadabhai presided over the Calcutta session in 1906, India was in a seething cauldron; the Partition of Bengal which was effected on the 16th of October 1905 was followed by the uprise of the New Spirit. East Bengal was seething with discontent. Hindu-Muslim troubles were being fomented. Ordinance rule came into existence. The quartering of the Military and of punitive Police became a new development in the maintenance of Law and Order, and the Provincial Conference at Barisal was dispersed "by the Police who wantonly broke the peace in order to keep the peace," to quote the words of Dr. Rash Behari Ghose. Dadabhai pointed out how, since 1893-94, the population grew 14 per cent., but the net Government administrative expenditure 16 per cent, while since 1884-85 the population grew 18 per cent., and the expenditure 70 per cent. The Military expenditure alone rose from 17 to 32 crores, 7 crores being spent in England. The recommendations of the Welby Commission in favour of an apportionment of the Military expenditure between England and India were honoured in letter but disregarded in spirit, for a certain contribution was made by England but the pay of the English soldier was raised so as to take away thrice the contribution made. The year that Dadabhai presided over the Calcutta Congress (1906) was the year when the Gaekwar visited the Congress. The spirit of boycott pervaded the atmosphere of the Congress. Babu Bepin Chandra Pal gave an extended application to the word boycott and interdicted all association with Government. Provinces other than Bengal sought to exempt themselves from the operation of the Resolution on Boycott. Swadeshi, which was its obverse, meant various things to various people. To Malaviya it meant the protection of indigenous industries; to Tilak it meant self-help, determination and sacrifice on the part of the Nation in order to end the sad spectacle of the middle classes using foreign goods. To Lalaji, it meant the conserving of capital. But to Dadabhai himself, the Spirit of the Times echoed itself in a cry for economic and educational reform, and the spread of Education created the craving for Swaraj. *The Englishman* fell foul of this old man of eighty coming from a distance of 6,000 miles and adding the new slogan of 'Swaraj' to the existing ones of Swadeshi, Boycott, and National Education. The way was preparing itself for the clarification of the Indian demand. In 1905, Gokhale had marked out the four lines of progress to

Self-Government which were embodied in the cardinal Resolution of 1906. We give below the four main resolutions of the Calcutta Congress passed under the presidency of Dadabhai Naoroji in 1906:—

SELF-GOVERNMENT

I. Resolved that this Congress is of opinion that the system of Government obtaining in the Self-Governing British Colonies should be extended to India and that, as steps leading to it, it urges that the following reforms should be immediately carried out:

(a) All examinations held in England only should be simultaneously held in India and in England, and that all higher appointments which are made in India should be by competitive examination only.

(b) The adequate representation of Indians in the Council of the Secretary of State and the Executive Councils of the Governors of Madras and Bombay.

(c) The expansion of the Supreme and Provincial Legislative Councils, allowing a larger and truly effective representation of the peoples and a larger control over the financial and executive administration of the country.

(d) The powers of local and municipal bodies should be extended and official control over them should not be more than what is exercised by the Local Government Board in England over similar bodies.

BOYCOTT MOVEMENT

II. Resolved that having regard to the fact that the people of this country have little or no voice in its administration, and their representations to the Government do not receive due consideration, this Congress is of opinion that the boycott movement inaugurated in Bengal by way of protest against the partition of that Province was, and is, legitimate.

SWADESHI

III. Resolved that this Congress accords its most cordial support to the Swadeshi movement and calls upon the people of the country to labour for its success, by making earnest and sustained efforts to promote the growth of indigenous industries and to stimulate the production of indigenous articles by giving them preference over imported commodities, even at some sacrifice.

National Education

IV. Resolved that in the opinion of this Congress the time has arrived for the people all over the country earnestly to take up the question of national education for both boys and girls, and organise a system of education, literary, scientific and technical, suited to the requirements of the country on National lines and under National control.

It is impossible to recount within the short space of a few pages the services of one who lived and worked incessantly for India's uplift, whose pen knew no rest and to whom Providence gave more than the proverbial three score years and ten. Dadabhai lived and laboured and has left behind him not only the noble example of a dedicated life, but also in flesh and blood his granddaughters who are maintaining the noble traditions created by him.

Ananda Charlu

When the first Congress was held in Bombay in 1885, Editor G. Subrahmania Aiyar and Mr. Ananda Charlu, Telang and Dadabhai Naoroji, Narendra Nath Sen and W. C. Bonnerjee, S. Subrahmania Aiyar and Rangaiah Naidu, Pherozeshah Mehta and D. S. White—all eminent men, founders and patriarchs of the Congress—gave an indication, in their speeches, of the forces that were gathering strength in Indian Politics. They constituted, in the march of time, the Moderates of India, but their language, however polite, was certainly not moderate. Ananda Charlu, who later became the President of the Nagpur Congress in 1891, began with his characteristic eloquence, describing the India Council as "the oligarchy of fossilized Indian administrators" who were "superannuated for service in India."

He presided over the Nagpur (7th) session in 1891 and made a stirring speech. "Take the case of the volunteers," said he. "We are excluded from the enrolment. Armenians, Negroes, West African Mulattoes and non-descripts of humanity who infest the back slums of Calcutta—these are all eligible as volunteers, these are our martial heroes, these are the defenders of our hearths and houses. These are invidious distinctions and I am sure they must disappear before the irresistible might of constitutional agitation. They are opposed to the spirit of British Law. They are opposed to the spirit of that law which is higher than all human laws, the law of Nature which is engraved on the hearts and consciences of the people of this country."

He was a shining light of the South Indian political firmament for nearly two decades, and though he never had a following or a school of thought behind him, he was a notable personality with a rugged eloquence all his own.

Amongst the earlier leaders, we could count a variety of men and temperaments. Men like G. Subrahmania Aiyar, D. E. Wacha, and G. K. Gokhale were of one type. Their forte was economics, their eloquence was the eloquence of facts; they never appealed to popular imagination by quoting ancient tradition or harping upon the golden age of India. Their arguments were clean cut, their logic was unassailable, their authorities above criticism.

D. E. Wacha

It is difficult to say which subject is the forte, and which the favourite, of this venerable patriarch of the Congress. His brilliant attainments showed themselves even at the first session of the Congress when he "made the first of many great speeches" and gave an able and exhaustive review of the Military position. At the second Congress he turned his attention to the property of the Indian population and drew attention to the annual tribute to Great Britain which was enriching England and impoverishing India.

He referred to "the increasing poverty of vast numbers of the population in India" and pointed out that "the condition of the ryot had steadily deteriorated since 1848 and that 40 millions of people had only one meal a day, and not always that." The main cause, he said, "was the tribute to Great Britain which is exported there, only to fructify and swell still further the unparalleled wealth of those distant isles, never in any shape to return here to bless the country from whose soil it was wrung, or the people the sweat of whose brows it represents."

At the fifth Congress (1889, Bombay), he dealt with the Excise policy and pointed out how the House of Commons, by a resolution, had directed the Government of India to modify their Excise policy so as to meet the wishes of the people, and after nine months, however, the Government had done nothing. He turned to the subject again at the 6th Congress, as well as to the question of Salt Tax. In 1892, the Congress at Allahabad was agitated over the Currency question and Mr. Wacha explained the effects of the demonetization of silver by Germany in 1873, the bearing of the 'Home Charges' on India, the Sherman Act of 1890, and the effect on India of a gold standard as jeopardising the interests of the masses. The 'State-regulated immorality' in India came up for severe censure at his hands at the 9th session. At the same session, Mr. Wacha moved a resolution against the stoppage of silver coinage and said:

"The hard working labourers, the overtaxed peasantry, are being impoverished in order that

Government officials and usurers may fatten at their expense. It robs the ryots; it entails an additional burden on them in order to actually compensate a microscopic minority, already in receipt of salaries which find no parallel in any part of the civilized globe."

Wacha's shrewdness led him to dwell upon the problems of Lancashire so early as in 1885, for he said, "If Military expenditure be not diminished, it should be met by a re-imposition of the import duties, the abolition of which had robbed poverty stricken India to enrich wealthy Lancashire."

Again in 1894, Wacha turned to "the injustice of imposing Excise duties on cotton goods, crippling the infant mill industry of India and sacrificing the interests of India to those of Lancashire." He praised the Government of India for its resistance to the Excise Bill and blamed the Secretary of State for this act of injustice. He deplored the helplessness of the former because "it was merely the registrar of the ukases of the Great Autocrat for the time being at Westminster." We shall not pause to mention in detail the various occasions—they are really many—on which Mr. Wacha dealt with his favourite themes, the Military problem, and the poverty of the people. Finance was still to the fore at the eleventh Congress (Poona, 1895), and Mr. Wacha exposed the serious misrepresentation of facts by Sir James Westland when he said that the increase in Civil and Military expenditure was due to the Exchange. Mr. Wacha proved the inaccuracy of the statement by quoting official figures. By the 11th Congress, Mr. Wacha earned the title of the "Firebrand of Bombay" and in a vigorous speech, full of facts and an intimate knowledge of his subject, he supported the import duties on cotton. He next distinguished himself by his brilliant evidence before the Royal

Commission on Expenditure, popularly known as the Welby Commission, and elicited the praise of the Congress and of scholars like Gokhale. The Frontier policy was a source of concern in the year 1897, and at the 13th session held at Amraoti that year, Mr. Wacha protested against the policy adopted, pointing out that if the Imperial policy required these trans-frontier excursions, the British Exchequer should bear most of the cost. The Indian Currency question became once more a burning question in 1898, i.e., between the reporting of the Herschell Commission and the appointment of the Fowler Committee. Mr. Wacha dwelt upon the wrong course pursued in closing the mints to silver coinage in 1898 and pointed out that the Amended Coinage Act of 1893 passed in half an hour by the Simla Legislature, without any representative of India being summoned, was the starting point. "It was the Home Charges that were the disease," said he, "not the currency. Then came attempts to fix exchange value and to prop it up by the Gold Bill. Frontier policy, famine and plague exhausted the cash balances." He followed up his attack on the Currency question by condemning the introduction of the gold standard into India at the 15th Congress (Lucknow, 1899). "The Congress had already discussed Currency Reform thrice. He condemned Lord Curzon's idea that gold would flow into India from all gold producing countries. The root of India's poverty was the yearly drain. Only indigenous wealth was fruitful. The silver of the rupee had been depreciated while its nominal value was enhanced. Silver had sold at a rupee per tola but now only at 10 or 11 annas. So silver jewels, the reserve fund of the poor, had diminished in market value." Mr. Wacha was called upon by the Nation to preside over the 17th session (1901, Calcutta), and delivered a marvellous address which should only be read and cannot be quoted from: We have given some extracts in other chapters. Mr. Wacha had been Joint General Secretary of the Congress since the year 1896 and continued to be such till 1913. His active association with the Congress reached its climax with his Presidentship, and thereafter he took only passive interest in the affairs of the Congress, occasionally moving a resolution or seconding it. Virtually his last appearance was in Bombay in 1915 when he was the Chairman of the Reception Committee. Mr. Wacha had been, for over a quarter of a century, one of the most oustanding figures of the Congress. For versatile talents, for mastery of facts, and for an intimate knowledge of obscure subjects like the Military question and of vague and widespread problems like the poverty of the people, there were few to equal and none to excel Mr. D. E. Wacha.

Presiding over the 17th Congress in Calcutta in 1901, Wacha asks in despair as well as derision: "Did England sit quiet while the Plantagenets were filling all the high offices to the great disadvantage of the English themselves? Was not England pauperized when the Papacy was rampant and abstracted millions from it annually, as history recorded? Would England refrain from complaining, supposing that the position of India and England was to-day reversed?" Is it any wonder that D. E. Wacha should have been dubbed 'the Firebrand of the Congress'? The extremist of one era becomes the moderate of a later era, and Wacha has lived to be a Knight, a nominated member of the Central Legislature and a much esteemed confidant of the British Government in India.

G. K. Gokhale

Gokhale was even more pronounced in his views and more severe in his language. His first appearance at the Congress was in 1889 along with Tilak. His *bete noire* in the Councils was the artificial surpluses during Lord Curzon's time which were the result of a manipulated exchange, and he put it to Government either to purify currency or reduce taxation. His attacks on the Salt Tax were profusely illustrated with facts and figures, as when he pointed out how a basket of salt costing 3 pies was made to cost 5 annas. If he spoke on the Public Services Commission and the orders of the Secretary of State on the Commission's recommendations, he showed how, instead of 125 posts legitimately due to Indians, they would get only 108, and how out of these, 93 were made by the Secretary of State discretionary. He, however, had the remarkable knack of saying the hardest things in the gentlest language. Condemning the open avowal in 1894 by Government that "the highest posts must for all time to come be held by Europeans," he says, "the pledges of equal treatment which England has given us, have supplied us with a high and worthy ideal for our Nation, and if these pledges are repudiated, one of the strongest claims of British Rule to our attachment will disappear." If Gokhale was pleasant in his criticism, he was nevertheless not given to mincing matters in any measure. His attack on Sir James Fitz-James Stephen was outspoken and stern. "An English Judge (the reference is to Sir James Fitz-James Stephen) famous or infamous in a way, did not scruple to accept this latter position (that England is prepared to break faith with us now) and propound the preposterous doctrine that the Proclamation of 1858 was never meant to be seriously taken." And he asks in utter despair whether we "should fling into the flames all these pledges as so much waste paper." Gokhale had a particularly euphemistic way of dealing with the bureaucracy. When the Reform Act of 1892 was passed, it was discovered that that Act did not give the right of election of members of Councils, but allowed the Viceroy to make rules subject to the approval of the Secretary of State, and Gokhale says, re. the rules, "I will not say that they have been deliberately so framed as to defeat the object of the Act of 1892, but I will say this, that if the officer who drafted them had been asked to sit down with the deliberate purpose of framing a scheme to defeat that object, he could not have done better." Gokhale always had a soft corner in his heart for the "starving, shrunken, shrivelled-up ryot, toiling and moiling from dawn to dark to earn his scanty meal, patient, resigned, forbearing beyond measure, entirely voiceless in the Parliament of his rulers and meekly prepared to bear whatever burdens God and man might be pleased to impose upon his back." And it was in the cause of such a ryot that he dealt with questions of taxation and expenditure. Even Gokhale's disciplined and proverbial moderation failed him on occasions, and the strain imposed upon it by the reactionary policy of Lord Curzon was really great. The Partition of Bengal, the curtailment of the rights of the Calcutta Corporation, the University Reform which, in the name of efficiency, officialized the Senates and made education expensive and even costly, the Official Secrets Act—all these more than counterbalanced Lord Curzon's good acts, such as his Famine Policy and his regulations re. passes to soldiers for shooting, the Ancient Monuments Preservation Act, and the punishment in the Rangoon and O'Hara cases, and provoked Gokhale into saying, "then, all I can say is 'Good-bye to all hope of co-operating in any way with the bureaucracy in the interests of the people'." "A great rush and uprising of the waters such as has been recently witnessed in Bengal cannot take place without a little inundation over the banks here and there. These little excesses are inevitable when large masses of men move spontaneously—especially when the movement is from darkness to light, from bondage towards freedom." Gokhale justified, as President of the Benares Congress

(1905), Boycott as a political weapon to be used only at the last extremity and with strong popular feeling behind it. Gokhale's courtesy for the opponent did not obscure his clarity of language or effectiveness of attack. "Four villages out of every five are without a school-house and seven children out of eight grow up in ignorance." This is far more telling than to say that literacy is only 12 per cent. It was in Gokhale's Presidential Address at Benares that he gave wide publicity to the confidential document of Lord Lytton in which the latter wrote:—

> "We all know that these claims and expectations never can or will be fulfilled. We have had to choose between prohibiting them (the Natives of India) and cheating them, and we have chosen the least straightforward course. . . . . Since I am writing confidentially, I do not hesitate to say that both the Governments of England and India appear to me up to the present moment unable to answer satisfactorily the charge of having taken every means in their power of breaking to the heart the words of promise they had uttered to the ear."

Gokhale was the chosen representative sent to England in two successive years, 1905 and 1906. Indeed he had visited England earlier in 1897. Gokhale's position between the people and the Government was an unenviable one. The former disparaged his moderation, the latter deprecated his extremism. This was largely due to the role that he filled as an intermediary between the two, a role which Chandavarkar as President of the Lahore Congress (1900) assigned to the Congress as the true interpreter between the rulers and the ruled. Gokhale interpreted popular aspirations to the Viceroy and the Government's difficulties to the Congress. This made him somewhat unpopular. Even Lord Minto wrote of Gokhale, when in October, 1907, a split occurred in the Congress at Surat, "as party manager he is a baby—he is always whining just like a second-rate Irishman, between Dan O'Connell and Parnell." Another incident indicating the attitude of the Viceroy towards Gokhale is set out in Minto's biography by Lady Minto. Gokhale had written a letter to a friend in England which Morley saw and he sent to Minto an extract therefrom. Minto remarked: "I can only call it mischievous and written with the intention to mislead. Gokhale would not have spoken in the same sense to me, and that is the worst of him, that one cannot rely upon his absolute good faith, although I know him well, admire him much, and am on most friendly terms with him."

It must also be admitted that as Gokhale advanced in years, he complained that "the bureaucracy was growing frankly selfish and openly hostile to National aspirations. It was not so in the past." What oppressed him was not capitalism but absentee capitalism super-added to the racial ascendancy of the West, the moral and material drain, the increasing death rate in India. And he formulated a definite programme embracing the demand for a larger share in administration and control by a steady substitution of Indians for Europeans, improvement in methods of administration, readjustment of financial arrangements and measures to improve the condition of the people.

Gokhale's great constructive work is the Servants of India Society, being an order of political workers pledged to work for the Motherland on a pittance and subject to rigid rules of discipline as well as loyalty to the Empire. Sastriar is his great Successor. As First Member of the Society, Gokhale may be regarded as the forerunner of the order of self-denying patriots established later by Mrs. Besant in the 'Sons of India' and of the still more ascetical and exacting order of *Ashramavasis* and

Ashrams, established by Gandhi in 1916, and others after the model of Gandhi's Ashram, since 1920.

After the Surat Split, Gokhale took a leading part in the Congress. He visited South Africa and rendered signal help to Gandhi in his campaign of Passive Resistance. At the Congress of 1909, he was in raptures over the cult of Passive Resistance and explained to an admiring audience the philosophy underlying it.[1] Later his activities were chiefly concentrated on the arena of the Central Legislature. In 1914 when there was an attempt to reunite the wings of the Congress, he agreed first to such a reunion but changed his mind afterwards. After a strenuous public career marked by a spirit of devotion to the country and intense sacrifice in its cause, Gokhale passed away on the 19th February, 1915.

G. Subrahmania Aiyar

One may ask out of curiosity as to who moved the first resolution of the first Congress. It was Mr. G. Subrahmania Aiyar of Madras, the Editor of *The Hindu*, popularly known as Editor Subrahmania Aiyar. The resolution was that the promised enquiry into the working of the Indian administration should be by a Royal Commission with adequate representation of Indians thereon. He made the pithy statement that "Parliament took control in theory but abandoned it in fact,—except where English Party interests were concerned—and the India Council took the place of the defunct Company, but ruled without enquiry." We do not hear of Mr. Subrahmania Aiyar till the 10th Congress which met in Madras in 1894, and at this session, he dealt with the question of Indian finance and the necessity for enquiry into it. He

[1] The passage is quoted in Chapter II entitled 'Review of Resolutions', Section 14—Indians Abroad.

pointed out how Sir William Hunter in *The Times* impugned the honesty of the Government of India, and where such accusations were made enquiry was needed. Another subject of interest at that session was the deprivation of the liberty of the Press in Indian States, and Mr. Subrahmania Aiyar entered a vigorous protest against it. At the twelfth session (1896, Calcutta), he dealt with the subject of simultaneous examinations as also the question of short settlements of Land Revenue. At the Amraoti Congress next year he protested against the Frontier policy. When the Congress met for the third time in Madras in 1898, Mr. Subrahmania Aiyar reverted to the question of Frontier policy, which he condemned as "mischievous, and dangerous.....a policy prompted by that spirit of aggression abroad and repression at home." He also spoke on the currency question pointing out how "Government looked only to exchange, Anglo-Indian merchants only to trade; none considered the people. Taxes were levied in silver and the ryot would have to sell 60 per cent. more of his produce to gain the inflated value of the rupee. The great flow of English capital into the country is not an advantage, for it increases the drain. Indian capital should be invested here, and then the gain would be real." Mr. Subrahmania Aiyar's favourite subject, however, was the economic condition of India, and at the sixteenth session (Lahore, 1900), he asked for an enquiry with a view to discovering and adopting remedies for the oft-recurring famines, and he also dealt with the question of the Public Services and the exclusion of Indians therefrom. At the seventeenth session (Calcutta, 1901), the sad story of the ryot and his poverty arrested his attention. He remarked that the reason for the ryot living at all was "the tropical climate where life can linger on the scantiest of subsistence." "But," he asked, "is the life's function of the Indian ryot to live and die merely like a brute? Is he not a human being endowed with reason, sentiment and latent capacity? There are nearly 200 millions of people living a life of chronic starvation and of the most abject ignorance, grim and silent in their suffering, without zest in life, without comfort or enjoyment, without hope or ambition, living because they were born into the world and dying because life could no longer be kept in the body." He also dealt with the question of famine at this Congress and pleaded for industrial independence. He made practical suggestions for founding technical institutions, foreign scholarships and a careful survey of indigenous industry. Mr. Subrahmania Aiyar's range of vision was as wide as his knowledge was deep. In 1902, at the 18th session at Ahmedabad, Mr. Subrahmania Aiyar dwelt upon the poverty of the people once again. He pointed out that "there had been a time when the population of India was so flourishing that foreign visitors envied it and when arts and industries flourished. The East India Company had deliberately sacrificed India to the commercial advantage of England, had discouraged industries and encouraged agriculture, so that India might produce raw materials for the manufacturing industries of England; that policy had destroyed Indian industries, and Government, which had inherited it, should reverse it. What is being done? The gold mines of Kolar are worked by European capital. They yield 20 crores of rupees' worth of gold annually, which is taken to another country. When, in another 20 or 30 years, all the gold is dug up and carried away, what will remain to the people of Mysore, but stones? Government ought to protect Indian wealth, not allow it to be carried away." Year after year Mr. Subrahmania Aiyar hammered away at subjects of not only economic, but also of cultural and administrative interest. The Tata Research Institute, the University Bill, Legislative Council Reform,—all these equally claimed his attention as well as his affection. The disposal of artificial surpluses, to which Gokhale drew public attention for the first time, and the currency problems under which the enhancement of the value of the rupee would be a new burden on the people and a silent addition to the taxes, were also his favourite themes. Subrahmania Aiyar was ultimately put into jail for his writings and only his physical disease got him his release. He was one of the most fearless and far-sighted politicians of his time and deserves the gratitude of posterity.

Budruddin Tyabji

Budruddin Tyabji was a staunch Congressman who rose to be the President of the Congress in its third year, (1887, Madras). Mr. Tyabji laid stress in his address on the representative character of the Congress and asserted its loyalty. It was at his instance that a Committee was appointed to consider the many suggestions sent in for discussion and to draw up a programme for the work of the Congress. The Committee was really the precursor of the Subjects Committee of later days. We do not hear of Mr. Tyabji in connection with the Congress till the 20th session held in 1904 in Bombay, as he had become a Judge of the Bombay High Court. In 1904, he took part in the discussion on the resolution dealing with Indians in Public Service. He passed away in 1906 and his demise was the subject of a resolution of intense grief, for, three ex-presidents died that year,—W. C. Bonnerjee, Tyabji and A. M. Bose. There was a peculiar appropriateness in Tyabji, a Muslim, presiding over the 3rd session, after the first had been presided over by a Hindu—W. C. Bonnerjee, and the second by a Parsee—Dadabhai Naoroji.

Justice Kashinath Trimbak Telang

He was "one of the most active founders of the Congress" and its "first hard-working Secretary in Bombay." At the very first session the Hon'ble Mr. K. T. Telang moved the resolution relating to the Supreme and Provincial Legislative Councils and outlined the electorates for members. At the fourth Congress, when Sir Auckland Colvin was looming large in the Congress horizon, the Hon'ble Mr. Telang effectively answered the hostile criticisms of Colvin and Dufferin. At the same session he had to intervene at a critical moment which arose in course of discussion on the subject of Permanent Settlement. Speaking at this very session Mr. Telang remarked that while Government had always money for its varied activities, it gave only one per cent. of its revenues to Education. He died a premature death in 1893 which was referred to by Dadabhai Naoroji at the ninth session.

W. C. Bonnerjee

For an authoritative statement of the objects of the Congress, one must necessarily turn to the first presidential address of the Congress, and W. C. Bonnerjee was the President of the first Congress who stated clearly these objects which have already been quoted in the account of the first session. He had the honour of proposing the President of the 3rd and the 5th Congress and was himself made again President of the eighth session (Allahabad, 1892). It may be remembered that in 1891 the Age of Consent Bill was the cause of considerable public agitation and Tilak made himself conspicuous by his opposition to it. Mr. W. C. Bonnerjee referred in his presidential address at Allahabad to the reasons for the non-interference by the Congress with social questions. There is, on the general question of political agitation, a striking passage in this address which we quote below:—

"Is our voice not to be listened to because, forsooth, to that voice has not been added the voice of our European fellow-subjects? We would welcome, welcome with open arms, all the support which we can get from our European fellow-subjects....... But apart from that, why is our voice to be despised? It is we who feel the pinch; it is we who have to suffer; and when we cry out, it is said to us: 'Oh, we cannot listen to you: yours is a contemptible and useless and a vile agitation, and we will not listen to you.' Time was when if we, natives of the country, agitated about any matter, with the help of non-official Europeans, the apologists of the Government used to say triumphantly: 'This agitation is not the agitation of the natives of the country, but has been got up by a few discontented Europeans; don't listen to them, it is not their true voice, it is the voice of these Europeans.' And now we are told: 'Don't listen to them; it is their own voice, and not the voice of the Europeans'."

W. C. Bonnerjee was a member of the delegation that went to England in 1890. He had taken part in the discussion on various resolutions, such as the appointment of a Parliamentary Committee (1888), the question of 'Grievances before supply' (1889), and the extension of the Jury system (1895). It was in connection with the Jury system that he made an excellent point in urging that "a judge, translating in his mind the vernacular of a rustic witness, was too engrossed with the language to attend properly to the witness. Indian jurymen understanding the language would watch the demeanour of witnesses and would distinguish truthful speech from false." He pleaded strongly for the maintenance of the British Committee at the seventeenth Congress (1901), and after meritorious services rendered to the national cause, passed away in the year 1906.

LOKAMANYA TILAK

Tilak and Gokhale go together. Broadly speaking, they between them had a certain kinship, though there were marked differences. When Lokamanya Tilak spoke, there was as much that was left unsaid as was actually said. That is how his writings and speeches were understood. They had a flair all their own. Lokamanya Tilak employed gentle satire in his remarks. "If you take away the produce of the land," said he, "and do not give it back to the land in some form more material than prestige and advice, the country must grow poorer and poorer." Talking of provincial contributions at the 12th Congress (Calcutta, 1896), he said: "The arrangement between the Supreme Government and the Local Governments is like that between an intemperate husband and his wife—that when the first had indulged all his extravagant habits, he asked his wife to surrender all her savings." In further illustration of this feature, we may quote the famous passage in his Amritsar speech where he said "give unto Caesar what is Caesar's and unto God what is God's." The implication was that it was our duty doubtless to obey the laws, but the duty to our country was not less imperative.

Lokamanya Tilak was the uncrowned king of Maharashtra, and later, of India during the Home Rule days. This position he attained by service and suffering. The outbreak of plague and the excesses of some of the officers in 1897 in Poona and Bombay led to great discontent and Dr. Besant considered that that was the birth of extremism. The murder of Mr. Rand and Lieutenant Ayerst while they were driving in a carriage, by a pistol shot from behind, ended in the execution of Damodar Hari Chapekar and his brother and the incarceration of the Sirdars Natu without trial.

Lokamanya Tilak was responsible for reviving the memory of Shivaji. Public meetings were organised and festivals held all over Maharashtra. The first public meeting so organised was attended by the leading Chiefs of the Maratha States as also by the leading Jagirdars and the Inamdars of the Deccan. We have referred to Lokamanya Tilak's sentence of 18 months' R. I. It was awarded on the 14th September 1897 for publishing a few verses (descriptive of an imaginary message of Shivaji) and a report of his speech at the Shivaji festival, and he was released on the 6th September 1898 as the result of an application signed by Prof. Max Muller, Sir William Hunter, Sir Richard Garth, Mr. William Caine, Mr. Dadabhai Naoroji and Mr. Ramesh Chandra Dutt. He was himself responsible for the condition that, if he should ever be convicted again for sedition, the six months now remitted should be added to the next sentence. It was while Tilak was in jail that sections 124-A and 153-A were added to the Penal Code so as to amplify the scope of the offences.

An attempt to pass a special resolution about Tilak's release at the Amraoti Congress in 1897 failed. What was lost in the Congress was gained in the speeches of the President, Sir Sankaran Nair, and of Surendra Nath Banerjea. Both of them paid an eloquent tribute to the great man and scholar who was wasting away in the jail. This raised Tilak's fame to the pinnacle of its glory, more so in contrast with the cloud that gathered over the head of Mr. Gokhale in the same year. Gokhale had gone to England in the summer of 1897 with a grand send-off. On his return he tendered an apology for certain statements he had made in England regarding the "violent acts of soldiers in the Rand regime." He could easily have substantiated his charges, but that meant the revealing of secret information as well as betraying his informants who were high placed men. Accordingly Gokhale chose the only honorable course open to him—of tendering an apology—and thus raised himself in the estimation of discerning judges.

Ever since 1896 Tilak was trying to induce the Congress to show a little more grit. In 1899, when he wanted to move a resolution condemning the regime of Lord Sandhurst, a storm of opposition was raised. He challenged the delegates to prove that Lord Sandhurst's regime had not been ruinous to the people. He quoted the misdeeds of the bureaucracy categorically and asked whether he was at all exaggerating. But Mr.R. C. Dutt, the President, and many other delegates were, it is said, violently against Tilak's propositions, and when Tilak began to quote chapter and verse to prove that he could not be restrained on the ground that provincial matters should not engage the attention of the Congress, the President threatened to resign if Tilak persisted. Mr. R. C. Dutt had only recently retired from the I. C. S. after holding the position of an Acting Commissioner.

The split in the Congress at Surat in 1907 was the subject of much bitter controversy at the time, and Lokamanya Tilak was described as the arch-offender who had brought about the ruin of the Congress which had been built up in more than 25 years. Varying versions were given by the two parties. There can be no doubt that the differences which had manifested themselves in Calcutta between the Moderate leaders and the Nationalists, and which had been somehow composed for the time being by the commanding personality of Dadabhai Naoroji, became acuter in 1907. The change of the venue of the Congress from Nagpur to Surat was due to these differences, and the Nationalists openly alleged that Surat had been purposely selected by the Moderates as a safe place where they could, with the help of local delegates, have their own way. The Nationalists wanted Lokamanya Tilak to preside, but the Moderates were opposed to this and Dr. Rash Behari Ghose was elected according to the constitution. The Nationalists put forward the name of Lala Lajpat Rai, thinking that the great prestige attendant on his recent return after deportation would carry his name without opposition. But Lala Lajpat Rai, with characteristic self-abnegation, declined the honour. When the delegates had arrived at Surat, the Lokamanya got the delegates of his way of thinking together in a separate camp. Attempts were made to compose the differences but misunderstandings went on increasing. The Nationalists were keen on getting the resolutions passed at Calcutta relating to Self-Government, Boycott and National Education to be repeated, if not extended, but they were under the impression that the Moderate leaders were keen on going back on them or, at any rate, watering them down. Unfortunately the draft of resolutions prepared by the Reception Committee was not available till the Congress actually met, and statements made to the effect that they were included in the draft were not accepted. Attempts were made by Lokamanya Tilak through intermediaries to bring about a compromise but these failed, and his effort to meet Mr. Tribhuvandas Malvi, the Chairman of the Reception Committee, met with no better success. When the Congress actually met on the first day, the 27th December, at 2-30, over 1,600 delegates were present, and after the Chairman of the Reception Committee had read out his address of welcome, the name of Dr. Rash Behari Ghose, who had been nominated by the Reception

Committee under the rules, was proposed as President. There were shouts and noise and when the proposition was being seconded by Surendra Nath Banerjea, the noise and disturbance were so great that the proceedings had to be adjourned till the next day. Fresh efforts appear to have been again made for a settlement with no result. On the 28th the Congress met again. When the Presidential procession was passing, a slip signed by Lokamanya Tilak was handed over to Mr. Malvi telling him that he wished "to address the delegates on the proposal of the election of President after it is seconded. I wish to move an adjournment with a constructive proposal. Please announce me." The proceedings started at the step at which they had been terminated on the previous day and Surendra Nath Banerjea completed his speech seconding the proposal for the election of Dr. Ghose. This slip was not attended to in spite of a reminder, and Lokamanya Tilak proceeded to the platform to assert his right of addressing the delegates. The Chairman of the Reception Committee and Dr. Ghose both thought Dr. Ghose was duly elected, and would not permit him to address the House. Shouting and confusion naturally followed which was intensified by the fact that a shoe was hurled from amongst the delegates which grazed Surendra Nath Banerjea and hit Sir Pherozeshah Mehta. Then a general melee ensued. Chairs were thrown and sticks were brandished and the Congress ended for the day. The Moderate leaders met and organised the Convention and fixed a constitution for the Congress which practically excluded the Nationalists. At this distance of time it is possible to form some opinion on the view-points of the two parties. That there were differences in outlook, and each party was anxious to have its outlook accepted by the Congress, cannot be gainsaid. But as matters stood at the time when the Lokamanya rose to speak, the point was a small one. He insisted that, under the constitution as adopted in Calcutta, the President was only nominated by the Reception Committee and it was the delegates assembled in Congress who finally and effectively elected the President. He was therefore entitled to move an amendment or even an adjournment of the House at that stage. He was not allowed to do so and he wanted to exercise his right of addressing the delegates on this unjust deprivation of his right. It is impossible to say that technically he was not correct. At the same time one cannot help saying that feelings had become exacerbated on account of pure misunderstanding which arose from a suspicion that the Calcutta resolutions were not included in the draft. Even if they were not, it was open to the Subjects Committee to include them, or if they were in a form not satisfactory to the Nationalists, it was open to the Subjects Committee to alter or modify them suitably, if they had a majority there. Their omission, by itself, even if it was a fact, need not have led to the situation as it developed. A frank discussion among the leaders of the two parties ought to have been sufficient to clear the position and the questions could have been dealt with on their merits. But this could not take place possibly on account of pique on the part of some Moderate leaders. It is, however, easy to be wise after the event, and when feelings run high even great men may, and do, lose their balance. It would be imprudent on our part to attempt any apportionment of blame between two such men as Lokamanya Tilak and Gokhale, and we pass over the unfortunate incident without allowing our reverence for them to be dimmed in the least.

Lokamanya Tilak was intensely nationalistic in his views but he recognised the limitations of the age. In 1904, when there was a demand for an enquiry into the state of India every 20 years and a deputation to urge this matter, because of the coming general election, Lokamanya Tilak seconded the motion and urged that "an agitation must be made in England, for there the judges sit who would decide our case and as the Government of India is impervious, they must reach the educated people and there should be a permanent political mission in England." Later he embarked on a big litigation in England in 1918 against Sir Valentine Chirol, who called him a seditionist, for defamation and when he went to England in this connection, he put so much faith in the Labourites and their power to emancipate India that he paid £3,000 to the Labour Party. The earlier politicians believed in the Liberals as against the Conservatives. The Nationalists of a later day believed in Labourites to the exclusion of Liberals and Conservatives alike. The result of his suit against Chirol was disappointing and it was expected that that at least should have opened his eyes to the real character of the British Rule in India and impelled him to change his plan of campaign against Government. But the moment the Bill of 1919 was passed he declared in favour of Responsive Co-operation, and when Non-co-operation was being discussed in the country he did not take active part in the conversations. He said he would be glad to help the Muslims in the Khilaphat troubles but passed away on the 1st August 1920. Non-co-operation itself was to begin on that date. Lokamanya Tilak was the one man in the old era who had suffered from persecution all along, and when the judge who convicted him in 1908 made bitter remarks against him and asked him what he would say, he gave a memorable reply which deserves to be enshrined in letters of gold in every home: "In spite of the verdict of the Jury I maintain I am innocent. There are higher powers that rule the destinies of things and it may be the will of Providence that the cause which I represent should prosper more by my suffering than by my remaining free." Indeed in a like spirit had he spoken in 1897 when, in the course of his trial for sedition, he was simply asked to declare the truth in the Court, namely, that the matter for which he was being prosecuted was not written by him (that was true of the articles of indictment in 1908 as well). He flatly refused and remarked: "There comes a stage in our lives when we are not the sole master of ourselves but must act as the representatives of our fellowmen." He took his sentences coolly and produced his magnificent works from behind the prison bars. *The Arctic Home of the Vedas* and the *Gita Rahasya* would not have been possibly left as a legacy to the Nation but for his incarcerations. Tilak was invited to the War Conference of Bombay in July 1918 and he attended. He had hardly spoken for two minutes when he was stopped from proceeding further. The fact was that he began to answer Lord Willingdon's remarks against Home Rulers.

The great part that the Lokamanya played in the Home Rule days and at Amritsar is described in the chapter dealing with the subject. Tilak is one of our patriarchs who passed away after much suffering for his country, but he will be remembered for ever for the rich and inspiring legacy that he has left to every citizen of his Nation which is contained in the thought "Swaraj is my birthright and I will have it."

When in 1896 Gandhi visited Poona and wanted to organise a meeting on the problem of 'Indians in South Africa,' he saw Lokamanya Tilak and, on his advice, Gokhale as well. Gandhi's estimate of the two is worth recalling. Tilak appeared to him like the Himalayas—great and lofty—but unapproachable, while Gokhale appeared like the holy Ganges in which he could confidently take a plunge. Tilak and Gokhale were both

Maharashtrians; they were both Brahmins; they both belonged to the same Chitpavan sect. They were both patriots of the first order. Both had made heavy sacrifices in life. But their temperaments were widely different from each other. Gokhale was a 'Moderate' and Tilak was an 'Extremist' if we may use the language in vogue at the time. Gokhale's plan was to improve the existing constitution; Tilak's was to reconstruct it. Gokhale had necessarily to work with the bureaucracy; Tilak had necessarily to fight it. Gokhale stood for co-operation wherever possible and opposition wherever necessary; Tilak inclined towards a policy of obstruction. Gokhale's prime concern was with the administration and its improvement; Tilak's supreme consideration was the Nation and its upbuilding. Gokhale's ideal was love and service, Tilak's was service and suffering. Gokhale's methods sought to win the foreigner, Tilak's to replace him. Gokhale depended upon others' help, Tilak upon self-help. Gokhale looked to the classes and the intelligentsia, Tilak to the masses and the millions. Gokhale's arena was the Council Chamber; Tilak's forum was the village *mandap*. Gokhale's medium of expression was English; Tilak's was Marathi. Gokhale's objective was Self-Government for which the people had to fit themselves by answering the tests prescribed by the English; Tilak's objective was Swaraj which is the birthright of every Indian and which he shall have without let or hindrance from the foreigner. Gokhale was on a level with his age; Tilak was in advance of his times.

Pandit Ayodhyanath

The names of several other elderly Congressmen occur to us. Pandit Ayodhyanath was a highly revered character in the early years, and his association began with his Chairmanship of the Reception Committee of the 4th Congress at Allahabad in 1888 over which Mr. George Yule presided. It was the melancholy duty of the eighth Congress that met once again in the same city in 1892 to bemoan the loss of both these Congressmen. When a memorial was sought to be raised in honour of the late Pandit Ayodhyanath, Mr. Hume gave a piece of advice which is well worth quoting: "For God's sake, waste no money on memorials or any other minor enterprise, but give every farthing you can spare to the general cause." But Pandit Ayodhyanath's best memorial and gift to the Nation is his son—Pandit Hridaynath Kunzru.

Surendra Nath Banerjea

In the Valhalla of Indian politicians there lies in a prominent niche the spirit of Surendra Nath Banerjea hovering over the destinies of India—Surendra Nath who had been for over four decades connected with the Congress and whose trumpet voice, resounding from the Congress platform in India, reached the farthest recesses of the civilized world. For command of language, for elegance of diction, for a rich imagery, for emotional heights, for a spirit of manly challenge, his orations are hard to beat; they remain unapproachable. The spice of his speeches was his avowal of loyalty. He developed this into a fine art. He presided over the Congress twice, first at Poona in 1895 and next at Ahmedabad in 1902. In the kaleidoscopic display of subjects and resolutions that came up before the Congress, in successive years, there was hardly any he was not feeling himself equal to. In the domain of the Military question, for years together towards the end of the 19th century, Russia was the bogey before England, as France had been in the 18th, and Germany is in the 20th. But Surendra Nath's answer is memorable: "The true scientific frontier against Russian invasion does not lie in some remote inaccessible mountain which has yet to be discovered, but it lies deep in the hearts of a loyal and contented people." Compare this utterance with the recent slogans which have become current from the popular side, namely, that the best safeguards for England, commercial or financial, lie in the goodwill of India and that you cannot sell British goods to Indians at the point of the bayonet. Surendra Nath went the length of suggesting that matters of Indian politics should be made party questions in the British Parliament—a consummation which even to-day is outside the pale of practical politics. "England," said he, "is our political guide and our moral preceptor in the exalted sphere of political duty." His ideal was to "work with unwavering loyalty to the British connection,—for, the object was not the supersession of British Rule in India but the broadening of its basis, the liberalising of its spirit, the ennobling of its character and placing it on the unchangeable foundations of a Nation's affections." "India," he hoped, "would in the fulness of time find its place in the great confederacy of free States, English in their origin, English in their character, and English in their institutions." What a contrast between this and the modern ideal of Complete Independence, with our own institutions and integrity! Protesting (in 1904) against Lord Curzon's declaration that by our environment, our heritage and our upbringing, we are unequal to the responsibilities of high office under British Rule, Surendra Nath said: "Never was a deeper affront offered to the people of India by a representative of the Sovereign. It is bad enough to repudiate the Proclamation but it is adding insult to injury to cast a slur on the people of this country." In this connection he pointed out how 14 per cent. of the posts carrying Rs. 1,000 per month and upward, and 17 per cent. of those carrying 500, represented the proportion of Indians, "although the country is ours, the money is ours and the bulk of the population is ours." At the 18th Congress, he pleaded for the permanence of British Rule in India. On another occasion he described the English civilization as "the noblest which the world has ever seen, the emblem of indissoluble union between England and India,—a civilization fraught with unspeakable blessings to the people of India and unspeakable renown to the English name." So early as in 1892, he was proud to declare that "We are the citizens of a great and free Empire and we live under the protecting shadow of one of the noblest constitutions the world has ever seen. The rights of Englishmen are ours, their privileges are ours, their constitution is ours. But we are excluded from them." If the spirit of Surendra Nath is able to follow the commercial safeguards to-day, it will see how reciprocity is established with a vengeance and what a mockery it is to speak of our rights and privileges and constitution. Surendra Nath was, in spite of these beliefs and this faith, *lathi* charged in Barisal during Lord Minto's Viceroyalty, but he lived to be a Minister of Bengal.

Pandit Madan Mohan Malaviya

The next great public character whom we may justly describe as yet another patriarch of the Congress is Pandit Madan Mohan Malaviya who, from the day that he made his maiden speech at the Calcutta Congress in 1886, continues, with unbroken zeal and unabating passion, to serve this National institution, now as a humble worker and now as a leader, now as whole-hogger and now as a part protestor, now as an opponent of Non-co-operation and Civil Disobedience, and now as a true Satyagrahi and civil resister in the British jails.

In the year 1918, the Viceroy convened a War Conference of Indian leaders on the 27th, 28th, and 29th of

April for the collection of men, material and money for the Great War. It was attended by Governors, Lieutenant-Governors, Chief Commissioners, Executive Councillors, European as well as Indian Members of the Imperial Council and the various Provincial Legislative Councils, Rulers of Indian States and various other distinguished European and Indian officials and non-officials. Sastriar, the Raja of Mahmudabad, Syed Hasan Imam, Sirdar Bahadur Sunder Singh Majithia, and Gandhi made speeches supporting the first resolution, moved by the Gaekwar of Baroda, declaring India's loyalty to the King-Emperor, who had sent a message to the effect that "the need of the Empire in India's opportunity.". Then Pandit Malaviya rose and asked the Viceroy "to take a lesson from recent Indian history. During the days of Aurangzeb, the Sikh Gurus contested his supremacy. Guru Govind Singh caught hold of the humblest classes of people who came forward and initiated them, obliterating all distinctions between the Guru and the disciple, and thereby won their hearts. Now, my Lord, I want you to do all that can be done to make the soldiers we enlist feel equal to any one else fighting alongside of them in the battle. It is the spirit of Guru Govind Singh that I want to be introduced at this juncture."

When the Non-co-operation movement was inaugurated, he kept himself aloof from it but never from the Congress. The Moderates had manned the Congress in their day and abandoned it; Mrs. Besant captured it and surrendered it. But through storm and sunshine, through good report and evil, Panditji has stuck to it; Panditji is the one man who has had the courage to be alone in what he considered to be the right. At one time he was on the crest of a wave of popularity, at another he was listened to with indifference on the Congress platform. He never yielded to the current forces, either by sheer inertia or by fear of popular reprobation. When all the Congressmen resigned their places in the Assembly in 1929, he remained and had a right to remain there as a member, because he had not gone there as a Congressman. And when in less than four months the time and occasion demanded it, he resigned in 1930. In 1921 he had opposed the Non-co-operation movement, but in 1930 he found himself a wholehearted civil resister. Altogether he holds a position that is unique. As a Hindu he is progressive in his ideas and leads the van; as a Congressman he is conservative and oftentimes leads the rear. Yet the Congress feels it a privilege to yield to him an uncontested place in the Councils of the Government and the Councils of the country. Of him it may well be said, what has been said of Gandhi, that he was a devoted friend of the Empire, but that in the later years of his public life, he found himself forced to resist its autocracy with all his strength and spirit. His utterances are numerous and spread over a full half-century, and on each occasion that he spoke he must have spoken for any time between an hour and two. His *magnum opus* is the Benares Hindu University, but he is an institution by himself. He epitomizes India in all her achievements and reverses, in all her hopes and delusions and disillusionments. The first time he presided over the Congress was in 1909 at Lahore over the 24th session, when he was suddenly called upon to take the place of Sir Pherozeshah Mehta who was the duly elected President but who, for certain unknown reasons, declined the honour six days before the due date. Ten years later, the Nation called upon the Pandit to preside over the 33rd session of the Congress at Delhi in 1918.

Lala Lajpat Rai

Another great public character in the older hierarchy of Congressmen was Lala Lajpat Rai. He was alike a philanthropist, social reformer and Congressman. He had appeared at the 4th Congress in Allahabad in 1888, and in seconding the main resolution of the day relating to the expansion of Councils, quoted the opinion of Sir Syed Ahmed, who was a strong opponent of the Congress, but who in his book entitled "Causes of the Indian Revolt", written in 1858, had stated that the people should have a voice in the Councils, for, that was necessary to the stability of the Government so as to "warn us of dangers before they burst upon and destroy us." Lalaji's sustained interest in the field of politics and social service easily gave him a foremost place not only in the Punjab but in the whole of India. The Benares Congress remembers him as an outstanding speaker and Nationalist. In 1907 he was deported along with Sirdar Ajit Singh under an obsolete regulation of which Lal Mohan Ghose, the President of the Madras Congress in 1903, said—"*Letters de Cachet* were abolished in France in 1789, but were introduced in India in 1818." Lalaji was the central factor round which the events of 1907 turned. The Nationalists proposed Lala Lajpat Rai as the President of the Congress of 1907, which was to have been held at Nagpur but whose venue was changed to Surat. Gokhale who was against the proposal plainly said, "if you flout the Government, Government will throttle you." Lalaji never cared for the position and magnanimously declined to have his name considered for the place. During the negotiations for a settlement at Surat, Tilak wanted a graceful reference to Lalaji's name in proposing the President of the Congress and Surendra Nath Banerjea readily agreed, but nothing materialized in the end that way.

In 1906 Lalaji was sent as a member of the Indian deputation to England along with Gokhale. In later years he was so much harassed by the C.I.D. that he preferred to stay abroad, and during the War he was in America, it was believed, under duress. Lalaji's turn to preside over the Congress came rather late. At the Special Session of the Congress in 1920 (September) he was like a fish out of water. He never saw eye to eye with the progenitors of the Non-co-operation movement and even in his concluding speech predicted only failure for it. He was a fighter, but not a Satyagrahi. To him Civil Disobedience did not mean more than Passive Resistance. He had a most arduous time of it all through. In his own Province, there was a section of younger men arrayed against him. The Council-entry programme found him back in his element, but alas, the brutality of a Police officer who laid his *lathi* on him ultimately cut short his life and carried him away from our midst. Lalaji was doubtless a man of true vision, for he spoke in Urdu at the Congress of 1888 and proposed that a half day be set apart for Educational and Industrial matters. The resolution was accepted and the industrial exhibitions since organised are a direct result of the recommendations of the Committee then appointed in that behalf.

Sir Pherozeshah Mehta

Sir Pherozeshah Mehta was one of those who had been associated with the Congress from its very inception and played a leading part in moulding its policy and programme. Mehta presided over the sixth session of the Congress held in Calcutta in 1890, and in his address he criticised Lord Salisbury's view that "Government by representation did not fit Eastern traditions or Eastern minds" and quoted Mr. Chisholm Anstey's statement that "the East is the parent of Municipalities. Local Self-Government, in the widest acceptation of the term, is as old as the East itself." Pherozeshah Mehta held that "the Congress was indeed not the voice of the masses, but it was the duty of their educated compatriots to interpret their grievances, and offer suggestions for their redress."

"History teaches us," he pointed out, "that such has been the law of widening progress in all ages and all countries, notably in England itself. That function and that duty, which thus devolve upon us, is best discharged, not in times of alarm and uneasiness, of anger and excitement, but when the heart is loyal and clear and the reason unclouded. It is, I repeat, the glory of the Congress that the educated and enlightened people of the country seek to repay the debt of gratitude which they owe for the priceless boon of education by pleading, and pleading temperately, for timely and provident statesmanship. I have no fears but that English statesmanship will ultimately respond to the call. I have unbounded faith in the living and fertilising principles of English culture and English education."

"All the great forces of English life and society, moral, social, intellectual, political, are if slowly, yet steadily and irresistibly, declaring themselves for the choice which will make the connection of England and India a blessing to themselves and to the whole world for countless generations..... I appeal to all true Englishmen—to candid friends as to generous foes—not to let this prayer go in vain."

Pherozeshah Mehta was really the power behind the Congress for a number of years, his work being largely done on the Committees, deputations and delegations of which he was elected a member. At the session of 1892 he was appointed a member of a Committee to draw up a petition intended to be presented to Parliament, regarding the Public Service Commission and the deep disappointment caused to the country over the orders passed on its recommendations. When in 1894 the Madras Congress decided upon sending a deputation to Lord Elgin, the Viceroy, in order to present certain Congress resolutions, Mehta was appointed a member thereof and a similar honour was shown to him at the Lahore Congress in 1900 (16th session). At the 15th session held at Lucknow in 1899 he was appointed a member of the Indian Congress Committee.

It was in 1907 that he took an active part on the Moderate side at Surat. Later he was almost out of view, and when he was duly elected President of the 24th session of the Congress held in Lahore (1909), he suddenly resigned six days before he was due to take his seat, and the result was that Pandit Madan Mohan Malaviya was elected in his place.

Ananda Mohan Bose

We have already seen how Ananda Mohan Bose was a famous social and religious reformer who occupied a foremost place in the progress of the Brahmo Samaj and how he led a protestant wing of that movement. The spirit of revolt which would not tolerate a reform movement that tends to run in a rut, would not remain subdued when in the political field the rights of the people were being daily encroached upon. That was why Ananda Mohan Bose, aptly described as "the brilliant star of East Bengal," became the first secretary of the Indian Association started in Calcutta in the year 1876 and an ardent coadjutor of Surendra Nath Banerjea. We do not hear of his having had any close connection with the Congress movement as such till the year 1896, when at the 12th session he protested against the new injustice perpetrated in the scheme for reorganising the Educational Service, as being calculated to exclude Indians from the higher grades of that service. Mr. Bose asked indignantly if "the cause of progress in India was not only not to advance but to be put back." The details of the downward course are given in the review of resolutions dealing with the Public Services. Ananda Mohan Bose soon became the President of the 14th session of the Congress in 1898 (Madras). His speech on the occasion was a remarkable oration full of unanswerable arguments, and his closing message to the Congress embodied the Gospel of Love and Service of the Nation. He suggested the direct representation of India in Parliament. And it was the country's misfortune that, when it needed his services most, the Fates should have taken him away in 1906.

Man Mohan Ghose

We first hear of Man Mohan Ghose in connection with the 5th session of the Congress held in Allahabad in 1888. He moved the resolution on the Public Services. He was the Chairman of the 6th session of the Congress held in Calcutta in 1890. In a powerful speech he defended the Congress from the various attacks made on it and defined its true position. Mr. Ghose made a special study of the question of Judicial *Vs.* Executive and when, at the 11th session held at Poona in 1895, he moved the resolution on the subject, he unearthed a statement by Mr. James, a Commissioner, that the "union was the mainstay of the British power in India." His death was bemoaned at the 12th session (Calcutta, 1896).

LAL MOHAN GHOSE

Lal Mohan Ghose appeared on the Congress platform at first in 1890 at the sixth session (Calcutta) and moved the resolution relating to Mr. Bradlaugh's Bill on the Government of India, emphasising the moderation of the proposals embodied therein. He was elected as the President of the nineteenth session of the Congress held in Madras in 1903, and his Presidential Address was one of the ablest addresses ever delivered from the Congress platform. He had been out of view from active politics for some years when he was summoned to this high office. We give below two extracts from his Presidential Address:—

"Coming to the case of our own country, although there is not a man amongst us who is not sincerely loyal to the British Government, yet, claiming the undoubted right of British subjects to criticise the acts of the Government, may we not respectfully ask our rulers—and in this connection I make no distinction between the different English political parties—may we not ask whether we are to believe that the policy which many years ago killed our indigenous industries, which, even only the other day and under a Liberal administration, unblushingly imposed Excise duties on our cotton manufactures, which steadily drains our national resources to the extent of something like 20 millions sterling per annum, and which, by imposing heavy burdens on our agricultural population, increases the frequency and intensity of our famines to an extent unknown in former times, are we to believe that the various administrative acts which have led to these results were directly inspired by a beneficent Providence?"

* * *

"We are not a Self-Governing Nation. We are not able, like the English people, to change one administration for another by our votes in the polling booths. We have to depend entirely upon the justice of the British Parliament; for, unfortunately, it is only too true that, as time advances, our Indian bureaucracy, instead of coming into line with popular ideas, seems to grow more and more unsympathetic. Do you think that any administration in England, or France, or the United States would have ventured to waste vast sums of money on an empty pageant, when Famine and Pestilence were stalking over the land, and the Angel of Death was flapping his wings almost within hearing of the light-hearted revellers?

"Gentlemen, a year has now rolled by since the great political pageant was held at Delhi against the almost unanimous protests of all our public and representative men both in the Press and on the platform. On what ground did they protest? They protested, not because they were wanting in loyalty to the Sovereign, whose coronation it was intended to celebrate, but because they felt that if His Majesty's Ministers had done their duty and had laid before him an unvarnished story of his famine-stricken subjects in India, His Majesty, with his characteristic sympathy for suffering humanity, would himself have been the first to forbid his representatives in this country to offer a pompous pageant to a starving people. And the great *tamasha* was celebrated with that utter recklessness of expense which you may always expect when men, no matter how highly placed, were dealing with other people's money, and were practically accountable to no one for their acts.

"We are all familiar with the financial jugglery which, by distributing the expenses under various and sometimes under the most unexpected headings, makes it so difficult for ordinary men to find out the total cost of such pageants. Still, whether you estimate that cost by a few lacs more or less, it cannot be denied that if even half of the vast sum spent in connection with the Delhi Darbar had been made over for the purposes of famine relief, it might have been the means of saving millions of men, women and children from death by starvation."

C. Vijiaraghavachariar

Mr. C. Vijiaraghavachariar of Salem is one of our earliest Congressmen, his name being found amongst those of the members of a Committee formed at the 3rd session (Madras, 1887) to draw up a constitution for the Congress. He was appointed next as a member of the Indian Congress Committee at the fifteenth session held in Lucknow in the year 1899, and the sixteenth at Lahore next year. He was at the Lahore Session in 1900 and seconded the proposition that the Hon'ble N. G. Chandavarkar should preside over the session. In 1901 and 1902, he shared the responsibility with three others for the collection of sums due for the copies of *India* assigned to the Madras circle. When in 1905 Gokhale was elected by the Congress at Benares as a delegate to England to urge the more pressing proposals of the Congress on Government, he seconded the resolution in an able speech. At the 22nd session held in Calcutta (1906) he moved the resolution relating to Permanent Settlement and protested against the view that the Land Tax was rent. His view was that "land in India had never belonged to the King; the sages had said that the world belonged to those who were born in it; private property was gained by cultivation, and the King, who was ordained for protection, received a share from the cultivators for his services. The idea that land belonged to the King was Western and fedual, not Indian."

He had virtually stood aloof from the Congress since the Surat Split. The Moderate Congress did not appeal to his judgment. He reappeared in the Congress after the Nationalists were admitted into the Congress by the Lucknow amendments of 1916, and took an active part in the Special Session of the Congress held in Bombay in 1918, and in the session at Amritsar (1919), dwelling at the latter at length upon the Fundamental Rights of the people. He was shortly after called on to preside over the Nagpur session of the Congress and he performed his duties there with great tact and ability.

Raja Rampal Singh

Amongst other Congressmen of eminence Raja Rampal Singh's was a most outstanding name for a long time in Congress circles. It is interesting to note that Raja Rampal Singh was the mover of the resolution on Volunteering at the 2nd Congress and administered a solemn warning to India:—

> "Despite the glories of *Pax Britannica*, despite the noble intentions of Great Britain, despite all the good she may have done or tried to do us, the balance will be against her, and India will have to regret rather than rejoice that she has ever had anything to do with England. This may be strong language, but it is the truth. Nothing can ever make amends to a Nation for the destruction of its National spirit, and of the capacity to defend itself and the soil from which it springs. Look where you will around you in the world and you will see gigantic armies and armaments. There is trouble in store for the whole civilized world, and sooner or later, a tremendous military struggle will commence, in which, assuredly, before it terminates, Great Britain will be involved. Great Britain, with all her wealth, cannot put one hundred men into the field for every thousand that several Continental Powers can. Then will England regret that, instead of having millions of brave Indians trained to fling back invaders, she has only her scanty legions to oppose to them."

He pointed out how people and crops were entirely at the mercy of wild beasts. In his grandson, the young Raja of Kalakankad, who has lately passed away at a premature age, Rampal Singh was truly reborn as a sincere patriot and as a true apostle of the Congress, at whose shrine he himself had offered incense while on earth in flesh and blood.

KALI CHARAN BANERJEE

In the first half of these fifty years of Congress activity it used to be the prevailing practice to group together important resolutions of more than one year's standing and call them the omnibus resolution. Men of versatile talents who could deal with the several subjects comprised in this resolution used to be selected to move it year after year, and in 1889 the choice fell upon Kali Charan Banerjee. He was an Indian Christian who had taken for years keen interest in Congress affairs, and in the year 1890 formed a member of the Indian delegation to England elected "to represent Congress views before the British Public." At the 9th Congress (Lahore 1893), he moved the resolution on the separation of the Judicial and the Executive and cited the "shocking case which had just occurred in which four men were sentenced to death and three to transportation for life, after a trial in which rules of Law were disregarded and the Magistrate acted as Prosecutor and Judge combined." Mr. Banerjee handled the subject of simultaneous examinations in the year 1895 at the eleventh session, Poona, and pleaded, the next year, in Calcutta for Teaching Universities in particular and the improvement of Universities in general. Government said the matter was not urgent and he prayed the Congress to make it so. As time advanced and political consciousness grew in the people, their liberties were notably curtailed, and when the prohibition was imposed on managers and teachers in aided institutions forbidding them from taking part in political movements or attending political meetings without the consent of the Director of Public Instruction, Mr. Banerjee entered a spirited protest against this invasion of elementary rights of citizens at the fifteenth session of the Congress (Lucknow, 1899). Two years later in Calcutta, in 1901, he urged that Indian lawyers should be added to the Judicial Committee of the Privy Council for Indian appeals. Babu Kali Charan Banerjee would undoubtedly have become the President of the Congress in the fulness of time if he had been spared long enough, and the Congress which had a Hindu as its first, a Parsee as its second, and a Muslim as its third President, would have had an Indian Christian also as the tribune of the people, but he was cut off before his time in 1908.

NAWAB SYED MAHOMED BAHADUR

The practice of coupling a Muslim Secretary with a Hindu Secretary started with the Madras Congress of 1914 at which Nawab Syed Mahomed Bahadur and Mr. N. Subba Rau Pantulu were elected Secretaries. But the Nawab had already become the President of the Congress, having been called to that high office at Karachi in 1913. He was however a Congressman first and a Muslim next. So early as in 1901 he was elected to the Indian Congress Committee, and earlier still in 1898, he had taken part in the deliberations of the Madras Congress, having seconded a resolution welcoming Lord Curzon. When the Congress met in Madras in 1903 (19th session) the Nawab was the Chairman of the Reception Committee, and at the 20th session (1904, Bombay), he was one of those elected to a Committee to draw up a constitution for the Congress. In 1906 he was elected to the Standing Committee of the Congress. When the Convention Congress sat in Madras in 1908, the honour of proposing Dr. Rash Behari Ghose to the Chair fell to the lot of the Nawab. His greatest service to the cause of the Congress was really rendered at

Karachi (1913) where he presided over the 28th session. Being a patriot not imbued in the least with communal consciousness, he struck a high note of Nationalism and urged that the various communities of India should advance together rather than in separate groups. He noted the *rapprochement* of Hindus and Muslims, as shown by the hope expressed by the All-India Muslim League that the Leaders on both sides should meet periodically "to find a *modus operandi* for joint and concerted action on questions of public good." It would be no exaggeration to say that the Hindu-Muslim concordat as well as the Congress League Scheme of Lucknow were the off-spring of the seed sown by the Nawab at Karachi in a spirit of lofty patriotism and with pure Nationalistic outlook.

DAJI ABAJI KHARE

Permanent Settlement and fixity of tenure of land were a favourite subject in the early years of the Congress and Mr. Khare moved a resolution on the subject at the 9th session at Lahore (1893). He had been earlier selected in 1890 as a member of the Congress deputation that was to go to England. He took an intimate part in the preparation of a constitution for the Congress, which was passed in the year 1906 on his motion and most of which was later incorporated in the constitution framed in 1908. Mr. Khare was the Secretary of the Congress from the year 1909 to the year 1913 along with Mr. D. E. Wacha, and in 1911 he moved the abolition of the countervailing Excise duties on Indian cotton goods handicapping the growth and expansion of the Indian cotton industry. When in 1913 the Muslim League adopted the ideal of Self-Government for India, Mr. Khare in seconding the resolution welcoming such a development said that Self-Government would be won by the brotherhood of Hindu and Muslim.

Munshi Ganga Prasad Varma

Amongst those early patriots who had graced the first session of the Congress was Ganga Prasad Varma from Lucknow. At the second session he was elected to the Committee appointed to consider the Public Service question and report to the Congress. So late as in 1906 he was elected to the Standing Committee of the Congress and in the *interim* period he had filled various positions in the Congress Committees.

R. N. Mudholkar

Amongst the hardworking Congressmen of the earlier era Mr. R. N. Mudholkar held a position second to that of none. His first association with the Congress was in 1888 at its fourth session (Allahabad) when in seconding the resolution on the Police, he pointed out "how the Policeman who ought to be loved was detested." Twenty-four years thereafter, the Nation chose him as the President of the Congress in 1912 at Bankipore, and during these long years, he was a laborious student of Indian politics covering a wide range of interests. Agricultural Indebtedness, Poverty and Economic uplift including Technical Education were his forte. It was as his coadjutor that Mr. C. Y. Chintamani underwent the necessary probation before he shot up in Indian politics by dint of his dynamic intellect.

Sir C. Sankaran Nair

Sir C. Sankaran Nair was a power in his own day. He was a stalwart in intellect as he was in stature and to his credit stand some big achievements. His labours in the Congress cause were early rewarded by the National body calling him to preside over the Amraoti session in

1897. Like Chandavarkar and Tyabji in Bombay, Sankaran Nair too was drafted to the Bench of the Madras High Court some time after. From the Bench he was translated to the Government of India as Member of the Executive Council in 1915 and his resignation, on the question of continuance of Martial Law in 1919, of his high office made him widely popular. But like a boomerang which bursts—no one knows where—his attacks were unexpected always and they sometimes recoiled on himself. Such was his attack on Gandhi in the book 'Gandhi and Anarchy,' which led to his being sued by Sir Michael O'Dwyer, Lieut. Governor of the Punjab and he had to pay 3 lacs of rupees altogether as damages and costs.

P. Kesava Pillai

Dewan Bahadur P. Kesava Pillai's connection began with the earliest days and continued till the year 1917, since when he resigned from the Congress. In the closing years of his connection, he was a Secretary of the Congress and an ardent coadjutor of Mrs. Besant.

Bepin Chandra Pal

From Bengal we have many names to recall. Bepin Chandra Pal, Ambika Charan Mazumdar, Baikunta Nath Sen, were all men of first rate position and abilities who were popular speakers of the Congress in their day. Bepin Babu's connection began fairly early. He was an orator of renown and he swept the country from end to end by his eloquence in preaching his new cult of Boycott, Swadeshi and National Education. His extended meaning of Boycott at the Calcutta session (1906) was dissented from by speaker after speaker. His speeches in Madras in 1907 were considered by Sir V. Bhashyam Iyengar, the

Advocate-General, as inflammatory but not seditious, and he was forced to quit the Presidency. He was once deported during Lord Minto's time and on another occasion when Aurobindo Ghose was being prosecuted as Editor of *Bandemataram,* Bepin Babu knowing that his evidence would be material against Aurobindo, declined to speak from the box and cheerfully took his six months' R. I. for it. Later when he returned from England he was prosecuted for his articles on 'Aetiology of the Bomb,' but he apologized. He was since feeling out of joint with the growing changes in the evolution of Indian Politics, and being an individualist of a marked type, naturally ceased to be the popular and prominent figure that he had been for years in the Congress arena. His last public appearance was at the All-Parties' Conference held at Lucknow in 1928. It must be admitted that Bepin Babu was one of the few men that exercised a magical influence, through his speeches and writings in *New India* and *Bandemataram,* on the young men of his time.

Ambika Charan Mazumdar

Babu Ambika Charan Mazumdar was a lawyer who steadily worked his way up to the Presidentship of the Congress at Lucknow in 1916. His flights of eloquence were of a rare order. We have already quoted from his speech in 1911, at the Calcutta Congress. He was the author of a fine and famous book on the Congress entitled 'Indian National Evolution.'

Bhupendra Nath Basu

Not less eloquent was Babu Bhupendra Nath Basu who was called upon to preside over the Congress in 1914 in Madras. Dealing with the *raison d'etre* of Indians' demand for Self-Government, Mr. Basu said:

> "The days of the lotus-eaters are gone. The world is swinging onward on the uplifting ropes of time, and in Europe, the War of Nations, now in progress, will knock off the last weights of medieval domination of one man over many, of one race over another. It is not possible to roll back the tide of wider life which is flowing like the warm gulf-stream through the gateways of the West into the still waters of the East. You may bend the Indian Universities to your will, if you like, fetter their feet with obstructive statutes, but you cannot bar the imponderable influences of an expanding world. If English rule in India meant the canonization of a bureaucracy, if it meant perpetual domination and perpetual tutelage, an increasing deadweight on the soul of India, it would be a curse to civilization and a blot on humanity."

Bhupen Babu was a successful solicitor in Calcutta with a large practice who gave his time to politics gladly and his oratory was undoubtedly of a highly cultured type. He was able almost to act his part and display considerable emotion, so much so that one big leader humorously described him as the man with a melodramatic countenance and chemical tears in his eyes. We would say the tears were physiological as well as psychological. He took up the position that the Congress should act as His Majesty's Opposition.

Maulvi Mazar-ul-Haq

Maulvi Mazar-ul-Haq is one of those stalwarts in intellect as well as in physique who gave the warmest support to the Indian National Congress from Bihar and who was a Nationalist every inch. Communalism was abhorrent to him and when at the 25th Congress in 1910 which met at Allahabad, Mr. Jinnah moved a resolution condemning communal representation, Maulvi Mazar-ul-Haq seconded it in an able speech in which he exhorted Hindus and Muslims to join hands. It will be remembered that the Minto-Morley Reforms had just come into operation and had embodied for the first time a scheme of communal representation in the Legislative Councils. It required the utmost sincerity of purpose and courage of conviction to be able to say, as Mazar-ul-Haq did, to the Muslims who were just then elated with their achievements, that their success was really injurious to the common interests of the two great communities, and that what the country wanted was that they should join hands and not remain apart in watertight compartments.

When in 1914, a deputation was sent to England by the Congress, Maulvi Mazar-ul-Haq was elected to serve on it along with Messrs. Bhupendra Nath Basu, M. A. Jinnah, N. M. Samarth, S. Sinha, B. N. Sarma and Lala Lajpat Rai. Thereafter he did not take active interest in Congress affairs but remained a staunch Nationalist to the end. The purity of his Nationalism was only excelled by the saintliness of his character which attracted public attention and endeared him to the people of India in general and to the people of Bihar in particular, and the latter days of his life he spent not only in retirement but in renunciation as a true *Faquir*.

Mahadev Govind Ranade

Mahadev Govind Ranade, popularly known as Justice Ranade, was a towering personality in the Congress. Within the strict meaning of the term, he could not be termed a Congressman, for he was a high officer in the Judicial Department of the Bombay Government, but he was for years together the power behind the throne. He furnished the inspiration for the Congress movement. His tall stature, the statuesque cut of his face and his Maharashtra turban, with his flowing robes of ancient Hindu style, marked him out at the various sessions of the Congress from the rest. His attainments as a scholar and savant, which have made him memorable both as an economist and a historian, have left the Nation a rich legacy in the *Rise of the Maratha Power* and in his *Essays in Indian Economics.* Social Reform was his forte, and for years the Social Conference, which had formed an adjunct of the Congress, was his pet child. When differences arose in the year 1895 at the Poona Session as to whether the Congress could concern itself with questions of Social Reform and with the Social Conferences, it was the "tolerant and wise action of Mr. Justice Ranade," as pointed out by Babu Surendra Nath Banerjea, that put an end to them and smoothed matters. Justice Ranade's services to the Nation during the outbreak of plague were inestimable and it is not time yet to describe them all to posterity. After fifteen years of indefatigable labours in the field of Social Reform and in the cause of the Congress, Ranade passed away in the year 1901 leaving memories which serve to help us hold his name in high veneration.

PANDIT BISHAN NARAYAN DHAR

Pandit Bishan Narayan Dhar is another of the earlier day politicians who made a mark on Congress history by his devotion to the National Congress.

In 1903 he moved the resolution on the Official Secrets Bill and said: "Lord Curzon is astonished that this should be described as Russianizing the administration. I am astonished that any one should be so imperfectly informed regarding the Russian Government as to think that it has got anything in its purely civil laws so arbitrary and so disastrous to the Civil Liberties of the people as Lord Curzon's Bill, if passed, would be in this country."

He was called upon to preside over the Calcutta Congress in 1911 over which it was hoped Mr. Ramsay MacDonald would preside, but the death of Mrs. MacDonald had called him away from India and Bishan Narayan Dhar was unexpectedly asked to take his place. He presided over the Congress just at a moment when the worst blow was dealt to the bureaucracy by the annulment of the Partition of Bengal. But long anterior to his attainment of the highest National honour, he gave proofs of his capacity and eloquence which really he shared with most of the earlier day stalwarts. Pandit Bishan Narayan Dhar had indeed figured prominently from the earliest Congress. He made a noble appeal at the 3rd Congress (Madras, 1887) saying: "England has moved us from our ancient anchorage. She has cast us adrift, against our will, upon the wide waters of a seething proletariat; and we turn back to England and ask her to grant us that compass of representative institutions by which, amidst a thousand storms, she has steered her prosperous course to the safe haven of regulated political freedom."

Bishan Narayan Dhar's description of the bureaucracy is alike picturesque and pungent and we make no apology for quoting it at length here:

> "The root-cause of most of our misfortunes which, if not corrected, forebodes serious disasters in the future, is the growth of an unsympathetic and illiberal spirit in the bureaucracy towards the new-born hopes and ideals of the Indian people. While a New India has gradually been rising up, that spirit too has been growing, and so a critical situation has arisen. On the one hand, the educated classes filled with new knowledge and conscious of new political rights, but hampered by the bars and fetters of a system perhaps good enough for other days but now obsolete; on the other, the bureaucracy with its

vested interests, its domineering habits, its old traditions of absolute and unquestioned authority, suspicious of knowledge and adverse to innovation, like every close corporation, cut off from the people by its racial exclusiveness and wedded to a paternal system of Government under which it has so long enjoyed power and pelf but which is discordant with the moral, liberal ideals of the present day."

RAMESH CHANDRA DUTT

Another outstanding character in the Congress politics towards the end of the last century was Ramesh Chandra Dutt. He was not a mere political agitator even in the sense of the London *Times* which derisively described Congressmen (1886) as men with little or no stake in the country, men of straw who were place-seekers. He had closed a career, having risen to the position of Commissionership. He cast in his lot with the Congress and brought to bear his rich experience and knowledge acquired over a long course of years spent as an I.C.S. officer, on the public questions of the day. He held that the causes of famine were the heavy assessments on land and the destruction of the village industries by free competition with English machinery. He regretted that a country which had organised Village Self-Government 3,000 years ago was being virtually ruled through the Police, "the hated link between the district officers and the people." He was a great authority on Land Revenue affairs, Economic questions and Famines. He presided over the Congress at Lucknow, 1890. He has made himself memorable by the statement that "there is no better way of creating sedition than by suppressing free discussion in newspapers and meetings."

N. Subba Rau Pantulu

Another of these venerable patriarchs of the Congress is Mr. N. Subba Rau Pantulu who is an active public man to-day at the age of four score and who, though he has not been quite a whole-hogger in respect of recent Congress programmes, continues to be an ardent Nationalist. His connection with the Congress began almost from its birth, for he was present and spoke at the 4th Congress (Allahabad, 1888) and ever since figured on the Congress platform moving, seconding or supporting resolutions relating to Salt Tax, the Judicial and the Executive, the admission of Indians into the Executive Councils, Trial by Jury and the position of Legal practitioners. As a member of the Imperial Legislative Council, he moved a resolution urging the appointment of a Public Services Commission which was accepted, and in the Congress of 1912 at Bankipore he moved the resolution of thanks for the appointment of a Royal Commission on Public Services.

He has not cared to accept a title or seek a job at the hands of Government, when his contemporaries were being rewarded with the one or the other. On the other hand, his Province chose him as the Chairman of the Reception Committee in 1898 and the Congress itself elected him as the General Secretary in 1914, '15, '16 and '17. But in 1917 he declined the honour with thanks when he saw that Mrs. Besant took a third Secretary in Mr. C.P. Ramaswami Aiyar as the real Working Secretary. He set the example, during his term, of touring India at his own expense and enthusing the people on Congress matters throughout the country.

LALA MURLIDHAR

We may not forget to record the name of Lala Murlidhar of Punjab who went to the second session of the Congress in Calcutta (1886) straight from prison released on bail, convicted without evidence "because I am considered a political agitator, because I have my own opinions and speak what I think without fear." Lala Malik Bhagwan Das from Dera Ismail Khan was the first to speak in Urdu at this very session. The first lady speaker of the Congress was Mrs. Kadimbini Ganguli who moved the customary vote of thanks to the President of the sixteenth Congress in 1900 (Calcutta).

MR. S. SINHA

Mr. Sachchidananda Sinha first made his appearance at the 15th session of the Congress, at Lucknow (1899), and spoke on the separation of the Executive and the Judicial functions, "a subject worn threadbare but necessarily brought up for the 15th time," as Mrs. Besant says. He reverted to the same subject at the next session, (Lahore, 1900) and gave a foretaste of his abilities and concluded by saying that "the Government must rest upon the affection of the people, and that could only be secured by conferring upon them the boon of justice, not the justice which we enjoy to-day, half milk and half water, adulterated justice, but real and righteous British justice." At the seventeenth session, an allied subject, namely, Police Reform, was handled by him. The next year too, Mr. Sinha was chosen to speak on the same subject and then he referred to the inadequacy of the representation of experienced Indians on the Police Commission which was appointed during Lord Curzon's time. There was a peculiar appropriateness in his remark that, of the two non-officials on the Commission, "One was a C. I. E.

always speaking to please Englishmen and the other a Maharaja, as yet untried." The appropriateness lies in the fact that though Mr. Sinha became later a Member of the Executive Council of Bihar he remains without a title. At the twentieth session he supported a resolution that a deputation should be sent to England on the eve of the General Election of 1905. At the same session he had the honour of moving the resolution urging the election to Parliament of Mr. Dadabhai Naoroji, Sir Henry Cotton and Mr. John Jardine. At the twenty-first Congress (Kashi, 1905) "Police Reforms were entrusted to the old champion," Mr. Sinha, and he pointed out how bitterly the Police Commission had disappointed them, constituting a special Police Service from which Indians were to be excluded. Mr. Sinha was present as an active member at the 1st Moderate Congress of 1908. By the year 1910, in which the Congress met at Allahabad, the outlook of the Indian politicians was widened by the appointment of an Indian to the Law Membership of the Viceroy's Executive Council but the range of choice was limited to the members of the English Bar, and the Hon. S. Sinha pointed out the unwisdom of the restriction and urged that the advocates and vakils should also be eligible. Next year when the Congress met in Calcutta Mr. Sinha pleaded for an Executive Council and a Governor for the U. P. He was again present in Madras in 1914 and received the thanks of the Congress for the good work that he had done as a member of the deputation to London composed of, besides himself, Messrs. Bhupendranath Basu, M. A. Jinnah, Samarth, Mazar-ul-Haq, the Hon. B. N. Sarma and Lala Lajpat Rai.

There are scores of public workers—many of them dead and a few still alive—who have made notable contributions to the National cause by their sincerity of purpose, services and sacrifices, to whom posterity owes

Surendra Nath Banerjea
1895 : Poona
1902 : Ahmedabad

Md. Rahimatullah Sayani
1896 : Calcutta

Sir C. Sankaran Nair
1897 : Amraoti

Ananda Mohan Bose
1898 : Madras

a deep debt. To enumerate them would only lead to invidious distinctions, however unmeant they be, and we shall be content to recall their memory with a feeling of sincere gratitude.

Part II

(1915 TO 1919)

SYNOPSIS

CHAPTER I

TOWARDS RE-UNION (1915)

Mrs. Besant advocates India's claim for Justice—Position in 1915—Tilak reappears—Proposals to re-unite the two wings of Congress fail—Gokhale passes away—Tilak's constructive work—The Bombay Congress.

CHAPTER II

A UNITED CONGRESS (1916)

Tilak's Home Rule League—Tilak's triumphs and reverses—Hindu-Muslim Concordat—The Nineteen Memorandum—Mrs. Besant's All-India Home Rule League—Tilak at the Lucknow Session—The Congress Resolutions.

CHAPTER III

TOWARDS RESPONSIBLE GOVERNMENT (1917)

Agitation and Repression—Internment of Mrs. Besant, Arundale and Wadia—Siva who cut his wife into 53 pieces—Imperial War Conference—Passive Resistance—A.I.C.C.'s statement—P. C. C.'s on Passive Resistance—Montagu's Announcement of August 20th—Congress-League Memorandum of India's equality with Dominions—Mrs. Besant's change of attitude—Gandhi's achievements by Satyagraha

—Champaran, Kaira, and Ahmedabad Mill labourers—Signatures to the Congress-League Scheme—a Permanent fund for the Congress—Mrs. Besant elected President—Her Presidential address—Congress resolutions—Appointment of Rowlatt Committee—Andhra Congress Circle—National Flag.

CHAPTER IV

MONTAGU-CHELMSFORD PROPOSALS (1918)

A.I.C.C. meetings—Mrs. Besant's strenuous work—Prohibitory orders against Pal and Tilak—War Conference at Delhi—Tilak's Wager—Montagu-Chelmsford Report published—Differences amongst Indians on it—The Curtis Episode—The Special Congress at Bombay—The Functions and Franchise Committees—The operation of the Defence of India Act—The Rowlatt Committee's Report—The Delhi Congress.

CHAPTER V

NON-VIOLENCE, A REALITY (1919)

The Rowlatt Bills—Gandhi appears on the scene—The Satyagrahic pledge—New values—Hindu-Muslim Unity—Happenings in the Punjab—Gandhi's arrest—Amritsar—General Dyer and the Hunter Committee—Lahore and Colonel Johnson—Gujaranwala and Colonel O'Brien—Doveton and Bosworth Smith, and Kasur—Withdrawal of Satyagraha—Law and Order—Indemnity Bill—A.I.C.C. meets, appoints a Committee of Enquiry—Gandhi's statement withdrawing Satyagraha—Deputations to England—Differences with the British Congress Committee, a double fight—The Albert Hall Meeting—Mr. Lansbury's good offices—A Comparative Study of the four schemes on hand—The Punjab Enquiry—The Hunter Committee—A grave situation—The Reform Bill—Tilak offers Responsive Co-operation—The Amritsar Congress—The main resolution—The compromise—Condemnation of mob violence—Gandhi's speech thereon—Other resolutions—Recall of Chelmsford—Sarma opposes—Royal amnesty—Mr. Neville attacked.

Part II

CHAPTER I

Towards Re-union (1915)

The year 1915 really is a landmark in the political history of India. Mrs. Besant's publication entitled 'How India Wrought For Freedom' has covered the period intervening between 1885, the year of the birth of the Congress, and 1914, the year of the outbreak of the Great War. It may be remembered that the Japanese victory in the Russo-Japanese War had filled the Asiatic Nations with a sense of renewed confidence in their own capacities and prowess at the beginning of this century. Likewise did the marvellous feats of endurance and bravery displayed by the Indian troops in the winter of 1914 in France and Flanders, and their successful stand against the onslaughts of German invasion in the Great European War create a new atmosphere alike in Europe and Asia and raise the Indians miles higher in the estimation of the Western Nations than ever before. Such an appreciation of the services of the Indian troops in the War who were taken abroad in anticipation of Parliamentary sanction, naturally had its repercussion on the minds of Indians. It kindled a sense of reward in the minds of some, such as Surendra Nath Banerjea, and a sense of rights in the minds of others, such as Mrs. Besant. Mrs. Besant had been working in the cause of the poor, the whole of her lifetime, and of India ever since the days of Mr. Bradlaugh. But it was in 1914 that she joined the Congress and speaking on the question of 'Reciprocity' said, "there had been talk of a reward due to India's loyalty; but India does not chaffer with the blood of her sons and the proud tears of her daughters in exchange for so much liberty, so much right. India claims the right, as a Nation, to justice among the peoples of the Empire. India asked for this before the War. India asks for it during the War. India will ask for it after the War; but not as a reward, but as a right does she ask for it. On that there must be no mistake." When Mrs. Besant jumped from Theosophy and the High Court where she had to face a litigation relating to Jiddu Krishnamurti and his brother, to the Congress and the spacious atmosphere of the Beach, she brought new ideas, new talents, new resources, and altogether a new method of organisation and a new outlook into the field of the Congress. She was already a great world character and had millions of followers in the East and the West, in the New Hemisphere as well as the Old. No wonder then that, with this mighty following and with her inexhaustible energy, she gave a new life to Indian politics.

What was the position of affairs in 1915? Gokhale had passed away on the 19th February 1915. Sir Pherozeshah Mehta had already gone out of view, having declined the Presidentship of the Congress in 1909, six days before he was due to take the chair, and followed Gokhale to the grave in November 1915. Infirmities of advancing years were creeping upon Mr. Wacha who stated at the Bombay Congress of 1915 that old age had its own penalties, for his vision was fast failing. Moreover he was all along only a great scholar and a good Secretary, never a General leading his forces from victory to victory. Sir Narayan Chandavarkar had retired as a judge and was a spent force in politics. Heramba Chandra Maitra, Mudholkar and Subba Rau Pantulu were excellent Lieutenants, Captains or Colonels in the army of the Congress, and nothing more. Surendra Nath Banerjea, eminent as he was, was not quite in tune with the new thought.

Pandit Motilal Nehru
1919 ; Amritsar
1928 ; Calcutta

C. Vijiaraghavachariar
1920 : Nagpur

Lala Lajpat Rai
1920 : Calcutta (Special)

Hakim Ajmal Khan
1921 : Ahmedabad

There was no Field-Marshal, no Generalissimo to lead the army. Lokamanya Tilak was released in June 1914 from Mandalay after nearly completing his full term. Mr. Srinivasa Sastri no doubt stepped into the shoes of Gokhale as the President of that great and noble order—the Servants of India Society, but by his inherent temperament as well as by the eternal conflict raging in his breast between his Extremist inclinations and Moderate 'conviction,' between principle and expediency, between the ultimate and the immediate, he was always content to remain a back-bencher, though he loved to praise the cross-bench mind. At any rate he never occupied the Front Bench nor cared for the limelight. Pandit Madan Mohan Malaviya was not in a position to lead the Congress on the Moderate lines, nor had he the grit to force his way forward. Gandhi himself had just arrived in India and, if we may say so, did not as yet start his public life on defined lines. He was under the advice of his political Guru—Gokhale, silently studying the conditions of the country which he had long ago left and to which he had paid two or three short visits at intervals. Lala Lajpat Rai was disgusted with the state of affairs in this country and notably in his Province, and during the War was virtually an exile in America. Satyendra Prasanna (later Lord) Sinha, who presided over the Congress of 1915 in Bombay, was altogether out of tune with the new spirit and ceased to interest himself in Congress politics after the Bombay Session. Leadership was almost passing from the Nation to the bureaucracy. Power had gone out of the Moderates. The Nationalists had not as yet come into their own. Attempts made by Mrs. Besant to bring the two wings of the Congress together failed in 1914 and 1915, and the story of the failure may briefly be studied.

In 1915 Lokamanya Tilak should have been the uncrowned king not only of Maharashtra, but of the whole of India, except for an unfortunate combination of forces to keep him out of what should legitimately have been his. He was released in June 1914 and ever since strenuous efforts were made by him to start a big Home Rule agitation, and by well-meaning friends to bring the two wings of the Congress together. Lokamanya Tilak himself wanted sedulously to avoid offending the susceptibilities of the Moderates but they did not respond to his approaches. Tilak's threefold programme was, (1) the Congress Compromise, (2) the re-organisation of the Nationalist Party, and (3) the setting on foot of a strong agitation for Home Rule. On the first of these items, Lokamanya Tilak and the Nationalists wanted the avenues to the election of Congress delegates to be widened. As things stood, the Articles of the Constitution restricted the right of election to certain organizations —"provided that no such political association or public body shall be recognized unless the said Association or Body, by a resolution of a general meeting of its members, expressed its acceptance of the principle embodied in Article I of this Constitution and makes the acceptance of the same condition precedent to new membership." The Article contemplated a Moderate creed with Colonial Self-Government as the goal. The election of Congress delegates was thus placed exclusively in the hands of the Moderate Associations and it was not to be expected that the Nationalists should seek admission, through the good-will of their opponents, to the Congress. Article XX had therefore to be widened and to this end Mrs. Besant and Mr. N. Subba Rau Pantulu, the General Secretary of the Congress, went to Poona in the first week of December, 1914 and conferred with Messrs. Tilak, Gokhale and others. An amendment was agreed upon. Then Mr. Subba Rau went to consult Sir Pherozeshah in Bombay and returned disappointed. Then he met Mr. Tilak and Mr. Gokhale. Mr. Gokhale was convinced that Mr. Tilak's re-entry into the Congress camp would only be a signal for a renewal of the old struggle. He therefore withdrew his support to the amendment proposed, in an oral message to Mrs. Besant. In reply to a letter from the President-elect of the 19th Congress of 1914, he wrote a confidential letter explaining the reasons of his change of view. The letter became public in no time. It was stated in it that Mr. Tilak had openly avowed his intention of adopting the 'Boycott of Government' and the obstructionist methods of the Irish if he entered the Congress. When Lokamanya Tilak repudiated it, on an enquiry by Mrs. Besant, an apology was no doubt offered to him, but the reconciliation was postponed. Mr. Subba Rau Pantulu published in *New India* (8-2-1915) a statement in which he said that the Bombay Conventionalist leaders were dead opposed to Mrs. Besant's amendment.

The story of Mrs. Besant's unsuccessful attempts to bring the Moderates and the Nationalists together in the Congress has just been told. Early in the year, India sustained a great loss in the premature death of Gokhale who passed away on the 19th February. Tilak had a great regard for his political opponent, and when Gokhale passed away, delivered the funeral oration which was intensely passionate:—

> "This is not a time for cheers. This is a time for shedding tears. This diamond of India, this jewel of Maharashtra, this prince of workers is laid to eternal rest on the funeral ground. Look at him and try to emulate him. Every one of you should place his life as a model to be imitated and should try to fill up the gap caused by his death, and if you will do your level best to emulate him in this way, he will feel glad even in the next world."

In the Provincial Conference (May 4, 1915), in moving the resolution of condolence to Mr. Gokhale's family, Tilak described how he was partially responsible for introducing Gokhale into the field of public life.

During the year 1915, and the year 1916 too, Tilak worked assiduously to organize his party. He held that "a strong party needs (1) a magnetic leadership, (2) a rallying point, and (3) a war-cry. In Mr. Joseph Baptista, Tilak found an able co-adjutor and under Mr. Baptista's Presidentship a thousand Nationalists met at Poona, and this Conference stood in marked contrast with the Moderate Conference which met shortly after with a poor attendance, but was graced by the presence of Lord Willingdon at it. The Poona Conference supplied the war-cry of Home Rule and Tilak's sole pre-occupation was how to advance India's cause to this goal. It was his intention to get a Bill introduced in Parliament through the good offices of Labour leaders and then concentrate his activities on a vast propaganda. (Account taken from Mr. Athalye's 'Life of Lokamanya Tilak.')

The Congress of 1915 was to meet in Bombay, and as all proposals for a compromise had failed, it was to be essentially a Moderate Congress. On the eve of the Congress, Sir Pherozeshah Mehta passed away in the month of November. The President chosen for the year was Sir Satyendra Prasanna Sinha,—whose position and learning were of an unchallengeable character. His touch with the Congress movement was indeed little, but he brought to the Bombay Session all the prestige that clings round the name of an ex-Law Member of the Government of India, who had not cared to stick to his high office even for half his term. But he was new to his new duties and was largely influenced by the elderly Congressmen by whom he was surrounded.

Sir S. P. Sinha made, from the Nationalist point of view, a most reactionary speech, in which he described India as a patient whose fractured limbs were in splints. According to his conception the need was "a reasoned ideal of India's future such as will satisfy the aspirations and ambitions of the rising generation of India and at the same time will meet with the approval of those to whom India's destinies are committed." In this view he demanded an announcement of policy. He was essentially an ultra-Conservative.

At the Bombay Congress of 1915, however, the first signs of that great revival in public interest in the Congress after the Surat imbroglio became visible, which made its influence felt from, and after, the next following Congress at Lucknow. No less than 2,259 delegates attended the Bombay Session and the resolutions that were passed covered a large variety of subjects. The first four recorded the Nation's grief at the passing away of three ex-Presidents of the Congress, *viz.*, Gopal Krishna Gokhale, Pherozeshah Mehta, Sir Henry Cotton, and of a friend, Keir Hardie, who "in and outside the House of Commons rendered valuable services to this country which will be gratefully cherished by the people of India." The fifth recorded the loyalty of the people. The sixth resolution recorded the abiding sense of the Congress in the righteousness of the cause espoused by Great Britain and her Allies and expressed gratification at the splendid achievements of the British Navy. The seventh resolution asked for an extension of term of office for Lord Hardinge as Viceroy. The eighth resolution re-affirmed the numerous previous resolutions of the Congress regarding the justice and expediency of admitting Indians to commissions in the Army and Navy, their training in existing Military and Naval schools and colleges and opening fresh ones in India. It also emphasised the necessity of re-organizing the system of volunteering with due regard to the rights of the people of this country to enlist themselves as Citizen soldiers without distinction of race, class or creed. The ninth resented the unmerited slur cast upon the people by the Arms Act (XI of 1878) and the tenth regretted the existing laws affecting Indians in South Africa and Canada. The eleventh resolution thanked the Viceroy for lending his statesmanlike support to the resolution of the Imperial Legislative Council demanding representation for India on the Imperial Conference and requested the Government to allow at least two members deputed to take part in the Conference to be elected by the elected members of the Imperial Council. The twelfth resolution reiterated the demand for an Executive Council for the United Provinces. The thirteenth asked for the abolition of indentured labour and the fourteenth repeated the oft-repeated demand for the separation of Executive and Judicial functions. The fifteenth asked for the establishment of High Courts in the Punjab, Burma and the Central Provinces with the status and powers of Chartered High Courts. The sixteenth supported the Swadeshi movement and the seventeenth protested against the continuation of the Press Act. The eighteenth resolution opined that in the best interests of the people of India it was necessary that complete fiscal freedom with special reference to import, export and excise duties should be conceded to the Government of India. The nineteenth resolution was important and demanded substantial measures of reform towards Self-Government so as to secure to the people an effective control over the Government by introduction of Provincial Autonomy, expansion and reform of Legislative Councils where they existed and their establishment in Provinces where they did not exist, the reconstruction of various existing Executive Councils and their establishment in Provinces where they did not exist, the reform or abolition of the India Council, and a liberal measure of Local

Self-Government. The resolution further asked the All-India Congress Committee to frame a scheme of reform and a programme of continuous work, educative and propagandist, and it authorised the Committee to confer with the Committee of the All-India Muslim League for the same purpose and to take such further measures as may be necessary.

The twentieth resolution opined that a reasonable and definite limit should be put to the demand of the State on land and that Permanent Settlement should be introduced in all areas, Ryotwari or Zamindari, creating fixity of tenure for occupants, and failing Permanent Settlement, a settlement for a period of not less than sixty years. The twenty-first resolution insisted on steps for industrial development of the country by making greater provision for industrial and technical education, grant of fiscal autonomy to India in regard to import and export duties, by the removal of unjust and artificial barriers like excise duties on cotton goods and differential rates for Railway consignment which favoured the foreign manufacturer at the expense of the indigenous manufacturer. The twenty-second resolution disapproved of the Indian Students' Department in England and expressed the growing discontent caused by the increasing tendency on the part of educational institutions in the United Kingdom to restrict the admission of Indian students and to accord differential and unfair treatment to them after admission. The other four resolutions were of a formal character, appointing the General Secretaries, appreciating the services of Sir William Wedderburn and other members of the British Committee and desiring the maintenance of *India,* amending the Constitution of the Congress and fixing the next Congress to be held at Lucknow.

We thus see that the Congress resolutions of 1915 are an epitome of the resolutions which had been passed from time to time by all the Congresses held ever since its birth in 1885.

In regard to the question of Self-Government, however, as we have seen, the Congress session held in Bombay in 1915 gave the lead by its resolution XIX instructing the All-India Congress Committee to confer with the Executive of the Muslim League and frame a scheme of Self-Government. That was the culmination indeed of the goodwill that had its origin at the Karachi Session in 1913.

An interesting feature of the Congress of 1915 was that Gandhi could not be elected to the Subjects Committee, and therefore he was nominated to the Committee by the President under the powers vested in him under the Constitution.

One achievement of the Bombay Session was that the Constitution of the Congress was suitably altered so as to throw the doors of entry practically open to the ingress of Nationalist delegates who were allowed to be elected by "public meetings convened under the auspices of any association which is of not less than two years' standing on 31st December, 1915, and which has for one of its objects the attainment of Self-Government within the British Empire by constitutional means" and this was followed by a hearty response from Tilak who forthwith publicly announced the willingness of his party to re-enter the Congress through the partially opened door.

CHAPTER II

A UNITED CONGRESS (1916)

The year opened under more auspicious circumstances for the healthy development of Congress activities than the previous year. But the country was the poorer for the loss of two great men—Gokhale and Mehta—both of whom had passed away in 1915. Tilak had as yet no place in the Congress, for under the compromise reached at the Bombay Session he had to wait a full year before he could influence the National organ to work on his lines. He, therefore, fell back upon his idea of a Home Rule League, and well was he qualified to take up leadership at this juncture by his culture and talents, by his services and sacrifices. He tried his best to induce the Congress to send a deputation to England, but that was not to be. He then started his Home Rule League first in India on 23rd April, 1916, some six months before Mrs. Besant started hers.

But the bureaucracy was his sworn enemy. While Tilak was pleading for students joining the Defence Force, he was served with an order from the Punjab Government prohibiting him from entering Delhi or the Punjab.

He accepted the Creed of the Congress for his Home Rule League and this, it seems, pleased Sastriar much. In 1916 he completed his *Shashtipurti* or 60 years of age, and a purse of one lac of rupees was presented to him which he dedicated to National work. The more Government repressed him, the more he was bounding up, and as a last resort "in order to silence him rather than imprison him" he was asked to be bound over for good behaviour for one year in a sum of Rs. 20,000 in his own recognizance and in two securities of Rs. 10,000 each. The Magistrate directed him after trial to enter into a bond accordingly, but the High Court reversed it, on the 9th November, 1916. This only served to increase his popularity. Tilak met with honours, received ovations and purses wherever he went, but physically he was frail—a circumstance which stood in the way of his undertaking energetic propaganda throughout India, moving on the wings of time and electrifying the people by an appeal to their emotions. This was left to be done by one older than himself in age, frail in sex, but enjoying a better start in life, not being under a cloud in the scene of her operations, better known to the world, and endowed with that dynamic energy which knows no fatigue and seeks no rest.

Here was India then in 1916, a Nation whose cause went unheeded, and whose leader remained yet to be found.

It was at such a juncture that Mrs. Besant stepped into the trench. She jumped from religion to politics, from Theosophy to Home Rule. She started a daily, *New India,* and later a weekly, *The Commonweal.* She was the first to popularise the cry of 'Home Rule' and she carried on a raging, tearing propaganda. The formation of a 'Home Rule for India League' was discussed in 1915 but was put off to see if the Congress of the year would take up work directly for Self-Government.

The Conference between the representatives of the Congress and the Muslim League enjoined by the Bombay Congress was duly held and the outcome was a complete agreement between the leaders of the two great communities. A joint Committee was appointed to frame a scheme and make all the arrangements necessary to promote the cause of Indian Self-Government within the Empire. The draft prepared by the Joint Committee was to be approved at Lucknow in 1916 by both the Congress and the Muslim League. Discussions were held at the All-India Congress Committee meeting at Allahabad on the 22nd, 23rd and 24th April, 1916 at the residence of Pandit Motilal Nehru, a member of the Committee, who at Surat had seconded the resolution proposing Dr. Rash Behari Ghose to the chair, but had not been heard of again till 1915. The proposals tentatively arrived at by the A.I.C.C. were considered at a joint meeting of the A.I.C.C. and the Council of the Muslim League in Oct. 1916 in Calcutta and the Hindu-Muslim Concordat was almost fully hammered out, the quotas of Punjab and Bengal alone being left to be finally agreed upon at Lucknow during the sittings of the year's Congress. The scheme, as finally agreed to by the Joint Committee in Calcutta, was approved by the Congress. The inner circle of politicians were also aware by the time of the Congress that what later came to be widely known as the 'Nineteen Memorandum' (see Appendix I) had been sent up to the Viceroy in Nov. 1916 and that it embodied the principles of a scheme of Self-Government for India, the nineteen signatories being all members of the Supreme Council. All the elected members of the Supreme Legislative Council except the two Anglo-Indians, the three who were away from headquarters and two Muslims and one Sikh, signed the Memorandum. It is believed that it was the result of information which the signatories had that the Government of India had sent up certain proposals on the subject which were reactionary.

Apparently Mrs. Besant was not satisfied with the tardy way in which Congress affairs were progressing. The British Committee of the Indian National Congress was no doubt attending to Congress work in England, but it was only holding 'a watching brief' to use its own phraseology. Mrs. Besant wanted a more dynamic body and organized an Auxiliary Home Rule League in London on 12th June, 1916, under the Self-Government Resolution of the Madras Congress of 1914. In India her Home Rule League was definitely founded in Madras in the Gokhale Hall on 1st September, 1916 and worked well without a hitch throughout 1917 on the simple lines suggested by Mrs. Besant, who was its President elected for three years by the founding branches. The first Home Rule League in India had really been formed, as already pointed out, by Lokamanya Tilak in Maharashtra with headquarters at Poona on the 23rd April, 1916, and to distinguish hers from it, Mrs. Besant christened the former the All-India Home Rule League in 1917.

Tilak joined, in accordance with his announcement in Jan. of the year, the Congress of 1916 at Lucknow. He succeeded in securing a vast majority of his party, the Nationalists, as the delegates from the Bombay Presidency to the Lucknow session. The Constitution of the time provided that the Subjects Committee should include the members of the A.I.C.C. from each Province, and an equal number, Province by Province, elected by the delegates of the Province assembled at the session. An interesting story is told of Gandhi's being found a place in the Subjects Committee of the Congress in 1916. It will be remembered that it was in that year that Tilak rejoined the Congress after the Surat Split. A proposal that Tilak had made to the Moderates in regard to the personnel of the elected members of the Subjects Committee having failed, Tilak decided to get the delegates of Bombay who were all Nationalists to elect only those of their own party. The names were put to the House in pairs, one a Nationalist and the other a Moderate. In every case it was the former that was elected. Likewise when a Nationalist name was pitted against Gandhi, the latter was voted down, but Tilak declared that Gandhi was elected.

The Lucknow session was presided over by Babu Ambika Charan Mazumdar, a tried servant of the Nation whose services to the National cause were fittingly rewarded by the honour conferred upon him at Lucknow. His Presidential Address was of a piece with the eloquent outpourings which the Congress had been accustomed to hear with real gusto for many years, and examples of which have been quoted in these pages. The great achievement of Lucknow was the completion of the Congress-League Scheme of Reforms (see Appendix II) with a full formation of the Hindu-Muslim Concordat.

It will be remembered that the preliminaries of this concordat were gone through at Joint Conferences of the League and the Congress Executives at Allahabad in April 1916, and in Calcutta in the following November. In working out the details of this agreement, the quotas of the Punjab and Bengal in respect of Muslim representation in the Legislatures remained to be settled, and settled they were at Lucknow. A full account of this concordat is given in the section dealing with Communal Representation in Part I, Chapter II. The essentials of the Congress-League Scheme itself were the subordination of the Executive to the Legislature, but it must be noted that the Legislature itself was still to consist of a 1/5 nominated element. The Secretary of State's Council was to be abolished. Altogether it was, judging from the rapid strides since taken by the Congress, a poor show. Yet, the Government fought shy of it and pitted against it a scheme of their own, as we shall see from the developments of the year 1917.

The Lucknow session of the Congress was altogether a unique one, for the fraternization of the Hindus and Muslims as well as for the formulation of a scheme of Self-Government. Not less important was the re-union of the two wings of the Congress which had been separated since 1907. It was truly an enlivening spectacle to see Tilak and Khaparde sitting side by side with Dr. Rash Behari Ghose and Surendra Nath Banerjea. Mrs. Besant was there with her two co-adjutors—Arundale and Wadia—and the banner of Home Rule in their hands. Amongst the Muslims were men like the Rajah of Muhammadabad, Mazar-ul-Haq, A. Rasul and Jinnah. Gandhi and Polak were there too. The Congress-League Scheme which was passed by the Congress was, immediately after, approved by the Muslim League.

The Lucknow Congress, like the Congress at Bombay, was largely attended. There were no less than 2,301 delegates, besides a large number of visitors who filled the spacious Pandal to its utmost capacity. The Congress sat for four days and the resolutions dealt with the same variety of subjects, namely, India's loyalty, the Arms Act, Volunteering and Commissions in the Army, the Press Act, Indentured Labour, Indians in the Colonies, Executive Council for U.P., India and the Imperial Conference, High Courts for the Punjab and other Provinces, the Swadeshi movement, and Trial by Jury—subjects which had been dealt with year after year at successive sessions of the Congress. The Congress recorded its sense of loss at the deaths of Pandit Bishan Narayan Dhar who had presided at the Calcutta Session in 1911, Mr. G. Subrahmania Aiyar, and Mr. D. A. Khare who had worked as its General Secretary for several years. The Congress passed two resolutions about Bihar—one dealing with the relation between the Indian ryot and the European planters in North Bihar, and urging the desirability of a mixed Committee of officials and non-officials to enquire into the causes of the agrarian troubles; and the other with the up-to-date Patna University Bill which was then pending before the Imperial Council.

The resolution regarding the ryots and planters in North Bihar was of great importance. Mahatma Gandhi in the following year visited Bihar for investigation into the causes of discontent among the ryots, which will be referred to later.

The resolution dealing with Self-Government for India declared that "(a) having regard to the ancient civilization of India, the progress made in education and the public spirit shown, His Majesty the King-Emperor should be pleased to issue a Proclamation announcing that it is the aim and intention of British policy to confer Self-Government on India at an early date; (b) that as a definite step in that direction the Congress-League Scheme should be granted; and (c) that in the reconstruction of the Empire, India should be lifted from the position of a dependency to that of an equal partner in the Empire with the Self-Governing Dominions."

It should also be noticed that the Lucknow Congress, in a resolution, viewed with alarm the extensive use made of the Defence of India Act and the Bengal Regulation III of 1818; and urged that in the application of the Defence of India Act, which was an emergency measure, the same principle should be followed as under the Defence of the Realm Act of the United Kingdom and the same procedure adopted in dealing with persons sought to be proceeded against under the Act, namely, that a statement in writing of the charge should be handed over to an arrested person, and an explanation obtained from him placed before a lawyer-Judge of the High Court, a non-official practising lawyer, and a judge belonging to the Indian Civil Service, and no internment ordered before the same had been considered and the arrested persons afforded proper facilities for legal assistance. The same procedure was to be followed as far as practicable in regard to persons detained under Bengal Regulation III of 1818 and similar Regulations in other Provinces. The movers and supporters of this resolution pointed out how extensive use had been made of the drastic provisions of the emergency measures and how the belief was honestly held that many innocent young men with bright prospects in life had been ruined by the application of the Act. It was said that in Bengal above 479 persons had been interned and more than sixty persons detained under Regulation III of 1818. The rigorous enforcement of the Defence of India Act and the old Regulations had thus begun to be deeply resented by the people.

The practice of holding the sessions of the Congress and the League in the same city had been inaugurated the previous year in Bombay and was continued at Lucknow. When the scheme of Self-Government was passed at Lucknow, the Congress followed it up by a resolution calling upon the various Congress Committees and other organized bodies and associations to start a propagandist and educative campaign throughout the country. The response to this call was marvellous. One Province vied with another in carrying on propaganda, and Madras, under the immediate guidance of Mrs. Besant, created a record for itself. The Lucknow session of the Congress had no easy time. Untold difficulties had been created in Lucknow when the 15th session of the Congress was to meet at the place in 1899. But these were put an end to by the wisdom of the Lieut. Governor, Sir Antony MacDonnell, at the time. A similar incident repeated itself in 1916. The Secretariat of the U. P. Government issued a warning to the Reception Committee against any spirit of sedition in the Congress speeches, and a copy of the letter was served upon the President-elect as well, through the Government of Bengal. The Reception Committee gave a fitting reply to this gratuitous insult while the President treated it with the contempt it deserved. Mrs. Besant just then was under orders of externment from Berar and Bombay, and not unnaturally some developments were apprehended at the Lucknow session. But once again the wisdom of Sir James Meston, the Lieut. Governor, averted all complications. Sir James and Lady Meston, with staff, attended the Congress session and to the welcome extended to them by the President, Sir James gave a suitable reply.

CHAPTER III

Towards Responsible Government (1917)

One great obstacle to the development of Indian polity has all along been the communal differences in India. These were inaugurated virtually during the time of Lord Minto, and when a scheme of Self-Government was about to be formulated in 1917, it was fortunate that the adjustments between the two great communities of India—Hindus and Muslims—were made not by force of authority from above, but by voluntary agreement between the two parties. This augured well for the coming political struggle, and political agitation was set on foot in 1917 with clear minds and clear hearts. The year 1917 witnessed a quickening of National consciousness throughout India and a widely popular agitation in favour of Home Rule, and this was followed by an ever increasing severity of Police repression.

The cry of Home Rule spread to the remotest corners of the land and Home Rule Leagues were established all over the country. In Mrs. Besant's hands, the Press became powerful in spite of repression under the Press Law, and Lord Pentland's Government promulgated G. O. No. 559 restraining students from taking part in political agitation. He had sent for Mr. Kasturi Ranga Iyengar, Editor of *The Hindu*, who had half an hour's plain talk with the Government on the situation, and told them frankly what he thought of the political situation.

But Mrs. Besant who had a daily, *New India*, and a weekly, *The Commonweal*, was called upon to furnish security for her press and papers, and altogether she deposited and forfeited a sum of Rs. 20,000.

In the meantime the Home Rule idea was spreading like wild fire. "The strength of the Home Rule movement was rendered ten-fold greater," as Mrs. Besant herself pointed out in her Presidential Address in Calcutta (1917), "by the adhesion to it of a large number of women who brought to its helping the uncalculating heroism, the endurance, the self-sacrifice, of the feminine nature. Our League's best recruits and recruiters are amongst the women of India; and the women of Madras boast that they marched in procession when the men were stopped and that their prayers in the temples set the interned captive free. Home Rule has become so intertwined with Religion, by the prayers offered up in the great Southern Temples,—sacred places of pilgrimage—and spreading from them to village temples, and also by its being preached up and down the country by Sadhus and Sanyasins." Another factor that largely contributed to the great success of the movement was that from its inception it recognised the integrity of language areas, and in organising the country, adopted the linguistic principle as determining the provincial delimitations. In this respect it went ahead of the Congress and was its forerunner in reality.

On June 15th, 1917, Mrs. Besant, Mr. G. S. Arundale and Mr. B. P. Wadia were served with a notice to choose one of six places mentioned where they should live in internment. Coimbatore and Ootacamund were the places chosen. With the internment of the three leaders, the Home Rule Leagues became more popular, Mr. Jinnah having joined the League immediately after. It is an open secret that Mrs. Besant, despite governmental orders and surveillance, was freely writing to her paper *New India*. A new weekly called *The Commonweal* was also started. Mr. P. K. Telang went over to Madras to take up the Editorship of *New India*. Mr. A. Rangaswami

Iyengar, who later became the Editor of *The Hindu*, was assisting in the conduct of the daily. Mr. C.P. Ramaswami Aiyar was devoting his time and talents to the work of Home Rule organisation as well as to journalism. Every month that the internees were kept under detention, agitation was growing in the country in geometrical progression. The situation in India became tense, but the authorities in England would not relent. Mr. Montagu in his *Diary* narrates a story and draws a lesson. "I particularly liked that Shiva who cut his wife into 52 pieces," says Montagu, "only to discover that he had 52 wives," and Montagu adds: "This is really what happened to the Government of India when it interned Mrs. Besant."

While a political storm was thus developing in India, an Imperial War Conference met in London in co-operation with delegates from the Dominions, and the Maharaja of Bikaner and Sir S. P. Sinha were sent over there as India's representatives. They made such a profound impression everywhere by the dignity of their bearing and the polish of their pronouncements that they were given public receptions, civic honours, and excellent Press, so much so that the British Committee which had earlier suggested a deputation from India, to deal with the question of Indian Reforms, revised their ideas and countermanded a fighting campaign in England just at that juncture. As a matter of fact, a meeting of the A.I.C.C. had been convened on 7-4-1917 to arrange a deputation to England and a session of the Congress in London. The following were asked to form the deputation: Surendra Nath Banerjea, Dr. Rash Behari Ghose, Bhupendra Nath Basu, Madan Mohan Malaviya, Sir K. G. Gupta, Raja of Muhammadabad, Tej Bahadur Sapru, V.S. Sastri, and C. P. Ramaswami Aiyar. The British Committee tried hard to get Mr. Austen Chamberlain, the Secretary of State, to make a pronouncement of policy and grant commissions to Indians in the

Army, but he would not do either. A small Conference was held in London on 8-5-1917, when Sir S.P. Sinha was present, and it was the deliberations of this body that led to the countermanding of an accredited deputation from India.

India was however planning a campaign of Passive Resistance in order to secure the release of the Home Rule internees. A joint meeting of the All-India Congress Committee and of the Council of the Muslim League was convened in July 1917, and when it met on the 28th, the very first resolution it had to pass was one bemoaning the death of India's Grand Old Man—Dadabhai Naoroji. A small deputation consisting of Messrs. Jinnah, Sastri (alternatively C. P. Ramaswami Aiyar), Sapru and Wazir Hassan was appointed to proceed to England, contingent on Sir W. Wedderburn's advice, in the middle of September to explain the general political situation in India and to promote the Scheme of Reforms adopted. On the question of adopting Passive Resistance, both as regards its principle and working, in carrying on political work, it was resolved to request the Provincial Congress Committees and the Council of the Muslim League to consider its advisability and to send their opinion to the General Secretaries within six weeks. The joint sitting also recorded its strong protest against the high-handed action of the Government of Bengal in prohibiting the public meeting which was to be held in Calcutta under the Presidentship of Dr. Rash Behari Ghose, to protest against the internments of Mrs. Besant and Messrs. Arundale and Wadia and trusted "that the people of Bengal will use every lawful means to vindicate their rights." A reasoned statement regarding the situtation was prepared and it makes interesting reading to-day. It pointed out how here in India Lord Chelmsford, referring to the recommendations of the 'Nineteen Memorandum' deprecated them as 'catastrophic changes,' and how there in England Lord Sydenham was speaking of 'the Danger in India' and condemned the 'Nineteen Memorandum' as embodying 'revolutionary proposals' and recommended repressive measures on the ground that "German intrigue was at work." Soon afterwards, the Government of India sent round a circular regarding the policy to be adopted *vis a vis* the popular agitation for Self-Government. The master's voice was echoed in the pronouncements of distant satraps like Sir Michael O'Dwyer of the Punjab and Lord Pentland of Madras, which warned the people against extravagant expectations and threatened repressive measures. The former declared that the changes proposed by the party of Reform would be as revolutionary and subversive as those of the Ghadr emissaries. What irritated Government was that while Delhi and Simla were sending secret despatches regarding Reforms, the Congress and the League and certain members of the Supreme Legislative Council should have over-reached them, the last sending up a Memorandum publicly and the first two formulating a whole scheme of Self-Government. These Provincial Governors did not see the impolicy of openly telling the public that the Reforms would be of a minor character, but if they were impolitic, they were at least honest. Then the statement protested against the internments and asked, as remedial measures, for (1) an authoritative pronouncement pledging the Imperial Government in unequivocal terms to the policy of making India a Self-Governing member of the British Empire, (2) for immediate steps to sanction the Scheme of Reforms conjointly framed, (3) for the publication of official proposals, and (4) for the reversal of the repressive policy.

The main portions of the lengthy statement were cabled to the Secretary of State, the Prime-Minister and

Sir William Wedderburn on the 30th July, and Sir William in reply cabled: "Had interview with Secretary of State; I feel justified in urging you earnestly to exercise patience. Will telegraph further when situation becomes clearer."

Let us turn our eyes once again towards India. The proposal for adopting Passive Resistance was seriously considered by the various Provincial Congress Committees in the months of August and September, 1917, and while Berar considered it advisable, and Bombay, Burma and the Punjab advised postponement in view of Mr. Montagu's expected visit to India, U. P. considered it inadvisable "in the existing situation." Bihar thought that "a date must be fixed within which the release of the Home Rule Internees as well as of the Ali Brothers and Moulana Abul Kalam Azad should be demanded; Bihar would herself intensify the demand by repeating it from different platforms, and redress failing, the public men of the Province shall betake themselves to actively preaching Passive Resistance to the people and be prepared to suffer all sacrifices and privations that it may involve." The Madras Provincial Congress Committee approved of the idea on the 14th August, 1917 in a resolution which we quote below:—

> "Resolved that, in the opinion of the Madras Provincial Congress Committee, it is advisable to adopt the policy of Passive Resistance in so far as it involves opposition to all unjust and unconstitutional orders against the carrying on of constitutional agitation, and also against the prohibition of public meetings peacefully and constitutionally conducted to protest against the unjust and unconstitutional orders of internment and against the Repressive Policy of Government."

It was further resolved that "a sub-committee be appointed to formulate and report within a fortnight on the practical steps by which effect may be given to the resolution of Passive Resistance adopted this day." In the City of Madras a pledge was drafted and Sir S. Subrahmania Aiyar, retired Judge of the Madras High Court, and Honorary President of the All-India Home Rule League and an old Congressman, was the first to sign the pledge. He had renounced his knighthood as a protest against the internment of Mrs. Besant and her co-workers, and addressed a letter to President Wilson, which he sent by Mr. and Mrs. Hotchner. The next to sign the pledge was Mr. S. Kasturi Ranga Iyengar, Editor of *The Hindu*, a most unostentatious worker in public life, who had been devoting his talents, energies and resources to the great daily he had taken up, only to make it the greater by his assiduous work and undiluted Nationalism. A few young men then signed the pledge. Mr. C. P. Ramaswami Aiyar had not made up his mind in Madras, but signed the pledge in Bombay. While matters were thus progressing, the situation in India changed by the announcement of Mr. Montagu, and the Madras Provincial Congress Committee passed on the 28th September, 1917, a resolution running as follows:—

> "That having regard to the altered circumstances in the political situation, the consideration of the question of Passive Resistance be deferred and that the All-India Congress Committee be communicated with accordingly, and the report of the sub-committee be recorded."

What was this altered situation to which repeated references are being made? In the conduct of the Great War, the Mesopotamian Campaign was mismanaged and a debate of first class importance took place in the House of Commons in which Mr. Austen Chamberlain, the

Secretary of State, was mercilessly criticised by Mr. Montagu for the Mesopotamian muddle which had resulted from an inadequate supply of men and materials from India. It was in the course of this debate that Mr. Montagu characterized the Indian Government as "far too wooden, far too iron, far too inelastic and far too antediluvian to subserve its purposes in modern times." The result was Mr. Chamberlain's resignation and Mr. Montagu's appointment as the Secretary of State. Mr. Montagu was quite a young man then, not being older than 36, yet he had been Under-Secretary for India for four budgets in succession already, and toured India extensively in 1912. His famous Guildhall speech at Cambridge on 'Prestige' on the 28th February was a remarkable utterance. Here is an extract from it:—

> "And as for prestige, Oh! India, how much happier would have been your history if that word had been left out of the English vocabulary. But there you have Conservative Imperialism at its worst; we are not there, mark you, to repair evil, to amend injustice, to profit by experience. We must abide by our mistakes, continue to outrage popular opinion for the sake of being able to say 'I have said what I have said'. I have in other places and at other times expressed freely my opinion on Prestige (The reference was to his budget speech of 1911 in the House of Commons). We do not hold India by invoking this well-mouthed word, we must hold it by just institutions, and more and more as time goes on, by the consent of the governed."

This speech was delivered in reply to Mr. Bonar Law's criticism of the transfer of Capital to Delhi and the annulment of the Partition of Bengal, on the ground of expense and loss of prestige. This was considered a first class victory for India, for Mr. Montagu was believed to be a statesman possessing goodwill, ability, courage and first-hand knowledge. True to public expectations, shortly after assuming office, Mr. Montagu on behalf of the Cabinet made the following authoritative pronouncement on the 20th August regarding Responsible Government as the goal of British Policy:—

> "The policy of His Majesty's Government, with which the Government of India are in complete accord, is that of the increasing association of Indians in every branch of administration, and the gradual development of self-governing institutions with a view to the progressive realisation of Responsible Government in India as an integral part of the British Empire. They have decided that substantial steps should be taken in this direction as soon as possible."

"I would add," proceeded Mr. Montagu's announcement, "that progress in this policy can only be achieved by successive stages. The British Government and the Government of India on whom the responsibility lies for the welfare and the advancement of the Indian peoples, must be the judges of the time and the measure of each advance and they must be guided by the co-operation received from those on whom new opportunities of service will thus be conferred, and by the extent to which it is found that confidence can be reposed in their sense of responsibility. Ample opportunity will be afforded for public discussion of the proposals which will be submitted in due course to Parliament." And as a practical token of trust in the people, he removed the racial bar which excluded Indians from the King's Commissions in the Army. Further he announced his intention to proceed to India in order to consult with the Viceroy and to give a hearing to all the interests concerned in India's advance towards Self-Government.

We have here recounted how agitation in India was growing apace and special Provincial Conferences were asked to be held throughout the country giving expression to the feeling in the country, how the various Congress Committees and the Council of the Muslim League were asked to canvass the question of Passive Resistance and send their opinions within six weeks from the 29th July, on which day the A. I. C. C. and League Council had met in Bombay. We have also noted the opinions of the Provincial Congress Committees. During the six weeks, however, much water flowed under the bridge in the Thames as well as the Jumna, the announcement of the 20th August was made, and in pursuance of the new policy, Mrs. Besant and her associates were released on the 16th of September.

There was again a joint session of the All-India Congress Committee and the Council of the Muslim League on the 6th October at Allahabad, at which there was a general consensus of opinion that the question of Passive Resistance should be dropped. Mrs. Besant herself was against the idea of Passive Resistance and the younger men were greatly disappointed at this unexpected termination of an effective programme. The joint meeting instead of pursuing Passive Resistance decided upon sending an All-India Deputation to the Viceroy and the Secretary of State with a reasoned representation in support of the Congress-League Scheme. To this end a Committee of twelve was appointed with Mr. C. Y. Chintamani as Secretary to prepare an address and the Memorandum. The deputation waited on Lord Chelmsford and Mr. Montagu in November 1917 with the Memorandum, extracts from which may be quoted here:—

"Grateful as the people of India are for the authoritative announcement that has been made in the name of His Majesty's Government and with the accord of the Government of India, they feel that it would be more satisfactory to them if action is taken such as is suggested here.

"At all times and in all circumstances the position of a mere Dependency is wounding to the self-respect of a people who, in the language of the Congress resolution, are the inheritors of ancient civilisations and have shown great capacity for government and administration. While this is so, there has arisen during the last two years a consideration of urgency which necessitates their insistence upon the elevation of their country to a status of equality with the Dominions in all inter-Imperial matters. It has become clear that the latter will in future have a potent voice in the settlement of Imperial problems. They are no longer to be in the position of daughter-States; they are referred to as sister-States, forming with Britain the five free Nations of the Commonwealth. If, as some writers suggest, a Parliament and (or) a Council of the Empire should be established with representation therein of the United Kingdom and the Dominions, and if all affairs of the Empire are to be disposed of by them (it), the present House of Commons and House of Lords concerning themselves exclusively with the affairs of Britain, it is obvious that there will result the Governance of India by the Dominions in conjunction with Britain. To any such development of Imperial polity, Indians cannot but offer a most resolute resistance. For even if the attitude of the Dominions towards India and Indians were unexceptionable, no assent can be given to the widening of the area of subjection which the change will involve. The indispensable condition, from the Indian standpoint, of such a 're-fashioning of the fabric of the Empire' is that India should be represented in an Imperial Council and (or) an Imperial Parliament by elected members, the extent of such representation being determined by the same criteria as will be applied to the Dominions.

"If no such Council or Parliament should be created, if all that will be done be to hold annual meetings of the Imperial Conference and to invite its members to special sittings of the British Cabinet, again it will be necessary to secure India's representation therein by means of elected members. Indians gladly acknowledge the step in advance that was taken early this year when His Highness the Maharaja of Bikaner, His Honour Sir James Meston and the Hon. Sir Satyendra Prasanna Sinha were deputed to the Imperial War Conference and the Imperial War Cabinet to represent the Government of India, nor are they insensible of the value of the resolution that was passed by the former in favour of India's representation at future Conferences. Their submission, however, is that for as long as the Government of India is a subordinate Government, not representative of, nor responsible to the people of India, the analogy with the Governments of the Dominions does not hold and Indians will derive what at best must be a very qualified satisfaction from the recognition that is accorded to their Government, as distinguished from themselves. There need be no doubt that whoever may be chosen by Government to attend the Imperial Conference on their behalf, will do their very best to do their duty honestly by this country, but they will labour under the initial disadvantage of owing no responsibility to the people, which will be a great drawback indeed.

"By common consent, the Maharaja of Bikaner, Sir James Meston and Sir S. P. Sinha acquitted themselves very creditably at the last Conference, but the Memorandum on Emigration which they laid before it did very partial justice to the claim and the view-point of Indians. An elected representative who made himself responsible for that document would have found it difficult to justify himself before his constituents.

"It is not demanded that the election should be made directly by the people or even by any very large electorate. It will suffice if the elected members of the Indian and Provincial Legislative Councils are given the right to elect the representative or representatives. This, it is hoped, will find acceptance."

In the meantime the rank and file of the Congress were not idle. They were obtaining signatures to the Congress-League Scheme, as has already been stated. Mrs. Besant sought interviews several times with the Viceroy soon after her release, but she was turned away. On the other hand Mr. Montagu's *Diary* shows that Lord Chelmsford wanted to book Mrs. Besant once again, for he complained that she had 'a sharp tongue'. Mr. Montagu wrote in reply to Lord Chelmsford that he would not tender any advice in the matter, but that he would support him in whatever steps he might feel impelled to take to curb Mrs. Besant and her activities. A mystery surrounded the attitude and activities of Mrs. Besant soon after her release.

Mrs. Besant was shunned by Lord Chelmsford while Mr. Montagu showed no great regard for her leadership. Soon after her release she repudiated Passive Resistance. Was there anything behind, which justified such an attitude on the part of the Viceroy? Mr. Montagu has an interesting note in his *Diary* on page 137 which runs as follows:—

> "Chelmsford tells me that he thinks he will have to take action about Mrs. Besant's speeches and promised to tell me what he is going to do. Perhaps it is well that I should not know. I had thought of writing, regretting the strength of her language, but I fear it will be no good. There will of course be an outburst of anger at her release, and jeers that my visit has not produced a calm atmosphere, and that she has violated her pledges."

What these pledges may be, when they were given, and to whom, we do not know!

In the closing months of the year 1917, the political atmosphere was charged with the Montford current of electricity. Mr. Montagu and Lord Chelmsford had been touring the whole country receiving deputations and granting interviews everywhere. Mrs. Besant said to certain friends towards the end of 1917, after her interview with Mr. Montagu, "We must support Mr. Montagu." The Moderates everywhere repeated the statement and added that Mr. Montagu could do nothing if he was disowned by the Extremists in India as well as the die-hards in England. Apparently Montagu's mission was to consult the conflicting interests in India and to formulate draft schemes for the consideration of Parliament in England. But the former was done by the Hindu-Muslim Concordat of Lucknow (1916) which he bodily accepted. In regard to the latter, it may be news to many that the whole of the Montagu-Chelmsford Scheme, so-called, was worked out in every detail by March, 1916. The fact was that Lord Chelmsford was a Major in the Army in the Territorial Force in India, when the order reached him of his appointment as Viceroy. When he went to England in March, 1916, he was shown the full-blown scheme ready made,—a fact which we learnt only in 1934,—which was to be associated with his name. No doubt Mr. Montagu gave a hearing even to persons like Mrs. Besant, Tilak and Gandhi. He must doubtless have heard of the classical statement made by Mrs. Besant on the publication of the Montford Report, that the Reform Scheme was unworthy of Britain to offer and of India to accept.

But what Mr. Montagu did in his Indian tour was to pitch upon his future Ministers, Executive Councillors and Advocates-General. He wanted to be sure of the men that would work his scheme. This was behind the chorus of remarks we met with everywhere in the early part of 1918,—namely, "we must support Mr Montagu." The saddest event, however, associated with

Mr. Montagu's visit to India was the somewhat unceremonious treatment he gave to Mrs. Besant, in spite of her readiness to co-operate soon after her release.

During this period, in 1917, when Mrs. Besant's Home Rule movement was at its height, Gandhi, with a band of select workers—including Rajendra Babu, Brij Kishore Babu, Gorak Babu, Anugraha Babu, from Bihar, Prof. Kripalani, and Dr. H. S. Dev of the Servants of India Society—was engaged in investigating the grievances of the tenants of Champaran against the indigo planters. He kept himself and his co-workers strictly aloof from the movement for a whole period of six months, till he had finished the enquiry and given proof of the remarkable potency of Satyagraha which was destined to inaugurate a new epoch in the later history of India.

Champaran is a district in the north-western corner of Bihar. Early in the nineteenth century, indigo began to be grown in the district by European planters who in course of time secured, on temporary and permanent leases, large tracts of land from the Zamindars of the districts, particularly the Maharajah of Bettiah who became involved in heavy debts. The planters, with the influence and status thus acquired, coupled with the influence which they possessed as being members of the ruling race, were soon able to get indigo grown by the tenants of the villages on portions of their holdings varying between 3/20th and 5/20th and later on they regarded this compulsory cultivation as a matter of right which they got recognised in the Bengal Tenancy Act. This system of growing indigo came to be known as *tinkathia* or the system of three *cottahs* *i.e.*, 3/20th of a bigha. It was the grievance of the tenants that growing of indigo was not at all profitable for them and that they were forced to do it to the detriment of other cultivation and that the wages that they got for labour were nominal. Their grievances came to a head several times and their risings were suppressed with a heavy hand, but resulted now and then in some increase in the price paid for the indigo by the planter to the cultivator. Early in the twentieth century, on account of the introduction of synthetic dyes, growing of indigo even under conditions which prevailed in Champaran became unprofitable to planters, and they began to close their factories. But instead of taking the losses on themselves, as they ought to have fallen in due course, they devised means to transfer them to the shoulders of the poor tenants. They adopted two methods. In the villages which they held under permanent lease and in which any increase in the rent paid by the tenants would accrue to their benefit as permanent lessees as against the superior landlord, the lessor, they took agreements from the tenants agreeing to enhancement of rent, agreeing on their (planter's) part to release the tenants from the so-called obligation of growing indigo for the benefit of the planters.

Thousands upon thousands of such agreements were taken, as was alleged by the tenants, forcibly, from them. The enhancements would be ordinarily illegal but were saved by a provision in the Tenancy Act which had been inserted at the instance of the planters. The Government, in spite of popular protests inside and outside the Legislature, helped the planters in completing such agreements by appointing special registrars for registering them. In villages where the planters had only temporary leases, and where consequently an increase in the rent roll would accrue to the benefit of the superior landlord after the term of the lease was over, the planters adopted the device of taking, or as the tenants alleged, extorting cash payment or its equivalent from the tenants, and agreeing to release them from the so-called obligation of growing Indigo which, even under the special provisions of the Tenancy Act, did not exist in such villages. In this way they realised something like 12 lacs from the tenants. As the whole district had come under the planters, they had divided it into various portions or spheres of action, each indigo concern holding sway over a particular portion of the district. Their influence with the Government and officials was so great that tenants dared not approach either the Judicial or the Executive officials without serious risks to their person and property. Beating and shutting up of Hindus of high caste in *murgikhanas*, impounding cattle, and harassments in a thousand and one ways, including looting of their houses, stoppage of services by barbers, washermen, *chamars*, and even the ingress into and egress from their houses, and collecting untouchables to sit at their doors, were an ordinary everyday affair. The planters used also to extort a large number of unauthorised and illegal perquisites in the form of taxes which were counted during the inquiry to be more than fifty in number. A few illustrations may be given. There was a tax on marriage, a tax on every hearth, a tax for *kolhu* or oil-mill. If the Sahib was ill and needed a visit to the hills, the tenants had to pay a special tax called *paparhi*. If he needed a horse or an elephant or a motor car, the tenants must bear the cost and pay special taxes known as 'ghorahi' 'hathiahi' or 'hawahi.' Besides those taxes heavy fines used to be imposed and realised for anything which offended the planter or for offences against others, thus replacing civil authority and Courts in the district.

All efforts on the part of the public men of the Province to secure redress had failed. The Local Government were aware of these grievances, admitted them and sympathised with the tenants, but found themselves helpless or unwilling to do anything substantial.

It was in this condition of things that Mahatma Gandhi was approached by some representative tenants and Bihar delegates at the time of the Lucknow Congress. He promised to visit Champaran and study the situation.

In April 1917 he reached Motihari, the headquarters of the district, and was going to see a village when he was served with a notice under Sec. 144, Cr. P. C., calling upon him to leave the district forthwith. He disobeyed this order, returned the Kaisar-i-Hind gold medal which had been granted to him by Government for humanitarian work and stood for his trial before the Magistrate. He pleaded guilty in one of those remarkable statements in Court with which the country has since become familiar, but which at the time struck an altogether new and unfamiliar note. The Government ultimately withdrew the prosecution and allowed him to continue his enquiry in the course of which, with the aid of friends, he got the statements of some 20,000 tenants and formulated their demand on the basis of those statements. The Government ultimately appointed a Commission consisting of representatives of landlords, planters, and the Government, and Mahatma Gandhi himself as representing the tenants. The Commission after an inquiry submitted a unanimous report practically accepting the complaints of the tenants as valid, and embodying a compromise reducing the enhancements of rent and refunding part of the money which the planters had taken from the tenants. The recommendations of the Committee were embodied in an act by which, among other things, growing of indigo or *tinkathia* was abolished. Within a few years after this, most of the planters sold their factories and lands and left the district. To-day one can see only the remains of what were once the palaces of the planters, and those that are still continuing are not subsisting on indigo at all but on other crops like other cultivators, shorn of all their illegal gains and most of the prestige which made them possible.

The grievances which had failed to secure redress at the hands of both the popular leaders of the day and the Government for a hundred years were thus in a few months removed; and no wonder Champaran is ever so faithful to whatever Gandhi says or does.

Equal in importance to the Champaran Satyagraha, from the point of view of the principles involved, though not of the results achieved, was the Satyagraha in Kaira in 1918. The Indian peasants had never known, before the entry of Gandhi in the public life of India, to question the Government's right to demand assessment from them, even in years of acute famine. Their representatives made petitions and memorials and moved resolutions in the local Council, but there their protests ended. In 1918 Gandhi inaugurated a new era. A condition approaching famine had risen in the Kaira district in the Bombay Presidency, owing to a widespread failure of crops, and the peasants felt that the situation entitled them to a suspension of the assessment. The usual remedies had been tried, and had failed. The peasants claimed that the crops did not exceed four annas in the rupee but were less; the Government officials said they exceeded four annas and that the peasants had no right to suspension under the Land Revenue Code. All petitioning and prayer had failed and Gandhiji had no alternative but to advise the peasants to resort to Satyagraha. He also appealed to the public for help by contributing volunteer workers for educating the peasants. The response was prompt and spontaneous; and prominent among those who offered their voluntary services was Sirdar Vallabhbhai Patel who suspended a splendid and growing practice at the Bar and cast in his lot with Gandhi. The Kaira Satyagraha was the occasion which brought the two great men together. It was the beginning of Sirdar Vallabhbhai's public life. He burnt his boats and gave Gandhi a co-operation and allegiance which have grown with the years. The peasants signed a pledge to the effect that they would rather let their lands be forfeited than allow their case to be considered false or their self-respect to be compromised by being coerced into paying the assessment; also that the well-to-do amongst them would pay if the poor were granted suspension.

Now began a unique education of the peasants,—an education into principles that they had never before heard of. They were to understand that it was their right to question Government's authority to tax them, that the officials were not their masters but their servants, that therefore they should shed all fear of officials and stand erect in defiance of coercion, intimidation and worse. They had also to learn the primary lesson of civility without which even the highest courage would be vitiated. From day to day Gandhi and Vallabhbhai Patel and other co-workers went about from village to village inculcating these principles, and asking them to stand firm in spite of attachment of cattle and other moveables and penalty notices and threats of confiscation of land. No money was needed for the campaign, but the Bombay merchants lavished more contributions than the organisers of the campaign could make use of.

The Satyagraha also afforded an occasion for the first instance of Civil Disobedience in Gujarat. With a view to steeling the hearts of the peasants Gandhi advised the people, under the leadership of the late Sjt. Mohanlal

Pandya, to remove the crops from a field which had been wrongly attached. This was a good opportunity for the people to learn the lesson of courting fines or imprisonment which was the necessary consequence of Civil Disobedience. Sjt. Mohanlal Pandya removed the crop of onion from the field and a few peasants also joined him. They were arrested and convicted and sentenced to brief terms of imprisonment. This was a unique experience for the people who hailed it with delight and lionised their leaders and took them in procession after their release.

The campaign came to an unexpected end. The authorities accepted the people's contention by the grant of suspensions to poor peasants, but they did this without making a public announcement or letting the people feel that they had done anything by way of a settlement. Very few got the benefit of the belated, unacknowledged and grudging settlement, and the triumph of Satyagraha, though it was one in principle, lacked the essentials of a complete triumph. But the indirect results were great. The campaign laid the foundation of an awakening among the peasants of Gujarat and of a true political education. "The lesson," says Gandhi in his Autobiography, "was indelibly imprinted on the public mind that the salvation of the people depends upon themselves, upon their capacity for suffering and sacrifice. Through the Kaira campaign Satyagraha took firm root in the soil of Gujarat."

We may next usefully add a note of the part played by Congressmen in the organisation of Labour in Ahmedabad, and the great lesson in Satyagraha taught us by Gandhi and his fellow-workers.

The story of the organisation of the textile workmen in Ahmedabad by Gandhi, who had not then assumed the leadership of the Congress, is a romance which would adorn the history of freedom of any Nation. For the very first time in history methods based on truth and non-violence were employed for the solution of industrial disputes, and with such sound and far-reaching results that the labour organisation in Ahmedabad has successfully stood the test of many an industrial storm and has been the wonder and admiration of Western visitors. Even a brief resume of the story would occupy a number of pages in this history. One should content oneself with indicating the part played by Gandhi and with mentioning the salient features of the organisation which distinguish it from similar organisations in India and the world.

Shrimati Anasuyaben Sarabhai had been since 1916 conducting educational work in labour areas, which brought her into contact with the workers' difficulties in the mills. The first section to benefit by her guidance were the warpers, but she soon saw that if all the workmen were to be organised and given effective help, she must seek the guidance of some one who commanded her confidence. A dispute between the weavers and the millowners in 1918 led her to seek Gandhi's advice, who instead of trying to force the hands of the millowners got them to accept the principle of arbitration,—an event of the greatest importance to the labour movement. He and Sirdar Vallabhbhai Patel consented to be two of the arbitrators on behalf of labour, but the arbitration fell through, as some of the workmen in a few mills went on strike. Gandhi expressed his regret and got the workmen to make amends. The breaches of understanding were on both sides, but the millowners refused to listen. Before advising the workmen to take any definite step, Gandhi went into the matter of dispute at very great length, examined the state of trade, the profits made by the mills, the rise in the cost of living on the one hand and the extent to which the cost of production of the industry had increased on the other. A careful examination of these factors led him to arrive at the conclusion that the minimum the workmen had a right to claim was a 35 per cent. increase in their wages. The labourers who were pitching their demands much higher were persuaded to accept this, and were educated into the healthy tradition, which has since been faithfully followed, of always limiting the demands to the barest minimum which can be legitimately claimed.

The demand thus formulated was communicated to the millowners who in their turn said that they were not prepared to go beyond 20 per cent. and declared a lock-out on 22nd February 1918. Thereupon Gandhi called a meeting of all the workmen and administered to them a pledge—under a tree, which is still held sacred,—not to resume work until they had secured their demand and not to do anything in breach of the peace during the lock-out. This was followed by an intensive educative propaganda and house to house visits by Shrimati Anasuyaben, and Srijuts Shankerlal Banker and Chaganlal Gandhi and leaflets issued and huge mass meetings addressed every day. These leaflets were drafted by Gandhi who explained to the workmen in a simple homely style that the struggle in which they were engaged was not a mere industrial dispute but a moral and spiritual struggle calculated to educate and uplift and ennoble them, besides enabling them to win an increase in their wage. The struggle went on for a fortnight, but the workmen unaccustomed to a loss of wage for any length of time showed signs of exhaustion, and the unreasoning element among them even began to grumble that it may be all right for Gandhi to exhort them to keep the pledge but no easy thing for them to do so, whilst they and their children were on the brink of starvation. That, to Gandhi, was the warning voice of God and he declared at the next evening's meeting that he would have no food and would use no conveyance until the workmen had been enabled to carry out their pledge. The news spread like wildfire throughout the length and breadth of India. It was a fast unto death, though the language used was different, but he staked his life for the great moral purpose of helping a mass of covenanters to adhere to their pledge. Critics and cavillers said that it was wrongful coercion of the millowners. Gandhi confessed that the fast was tainted to the extent that the millowners might be compelled to yield against their will, but that, he said, would be the indirect and not the direct result of the fast, which was aimed at helping a community of men to adhere to a pledge solemnly taken. Nothing moves Gandhi so deeply as the sanctity and faithful observance of a pledge, however small, and nothing pains him more than the violation of a pledge. The workmen pleaded with him in vain; his decision was irrevocable. But he now appealed to them not to while away their time, but to earn an honest penny by taking up any work that could be found for them. Gandhi could easily have made a successful appeal for funds in order to sustain the workmen with doles, but he would not brook the suggestion. The workmen's suffering would lose all its value if it was backed up by doles. Work was found for hundreds of workmen on the grounds of the Satyagraha Ashram, Sabarmati, where buildings were under construction, and they worked merrily with the members of the Ashram, who joined them with Anasuyaben at their head, in carrying loads of earth and bricks and mortar. The moral effect of this was tremendous. It strengthened the workmen in their resolve, and it also moved the hearts of the millowners. Appeals were made to them by leaders from various parts of the country, the most prominent among them being the late Dr. Besant who sent them an urgent wire to "yield for India's sake and save Gandhiji's life." Shrimati Saraladevi, the cultured wife of Seth

Ambalal Sarabhai, was moved as much by the suffering of the workmen as by the impending danger to one whom she revered, and she played no little part in persuading the millowners to find out a solution. On the fourth day of the fast, a solution was found enabling the workmen to keep the pledge and the millowners to concede to them justice consistently with honour. Both agreed to submit to arbitration for the ultimate settlement of the wage increase, and the arbitrator's Award gave the workmen a 35 per cent. increase as originally demanded.

This peaceful settlement of the dispute laid the foundation of an indissoluble union between Congress leaders and workmen, and of a permanent organisation called the Textile Labour Association, which has grown during these fifteen years under the fostering care of Shrimati Anasuyaben and Shankerlal Banker, both prominent members of the Congress. It has helped the workmen to tide over several crises and saved the city of Ahmedabad from industrial troubles of a serious nature. The workmen are so well organised, and the education imparted to them by the permanent staff of the Union, with Sjt. Gulzarilal Nanda at their head, is of such a solid character that the workmen have frequently rendered public service of a far-reaching character. Under Gandhi's advice the Labour Association engaged itself in the relief of distress caused by heavy rain and floods in 1927. During the Civil Disobedience campaign of 1930 the workmen conducted an intensive temperance campaign, and nearly 200 volunteers from amongst them responded to the call of the Congress by working as pickets and 162 of them were sentenced to various terms of imprisonment. There have since been disputes between them and the millowners of a rather serious character, but thanks to their wonderful discipline, they kept peace during arbitration proceedings extending over a period of 16 months and carried on by Gandhi who worked throughout the period as their permanent arbitrator. The Labour Association, Ahmedabad, is perhaps the only one in the world with a constitution which pledges it to the observance of truth and non-violence and which has as its ultimate goal the nationalization of the textile industry. The Association has at present nearly 30,000 paying members, it handled nearly 4,000 complaints in 1934 of which nearly 80 per cent. were successful, and dealt with 39 strikes of which 23 ended in favour of the workers. The Association secured maternity benefit for 1185 women, amounting to Rs. 29,000 and Rs. 18,074 as accident compensation, and Rs. 9,856 as victimization benefit to 164 operatives. Its special uplift work includes medical aid, education, physical culture and recreation, municipal facilities, temperance and social reform.

Gandhi, who had given proofs of his magical powers in Champaran, liberated the simple but effective proposal that the Congress-League Scheme should be translated into the Indian languages, explained to the people and their signatures taken in support of the Reforms outlined therein, and it was welcomed throughout the country and up to the end of 1917 over a million persons subscribed to the scheme. This was almost the first Nation-wide organization that had been attempted by the Congress, but reference may here be made to an earlier attempt to organize the country for Self-Government and, to that end, gather funds for continuous work in England and India. At the Bombay Session of the Congress in 1915 presided over by Sir S. P. Sinha, the A.I.C.C. had resolved to raise a permanent fund for the Congress on the 30th December, 1915, and appointed a sub-committee consisting of Surendra Nath Banerjea, Bhupendra Nath Basu, S. Srinivasa Iyengar, Samarth, Wacha and Malaviya to devise the best means of raising a

Permanent Fund for the support of the British Congress Committee in England and its organ *India*, and for Congress work in India. It was widely talked about that Sinha himself offered to give a lac of rupees to the Fund. The Committee met in Calcutta on the 17th November, 1916, and recommended that a sum of three lacs and a half be raised and the same be invested as a Permanent Fund. A Board of Trustees with Dr. Rash Behari Ghose as Chairman was appointed at Lucknow on the 30th December, 1916 to receive and administer the same. The Board met subsequently in Calcutta in April, 1917 and appointed the Hon. V. S. Srinivasa Sastri as the Secretary and postponed the question of allocating the Fund to the Provinces. Nothing was however done in the direction.

In this connection we may recall a similar attempt made in the early years of the Congress. So early as 1889 it was proposed to establish a permanent Congress Fund and a sum of Rs. 50,000 was voted to form the nucleus of such a fund. Out of this a small sum of Rs. 5,000 only was realised and deposited with the Oriental Bank which was then considered as the strongest Exchange Bank in India. In the Bombay crisis of 1890, the Bank, however, went into liquidation and the small sum thus credited to the Fund was lost.

Before dealing with the Congress session of the year 1917, we have to make reference to one important matter. The Congress of the year was to take place in Calcutta, and in that city opinions were keenly divided between the old Moderates for whom it was a stronghold, and the new Home Rulers and Nationalists who made Calcutta their 'stronger hold.' The old guard was represented by Rai Baikunta Nath Sen, Ambika Charan Mazumdar, Surendra Nath Banerjea and Bhupendra Nath Basu. Mr. C. R. Das began to interest himself in Congress work and cast in his lot with the younger folks—B. K. Lahiri, I. B. Sen and Jitendralal Banerjee.

Although the majority of the Provincial Congress Committees had recommended Mrs. Besant as the President of the ensuing Congress, there was a keen division in the Reception Committee which, in those days, had to accept the majority recommendation. But the meeting of the Reception Committee held on the 30th of August, 1917 became the scene of acute controversy. The Joint Honorary Secretaries—Fazl-ul-Haq, Lahiri and Jitendralal Banerjee, claimed that the majority recommendation was accepted by an overwhelming majority of the members of the Reception Committee at the meeting. Rai Bahadur Baikunta Nath Sen and 30 others left the meeting at an early stage owing to some unpleasantness. A statement was submitted to the A.I.C.C. by the Secretaries in which it was claimed that Mrs. Besant was elected. On the contrary the Rai Bahadur sent a telegram that the Reception Committee "failed to elect President within month of August. As Chairman of Reception Committee refer the matter to the A.I.C.C." To make a long story short, Mrs. Besant was elected by the A.I.C.C. easily, by circulation, while yet she was under the heavy ban of Government displeasure. The record of the Congress of 1917 may shortly be stated.

Mrs. Besant's Presidential Address is an elaborate thesis of India's Self-Government. Her summary of the Military and Mercantile problems is comprehensive as well as detailed, and constitutes a splendid source of reference to students in quest of knowledge. In effect she demanded, "A Bill during 1918 establishing Self-Government in India on lines resembling those of the Commonwealth on a date to be laid down therein, preferably 1923, the latest 1928, the intermediate five or ten years being occupied with the transference of the

Government from British to Indian hands, maintaining the British tie as in the Dominions." At the end of the address, she gave copious extracts from Bernard Houghton's 'Bureaucratic Government' and a detailed Bill regarding Village Government. With Mrs. Besant, the Presidentship of the Congress was not a passing show or a three-day festivity. It was a day-to-day responsibility, and in that view Mrs. Besant was the first to claim Presidentship of the Congress throughout the succeeding year. The claim was not new but its enforcement was not known in the previous history of the Congress. The Calcutta Session was attended by 4,967 delegates and about 5,000 visitors.

The resolutions of the Calcutta Session of the Congress of 1917 were, with some exceptions, again of the same stereotyped sort and after recording the grief of the Congress at the deaths of the Grand Old Man Dadabhai Naoroji and Mr. A. Rasul of Calcutta, and India's loyalty to the Throne and welcome to Mr. Montagu, proceeded to ask for the release of Messrs. Mahomed Ali and Shaukat Ali who had remained incarcerated since October, 1914. The Congress again urged as usual the necessity and justice of adequate provision for giving Military training to Indians and while expressing satisfaction at the removal of the racial bar against admission of Indians to the Commissioned ranks of the Army and the appointment of nine Indians to such ranks, expressed the hope for a larger proportion of Commissioned posts to Indians and urged improvement in the pay, prospects and equipment of Indian soldiers. The Congress reiterated its protest against (a) the wide and arbitrary powers conferred by the Press Act of 1910 upon the Executive, (b) the Arms Act, (c) the treatment and disabilities of Indians in the Colonies. The Congress asked for complete abolition of the system of indentured labour and a Parliamentary Commission to inquire into the working of the special coercive legislation restricting freedom of speech, writing, association and meetings and the use of the Defence of India Act for similar purposes. The Government had, on the 10th December, announced the appointment of the Rowlatt Committee and the Congress condemned it "inasmuch as the avowed object of the appointment is not to give relief but to introduce fresh legislation arming the Executive with additional powers to deal with alleged revolutionary conspiracy in Bengal. By the same resolution the Congress expressed alarm at the extensive use made of the Defence of India Act and Regulation III of 1818, and in view of the widespread discontent on account of the indiscriminate operations of the Act asked for a general amnesty to all political prisoners.

The Congress by a resolution asked for intervention of the Government of India to save the life of Lala Arjunlal Sethi who was in danger of death by starvation in Vellore Jail on account of his religious principles, and, by another, recommended the formation of Boy Scouts' Associations in every Province, under Indian control. The main resolution was that dealing with the question of Self-Government and ran as follows:—

> "This Congress expresses its grateful satisfaction over the pronouncement made by His Majesty's Secretary of State for India on behalf of the Imperial Government that its object is the establishment of responsible Government in India.
>
> "This Congress strongly urges the necessity for the immediate enactment of a Parliamentary Statute providing for the establishment of responsible Government in India, the full measure to be attained within a time-limit to be fixed in the statute itself at an early date.
>
> "This Congress is emphatically of opinion that the Congress-League Scheme of Reforms ought to be immediately introduced by the Statute as the first step in the progress."

A new resolution accepted by the Calcutta Congress was the one relating to Andhra being recognized as a separate Congress circle, and in this connection we may make a reference to a National or sub-national movement which was inaugurated in the Andhradesa in 1913 and which travelled on to the Congress of 1915. The movement related to the question of redistributing the Indian Provinces on linguistic lines. It had its origin really in the efforts made by Mahesh Narayan of Bihar in 1894 to get his Province separated from Bengal. The Congress created Bihar into a separate Province in 1908, and the principle was approved in the scheme of Provincial Autonomy set forth in the Government of India's Despatch of August 25th, 1911, and Bihar separated from Bengal as the result of that despatch. Wide and strong was the belief that for Provincial Autonomy to be successful, the medium of instruction as well as administration must be the provincial languages, and that the failure of the British administration, notably in the domain of Local Self-Government, is undoubtedly due to the pell-mell admixture of populations in British Provinces which are carved out on no logical or ethnological, but on a chronological basis. In 1915 the Congress was not prepared to deal with the question but it was pressed to the fore in 1916 by the Andhra Conference, and to anticipate events, we may say that on the 8th of April, 1917, the All-India Congress Committee to which it was referred by the Lucknow Congress, 1916, accepted the principle after duly consulting the Provincial Congress Committees of Madras and Bombay, and resolved that the "Telugu speaking districts of the Madras Presidency be constituted into a separate Congress Province." Sindh followed suit and Karnataka came later. The subject was hotly contested in the Subjects Committee of the Calcutta Congress (1917). Even Gandhi thought that the question might await the implementing of the Reforms, but Lokamanya Tilak saw the point, namely, that Linguistic Provinces were an essential condition pre-requisite to real Provincial Autonomy. Mrs. Besant presided over the Calcutta Congress (1917), and the idea was opposed vehemently by her as well as by some Tamil friends from the South. The subject held the field for over two hours in Calcutta, and was ultimately accepted late at night at 10-15 p.m. Sindh was recognised as a separate Congress circle by the A.I.C.C. on 6th October, 1917. The principle which was then accepted became the guiding principle for a redistribution immediately after the Nagpur Congress, and we have now twenty-one Congress circles as against the nine British Provinces.

In Calcutta Mrs. Besant was anxious to appoint Mr. C. P. Ramaswami Aiyar as Secretary and therefore asked for three Secretaries at the point of having to amend the constitution. It was agreed to, and Mr. Subba Rau Pantulu, though re-elected, forthwith resigned his secretaryship. The Presidentship of Mrs. Besant over the Calcutta Session brought nearer together the Congress and the Home Rule League and the constitution of the League was made so rigid in Calcutta that it brought about a complete paralysis of the organization. The Calcutta session was memorable for the question of the National flag being formally raised. Indeed the Home Rule League had already adopted and popularized the Tricolour flag, and a committee was appointed to recommend a design including on its personnel Abanindra Nath Tagore. But the committee never met and the old Home Rule flag virtually became the Congress flag, with the Charkha added on it later on, until the Flag Committee of 1931 substituted the saffron colour for the red.

CHAPTER IV

THE MONTAGU-CHELMSFORD PROPOSALS (1918)

Mrs. Besant, it has already been noted, took the view that the President of the year's session of the Congress was President for the whole year. This was not a new idea by any means, but she was the first to act upon it.

At the very first meeting of the All-India Congress Committee held immediately after the Congress on 30th December, 1917, the question of raising a permanent fund for the Congress was considered, and further, Provincial Committees were called upon to appoint a Working Committee for carrying on educative and propagandist work in India and in England. The months that followed were months of incessant activity, especially in Madras where lacs of leaflets explaining the Congress-League Scheme were circulated, and more than 9 lacs signatures obtained in its support and presented to Mr. Montagu when he visited Madras.

The All-India Congress Committee met again on 23rd February, 1918 at Delhi, and after recording its sense of sorrow at the death of Sir William Wedderburn, appointed a Deputation to urge on the Viceroy the cancellation of the order excluding Lokamanya Tilak and Babu Bepin Chandra Pal from the Punjab and Delhi Provinces.

The Deputation waited on the Viceroy but without any result. Lord Chelmsford and Mr. Montagu were expected to issue their Report on Constitutional Reforms, and the A.I.C.C. resolved to have a special session of the

Congress at Allahabad or Lucknow soon after the publication of the Report and to send a Deputation to England after the special session.

A third meeting of the A.I.C.C. held on 3rd May 1918, protested against the action of the Government in turning back the deputations of the two Home Rule Leagues on their way to England, from Gibralter and Ceylon. The Committee insisted that nothing short of an authoritative pronouncement that India should have Responsible Government as the issue of the War would inspire the youth of the country to flock to the colours in sufficient numbers to ensure success.

The first five months of 1918 were a period of restless activity for Mrs. Besant. An idea of her continuous tours is given in the pamphlet on 'Home Rule Leagues' (See Appendix III). Mrs. Margaret E. Cousins and Mrs. Dorothy Jinarajadasa addressed letters to her respecting the grant of franchise to women under the Congress-League Scheme. Mr. John Scur wrote to her from England suggesting that the Congress should invite the Labour Conference in June 1918 to send a fraternal delegate to the Indian National Congress of 1918, and the A.I.C.C. did so. This idea and this language were fast becoming familiar and were peculiarly befitting the democratic organisations of the day. "The Home Rule Leagues had just then appointed Mr. Baptista as their fraternal delegate to the annual Labour Conference next month," said Mrs. Besant in her Presidential Address, "and Major Graham Pole comes to us from them." She was a great believer in the Indo-British connection. Indeed her vision had not travelled beyond the conception of Home Rule, as understood in those days; even a Dominion of those times was, in status, far behind the Dominions of 1926, and certainly could not be compared to the Dominions of the present day with the Statute of Westminster behind them. In any case, Mrs. Besant was soon feeling out of tune both with Government and with the people. The former deprecated her forwardness, the latter, her backwardness. While she had a good following and abundant influence at the Special Congress of Bombay (Sep. 1918), it was seen that she became a back number at the Delhi Congress (December 1918). Between the two she was rapidly losing ground.

The Defence of India Act was vigorously at work everywhere. Even in 1917, orders of externment had been passed against Bal Gangadhar Tilak and Bepin Chandra Pal from the Punjab and Delhi. But popular agitation was not cowed down by these repressive measures. When the Governor of Bombay held a War meeting of leaders, Tilak raised the question of Self-Government, but was not allowed to speak for more than two minutes. When the Viceroy held a meeting in Delhi, Gandhi was present though he had at first declined the invitation, not merely on the ground that Tilak and Mrs. Besant were not invited but on the higher ground that there were secret treaties which Britain had entered into regarding the Cession of Constantinople to Russia and other matters. He had an interview with Lord Chelmsford who bore it in upon him that the news emanated from interested quarters (Russia) which had by that time emerged out of the War, a fact which, by the way, made the question no longer a live issue, that he himself could not believe that the Cabinet would enter into such a treaty, and finally, that, in any case, such a question could not possibly be raised or discussed in the midst of the War. Therefore Gandhi agreed to join the War Conference and he wired to the Lokamanya to go to Delhi, although there was no invitation to the latter; but Delhi being an area from which he had been externed, he declined to go unless the orders against him were expressly cancelled. Government were too proud to do that.

In August 1918, Tilak was served with an order prohibiting him from lecturing without the previous permission of the District Magistrate. Only a week before, we are told he was engaged in a recruiting campaign and "as guarantee of good faith he had sent to Mahatma Gandhi a cheque for Rs. 50,000, the amount to be forfeited as penalty if certain conditions were not fulfilled by him. This was in the nature of a wager. The wager was that Tilak undertook to recruit 5,000 persons from Maharashtra if Gandhi could secure a promise from Government beforehand that Indians would get Commissioned ranks in the Army. Gandhi's position was that the help should not be in the nature of a bargain and therefore returned the cheque to Tilak. In 1917-1918, the Congress was suspicious of Tilak. The Bureaucracy was positively persecuting him. Mrs. Besant alone was in alliance with him.

The Montagu-Chelmsford Report was published in June 1918. It was a masterpiece of literature and, like other political documents produced by British Statesmen, it contained a dispassionate statement of India's case for Self-Government. Only, the obstacles to Reform are described with equal lucidity, and in the end the latter triumph. In the case of the Report in question, there was an additional circumstance. The Congress Scheme prepared by the two great bodies representing India had provided for fixed Executives responsible to the Legislature. Here was a more fascinating scheme of Responsible Government with replaceable Cabinets, possessing corporate responsibility and subject to the vote of the Legislatures, the very reproduction of the British type of Self-Government. What else should the people of India want? Their Legislatures would no longer be the arena for the training of Indian politicians, but the forum in which ministers should justify their conduct to their constituencies and stand or fall upon the vote of their colleagues in Parliament. Many in India were taken in by such a scheme and a chorus of praise was to be heard from them. The centre of gravity shifted from the Congress-League Scheme to the Montford Scheme. We have it on the authority of Mr. Montagu's *Diary* that Mrs. Besant promised to accept anything that Sir Sankaran Nair accepted, and Sir Sankarn Nair accepted this scheme. "Extremists who do not mean well to Government must be separated from those who do." About Mr. C. P. Ramaswami Aiyar, Montagu says, "I asked him point-blank what he would accept. He accepted Sastri's four criteria, and I am afraid he would never accept periodic inquiries. What he wants is a time-limit, and there is much more in this time-limit than people really believe. He pathetically said that their confidence in me was everything and he begged me not to be persuaded to desert them." (P. 129). Then comes Mr. S. Srinivasa Iyengar: "After I had finished with Lord Pentland the Advocate-General of the Presidency, Srinivasa Iyengar, came to see me. He assured me that nobody really expected the whole of the Congress-League Scheme and if they are certain that it will develop they will not much mind. He thinks the Curtis scheme is the best. He tells me that there is great bitterness against the Government but he had nothing very much to say." In justice to Mr. S. S. Iyengar, it must be said that he was not a Congressman at the time. After these statements we need hardly be told by Mr. Montagu that "Setalvad, Chandavarkar and Rahimtoola approved of the Reservation scheme." Montagu's strategy has already been described. Government was to form a Department to help the Moderates to organise themselves. "There was a proposal,—27th proposal," says Montagu, "in favour of a new organisation of Indians, assisted in every way by Government, for propaganda on behalf of our proposals and to send a Delegation to England and to assist us." "Proposals No. 30 and 31 contemplated," adds Mr. Montagu, "that Sir S. P. Sinha should succeed Mr. Montagu,—Montagu to be Under-Secretary." Mr. Montagu's observations on this are interesting: "It will teach the I.C.S. that a British statesman who, however undeservedly, has reached Cabinet rank, finds nothing derogatory in assisting, rather than controlling India. It will fire the imagination of India." On the other hand, the Nationalists left no doubt whatever in Mr. Montagu's mind as to what they wanted. "Motilal Nehru would be satisfied if he could get Responsible Government in 20 years." (P. 62). "C.R. Das anticipated the failure of Dyarchy and wanted real, Responsible Government in 5 years hence, and promise of it now." (Page 91) Mr. Montagu had secured the support of Surendra Nath Banerjea. "Then Basu (Bhupendra Nath Basu) said that he thought the Congress would pass a resolution accepting it, leaving all my amendments to subsequent negotiation so as not to provide their enemies with a handle for saying that they had been captious."

The general belief about the Report was that it was largely drafted by Sir James (later Lord) Meston and Mr. (later Sir Wm.) Marris, while Mr. Lionel Curtis greatly assisted in the task. Mr. Curtis belonged to a group of Round Tablers who had a scholarly bent of mind and who were touring various countries in order to "serve the Empire." A letter that he had drafted on Indian Reforms miscarried and fell into the hands of Indian publicists and *The Bombay Chronicle* and *The Leader* published it. This act of audacity exposed the bureaucratic intrigues and roused the ire of officialdom against Nationalist India.

The fact was that, in a private letter to Mr. Philip Kerr, then Secretary of the Round Table, Mr. Lionel Curtis discussed the possibility of India being made subordinate, in her external and internal affairs, to an Imperial Council on which the Self-Governing Dominions would be represented, but she would not be represented. He added that this would perhaps lead to bloodshed, but if it were the right thing to do, that would have to be faced. The writer stated in his letter that his views expressed in it were generally approved by "Meston, Marris and Chirol." Copies of this letter, for circulation among the Round Table Confederates, were actually printed in the Government Press at Allahabad, and when one fell into Indian hands it was promptly published on the eve of the Lucknow Session of the Congress in 1916. Mr. Curtis later addressed "A letter to the People of India" explaining his position. He was originally an official in South Africa, and, soon after the Boer War, when the British Government borrowed the services of Sir James Meston and Mr. Marris to organise the Civil Service in South Africa, he made their acquaintance for the first time. Ever since they studied the problems of the Commonwealth of British Nations in South Africa, Canada, and India, and Sir James Meston invited Mr. Curtis to go to India in 1916 to study the Indian problems of the Empire and publish in a quarterly, *The Round Table*, their studies from time to time. The letter in question was one such study, meant for publication and for being sent to England, which unfortunately miscarried. It was alleged that Mr. Curtis was engaged in a conspiracy with Indian officialdom to place India, in a scheme of post-War reconstruction, not only under England but under the Dominions as well. "The root of the present trouble is," says Mr. Curtis in his "Letter to the People of India," "that this insistence of mine on the doctrine that you cannot at present divide the control of India, and the control of foreign affairs, has led to a false impression here that the Dominions want to control Indian affairs: There is nothing they less desire." He finally explained from documents of earlier origin how he held "that it is the duty of those who govern the whole British Commonwealth to do everything in their power to enable Indians to govern themselves as soon as possible, and that Indians must also come to share in the Government of the British Commonwealth as a whole." The fact was that Mr. Montagu gathered around him the pick of the I.C.S. men in India besides the six colleagues that accompanied him from England. Amongst the former were Sir Malcolm Hailey, Sir James Meston and Mr. Marris, the last of whom was Inspector-General of Police in U. P. at the time.

It is therefore not surprising that soon after the publication of the Report, markedly different opinions regarding the attitude to be adopted towards it began to be expressed all over the country by various leaders, and it became apparent that the Special Session of the Congress, which the A.I.C.C. had already decided to convene, should be held. It was found that Lucknow and Allahabad would not be suitable places and the venue was changed to Bombay which made elaborate arrangements for the Congress in a short time. The differences among Congressmen had become acute. While no party was fully satisfied with the scheme as it stood, there were naturally differences in the tone of the criticism, and it seemed as if one party which was more radical in its views would press at the Special Congress for its total rejection, and the other only for amendments to improve it. Just a few days before the Congress, an attempt was made to reconcile all the differences at a Conference, but the attempt failed and the Congress met on the 29th August 1918 under the Presidentship of Mr. Hasan Imam. It was very largely attended and there were no less than 3,845 delegates present, Mr. Vittalbhai Patel acting as the Chairman of the Reception Committee. Veteran leaders like Dinshaw Wacha, Surendra Nath Banerjea, Bhupendra Nath Basu, Ambika Charan Mazumdar were absent from the Congress. After four days' discussion the Congress re-affirmed the principles of Reform contained in the Congress-League Scheme and declared that nothing less than Self-Government within the Empire would satisfy the legitimate aspirations of the Indian people. It dealt with the Montagu proposals at great length. It declared that the people of India were fit for Responsible Government and repudiated the assumption to the contrary contained in the Report. It asked for simultaneous advance in the Provinces and the Government of India and disagreed with the formula that the Provinces are the domain in which the earlier steps should be taken towards the progressive realisation of Responsible Government, leaving the authority of the Government of India in essential matters indisputable, pending experience in the Provinces. It conceded, however, that subject to a Declaration of Rights of the people of India,—(a) guaranteeing to them liberty of person, property, association, free speech and writing, except under sentence of an ordinary court of justice as a result of lawful and open trial, (b) entitling Indians to bear arms, subject to the purchase of a licence as in Great Britain, (c) guaranteeing freedom of Press, dispensing with licence and security, on the registration of a Press or newspaper, and (d) guaranteeing equality to Indians before the law,—the Government of India should have undivided administrative authority on matters directly concerning peace, tranquillity and defence of the country.

Another resolution was strongly of opinion that the Indian Legislature should have the same measure of fiscal autonomy as the Self-Governing Dominions of the Empire possessed. The resolution dealing directly with the Reform Scheme appreciated the earnest attempt on the part of the Secretary of State and the Viceroy to inaugurate a system of Responsible Government, and while it recognised that some of the proposals constituted an advance in some directions, it was of opinion that the proposals were 'disappointing and unsatisfactory' and went on to suggest modifications which were considered absolutely necessary to constitute a substantial step towards Responsible Government. Dealing with the proposals relating to the Government of India, the Congress desired the same system of reserved and transferred subjects for the Central Government as had been proposed for the Provinces, the subjects reserved being Foreign Affairs, excepting relations with the Colonies and Dominions, Army, Navy and relations with Indian ruling Princes, all the other subjects being transferred subjects. After the first term of the reformed Assembly, the position of the Viceroy in the Legislative Assembly in regard to transferred subjects should be the same as that obtaining in the Self-Governing Dominions. All legislation should be by bills introduced in the Legislative Assembly, provided that, in case the Legislature refused to pass any measures regarding reserved subjects which the Government deemed necessary, the Governor-General might provide for the same by regulations which would remain in force for one year but could not be renewed unless 40 per cent. of the members of the Assembly present voted for them. There should be no Council of State, but if one was constituted at least half of the total strength should be elected. The procedure by certification should be confined to reserved subjects. At least half the members of the Executive Committee (if more than one) in charge of reserved subjects should be Indians. The Legislative Assembly was to consist of 150 members, four-fifths of whom were to be elected and it should have the right to elect its own President and Vice-President and make its own rules of business. A statutory guarantee was demanded that full Responsible Government should be established in the whole of British India within a period not exceeding 15 years.

As regards the Provinces, the Congress resolved that (a) there should be no additional members of the Executive without portfolios, (b) that after the first term of the reformed Councils the Governor should have the same relation with the Ministers in regard to transferred subjects as in the Self-Governing Dominions, (c) that the status and the salary of Ministers should be the same as that of Executive Councillors, (d) that half the Executive Committee should be Indians, and (e) that the budget should be under the control of the Legislature subject to the allocation of a fixed sum for the reserved subjects; if fresh taxation became necessary it should be imposed by the Provincial Government as a whole. The Congress while holding that the country was ripe for full Provincial Autonomy was yet prepared, with a view to facilitating the passage of the Reforms, to leave the departments of Law, Police and Justice (prisons excepted) in the hands of the Executive Government in all Provinces for a period of six years. Executive and Judicial departments must be separated at once. As in the case of the Central Legislature, the Provincial Councils would elect their Presidents and Vice-Presidents. The proposal to institute a Grand Committee should be dropped. But if it was to be instituted, no less than one-half of the strength should be elected. The proportion of elected members in the Provincial Councils should be four-fifths.

The Provincial Council should legislate in respect of all matters including Law, Justice and Police, but if the Government was not satisfied with its decisions in respect of Law, Justice and Police, the Provincial Government could refer the matter to the Government of India, which in its turn would place it before the Indian Legislature where the ordinary procedure should be followed.

The control of Parliament and the Secretary of State must only be modified and the responsibility of the Indian and Provincial Governments to the electorates increased. The India Council should be abolished. There should be two Under-Secretaries to assist the Secretary of State for India, one of whom should be an Indian.

As regards communal representation, the Congress resolved that the proportion of Muslims in the Indian and Provincial Legislatures should be as laid down in the Congress-League Scheme. Women should not be disqualified on account of sex. The Government of India should have complete freedom in all fiscal matters.

As regards the place of Indians in the Army, the Congress recorded its deep disappointment at the altogether inadequate response of the Government to the demand for the grant of commissions to Indians in the Army and opined that steps should be immediately taken so as to enable the grant of at least 25 per cent. of the commissions to Indians, to be increased to 50 per cent. within fifteen years.

The Congress decided to send a Deputation to England, and appointed a Committee of selection for the purpose.

It will thus be noticed that the Special Session, which had threatened at one time to create a schism on the question of Reforms in the Congress, passed off successfully and after considerable discussions came to conclusions which reconciled various conflicting views and commanded the unqualified support of the large majority of Congressmen all over the country. A session of the Muslim League had been held at the same time under the Presidentship of the Rajah of Mahmudabad and had adopted a resolution on practically the same lines as the Congress with whose committee there had been complete collaboration.

One thing more, however, remained to be done to complete the Reform proposals, namely the division of functions between Provincial and Central Governments and the determination of Franchises and Constituencies. Accordingly two commissions came out from England,—the Southborough Commission to deal with Franchises, and the Featham Commission to deal with Functions. Deputations were profusely received. In the South of India the Non-Brahman movement which had been brought into existence in February 1917, became quite vocal and irresistible by November 1918, and suspecting that Mr. Sastri who was a member of the Southborough Committee was influencing Lord Southborough against separate representation to their community, the Non-Brahman leaders boycotted the Committee to mark their protest against Mr. Sastri's inclusion on the Commission and threatened to carry their case to England. Carry they did, and succeed too. But India's woes did not end. The Defence of India Act, the counterpart of the British Defence of the Realm Act (D.O.R.A.) which could call upon any one in the country to do anything or to refrain from doing anything, was vigorously at work. We have already referred to the internment of the Ali Brothers, and Maulana Abul Kalam Azad. The Ali Brothers were never Congressmen until they appeared at the Amritsar Congress on their release in 1919. Mahomed Ali was editing a powerful and spicy weekly—*The Comrade*—and Shaukat Ali, his elder brother, was editing the *Hamdard*, an Urdu daily. Soon after the outbreak of the War and the pompous announcement of its cause as being the protection of the weaker Nationalities, Mahomed Ali published an article headed 'Evacuate Egypt.' The brothers and the Maulana were all presently interned and they remained in their confinement till, under the amnesty granted by the Royal Proclamation, they were released on the 25th December, 1919.

The methods employed for recruiting soldiers into the Army as well as collecting money for War Loans were highly objectionable. The methods of 'pressure and persuasion'—a phrase used by Lord Willingdon's Government in description of the methods employed for these purposes—was only a euphemism for the excesses which were destined to lead later to serious developments in the Punjab and elsewhere. In the country districts what was called the 'Indent system' prevailed, under which local officials had to make a return of the lending capacity of the areas in their charge, and it was left to the subordinates to maintain their reputation and obtain as much money as possible for War Loans by methods of 'pressure and persuasion.' These methods ultimately led to an angry crowd surrounding the bungalow of a Mamlatdar and after allowing his family to escape, burn it to the ground with him in it.

In the domain of pure politics, the repressive policy adopted during the days of Lord Chelmsford chiefly centred round the Press Act which was used often and with severity. Mrs. Besant was prohibited from entering the Bombay Presidency by Lord Willingdon under the Defence of India Act. In Bengal, the number of youngmen interned ran up to nearly three thousands. Then followed the internment of Besant, and the next year witnessed the Rowlatt Bills and the agitation centering round them.

It would be recalled that in the previous year the Government had appointed a Committee of which Sir Sidney Rowlatt was President and Mr. Kumaraswami Sastri and Provash Chandra Mitter were members, "to investigate and report on the nature and extent of the criminal conspiracies connected with the revolutionary movement, to examine and consider the difficulties that have arisen in dealing with such conspiracies and to advise as to the legislation, if any, necessary to enable Government to deal effectively with them." The Committee had enquired and submitted a Report. The Report suggested legislation which was subsequently introduced into the Imperial Council and led to a widespread protest all over the country. At the time of the Special Congress, only the Report had been published and the Congress "condemned the recommendations of the Rowlatt Committee which, if given effect to, would interfere with the fundamental rights of the Indian people and impede the healthy growth of public opinion."

The Special Session concluded at the end of August. The ordinary session of the Congress was to be held at Delhi in the following December. The Provincial Congress Committee and the Reception Committee elected Lokamanya Tilak as the President of the Delhi Session. But as he had to proceed to England in connection with the litigation between himself and Sir Valentine Chirol, he expressed his inability to preside, and Pandit Madan Mohan Malaviya was elected instead.

The thirty-third session of the Congress was held at Delhi on 26th December with Hakim Ajmal Khan as the Chairman of the Reception Committee and Pandit Madan Mohan Malaviya as the President. The War had come to an end with the Armistice on November 11, 1918. The Allies had been completely successful and the principle of self-determination had been declared by President Wilson, Mr. Lloyd George and other allied statesmen. It was therefore but natural that the Congress should consider the Reform Scheme once again in the light of these declarations and the criticism of the Montford Report which had been made since the Special Session of the Congress. At the Delhi Congress also the attendance was very large and there were no less than 4,865 delegates present.

The Congress conveyed its loyalty to the King and congratulations on "the successful termination of the War" which was waged for the liberty and freedom of all the peoples of the world. Another resolution recorded the appreciation of the Congress of the gallantry of the allied forces and "particularly of the heroic achievement of the Indian troops in the cause of freedom, justice and self-determination." Another resolution asked for the recognition of India by the British Parliament and by the Peace Conference as "one of the progressive nations to whom the principle of self-determination should be applied," and as a first step the "immediate repeal of all laws, regulations and ordinances restricting the free discussion of political questions, and conferring on the Executive the power to arrest, detain, intern, extern or imprison any British subject in India outside the processes of ordinary civil or criminal Law, and the assimilation of the law of sedition to that of England." The Congress further demanded an Act of Parliament establishing at an early date complete Responsible Government in India and a place for India similar to that of the Self-Governing Dominions in the reconstruction of Imperial policy. The Congress also wanted to be represented by elected representatives at the Peace Conference and nominated Lokamanya Tilak,

Mahatma Gandhi and Mr. Hasan Imam as its representatives.

Dealing with the Reforms, the Congress reaffirmed the resolution passed at the Special Session at Bombay regarding the Congress-League Scheme, the fitness of India for Responsible Government, and the resolution of undivided authority to the Government of India concerning the peace, tranquillity and the defence of the country, subject to the Declaration of Rights. By another resolution, the Bombay resolution regarding other points was affirmed, except that in the Provinces full Responsible Government should be granted at once and that no part of British India should be excluded from the benefit of the proposed constitutional reforms. The Rowlatt Committee's Report came up again for review, and after reiterating the Bombay resolution, the Congress also expressed the view that it would prejudicially affect the successful working of the constitutional Reforms. The Congress urged on the Government the immediate repeal of the Defence of India Act, the Press Act, the Seditious Meetings Act, the Criminal Law Amendment Act, the old Regulations and other similar repressive measures and the release of all detenus and all political prisoners.

The Report of the Industrial Commission, of which Pandit Madan Mohan Malaviya had been a member, also came in for consideration and the Congress passed a resolution welcoming its recommendations and the policy that the Government must play an active part in promoting the industrial development of the country, and hoping that encouragement would be given to Indian Capital and enterprise, and protection against foreign exploitation. The Congress regretted that the question of tariffs had been excluded from the scope of the Commission's enquiries. The Congress supported the recommendation of the

Committee that industries should have separate representation in the Executive Council of the Government of India and that there should be Provincial Departments of Industries. The Congress also suggested the constitution of Imperial and Provincial Advisory Boards consisting of Indians elected by Indian industrial and trade associations and Chambers of Commerce. It further was of opinion that the proposed Imperial Industrial and Chemical Services should be constituted with adequate salaries and that Universities should establish Commercial Colleges with help from Government. The Congress regretted the absence in the Report of recommendations for adequate organisation for financing industries, and urged the starting of industrial banks.

Another resolution of the Congress requested the Government to release the Ali Brothers. The Congress also asked, in view of the unprecedented economic strain and the cessation of hostilities, that India should be relieved from the burden of contributing 45 millions for war purposes. An interesting resolution related to Ayurvedic and Unani systems of medicine and recommended to the Government of India the desirability of securing to them the advantages vouchsafed to the Western system.

While the Congress thus practically reiterated the Special Session resolutions, it carried them further, and it was found that the harmony that had prevailed at Bombay (in September, 1918) disappeared. A split ensued on the 'narrow' issue, as Mrs. Besant said later, as to whether Provincial Autonomy must be whole and immediate, or whether the Bombay deductions should still stand. While "Madras and other Moderates" stood for the Bombay resolution, the majority favoured the rejection of the Bombay compromise. And when it came to a question of a Deputation to England, it was resolved that the members of the Deputation must advocate and press the Delhi demand, thus excluding those who held to the Bombay compromise. Mr. Sastri moved an amendment objecting to the words 'disappointing and unsatisfactory' and asking that the 15 years' limit should be deleted. But the original resolution held the field. Finally, a resolution offering welcome to the Prince of Wales was dropped.

CHAPTER V

Non-Violence, a Reality (1919)

The Delhi Congress brought no peace to the country. The Rowlatt Bills made their appearance early in 1919 (February). They were two in number,—one of them being meant to be introduced in the Spring session. One was a temporary measure, intended to deal with the situation arising from the expiry of the Defence of India Act, six months after the formal conclusion of peace. It was framed to enable anarchical offences to be tried expeditiously by a strong Court of three High Court Judges with no right of appeal, in areas where offences of a revolutionary character were prevalent. It also provided for powers to order persons suspected to be concerned in movements likely to lead to the commission of offences against the State, to furnish security, to reside in a particular place, or to abstain from any specified act. And as a safeguard, an investigating authority composed of one Judge and one non-official was to examine the material upon which orders against any person were framed. Thirdly, Local Governments were given powers to arrest persons reasonably believed to be connected with certain offences, the commission of which threatened public safety, and to confine them in such places and under such conditions as were prescribed. Further, dangerous characters already under control or in confinement could be continuously detained under the Bill. The second Bill was meant to cause a permanent change in the ordinary Criminal Law of the land. The possession of a seditious document with the intention to publish or circulate it, was to be made punishable with imprisonment.

Promise of official protection against violence was to be allowable in the case of an accused willing to turn

'King's evidence.' District Magistrates were to be authorized to direct a preliminary enquiry by the Police in the case of certain offences for which a prosecution could not then be launched without the sanction of a Local Government. Finally, persons convicted of an offence against the State might be ordered by the Court to execute a bond of good behaviour for a term not exceeding two years after the expiration of their sentence.

Following the Rowlatt Report which had been published on 19-1-1919, the Rowlatt Bills were introduced into the Supreme Legislative Council by Sir William Vincent on the 6th of February, 1919, and while the second was dropped, only the first was passed in the 3rd week of March, 1919. Gandhi notified his intention of meeting the situation with a campaign of Satyagraha, if the Rowlatt recommendations should be embodied into Bills. To this end he had toured the country extensively and was received with great respect everywhere. What was it that had endeared this comparative stranger in the country to all Provinces and commended his equally strange programme of Satyagraha to the people all over? Let the Government answer. (*Vide* 'India, 1919'):—

"Mr. Gandhi is generally considered a Tolstoyan of high ideals and complete selflessness. Since his stand on behalf of the Indians in South Africa, he has commanded among his countrymen, all the traditional reverence with which the East envelops a religious leader of acknowledged asceticism. In his case he possesses the added strength that his admirers are not confined to any religious sect. Since he took up his residence in Ahmedabad, he has been actively concerned in social work of varied kinds.

"His readiness to take up the cudgels on behalf of any individual or class whom he regards as being oppressed has endeared him to the masses of his countrymen. In the case of the urban and rural population of many parts of the Bombay Presidency his influence is unquestioned, and he is regarded with a reverence for which 'adoration' is scarcely too strong a word. Believing as he does in the superiority of 'Soul Force' over material might, Mr. Gandhi was led to believe that it was his duty to employ against the Rowlatt Act that weapon of Passive Resistance which he had used effectively in South Africa. It was announced on the 24th February that he would lead a Passive Resistance or Satyagraha movement if the Bills were passed. This announcement was regarded as being of the utmost gravity both by Government and by many of the Indian politicians. Some Moderate members of the Indian Legislative Council publicly affirmed their apprehension as to the consequences of such a step. Mrs. Besant, with her remarkable knowledge of the psychology of the Indian temperament, warned Mr. Gandhi in the most solemn manner that any such movement as he contemplated would result in the release of forces whose potentialities for evil were quite incalculable. It must be clearly stated that there was nothing in Mr. Gandhi's attitude or pronouncements which could have justified Government taking any steps against him before the inception of the movement. Passive Resistance is a negative and not a positive process. Mr. Gandhi expressly condemned any resort to material force. He was confident that he would be able by a process of passive disobedience to civil Laws to coerce the Government into abandoning the Rowlatt Act. On the 18th March he published a pledge regarding the Rowlatt Bills which ran as follows: 'Being conscientiously of opinion that the Bill known as the Indian Criminal Law Amendment Bill, No. 1 of 1919, and the Criminal Law Emergency Powers Bill, No. 2 of 1919, are unjust, subversive of the principles of liberty and justice and destructive of the elementary rights of an individual on which the safety of India as a whole and the State itself is based, we solemnly affirm that in the event of these Bills becoming Law and until they are withdrawn, we shall refuse civilly to obey these laws and such other laws as the Committee, hereafter to be appointed,

> may think fit, and we further affirm that in the struggle we will faithfully follow truth and refrain from violence to life, person or property."

Most people did not understand why he should have chosen the petty and collateral issue of Rowlatt Bills for the inauguration of Satyagraha, although there was before India the mammoth issue of Self-Government. The same doubt was expressed in 1920 when the Punjab tragedy and the Khilaphat wrong were made by him the issue on which to inaugurate the Non-co-operation movement,—not Swaraj. But to this point we shall revert later. Nevertheless there was a good response from all parts of India except, at first, Bengal. The South responded unexpectedly well. There was some doubt whether Satyagrahis could alienate their property so as to avoid attachment and sale by Government. It was reported that Gandhi did not object to the idea, as it was up to people to fix the limit to which they could surrender their person and property. Gandhi inaugurated the movement with a fast—an idea cavilled at by the neo-social Reformers but one quite in consonance with the traditional beliefs in the country.

The idea of self-purification itself jarred on the ears of politicians, for, "what had purity to do with politics?" they asked in derision. The 30th of March, 1919, was fixed to be a day of *hartal*, a day of fasting and prayer and penance and meetings all over. The date was changed to 6th April, but the change not being notified in Delhi in time, processions and *hartals* were held in Delhi, and as the Fates would have it, shooting took place there. The procession of the day was being led by Swami Shraddhananda whom some European soldiers threatened to shoot, and he bared his chest for the promised bullets and thus paralysed the threats. But at the Delhi Railway

Station, a scuffle arose ending in shooting, causing five deaths and a score or so of casualties. The demonstrations on the 6th April were held on a country-wide scale. "One noticeable feature of the general excitement," says 'India, 1919,' "was the unprecedented fraternization between the Hindus and the Muslims. Their union, between the leaders, had now for long been a fixed plan of the nationalist platform. In this time of public excitement, even the lower classes agreed for once to forget their differences. Extraordinary scenes of fraternization occurred. Hindus publicly accepted water from the hands of Muslims and *vice versa*. Hindu-Muslim unity was the watchward of processions indicated both by cries and by banners. Hindu leaders had actually been allowed to preach from the pulpit of a (Cathedral) Mosque." The one immediate cause for such a unity was the disgust that Muslims felt at the position of Turkey being unsettled after the War and the danger to the Khilaphat, and the Hindus fully sympathised with those feelings.

The country took to the new idea readily and wholeheartedly. Gandhi was already a *persona grata* both with the country and the Congress. The omission of his name from the list of Indian delegates to the Peace Conference to be chosen at the Delhi Congress, 1918, was repaired then and there on the suggestion of Mr. B. Chakravarti and the amendment was accepted reverently and apologetically by Mr. C. R. Das, the mover of the Resolution. He had also been elected as a member of the Deputation to England. The month of April, 1919 began a new chapter in Indian History.

The scene of India's struggles and sufferings shifts now to the Punjab, the gateway of India for foreign industrial and commercial invasions. The Punjab is the home of the Sikhs and other martial races of India. Is the Punjab to be exploited by the educated classes and their Congress movement, and all their high falutin of Self-Government? It is sufficiently hard that these educated classes should be seeking Military careers and pleading for Military Colleges as well. What should happen if the military races should seek political education and entertain political ambitions? That would be the end of the British Government in India! Had not the Indian troops just returned from the various war-fronts where, by their superior prowess and self-sacrifice, they had helped to defeat the highly disciplined troops of Germany, Austria, Russia and Turkey? The Russo-Japanese war itself had sufficiently disillusioned the Asiatics of ideas of European superiority on the battlefield. The Great War obliterated any lingering fragments of that erstwhile faith. So, the Iron Man of the Punjab, Sir Michael O'Dwyer, was determined to prevent the contamination of the Punjab by the spread of the Congress movement, and it was a tussle between him and the Congress as to whether the Congress which was invited to Amritsar in 1919 should be held in the Punjab. Dr. Kitchlew, an advocate, and Dr. Satyapal, a medical practitioner, who were organising the Congress, were sent for by the District Magistrate of Amritsar to his house one fine morning (10-4-1919) and were spirited away to some unknown place. The report soon spread far and wide, and crowds of people gathered together and wanted to meet the District Magistrate to ask for their whereabouts. They were prevented by military pickets posted at the level crossing, between the city and the Civil Lines, from marching to the Civil Lines, and of course the story of the never failing brick-bat now comes in. The crowd was fired upon, and there were several casualties with one or two deaths. The crowd turned back into the city carrying their victims in procession, and on their way set fire to the National Bank buildings and killed its European manager. Altogether the mob violence was responsible for the deaths of five Englishmen and for the destruction by fire of a Bank, a Railway goods-shed and some other public buildings. Naturally, the officers of the place took umbrage at the events and vowed red-vengeance. The town was made over by the Civil to the Military authorities on the 10th April on the initiative of local officials and in anticipation of sanction from the higher authorities. The behaviour of the masses was not less reprehensible at Gujaranwala and Kasur.

At Gujaranwala and Kasur there was serious violence. At the latter place, on April 12th, crowds did considerable damage to the railway station, burnt a small oil shed, damaged signal and telegraph wires, attacked a train in which were some Europeans and beat two soldiers to death, a branch post-office was looted, the main post-office burnt, the Munsiff's Court set on fire, and other damage done. That is the official version summarised. The popular version alleges previous provocation of the crowd.

At Gujaranwala, on April 14th, crowds surrounded and stoned a train, burnt a small railway bridge and fired another railway bridge where a calf had been killed by the police, as alleged, and hung up on the bridge as an insult to Hindus, to whom the cow is sacred. The telegraph-office, post-office and railway station were subsequently set on fire, as well as the Dak Bungalow, Kutcheri (Collector's office) a church, a school, and a railway shed.

These were the chief incidents. There were minor outbreaks elsewhere in smaller places, such as stoning of trains, cutting of wires, and setting fire to railway stations.

In the meantime there were sporadic outbreaks of violence in different parts of the country. In Lahore shootings and reprisals took place. Bad news came from far-off Calcutta. Hearing of the trouble in the Punjab, and on the invitation of Dr. Satyapal and Swami Shraddhananda, Gandhi started for Delhi on the 8th April. On his way however he was served with an order not to enter the Punjab or Delhi, and on his refusal to obey the order he was arrested and turned back from a way-side railway station, Palvel, by a special train to Bombay on the 10th April.

The news of the arrest created disturbances in Ahmedabad where some English and Indian officers were killed. Viramgam and Nadiad were also the scenes of some trouble on the 12th April. In Calcutta, likewise, the result of the disturbances was that five or six men were killed and twelve others were wounded due to firing. Gandhi after reaching Bombay helped in calming the populace and proceeded to Ahmedabad where his presence was helpful in restoring quiet. On account of these disturbances, he issued a statement suspending Satyagraha.

While matters stood thus, tragic events were fast developing in Amritsar. It may be noted that Martial Law was not declared as yet on the 13th April, though as the Government Report admits, *de facto* Martial Law was in force since the 10th April. As a matter of fact, Martial Law was formally proclaimed in Lahore and Amritsar on the 15th April, and shortly after in two or three other districts. On the 13th April, which was the Hindu New Year's Day, a large public meeting was advertised and held in the Jallianwala Bagh, which is an open ground in the midst of the city enclosed with walls which form the boundaries of houses overlooking it. It has a bottle-neck that forms the only entrance to it, and so narrow that a carriage cannot pass along it. When twenty thousand people,—men, women and children,—gathered at the Bagh, Genéral Dyer entered the place at the head of a force composed of 100 Indian troops and 50 British, while one Hánsraj was lecturing to the audience, and gave orders forthwith to fire. His own version as given later before the Hunter Commission was that he ordered the people to disperse and then fired, but he admitted that he fired within two or three minutes of the order. In any case, it was obvious that 20,000 people could not disperse in 2 or 3 minutes especially through that narrow outlet, and when 1,600 rounds were fired,—and the firing stopped only when the ammunition had run out,—the casualties were, even according to Government's version, about 400 dead, while the wounded were estimated at between a thousand and two. The firing was done by the Indian troops, behind whom were placed the British troops,—all on an elevated platform in the Bagh. The greater tragedy really was that the dead and dying were left to suffer the whole night without water to drink, or medical attendance, or aid of any character. Dyer's contention—as it came out later—was that "the city having passed under the Military, he had tomtomed in the morning that no gatherings would be permitted and as the people openly defied him, he wanted to teach them a lesson so that they might not laugh at him. He would have fired, and fired longer, he said, if he had had the required ammunition. He had only fired 1,600 rounds because his ammunition had run out." "As a matter of fact," he said, "he had taken an armoured car but found that the passage to the Bagh would not admit it, and so he left it behind."

General Dyer's regime witnessed some unthinkable punishments. The water supply and the electric supply of Amritsar were cut off. Public flogging was common.

But the 'crawling order' surpassed the rest of his achievements. A missionary lady doctor named Miss Sherwood had been attacked while she was cycling in a lane by the people, and every one passing through the lane was ordered to crawl with belly to the ground. And all who lived in the street had to obey this order, despite the fact that Miss Sherwood was protected in that very lane by decent citizens. The incident became an object of merriment and joking at the hands of Quarter-Master-General Hudson in the Imperial Legislative Council.

The issue of third-class tickets on the railway was prohibited, which involved a general suspension of travelling by the Indian public. More than two persons were prohibited from marching on side-walks or pavements. Bicycles, "other than those owned by Europeans," were commandeered. People who had closed their shops were forced to open them, under severe penalties. Prices of commodities were fixed by military officers, carts were commandeered. A public platform for whippings was erected near the fort, and a number of triangles for floggings were erected in various parts of the city.

Let us now give some figures of the cases dealt with by the Tribunal at Amritsar. On major charges 298 people were put before the Martial Law Commissioners, who tried cases unfettered by the ordinary recognised rules of procedure or laws of evidence. Of these, 218 were convicted, 51 were sentenced to death, 46 to transportation for life, 2 to imprisonment for ten years, 79 for seven years, 10 for five years, 13 for three years and 11 for lesser periods. This does not take account of the cases dealt with summarily by military officers, numbering 60 persons, of whom 50 were convicted, and 105 persons convicted under Martial Law by Civil Magistrates.

In answer to a question by Justice Rankin, a Member of the Hunter Committee who asked, "Excuse me putting it in this way, General, but was it not a form of frightfulness?", General Dyer replied :

> "No, it was not. It was a horrible duty I had to perform. I think it was a merciful thing. I thought that I should shoot well and shoot strong, so that I or anybody else, should not have to shoot again. I think it is quite possible I could have dispersed the crowd without firing, but they would have come back again and laughed, and I should have made what I consider to be a fool of myself."

And General Dyer's action was immediately approved by Sir Michael O'Dwyer in a telegram sent to him with Sir Michael's approval: *"Your action correct. Lieutenant Governor approves."*

All these facts are admissions made by General Dyer before the Hunter Commission in the early part of 1920. The full facts however were quite unknown for a year after the event, even the bare news being unknown at the time, and for months together later. The censoring of news was so strict and the ingress and egress of people to and from the Punjab was so rigidly regulated, that the All-India Congress Committee learnt, in any detail, the news of the Amritsar tragedy only when it was broken to it in July 1919 in Calcutta (at one of its meetings held at the Law Association chamber), not only with bated breath and in whispering tones but with the charge that it should be kept strictly confidential. The tragedy of the Punjab was not confined to Amritsar. Lahore, Gujaranwala, Kasur and other places shared the scenes of confusion and carnage and the gruesome details of the events and the atrocities, the barbarities and inhuman acts perpetrated by Col. Johnson, Bosworth-Smith, Col. O'Brien and other officers, both Civil and Military, are really blood-curdling.

According to the official Report contained in the White paper issued to Parliament, the administration of Martial Law was 'more intensive' in Lahore than elsewhere.[1] The Curfew order, of course, was immediately put in force and people out after 8 p.m. were liable to be shot, flogged, fined, or imprisoned or otherwise punished. Those whose shops were closed were ordered to open them; the alternatives were either being shot or have the shops publicly opened and their contents distributed free to the public.

"Lawyers' agents and touts" were ordered to be registered and forbidden to leave the city without permit. Occupiers of premises on whose walls Martial Law notices were posted were ordered to protect them and were liable to punishment if in any way they were defaced or torn, although they could not stay out at night to watch them. More than two persons abreast were not allowed on the side-walks. Students of colleges were ordered to report themselves four times a day to the military authorities at varying places of assembly. *Langars* or public food kitchens, which had been opened by philanthropic persons for the feeding of those who could not purchase food were ordered to be closed; motor cars and motor bicycles belonging to Indians were ordered to be delivered up to the military authorities and were handed over to officials for their use. Electric *punkas* and other electric fittings belonging to Indians were commandeered and stripped from the houses for the use of British soldiers. Public conveyances were ordered to report themselves daily at places a considerable distance from the city. There was one case of an elderly man who was caught tending his cow outside his shop door in a side lane after 8 p.m. He

---

[1] This and the succeeding accounts are taken from *Amritsar*, by B. G. Horniman.

was seized and flogged for the breach of the Curfew order. Drivers of *tongas* (hackney carriages) had participated in the *hartal.* To teach them a lesson, 300 tongas were commandeered. Of those who were permitted to ply for hire, orders to report themselves at certain times at places distant from the busy parts of the city, and their detention at the pleasure of the military officials concerned, effectually destroyed their chances of a day's earnings. Colonel Johnson admitted that many of his orders were directed against the educated and professional classes, lawyers etc. He considered they were the classes from which the political agitators were drawn. Professional men and other residents on whose premises Martial Law orders were posted had to set servants to watch them lest they should be torn or defaced, perhaps by a police agent: one such case was detected. When they applied for permits for such guardians of the placards to be out after 8 p.m., they were told they could have passes for this purpose for themselves but not for their servants. Students, boys of 16 to 20, were the objects of special attention. The students of several colleges in Lahore, which is a large University town, were ordered to report themselves four times daily at a place, in one case four miles distant from their college. In the burning sun of Lahore in April, the hottest time of the year, when the temperature is often over 108 in the shade, these youths had to walk 19 miles daily. Some of them fainted by the wayside. Colonel Johnson thought it did them good, it kept them out of mischief. A Martial Law notice was torn from one of the walls on one college. The whole professional staff, including the Principal, were arrested, and marched under military escort to the fort, where they were kept in military custody for three days. They were given "a corner in the fort" for their accommodation and allowed to sleep on the roof. The closing of the *langars* or public kitchens which had been opened by philanthropic persons, was explained by Colonel Johnson on the ground that they were used for seditious propaganda. Under cross-examination he could produce no justification for this assertion. He had no evidence and he could not say who gave him the information.

The headman (a person of high status in the village) was tied to a tree and publicly flogged for his own punishment and the edification of the village. There was apparently no court or pretence of judicial procedure, summary or otherwise. There was only summary flogging.

Colonel Johnson, however, was quite pleased with what he did in this respect, and the Europeans of Lahore entertained him at a farewell dinner and lauded him as the "protector of the poor"—the poor people who suffered a six weeks' agony under his rule. Colonel O'Brien who administered Martial Law in Gujaranwala, Captain Doveton who had charge of Kasur, and Mr. Bosworth Smith, a Civilian officer who was in command at Sheikhupura, particularly distinguished themselves.

Regarding the bombing at Gujaranwala, the public are asked to believe that this promiscuous dropping of bombs and the firing of altogether 255 rounds of a machine-gun, apparently at close quarters, into crowds of people, resulted in the killing of nine and wounding of only about sixteen people.

Colonel O'Brien in his evidence before the Committee said the crowd was fired on "wherever found." This was referring to the aeroplanes. Once it was 'found' by an aeroplane in charge of Lieut. Dodkins R.A.F. in the form of twenty peasants in a field. Lieut. Dodkins said he machine-gunned them till they fled. He saw another party in front of a house being addressed by a man, so he dropped a bomb on them because he "had no doubt in his mind that they were not a marriage or funeral party." Major Carbey R.A.F. was the gentleman who bombed a party of people because he thought they were rioters going or coming from the city. Major Carbey's state of mind may be gathered from some further extracts from the report of his evidence.

> "The crowd was running away and he fired to disperse them. As the crowd dispersed, he fired the machine gun into the village itself. He supposed some shots hit the houses. He could make no discrimination between the innocent and the guilty. He was at a height of 200 feet and could see perfectly what he was doing. His object was not accomplished by the dropping of bombs alone."
>
> "The firing was not intended to do damage alone. It was in the interests of the villagers themselves. By killing a few, he thought he would prevent the people from collecting again. This had a moral effect."
>
> "After that he went over the city, dropping bombs, and fired at the people who were trying to get away."

Gujaranwala, Kasur, and Sheikupura, like Amritsar and Lahore, had their Curfew order, prohibition of travelling for Indians, floggings public and private, wholesale arrests and punishments by Summary Courts and Special Tribunals.

Colonel O'Brien was responsible for an order that when Indians met British officers they must salute, alight from their carriages, or dismount if they were riding or driving, and lower their umbrellas if they were carrying any. This order, Colonel O'Brien told the Committee, "was good by way of bringing home to the people that they had new masters." People were whipped, fined, and otherwise punished for disobedience of this monstrous order. He was responsible for the arrest of numbers of people, who were kept in gaol for as long as six weeks without being brought to trial. In one case a number of leading citizens were summarily arrested, put in a goods truck, where they were huddled together after being marched several miles in the burning sun, some of them half-clad, and sent by train to Lahore. They were refused permission to answer the calls of nature, and were kept in the truck in these conditions for about forty-four hours. Their horrible plight hardly needs description. As they were marched through the streets, an ever-growing crowd of prisoners,—for Colonel O'Brien went on making arrests indiscriminately as he proceeded, —they were handcuffed and chained together. Hindus and Muslims were chained together. This was regarded by the populace as a jibe at Hindu-Muslim unity. Colonel O'Brien said it was accidental. As an example of the spirit of the whole proceeding, it may be mentioned that one of the victims, an elderly citizen, was a noted benefactor of the town, who gave a lakh of rupees (£10,000) to found the King George School in commemoration of the King's visit, and had contributed largely to War Relief Funds and War Loans.

Another example of Colonel O'Brien's methods is the arrest of an elderly farmer, as a hostage for his two sons, whom he was unable to produce. Colonel O'Brien ordered this man's property to be confiscated, and issued a warning that anybody attempting to help him with his crops would be shot. He admitted the man had committed no offence himself, but "he did not say where his sons were."

These are only incidents in Colonel O'Brien's lengthy record. Two hundred persons were convicted by Summary Courts, and received sentences of whipping, or from one month up to two years' imprisonment. The Commission convicted 149 people, of whom 22 were sentenced to death, 108 to transportation for life, and others to sentences varying from ten years downwards. Colonel O'Brien's final achievement was to rush a large batch of cases through in about twenty-four hours, when he heard that Martial Law was to terminate the next day. The people concerned were given little opportunity of defending themselves, and cases fixed for some days ahead were rushed into the Court post-haste, so anxious was Colonel O'Brien that none should escape his justice by reason of the lapse of Martial Law.

Captain Doveton was in a sort of independent command in the Kasur sub-division, the headquarters of which is the fairly large town of Kasur. At this place a public gallows was erected for hangings, though apparently it was never used, and was taken down by order of the superior authorities. It was there, however, for some days to the terror of the inhabitants. A large public cage was also erected near the railway station, designed to accommodate 150 persons, and here suspects were incarcerated before the public gaze. The whole male population of the town was paraded for identification.

Floggings took place in public, and photographic records of these disgusting incidents are in existence, showing that the victims were stripped naked to the knees, and tied to telegraph poles or triangles. Publicity was not casual, or accidental, but designed. A sort of levee of the 'bad characters' of the town was held for the purpose by Captain Doveton's order, and on at least one occasion prostitutes were brought to witness the floggings. Just as Colonel Johnson had his 'one regrettable incident,' when a wedding party was flogged, this flogging in the presence of prostitutes was the one thing which seemed to excite Captain Doveton's shame when he was taxed with it, while giving evidence before the Hunter Committee. His explanation was that he had ordered the Sub-Inspector of Police to round up the bad characters, and bring them to witness the floggings, but was 'horrified' when he saw these women there. But he could not send them away, because he was unable to find an escort for them. So they remained to witness the floggings.

Captain Doveton was a prolific inventor of 'minor punishments.' His sole object in inventing minor punishments, he told the Committee, was to make things, "as mild as circumstances would permit." Offenders against Martial Law were set to work at loading and unloading goods waggons in the station yard. He instituted a system of making people touch the ground with their foreheads, —a sort of variation of Colonel Dyer's crawling order.

Mr. Bosworth-Smith was a civilian officer who administered Martial Law in the sub-division of Sheikupura. He admitted that Martial Law was not 'essential,' but he thought it was 'desirable' and keeping it on was 'a good thing.' He tried all the cases in his area, and, as elsewhere, sentences of flogging were inflicted, which were carried out at the rising of the Court. He tried 477 persons between May 6 and May 20.

An order was issued by the military authorities, compelling schoolboys to parade three times a day to salute the flag. The order applied to the infant classes and children of five and six years of age were included. It is actually alleged that there were fatal cases of sunstroke resulting from this, and it is admitted that children fainted from undue exposure to the sun. It is alleged too, that in some instances the boys were made to repeat: *"I have committed no offence. I will not commit any offence. I repent, I repent, I repent."*

"Major Smith, Administrator of Martial Law in Gujaranwala, Gujrat, and Lyallpur, was asked by Sir Chimanlal Setalvad whether the order was enforced in all places in his area and whether it applied to all classes, including infant-classes. The Major replied that it applied to all places in his area where there were troops, and that even infant-class boys of the ages of five and six were required to attend the parade, but the little boys were exempted from the evening parade.

Colonel O'Brien, in his evidence, said that "one day when he was at Wazirabad, he saw a boy fainting during his march to the flag, and wrote to the military authorities." He did not know if the next day this duty was increased from two to three times. Questioned, if it was so done, would it not be hard on the boys, Colonel O'Brien said, 'No.'

The idea of repentance, however, was greatly to the fore in the mind of Mr. Bosworth-Smith. He admitted that he had suggested the erection of a 'House of Repentance' at Sangla. "His idea was good," he said, but he denied that it was his object to build this house at a cost of Rs. 10,000.

For a detailed account, however, the reader is referred to the Congress Committee's evidence and reports on the subject. The former contains nearly 1,500 affidavits given by sufferers.

Gandhi was doubtless greatly shocked by the unexpected turn events had taken and admitted that he had made "a blunder of Himalayan dimensions which had enabled ill-disposed persons, not true passive resisters at all, to perpetrate disorders," and while declaring his readiness to assist in every possible way to restore normal conditions, he announced the suspension of Passive Resistance. Now was the turn of Government to restore order. Lord Chelmsford published a Resolution dated 14th April 1919, in which Government's intention was announced in the plainest terms to employ all available forces to put a speedy end to disaster. Meanwhile the outbreak of the 3rd Afghan War complicated the situation in the Punjab, and the mobilization of troops took place on the 4th May and Martial Law dragged on its bloody length until the 11th June, except as regards Railway land in which it was continued for long afterwards. The undue prolongation of Martial Law led to Sir Sankaran Nair resigning his membership of the Executive Council of the Viceroy on the 19th July as a protest. All this time the Punjab was isolated by a rigorous censorship of news and control of traffic. The Rev. C. F. Andrews was prohibited from setting foot in the Punjab, kept in remand for a day and then deported and arrested at Amritsar early in May, and Mr. Eardley Norton, Barrister-at-Law, was prohibited from entering the Punjab to which he wanted to go in order to take up the cause of the prisoners. There was a universal cry for an enquiry into the Punjab wrongs and for the mitigation of the barbarous sentences meted out by Martial Law tribunals. Lala Harikishen Lal, a distinguished Congressman and financier, was sentenced to transportation for life and forfeiture of property (worth 40 lakhs). It was in September 1919 that the Viceroy, to anticipate later events, announced the appointment of the Hunter Committee to enquire into the Punjab disorders, but forthwith followed it up on the 18th September by the Indemnity Bill which usually comes in the wake of

Martial Law. Pandit Madan Mohan Malaviya vigorously pleaded for its postponement in a 4¼ hours' speech, but the defence was that the Bill only indemnified from legal, as apart from departmental penalties, actions taken "in good faith and in a reasonable belief that they were necessary for maintaining or restoring order", while it left the ordinary courts to judge, according to the usual legal standards, whether these conditions were fulfilled.

Sir Dinshaw Wacha "declared himself convinced that Government was justified in the attitude it had assumed towards the Indemnity Bill." Mrs. Besant who had all along been fighting Gandhi said that the Rowlatt Bill contained nothing which an honest citizen should object to and wrote on April 18th that "when the mob begins to pelt them (soldiers) with brick-bats, it is more merciful to order the soldiers to fire a few volleys of buckshot." This gave rise to the expression, "Bullets for Brick-bats" which since became associated with her name, and Mrs. Besant was virtually at the nadir of her popularity since that time. A definite cleavage of parties, the germs of which were already noticeable at Delhi, came thus into existence since April 1919.

The All-India Congress Committee met on the 20th and 21st April and protested against the Externment orders passed on Gandhi by the Punjab and Delhi Governments and urged an enquiry into the Punjab wrongs. A Deputation composed of Mr. Vittalbhai Patel and Mr. N. C. Kelkar was appointed, to sail at once to England, in view of the seriousness of the political situation. They actually did so on the 29th April 1919. On the 8th June a second meeting of the A.I.C.C. took place at Allahabad which was occasioned by an Ordinance of the Governor-General dated 21st April, delegating powers to the Punjab Government, whereby any offence committed on or after the 30th March could be transferred for trial to Martial Law Tribunals. Obviously this date was fixed because *hartals* began that day. Prisoners were not allowed to choose their own counsel. Mr. C. F. Andrews who had been pressed by all the leading Editors in India, including Mrs. Besant and Babu Surendra Nath Banerjea, to make an independent Enquiry into the Punjab affair was arrested, as we have already related, when he tried to visit the Punjab, and Martial Law was continued. These and other matters were considered at the meeting of the 8th June, and it was suggested that the scope of the enquiry by the Committee to be appointed should include Sir Michael O'Dwyer's regime in the Punjab, with special reference to the method of recruitment for the Indian Army and the Labour Corps during the War, the raising of the War Loan, and the administration of Martial Law. Mr. B. G. Horniman had been deported for his strong condemnation of Government's policy in the Punjab in the columns of *The Bombay Chronicle*, and the A.I.C.C. urged the cancellation of the orders against his return to India.

Incidentally, it may be noted that with the exit of Mr. Horniman, people felt the want of an organ and found it in *Young India*.

Young India had been originally started by Jamnadas Dwaraka Das during the Home Rule days, and later came into the hands of a Syndicate of whom Mr. Shankerlal Banker was a member. When Mr. B. G. Horniman was deported and *The Bombay Chronicle* was put under censorship, Gandhi took over charge of *Young India*.

To resume the story. A Committee was appointed to arrange for the conduct of an enquiry into the Punjab occurrences, to take all necessary legal proceedings in India or England in relation thereto and to collect funds for the purpose. Into this Committee were co-opted later, on October 16th, Gandhi, Andrews, Shraddhananda Swami and others. In the beginning of November Mr. Andrews was suddenly called upon to go to South Africa at a critical moment. He left all the evidence he had collected with the Congress Committee. It was resolved to secure the services of Messrs. Neville and Captain, solicitors of London and Bombay respectively, to assist in the work of the Sub-Committee. A cable was sent by the Hon'ble Pandit Malaviya on behalf of the A.I.C.C. to the Premier, the Secretary of State and Lord Sinha, asking for the suspension of the "execution of all sentences passed under Martial Law, pending proposed enquiry." By this time Sir Satyendra Prasanna Sinha had become a member of the Privy Council, a K. C., and a Baron, as the result of which he took the name of Lord Sinha of Raipur. He was also appointed Under-Secretary of State for India, and later on, it was he that piloted the Government of India Bill through the House of Lords. The A.I.C.C. next met in Calcutta on July 19th and 20th, primarily to consider the question of the venue of the Congress, but it was resolved that the Congress should be held at Amritsar. The demand for a committee of enquiry directly by His Majesty's Government was reiterated, and legal authority was sought for it to revise, annul or suspend Martial Law sentences. It was on July 19th, it will be remembered, that Sir Sankaran Nair resigned his membership of the Governor-General's Executive Council as a protest against the continuance of Martial Law, and the A.I.C.C. recorded its grateful appreciation of his resignation and requested him to proceed to England to lay the case of the Punjab for speedy redress of its grievances. A sum of Rs. 10,000 was collected for the Punjab Committee. On the 21st July the A.P.I. published the following statement by Gandhi dropping Civil Resistance for the time being :—

> Bombay, July 21. "In the course of a letter to the Press Mr. M. K. Gandhi writes: 'The Government of India had given me, through His Excellency the Governor of Bombay, a grave warning that the resumption of civil disobedience is likely to be attended with serious consequences to public security. This warning has been reinforced by His Excellency the Governor himself at the interviews to which I was summoned. In response to these warnings and to the urgent desire publicly expressed by Dewan Bahadur L. A. Govinda Raghava Aiyar, Sir Narayan Chandavarkar and several Editors, I have, after deep consideration, decided not to resume civil resistance for the time being. I may add that several prominent friends belonging to what is called the Extremist Party have given me the same advice on the sole ground of their fear of a recrudescence of violence on the part of those who might not have understood the doctrine of civil resistance. When, in common with most other Satyagrahis, I came to the conclusion that the time was ripe for the resumption of civil resistance as part of Satyagraha, I sent a respectful letter to H. E. the Viceroy, advising him of my intention so to do and urging that the Rowlatt Legislation should be withdrawn, that an early declaration be made as to the appointment of a strong and impartial Committee to investigate the Punjab disturbances, with power to revise the sentences passed, and that Babu Kalinath Roy, who was, as could be proved from the record of the case, unjustly convicted, should be released. The Government of India deserve thanks for the decision in Mr. Roy's Case, (Mr. Roy was the Editor of *The Tribune*). Though it does not do full justice to Mr. Roy, the very material reduction in the sentence is a substantial measure of justice. I have been assured that the committee of enquiry, such as I have urged for, is in the process of being appointed. With these indications of good will, it would be unwise on my part not to listen to the warning given by the

Government. Indeed, my acceptance of the Government's advice is a further demonstration of the nature of civil resistance. A civil resister never seeks to embarrass the Government. I feel that I shall better serve the country and the Government and those Punjabi leaders who, in my opinion, have been so unjustly convicted and so cruelly sentenced, by the suspension of civil resistance for the time being. I have been accused of throwing a lighted match. If my occasional resistance be a lighted match, the Rowlatt Legislation and the persistence in retaining it on the Statute Book is a thousand matches scattered throughout India. The only way to avoid civil resistance altogether is to withdraw that legislation. Nothing that the Government have published in justification of that Bill has moved the Indian Public to change their attitude of opposition to it.' In conclusion, Mr. Gandhi advised his fellow Satyagrahis to seek the co-operation of all in the propagation of pure Swadeshi and the promotion of the Hindu-Muslim unity."

The Joint Parliamentary Committee under the Chairmanship of Lord Selborne was at this time sitting in England and we may take up the question of the several Deputations that went to England, though we are primarily concerned with the Congress Deputation, which was ably represented by Mr. Vittalbhai J. Patel and Mr. V. P. Madhava Rao. These, along with Messrs. Lokamanya Tilak, B. C. Pal, G. S. Khaparde, Dr. P. J. Mehta, A. Rangaswami Iyengar, N. C. Kelkar, Syed Hasan Imam, Dr. Sathaye, Mr. B. G. Horniman and Mr. P. Chenchia formed a Congress Delegation to lay India's claims before the British public. Mr. V. P. Madhava Rao, ex-Dewan of Mysore, by the dignity of his bearing, his independence and straightforwardness raised the Congress in public estimation and earned the encomiums of Mr. Ben Spoor, M. P., who on behalf of the Labour

Party was looking after Congress interests in England and who was the Secretary of the British Congress Committee at the time. Other deputations that went to England were the Moderate Deputation, the Justice Party and the two Home Rule Deputations, the minority and the majority ones, for, by this time the All-India Home Rule League became split into two, composed of those who swore by the Delhi Resolution of the Congress and those who still harked back to the Bombay (Special) Congress. Mr. C. P. Ramaswami Aiyar represented the minority wing, while Mrs. Besant carved out a new organization called the National Home Rule League and represented it. It may be noted that the Maharashtra Home Rule League Deputation was turned back from Colombo and not permitted to proceed to England, though the Lokamanya had to be given passports shortly after in connection with his case against Sir Valentine Chirol. The British Committee of the Indian National Congress did not at this time see eye to eye with the protagonists of the Delhi Congress and inclined more favourably to the Bombay compromise. There was a veritable tug of war between Mr. Vittalbhai J. Patel and the Committee and a sharp exchange of letters in which "he who paid the piper claimed, and ultimately got, the right to call the tune," and the British Committee had to yield. At first the Committee took the view that each of the five Delegations then in England should send a representative and that they all should meet and define their course of conduct at an ordinary meeting of the Committee, which they were asked to attend as visitors. This provoked a sharp reply from Vittalbhai who expressed his surprise that the Committee should have recognised other Deputations than the Congress one, and who, point-blank, asked those members of the Committee who were not prepared to carry out the mandate of the Congress to sever their connection with the Committee. The Committee was also called upon to draw up a written Constitution for itself and present it to the Congress, which it did. Opportunity was taken of the presence of Indian delegates to organize meetings of propaganda in various counties in England and a farewell dinner was given by the Labour Party at the House of Commons and a message was sent to the Indian National Congress. The Independent Labour Party at its Glasgow Conference passed a Resolution supporting self-determination for India along with Ireland and Egypt. Likewise did the National Peace Council pass a Resolution at its Annual Conference and the Labour Party, at its Annual Conference at Scarborough, demand that "the principle of democratic self-determination should be applied to the reorganization of the Indian Government with adequate protection to minorities." All the organizations condemned the Punjab atrocities equally vehemently.

Vittalbhai J. Patel and the Congress Deputation were called upon in England to face a double fight. On the one hand they had to settle up with the British Committee of the Congress, and on the other with Mrs. Besant who was indefatigable in her energies and in her opposition to the Congress.

While the Deputations were in England, an acute and unseemly controversy took place between the Congress Deputation and Mrs. Besant which led to mutual recriminations and even accusations of uttering falsehood against one another. Both the Congress Deputation and Mrs. Besant, we have already explained, looked to the Labour Party to have their views represented in the House of Commons. Mrs. Besant was for supporting the Montagu Scheme with certain modifications: The Congress Deputation was for the Delhi Resolution with its emphasis on self-determination and full Responsible Government. Woman suffrage was intended by Mr. Montagu to be left to the decision of the Local Legislatures, but the Congress Deputation wanted its acceptance to be incorporated in the Act. Then there was the Albert Hall meeting held on the 25th of October, 1919, at which the open differences between the two wings created an awkward position for the Chairman, Mr. Lansbury. The meeting was held under the auspices of the Home Rule League for India Branch established by Mrs. Besant in London. However, the Resolution, as eventually passed, was unobjectionable in that, "this mass meeting of the British Commonwealth which insists upon the right of self-government being conferred on each of the nations within its boundaries, hereby declares that the Indian people are entitled to receive at the earliest opportunity the full right of self-determination."

Mr. Lansbury was the Chairman-Elect and his intervention brought about this form which replaced the original draft intended to support Mr. Montagu's Bill as a first step towards the fulfilment of the declaration made in the House of Commons on August 20th, 1917. Mrs. Besant, nevertheless, in her speech supported Mr. Montagu's Bill in unmistakable terms and Vittalbhai J. Patel had to contradict her. Finally, in connection with these recriminations, Mr. G. S. Khaparde with his pungent humour described Mrs. Besant as *Putana* to which she seriously objected, but which description was in detail justified by Vittalbhai. At this distance of time, and knowing as we do Mrs. Besant's great services to the Nation, we cannot help saying that the description was unfortunate and undeserved, in spite of Mrs. Besant's unconcealed antipathy to the Congress and its activities in London in 1919. It is to be feared that there was something worse which should account for this irrepressible anxiety on Mrs. Besant's part to support Mr. Montagu in spirit and in letter. Gandhi always treated her with reverence and was always in the habit of rising from his seat to receive her, such was the regard shown towards her by Gandhi and the Congress, but she treated them contemptuously (refer to the events of 1930). Even at that, one should say that Mr. Khaparde's description of her was not only in bad form, but in bad taste and worse spirit. Let us take this opportunity to state this much.

The Punjab Enquiry

Affairs in India now demand our attention. In pursuance of the Resolution of the A.I.C.C., Swami Shraddhananda, Pandit Motilal Nehru and Pandit Malaviya went to the Punjab in the last week of June to enquire into the happenings in the Punjab. Mr. Andrews went there shortly after. Both the Pandits returned, then Motilalji visited Punjab again later. Jawaharlal and Purushottam Das Tandon joined Mr. Andrews. Gandhi joined the party on October 17th, as soon as the order against him was withdrawn. The people of the Punjab were filled with panic, but confidence came back when Gandhi was present in their midst. His arrival was nothing less than a triumph both at Lahore and at Amritsar. Meanwhile the official enquiry was announced. Its terms of reference fell short of the Congress demand. Nevertheless, it was considered advisable to co-operate with the official Committee. Mr. C. R. Das arrived from Calcutta presently and appeared on behalf of the Congress before Lord Hunter's Commission, but unexpected difficulties faced the Congress Sub-Committee and it was obliged reluctantly to withdraw co-operation from the Disorders Enquiry Committee. The history of the situation was set forth in a memorandum. The Sub-Committee wanted some of the Martial Law prisoners to be brought under custody to attend and assist in the enquiry but was refused permission. It therefore appealed against the Punjab Government to the Government of India and the Secretary of State, but they declined to interfere. The prisoners in the gaol endorsed the decision to withdraw. Later experience only proved the wisdom of the course adopted. Amongst other things, there was this fact, that the restricted terms of reference would not have allowed the Hunter Commission to entertain matters which justly came under the events of April 1919, but which were unjustly excluded from the reference. Accordingly, the Congress undertook a separate enquiry by a Committee composed of Messrs. Gandhi, Motilal Nehru, Das, Fazl-ul-Haq and Abbas Tyabji with Mr. K. Santanam as Secretary. But soon after, Pandit Motilal, having been elected President of the Amritsar Congress, resigned and was relieved of his membership of the Committee, Mr. Jayakar taking his place. Mr. Neville, the London solicitor, who was in charge of the Privy Council appeals was with the Committee. It was also resolved to acquire the Jallianwala Bagh and raise a memorial, for which a committee was appointed with Pandit Malaviya as President. To anticipate matters, that Bagh has been acquired for the Nation. The non-official Report, however, could not be ready for the Amritsar Congress, and at the time it was even contemplated that a special session of the Congress might have to be held to consider it when ready, in detail and at leisure, but this much the Committee stated, namely, that "the admissions made by General Dyer before the Hunter Commission established beyond dispute that his action of the 13th April was nothing but a cold-blooded, calculated, massacre of innocent, unoffending, unarmed men and children, unparalleled for its heartless and cowardly brutality in modern times." Judged by the happenings of April and May in the Punjab, we can readily understand the rumour prevalent at the time that it was General Dyer's intention at first to raze Amritsar to the ground as a fitting punishment for the horrors of the 10th April committed by the populace. Alogether, towards the latter half of the year 1919, the situation in India,—what with the appointment of the Hunter Committee with no Congress representative thereon, and with a Reform Bill which was but a poor performance of a vast promise,—was not merely gloomy but portentous. We extract below in full a "Manifesto on the Situation in India unanimously adopted by the Delegates from the Indian National Congress (to England), and the British Committee of the Indian National Congress in the autumn of 1919," soon after the appointment of the Hunter Commission and when the Reform Bill was before Parliament.

MANIFESTO ON THE SITUATION IN INDIA

"It is time that the British public had a clear vision regarding India, where, through the folly of the Government a cloud bigger than a man's hand has already gathered, threatening to break into a storm, the dimensions of which no one can foresee.

"In moving a Resolution conveying the thanks of Parliament to the Forces engaged in the Great War, Mr. Lloyd George said, 'As to India, by her remarkable contribution to our triumph, notably in the East, she had won a new claim to our consideration, a claim so irresistible that it ought to overpower, and must overpower, all the prejudice and timidity which might stand in the way of her progress.' So far as 'a new claim' is concerned, the Government of India since the Armistice has requited India's glorious services by legislative and administrative repression, depriving India of freedom of the Press, freedom of speech, freedom of the person, provoking public protest and riots, particularly in the Punjab, with Martial Law, deportation of leaders beloved by the people, confiscation of property, suppression of newspapers, execution, public flogging, imprisonment of prominent and patriotic citizens on fantastic charges, refusal of permission to choose counsel for their defence before Military Tribunals, shooting by machine-guns and bombing by military planes of defenceless men and women,—a regime of blood and iron which, if practised by Germans, would have filled Englishmen with horror and indignation.

"To make matters worse, a whitewashing Commission of Enquiry has been appointed without any representation from the Indian National Congress and the Indian Muslim League, and an Indemnity Bill passed by the Government of India which will prevent those officials who may be found guilty from being properly punished. Prussianism could no further go."

If the British Committee of the Indian National Congress was, as we have seen, so deeply impressed with the seriousness of the situation in India, as to publish the Manifesto herein extracted, imagine what should have been the feeling in India. The feeling was aggravated by the inadequacy of the Reform Bill which embodied the Montford Scheme. Only the Grand Committees were not there. But Dyarchy, nominated membership of Legislatures, the Council of State, powers of certification and veto, ordinance-making powers,—and all those reactionary aspects of a constitution which the country had protested against all these years, but which have been embodied in an aggravated form in the Act of 1935—these were the malformations and monsters that the Amritsar Congress was called upon to fight. It must be evident to the reader that by this time the fissiparous forces always operating in Indian politics and altogether inevitable under a foreign rule, must have been vigorously at work in India. They had manifested themselves in the Home Rule League itself. At Amritsar they appeared in their full strength. Lokamanya Tilak had by this time returned from England where he lost his

Case against Sir Valentine Chirol for defamation. The opinions that he had expressed in England were that he would take whatever was given and fight hard for the rest. They did not appear so hostile to the Scheme as those indicated by him as soon as he landed in India. Here he was sure that the Reform Scheme was quite inadequate. Nevertheless, he wired his congratulations to the King (or Cabinet) on the passing of the Reform Bill on behalf of the Indian people, while on his way to the Amritsar Congress, from a Railway Station (Gangapur) and offered 'Responsive Co-operation' in the matter of working the Reforms. The phrase was coined by Mr. Baptista and the telegram was drafted by Mr. Kelkar. This was quite unexpected in Congress circles and the Amritsar Congress became the scene of a battle royal between the contending parties.

At Amritsar, Mr. C. R. Das was greatly in evidence before the Congress. He had shot up into prominence easily even in 1917 when he had espoused the cause of Mrs. Besant for the Presidentship of the Calcutta Session. At the Delhi Congress (1918), he took a leading part in demolishing the compromise of the Bombay Special Session (1918). At Amritsar, naturally, it was a measuring of strength between the rapidly vanishing Old Guard of orators, whose ranks were by this time reinforced by Mrs. Besant's accession to them, and the new Nationalists who were irrepressible. Das came to the Congress with his resolutions ready and adopted the strategy of moving his, before the official ones were even put forward. The Resolution on Reforms placed before the Amritsar Session was Mr. Das's draft as approved of by the Subjects Committee. This Resolution underwent a serious change in the open session by the incorporation of a paragraph at the end stating that "pending the introduction of Responsible Government, the people would so work the Reforms as to secure its early establishment."

The implication here was that the co-operation offered would be responsive, in the measure in which Government would co-operate with the people. It will be remembered that the famous Announcement of August 20th, 1917, by Mr. Montagu embodies a reference to this bilateral co-operation. Mr. Das omitted all reference to it. Gandhi suggested an elaborate reference in a separate paragraph.

The Amritsar Congress (1919) was a triumph for national self-respect. At that Congress, the Indian politicians were keenly divided in views. Pandit Madan Mohan Malaviya and Gandhi wanted to work the Reforms on the basis of offering co-operation in the measure in which Government co-operated with the people. Mr. C. R. Das was for rejecting the scheme. He moved the main Resolution of the day which ran as follows:—

> "1. That this Congress reiterates its declaration of last year that India is fit for full Responsible Government and repudiates all assumptions and assertions to the contrary.
>
> "2. That this Congress adheres to the Resolution passed at the Delhi Congress regarding Constitutional Reforms and is of opinion that the Reforms Act is inadequate, unsatisfactory and disappointing.
>
> "3. That this Congress further urges that Parliament should take early steps to establish full Responsible Government in India in accordance with the principle of Self-determination."

Gandhi moved an amendment omitting the word 'disappointing' and adding a fourth paragraph which ran as follows:—

"4. Pending such introduction, this Congress begs loyally to respond to the sentiments in the Royal Proclamation, namely, 'Let the new era begin with a common determination among my people and my officers to work together for a common purpose,' and trusts that both the authorities and the people will co-operate so to work the Reforms as to secure the early establishment of full Responsible Government.

"And this Congress offers its warmest thanks to the Rt. Hon. E. S. Montagu for his labours in connection with them."

Finally, a formula was evolved which was accepted by the Congress. In the final form, the Resolution embodies the original Resolution moved by Mr. Das with the replacement of Gandhi's extra paragraph by the following:—

"Pending such introduction, this Congress trusts that, so far as may be possible, the people will so work the Reforms as to secure an early establishment of full Responsible Government, and this Congress offers its thanks to the Rt. Hon. E. S. Montagu for his labours in connection with the Reforms."

Mrs. Besant's alternative proposition was lost and Mr. Das's, as finally agreed to, was passed.

The compromise effected was however not an indubious one, although it must be said that Mr. Das's speech made it clear that he reserved for the Nation the right of pursuing a policy of obstruction if necessary and co-operation if possible. The Resolution was a triumph neither for Das nor for Gandhi exclusively. It was a triumph for both, the addition of the rider for Gandhi, and its amended form for Das. By that time it was clear that the stalwarts of the Indian Congress could not always see eye to eye. That was only to be expected.

But the irony of the position was that while Das was inclined to obstruction and rejection—shall we say, Non-co-operation?—Gandhi was there as the apostle of co-operation. Yes, that he was. Whatever the verdict of posterity be upon the Resolution on Reforms at Amritsar, there is no manner of doubt whatever that the whole Congress was a triumph for Gandhi. He had already impressed the Congress with his personalty, his point of view, his principles and philosophy, his code of ethics, his cult of Truth and Non-violence. We shall presently see how. The Amritsar Congress passed 50 resolutions which embrace a wide variety of topics, ranging from a demand for the recall of Lord Chelmsford to the call for an investigation of the Land Revenue system, Labour conditions, and the woes of third-class passengers. The Congress itself was attended by 36,000 people, of whom over 6,000 were ordinary delegates and there were besides these some 1,200 Tenant delegates. The rest were visitors. The atmosphere of the Congress was charged with electricity. Punjab and its atrocities naturally claimed the greatest attention. Gandhi was anxious that the mob violence in the Punjab and Gujarat should be condemned. The Subjects Committee threw out the Resolution. Gandhi was disappointed. It was late at night. He firmly, but politely and respectfully, expressed his inability to be in the Congress if the Congress could not see its way to accepting his view-point. The next morning, amidst the whinings and whimperings of the bulk of delegates, Resolution V was approved which, "while fully recognizing the grave provocation that led to a sudden outburst of mob frenzy, expressed the deep regret of the Congress at, and its condemnation of, the excesses committed in certain parts of the Punjab and Gujarat resulting in the loss of lives and injury to person and property during the month of April last." Gandhi's speech on the subject was superb.

It encompassed within a short range his whole plan of campaign and his future policy.

> "There is no greater Resolution before this Congress than this one. The whole key to success in the future lies in your hearty recognition of the truth underlying it, and acting up to it. To the extent we fail in recognizing the Eternal Truth that underlies it, to that extent we are bound to fail. I say if there was no violence on our part,—we have abundant proof of it, and I can produce before you, chapter and verse from Viramgam, from Ahmedabad and from Bombay that there was violence on our part intended and committed. I agree that there was grave provocation given by the Government in arresting Dr. Kitchlew and Dr. Satyapal and in arresting me who was bent on a mission of peace at the invitation of Dr. Satyapal and Swamiji,—these troubles would not have arisen. But the Government went mad at the time; we went mad also at the time. I say, do not return madness with madness, but return madness with sanity and the whole situation will be yours."

Ringing, soul-stirring words these! Only, the wonder is whether people understood their full significance then. Really, this Resolution set the tone for the Congress. Gandhi was not willing or ready to break with Government yet. That was why a Resolution was passed offering welcome to the Prince of Wales, thus repairing the omission at Delhi. That was why the rider to the Reforms Resolution offering co-operation was passed at Amritsar, though it was greatly diluted by the compromise. Of a piece with this avowal of Truth and Non-violence, or allied to it, were the Resolutions on (1) Swadeshi, "recommending a revival of the ancient industry of hand-spinning and hand-weaving" (few people would have noticed the expression 'handspinning'), (2) on the prohibition of export of milch cows and breeding bullocks, (3) on the Liquor Policy of the Provinces, and

(4) on the amelioration of the grievances of Third and Intermediate class passengers. Not far removed from this batch comes the batch relating to gratitude to Muslims for recommending the discontinuance of cow-slaughter at Bakrid and the protest against the hostile attitude of some of the British ministers towards the Turkish and Khilaphat questions. The Amritsar Congress turned its attention to the lot of peasants after a number of years. The labourers also claimed its attention equally. The Unani system as well as the Ayurvedic system were commended to the attention of Government. The British Committee was thanked for its services and so was the Labour Party in England in general, and Mr. Ben Spoor in particular. The Lokamanya had just returned from England after befriending the Labour Party to which he gave a donation of £3,000. The Lokamanya was responsible, very likely, for the assertion that a permanent mission be established in England and elsewhere for Congress propaganda. Lala Lajpat Rai was thanked for his services to the country, in America, and the Congress Deputation for their services in England. 'Indians overseas' were not to be missed, the settlers in the Transvaal were still being deprived of their rights of property and trade till then enjoyed by them. Indian agitation raised its head in East Africa. Mr. Andrews's services to Indians abroad were not less entitled to the thanks of the country, than his services in the Punjab. The Congress, for the first time and publicly, explained why it was forced to boycott the Hunter Commission. The Lieutenant-Governor had "refused permission even to a few of the Punjab leaders undergoing imprisonment to attend and sit in the Committee Rooms even as prisoners under custody, to assist and instruct counsel in the same manner as the Government Counsel was instructed by the Commission." The Congress accordingly endorsed the boycott as a fitting and dignified action

and called upon the Sub-Committee to make an independent Report. The Congress congratulated Sir Sankaran Nair on his resignation and demanded the recall of Lord Chelmsford, the removal of General Dyer from his command, and of Sir Michael O'Dwyer from his membership of the Army Committee. There is a story relating to the Resolution of the recall of Lord Chelmsford which may be told here. He was hoping that if the Congress should table a Resolution asking for his recall, it would be opposed by some leading Moderate Congressman such as Mr. Sastri. But on the second day of the Congress, both Mr. Sastri and Mr. C. P. Ramaswami Aiyar left for Calcutta where the first sitting of the Liberal Federation was to be held. So Mr. Sastri was not there at the Congress when the Resolution came up, and Mr. B. N. Sarma jumped into the gap. He was too forward for the Liberals and so would not go to Calcutta. But he was too backward for the Nationalists and so would not endorse the recall of the Viceroy, and amidst a hostile demonstration managed to oppose the motion before the House. He only performed what he considered to be a duty. It was but recently that he had tendered his resignation of membership of the Supreme Legislative Council as a protest against the introduction into it of the second Rowlatt Bill, but forthwith withdrew it that very evening after attending a Viceregal party. At Amritsar he opposed the recall Resolution. Altogether he did notable service to Lord Chelmsford who rewarded him handsomely by appointing him to the Executive Council six months later in June 1920[1]. Dealing with the question of the Punjab wrongs, the Amritsar Congress asked for the cancellation

[1] Lord Chelmsford had at first recommended the name of the Maharaja of Burdwan to the vacancy, but Mr. Montagu wanted a man of Legislative experience and mentioned the name of Mr. Sastri

of the indemnities levied upon the people in certain places for injuries done to person and property, as well as the punishments meted out to University and School students under the Martial Law. The Reforms Resolution was reinforced by another on Fundamental Rights which was pressed for by the Grand Old Man, Mr. C. Vijiaraghavachariar at 10 o'clock in the night. Then the Congress pleaded for the repeal of the Press Act and the Rowlatt Act and the release of various prisoners who were still in jails despite the Royal Proclamation.

Mr. Horniman's deportation was the subject of a protest and its cancellation was urged strongly . It was also urged that the Reforms should be extended to Burma and that Delhi and Ajmer-Merwara should be made full blown Provinces. Audit and accounts, and recovery of Funds from various people, formed the subjects of two other resolutions and the session terminated. It put a great strain upon its President—Pandit Motilal Nehru who lost his voice and was greatly tired by the strain of the week. The sittings of the Subjects Committee ran into the early hours of the morning, night after night, and the unbearable cold of the Punjab proved too much for many delegates and added to their difficulties.

Two incidents may be narrated here which are of interest. The Royal Proclamation granting amnesty to political prisoners, couched in the sweetest language imaginable, reached Amritsar a day before the Congress was held and with it came the Ali Brothers to the city in the midst of a tumultuous enthusiasm of multitudes of people. They had a grand procession and Mahomed Ali appearing on the platform stated that he came from the Chhindwara gaol 'with a return ticket,' an expression which has become classical since. The other incident relates to Mr. Reginald Neville, the London solicitor who had been in India for some time and who was in Amritsar during the Congress week. The room in his hotel was broken into at dead of night on the 25th December, 1917, by some 20 European soldiers from the garrison at Jullunder, and he was insulted and asked how, being a white man, he dared to work against Dyer. One of them said "We have shot the whole seething mass of sweaty natives," and that he was one of those who formed Dyer's contingent that did this. We learnt later that the soldiers were made to apologize to Mr. Neville.

R. C. Dutt
1899 ; Lucknow

N. G. Chandavarkar
1900 : Lahore

D. E. Wacha
1901 : Calcutta

Lal Mohan Ghose
1903 ; Madras

Part III

SYNOPSIS

CHAPTER I

The Birth of Non-co-operation (1920)

The Khilaphat wrong—Gandhi's Manifesto, Tilak's views—Gandhi on 'Tilak and N. C. O'—Gandhi's achievements—Abolition of Indentured Labour—Hunter Report —A. I. C. C. meets—Leaders and N. C. O.—Tilak passes away—Muslim Hijrat—N.C.O. inaugurated—P.C.C.'s on N.C.O.—The Calcutta Special Session—The Resolution on N.C.O.—Government's reaction—Khaparde opposes N.C.O.—Bengal's Resistance to N.C.O.—Das's Conversion —Better support for Gandhi at Nagpur—Colonel Wedgwood's warning—Congressmen's replies to Colonel Wedgwood—Other resolutions—Change of Constitution.

CHAPTER II

Non-co-operation Galore (1921)

A New Era—The Duke's regret over the Punjab Occurrences—Government of India's regret—People's response to N.C.O., (1) Lawyers (2) Students—Provision for Non-co-operators—The Bezwada Programme—Orders of Restraint—Nankana Tragedy—The Budget—Gandhi-Reading Conversations—Ali Brothers' apology—The success of the Bezwada Programme—Boycott of foreign cloth—Picketing—Non-violence under grave provocation —Dharwar shooting—Moplah Rising—Karachi Khilaphat Conference—Working Committee's resolutions to be repeated by Congress Committees—Boycott of the Prince

—Foreign policy—Arrest of the Ali Brothers—Gandhi repeats the speech—Civil Disobedience sanctioned—Conditions prescribed—Chirala-Perala—Some details of the Moplah rebellion—The Prince arrives—Bonfire of foreign cloth—Consolidation of Volunteer Movement—Peace Negotiations in December 1921—Pandit Malaviya sees Das in Prison—Das's terms—Gandhi's terms—Negotiations fail—The Royal Message—President-elect of Ahmedabad Congress in Jail—Hakim Ajmal Khan officiates—Thirty thousand in jail under individual Civil Disobedience—Mass Disobedience under contemplation—Nation sheds fear—Notable features of the Ahmedabad Session—Rev. C. F. Andrews delivers message opposing burning of foreign cloth—The Session—Das's Address read by Sarojini Devi—The main resolution—A thesis on Non-co-operation—The resolution—Hasrat Mohani's amendment in favour of Complete Independence—Gandhi opposes—Other resolutions—The Congress and the Ulemah.

CHAPTER III

Gandhi Bound (1922)

The All-Parties' Conference, Bombay—Gandhi's Speech—Suffering not enough—Sir Sankaran Nair's walk-out—Working Committee confirms the Resolution of the Conference—No-tax campaign in Guntur—Mass Civil Disobedience at Bardoli—Gandhi's letter to the Viceroy—Chauri Chaura—Firing in Madras—The Bardoli withdrawal—Reaction of A. I. C. C.,—I. C. D. sanctioned—Government's Reaction to Delhi decisions—Imprisoned leaders on the withdrawal of C. D.—The Great Trial—Sarojini Devi on the Trial—Gandhi and Banker plead guilty—Gandhi takes full responsibility—The written statement—The Judgment—After Gandhi's conviction—Re-adjustments—The Moplah Enquiry Committee—

A.I.C.C. meets at Lucknow—N.C.O. re-assessed—The Civil Disobedience Committee—Personnel—Montagu's resignation—Sections 108 *and* 144 *Cr. P. C.—Lloyd George's 'Steel Frame' speech—The Borsad Satyagraha—The Guruka Bagh affair—C. D. Committee's tour—C. D. Committee's recommendations—Hindu-Muslim disturbances—Two strings to the bow of N.C.O.—From the firing line to the Chess Board—A.I.C.C.'s historic gathering in Calcutta in Nov.* 1922*—Question of Council-entry postponed to the Gaya Session—18th Observed as Gandhi Day —Jawaharlal's Conviction—The Gaya Session—Challenge to Gandhism—Das's speech—N.C.O. from inside the Councils—The resolutions—A.I.C.C.'s resolution on C. D. ratified—Das resigns and forms the Swaraj Party—Volunteer organization.*

CHAPTER IV

N. C. O. FROM WITHIN COUNCILS (1923)

Unexpected end of Khilaphat—The Gaya Programme —A.I.C.C. meets in February—The Compromise—Jawaharlal—C. D. not seriously taken up—A National Convention—The Deputation on tour—A.I.C.C. prohibits propaganda against Council-entry—A Special Session of the Congress resolved upon at Nagpur—The revolt of Tamil-nadu—A.I.C.C. meets at Nagpur—Special Congress idea opposed—Special meeting of A.I.C.C. called—Special Congress Confirmed—To meet at Delhi—The Nagpur Satyagraha—Indians Abroad—Special Session at Delhi—Delhi Resolution permissive—Swaraj Party's Manifesto—On the eve of the Cocanada Session—Gandhi's message —The main resolution—The Cocanada Session—Other resolutions—Congress Departments—The Akali movement—Fight over Gurudwara Temples—Guruka Bagh affair—Mr. Macpherson's testimony—Reading of Akhand Pant, a crime.

CHAPTER V

Congress at the Cross-Roads (1924)

Gandhi's illness—The Juhu Conversations—Achievements of the Swaraj Party—Hailey's interpretation of Dominion Status—Statements of Gandhi and of Das and Nehru—A. I. C. C. meets—Yarn franchise of elected Congress Members—Other resolutions of A. I. C. C. at Ahmedabad—Communal troubles—All-Parties' Conference, November, 1924—The Belgaum Session—Revolt against Gandhi incomplete—All boycotts lifted except the boycott of violence and of foreign cloth—The spinning franchise—Essentials of Swaraj Scheme—Independence—Belgaum Resolution—Indians Abroad.

CHAPTER VI

Partition, or Partnership ? (1925)

Swarajists' achievements—Gandhi's tour—Psychology of Das—Das's Faridpur speech—Das's faith in Birkenhead—Das's last letter—Das's successor in Bengal—Gandhi's offer of resignation—The Muddiman Committee—Government's efforts to cajole Swaraj Party—Motilalji's appreciation of Gandhi's offer of self-effacement—Wanted a Middle Course—A. I. C. C. meets at Patna—The Partition—The Discussion—Motilalji ablaze—Motilalji makes amends—A point of honour—Partition or Partnership—Threats to arrest Das—The Cawnpore Session ahead—A loyal daughter's task—The Congress motor lacks momentum—Interest in Local Bodies—Internal revolt in the Swaraj Party—Kelkar's Criticism—The three resignations—The rising in Andhra Agency—The Cawnpore Session—Gandhi hands over charge to Sarojini Devi—Sarojini Devi takes charge—The battle for liberty—The deliberations of the Session—The main resolution—Pandit Malaviya's amendment—Other resolutions—Holmes attends the Session—Hindu-Muslim Riots—The Gurudwara question.

CHAPTER VII

THE COUNCIL FRONT (1926)

Responsive Co-operation—Assembly walk-out—President Patel—Conditions for accepting office—The Sabarmati Pact—Pandit Nehru clears position—Strained relations between Responsivists and Swarajists—Breakdown of Negotiations—Panditji's departure to England—The Bengal Swarajists—Calcutta Riots—Exchange Ratio—Lalaji v. Motilalji—Irwin replies to Sir Abdur Rahim on the appointment of a Muslim to his Cabinet—The General elections.

The Gauhati Congress—Shooting of Swami Shraddhananda—Presidential Address—The resolutions—Gandhi on the murder—The main resolution—Distinguished visitors—Motilalji on Nabha—Election Programme of 1926*—Progress of Khadi.*

CHAPTER VIII

THE COUNCIL FRONT (1927)—A STALEMATE

Congress fight in the Assembly—Adjournment motion re. S. C. Mitra—A series of Clashes—The ratio question—Saklatwalla's visit—President Patel's Trust—Panditji v. Iyengar—Panditji resigns his seat on the Skeen Committee—South Africa—A new atmosphere—Lalaji sails for Europe—A. I. C. C. meets in Bombay—Decision to draw up a Constitution—Other A. I. C. C. resolutions—The Madras Council party in the pillory—Subash

Chandra Bose released—Communal Riots—New law to punish offences relating to outraging religious feelings—Unity Conference of October—Its resolution—A. I. C. C. meets in October—Confirms Unity Conference Resolutions—Other resolutions—Announcement of the Simon Commission—Dr. Besant on the Commission—Pandit Motilalji on the Commission—The Commission's duty—The Madras Congress—Doctor Ansari's Presidential Address—The main resolution—Boycott of the Statutory Commission—The Kakori Case—Creed of Independence—The exhibition—Admits Mill-cloth.

CHAPTER IX

THE RENDITION OF THE CONGRESS (1928)

Boycott of Simon Commission—Effects of Simon Boycott—Lahore—Lucknow—Patna—The Procedure—All-Parties' Conference—Three burning questions, (1) Panditji to preside over Calcutta Congress, (2) The character of the Calcutta Exhibition, (3) The Bardoli ryots—The Bardoli struggle—Congress invited to guide it—Attachments galore—President Patel's threat—Government's bluff—The settlement—The Nehru Report—The Council front again—The Reserve Bank Bill—Public Safety Bill—The Calcutta Session—Panditji's Address—Resolutions—The States' Resolution—The main resolution—An ultimatum—Condemnation of Mr. Johnson's deportation—The Youth Movement—The main resolution—A compromise—Call to Gandhi—Gandhi's Speech—Parties secede from the Conference—The All-Parties' Conference—A sad failure—The A.I.C.C. warns the Council Party—Gandhi fed up, but gives up his European tour—Does not lose faith in his workers.

Part III

CHAPTER I

The Birth of Non-co-operation (1920)

The year 1920 opens with a definite cleavage of parties in Indian politics. The Liberals had definitely cut themselves off from the Congress and met in Calcutta in December, 1919. In the Congress itself, the events that were fast developing themselves were tending to create a further schism amongst the Congressmen left behind. At Amritsar, the central issue was co-operation or obstruction. A few months after the new year had opened, the position of the Amritsar parties was reversed. Gandhi stood for Non-co-operation, and those who had opposed his co-operation at Amritsar ranged themselves once again against him. What brought about such a sudden change of front? The fact was that anxiety was growing in the public mind over the Punjab atrocities as well as the Khilaphat question.

The events of 1920 centre round a great movement called the Khilaphat movement, and it is necessary to give in outline the genesis of the Khilaphat trouble. During the Great War, Mr. Lloyd George, the Premier of England, had made solemn promises to Indian Muslims who depending upon them went and fought against their brothers in Islam. When the war came to a close, a curious interpretation was put upon the promises, evidently to avoid fulfilment. If there was anything that exasperated the Indian Muslims, it was this perfidy of the British Premier. The pledges given by Lloyd George declared unequivocally in these words: "Nor are we fighting to deprive Turkey of the rich and renowned lands of Asia Minor and Thrace which are predominantly Turkish in race." These pledges were unredeemed and the promises were heartlessly broken. The Muslim contention was that the Jazarat-ul-Arab including Mesopotamia, Arabia, Syria and Palestine, with all the Holy Places situated therein, must always remain under the direct suzerainty of the Khalif. But as a result of the terms of the armistice, Turkey was deprived of her homelands. Thrace was presented to Greece. Both Great Britain and France divided the Asiatic portions of the Turkish Empire among themselves under the guise of Mandatories. A High Commission was appointed by the Allied Powers, who, to all intents and purposes, were the rulers in Turkey, with H. M. the Sultan as nothing better than a prisoner. Not only the entire Muslim population in India but other communities as well were in rage against what was rightly termed as the British Premier's 'betrayal,' and it was at Amritsar that the leading Congress and Khilaphat men discussed the situation in the country caused by Lloyd George's doings, and decided to organise the Khilaphat work under the guidance of Mahatma Gandhi.

In the middle of January, 1920, Mr. Mahomed Ali issued, along with his brother, a Manifesto to the country in the course of which, after formally thanking the public for their sympathy and support, he outlined his future course of action. "We expect to hear from His Excellency the Viceroy in a day or two," wrote Mr. Mahomed Ali and his brother in that Manifesto, "when he would be pleased to receive the Khilaphat Conference Deputation of Indian Muslims." A deputation waited upon the Viceroy on the 19th January, 1920, headed by Dr. Ansari and impressed him with "the necessity for the preservation of the Turkish Empire and of the Sovereignty of the Sultan as Khalif." They stated the Khilaphat issue in a word, when they laid down the principle "that the continued existence of the Khilaphat as a temporal no less than spiritual institution was the very essence of their faith."

The Viceroy's reply to the Deputation was disappointing to a degree, and the Muslim leaders issued a statement recording their firm conviction that "should the peace terms result unfavourably to Muslim religion and sentiments, they would place an undue strain upon Muslim loyalty" and demanding that "Arabia, as delimited by Muslim authority, and the Holy Places of Islam must remain under the control of the Khalif," and that the pledge given by Mr. Lloyd George should be fulfilled. The third Khilaphat Conference met at Bombay in February, 1920, and expressed its confidence in the Deputation going to England and issued a very important Manifesto, laying down the Muslim demands and declaring that "any reduction of the claim would not only be a violation of the deepest religious feelings of the Muslims, but also a flagrant violation of the solemn declarations and pledges made or given by responsible statesmen, representing the Allied and Associated Powers and given at a time when they were desirous of enlisting the support of the Muslim people and soldiery, and warning them against the consequence of a wrong decision, particularly when not only the Muslim but also the entire Hindu population was joining them in their demand."

Lord Chelmsford's emphasis on the fact that the question did not lie in the hands of Great Britain alone was not reassuring, and virtually neutralized his 'profound sympathy' with the Muslim view point. The militant tone of certain sections of the French, English and American Press regarding the desirability of settling the Eastern Question once for all, only strengthened the apprehensions of the Muslims. Influential sections of English and American opinion demanded that the Turks should be expelled from Constantinople, and reduced to the status of a fourth-rate Power. The Khilaphat question came more and more to the fore, during the months of February and March in Indian politics. A Muslim Deputation left for England early in March, 1920. The Deputation which was headed by Maulana Mahomed Ali was received by Mr. Fisher on behalf of the Secretary of State for India, and it also waited upon the Prime-Minister. It further requested permission to place its views before the Supreme Council of the Peace Conference but was refused.

Lloyd George's reply to the Muslim Deputation in England on the 17th March, insisting on the fact that Turkey could not be treated on principles different from those that were applied to Christian countries, and asserting the doctrine that while Turkey was to be allowed to exercise temporal sway over Turkish lands, she was not to be permitted to retain those lands which were not Turkish, struck at the root of the whole Khilaphat sentiment in India. On this, the 19th March was fixed as a day of National mourning,—a day of fasting and prayer and *hartal*. Gandhi once again appeared on the scene with the announcement that he would lead a movement of Non-co-operation if the terms of peace with Turkey did not meet the sentiments of the Muslims in India. Shaukat Ali tabled a resolution for the 19th March that if the peace terms were not acceptable, Muslims would be forced to sever their loyal connection with the British Throne. This evoked a resolution from the Government of India in the beginning of March, pointing out the impossibility of Government servants joining the celebration of the 19th March. Gandhi's ideas were embodied in a Manifesto dated the 10th March, which ran thus, and in which he had indicated his plans of Non-co-operation for the first time:

> "Now a word as to what may be done if the demands are not granted. The barbarous method is warfare, open or secret. This must be ruled out, if only because it is impracticable. If I could but persuade every one that it is always bad, we should gain all lawful ends much quicker. The power that an individual or a nation forswearing violence can generate, is a power that is irresistible. But my argument to-day against violence is based upon pure expediency, is utter futility. Non-co-operation is, therefore, the only remedy left open to us. It is the clearest remedy, as it is the most effective, when it is absolutely free from all violence. It becomes a duty when co-operation means degradation or humiliation, or an injury to one's cherished religious sentiment. England cannot expect a meek submission by us to an unjust usurpation of rights which to Muslims means a matter of life and death. We may therefore begin at the top as well as the bottom. Those who are holding offices of honour or emoluments ought to give them up. Those who belong to the menial services under Government should do likewise. Non-co-operation does not apply to service under private individuals. I cannot approve of the threat of ostracism against those who do not adopt the remedy of Non-co-operation. It is a voluntary withdrawal alone that is a test of popular feeling and dissatisfaction. Advice to the soldiers to refuse to serve is premature. It is the last, not the first step. We should be entitled to take that step when the Viceroy, the Secretary of State and the Premier leave us. Moreover, every step withdrawing co-operation has to be taken with the greatest deliberation. We must proceed slowly so as to ensure retention of self-control under the fiercest heat."

Let us quote Government's opinion from 'India, 1920' on this: "There was no doubt that Gandhi's advocacy of soul force commended itself to a populace who shared his religious belief and believed in his doctrines of self-abnegation and admired his asceticism. He stood like a 'rock of salvation' before the injured national pride of many of his countrymen. His behests had the influence of semi-divine commands." Lokamanya Tilak did not share Gandhi's views at first. His subtle intellect and world-conquering will stood in contrast with Gandhi's spiritual fervour and heaven-aspiring soul. It was in the midst of an atmosphere charged with unrest that the non-official Report on the Punjab atrocities was published (25th March). The Hunter Commission's inability to examine the Congress Sub-Committee's evidence made a separate Report inevitable, and at the same time antagonized the public to the Hunter Commission and its findings yet to be published. Sir Michael O'Dwyer was the *bete noire* of the Congress Report. His studied contempt of the educated classes, his pressure for recruits and contributions by high-handed methods, and his suppression of public opinion, were naturally the subjects of popular accusation against him. The events of the year 1919 began, it will be remembered, on the 6th April and found their culmination in the Jallianwala Bagh massacre on the 13th. So the week was observed as a National Week in 1920 and continues since to be so observed to this day. In the month of May the peace terms with Turkey were published and they only served to stimulate the Khilaphat agitation. Soon after, Gandhi declared his resolve to organize the Non-co-operation movement in order to get the terms modified. The Lokamanya did not sympathise whole-heartedly with this movement, but he did not oppose it.

The policies of the two great leaders may be studied side by side. Both had published valuable manifestoes in the third week of April. Gandhi had just then accepted the Presidentship of the All-India Home Rule League from which Mrs. Besant seceded, and he published a statement in doing so. Tilak had published a Manifesto enunciating his policy in relation to the new Reforms.

Gandhi's Statement

"It is a distinct departure from the even tenor of my life for me to belong to an organization that is purely and frankly political. But, after careful deliberation with friends, I have joined the All-India Home Rule League and accepted the office of its President. Some friends whom I consulted told me that I should not join any political organization and that, if I did, I would lose the position of splendid isolation I enjoy at present. I confess that this caution had considerable weight with me. At the same time, I felt that if I was accepted by the League, as I was, I should be wrong in not identifying myself with an organization that I could utilise for the advancement of causes in which I had specialised, and the methods which, experience has shown me, are attended with quicker and better results than those that are usually adopted. Before joining the League, I endeavoured to ascertain the opinion of those who were outside the Presidency and with whom I had not the privilege to come in such close contact as with co-workers in the Bombay Presidency. The causes referred to by me are Swadeshi, Hindu-Muslim Unity with special reference to Khilaphat, the acceptance of Hidustani as the *lingua franca,* and a linguistic re-distribution of the Provinces. I would engage the League, if I can carry the members with me, in these activities so that they occupy the largest part of the Nation's time and attention.

"I freely confess that reforms take a secondary place in any scheme of national reorganization. For, I feel that the activities chosen by me, if they could but absorb national energy, would bring about all the reforms that the most ardent Extremist can ever desire, and so far as the desirability of getting full Self-Government can be best accelerated by developing the activities that I have mentioned, I keep them in the forefront of the national programme I shall not treat the All-India Home Rule League as a party organization in any sense of the term. I belong to no party and I wish to belong to none hereafter. I am aware that the constitution of the League requires it to help the Congress, but I do not consider the Congress as a party organization, even as the British Parliament, though it contains all parties, and has one party or other dominating it from time to time, is not a party organization. I shall venture to hope that all parties will cherish the Congress as a national organization providing a platform for all parties to appeal to the Nation, with a view to moulding its policy, and I would endeavour so to mould the policy of the League as to make the Congress retain its no-party national character.

"This brings me to my methods. I believe that it is possible to introduce uncompromising truth and honesty in the political life of the country. Whilst I would not expect the League to follow me in my Civil Disobedience methods, I would strain every nerve to make truth and non-violence accepted in all our national activities. Then we shall cease to fear or distrust Government and their measures. I do not wish, however, to develop the theme any further, but I would rather let time solve the many questions that must arise from the bold statement I have here made. My purpose just now is not to demonstrate the propriety of my action or the truth of the policy herein adumbrated but to take the members of the League into my confidence and to invite their criticism of the programme therein set forth, and any suggestion they may wish to make for the advancement and the welfare of the League."

Tilak's Programme

Here is Tilak's Manifesto:

"The Congress-Democratic Party, as the name denotes, is a party animated by feelings of unswerving loyalty to the Congress and faith in Democracy. It believes in the potency of democratic doctrines for the solution of Indian problems, and regards the extension of education and political franchise as two of its best weapons. It advocates the removal of all civic, secular, or social disabilities based on caste or custom. It believes in religious toleration, the sacredness of one's religion to oneself and the right and duty of the State to protect it against aggression. This party supports the claim of the Muslims for the solution of the Khilaphat question according to Muslim dogmas and beliefs and the tenets of the *Koran.*

"This party believes in the integration or federation of India in the British Commonwealth for the advancement of the cause of humanity and the brotherhood of mankind, but demands autonomy for India and equal status as a sister-State with every partner in the British Commonwealth, including Great Britain. It insists upon equal citizenship for Indians throughout the Commonwealth and effective retaliation whenever it is denied. It welcomes the League of Nations as an instrument for enforcing the peace of the world, the integrity of States, the freedom and honour of nations and nationalities, and for ending the exploitation of one country by another.

"This party emphatically asserts the fitness of India for Representative and Responsible Government and claims for the people of India, on the principle of self-determination, the exclusive right of fashioning the form of government and determining the most appropriate constitution for India. It regards the Montagu Reforms Act as "inadequate, unsatisfactory and disappointing" and will strive to remedy the defect by introducing, with the aid of the members of the Labour party and other sympathisers in the British Parliament, at the earliest opportunity, a new Reform Bill for establishing full Responsible Government in India, including full Military control and full fiscal freedom, and an exhaustive Declaration of Rights with constitutional guarantees. To achieve this object, it contemplates and recommends a resolute and energetic campaign in India and in the countries represented on the League of Nations. In this matter, the party's watchword will be 'Educate, Agitate and Organize.'

"This party proposes to work the Montagu Reforms Act for all it is worth and for accelerating the grant of full Responsible Government, and, for this purpose, it will without hesitation offer co-operation or resort to constitutional opposition, whichever may be expedient and best calculated to give effect to the popular will.

"Apart from the foregoing aims and principles, the party platform will contain the following planks, but it does not profess to be exhaustive:

IMPERIAL

1. Repeal of all repressive legislation *e.g.*, (Rowlatt Act, the Press Act, the Arms Act, etc.), the introduction of trial by Jury of one's own countrymen, especially in cases of offences against the State; the abolition of rigorous imprisonment for such offences, and jail reform with a view to placing offenders of all classes on a par with similar offenders in Great Britain.

2. Securing for the labouring classes, agricultural and industrial, a fair share of the fruits of labour, a minimum wage, relationship between capital and labour on equitable basis, and promoting organizations suitable for the purpose.

3. Control of the export of foodstuffs and other necessaries of life by tariff or by other methods, with a view to reducing the prices thereof and conserving supplies.

4. Promotion of Swadeshism and development of industries by all recognised methods, including State subsidies and protective tariff.

5. Nationalisation of railways and regulation of railway tariffs by legislation, with a view to assist industrial development and to abolish privileges and favouritism in their working.

6. Retrenchment first and foremost in every department, especially in the Military expenditure, and taxation when imperative or desirable, but taxation graduated according to the capacity of various classes, corporations or individuals, so that the burden may be proportionate to the means or wealth of the tax-payers.

7. Creation of a Citizen Army, officered by Indians; naval, aerial and military education; Commissions for Indians in all Military services without racial discrimination.

8. Recruitment of all services by open competitive examination in India.

9. Promotion of national unity by such means as the establishment of a *lingua franca* for all India, betterment of relations between followers of different religions, and especially a Hindu-Muslim *Entente*.

10. Re-adjustment of Provinces on linguistic basis.

PROVINCIAL

1. Immediately securing full popular autonomy for the Provinces.

2. Permanent Ryotwari settlement on the basis of an equitable assessment.

3. Village control over reserved and protected forests in regard to pasturage, fuel, dealwood, and use of minor products.

4. Absolute prohibition of *Veth*, *Begar* and *Sarbarai*.

5. Education through the vernacular as high as possible.

6. Free and compulsory education without distinction of sex, special contributions and increased grants-in-aid from State funds to Municipalities and Local Boards to carry out this object immediately.

7. Restoration of Village Panchayats with administrative and judicial powers.

8. Abolition of drink.

9. Extension of the franchise without sex distinction.

10. Sanitation upon a systematic basis under a Minister of Health.

11. Carrying out of departmental reforms already enunciated and approved by popular opinion, *e.g.*, agricultural development, extension of irrigation, the co-operative movement, industrial and technical education suitable to the needs of the country, organised medical relief, and encouragement to indigenous system of medicine.

"Under this programme, the party appeals for votes and support for candidates pledged to these principles, with the fullest confidence of receiving an enthusiastic response so as to ensure victories in the coming election battles."

While the Deputation was still in Europe, the proposed terms of peace with Turkey were made public on 14th May, 1920, and in India, they were accompanied with a message from the Viceroy to the Muslims of India, explaining those terms. The message recognised that the terms were such as must cause pain to the Muslims of India, but asked them to brace themselves to bear with patience and resignation the misfortunes of their Turkish co-religionists. The publication of the proposed peace terms caused the deepest indignation, and synchronising as it did with the publication of the Hunter Committee's Report, the whole country was ablaze. The Khilaphat Committee met at Bombay to deliberate upon Gandhi's Non-co-operation project and adopted it on the 28th May, 1920, as the only means now left to the Muslims. On the 30th May, the All-India Congress Committee met at Benares to discuss the Hunter Report and the Turkish Peace terms, and after a long debate decided to hold a Special Session of the Congress to consider the question of Non-co-operation.

Gandhi himself recorded his impressions of Tilak's attitude towards Non-co-operation in his reminiscences about Tilak (Vol. 1. p. 253): "About Non-co-operation Tilak significantly repeated what he said to me before. 'I like the programme well enough, but I have my doubts as to the country being with us in the self-denying ordinance which Non-co-operation presents to the people. I will do nothing to hinder the progress of the movement. I wish you every success, and if you gain the popular ear you will find in me an enthusiastic supporter.' "

Before we proceed to narrate the events of 1920 in the sphere of Indian politics, we must refer to the celebration on the 1st January, 1920 of the abolition of the system of Indentured Labour in the Colonies, which had been prevalent for well-nigh a century and by which India was directly affected. In Natal, the Indentured Labour system was brought to an end by the refusal of the Indian Government to allow any more recruiting. In Mauritius, Indentured Labour ceased in 1911 because no more labour was required. But in other Colonies in different parts of the world, the Indenture system was still being carried on. During 1914 and 1915, the Government of India made an enquiry from the Governments of those Provinces from which Indentured Labour was taken, and it was found that the villagers were already up in arms against the Indenture system which was open to the gravest abuses. In 1915, Mr. C. F. Andrews and Mr. W. W. Pearson went out to Fiji and brought back information of the most damaging character which was issued in the form of a Report. This enabled Lord Hardinge to accept Pandit Madan Mohan Malaviya's motion in the Imperial Legislative Council for the abolition of Indenture. But he added the ominous words that some delay must be allowed while adjustments were being made. Later in the year, it was found out that he had privately agreed with the Colonial Office that recruiting should go on in India for another five years. Since it was clearly proved that such recruiting led to grave moral evils and even suicides, the Government of India was challenged by Mr. Andrews whether such a private understanding did or did not exist. And when it was made public that such an understanding had been signed between the two Offices at Whitehall,—Indian and Colonial,—a wave of moral indignation swept the country. And Gandhi himself took up the challenge and started the anti-Indenture campaign in the North and the West of India. Mrs. Besant carried on the campaign in Madras. This campaign was at its height in the months of March and April, 1917, and possibly Mrs. Besant's activity in this behalf was one of the governing reasons of her internment which took place on the 15th June, 1917. Lord Chelmsford called Gandhi and realised the seriousness of the situation. A deputation of Indian ladies from every Province went also to Lord Chelmsford on behalf of their Indian sisters. A date was fixed—31st May, 1917—by Gandhi, within which the system had to be brought to an end; otherwise a Satyagraha campaign would be started in order to prevent further recruitment. On April 12th (1917), Lord Chelmsford announced that all recruitment would be stopped as a special war-measure under the Defence of India Act. It was clear, however, that at the end of the war the whole question would be revived by the Colonies concerned, because vast financial interests were involved. Therefore Mr. Andrews, on the advice of Gandhi and with the cordial consent of the Poet Rabindra Nath Tagore, went out to Fiji again, in order to collect further facts which could be used when the question might be resuscitated at the end of the war. He spent nearly a year in Fiji and gathered far more damaging facts than on his previous visit. He also greatly interested the women of Australia in the moral question involved, and gained strong support for the abolition of the Indenture system. In March, 1918, he met Mr. Montagu at Delhi and was able to put before him the facts he had in his possession and to convince him that the system was altogether immoral. In 1919, the Government of India were able to announce that no further Indenture would be allowed and that all Indentured labourers whose five years' term had not expired should be set free. Therefore on January 1st, 1920, there was universal rejoicing among Indians in Fiji, British Guiana, Trinidad, Surinam, and Jamaica, where Indenture was still lingering, because on that day of emancipation every Indian labourer who had come out under Indenture was set free. It may be noted that this whole system was started as early as 1835 in order to supply labour to the old sugar plantations in the Colonies, which the African slaves had worked until slavery itself was abolished in 1833. It was thus a device to carry on the sugar plantations in a manner not far removed from slavery itself. Sir W. Wilson Hunter, the historian, called it 'semi-servile labour' and that description is accurate.

The Hunter Report was published on the 28th May, 1920, and its findings filled the country with disappointment and disgust. The Report was not unanimous, the Indian members differing from the English. The difference centred round the issue whether the outbreak in the Punjab was a premeditated revolt or an accidental outburst. The English members took the former view and the Indian the latter. Accordingly the latter thought that Martial Law was not called for. Moreover they put down the outbreak to O'Dwyer's *Zulum* in collecting money and recruiting soldiers. They took Government to task for suppressing news which gave rise to misrepresentation. Government accepted the view that "the administration of Martial Law was marred in particular instances by misuse of power, by irregularity and by injudicious and irresponsible acts; that General Dyer acted beyond what any reasonable man could have thought it to be necessary, and that he did not act with such humanity as the case permitted." His Majesty's Government also expressed strong disapproval of certain specified instances of undue severity and of improper punishments and orders during the Martial Law Regime, and instructed the Government of India to see that this disapproval "was unmistakably marked by censure or other action upon officers responsible for them". Mr. Montagu, however, remarked that "General Dyer acted to the best of his lights and with a sincerity of purpose, but that he committed an error of judgment." It was no consolation to India that instructions were issued to the Government of India to prepare a code of Martial Law regulations for future use! Nor was the fact that by the time "the cases of the officers concerned were examined with great care," many of those whose conduct had been censured by the Hunter Committee had left India or Government service, any source of comfort or satisfaction to the people of the Punjab or India.

Soon after the publication of the Hunter Commission Report, the All-India Congress Committee met at Benares on the 30th May, and recorded the country's indignant protest on all the questions and decided to have a Special Congress to consider the matter. Although Lokamanya Tilak passed Benares at the time, he did not attend the Benares meeting, for his heart was not wholly in the Khilaphat agitation. But he had the fairness and patriotism to say that he would act up to the behests of the A. I. C. C. It was about this time that Gandhi resolved to refer the question of Non-co-operation, which was mainly concerned at this time with the Khilaphat movement, to a conference of leaders of all parties which met at Allahabad on the 2nd June, 1920. At this conference the policy of Non-co-operation was decided upon, and a Committee was appointed, composed of Gandhi and some Muslim leaders, to draw up the programme. The Committee published their programme which comprised the boycott of schools and colleges and Law Courts. As a matter of fact, the All-India Khilaphat Conference held at Delhi in November, 1919 had resolved to withdraw co-operation from Government under Gandhi's advice,—a decision which was reaffirmed by Muslim meetings in Calcutta and elsewhere, as well as by the Madras Khilaphat Conference on 17-4-1920, where the progressive scheme of Non-co-operation was further defined as renunciation of titles and posts under Government, honorary posts and memberships of the Councils, appointments in the Police and Military, and refusal to pay tax. By the summer of 1920, the situation became acute. The 'Triveni' of the Khilaphat and Punjab wrong, and the invisible flow of inadequate Reforms, became full to the brim, and by their confluence enriched both in volume and content the stream of national discontent. Everything was ripe for Non-co-operation. Even the Lokamanya promised to abide by the decisions of the All-India Congress Committee, but alas! he passed away on the midnight of July 31st, leaving Gandhi without that towering strength which would have been his if he had been by his side.

In the meantime the Muslims embarked upon a plan of *Hijrat* (flight) to Afghanistan as they felt they could not stay in India under the British after the peace with Turkey. The movement started in Sindh and spread to the N. W. F. A ghastly collision took place between the emigrants and the Military at Kacha Garhi which exasperated the people, and in the month of

August it was estimated that 18,000 people were on their way to Afghanistan.

·But very soon the Afghan authorities forbade the admission of the pilgrims and a set-back was given to the idea, after considerable loss of life and sufferings. When in August the Supreme Legislative Council met, the Non-co-operation movement had already begun and some members of the Council resigned their seats. The Viceroy declared that the policy of N.C.O. must inevitably lead to disorder and asked whether anything could be more futile or ill-advised. He finally characterised the movement as the "most foolish of all foolish schemes." But the proposed visit of the Prince of Wales to India to open the new Assembly, which was opposed even by Sastriar at the Bombay Liberal Conference, was given up in the month of August and the Duke of Connaught was to take his place. It was in August too, that Dr. Sapru was appointed Member of the Viceroy's Executive Council.

The scheme of N. C. O. was formally inaugurated on the 1st of August. Gandhi and the Ali Brothers toured the country. It was the one study of Gandhi to discipline the people and regulate their obvious enthusiasm. As usual, Gandhi's administration of a reprimand to his following was always quoted by Government as proof of the rule of the mob. This proposed departure of the Congress from the traditional, constitutional paths was considered an issue big enough for a Special Congress, and the Special Session which had been decided upon already in May was held on the 4th to the 9th of September, 1920, in Calcutta.

By this time, the various Provincial Congress Committees gave their opinions on the burning question of the day—N.C.O.

The Andhra Congress Committee and the Punjab Committee recommended to the Special Congress the adoption of the *policy* of N.C.O., but would defer the *programme* till after the Special Session. Bengal held that under the conditions N.C.O was the only effective weapon left to the people, but the Committee, in common with C.P., did not consider a boycott of the new Legislative bodies was called for. On the contrary, the presence of a large number of members who would be prepared to resort to N.C.O. within the Council was demanded. Bihar and Orissa approved of the principle and appointed a Committee to recommend a programme suitable for the Province. Bombay wholeheartedly accepted the principle and would entrust the details to a committee to be appointed by the Special Congress. Burma approved, but believed that the movement was not practicable in that Province. The Madras P. C. C. approved a policy of N.C.O. but voted against Mr. Gandhi's programme. Sindh approved and framed a programme in detail in four steps, but objected to the Military being asked to withdraw. The U. P. approved and formulated a detailed programme, adding boycott of the welcome to H. R. H. the Duke of Connaught.

Buttressed by these opinions from all Provinces, the Calcutta Session met. It was a momentous session. Bengal did not see eye to eye with Gandhi, and C.R. Das stood foursquare against Gandhi's programme of N.C.O. The boycott of Councils and Law Courts evoked no sympathy in him, nor in the majority of delegates. Yet, by a narrow though conclusive majority of seven votes, the Subjects Committee passed Gandhi's Resolution in which a graduated scale of boycott was advocated. The atmosphere then prevalent was such that Non-co-operation was inevitable. The Government of India had blindly accepted the findings of the majority in the

Hunter Committee Report and was inclined to throw a veil of oblivion over the misdeeds of officials. They had slurred over Dyer's conduct as amounting only to "a grave error of judgment which exceeded the reasonable requirements of the case," and held that "it was based upon an honest but mistaken conception of duty." Montagu himself tamely acquiesced in those recommendations and practically condoned the misdeeds of the Punjab officials and aggravated matters by adding that Dyer was actuated by "honesty of purpose and unflinching adherence to duty." The debate in the House of Commons itself turned upon the supposed wrong and injustice of the punishment inflicted upon Dyer, while in the House of Lords, Lord Finlay's motion which was accepted was inaccurate, onesided, and false in spirit and substance. Altogether, the discussions betrayed the rights and liberties of the Indian people. These and the Khilaphat wrongs and the Reforms formed the subjects of strongly worded resolutions at the Calcutta (special) Session.

The Special Session of the Congress was held in Calcutta from 4th to 9th September, 1920 in the midst of the most enthusiastic scenes. Mr. B. Chakravarti was the Chairman of the Reception Committee and Lala Lajpat Rai, who had only recently returned from America was elected the President. The first resolution placed on record the deep and profound sorrow of the Congress at the death of Bal Gangadhar Tilak, "whose stainless purity of life, services and sufferings in the cause of his country, whose deep devotion to the welfare of the people, whose arduous endeavours in the fight for National Autonomy would enshrine his memory in the grateful recollection of our people and would be a source of strength and inspiration to countless generations of our countrymen." The Congress also recorded its grief at the loss sustained by the country in the death of Dr. Mahendra Nath.

The second resolution was moved by Sir Asutosh Chaudhuri who had recently retired from the Bench of the Calcutta High Court as a Judge and ran as follows:—

"That the thanks of the Congress be conveyed to the members of the Punjab Enquiry Sub-Committee and the commissioners appointed by them, for the great industry and judicial care with which they have collected the evidence and written their Report, which is supported not only by the evidence recorded by them but also by the evidence given before the Hunter Committee, and expresses its concurrence with the findings of fact arrived at by the said commissioners.

(a) This Congress expresses its deep and bitter disappointment at the drift, tone and tendency, and final conclusions of the Majority Report of the Hunter Committee and begs to express its complete and total dissent from the findings and recommendations of the deliberate opinion,

(b) This Congress further places on record its deliberate opinion,

(i) that the Report submitted by the Majority of the Hunter Committee is tainted by bias and race-prejudice, based on insufficient consideration of evidence, and characterised by a too obvious desire to slur over the proved, manifest iniquities of the Government officials concerned, and to whitewash the conduct of the Punjab Government and the Government of India;

(ii) that the said Report is unacceptable and unreliable inasmuch as it is based upon evidence which is incomplete, one-sided and biassed by self-interest;

(iii) that the findings arrived at in the Majority Report are not justified even from the evidence actually on record, and in any case, their recommendations fall far short of the minimum legitimate requirements of the case:

(c) That with reference to the Government of India's review of the two Reports of the Hunter Committee, this Congress records its deliberate opinion:

(i) that the said review accepts the findings of the Majority without sifting or discrimination;

(ii) that it pays scant and inadequate consideration to the arguments and findings of the Minority Report, even when such arguments and findings are amply borne out by the evidence on record;

(iii) that the whole drift and tendency of the said review is not to arrive at a just and impartial finding on facts, but to hush up the whole affair and to throw a veil of oblivion upon the misdeeds of the officials concerned;

(iv) that the action proposed to be taken in the review with reference to the conduct of guilty officials is grossly and utterly inadequate to the gravity of the state of things disclosed, and has shaken all confidence in the fairness of British justice.

The third resolution also dealt with the Punjab and expressed the "deep sense of bitter disappointment at the British Cabinet's failure to take adequate action with reference to the atrocities of the Punjab, at their acquiescence in the recommendations of the Government of India and their practical condonation of the misdeeds of the Punjab officials. The Congress was further of opinion that "in spite of the fine and lofty sentiments expressed in their Despatch, the British Cabinet by their failure to take adequate action have forfeited the confidence of the people of India."

But *the* resolution of the session was that dealing with Non-co-operation which was moved by Gandhi, and carried by 1886 delegates against 884. It ran as follows:—

"In view of the fact that on the Khilaphat question both the Indian and Imperial Governments have signally failed in their duty towards the

Muslims of India and the Prime-Minister has deliberately broken his pledged word given to them, and that it is the duty of every non-Muslim Indian in every legitimate manner to assist his Muslim brother in his attempt to remove the religious calamity that has overtaken him;

"And in view of the fact that, in the matter of the events of the April of 1919, both the said Governments have grossly neglected or failed to protect the innocent people of the Punjab and punish officers guilty of unsoldierly and barbarous behaviour towards them, and have exonerated Sir Michael O'Dwyer who proved himself directly responsible for most of the official crimes and callous to the sufferings of the people placed under his administration, and that the debate in the House of Lords betrayed a woeful lack of sympathy with the people of India, and systematic terrorism and frightfulness adopted in the Punjab, and that the latest Viceregal pronouncement is proof of entire absence of repentance in the matters of the Khilaphat and the Punjab;

"This Congress is of opinion that there can be no contentment in India without redress of the two aforementioned wrongs, and that the only effectual means to vindicate national honour and to prevent a repetition of similar wrongs in future is the establishment of Swarajya.

"This Congress is further of opinion that there is no course left open for the people of India but to approve of and adopt the policy of progressive non-violent Non-co-operation inaugurated by Mahatma Gandhi, until the said wrongs are righted and Swarajya is established;

"And inasmuch as a beginning should be made by the classes who have hitherto moulded and represented public opinion and inasmuch as Government consolidates its power through titles and honours bestowed on the people, through schools controlled by it, its Law Courts and its Legislative Councils, and inasmuch as it is desirable in the prosecution of the movement to take the minimum risk and to call for the least sacrifice compatible with the attainment of the desired object, this Congress earnestly advises,

(a) surrender of titles and honorary offices and resignation from nominated seats in Local Bodies;

(b). refusal to attend Government levees, durbars, and other official and semi-official functions held by Government officials, or in their honour;

(c) gradual withdrawal of children from schools and colleges owned, aided or controlled by Government, and, in place of such schools and colleges, the establishment of national schools and colleges in the various Provinces;

(d) gradual boycott of British Courts by lawyers and litigants, and the establishment of private arbitration courts by their aid for the settlement of private disputes;

(e) refusal on the part of the military, clerical and labouring classes to offer themselves as recruits for service in Mesopotamia;

(f) withdrawal by candidates of their candidature for election to the Reformed Councils, and refusal on the part of the voters to vote for any candidate who may, despite the Congress advice, offer himself for election;

(g) boycott of foreign goods;

"And inasmuch as Non-co-operation has been conceived as a measure of discipline and self-sacrifice without which no nation can make real progress, and inasmuch as an opportunity should be given in the very first stage of Non-co-operation to every man, woman and child for such discipline and self-sacrifice, this Congress advises adoption of Swadeshi in piece-goods on a vast scale, and inasmuch as the existing mills of India with indigenous capital and control do not manufacture sufficient yarn and sufficient cloth for the requirements of the Nation, and are not likely to do so for a long time to come, this Congress advises immediate stimulation of further manufacture on a large scale by means of reviving hand-spinning in every house and hand-weaving on the part of the millions of weavers who have abandoned their ancient and honourable calling for want of encouragement."

The Resolution was hotly contested, and Babu Bepin Chandra Pal moved an amendment, which was supported by Deshbandhu C. R. Das, by which the Prime-Minister was asked to receive a mission from India to lay before him the statement of India's grievances coupled with a demand for immediate Autonomy, and in case of his failure to receive the mission or to replace the Reforms Act of 1919 by a measure granting full Autonomy to India, a policy of such active Non-co-operation be adopted as would leave no doubt in the minds of the British people that India could no longer be governed as a Dependency. In the meantime the country was recommended to give consideration to Mahatma Gandhi's programme through a representative Committee and carry on preparatory propaganda in that behalf.

After a long and earnest consideration, the Resolution of Mahatma Gandhi was passed.

It may be incidentally mentioned that Gandhi had at first included the boycott of Local Bodies as well, but withdrew it in deference to the wishes of friends. The Nationalist party once again remained loyal to the Congress in spite of some of their differences with the programme. Particular mention should be made of the fact that nearly all Nationalist candidates who, in obedience to the Amritsar Congress Resolution, had announced their candidature for the Reformed Councils, and spent considerable time, labour and money on the campaign, immediately withdrew from the contest. The voters themselves—at least 80%—accepted the decision of the Congress and refrained from voting, and from not a few places empty ballot boxes were sent. Government themselves admitted, "It is rather in connection with the boycott of the new Councils that Mr. Gandhi's campaign of N.C.O. seems destined to exercise a potent influence upon the history of the next few years. It has prevented the inclusion in the new Legislatures of certain advanced thinkers who figure prominently in the public eye, and has left the Moderates a clear field."

In the beginning of November, Government found it desirable to make plain what exactly its policy was towards this movement: "They have instructed Local Governments to take action against those persons only, who in furtherance of the movement have gone beyond the limits originally set by its organizers, and have, by speech or writing, openly incited the public to violence, or have attempted to tamper with the loyalty of the Army or the Police." Government further expressed their trust and belief that "the sanity of the classes and masses alike would reject N.C.O. as a visionary and chimerical scheme, which if successful could only result in wide-spread disorder, political chaos and ruin of all those who have any real stake in the country." "The appeal of N.C.O. is to prejudice and ignorance," they said, "and its creed is devoid of any constructive germs."

A new atmosphere soon pervaded the country. The attitude of people to the established and age-long methods of political agitation changed. The Sub-Committee appointed by the A. I. C. C., in May, 1920, to present a Petition to Parliament on the Punjab Tragedy never moved in the matter. The Congress had stopped payment to the British Committee since 1918, owing to differences between the Congress and the Committee on the question of the Reforms. The same differences had led to an acrimonious controversy in England, in 1919, between the Congress Deputation and Mrs. Besant. The Labour Party and the English friends were lost between the contentions and view-points of the two schools of thought. The British Committee, we saw, was at last reduced to terms and the Congress gained control. Nevertheless, the British Committee disregarded the agreement reached between the Deputation and itself,—to the effect that it should appoint an Indian selected by the A. I. C. C. on its staff, and the Committee chose an Indian direct; and despite protests from the Congress, declined to yield. It was definitely recommended that the paper *India* should, therefore, be discontinued.

While this was so in regard to work in England, affairs in India claim our attention. On the 2nd October, 1920, the A. I. C .C. met and resolved to raise two funds, (1) the All-India Tilak Memorial Fund, and (2) Swarajya Fund, but the resolution remained a dead letter till December, 1920. The new resolutions on N.C.O. were not taken to kindly either in Bengal or Maharashtra. Mr. G. S. Khaparde, a co-worker of the Lokamanya, published a short Memorandum contrasting in parallel columns how the Calcutta (special) Resolutions sought to "divert the energies of the Congress into directions of attaining soul force and moral excellence, and loses sight of the political aspects of affairs." "By avoiding contact with the *de facto* Government," it proceeded, "it affords no training ground for acquiring the kind of political-mindedness and temper necessary to carry on a substantial struggle in a peaceful, and yet firm and orderly manner. The N.C.O. as preached now may develop powers of endurance, but cannot breed the energy and resourcefulness and practical wisdom necessary for a political struggle. The three boycotts at present recommended are futile and have not at all a distinct political aspect, and the tendency of the whole, as evidenced in the proceedings for alteration of the Creed of the All-India Home Rule League, now re-named Swaraj Sabha, would appear to be towards a return to autocracy and personal rule, which is objectionable and against the spirit of the age, though entrusted to a highly developed and moral individual."

This was dated 10th December, 1920. It was published on the eve of the Nagpur Congress. It calls attention to the change of the Creed of the Home Rule League, and the formation of the Swaraj Sabha by Gandhi. The fact was that, in Calcutta, while the fate of N.C.O. was hanging in the balance, Gandhi assembled the old Home Rulers, from whom Mrs. Besant virtually seceded, under a common banner and changed the Creed of the League into a form since adopted by the Congress at Nagpur, as also the name of the League into Swaraj Sabha. But this Sabha never had occasion to function, as Calcutta accepted the cult of N.C.O. and Nagpur confirmed it. It is by a strange irony of fate and of politics that the Resolution of N.C.O. should have been accepted at two successive Congresses held in the Headquarters of the two Provinces that strenuously opposed the new movement.

Nagpur Congress, 1920

The Nagpur Congress was to be the next place where the programme of Non-co-operation was to be finally discussed and decided. The number of delegates who attended the Congress was immense, and no Congress before or after Nagpur can claim to its credit as many delegates as did Nagpur. Their number was 14,582, of whom no less than 1,050 were Muslims, and 169 women. It was presided over by that veteran Congress leader from the South, Mr. C. Vijiaraghavachariar of Salem. Col. Wedgwood, Mr. Holford Knight and Mr. Ben Spoor attended the Congress as fraternal delegates from the Labour Party of England and conveyed the Labour Party's greetings and sympathy.

The Calcutta Special Session was presided over by an avowed opponent of N.C.O. Lala Lajpat Rai was a great Social and Educational Reformer, but his creation was the Dayanand Anglo-Vedic College, not the Gurukula. He never believed in cutting off from Government, though all his life he was cut off by Government, suspected, kept under surveillance and virtually externed during the war. Swami Shraddhananda, however, threw himself heart and soul into the new movement.

Likewise, it was the President of the Nagpur Congress, Mr. C. Vijiaraghavachariar, that demanded that Swaraj, not merely the Punjab tragedy and the Khilaphat wrong, should be the motive for N.C.O. Gandhi readily agreed. His point was that if once, on a moral issue, however limited it be,—be it the Rowlatt Act, the Khilaphat wrong or the Punjab atrocity,—we won on the ticket of Satyagraha, Passive Resistance or Non-co-operation, then the success would fill the Nation with self-confidence such as was generated by the success in the Transvaal and in Champaran. Intellectual India was inclined to be logically-minded; and an intellectual giant like Mr. Vijiaraghavachariar could not help being rigidly logical in his view of affairs. At Nagpur, however, Gandhi had one advantage, namely, that Mr. Achariar, in spite of his lukewarm attitude towards Non-co-operation, co-operated with Gandhi passively, and always made a point of vacating the Chair whenever a resolution came up before the open House with which he was not in agreement.

Mr. C. R. Das brought a contingent of about 250 delegates from East Bengal and Assam, bore their expenses to and fro, and spent Rs. 36,000 from his pocket to undo what was done in Calcutta. There was even a small fight between his men and those of Jitendralal

Banerjee, his opponent. Maharashtra's opposition was not less intense, nor less well-organized. Colonel Wedgwood attended the meeting of the Subjects Committee and so did Messrs. Ben Spoor and Holford Knight. Col. Wedgwood put all his force into his arguments against N. C. O. Nothing availed. The Khaddar clause was made tighter, the N. C. O. Resolution was re-affirmed, the Creed of the Congress was changed "in such a fashion as to eliminate the declared adherence of that body to the British connection and to constitutional methods of agitation." That was how Government viewed the change. The session was a personal triumph for Gandhi. It left every one of the older Congressmen,—seniors, leaders and patriarchs,—aghast, asking themselves and each other, "Who is this man that speaketh with a tone of authority and whence doth he come?" Seasoned men like Pal and Malaviya and Jinnah and Khaparde, stalwarts like Das and Lalaji were simply overpowered. If the situation did not give rise to feelings of jealousy, it must be due to the splendid character of our political leaders.

Let us study the events connected with the Nagpur Congress and the radical changes it introduced into the Creed and Constitution, as well as into the ideals and outlook of the National Congress. The acceptance of the Resolution on N. C. O. was an event by itself, but the great point about it is that the Resolution was moved by Mr. C. R. Das and seconded by Lala Lajpat Rai.

The support that Gandhi obtained at Nagpur was undoubtedly greater than what he had in Calcutta. In Calcutta, the only top-notch politician that had lent a helping hand to Gandhi, and that, rather late in the session, was Pandit Motilal Nehru,—after Gandhi had accepted his amendment to make the boycott of Law Courts and colleges gradual. Else the stool of the N. C. O.

was resting on but one leg. At Nagpur, it stood on all its four legs with perfect equipoise. Gandhi and Nehru, Das and Lalaji were all for it. The Resolution itself is a long and comprehensive one, sharing the characteristic features of all Gandhi's resolutions on the subject of N. C. O., in which he would not admit of any amendment generally. It was the fashion of those days for the more intellectually-minded delegates to table verbal and other amendments to all resolutions,—and to Gandhi's resolutions as well,—but it did not take long to discover that, alike in terseness and comprehensiveness, Gandhi's drafts could not be improved. That does not mean that he would reject any reasonable suggestion. Never was he more pleased than when a bright suggestion was made, and he would readily grasp it. The N. C. O. Resolution of Nagpur virtually reaffirmed that passed in Calcutta, covering the whole field, from the renunciation of titles at one end to the refusal to pay taxes at the other. It called upon merchants gradually to boycott foreign trade relations and encourage hand-spinning and hand-weaving, exhorted the country to make the utmost possible contribution of self-sacrifice to the National movement, urged the Congress to organize the Indian National Service, promote the All-India Tilak Memorial Fund which had already been resolved upon in the previous October, but which was an amalgamation of the two funds then contemplated, namely, the All-India Lokamanya Memorial Fund and Swarajya Fund, requested those elected to Councils to resign their seats and the electors to refrain studiously from asking for any political service from such Councillors, recognised the growing friendliness between the Police and soldiery and the people, appealed to all Government servants to help the national cause by importing greater kindness and stricter honesty in their dealings with the people and fearlessly and openly to attend all popular gatherings, laid emphasis on non-violence as an integral part of the N. C. O. movement. The Resolution emphasises non-violence in word and deed as essential, "as the spirit of violence is not only contrary to the growth of a true spirit of democracy but actually retards the enforcement (if necessary) of the other stages of N.C.O." and finally, urged upon all public bodies to devote their exclusive attention to the promotion of non-violent Non-co-operation with the Government, and promote complete co-operation amongst the people themselves. In this changed atmosphere, arrangements were made to wind up *India*, the Weekly published in England, while recognising the necessity of disseminating correct information in India, and in foreign countries. Homage was paid to the sacred memory of the late Mac Swiney of Ireland who had met with his end after a fast unto death extending over 65 days for the sake of Irish emancipation.

Incidentally, it must be mentioned that Ireland and its grim fight, though on violent lines, and the complete boycott of the Milner Mission in Egypt, nerved India for a fight equally grim, but on the plane of non-violence. Col. Wedgwood who was at the Subjects Committee at Nagpur and obtained permission to speak, gravely warned the Congress against the cult of Non-co-operation. "You will make it difficult for your friends in England to take up your cause," said he. "You will be hampered in your work. The Police will be after you. The lawyers sign a pledge that they would be loyal to the Crown and cannot therefore work for Non-co-operation. You are going into the wilderness. You must pursue a constructive programme." In this strain did he go on for a quarter of an hour with transparent sincerity and unmistakable friendliness. Hardly had he resumed his seat when up rose a voice in reply, and, in five minutes, answered his objections: "We have no friends outside India; let there be no mistake about that. Our salvation lies in our own hands. We must make or mar our future. We have realised that, and taken to this programme. The Police are not a new element in Indian politics. If we have opened a small school, every rupee we have collected, we have gathered only under the shadow of the red turban during the past fifteen years. Yes, the lawyers have to sign an undertaking to be loyal, so it is that they are asked to tear up their 'sanads.' We are going into the wilderness, we know, because the way to the 'land flowing with milk and honey,' the land of Canaan, from the land of our bondage, lies only through a wilderness. And we trust to the leadership of a Moses or an Aaron to lead us from untruth to truth, from darkness to light, from death to life."

The rise in Exchange and the 'loot' thereby effected in our Gold Exchange Standard Reserve, and Paper Currency Reserve, through Reverse Councils became the subject at Nagpur of a vigorous demand that the British Government should make good the loss. It was also stated in Resolution V that "dealers in British goods would be entirely justified in refusing to complete their contracts at the present rates of exchange." The country was asked to refrain from taking any part in functions or festivities in honour of H.R.H. the Duke of Connaught. Labour was encouraged and sympathy was extended to it in its struggles through Trade Unions. The export of food-stuffs was condemned. Sympathy was also offered to political workers, who were arrested and imprisoned with or without regular trial. The renewal of repression in the Punjab, Delhi and elsewhere was noted, and people were asked to bear it up with fortitude. The Congress requested all sovereign Princes to take immediate steps to establish full Responsible Government in their States. The policy of Government in still keeping Mr. B. G. Horniman removed from the Indian people was condemned and India's gratitude was expressed to him. The Esher Committee and its recommendations were also condemned as "calculated to increase India's subservience and impotence and constituting an additional ground for N.C.O." The Muslims were thanked for their resolution against cow-slaughter; and export of cattle and hides was asked to be discouraged by the people. Free education and indigenous medicine were the subjects of two resolutions.

Finally, we come to the Constitution of the Congress. Under it, the Creed of the Congress was changed. Its object was declared to be "the attainment of Swaraj by peaceful and legitimate means." Congress circles were reorganized on a linguistic basis. A cardinal change was the advancing of the Subjects Committee's sittings to two or three days before the open sittings of the Congress, and the limitation of its composition to the members of the A.I.C.C., whose strength, however, was increased to 350. The appointment of a Working Committee of the A. I. C. C., composed of 15 members, including the Secretaries, the Treasurers and the President, was a feature of the new Constitution which has revolutionized the day-to-day work of the Congress and made the National Congress to-day a continuous organization for carrying out the Congress behests. Before closing, let us add that the Congress offered its support to Indians in East Africa and South Africa in their heroic and noble struggle against the treatment meted out to them, approved of the policy of peaceful N.C.O. initiated by the Indians in East Africa, and deplored the inability of India to render any help to the Indians in Fiji who had been compelled to return to India, and lastly, the Congress recorded its vote of thanks to Mr. C. F. Andrews for his services to Indians Abroad.

CHAPTER II

Non-co-operation Galore (1921)

The Nagpur Congress really marked a new era in recent Indian history. The old feelings of impotent rage and importunate requests gave place to a new sense of responsibility and a spirit of self-reliance. People realized that if they would be free they must strike the blow themselves. It was a definite call to them to cross the Rubicon and burn their boats. They cheerfully agreed to the course and began to march forward. The Nagpur Congress laid a heavy duty upon the Nation, and the A.I.C.C., under the advice of the Working Committee, set itself seriously to its task. Let us, for a moment, study the position of affairs in India, towards the end of 1920 and the beginning of 1921. By the end of the year 1920, the Moderates once for all cut themselves off from the Congress. Mr. C. Y. Chintamani made a grand speech at the second annual session of the Liberal Federation. Surendra Nath Banerjea became knighted. Lord Sinha became the first Indian Governor of Bihar and Orissa. Early in 1921, the new Ministers included a man like Lala Har Kishen Lal who had been condemned a few months earlier to transportation for life and forfeiture of property, in the Punjab. The Duke of Connaught, uncle of King George, was sent over to assuage feeling in India and open the new era. He made a fine speech:—

> "I have reached a time of life when I most desire to heal wounds and reunite those who have been disunited. An old friend of India, I appeal to you all —British and Indians—to bury along with the dead past the mistakes and misunderstandings of the past, to forgive where you have to forgive and to join hands and to work together to realise the hopes that arise from to-day."

Later on, when the Punjab tragedy was raised by a resolution in the Supreme Council, Sir William Vincent, who led the debate on the question from the Government benches, made plain "the deep regret of the administration at the perpetration of those improper actions, and their firm determination that, so far as human foresight could avail, any repetition would be for ever impossible." Having stated this much, Government cleverly managed to get the mover of the Resolution to withdraw the third clause calling for deterrent punishment. The fact, however, was that though General Dyer was relieved of his command, and thereby perhaps lost his pension, a collection was made by the English ladies in India who looked upon him as their saviour, and £20,000 was paid to him, and more than the money, the honour publicly done to him in England and in India in the presentation of a sword was enough to compensate him for any loss otherwise sustained. Col. Johnson, the next arch-offender, secured a commercial appointment in India and found himself amply compensated for his 'losses.' Neither the appeal of the Duke nor the "regret of the administration" expressed by the Home Member, Sir William Vincent, helped to appease the feelings of Indians. N.C.O. came to stay. There was however one redeeming feature, and that was that the Central Legislature appointed a Committee early in 1921 to examine the Repressive Laws which were, with the exception of the Criminal Law Amendment Act, actually repealed early in 1922, but all these palliatives left the sore unhealed. It continued to be festering and the Congress had to do its own doctoring, instead of depending upon the time-honoured remedies of Royal Pronouncements or Legislative repeals.

The response to the Nagpur Congress was ample. The No-vote campaign had been a remarkable success. Less successful was the boycott of courts and colleges, though their prestige was greatly damaged. Numerous lawyers had left their profession throughout the country and thrown themselves heart and soul into the movement. An unexpected measure of response however was noticeable in the field of National Education. Though the number of students that non-co-operated was not large, there was an earnest move towards National Education.

The fact was Mahatma Gandhi's appeal to the finer instincts of the youth of the country to devote themselves to its service, and to shun the institutions which had been created and maintained to kill all manliness in them, was responded to with enthusiasm. Nor was the work confined to merely to boycott. National Universities, National Colleges, and National Schools of all grades were started in different parts of the country. The student movement in the U.P., the Punjab, and the Bombay Presidency was in full swing. Bengal was not behind-hand, and Calcutta witnessed one of those thrilling scenes which were not few or far between in the course of that memorable year and a half. About the middle of January, on an appeal by Deshbandhu C. R. Das, thousands of students left their colleges and examinations. Gandhi visited Calcutta and opened the National College on the 4th of February. He also visited Patna for a second time and formally opened the National College and inaugurated the Bihar Vidyapith. Thus in the course of less than four months, the National Muslim University of Aligarh, the Gujarat Vidyapith, the Bihar Vidyapith, the Kashi Vidyapith, the Bengal National University, the Tilak Maharashtra Vidyapith, and a large number of National Schools of all grades, with thousands of students on the rolls, were started in all parts of the country as a result of the great impetus given to National Education. In the Andhradesa, the torch of National Education which was lighted in 1907 and which was now dim and now luminous, once again began to shine bright and clear: The students that non-co-operated with the Regulation institutions were many, and not a few of the Provincial and District leaders of to-day are from amongst the lawyers and students who had non-co-operated in 1920-21.

In pursuance of the Nagpur Resolution, the Working Committee of the All-India Congress Committee met almost from month to month in the year 1921 at different centres. The first meeting of the A.I.C.C. took place at Nagpur to elect the Working Committee and to allocate seats in the A.I.C.C. to the twenty-one Provinces. Gandhi had already taken over *Young India* from the Home Rulers who were glad to part with this splendid English Weekly, which was the organ in Bombay of the Home Rule movement, for the purpose of helping the cause. The Home Rule League itself had been disorganized and disrupted. In January, 1921, Seth Jamnalal Bajaj, who was the Chairman of the Reception Committee of the Nagpur Congress and who shed his title of Rao Bahadur, donated one lac of rupees to the Tilak Swaraj Fund for the purpose of supporting non-co-operating lawyers. The Working Committee met in Calcutta on 31st January, 1921 and framed rules for the allocation of the Tilak Swaraj Fund, 25% being required to be sent to the Working Committee from the Provincial collections. No lawyer was to receive more than Rs 100 per mensem and no member of the National Service more than Rs 50. Indebtedness was made a disqualification for such service. Pending the evolution of a detailed curriculum of studies in the field of National Education, Hindustani and spinning were required to be taught, and a course of training was to be given for village workers. Mr. C.R. Das was requested to look after Labour organization and Mr. L. R. Tairsee was appointed Convener of the Economic Boycott Committee.

The Working Committee next met at Bezwada on the 31st March and 1st April, 1921, as also the All-India Congress Committee. The Working Committee felt unanimously that the time had not arrived yet for non-payment of taxes. It was at this meeting of the A.I.C.C. at Bezwada that collection of one crore of rupees for Swarajya Fund, enlistment of one crore of Congress members and introduction of 20 lacs of *charkas* were enjoined upon the Nation, quotas being fixed in the proportion of provincial population. The organization of Panchayats and the discouragement of drink were singled out for commendation. Even though only harmless reforms such as these were being preached by the people, Government had already begun to serve orders under Section 144 and Section 108, and the A.I.C.C. held that the country was not yet sufficiently disciplined, organized and ripe for the immediate taking up of Civil Disobedience, and called upon all to conform to orders served upon them. The Committee expressed its sense of horror over the Nankana massacre and assured the Sikhs of its sympathy with them in the heavy losses suffered by them. The fact was that even by the second week of March, the country was in a state of excitement. Orders of restraint were passed against Mr. C. R. Das entering Mymensingh, Babu Rajendra Prasad and Maulana Mazar-ul-Haq entering Arrah, Yakub Hasan entering Calcutta, and Lajpat Rai entering Peshawar. A host of other orders were passed against others. Lahore was proclaimed under the Seditious Meetings Act.

But all these were nothing compared to the Nankana tragedy. In the first week of March, peaceful pilgrims assembled in that Gurudwara were suddenly pounced upon and shot down, the casualities aggregating to 195 killed as estimated by the people, but 70 according to Government. The Mahant, a loyal subject, had stored 4,000 cartridges and 65 revolvers in his house. There was a pit dug with a big fire burning. A conference on public affairs was to assemble there on the 5th March. A number of *budmashes* perpetrated this crime. Major Currie, who was the same officer as was in Delhi two years previously on the Clock Tower tragedy day, and Mr. King, were transferred from the locality to another district forthwith. It is not known against whom the Mahant meant to direct his wrath. But the circumstances were inexplicable. There was a motion before the Council of State regarding the incident, which was explained by Government as a fight between two sections of the Sikhs. Mr. Man Singh while speaking on Bakshi Sohan Lal's amendment hinted that the officials of the locality should have been, for sometime previously, acquainted with possibilities of the projected crime of such magnitude. At this stage in the council, Sir William Vincent walked up to the seat of Mr. Hailey and whispered in his ear. Mr. Hailey got up and, in angry tones, vehemently condemned the speaker who attempted to assert the implication of the officials in the ghastly affair. The Nankana tragedy was an unprecedented event in which the pilgrims were shot down and, while yet life was lingering, thrown into the burning pit.

In the history of the earlier years of the Congress we saw how the British Committee was the real centre of work and how expensive were its establishment and other requirements. Sums aggregating to Rs. 60,000 a year were sanctioned in several years. Now the centre of gravity had shifted to India. At Bezwada it was resolved that a sum of Rs. 17,000 be sanctioned for the remainder of the 'current year' for the expenses of the office of the President, the Secretary and the Cashier. A sum of 1,000 dollars was cabled to Mr. D. V. S. Rao of the Indian Home Rule League of America on the recommendation of Lalaji and Mr. Kelkar. The sixth and the 13th of April were required to be observed as days of fasting and prayer. The representation of the Congress circles on the A.I.C.C. was readjusted so as, however, not to disturb the total strength of 350 members, excluding ex-Presidents. When the Working Committee next met at Allahabad in May on the 10th, there were already invitations to it from Tanjore and Sholapur. Nothing of importance transpired at this meeting. The Committee later met in Bombay on the 15th June, when Gandhi made a statement regarding his interview with the Viceroy.

At this interview which was brought about by Pandit Madan Mohan Malaviya, Lord Reading who became the Viceroy in April, 1921, had an opportunity of judging Gandhi's sincerity and discovered how unwise it would be on his part to take action against the N.C.O. movement as such. But he incidentally drew attention to the speeches of the Ali Brothers as falsifying the view of the Non-co-operation movement put forward by Gandhi. These speeches, it was pointed out to Gandhi, might be construed as subtle incitements to violence, and being the scrupulously fair man that Gandhi always is, he agreed that such a misconstruction of the speeches was possible. He therefore wrote to the Ali Brothers and secured from them a statement repudiating any such intention on their part.

This 'apology' was an epoch-making event in the history of the movement. Anglo-India was jubilant over Government's victory. Lord Reading was satisfied with the 'apology' and gave up the idea of prosecution.

At the Bombay meeting of the Working Committee the position in regard to defence in political cases was made clear. The Working Committee laid down that "in the event of prosecution or a civil suit being brought against Non-co-operators, they should not participate in the proceedings beyond making before the Court a full statement of facts in order to establish their innocence before the public. Where security is demanded from them under the Criminal Procedure Code, they shall refuse furnishing such security and offer to undergo imprisonment in default." Further it was laid down that non-co-operating lawyers were precluded from appearing as counsel, with or without payment. At that time there was an apprehension of hostilities being reopened with the Turkish Government at Angora and the Working Committee was of opinion that it was the duty of every Indian to refrain from helping the British Government in the prosecution of such hostilities in direct defiance of Muslim opinion, and it was therefore the duty of Indian soldiers to decline to serve in connection therewith.

An important sitting of the A.I.C.C. took place in July, 1921, in Bombay on the 28th, 29th and 30th. The feeling of the country was one of universal jubilation at the success of the Bezwada programme. The Tilak Swaraj Fund was over-subscribed by about 15 lakhs of rupees. The membership did not reach much over half the prescribed figure but the *charkas* came up nearly to the figure of 20 lakhs. The next thing was naturally to turn the country's attention to weaving and the accessory crafts of spinning and carding. To this end, a complete boycott of foreign cloth was the subject for the country to concentrate on, coupled with the manufacture of khaddar. The A.I.C.C. further advised that "all persons belonging to the Congress shall discard the use of foreign cloth, as from the 1st day of August next." The millowners of

Bombay and Ahmedabad were requested "to regulate the prices of their manufactures so as to bear proportion to the wages of mill hands and so as to be within the reach of the poorest, and in no case to raise the price beyond the prevailing rates." Importers of foreign cloth were asked to stop all foreign orders and to endeavour to dispose of their stock outside India.

The A.I.C.C. expressed the opinion that "it was the inherent right of a citizen to pronounce his opinion upon the advisability or otherwise of Government servants leaving Civil or Military service, and that it was the inherent right of every citizen to appeal in an open manner to every soldier or civilian to sever his connection with a Government which had forfeited the confidence and support of a vast majority of the population of India." The resolution on foreign policy submitted by the Working Committee was approved of by the A.I.C.C.

On the question of anti-drink propaganda, troubles had already arisen at Dharwar, Matian and other places by undue and improper interference from the authorities with attempts to wean weak members from visiting drink shops, and the A.I.C.C. warned that it would be prepared to recommend the continuance of picketing in disregard of such interference. The Thana District Board was congratulated on its resolution re. picketing and its determination to continue it, and the A.I.C.C. called upon other Local Boards and Municipalities in India immediately to follow the splendid lead of Thana. It may be noted here that the Congress had not up to that time tabled any resolution on picketing and even then it confined itself to public bodies. An appeal was made to traders that they should discontinue trade in intoxicants. The Congress was keenly alive to the duty of the Nation to maintain perfect non-violence, but excesses having been committed by some people in parts of the city of Aligarh even though under grave provocation, the A.I.C.C. advised Congress organizations to inculcate the spirit of complete non-violence, and congratulated the people on their self-control despite the grave provocation at Dharwar, Matian, Guntur, Chirala, Perala, Kerala, N. W. F. Province, Keonjhar and elsewhere.

Repression was going on particularly in U. P. in a serious and widespread manner. In several places people were wounded by firing. Many were under imprisonment without offer of defence, and to all congratulations were offered on the score that "only through voluntary suffering and through imprisonment of innocent people without defence or bail the way to freedom lay." The situation was such that from different parts of the country arose a demand for taking up Civil Disobedience in answer to the repressive measures of Local Governments. The administration in N. W. Frontier Province had even prohibited the entry into that Province of the members of the Frontier Enquiry Committee to enquire into the outrages alleged to have been committed by the local officials at Banu. Nevertheless, "to ensure greater stability of non-violent atmosphere throughout India, and in order to test the measure of influence attained by the Congress over the people and further in order to retain on the part of the Nation an atmosphere free from ferment necessary for the proper and swift prosecution of Swadeshi, the All-India Congress Committee is of opinion that Civil Disobedience should be postponed till after the completion of the programme referred to in the resolution on Swadeshi." Moreover a big event was about to take place in connection with the visit of H.R.H. the Prince of Wales. The A. I. C. C. resolved that "it is the duty of every one to refrain from participating in or assisting in any functions organized officially or otherwise in connection with his visit." And with the immense possibilities ahead, the A.I.C.C. wisely decided in favour of patience on the question of Civil Disobedience. The Working Committee appointed Sjt. Bhawani Shankar Niyogi, a non-co-operator lawyer of Nagpur (now a Judge of the C. P. High Court), Abbas Tyabji, retired Judge of Baroda, and Setlur, sometimes Judge of Mysore, to enquire into the firing by the authorities on the crowd at Dharwar on the 1st July, 1921 and to make a full report thereon. Provincial Congress Circles being carved out under the Constitution on a linguistic basis, the question of bilingual districts naturally became a contentious one, and Bellary was one such as between Karnataka and Andhra. The matter was required to be adjusted by an Arbitration Board appointed in that behalf as also later in respect of Ganjam between Andhra and Utkal. Power was given in regard to applications for the Congress funds to a Committee consisting of Mahatma Gandhi, Motilalji, and Seth Jamnalal Bajaj. When the Working Committee met at Patna on the 16th August, the letter of request for permission to start Civil Disobedience of orders under Section 144 from the District of Hardoi in the U. P. was adjourned to the next meeting of the Committee. For an effective boycott of foreign cloth before the 30th September, the Working Committee pointed out the necessity to collect foreign cloth from every home and to set apart volunteers under proper control for the purpose. Not less than one-fourth of the whole of the collections made in the Province for the All-India Tilak Swaraj Fund was required to be set apart, to organize the spread of hand-spinning, the collection of hand-spun yarn and the weaving and distribution of khaddar. Some Provinces not having sent 25 per cent. of the T.S.F. to the Working Committee, the latter withheld grants to defaulting Provinces. The next meeting met shortly after in Calcutta on the 6th, 7th, 8th and 11th September. It was an important meeting. Reports on the firing at Dharwar and on the Moplah outbreak were before it. On the latter the following resolutions were passed:

> "25. The Working Committee places on record its sense of deep regret over the deeds of violence done by Moplahs in certain areas of Malabar, these deeds being evidence of the fact that there are still people in India who have not understood the message of the Congress and the Central Khilaphat Committee, and calls upon every Congress and Khilaphat worker to spread the said message of non-violence even under the gravest provocation throughout the length and breadth of India.
>
> "Whilst, however, condemning violence on the part of the Moplahs, the Working Committee desires it to be known that the evidence in its possession shows that provocation beyond endurance was given to the Moplahs and that the reports published by and on behalf of the Government have given a one-sided and highly exaggerated account of the wrongs done by the Moplahs and an understatement of the needless destruction of life resorted to by the Government in the name of peace and order.
>
> "The Working Committee regrets to find that there have been instances of so-called forcible conversion by some fanatics among the Moplahs, but warns the public against believing in the Government and inspired versions. The Report before the Committee says: 'The families which have been reported to have been forcibly converted into Mohamedanism lived in the neighbourhood of Manjeri. It is clear that conversions were forced upon Hindus by a fanatic gang which was always opposed to the Khilaphat and Non-co-operation movement and there were only three cases so far as our information goes.'

"It has been reported to the Working Committee that the disturbances took place only in areas in which Congress and Khilaphat activities were prohibited and that the Congress and the Khilaphat workers tried their best at considerable risk to themselves to check the mob-fury and prevent violence."

Events were moving fast. The All-India Khilaphat Conference of 1921 took place at Karachi on the 8th July at which Mahomed Ali, the President, made a daring speech which since then became known as the Karachi speech. The proceedings of the Conference formed later the subject matter of the prosecution of the Ali Brothers, Dr. Kitchlew, Jagatguru Shri Shankaracharya of Sarada Peeth, Maulana Nisar Ahmad, Pir Gulam Mujadid and Maulvi Hussain Ahmed. While reiterating the Muslim demands, the Conference also passed a resolution declaring it "unlawful for any faithful Muslim to serve from that day in the army or help or acquiesce in their recruitment." It also declared that if the British Government fought the Angora Government, the Muslims of India would start Civil Disobedience and establish their Complete Independence and hoist the flag of the Indian Republic at the Ahmedabad Session of the Indian National Congress.

Mahomed Ali's speech on the occasion was repeated on the 16th October, 1921 from thousands of platforms in India in accordance with instructions from the Congress high command as a challenge to Government who had ordered the prosecution referred to. The resolution occasioning the speech was one regarding Military service under Government, which "virtually reaffirmed the principle laid down by the Congress both in Calcutta and at Nagpur." The Working Committee of the Congress having met in Bombay on the 5th October made a statement in the course of which it said:—

> "That it is contrary to the National dignity and National interest for any Indian to engage or remain in the service of a Government in any capacity whatever, a Government that has used the soldiers and the Police for repressing the just aspirations of the people, as during the Rowlatt Act agitation, and that has utilized the soldiers for the purpose of crushing the National spirit of the Egyptians, the Turks, the Arabs, and other nations."

The Ali Brothers and their comrades were ordered to be prosecuted and the Working Committee, while congratulating them on the prosecution, declared that the reason given for the prosecutions constituted an undue interference with religious liberty, and added the following rider:—

> "The Working Committee has been only deterred from calling out the soldiers and the civilians in the name of the Congress, because the Congress is not yet ready to support those Government servants who may leave Government service and who may not be able themselves to find means of livelihood. The Working Committee is, however, of opinion that in pursuance of the spirit of the Congress Resolution on N.C.O., it is the clear duty of every Government employee, whether soldier or civilian, who can support himself without Congress assistance, to leave such service."

Carding, weaving and spinning were pointed to the soldiers and the Police as affording honourable means for an independent livelihood. The Congress Committees were asked to adopt the above resolution at meetings all over the country, and this was carried out on the 16th October. The boycott of foreign cloth was as yet incomplete and unless it was effected, the Working Committee said, general Civil Disobedience in any District or Province, would not be possible. Nor would it be permitted unless hand-spinning and hand-weaving were developed so as to produce sufficient khaddar for the wants of the area—whether District or Province. The Working Committee, however, authorised Civil Disobedience by individuals who might be prevented in the prosecution of the Swadeshi propaganda, provided it was done under the authority of the Provincial Congress Committee which was to be assured of a non-violent atmosphere being retained. The detailed programme for the boycott of the visit of the Prince of Wales was worked out, and on the day of his landing, it was laid down, there should be general voluntary *hartal* throughout India, and as to the effective boycott of any public welcome to H.R.H. during his visit to the different cities of India, the Working Committee left arrangements in the hands of the respective Provincial Congress Committees. An important announcement was then made to all foreign States that the Government of India in no way represented Indian opinion, that India, as a Self-Governing country, had nothing to fear from the neighbouring States or any State, as her people had no design upon any of them and hence no intention of establishing any trade relations, hostile to or not desired by, the people of such States. Further, the neighbouring States not ill-disposed towards India, were warned against entering into any treaty with the Imperial power, and the Muslim States were assured that when India attained Self-Government, her foreign policy would naturally be so guided as to respect the religious obligations imposed upon Muslims by Islam. These were the views of the Working Committee and they did not want them to go forth in the name of the A.I.C.C. until they were thoroughly discussed by the public and adopted at a meeting by the former.

At this time the Ali Brothers were taken under custody, Maulana Mahomed Ali being arrested in the course of his tour, at Waltair, on his way from Assam to

people of Chirala suffered much, and suffered long. They were in huts outside the municipal limits for over ten months. In the meantime, the leaders were arrested for one reason or another. A few who were not non-co-operators were cajoled and coaxed into submission, and after nearly a year's abandonment of hearths and homes, they returned to the village and submitted to the Municipality. Another mighty undertaking was the strike in Chittagong. Chittagong is a port in East Bengal and the labour strike, organised by Sen Gupta, cost the Congress over a lac of rupees. The difficulty in regard to such undertakings is that men in authority can wear out the energies of the strikers. The Congress cannot always remain behind these movements. Its resources of money are limited. Its man-power, however, is great but Government have a complete hold on the men that conduct the movements of the Congress. When the strong personalities of a place are once removed and put into prison under some law or other, the forces of disruption add themselves to the forces of corruption, and movements give way.

In passing, we must also state the circumstances which led to the origin of the Moplah trouble in Malabar. The Moplahs are Muslims who were originally the off-spring of Arab immigrants in Malabar that had settled in this beautiful land and contracted marital alliances locally. They are, generally speaking, petty traders and cultivating peasants. But under the stress of religious excitement, they display a certain degree of fanaticism and do not care for life or comfort. The periodical outbreaks of Moplah riots have led to special legislation known as the Moplah Outrages Act. Government were from the outset anxious that the 'inflammable' Moplahs should not be charged with the spark of Non-co-operation. Yet the movement spread into Kerala as to any other place. Only, Kerala received it with the added enthusiasm of a newly integrated Congress Province. In the month of February, distinguished leaders like C. Rajagopalachariar and Yakub Hassan visited the Province, with the avowed object of preaching the cult of non-violence. Yakub Hassan expressly stated that he would not speak about N.C.O. Nevertheless prohibitory orders were passed. And four leaders—Yakub Hassan, Madhavan Nair, Gopala Menon and Moideen Koya were arrested on the 16th February, 1921. This incident only gave an impetus to the cause of N.C.O. movement in Malabar. At Ottapalem, a small town, the Kerala Provincial Conference was organised and with it a number of allied conferences were held. When the main conferences had concluded, and while the students' conference was sitting, the Reserve Police laid hands on some leading Congressmen and Khilaphatists, as well as on bazaar men. But people exhibited complete non-violence in a wonderful manner. Thereafter the whole of Malabar was organised on the lines indicated by the Bezwada resolutions.

The Moplahs are chiefly concentrated in Walvanad and Ernad talukas and Government proclaimed them under Sec. 144. By the month of August, the complexion of affairs changed and the Moplahs, writhing under insults offered to their Thangals or religious priests in mosques, broke into violence. Soon hostilities developed on a military scale. The Moplahs had few fire-arms, but plenty of swords. They practised guerilla warfare to which the country round about admirably lends itself. By the middle of October, a severer form of Martial Law was introduced than in the earlier months. The Moplahs in their turn were guilty of acts of compulsory conversion, looting of Hindus, arson and murder, besides looting and destroying public offices. The lives of Englishmen were at stake. Mr. M. P. Narayana Menon, a Congressman who had done much to organise Congress Committees all over Malabar, used his influence with the Moplahs and saved the Englishmen. This very worker was later hauled up and at first made a State prisoner in November, 1921, but in 1922 was tried for treason and sentenced to transportation for life. He was released only in September, 1934 after serving his full term. He could have been released earlier if he had only given an oral undertaking that he would not enter Walvanad Taluk for three years, but he would not and, therefore, served his full term heroically and voluntarily. The further course of the Moplah rebellion or even its developments since August on violent lines do not concern us, except to the extent to which the A.I.C.C. had to protest against their excesses at its November meeting.

The Prince of Wales arrived in India on the 17th of November. The Prince was to have opened the new Assembly, but the atmosphere in India of August, 1920 led Government to replace him by the Duke. He was therefore sent in November, '21 to India, to keep up the prestige of the British Government. The Congress had already resolved upon the boycott of all celebrations connected with the Prince's visit, which was duly carried out together with bonfires of foreign cloth. The very day of his arrival in Bombay, there were not merely clashes and conflicts in Bombay but rioting and bloodshed which extended over three or four days, resulting in the death of 53 persons and the wounding of 400 approximately, and which could not be put down in spite of Sarojini Devi, Gandhi and other leaders entering into the thick of the crowds and exhorting them to disperse. Numerous people were injured in the melee and Gandhi fasted for 5 days pending the restoration of order, as a penance for the excesses of the people. It was then that

Gandhi made the statement that Swaraj stank in his nostrils. The arrival of the Prince caused the Volunteer Movement all over India to consolidate itself. Till then Congress volunteers were only a kind of social service workers, helping pilgrims at fairs and festivals, patients in epidemics and victims of local catastrophes, also providing the retinue at conferences and other national public functions. The Khilaphatist volunteers were however, more 'militant,' as Government would say, and "they drilled and marched in mass formation," and they "wore uniform." Both sets of volunteers organised *hartals* and boycott of foreign cloth. These two wings coalesced and became civil resisters, subject to the conditions laid down by the All-India Congress Committee (*vide supra*). Arrests took place by the thousand. The Prince was to visit Calcutta on the 25th December, and the Government of Bengal, unlike that of Bombay, proclaimed enrolment of volunteers illegal under the Criminal Law Amendment Act, and a large number of persons were arrested, including Mr. and Mrs. Das and their son. Soon after, the U. P. and the Punjab followed suit. By the Ahmedabad Congress, Lalaji, Pandit Motilal Nehru, Jawaharlal Nehru, C. R. Das and family, were all in jail under the Criminal Law Amendment Act, or under Secs. 144, and 108, I.P.C. These sections were discovered and their application to politicals was advised, it seems, by Sir Tej Bahadur Sapru who became the Law Member of the Viceroy's Executive Council in August, 1920. While Bombay had acted under the ordinary Law, Bengal, the U. P. and the Punjab invoked the Repressive Laws.

It was at this juncture that negotiations were opened between Congress and Government. The Viceroy, under the arrangements made in shifting the metropolis from Calcutta to Delhi, resides in Calcutta for three or four weeks every year during the Christmas season and the Prince of Wales was to spend his Christmas in Calcutta. Lord Reading's presence in Calcutta under the circumstances was taken advantage of by intermediaries like Pandit Madan Mohan Malaviya to bring about an understanding between Government and the people, and Lord Reading was willing—if only to avoid the boycott of the celebrations on the 25th December in Calcutta. A deputation headed by the Pandit waited on the Viceroy on the 21st December. Mr. Das was in the Alipore jail in the city of Calcutta and telephonic communications took place between him and the intermediaries. Soon Gandhi had to be consulted. He was in Ahmedabad and by telegraphic communications it was agreed to by Government that the Civil Disobedience prisoners should be released and a Round Table Conference was to be held in March with 22 representatives for the Congress to consider the Reform Scheme.

Das's demand was for the release of all prisoners under the new law (Criminal Law Amendment Act). This would have left men like Lalaji in jail, besides the Karachi and the *Fatwa* prisoners who included, Maulana Mahomed Ali and Shaukat Ali, Dr. Kitchlew and various others. The Karachi prisoners were those who were convicted on November 1, 1921, for having participated in the All-India Khilaphat Conference held at Karachi in July, 1921, where the resolution regarding Military service had been passed. Some Ulemahs endorsed this resolution in a *Fatwa*—which is a decree issued by the learned Divines amongst the Muslims prescribing or proscribing certain acts under certain conditions. (For full details relating to the peace negotiations of December, 1921, the reader is referred to "Seven months with Mahatma Gandhi" by Krishnadas,—a book well worth-reading).

But Gandhi demanded the release of the Karachi prisoners which was also partly agreed to. His demand for the release of the *Fatwa* prisoners and for the continuance of the right of picketing was refused. Before Gandhi's telegraphic reply on this position could reach Lord Reading in Calcutta,—and unfortunately this message was delayed in transit,—his colleagues had left Calcutta (on the 23rd December) and the negotiations failed. Mr. Jinnah and Pandit Madan Mohan Malaviya were the intermediaries. Negotiations having failed, the boycott programme of the Prince's visit was observed by the rest of India. In Calcutta the *hartal* was complete, even the butchers' shops being closed, and this exasperated the Europeans. The civil resisters continued to be in jail till they were released in the usual course. The last week of December, 1921 finds us in the midst of the Ahmedabad Session of the Congress at which the Non-co-operation programme reached its acme. The political situation had not changed at all since the Nagpur Session. The inauguration of the Montford Reforms by the Duke of Connaught was made the occasion for a Royal message in the course of which it was said:—

> "For years, it may be for generations, patriotic and loyal Indians have dreamed of Swaraj for their Motherland; to-day you have the beginnings of Swaraj within my Empire and the best scope and ample opportunity for progress to the liberty which my other Dominions enjoy."

Neither this half-hearted reference to the term 'Swaraj' nor the Duke's appeal to bury the dead past and to forgive, nor the debates in the Assembly relating to the Punjab tragedy in which Sir William Vincent made plain the deep regret of the administration at the excesses of certain individual officers, and their firm determination to make any repetition impossible, assuaged the public feeling or restored confidence in the mind of the Nation. The N.C.O. programme had, therefore, been published and at the Ahmedabad Session its details were perfected. The President-Elect, Mr. C. R. Das,—Deshbandhu Das, as he came to be known by this time,—was in jail and Hakim Ajmal Khan was elected in his place.

The atmosphere was tense. "Swaraj inside a year" was the thought uppermost in every man's mind. Gandhi had promised Swaraj inside a year, if his programme was adhered to and carried out. The year was about to close and everybody was looking up to the political firmament to see some miracle bringing Swaraj down to his feet. But every one was prepared to do his best, to suffer his worst in order to "hasten the advent of that (no longer) far-off divine event." No sacrifice would be too much for popular endurance. Every one was anxious to have a programme of mass Civil Disobedience. Over twenty thousand individual civil resisters were already in jail. Their numbers were soon to swell to 30,000. But mass disobedience was the thing that was luring the people. What was it, what would it be? Gandhi himself never defined it, never elaborated it, never visualized it even to himself. It must unfold itself to a discerning vision, to a pure heart, from step to step, much as the path-way in a dense forest would reveal itself to the wayfarer's feet as he wends his weary way until a ray of light brightens the hopes of an all but despairing wanderer. Mass disobedience was to be undertaken by competent men in a suitable area with strict regard to conditions laid down in that behalf without haste and without rest. So Gandhi wanted to organise a No-tax campaign in Gujarat, but friends in Guntur had already been preparing the District for a No-tax campaign with equal warmth, enthusiasm and preparedness for sacrifice and suffering. The state of the country at the time as well as the duty of the Congress were aptly described in the opening paragraph of the main resolution of the Ahmedabad Session.

Fear had been cast off by the people. A sense of self-respect developed in the Nation. Congressmen realized that service and self-sacrifice were the only means of winning public confidence. The prestige too of Government was materially shaken, and people had received good lessons regarding the ideology of Swaraj.

The Ahmedabad Session is noteworthy for more than one reform. Apart from the elimination of the chairs and benches for delegates which had cost the Nagpur Session some seventy thousand rupees, the Congress had the shortest address from Vallabhbhai J. Patel, the Chairman of the Reception Committee, as also the smallest number of resolutions—altogether nine. Hindi was the language of the Congress mainly and khaddar worth over two lakhs was used for the tents pitched for the Congress.

Gandhi had asked the Rev. C. F. Andrews to be present at the Ahmedabad Session in order to give a religious message. He consented to do so but explained first of all to Gandhi that he was opposed to the burning of foreign cloth, because he feared that it would inculcate violence. Contrary to his usual custom, he appeared in European dress in order to make clear his opposition to the policy of burning. In his address he explained why he was not wearing khaddar on that occasion. It is noteworthy that he was received with the utmost respect and affection by the audience, though they could not be expected to agree with his opinion on the point at issue. Mr. Andrews announced at the end of his speech that he was leaving

Ahmedabad that night at the request of Gandhi, to the Moplah area as a peace-maker.

Let us now briefly review the events that engaged the attention of the Congress. Hakimji was elected in the absence of Deshbandhu Das for he was the embodiment of Hindu-Muslim unity. As a matter of fact, at a conference of the Hindu Mahasabha held in Delhi he was elected its President. He had all the suavity, polish and courtesies of a Padsha, his culture was of a high order and his character was its twin-sister, which made up the excellence of his equipment in the moral no less than the intellectual and social spheres of life. He made a simple but striking speech at Ahmedabad as the *locum tenens* of the Deshbandhu. Deshbandhu's own speech was read by Sarojini Devi with all the eloquence which the speech itself possessed in language and sentiment. As was to be expected Deshbandhu Das gave a correct and comprehensive review of Indian Nationalism that is primarily rooted in culture and for the recovery of which he said, "first we must have a house of our own before we can receive a guest, and secondly Indian culture must discover itself before it can be ready to assimilate Western culture." Then he examined the Government of India Act and asked in despair, "Now, is there anything in the Preamble to compel the British Parliament to recognize India, at any time, as a free and equal partner of the British Empire?" "I think not," was his brief reply. He was "quite willing to co-operate with England but on one condition only, that she recognized this inherent right of India"—freedom. "I cannot recommend to you the acceptance of the Act as a basis for co-operation with the Government. I will not purchase peace with dishonour, and so long as the Preamble to the Act stands, and our right, our inherent right to regulate our own affairs, develop our own individuality, and evolve our own destiny is not recognized, I must decline to consider any terms of peace." After this declaration he examined the oft-repeated statement of Lord Reading that he was 'perplexed and puzzled' by the policy of the Non-co-operators and answered it by saying that Lord Reading's claim that the resistance to N.C.O. was not repression, as all the proceedings were being taken under the ordinary Law which the Sapru Committee considered and whose repeal it declined to recommend.

The noble and dignified address of the Deshbandhu provided the proper perspective for the magnificent resolutions of the Ahmedabad Session. The main resolution was really a thesis on Non-co-operation, its philosophy and programme alike, so much so that Gandhi pointed out in moving it that it had taken him, 35 minutes minutely to read it in English and Hindustani and added that the resolution explained itself. This resolution, he said, "was absolutely the natural result of the National activities during the past fifteen months." The resolution did not bar, bolt and bang the door of negotiation, but kept it quite wide open if the Viceroy meant well, "but the doors closed in his face if he means ill, no matter how many people go to their graves, no matter what wild career this repression is to go through. There is every chance for him to hold a Round Table Conference, but it must be a real conference. If he wants a conference where only equals are to sit and where there is not to be a single beggar, then there is open door and that door will always remain open. There is nothing in this resolution which any one who has modesty and humility need be ashamed of." "This resolution," he added, "is not an arrogant challenge to anybody but it is a challenge to the authority that is enthroned on arrogance. It is a humble and an irrevocable challenge to authority which, in order to save itself, wants to crush freedom of opinion and freedom of association,—the two lungs that are absolutely necessary for a man to breathe the oxygen of liberty." We give below the main Resolution on N.C.O. and the duty of the country:—

Main Resolution

"Whereas, since the holding of the last National Congress, the people of India have found from actual experience that by reason of the adoption of non-violent Non-co-operation the country has made great advance in fearlessness, self-sacrifice and self-respect, and whereas the movement has greatly damaged the prestige of the Government, and whereas on the whole the country is rapidly progressing towards Swaraj, this Congress confirms the resolution adopted at the Special Session of the Congress at Calcutta and re-affirmed at Nagpur, and places on record the fixed determination of the Congress to continue the programme of non-violent Non-co-operation with greater vigour than hitherto in such manner as each Province may determine, till the Punjab and the Khilaphat wrongs are redressed and Swarajya is established and the control of the Government of India passes into the hands of the people from that of an irresponsible corporation.

"And whereas by reason of the threat uttered by His Excellency the Viceroy in his recent speeches, and the consequent repression started by the Government of India in the various Provinces by way of disbandment of Volunteer Corps and forcible prohibition of public and even Committee meetings in an illegal and high-handed manner, and by the arrest of many Congress workers in several Provinces, repression is manifestly intended to stifle all Congress and Khilaphat activities and deprive the public of their assistance, this Congress resolves that all activities of the Congress be suspended as far as necessary, and appeals to all, quietly and without any demonstration, to offer themselves for arrest by belonging to the Volunteer Organisations to be formed throughout the country in terms of the Resolution of the Working Committee arrived at in Bombay on the 23rd day of November last, provided that no one shall be accepted as volunteer who does not sign the following pledge:

With God as witness I solemnly declare that.

(1) I wish to be a member of the National Volunteer Corps.

(2) So long as I remain a member of the Corps, I shall remain non-violent in word and deed and shall earnestly endeavour to be non-violent in intent since I believe that, as India is circumstanced, non-violence alone can help the Khilaphat and the Punjab and result in the attainment of Swaraj and consolidation of unity among all the races and communities of India whether Hindu, Muslim, Sikh, Parsee, Christian or Jew.

(3) I believe in, and shall endeavour always to promote, such unity.

(4) I believe in Swadeshi as essential for India's economic, political and moral salvation, and shall use hand-spun and hand-woven khaddar to the exclusion of every other cloth.

(5) As a Hindu I believe in the justice and necessity of removing the evil of untouchability and shall on all possible occasions seek personal contact with, and endeavour to render service to, the submerged classes.

(6) I shall carry out the instructions of my superior officers and all the regulations not inconsistent with the spirit of this pledge prescribed by the Volunteer Board or the Working Committee or any other agency established by the Congress.

(7) I am prepared to suffer imprisonment, assault, or even death for the sake of my religion and my country without resentment.

(8) In the event of my imprisonment, I shall not claim from the Congress any support for my family or dependants.

"This Congress trusts that every person of the age of 18 and over will immediately join the Volunteer Organisations.

"Notwithstanding the proclamation prohibiting public meetings, and inasmuch as even Committee meetings have been attempted to be construed as public meetings, this Congress advises the holding of Committee meetings and of public meetings, the latter in enclosed places and by tickets and by previous announcements at which, as far as possible, only speakers previously announced shall deliver written speeches, care being taken in every case to avoid risk of provocation and possible violence by the public in consequence.

"This Congress is further of opinion that Civil Disobedience is the only civilised and effective substitute for an armed rebellion whenever every other remedy for preventing arbitrary, tyrannical and emasculating use of authority by individuals or corporations has been tried, and therefore advises all Congress workers and others who believe in peaceful methods and are convinced that there is no remedy, save some kind of sacrifice, to dislodge the existing Government from its position of perfect irresponsibility to the people of India, to organise individual Civil Disobedience and mass Civil Disobedience when the mass of people have been sufficiently trained in the methods of non-violence and otherwise in terms of the resolution thereon of the last meeting of the All-India Congress Committee held at Delhi.

"This Congress is of opinion that, in order to concentrate attention upon Civil Disobedience, whether mass or individual, whether of an offensive or defensive character, under proper safeguards and under instructions to be issued from time to time by the Working Committee or the Provincial Congress Committee concerned, all other Congress activities should be suspended whenever and wherever, and to the extent to which, it may be found necessary.

"This Congress calls upon all students of the age of 18 and over, particularly those studying in the National institutions and the staff thereof, immediately to sign the foregoing pledge and become members of National Volunteer Corps.

"In view of the impending arrest of a large number of Congress workers, this Congress whilst requiring the ordinary machinery to remain intact and to be utilised in the ordinary manner whenever feasible, hereby appoints, until further instructions, Mahatma Gandhi as the sole Executive authority of the Congress and invests him with the full powers of the All-India Congress Committee, including the power to convene a Special Session of the Congress or of the All-India Congress Committee or the Working Committee, such powers to be exercised between any two sessions of the All-India Congress Committee, and also with the power to appoint a successor in emergency.

"This Congress hereby confers upon the said successor, and all subsequent successors appointed in turn by their predecessors, all his aforesaid powers.

"Provided that nothing in this resolution shall be deemed to authorise Mahatma Gandhi or any of the aforesaid successors to conclude any terms of peace with the Government of India or the British Government without the previous sanction of the All-India Congress Committee to be finally ratified by the Congress specially convened for the purpose, and provided also that the present Creed of the Congress shall in no case be altered by Mahatma Gandhi or his successors except with the leave of the Congress first obtained.

"The Congress congratulates all those patriots who are now undergoing imprisonment for the sake of their conscience or country, and realises that their sacrifice has considerably hastened the advent of Swaraj."

RESOLUTION 2

"This Congress appeals to all those who do not believe in full Non-co-operation or in the principle of Non-co-operation, but who consider it essential for the sake of national self-respect, to demand and insist upon the redress of the Khilaphat and the Punjab wrongs, and, for the sake of full national self-expression, to insist upon the immediate establishment of Swaraj, to render full assistance to the Nation in the promotion of unity between different religious communities, to popularise carding, hand-spinning and hand-weaving from its economical aspect and as a cottage industry necessary in order to supplement the resources of millions of agriculturists who are living on the brink of starvation, and to that end preach and practise the use of hand-spun and hand-woven garments, to help the cause of total prohibition and, if Hindus, to bring about removal of untouchability and to help the improvement of the condition of the submerged classes."

We must now refer to a debate initiated by Maulana Hasrat Mohani, who proposed to define 'Swaraj' in the creed as "Complete Independence, free from all foreign control." At this distance of time, one is apt to look upon it as the most natural sequence of all that had happened, and may even wonder why it should have been resisted at all by the Congress or by Gandhi. But, at the time, Gandhi was obliged to speak out frankly:—

> "The levity with which the proposition has been taken by some of you has grieved me. It has grieved me because it shows lack of responsibility. As responsible men and women, we should go back to the days of Nagpur and Calcutta."

The language employed by Gandhi may strike us now, as we read it, as strong, but strong it was meant to be. Was it also too strong?, is the question. Gandhi had evolved a new movement, shaped a new Creed and planned a new attack. It was a perfect campaign in which the objective and the strategy were all clearly defined. The troops were in the midst of skirmishes and engagements. A huge battle was about to take place. Just then for a soldier to come up to the General and the army and say that the objective should be re-defined was to disturb the forces arranged for battle. There was no doubt that the time chosen was utterly inopportune and the spirit displayed unhelpful. No wonder, then, if the General was distressed or even became indignant. But some of the arguments employed by Gandhi on this occasion sound very much, it was pointed out at the time, *mutatis mutandis* like the arguments of the opponents of the existing Creed at the time of its evolution at Nagpur. "We shall be charged by the thinking portion of the world that we do not know really what we are. Let us understand too our limitations. Let Hindus and Muslims have absolute, indissoluble unity. Who is here who can say to-day with confidence: 'Yes, Hindu-Muslim unity has become an indissoluble factor of Indian Nationalism.' Who is here who can tell me that the Parsees and the Sikhs, and the Christians and the Jews and the untouchables about whom you heard this afternoon, who will tell me that those very people will not rise against any such idea?" The argument however that appealed was, "Let us first of all gather up our strength, let us first of all sound our own depths. Let us not go into waters whose depths we do not know, and this proposition of Mr. Hasrat Mohani leads you into depths unfathomable." This argument was clinching. A general cannot take an army into depths unfathomable to himself. And the proposition was thrown out, and to anticipate events, was pressed year after year until it was accepted as a resolution of the Congress in 1927 in Madras and was embodied in the Creed itself in 1929 at Lahore.

Of the other resolutions, one related to the Constitution and two to the appointment of office-bearers. Of the remaining, one relates to the Moplah disturbance and declares that the N.C.O. or the Khilaphat movement had nothing to do with it, that preachers of non-violence were denied opportunity of carrying the gospel for six months prior to the outbreak, and that, in any case, the movement would not have been prolonged if leading Non-co-operators like Yakub Hassan and Mahatma Gandhi himself had been permitted to visit the area. Horror and indignation were expressed at the inhumanity of confining nearly a hundred Moplah prisoners in a goods waggon on their transfer to Bellary, which ended in the death by suffocation of seventy of them on the night of November 19th, 1921. The Congress deplored the occurrences in Bombay on the 17th November and assured all parties and all communities that it was the desire and determination of the Congress to guard their rights to the fullest extent. Congratulations were then offered to Kemal Pasha on his victory over the Greeks which led to the revision of the Treaty of Sevres, and to Baba Gurudutt Singh of the *Komagatamaru* who, after being a fugitive for seven years, had delivered himself to the Police voluntarily, and to the Sikhs who remained non-violent on this occasion, as well as on other occasions, despite the great provocation by the Police and the Military.

One notable feature of the Ahmedabad Session was the prominent part played by the Muslim Divines in advising the Congress on the political matters that came up before it. Regarding the conditions of Individual and Mass Civil Disobedience, there was considerable discussion over the question of non-violence,—whether it should be in thought, word and deed. It will be remembered that the Calcutta resolution included 'word and deed' only. The Muslims objected to the addition of the word 'thought' in the volunteers' pledge as opposed to the *Shariat* and therefore '*intent*' was substituted for the word 'thought'. In all these matters, the Ulemah played a notable part in interpreting political ideas in the light of *Al Quoran*, the *Shariat* and the *Hadis*. We shall see later on that their aid was invoked on matters of Council-entry as well, and conduct of affairs thereafter. Finally, attention has to be invited to the penultimate paragraph in which Gandhi was appointed as the sole Executive authority of the Congress with power to appoint a successor, in case the ordinary machinery broke down. Only two limitations were placed in respect of powers so conferred on him, namely, that neither he nor his successors could conclude peace or alter the Creed. That could be done only with the leave of the Congress.

A new departure took place at the Ahmedabad Session which deserves to be noted. The delegates were not willing to disperse soon after the conclusion of the sittings. Gandhi walked up to each camp and explained the technique of Civil Disobedience. In the Andhra camp, he took pains to point out how, in any area where a No-tax campaign was contemplated, volunteers must go about the villages and take the signatures of the ryots agreeing to the campaign. This was of course to be done in addition to the enforcement of the conditions of mass and individual Civil Disobedience.

CHAPTER III

GANDHI BOUND (1922)

Hardly had the year 1921 closed when well-meaning friends of the Congress, who had not, however, accepted its new programme, were anxious to bring about an understanding between the Congress and Government. On the 14th, 15th and 16th of January, before the ink of the Ahmedabad resolutions was dry, an All-Parties' Conference was convened in Bombay which was attended by about 300 persons belonging to all parties.

At the Representative Conference, the convenors planned a draft resolution embodying the terms on which a truce could be asked for. Gandhi, explaining the position of the Non-co-operators, said that while it would not be possible for him formally and officially to join the Conference, he would assist the Conference informally. The reason for not participating formally was, as given by him, that the Government were still carrying on their repressive policy and any Round Table Conference would be futile unless there was repentance on their part. The Conference appointed a Subjects Committee of twenty which Gandhi alone joined from amongst the Non-co-operators. The draft prepared by the Subjects Committee was placed before the Conference on the following day and Gandhi again explained the position of the Non-co-operators. Sir Sankaran Nair who had been acting as Chairman disapproved of the draft resolution and retired from the Conference, which proceeded under the Chairmanship of Sir M. Visvesvarayya and passed a resolution unanimously condemning the repressive policy of the Government, suggesting that, pending negotiations, the Civil Disobedience contemplated by the Ahmedabad resolution should not be proceeded with, supporting an early convening of a Round Table Conference with authority to make a settlement on the questions of Khilaphat, the Punjab and Swaraj, and with a view to provide a favourable atmosphere, asking for withdrawal of notifications under the Criminal Law Amendment Act banning organisations, and the Seditious Meetings Act, and release of all prisoners convicted or under trial under them as also of the *Fatwa* prisoners. It further asked for a Committee to investigate the cases of persons convicted in connection with the movement under ordinary Law. After the Conference, Sir Sankaran Nair issued a statement to the Press containing some misstatements bitterly attacking Gandhi, to which Messrs. Jinnah, Jayakar and Natarajan, as Secretaries, and others had to issue contradictions.

The resolutions of the Representative Conference applicable to the Non-co-operators were virtually confirmed by the Working Committee at its meeting held on the 17th January, which postponed the starting of Civil Disobedience till the end of the month. A perusal of the correspondence reveals that Lord Reading received the communications from the Conference with apathy and nothing resulted from it. This, if nothing else, made it clear that the approaches for a settlement made in Calcutta by Government,—and even the sweet words that Lord Reading had employed in Calcutta when he said that neither side should claim victory for itself,—were not as sincere as the intermediaries imagined. Government were anxious to see that the sojourn of the Prince was not disturbed by the hostile demonstrations of Non-co-operators. The attempts of well-meaning intermediaries failed. The Viceroy summarily rejected the terms offered by the Conference. It was after this that Gandhi sent to the Viceroy, on

1-2-'22 a letter intimating his intention to start Civil Disobedience in Bardoli. The Congress did not regret the result, as the Congress fully shared Gandhi's belief that Government had not done its worst and the country had not shown its best in the new line of suffering and civil resistance, and it was premature to enter into a settlement.

While these negotiations were thus progressing, the country's attention was really rivetted on the campaign of No-tax, which Gandhi had decided to organize in the Bardoli Taluka in Gujarat. He was anxious to make the first experiment in mass Civil Disobedience under his own direct supervision. In that Taluka there were many South-Africa returned emigrants who were familiar with the ways of Gandhi, and it was Gandhi's earnest wish that the rest of India should watch his experiment and infuse strength and spirit into him. He was anxious that nothing should be done to distract or disturb his attention or endeavours. The same position was incorporated in a resolution of the Working Committee dated 31st January, 1922. Soon after the Ahmedabad Session, however, the Andhra P.C.C. met on the 7th January at Bezwada and decided to give power to District Congress Committees to explore their respective areas with a view to carrying on a No-tax campaign. Four Districts sought and obtained permission in this behalf. Krishna, Godavari, Guntur and Cuddapah were the Districts concerned. The Executive Committee of the A.P.C.C. had passed a resolution a fortnight before the Congress, on 15-12-'21, at Guntur calling upon the Andhradesa to withhold the payment of taxes. This step was taken in advance of the Congress decision, but in anticipation of it. While the other Districts began to investigate local conditions and take signatures of ryots as desired by Gandhi in his camp-talks after the Congress session at

Ahmedabad, Guntur alone declared a No-tax campaign outright on the 12th January, 1922. Gandhi having acquainted himself with the facts of the case by personal talks with two representatives from Andhra, in Bombay during the sittings of the All-Parties' Conference, sent a letter on the 17th January to the President, A.P.C.C., and a note to the Press saying that he would be glad to hear that all taxes were paid by the 25th. The Press note was not published for some reason or other. The letter gave rise to correspondence between Gandhi and friends in Guntur. The news of Gandhi's attitude, when broken to the other Districts, led to the taxes being paid up as desired. But in Guntur the campaign was continued. In answer to pressing requests for permission, Gandhi telegraphed as follows:—

> "If the Delhi conditions of mass Civil Disobedience are satisfied, and if you think Guntur has reasonable chances of success, then all that I can say is I do not wish to stand in your way. God help you."

This was interpreted into assent incorrectly. But a Committee was appointed to tour the District and investigate how far the Delhi conditions were fulfilled and to report on the advisability of continuing the campaign. The campaign took the form of withholding the payment of Revenue taxes in the plains, and of grazing fees in the forest areas. In one of those areas a Sub-Inspector who went to a village to impound certain cattle, and in impounding separated the calf from the dame, met with some protests and shot down a leading villager. The Military quartered themselves in Guntur (town) and the Governor's cavalry (bodyguard) visited villages where the men were gathered outside the village and taxes were attempted to be collected, though in vain, under threat of distraint and arrest. The state of affairs under such conditions could more easily be imagined than described.

By this time the Working Committee meeting on the 31st January, 1922 had received and considered the resolution of the Bardoli Taluka Conference regarding mass Civil Disobedience, and congratulated the people of the Taluka on their self-sacrificing resolve to offer mass Civil Disobedience. The Working Committee advised all other parts of India to co-operate with the people of Bardoli Taluka by refraining from mass or individual Civil Disobedience of an aggressive character, except upon the express consent of Mahatma Gandhi previously obtained. The Working Committee further advised the people throughout the Provinces to pay up the taxes due by them to the Government whether directly, or indirectly through Zamindars or Talukdars,—except in such cases of direct payment to the Government where previous consent had been obtained from Mahatma Gandhi for suspension of payment preparatory to mass Civil Disobedience.

Let us for a moment travel to Gujarat and other Provinces. Gandhi had made up his mind to run his No-tax campaign in Gujarat,—the campaign which, after the All-Parties' Conference of Bombay, he had postponed to 31st January. Accordingly, he sent to the Viceroy a letter on the 1st February, which roused adverse criticism from Mr. Jinnah and others. Gandhi explained in his letter how the campaign should have taken place even earlier, but for the unfortunate and regrettable riots in Bombay on the 17th November, 1921, resulting in the postponement of the step contemplated by Bardoli. He referred to the looting of property, assaults on innocent people, brutal treatment of the prisoners in jails, including flogging. He admitted intimidation. He pointed out that his task was to rescue from paralysis freedom of speech, of association and of Press. "The Working Committee of the Congress has restricted mass disobedience only to certain areas to be selected by me from time to time, and at present it is confined to Bardoli. I may, under the said authority, give my consent at once in respect of a group of 100 villages in Guntur in the Madras Presidency, provided they can strictly conform to the conditions of non-violence, unity amongst different classes, the adoption and manufacture of hand-spun khaddar and untouchability." Gandhi gave seven days' time to Lord Reading within which to release the prisoners and free the Press from administrative control. Gandhi's letter to the Viceroy is given below:—

Bardoli, 1st February, 1922.

To

His Excellency
The Viceroy,
Delhi.

Sir,

Bardoli is a small Tehsil in the Surat District in the Bombay Presidency, having a population of about 87,000 all told.

On the 29th ultimo, it decided under the Presidency of Mr. Vittalbhai J. Patel to embark on mass Civil Disobedience, having proved its fitness for it in terms of the resolution of the All-India Congress Committee which met at Delhi during the first week of November last, but as I am perhaps chiefly responsible for Bardoli's decision, I owe it to Your Excellency and the public to explain the situation under which the decision has been taken.

It was intended under the resolution of the All-India Congress Committee, before referred to, to make Bardoli the first unit for mass Civil Disobedience, in order to make the national revolt against the Government's consistently criminal refusal to appreciate India's resolve regarding the Khilaphat, the Punjab and Swaraj.

Then followed the unfortunate and regrettable riots on the 17th November last in Bombay, resulting in the postponement of the step contemplated by Bardoli.

Meantime repression of a violent type has taken place, with the concurrence of the Government of India, in Bengal, Assam, the United Provinces, the Punjab, the Province of Delhi and in a way in Bihar and Orissa and elsewhere. I know that you have objected to the use of the word 'repression,' for describing the action of the authorities in these Provinces. In my opinion, when an action is taken which is in excess of the requirements of the situation, it is undoubtedly repression. The looting of property, assaults on innocent people, brutal treatment of the prisoners in jails, including flogging, can in no sense be described as legal, civilised or in any way necessary. This official lawlessness cannot be described by any other terms but lawless repression.

Intimidation by Non-co-operators or their sympathisers, to a certain extent, in connection with *Hartals* and picketing may be admitted, but in no case can it be held to justify the wholesale suppression of peaceful volunteering or equally peaceful public meetings, under a distorted use of an extraordinary law, which was passed in order to deal with activities which were manifestly violent both in intention and action, nor is it possible to designate as otherwise than repression, action taken against innocent people under what has appeared to many of us as an illegal use of the ordinary law, nor again can the administrative interference with the liberty of the Press under a Law that is under promise of repeal be regarded as anything but repression.

The immediate task before the country, therefore, is to rescue from paralysis freedom of speech, freedom of association, and freedom of Press.

In the present mood of the Government of India, and in the present unprepared state of the country in respect of complete control of the sources of violence,

Non-co-operators were unwilling to have anything to do with the Malaviya Conference whose object was to induce Your Excellency to convene an R. T. C. But as I was anxious to avoid all avoidable suffering, I had no hesitation in advising the Working Committee of the Congress to accept the recommendations of that conference.

Although, in my opinion, the terms were quite in keeping with your own requirements, as I understood them through your Calcutta speech and otherwise, you have summarily rejected the proposal.

In the circumstances, there is nothing before the country but to adopt some non-violent method for the enforcement of its demands including the elementary rights of free speech, free association and free Press. In my humble opinion, the recent events are a clear departure from the civilised policy laid down by Your Excellency at the time of the generous, manly and unconditional apology of the Ali Brothers, *viz.*, that the Government of India should not interfere with the activities of the Non-co-operators so long as they remain non-violent in word and deed. Had the Government policy remained neutral and allowed public opinion to ripen and have its full effect, it would have been possible to advise postponement of the adoption of Civil Disobedience of an aggressive type till the Congress had acquired fuller control over the forces of violence in the country and enforced greater discipline among the millions of its adherents. But the lawless repression (in a way unparalleled in the history of this unfortunate country) has made immediate adoption of mass Civil Disobedience an imperative duty. The Working Committee of the Congress has restricted it only to certain areas to be selected by me from time to time, and at present it is confined only to Bardoli. I may, under said authority, give my consent at once in respect of a group of 100 villages in Guntur in the Madras Presidency, provided they can strictly conform to the conditions of non-violence, unity among different classes, the adoption and manufacture of hand-spun khaddar and untouchability.

But before the people of Bardoli actually commence mass Civil Disobedience, I would respectfully urge you as the head of the Government of India finally to revise your policy and set free all the Non-co-operating prisoners who are convicted or under trial for non-violent activities, and declare in clear terms the policy of absolute non-interference with all non-violent activities in the country, whether they be regarding the redress of the Khilaphat or the Punjab wrongs or Swaraj or any other purpose, and even though they fall within the repressive sections of the Penal Code or the Criminal Procedure Code or other repressive laws, subject always to the condition of non-violence. I would further urge you to free the Press from all administrative control and restore all the fines and forfeitures recently imposed. In thus urging, I am asking Your Excellency to do what is to-day being done in every country which is deemed to be under civilized government. If you can see your way to make the necessary declaration within seven days of the date of publication of this Manifesto, I shall be prepared to advise postponement of Civil Disobedience of an aggressive character till the imprisoned workers have, after their discharge, reviewed the whole situation and considered it *de novo*. If the Government make the requested declaration, I shall regard it as an honest desire on its part to give effect to public opinion and shall, therefore, have no hesitation in advising the country to be engaged in further moulding public opinion without violent restraint from either side, and trust to its working to secure the fulfilment of its unalterable demands. Aggressive Civil Disobedience in that case will be taken up only when the Government departs from its policy of strictest neutrality or refuses to yield to the clearly expressed opinion of the vast majority of the people of India.

I remain,
Your Excellency's
Faithful servant and friend,
(Sd.) M. K. Gandhi

The Government of India promptly published a reply to Gandhi's Manifesto justifying their repressive policy as being only the result of the Bombay riots and the dangerous manifestations of lawlessness in many other places, as well as a systematic campaign of violence, intimidation and obstruction by volunteer associations. The reply further pointed out that Government's policy was not at variance with that laid down by His Excellency at the time of the apology of the Ali Brothers, for, there it was made plain that Government would "enforce the Law relating to offences against the State, as and when they may think fit." Nor did the Government of India summarily reject the proposal of a conference, stated the reply, for, the fundamental condition of the discontinuance of the unlawful activities of the N. C. O. party was not amongst the proposals of the All-Parties' Conference. Only *Hartals,* picketing and Civil Disobedience would cease and other illegal activities, it was claimed, would continue. Those referred to apparently were the enrolment of volunteers in prohibited associations and the preparations for Civil Disobedience as stated by Gandhi. Moreover "Mr. Gandhi also made it apparent that the proposed Round Table Conference would be called merely to register his decrees." His demands comprised (1) the release of all prisoners 'convicted' or under-trial for non-violent activities, and (2) a guarantee that the Government refrain from interference with all non-violent activities of the Non-co-operation party even though they fell within the purview of the I. P. C.

There was, however, a fatality hanging over the Congress. On the 5th February, when a Congress procession was taking place at Chauri Chaura, near Gorakhpur, U.P., 21 constables and a Sub-Inspector were rushed by the mob into a Police Station, and the station and the men in it were set fire to. They all perished in the flames. Moreover, the scenes of Bombay on the 17th November, in which 53 persons died and 400 were wounded, had repeated themselves on the 13th January in Madras during the Prince's visit to the city, though on a miniature scale, and these two events were made the reason for suspending mass Civil Disobedience at a meeting of the Working Committee which met at Bardoli on the 12th February, 1922. Congressmen were asked to stop all activities designed to court arrest and imprisonment, all volunteer processions and public meetings merely for the purpose of defiance of notifications. Then a constructive programme was drawn up which included the enlisting of a crore of members, the popularising of the *charka*, organising of National schools, temperance and Panchayats. Just then, the Committee that had been appointed to tour the Guntur District and report on the conditions had published its recommendation to the people to pay up the taxes, and they were duly paid by the 10th February. It must be owned that the non-payment campaign in the Andhradesa was a thorough success, so far as the campaign went, for not even five per cent. of the taxes were collected so long as the Congress ban was operative.

The Bardoli resolutions gave rise to a variety of feelings in the country. There were many who placed implicit trust in Gandhi and his decision. There were also a few who would not lose an opportunity of questioning them. When the All-India Congress Committee met in Delhi on the 24th and 25th February, it virtually endorsed the Bardoli resolutions of the Working Committee, except that it permitted individual Civil Disobedience in respect of particular places of particular laws under the authority of the P.C.C.'s and in strict conformity to the conditions laid down in that behalf by the Congress. The picketing of foreign cloth was expressly permitted on the same terms as liquor picketing mentioned in the Bardoli resolutions. The A.I.C.C. reiterated its faith in Civil Disobedience and considered that an atmosphere of necessary non-violence could be established by the workers concentrating upon the constructive programme.

The A.I.C.C. proceeded to define Individual Civil Disobedience (I.C.D.) as "disobedience of orders or laws by a single individual or group of individuals." "Therefore, a prohibited public meeting where admission is regulated by tickets and to which no unauthorised admission is allowed is an instance of Individual Civil Disobedience, whereas a prohibited meeting to which the general public is admitted without any restriction is an instance of Mass Disobedience. Such a Civil Disobedience is defensive, when a prohibited public meeting is held for conducting a normal activity, although it may result in arrest. It would be aggressive if it is held not for any normal activity but for arrest and imprisonment."

There was great perturbation in Delhi when the A.I.C.C. passed its resolution advocating Individual Civil Disobedience, amongst the intermediaries who were not hopeful of any readjustment of relations between Government and Congress, but now were anxious to avoid the impending disaster of Gandhi's arrest. Very likely, Government would not have taken action if the A.I.C.C. had not still harped upon Civil Disobedience as the ultimate resort and Individual Civil Disobedience as an immediate practical programme. On the other side, there was an outcry against Gandhi that he should have switched off the whole current and made the movement no longer a live wire. Long letters were written from behind the bars by Pandit Motilal Nehru and Lala Lajpat Rai. They took Gandhi to task for punishing the whole country for the sins of a place. Why should, Panditji asked, a town at the foot of the Himalayas be penalised, if a village at Cape Camorin failed to observe non-violence? Isolate Chauri Chaura and if need be, Gorakhpur, but go on with Civil Disobedience, individual and mass. That was the burden of the complaints of Panditji as well as Lalaji and two other younger friends who too made no secret of their displeasure and disappointment and disgust at the sudden termination of the movement. These letters were read to an informal gathering of friends of the A. I. C. C. at Dr. Ansari's place on the 24th February, 1922. And strangely enough, C. I. D. men got mixed with the audience and were carefully following them. In reply Gandhi had but one word to say, namely, that those who went to jail were civilly dead and could not claim or be expected to advise those outside. But the storm blew with unexampled fury when the A.I.C.C. had a regular sitting. Gandhi was assailed on all sides. He was taken to task for resiling from the movement, and for the Bardoli resolutions in general. Bengal and Maharashtra tore him to pieces. Why should Individual Civil Disobedience not be continued? "Bengal is not going to pay the Chowkidari tax, say what you will." Even devoted men like Babu Hardyal Nag raised the standard of revolt. Why should civil resisters wear khaddar? Dr. Moonje had already confronted the Working Committee on 11th January, with a resolution of the Nagpur District Congress Committee permitting reservation in untouchability and Swadeshi. These were the questions put to Gandhi. Every line of the Bardoli resolutions was subjected to a scathing attack. The meeting reduced itself to attacks from Maharashtra and Bengal. A vote of censure on Gandhi was moved by Dr. Moonje at the A.I.C.C. meeting. Some speakers supported it by their speeches, but when it was put to vote only those who had spoken in favour voted for it, the rest of the House voting against it. Gandhi did not permit any one to oppose the motion of censure by speech. The storm blew over and Gandhi, like the proverbial reed, remained unmoved.

Gandhi's Arrest

The die was cast. Now was the turn of Government to pounce upon Gandhi. No administration would select a moment of high popularity of a leader in the country for its attack on him. It bides its time patiently, and it is when the army retreats fighting a rearguard action that the enemy comes down with all his fury "like a wolf on the fold." On the 13th March, Gandhi was arrested,—his arrest being virtually decided upon even in the last week of February,—and committed to sessions on a charge of sedition.

'The Great Trial' began on the 18th March at Ahmedabad, and, to quote from Sarojini Devi's Foreword to a little brochure bearing that title: "A convict and a criminal in the eyes of the Law: nevertheless the entire Court rose in an act of spontaneous homage when Mahatma Gandhi entered,—a frail, serene, indomitable figure in a coarse and scanty loin cloth, accompanied by his devoted disciple and fellow-prisoner, Shankerlal Banker."

When you go to a big textile shop or a jewellery mart for your dress and diamonds, your puzzle is what to buy with your limited purse. Even so might the Law officers of the Crown have been 'puzzled and perplexed' as to the choice of Gandhi's articles published from week to week for their indictment against him. Which was not seditious? Gandhi always held that it was his duty to propagate sedition, and if his articles were not sufficiently seditious, it meant his pen was weak. In the end they selected three of them, headed 'Tampering with Loyalty, 'The Puzzle and its Solution' and 'Shaking the manes.' As soon as the charge was read, Gandhi rose to plead guilty, remarking, "I observe the King's name has been omitted from the charges, and it has been properly omitted." Mr. Banker also pleaded guilty. The trial might have ended forthwith with the pronouncement of sentence, but the Advocate-General urged a full trial. The Judge disagreed and wanted only to decide the sentence. Gandhi made a statement and prefaced it by saying that his preaching disaffection had begun long before his connection with *Young India*. He took full responsibility for the occurrences in Madras and Bombay and Chauri Chaura and added:—

> "I knew I was playing with fire. I ran the risk and if I was set free, I would still do the same. I would be failing in my duty if I do not do so. It is the last article of my faith. But I had to make my choice. I had either to submit to a system which I considered has done an irreparable harm to my country, or incur the risk of the mad fury of my people bursting forth when they understood the truth from my lips. I know that my people have sometimes gone mad. I am deeply sorry for it; and I am, therefore, here to submit not to a light penalty but to the highest penalty. I do not ask for mercy. I do not plead any extenuating act. I am here, therefore, to invite and submit to the highest penalty that can be inflicted upon me for what, in Law, is a deliberate crime and what appears to me to be the highest duty of a citizen. The only course open to you, Mr. Judge, is, as I am just going to say in my statement, either to resign your post or inflict on me the severest penalty, if you believe that the system and law you are assisting to administer are good for the people. I do not expect that kind of conversion. But by the time I have finished with my statement, you will, perhaps, have a glimpse of what is raging within my breast to run this maddest risk which a sane man can run."

THE WRITTEN STATEMENT

"I owe it perhaps to the Indian public and to the public in England, to placate which this prosecution is mainly taken up, that I should explain why from a staunch loyalist and co-operator I have become an uncompromising disaffectionist and non-co-operator. To the Court too, I should say why I plead guilty to the charge of promoting disaffection towards the Government established by law in India.

"My public life began in 1893 in South Africa, in troubled weather. My first contact with British authority in that country was not of a happy character. I discovered that, as a man and an Indian, I had no rights. On the contrary, I discovered that I had no rights as a man because I was an Indian.

"But I was not baffled. I thought that this treatment of Indians was an excrescence upon a system that was intrinsically and mainly good. I gave the Government my voluntary and hearty co-operation, criticising it fully where I felt it was faulty, but never wishing its destruction.

"Consequently when the existence of the Empire was threatened in 1890 by the Boer challenge, I offered my services to it, raised a volunteer ambulance corps, and served at several actions that took place for the relief of Ladysmith. Similarly in 1906, at the time of the Zulu revolt, I raised a stretcher-bearer party and served till the end of the 'rebellion.' On both these occasions, I received medals and was even mentioned in despatches. For my work in South Africa, I was given by Lord Hardinge a Kaisar-i-Hind Gold Medal. When the war broke out in 1914 between England and Germany, I raised a volunteer ambulance corps in London consisting of the then resident Indians in London, chiefly students. Its work was acknowledged by the authorities to be valuable. Lastly in India, when a special appeal was made at the War Conference in Delhi in 1917 by Lord Chelmsford for recruits, I struggled at the cost of my health to raise a corps in Kheda, and the response was being made when the hostilities ceased and orders were received that no more recruits were wanted. In all these efforts at service, I was actuated by the belief that it was possible by such services to gain a status of full equality in the Empire for my countrymen.

"The first shock came in the shape of the Rowlatt Act, a law designed to rob the people of all real freedom. I felt called upon to lead an intensive agitation against it. Then followed the Punjab horrors, beginning with the massacre at Jallianwala Bagh and culminating in crawling orders, public floggings and other indescribable humiliations. I discovered too that the plighted word of the Prime-Minister to the Muslims of India regarding the integrity of Turkey and the holy places of Islam was not likely to be fulfilled.

"But in spite of the foreboding and the grave warnings of friends, at the Amritsar Congress in 1919, I fought for co-operation and working the Montagu-Chelmsford Reforms, hoping that the Prime-Minister would redeem his promise to the Indian Muslims, that Punjab would be healed, and that the Reforms, inadequate and unsatisfactory though they were, marked a new era of hope in the life of India.

"But all that hope was shattered. The Khilaphat promise was not to be redeemed. The Punjab crime was whitewashed and the semi-starved masses of Indians are slowly sinking to lifelessness. Little do they know that their miserable comfort represents the brokerage they get for the work they do for the foreign exploiter, that the profits and the brokerage are sucked from the masses. Little do they realise that the Government established by law in British India is carried on for this exploitation of the masses. No sophistry, no jugglery in figures can explain away the evidence the skeletons in many villages present to the naked eye. I have no doubt whatsoever that both England and the town-dwellers of India will have to answer, if there is a God above, for this crime against humanity which is perhaps unequalled in history. The law itself in this country has been used to serve the foreign exploiter. My unbiassed examination of the Punjab Martial Law cases has led me to believe that at least ninety-five per cent of convictions were wholly bad. My experience of political cases in India leads me to the conclusion that, in nine out of every ten, the condemned men were totally innocent. Their crime consisted in love of their country. In ninety-nine cases out of hundred, justice has been denied to Indians as against Europeans in the Courts of India. This is not an exaggerated picture. It is the experience of almost every Indian who has had anything to do with such cases. In my opinion the administration of the law is thus prostituted, consciously or unconsciously, for the benefit of the exploiter.

"The greatest misfortune is that Englishmen and their Indian associates in the administration of the country do not know that they are engaged in the crime I have attempted to describe. I am satisfied that many English and Indian officials honestly believe that they are administering one of the best systems devised in the world, and that India is making steady though slow progress. They do not know that a subtle but effective system of terrorism and an organised display of force on the one hand, and the deprivation of all powers of retaliation or self-defence on the other, have emasculated the people and induced in them the habit that has added to the ignorance and the self-deception of the administrators. Section 124-A, under which I am happily charged, is perhaps the prince among the political sections of the Indian Penal Code designed to suppress the liberty of the citizen. Affection cannot be manufactured or regulated by Law. If one has no affection for a person or thing, one should be free to give the fullest expression to his disaffection, so long as he does not contemplate, promote or incite to violence. But the section under which Mr. Banker and I are charged is one under which mere promotion of disaffection is a crime. I have studied some of the cases tried under it, and I know that some of the most loved of India's patriots have been convicted under it. I consider it a privilege, therefore, to be charged under it. I have endeavoured to give in their briefest outline the reasons for my disaffection. I have no personal ill-will against any single administrator, much less can I have any disaffection towards the King's person. But I hold it to be a virtue to be disaffected towards a Government which, in its totality, has done more harm to India than any previous system. India is less manly under the British rule than she ever was before. Holding such a belief, I consider it to be a sin to have affection for the system. And it has been a precious privilege for me to be able to write what I have in the various articles tendered in evidence against me.

"In fact, I believe that I have rendered a service to India and England by showing in non-co-operation the way out of the unnatural state in which both are living. In my humble opinion non-co-operation with evil is as much a duty as is co-operation with good. But in the past, non-co-operation has been deliberately expressed in violence to tax the evil-doer. I am endeavouring to show to my countrymen that violent non-co-operation only multiplies evil, and that, as evil can only be sustained by violence, withdrawal of support of evil requires complete abstention from violence. Non-violence implies voluntary submission to the penalty for non-co-operation with evil. I am here, therefore, to invite and submit cheerfully to the highest penalty that can be inflicted upon me for what, in Law, is a deliberate crime and what appears to me to be the highest duty of a citizen. The only course open to you, the Judge and the Assessors, is either to resign your posts and thus dissociate yourselves from evil if you feel that the law you are called upon to administer is an evil and that in reality I am innocent, or to inflict on me the severest penalty if you believe that the system and the law you are assisting to administer are good for the people of this country, and that my activity is therefore injurious to the public weal.

M. K. GANDHI"

The judge passed judgment sentencing Gandhi to six years' imprisonment, on the analogy of Lokamanya Tilak who had been similarly sentenced, and Mr. Shankerlal to one year's simple imprisonment and a fine of Rs. 1,000, or six months' imprisonment in default of payment. Gandhi made a short reply saying that he considered it a proud privilege to have his name associated with that of the Lokamanya and thanked the judge for his considerateness in passing the sentence and for his courtesy. All those present in Court bade him good-bye, most of them with tears in their eyes.

Gandhi was thus convicted and spirited away from the Nation. That was not unexpected. On the 9th of March, he had published an article in *Young India* headed 'If I am arrested,' where he reiterated his discovery that there was a spirit of violence abroad, that Kunzru's report about Chauri Chaura was clinching, that the Congress Secretary's report from Bareilly was clear that in the volunteer procession there might not be violence, but there was the spirit of violence. Accordingly, he had ordered the suspension of Civil Disobedience and explained that disobedience under the conditions would be not 'Civil' but 'Criminal.' He could not understand, however, the Englishman's dead-set against the very theory of Civil Disobedience, as if it was something immoral, when he had glorified even armed rebellion. It would be a sad commentary if his arrest was to be a signal for a storm all over the country. Let all the workers show that Government's fears are wholly wrong. Let there be no *hartals,* noisy demonstrations, no procession. The Bardoli programme, if fulfilled, would not only release him but inaugurate Swaraj. It was with these words that he had welcomed his arrest, because it powers, disprove the theory that people had accepted would explode the superstition about his supernatural

N. C. O. under his influence, prove our capacity for Swaraj and finally give him a quiet and physical rest which perhaps he deserved. And well did the country respect his wishes and observe perfect peace on his arrest and conviction.

About the same time that Gandhi was arrested, a fairly large number of arrests took place in Andhra in connection with the No-tax campaign. But the really noticeable feature was that as the Congress relaxed its Civil Disobedience movement, Government tightened its repression. That was but to be expected, for Government having sent out the leader of the Non-co-operation movement, the General of the Army, it was but natural that they should seek to disperse or even destroy the force. It is equally natural for the forces to muster together and carry on with a substitute for the departed leader. That is one position. The other position is that with the removal of Gandhi, there was created a chasm in the public life of the country. The one experiment that should have been made on the 23rd of November but was postponed by the Bombay riots to the new year, and postponed again to the 31st January, on account of the All-Parties' Conference of Bombay (14th and 15th January, 1922), was ultimately postponed *sine die*. Who was to attempt this stupendous and novel experiment during the six years of Gandhi's absence?

The Working Committee was busy for three months after Gandhi's conviction with adjusting affairs. The khaddar department was entrusted to Seth Jamnalal Bajaj and five lacs of rupees were asked to be placed in his charge. For relief in Malabar, the Committee voted Rs. 84,000. Seth Jamnalal Bajaj generously paid another lac of rupees as a donation for the maintenance of lawyers. The compulsory 'use' of khaddar was interpreted to mean 'personal wear.' Non-co-operating lawyers were once again warned not to appear in cases, and Non-co-operators were not to enter defence. A Committee was appointed for investigating and reporting upon, (1) the causes which led to the outbreak of the Moplah rebellion, (2) the extent of the outbreak, (3) the measures adopted by Government for suppressing it, including the declaration of Martial Law, (4) Forcible conversions by the Moplahs, (5) Destruction of property, and (6) steps, if any, necessary to restore and strengthen Hindu-Muslim unity. The C. P. Marathi Provincial Congress Committee already suggested certain modifications in the N. C. O. programme. A Committee was appointed to formulate a scheme regarding the removal of untouchability. All these and other recommendations were soon considered by the A. I. C. C. which met at Lucknow on the 7th, 8th, 9th, of June, 1922. The fact is that in this world, whenever there is a failure in business or death of the head of a family, the calamity is followed by an immediate bustle and excitement incidental to readjustment, which in turn gives rise to a feeling of void and vacuum. Into this void and vacuum, there is a rush of multiple thoughts and divided counsels ending in some confusion. Even so was the conviction of Gandhi followed by three months of readjustment of affairs, payments of money, collection of dues, interpretation of terms, appointment of committees, reassertion of principles, statement of policies, filling of casual vacancies, recording of services and such other things. Then came the time in June for a re-examination of fundamentals.

The task of the A.I.C.C. was really to re-assess the theory and practice, review the science and art of Non-co-operation, Passive Resistance, and Civil Disobedience. We need not make an unnecessary secret of the simple fact that the top-notch politicians, notably Deshbandhu Das and Vittalbhai J. Patel, who were reluctant converts but warm apostles of Non-co-operation, were in favour of changing faith on its orthodox lines and professing a protestant creed that would carry Non-co-operation into the very aisles and chancel of the Bureaucratic Church. They wanted to beard the lion in its own den and carry Non-co-operation into the very citadels of Provincial Governments. Accordingly, the A. I. C. C., after placing on record Gandhi's services to the cause of humanity by his message of peace and truth, reiterated its faith in the principles of non-violent Non-co-operation, and carried the Working Committee's resolution moved by Pandit Motilal Nehru, who had just been released, as amended by Pandit Malaviya. It condemned the continued repression by Government and recognised the necessity of some form of Civil Disobedience to combat it. It held the constructive programme to be the best preparation for even mass Civil Disobedience. It adjourned, to the month of August, the consideration of the question "whether Civil Disobedience in some form, or some other measure of similar character, should be adopted," and in the meantime requested the President to nominate and authorize a few gentlemen to tour round the country and report on the situation to the next meeting. Accordingly, Pandit Motilal Nehru, Dr. Ansari, Syts. V. J. Patel, Jamnalal Bajaj, C. Rajagopalachariar and Seth Chothani were appointed by the President, Hakim Ajmal Khan, who was to be the Chairman of the Committee.

In place of Seth Jamnalal who could not accept the offer, Mr. S. Kasturi Ranga Iyengar was appointed. Seth Chothani could not join at all.

Before we proceed to deal with the Civil Disobedience Committee's activities and their report, let us go back to the month of March. Montagu was forced to resign his ministership on the 23rd of March, 1922, for revealing the contents of a certain document relating to the revision of the Treaty of Sevres with Turkey which scored a first class victory just then against the Greeks. Prosecutions and convictions were raging everywhere. In the Punjab it was the Lawrence Statue that was the object of the attack. In Andhra, it was the hoisting of the National Flag in Godavari that was the red rag to the bureaucratic bull. The No-tax campaign was of course there. The reign of Law reduced itself to the reign of Sections 108 and 144. The Indian Members of the Executive Councils expressed helplessness as the Collectors (Deputy Commissioners) were all-powerful in the matter, and only a Judicial appeal—which the non-co-operators would not resort to—could remedy the obvious wrong. Another source of irritation to the people of India arose from the 'steel frame' speech of Lloyd George, the Premier. It was occasioned by a circular known as the O'Donnell circular to Provincial Governments, inviting their opinions on the various considerations involved in the question of Indianization, in order that the Government of India might consider the whole position. This got wind and roused the ire of the officers in England and India, whereupon, to reassure them, Lloyd George made a speech in which he declared that "the Civil Services of India were the steel frame of the whole structure of administration." He added that he could see no period when India could dispense with the guidance and assistance of a nucleus of the British Civil Services, whose continued assistance was necessary to bring about the discharge of Britain's great trust in India, and it was not to relinquish this trust but to bring it into partnership in its discharge, that the Reforms had been introduced. The Viceroy, however, to appease apprehensions in India, obtained at the time, from Mr. Lloyd George, a clear authorization to say that nothing in that speech was intended to conflict with earlier pledges and proclamations. One thing after another helped to keep up excitement.

We must now refer to another instance of Satyagraha with which the name of Borsad was associated. The Satyagraha at Borsad took place in the year 1922. It was organized under circumstances which seem to us almost incredible. For some time past, an arch-dacoit named Devar Baba had been carrying on his exploits in the Borsad Taluka. He would come in his usual dress to the schools in the day-time and distribute sweets to children. He hit upon this device in order to ascertain who was rich in the village, and then in the nights he would descend with his men upon his intended victim, kidnap him and negotiate a ransom for his release. This went on for a month, and there was no help. While these exploits were progressing, a rival rose in the person of a Muslim who had a quarrel with a pleader and, having murdered him, had disappeared and become an outlaw. He gathered a band of men and was carrying on his depredations in the Taluka as a rival to Devar Baba. The Police were helpless. Government posted to the place their best officer, but his labours met with no success. The Baroda Police were also interested in the detection of the criminals, as similar mischief was going on in their territory adjoining the Borsad Taluka. The Police and the Revenue officers concerned, of the State and the Taluka, put their heads together and evolved a clever plan of detecting the criminals. They entered into a pact with the Muslim outlaw, who undertook to catch Devar Baba and deliver him to the authorities, provided he was well-armed and, further, received the assistance of four or five constables with rifles and cartridges. This was agreed to. A thief was set to catch a thief, but the new ally of the Police only used his men and munitions to intensify his campaigns in the Taluka for his own ends.

Crime increased and, as the last resort, Government thought that the villagers themselves were privy to these crimes and posted Punitive Police on the Taluka, levying a heavy punitive tax which they began to collect with the usual relentlessness that prevails under such circumstances. In the meantime, public men in Gujarat learnt about the pact between the Police and the Muslim dacoit, and Vallabhbhai J. Patel challenged Government on the matter. He went to Borsad and asked the people not to pay the punitive tax. The shots that were taken out of the bodies of persons injured in the dacoities proved to be Government shots and left no doubt that the Police rifles and ammunition were being used by the dacoits. Vallabhbhai J. Patel posted 200 volunteers in the Taluka and they kept watch day and night. He succeeded in persuading the people not to lock up their doors from the evening time, as they had been wont to, for weeks together previously, but keep them open. The villagers proved by the aid of photographs that the officers of the punitive Police posted in the Taluka were themselves locking up their doors inside, as well as getting them locked outside. in order to put the dacoits off the scent and make them believe that the houses were abandoned. On the slightest noise outside, the Police were crouching under their cots. All these allegations were proved to the hilt by photographs taken, and when the charges were publicly brought against the authorities, they had only two alternatives left to them,—either to prosecute those that had brought them forward or to plead guilty by silence.

When these revelations were made, the Baroda Police was quickly withdrawn from the villages in the State, but the British Police continued to remain and attachments of property went on merrily for collection of the punitive tax.

In the meantime Lord Lloyd, the Governor of Bombay, left India and his successor, Sir Leslie Wilson, took charge of the Province. On hearing of the happenings in Borsad, he at once sent the Home Member to Borsad, who verified the allegations and withdrew the Police on the spot. Devar Baba himself had disappeared the moment Vallabhbhai and the volunteers appeared on the scene.

Two events of the year now claim our attention. The first of them was the tour of the Civil Disobedience Committee in the summer in the country. The second was the great event known as the Guruka-Bagh affair which took origin in August. We shall describe the latter first. The Shiromani Gurudwar Prabandhak Committee was a reformist group of Sikhs who called themselves Akalis—as opposed to the Udasis who were conservatives and whom the Mahants or the Abbots in power at the Sikh shrines favoured. The reformists wanted to capture the shrines by Satyagraha and some Akalis serving the shrine cut down a tree in August on the land of the Guruka-Bagh shrine. The Mahant complained to the Police, who afforded protection, but batches of Akalis pledged to non-violence passed the Police Pickets and were severely beaten as unlawful assemblies. No resistance was made to these attacks by the Police and the spectacle aroused considerable excitement in the country. It was an object lesson in non-violence displayed by a martial race of India who had fought the Germans and won victories for the British in Europe.

The self-control exhibited by the Akalis has been freely acknowledged by Government, and Government's only regret was that "while this fact was emphasized and indeed praised to the skies as a triumph of Gandhism in various sections of the Indian Press, scarcely a word of commendation was given to the remarkable good temper and excellent discipline shown by the Police in the discharge of their peculiarly unpleasant duty." Indeed, it was at Guruka-Bagh that the Police, it was said, perfected the technique of *lathi*-charge which was destined, a decade later, to play so prominent a part in Indian politics. Even the Police abominated their thankless task and ere long Government were forced to abandon the dispersion of the Akali *jathas* and, instead, to arrest individual members and in November, 1922, a public-spirited gentleman, Sir Ganga Ram, stepped in to take on lease the lands in question from the Mahant and made no objection to the Akalis cutting the wood thereon.

The Civil Disobedience Committee undertook its tour throughout India. The spirit of the people was not dead. Wherever they went, they received a warm welcome. At Guntur, the Municipality presented an address to the Committee wishing them success in their object. On their arrival at the Railway station. 200 volunteers were arrested by the Police,—a fact worth more by way of evidence than the arguments presented to them. The Committee finished their labours and presented their Report. At first, it was the intention of the A.I.C.C. to discuss this at a meeting to be held on the 15th August. No meeting could be held but, apparently, private discussions took place about the time when some of the prominent men of India met in Calcutta in connection with the wedding of Deshbandhu Das's second daughter. It was then, we were told at the time, that Pandit Motilal Nehru was weaned away from Civil Disobedience and converted to Council-entry. Later, when the Report was published, it transpired that all the members discussed the question whether the Congress should or should not contest Council elections. A little later, a parallel Committee appointed by the Khilaphat Committee reported predominantly in favour of continuing the Council Boycott. Without dwelling at greater length upon the forces that were at play in the production of the Report,—and there must, doubtless, have been many legitimate forces operating,—we quote below the recommendations of the Civil Disobedience Committee :

Civil Disobedience Committee's Recommendations

1. CIVIL DISOBEDIENCE

(a) The country is not prepared at present to embark upon general mass Civil Disobedience of a limited character *e.g.*, the breaking of a particular law or the non-payment of a particular tax for which the people are ready. We recommend that Provincial Committees be authorised to sanction such limited mass Civil Disobedience on their own responsibility, if the conditions laid down by the All-India Congress Committee in that behalf are fulfilled.

(b) We recommend the restoration of the resolution No. 2 passed by the All-India Congress Committee at Delhi on the 14th and 15th November, which gives Provincial Committees all the powers necessary to determine upon a resort to Civil Disobedience of any kind whatever, by cancelling Resolution I. Cl. 1, passed on the 24th, 25th February, to the extent it conflicts with that resolution; provided that general mass Civil Disobedience is not permissible.

2. ENTRY INTO LEGISLATIVE COUNCILS

(a) The Congress and the Khilaphat at their Gaya Session should declare that, in view of the fact that the working of the Legislative Councils during their first term has, besides proving a great obstacle to the redress of the Khilaphat and the Punjab wrongs and the speedy attainment of Swarajya, caused great misery and hardship to the people, it is desirable that the following steps should be taken in strict accordance with the principles of non-violent Non-co-operation to avoid the recurrence of the evil:

1. Non-co-operators should contest the election on the issue of the redress of the Punjab and Khilaphat wrongs and immediate Swarajya, and make every endeavour to be returned in a majority.

2. If the Non-co-operators are returned in a majority large enough to prevent a quorum, they should after taking their seats leave the Council Chamber in a body and take no part in the proceedings for the rest of the term. They should attend the Councils occasionally, only for the purpose of preventing vacancies.

3. If Non-co-operators are returned in a majority which is not large enough to prevent a quorum, they should oppose every measure of the Government including the budget, and only move resolutions for the redress of the aforesaid wrongs and the immediate attainment of Swarajya.

4. If the Non-co-operators are returned in a minority they should act as pointed out in No. 2; and thus materially reduce the strength of the Council.

As the new Councils will not assemble till January, 1924, we further propose that the Congress Session of 1923 be held during the first instead of the last week of December and the matter be again brought up for the issue of a final mandate by the Congress in view of the election.

(Recommended by Hakim Ajmal Khan, Pandit Motilal Nehru, V. J. Patel).

(b) There should be no change of the Congress programme in respect of the boycott of Councils.

(Recommended by Dr. M.A. Ansari, Syt. C. Rajagopalachari, Syt. S. Kasturi Ranga Iyengar.)

3. LOCAL BODIES

We recommend that in order to clear the position it should be declared that it is desirable for Non-co-operators to seek election to Municipalities and District or Local Boards with a view to facilitate the working of the constructive programme, but that no hard and fast rules be at present laid down to regulate or restrict the activities of non-co-operating members beyond advising them to act in harmony with Local or Provincial Congress organisations.

(Unanimous)

4. BOYCOTT OF GOVERNMENT EDUCATIONAL INSTITUTIONS

We recommend a strict adherence to the Bardoli resolution in regard to these by suspending for the present active propaganda calling upon boys to come out of schools and colleges. As required by that resolution, reliance should be placed upon the superiority of National schools for drawing scholars from Government institutions and not upon picketing or other aggressive propaganda.

(Unanimous)

5. BOYCOTT OF COURTS BY LITIGANTS AND LAWYERS

Effort should be concentrated on the establishment of Panchayats and cultivation of a strong public opinion in their favour.

We further recommend that all existing disqualifications imposed on practising lawyers should be removed.

(Unanimous)

6. ORGANISATION OF LABOUR

Resolution No. 8 passed by the Nagpur Congress should be carried out without further delay.

(Unanimous)

7. RIGHT OF PRIVATE DEFENCE

(a) We recommend that individuals should be given full freedom to exercise the right within the limits defined by Law, except when carrying on Congress work or on occasion directly arising therefrom, subject always to the condition that it is not likely to lead to a general outburst of violence. Using force in private defence in gross cases, such as insults to religion, outrages on modesty of women, or indecent assaults on boys and men, is not prohibited under any circumstances.

(All members except Syt. V. J. Patel).

(b) Full freedom to exercise the right within the limits defined by Law should be reserved to Non-co-operators, subject only to the condition that it is not likely to lead to a general outburst of violence, and to no further conditions.

(Syt. V. J. Patel).

8. BOYCOTT OF BRITISH GOODS

(a) We accept the principle and recommend that the whole question be referred to a committee of experts for a full report to be submitted before the Congress meets.

(All members except Syt. C. Rajagopalachari).

(b) There is no objection to the collection and examination of facts by experts, but the acceptance of the principle by the All-India Congress Committee would mislead the Nation and injure the movement.

(Syt. C. Rajagopalachari).

It will be evident to the reader that the forces of orthodox and heterodox Non-co-operation were equally arrayed against each other. But both were really forces of N.C.O., neither plumping for co-operation with Government. Only with the heterodox school the bow of Non-co-operation was to work with a second string by which arrows could be better flung at the citadel of Bureaucracy from inside the Council Chamber. The recommendation regarding Local Bodies was but to be expected. Already Congressmen and Non-co-operators had begun to contest elections of Municipalities and Local Boards and give pin-pricks to Government, as the latter thought, by advocating the use of khaddar in hospitals and for uniforms for servants, by urging the hoisting of the National Flag upon their offices, by recommending the introduction of charkha and Hindi in 'Local' and Municipal Schools, and occasionally by urging the boycott of Governors' visits and the visits of Ministers. But, except that they were indications of an attitude, there was not much in the way of real achievement.

The diversion of the national mind—be it even of a section—from the dynamic and destructive programme of boycott and the offensives of Civil Disobedience to the milder spheres of Local Self-Government and Legislatures is perhaps like a diversion from the firing line of the battle-field to the chess-board of the drawing-room. Yet, the fact must be recognized that by the winter of 1922, there was a schism which it was no longer possible to conceal, and which was destined to develop into a split at the Gaya Congress. The meeting of the A.I.C.C. which should have been held on August 15th, had necessarily to wait till the month of November. In that month, a truly historic gathering of the Committee met in Calcutta on the 20th, 21st, 22nd, 23rd and 24th November, 1922. It was a gala session, extending over five days, much like the field-day of Budget debates in Legislative Councils, when members could speak on subjects, all and sundry, without time-limit. The Congress discussions in Calcutta were like a tournament in which the rounds were all well marked out, and pairs of opposing speakers were carefully selected. The first day's sittings were held in the Indian Association Rooms, but the atmosphere was suffocating and the next four days were spent under a *shamiana* that was erected for the occasion on the premises of 148, Russa Road, Bhawanipore, the magnificent residence of Mr. C. R. Das, which was bearing on its forehead the marks of ten months' neglect. Nor could it be said that the Calcutta performance was a mere feat of intellectual levity. Although towering personalities like Nehru, the Elder, and Das were supporting the Council programme and were briskly aided by their old ally, Maharashtra, yet the recent incarceration of Gandhi and the spirit of loyalty and reverence which his following always bore towards him, the attractiveness of a programme of revolt, the absence of a programme of equal attractiveness, the proximity of the goal in sight, in spite of the crags and chasms that intervened but were hidden from view by the carpet green of tree-tops, and above all, the crossing of the Rubicon and the burning of the boats by most Non-co-operators,—all these constituted a formidable opposition which could not be overawed either by the intellectual eminence of Motilal or the dominating personality of Das. At the end of five days' analysis, criticism, invective and diatribe, the Committee resolved that the country was not prepared for mass Disobedience but it authorized P. C. C.s to sanction on their own responsibility limited Civil Disobedience that may be demanded by any situation, subject to the fulfilment of the conditions laid down in that behalf. The harder question of Council-entry was held over till Gaya, and likewise were postponed the questions of Boycott of British goods, the recommendation of entry into Local Bodies with a view to facilitating the constructive programme, the boycott of schools and colleges and Law-Courts, and the right of private defence within the limits of Law except when carrying on Congress work. Thus ended the deliberations of the Civil Disobedience Committee which cost the Congress Rs. 16,000.

Before we pass on to the Gaya Congress, let us bring the deliberations of the Working Committee up to date. In 1922, the Committee had met thrice in January, twice in February, once in March, once in April, once in May for four days on end, twice in June, once in July, once in September, once in November, and once in December. An influential Committee had been appointed to investigate the Guruka-Bagh affair, the grief of the Congress was expressed over the death of the venerable old patriot, Motilal Ghose of the *Amrita Bazaar Patrika*, a Committee was appointed to visit Multan with a view to bringing about the restoration of good feelings between Hindus and Muslims.

It was unfortunate that the Hindu-Muslim unity which was a remarkable feature of the history of the previous two years should have been broken in the Muharram of 1922, in which communal feeling in Multan reached serious heights, leading to extensive destruction of life and property. Strenuous efforts made to restore unity proved unavailing. "The structure so painfully erected by Mr. Gandhi," says 'India, 1922-23,' "had crumbled hopelessly."

In fact, the 18th of every month was being observed ever since the 18th April, throughout the country as the Gandhi Day, even as the 15th of every month was being observed in 1917 as the Besant Day, till her release in September that year. Another important event was the arrest and conviction of Jawaharlal in May, 1922, some time after his release from imprisonment in connection with the boycott of the Prince's visit. The warrant of his arrest bore the 'familiar' Section 124-A. But he was not tried under it. He stood charged with "criminal intimidation and abetment of an attempt to extort." He had really declared his intention in a public speech to picket foreign shops. He had also presided at a Committee meeting at which letters were agreed to be sent to certain cloth merchants to pay the fines imposed by their own association under their own rules. The conviction was under Sec. 385 I.P.C. The fact was that he was really being tried for picketing foreign cloth shops. He made an exquisite statement in Court on the 17th May, 1922, in which he explained how he, who ten years before was virtually an Englishman who had imbibed all the prejudices of Harrow and Cambridge, was transformed in the space of ten years into "a rebel against the present system of Government in India." "I marvel at my good fortune," he concluded. "To serve India in the battle of freedom is honour enough. To serve her under a leader like Mahatma is doubly fortunate. But to suffer for the dear country! What greater good fortune could befall an Indian unless it be death for the cause, or the full realization of our glorious dream."

The Gaya Congress of 1922 was in every sense a remarkable one. The towering personality of Deshbandhu Das, the President, would, if nothing else, make it remarkable. It was not, however, merely the men who conducted the Congress, but the matters relating to the Congress which made the Congress remarkable. The fight at Gaya was really a tri-partite one,—between those that raised politics to a spiritual level and those that worked politics on the intellectual and the material plane. That the leader of the former group was not present in flesh and blood made no difference. His ideals of truth and non-violence, his philosophy of suffering and sacrifice, his religion of politics based on the Sermon on the Mount and the Beatitudes,—all these were there imperfectly lisped by his followers, but perfectly shining forth from the aureole that surrounded his benign portrait.

The question which caused the greatest excitement and difference among the delegates was the question of entry into Councils. It will be remembered that the A.I.C.C. meeting in Calcutta had left this question over for the Congress, and the Congress had to sit for five days, to come to conclusions on this and other matters. There were those who felt strongly that the scheme of Non-co-operation would be upset if entry into Councils was permitted, and they insisted that the ban on Council-entry should not be lifted. There were a few intellectuals who would enter Councils and not take seats or Oaths of Allegiance and would, that way, beat the enemy altogether. Finally, there were the passionate politicians who would sweep the Councils and make short work of Cabinets and Ministers, who would beard the lion in his den, who would withhold supplies and move Votes of Censure, who would create deadlocks and bring the Government machinery to a standstill.

Deshbandhu Das delivered his speech, a marvel of logic, erudition and practical idealism. But the reaction against the change of direction of the ship of N.C.O. gathered volume and force, and despite the high intellectualism of S. Srinivasa Iyengar and Pandit Motilal Nehru, the ship pursued its own old course. Mr. S. Srinivasa Iyengar tabled an amendment to the effect that Congressmen should contest seats but refuse to take their seats, and Pandit Nehru gave his qualified assent to it. Mr. Srinivasa Iyengar had resigned his membership of the Madras Legislative Council, his Advocate-Generalship and his 'C.I.E.,' and come into the movement more than a year earlier in the midst of universal congratulations. The Khilaphatists were under-the influence of the Jamiat-ul-ulemah, who had published a Fatwa declaring Council-entry as *mamnoon*, not *haram*. But nothing availed at Gaya. The spirit of Gandhi was all-pervading. Every one took it to be an act of disloyalty to the Master to turn his back on him, the moment he was found to be absent from the Congress. After doing honour to the memory of Motilal Ghose and A. C. Mazumdar, a handsome tribute was paid to Gandhi and his principles. The unexampled bravery of the Akali Martyrs and the noble example of non-violence set by them as well as other political prisoners were admired. Kemal Pasha was congratulated on his success. Councils were asked to be boycotted. A solemn warning was administered to Government not to incur any more National Debt, and to the people not to contribute any further to National Debts floated by the bureaucracy under the authority of the so-called Legislatures. The A.I.C.C.'s resolution of November on Civil Disobedience was virtually ratified, the Nation being called upon to get ready money and men in the meantime for the purpose. The boycott of colleges and courts was to be continued, the right of private defence as already defined in November was conceded. Labour was to be organised by a Committee including Mr. Andrews, Sen-Gupta and four others with power to co-opt. Congress Bodies in South Africa and Kabul were affiliated with rights to send 10 and 2 delegates respectively to the Congress.

Deshbandhu Das really had two precious documents in his pocket when he presided over the Gaya Congress,—one was the Presidential Address, and the other his resignation of the Presidentship, together with a constitution of the Swaraj Party.

The Bengal Provincial Congress Committee had formulated some such thing in 1920. At the Special

Congress of Calcutta, Bengal and Maharashtra leaders had opposed boycott of Councils. At Nagpur, Das had spent Rs. 36,000 to undo Calcutta, and when he failed, he magnanimously moved the resolution of the day. At Ahmedabad, we know not what he would have done if he had been present in person. The Gaya Congress was a battle-royal between the two contending parties. It was not to be expected that a man of Das's personality—with the support of eminent men like Motilal and Vittalbhai—would tamely succumb to the spirit of the masses and submit to Council-Boycott. A party was, therefore, organized and a programme was drawn up. Das was to capture the Provincial Council of Bengal and Motilalji was to mountguard over Delhi and Simla. Maharashtra would look after Nagpur. If Bardoli's successful No-tax campaign would obviate similar campaigns of suffering and sacrifice in India, why not the success in Calcutta and Nagpur of the programme of wrecking the formation of Ministries set an example to and save the troubles and sufferings of the rest of India? Das had immense faith in his Province. Indeed, if the choice were given to him, he would be happy with schemes of village reconstruction, provided he had facilities therefor. His tastes and tendencies were to narrow down the sphere of activity for intensive work, and not to diffuse his energies over an extensive area. The Non-co-operation movement was shortly to be shunted to the side-line of legislative activities.

Before we close the year 1922, we have to refer to two matters, though they are not directly germane to our subject. Government was not unmindful of the growing passion of young men for volunteering. The volunteer organization was really growing in numbers and strength, and the tour of the Congress party met with reactionary orders in Jubbulpore and other places. The Khilaphat volunteers and their quasi-military equipment and dress were such as to strike the imagination of young India; and Government, as if to take the wind out of the sails of the national movement, started a territorial organization for different parts of India and Burma. A scheme was also initiated for the training of Indian lads for Sandhurst in an Indian Military College. The second matter relates to the relation of jail rules in respect of 'political prisoners.' This term was not avoided by Government then, as it was in the later years. Their treatment was sought to be regulated along certain broad lines. Of course, this category of prisoners excluded all those convicted of offences involving violence, or against property, all persons convicted of attempts to seduce soldiers or Police from their allegiance, and of offences directly involving criminal intimidation. The cases were to be considered, each on its merits and selection, for differential treatment which was to be based upon the status, character and education of the prisoner and the nature of his offence. Prisoners so selected were to be separated from ordinary prisoners, might get their own food and bedding and wear their own clothes, might possess books and magazines, receive visitors and letters at stated intervals, and enjoy exemption from labour and from menial duty. We have described at length these instructions issued by the Government of India, only to show that they had not been then or later observed by the jail authorities in relation to the vast bulk of political prisoners. Indeed, Government have latterly refused to recognize the term 'political' itself, as qualifying prisoners.

CHAPTER IV

N.C.O. FROM WITHIN COUNCILS (1923)

The political atmosphere of the country at the commencement of 1923 was beginning to get polluted once again by communal differences. The year 1922 had already witnessed the Multan riots. The Muharram of 1923 was attended with serious riots both in Bengal and the Punjab. In the year 1922, the Khilaphat question met with an unexpected end. After the signing of the Armistice at Mudania early in October, 1922, a conference of the Allied Powers was convened at Lausanne, on the 20th November, where a two months' discussion was held. It was then that representatives of the Angora Government took over the civil administration of the city, with the result that the Turkish Sultan was compelled to flee for his life secretly on a British warship which conveyed him to Malta. No sooner had he departed than he was deposed, not only as Sultan but also as Khalifa. A new Khalifa was elected in the person of his nephew Abdul Majid Effendi and the Sultan ceased to exist, Turkey having become a Republic. Thus had the Khilaphat been vaticanized.

The victory of the no-changers at Gaya was destined to be short-lived. The A.I.C.C. resolved on the 1st January, 1923, that a sum of 25 lacs be collected and 50,000 volunteers be enrolled before the 30th April, 1923, and the Working Committee was authorized to take all necessary steps. It was also empowered to relax any of the Delhi conditions for Civil Disobedience in order to meet any grave emergency that might arise out of the Turkish situation. Dr. Ansari was requested to get a scheme of National Pact prepared for the next meeting. But the most important matter before the Committee was the President's resignation. That was inevitable, for he had already intimated to the Subjects Committee his plans regarding the new Swaraj Party. The question of the resignation was held over to the next meeting of the A.I.C.C. which was held at Allahabad on the 27th February, 1923. At this meeting a compromise was arrived at, under which Council propaganda was to be suspended on both sides till the 30th April, and both parties were to be at liberty to work the remaining items of their respective programmes in the interval without interference with each other, and each party was to adopt such course after the 30th April as it might be advised.

By this time, both Maulana Abul Kalam Azad and Pandit Jawaharlal Nehru were released and the A.I.C.C. recorded their grateful thanks to both for their services in effecting the settlement.

It did not look as though Civil Disobedience would be seriously taken up as a national programme. The split itself would be a potent cause for its not being resumed. Again, a splendid opportunity arose in the budget of the year. The Salt Tax was proposed to be raised in the budget session of 1923, but the Assembly threw the proposal out. The Viceroy of course certified the higher figure. Although the members of the Assembly had urged that the imposition of the enhanced tax would only place a premium upon Non-co-operation, although the restoration of the duty by the Viceroy,—after it had been condemned by men like Mr. Montagu Webb and Mr. E. D. Sassoon,—was received with alarm and indignation, although it was felt at the time that "if only the N.C.O. party had been possessed of any thing like its former vigour, it is quite possible that the certification of the Salt Tax might have provided it with a fresh lease of life," yet, the fact remained that this opportunity made no impression on the Congressmen's minds. It did not occur to them, as it occurred seven years later to their Master, that salt would be a splendid point at which to begin Satyagraha. In fact the author of *India*—a Government officer, twitted the Congress then and there, saying that the Viceroy's certification was not availed of to renew C. D. in some form. The autocratic action of Lord Reading had, however, a collateral result. Mrs. Besant had been talking, for some time earlier, of a National Convention to rally together all the constitutionalists. Dr. Sapru had just resigned his office of Law Member of the Government of India and a Conference was convened under his presidency to discuss a practical programme for achieving self-governing status within the Empire and the Conference appointed several committees to consider various details.

The constructive programme was vigorously preached and popularised by a deputation composed of Babu Rajendra Prasad, C. Rajagopalachari, Seth Jamnalal Bajaj and Devidas Gandhi, which toured the country widely and made a good collection for the T. S. Fund. They submitted a report of their work to the Working Committee that met in Bombay on the 25th, 26th, and 27th May, 1923. There took place an important meeting of the A.I.C.C. as well, at which it was decided that no propaganda be carried on amongst voters in furtherance of the resolution passed at the Gaya Congress relating to the Boycott of Councils. It was just a month previous to that, that the Deshbandhu had made a suggestion that the work of the Congress should be divided into various sections including the capture of the Councils, and that each section be entrusted to persons interested in it and that five to six crores of rupees be collected for the purpose. This proposal was explained to the Working Committee by Messrs. C. Rajagopalachari and Babu Rajendra Prasad, but was dropped as impracticable and opposed to the Gaya Congress resolutions, so far as the Councils were concerned. The moment the A.I.C.C. passed the aforesaid resolution, and on account of it, six members of the Working Committee tendered their resignations of membership of the Committee. These were Messrs. C. Rajagopalachari, Vallabhbhai J. Patel, Rajendra Prasad, Brij Kishore Prasad, G. B. Deshpande, and Jamnalal Bajaj. After some parley for a reconsideration, at the instance of Jawaharlal Nehru, the resignations were accepted and so was the President's resignation. The Committee was reconstituted and work was carried on under Dr. Ansari's chairmanship. There was nothing further of any importance done at this meeting. Only, we must pause at the Committee's congratulations offered to the volunteers of the Central Provinces carrying on their Flag Satyagraha and the call to the volunteers throughout India to be ready to join the struggle when required.

The Bombay compromise was obviously resented by a number of Provincial Committees and the A.I.C.C. that met later at Nagpur felt it necessary "to declare in express terms the adherence to, and insistence on, the propriety and validity of the compromise resolution passed by this Committee on the 26th of May and this Committee makes the said declaration." It further resolved "that the attempt of certain Provincial Congress Committees to act contrary to the said resolution is deplorable," and it hoped that such conduct would not be persisted in. The Tamil Nadu Congress Committee was sought to be condemned for indiscipline. This was objected to by a section of the A.I.C.C. as the material was not sufficient for such condemnation. The House agreed in the latter view and this led to the resignation of Jawaharlal who had moved the proposition and those of his persuasion; from the Working Committee, including Dr. Ansari. The resignations were accepted by the A.I.C.C. and a new Working Committee was elected on the spot.

But really quite an unexpected resolution, and one in respect of which no notice was given, was sprung on the Committee at Nagpur when "a Special Session of the Congress to consider the question of the Boycott of Councils" was decided upon. It was to meet in Bombay in the month of August and Maulana Abul Kalam Azad was elected President and the Working Committee was empowered to take all necessary action in this behalf.

As was to be expected, the unexpected decision at Nagpur in favour of a Special Congress naturally aroused some opposition which was strengthened by another circumstance, namely, the closeness of voting on the resolution itself, and these two reasons were cited in a requisition for a special meeting of the A.I.C.C. in the month of August at Vizagapatam. At this special meeting which was held on the 3rd of August, "the President asked;" says the official Report of the proceedings; "if any member wanted to move a resolution in pursuance of the requisition. None coming forward, Mr. C. Rajagopala-chari moved the following resolution which, being duly seconded, was carried."

The resolution voted for a Special Session in September (not August) and if there was any difficulty regarding the venue, the President was authorized to arrange for the session being held in any other place. There is something striking in the mover being Mr. Rajagopalachari. It may be noted incidentally that the President was Desabhakta K. Venkatappayya, a pronounced no-changer. Was it intended to thresh out the question at a Special Session, or was it intended to facilitate the passage of the Congress train along the new direction?

Before we proceed to the Special Session which was ultimately held in Delhi—not Bombay, as originally intended—we may as well review the events of the day. The Nagpur Satyagraha claims our first attention. The movement at Nagpur arose from the Police objecting to a procession carrying the National Flag, proceeding in the direction of the Civil Lines of the City, by the promulgation of S. 144 on the 1st May, 1923.

The volunteers insisted on their right to carry the flag where they willed. They were arrested and sentenced. This developed soon into a movement earning the blessings of the Working Committee, as we have already seen, and later of the All-India Congress Committee held on the 8th, 9th, and 10th of July, 1923 at Nagpur. The Committee resolved to give assistance to the Nagpur Satyagraha Committee in carrying the campaign to a successful issue, and further called upon the country to observe the next Gandhi day (18th) as a flag day, the Provincial Committees being instructed to organize flag processions and public display of the flag by the people. By this time Seth Jamnalal Bajaj also had been arrested in connection with this Satyagraha movement. That was really why the A.I.C.C. met at Nagpur and the Committee appropriately congratulated Sethji on his incarceration and "assured him of its whole-hearted support of the said campaign." Sethji's car was attached for realizing the fine of Rs. 3,000 imposed upon him, but the car would not sell in Nagpur; so, it was taken to Kathiawar for sale. Numerous were the sufferings of the prisoners in the Nagpur Satyagraha who came from all the Provinces of the country in response to the call of the Working Committee and the A.I.C.C. to support the campaign at Nagpur.

The Nagpur Flag Satyagraha soon developed into an All-India movement and Syt. Vallabhbhai J. Patel was asked to be in charge of it as from the 10th July. Volunteers were being sent from several parts of India; some Congress Committees appealed for funds. The Working Committee met at Vizagapatam early in August and recorded "its grateful appreciation of the help rendered by Syt. Vittalbhai Patel in the conduct of the Nagpur Satyagraha and requested him to continue to be on the spot and help to guide the movement along with the member-in-charge, (Vallabhbhai J. Patel). Virtually then, the Patel Brothers were looking after the campaign, and to them is due the credit for bringing it to an honourable termination. Government's contention was that the processionists should apply for permission. Congress claimed the right to proceed along any public road without let or hindrance. A vigorous campaign was contemplated and the public were taken into confidence by Vallabhbhai who cleared all misunderstandings and proclaimed the time and route of the March for the 18th. The prohibitory section was there, in fact it had just been renewed, but on the 18th the flag procession was allowed to pass. Later, a controversy arose out of this, Anglo-Indian papers claiming victory for Government on the allegation that the Congress had applied for permission, and the Congress rightly contending that it never did so. This is not the only struggle in which a settlement has given rise to different comments by opponents of the National movement. Suffice it to say that the Delhi Congress offered its "hearty congratulations to the organizers of the Flag Satyagraha movement at Nagpur and the Volunteers for having, by their heroic sacrifice and suffering, upheld the honour of the country by carrying the fight to a successful finish."

There remains an important development relating to Indians abroad which arrested the attention of the Congress in the months of July, August and September. Affairs in Kenya were going from bad to worse and merited a pronouncement by the A.I.C.C. early in August at its Vizagapatam sitting. The position in the years 1922-23 may briefly be reviewed. With the exception of New Zealand and Newfoundland, Indians resident in other parts of the British Empire had for long been subject to certain humiliating conditions. In 1921, the Dominion representatives assembled at the Imperial Conference of 1921, South Africa alone dissenting, passed a resolution admitting the justice of Indian claims saying "that in the interests of the solidarity of the British Commonwealth, it is desirable that the rights of Indians (lawfully domiciled in some other parts of the Empire) should be recognized." It was also agreed that thenceforth India should directly negotiate with South Africa in matters in which her Nationals were concerned. In South Africa the rights of Indians secured to Indians by the Smuts-Gandhi Agreement of 1914, were endangered early in 1920 by a decision of the Transvaal Provincial Court. In Transvaal, Indians were politically helpless. In Natal, they no doubt possessed the municipal franchise, but their position had lately been the subject of serious attack. In the Orange River Free State, Indians are not allowed at all, while in the Cape Province, Cecil Rhodes' "equal rights for every civilized man" prevails. A Commission appointed by the South African Government in 1920 to enquire into the question of Asiatics trading and holding land in the several South African Provinces, and before which Sir Benjamin Robertson appeared as the representative of the Government of India, recommended, it is true, the retention of the law prohibiting the ownership of land by Asiatics but declined to recommend a compulsory segregation. In Natal, however, the right of Indians to acquire and own land was confined to the coast belt, but on the protest of the Government of India, the Union Government abandoned the proposal. Natal, however, issued two Ordinances shortly after, which endangered still further the position of Indians, but which were vetoed by the Governor-General of South Africa. These two and a third Ordinance were once again introduced in 1922-23, but the Union Government once again vetoed the first two and pressed for certain changes in the third. The third is the Natal Retail Dealers Licensing Ordinance. All along, Lord Reading's Government took a just view of the matter and explained the same to a deputation of the Central Legislature. Let us recall the fact that at the Imperial Conference of 1921, it was suggested that a deputation from India should visit Canada, New Zealand and Australia to assist the Governments concerned to implement the resolution of the Conference recognizing the rights of Indians. The proposal being officially endorsed by the several Dominion Governments, the Hon'ble V. S. Sastri, accompanied by Mr. G. S. Bajpai, left India in May, 1922, for the three Dominions.

We need not go into the small grievances of Indians in these places and the success that attended Sastriar's good offices. It is to Kenya that we must now turn our attention. The position of Indians there had long been most unsatisfactory. This Colony owed much to Indian labour and Indian capital. Indians were the pioneers in many directions and they outnumbered the European population.

Winston Churchill's testimony to the Sikh soldier, the Indian trader, the Indian banker who advanced financial aid even to the white settlers, and his protest against a policy of deliberately squeezing out the native of India from regions in which he had established himself under every security of public faith, were largely quoted by Moderate politicians in the Indian Central Legislature. Indians resented the prohibition against the transfer to Indians of agricultural lands in the highlands of the Colony, the region which stretches across the road to Uganda with its cotton fields, where Indian interests are already considerable. Compulsory segregation, the denial of franchise to Indians, and the prohibition of Indian immigration, it was feared, may be forced on Kenya, by the intolerance of the European community. The very Churchill who had "accepted the recognition of the Imperial Conference that there is an incongruity between the position of India as an equal member of the Empire and the existence of disabilities upon Indians lawfully domiciled," was the Colonial Secretary in 1921. Early in 1923, the Colonial Office sent for the Governor of Kenya and he proceeded to London along with European and Indian delegations, for the purpose of discussing the terms of a final settlement. Likewise the Indian Central Legislature sent a delegation of which Sastriar was the leader. The Kenya Indian delegation asked Mr. C. F. Andrews to accompany them as their adviser. In this capacity he rendered to the cause of Indians in Kenya notable help for which the Working Committee thanked him in April, 1923.

The problem became more urgent in view of proposals in the air to carve out one great union of Rhodesia, Tanganyika, Nyassaland, Uganda and Kenya. The position of Indians in Uganda was dependent upon the settlement of the Kenya problem. 'Segregation' was infecting this Colony as well. In the township of Kampala, a residential site, away from European quarters, was assigned to Asiatics in Uganda. The Government of India's representations were of no avail. In Tanganyika, on the assurances of Lord Milner in 1921, Indians bought enemy property, and the equal rights promised were sought to be set aside by the three Ordinances introduced by Government "for fiscal purposes." An extensive *hartal* was organised which persisted up to the middle of April, 1922. Restrictions on travel by 1st class in Railways were imposed, but were withdrawn.

We have given all these details because the Congress took a definite step early in August, 1923 on the question. The resolution passed by the A.I.C.C. runs as follows:—

> "The decision of the British Government on the Kenya question having made it clear that it is not possible for India to have an equal and honourable place in the British Empire, the A.I.C.C. of the Indian National Congress is of opinion that there should be a solemn demonstration throughout India to mark the event."

The Committee then prescribed a peaceful *hartal* on the 26th of August with meetings everywhere calling upon people to abstain from participation in the British Empire Exhibition, the Imperial Conference, the Empire Day celebrations and all other Imperial functions.

Delhi Special Congress, 1923

Now we pass on to the Special Session of the Congress at Delhi convened in the 3rd week of September, 1923. The President, Maulana Abul Kalam Azad, is a great Muslim Divine who commands respect and popularity in Bengal as well as Delhi, and whose clear head and impartial judgment were trusted to by both parties alike. There was not much difficulty in the pro-Council party getting the Congress to register their wishes in a permissive resolution which declared that "such Congressmen as have no religious or other conscientious objections against entering the legislatures are at liberty to stand as candidates and to exercise their right of voting at the forthcoming elections. And this Congress, therefore, suspends all propaganda against entering the Councils." Of course, a rider was added urging that redoubled efforts be put forth in behalf of the constructive programme. The death of Pandit Rambhuj Dutt Choudhri, the earthquake in Japan, forced abdication of Nabha, and floods in Bihar, Kanara and Burma were the subjects of suitable resolutions of condolence and sympathy. Then a Committee was appointed to organise an effective campaign of Civil Disobedience and to advise and regulate the action of Provinces in this behalf. Another Committee was appointed to revise the Constitution, and still another to prepare a draft of the National Pact. The Press was warned to observe great restraint in dealing with matters relating to inter-communal relations, and the appointment of District Conciliation Committees was advised. The Akalis were once again congratulated on their courageous and non-violent stand against repression, culminating in the arrest of the Enquiry Committee sent by the Siromani Gurudwara Prabandhak Committee. The boycott of foreign cloth through khaddar was urged and a Committee was appointed to determine the most feasible methods of encouraging Indian manufactures and the boycott of British goods in particular. The Flag Satyagraha campaign received congratulation on its successful finish and the released prisoners, notably Lalaji and Maulana Mahomed Ali were welcomed.

Kenya became the subject of indignation, and Turkey for jubilation. Two more Committees were appointed, one to recommend measures to prevent the Hindu-Muslim dissensions which had recently shown a recrudescence and the other to investigate allegations of force in respect of *Suddhi* and anti-*Suddhi* movements. The formation of Civic Guards and the promotion of physical culture were finally urged on the Nation for the maintenance of peace and order.

The way was cleared at Delhi for a realignment of the course of the Congress. The revolt at Gaya had nearly borne fruit. Nay, the Delhi resolutions bear testimony to a complete change in the outlook of those that had the ordering of things in their hands. The large number of Committees—altogether five, was itself an indication of leisure created anew which could not be better occupied than in a re-examination of the several questions committed to their care. "Civic Guards and physical culture" wound up the deliberations, while the question of Council-entry opened them. There was, perhaps, a tinge of a taint in that the resolution regarding Council-entry was only permissive, but the feeling of the mass of the population on the subject had to be respected. The way was, however, clear to those who were inclined to take part in the ensuing elections, and Congressmen were for the first time divided in their attention to a programme which itself was divided in its course. The principles and policy to be followed by the Swaraj party were set forth in a manifesto.

The next annual session of the Congress was to meet at Cocanada. There were lingering hopes in the minds of a few no-changers that, though Cocanada might not be able to undo what Delhi had done, for the elections would be over by that time, still the banner of orthodox

Non-co-operation should be kept raised at an annual session. Maulana Mahomed Ali was chosen as the President of the year. He had coined a phrase even at Delhi that a bird was whispering in his ears that Gandhi himself would not object to Council-entry, and the phrase was literally taken by not a few in the country. The basis for such a statement was a message, to which related the veiled reference, sent by Gandhi in prison to Mahomed Ali free, through Devidas Gandhi, which is available to the public. "I can send you no message," said Gandhi, "because I am in prison. I have always disapproved of people sending messages from prison. But I may say that I am deeply touched by your loyalty to me. I would, however, ask you not to allow your loyalty to me to weigh with you so much as your loyalty to the country. My views are very well known. I expressed them before I went to jail and there has been no change in them since. I may assure you that if you chose to differ from me, it will not affect by one jot the sweetness of the relations between you and me." Does this sound like supporting Council-entry? Mahomed Ali was anyway for peace and Shaukat Ali, who presided over the Khilaphat Conference of the year, was equally for peace. Their aged mother's exhortations in the open Congress *'ettifaq se raho'* could not be easily ignored. Yet, at Cocanada a strong resistance was put up. Only some of the pronounced No-changers had disappeared from the leadership of the party. Rajendra Babu could not attend the Cocanada Session owing to ill-health and Mr. C. Rajāgopalachari cast his weight on the side of the Delhi resolution. Syt. Vallabhbhai was present, but his assent to the Delhi settlement had been wrung out of him at the Delhi Session. Shyam Sunder Chakravarti, the woe-struck man of Bengal, who had suffered years of deportation and imprisonment, of poverty and misery, was the man who moved the mighty audience of Cocanada to tears by his speech opposing Council-entry. But the die was cast. The fate of the Council-Boycott was sealed. We give below the main resolution:—

> "This Congress reaffirms the Non-co-operation resolutions adopted at Calcutta, Nagpur, Ahmedabad, Gaya and Delhi.
>
> "Since doubts have been raised by reason of the Non-co-operation resolution adopted at Delhi with regard to Council-entry, whether there has been any change in the policy of the Congress, this Congress affirms that the principle and policy of that boycott remain unaltered.
>
> "This Congress further declares that the said principle and policy form the foundation of constructive work and appeals to the Nation to carry out the programme of constructive work as adopted at Bardoli and prepare for the adoption of Civil Disobedience. This Congress further calls upon every P.C.C. to take immediate steps in this behalf with a view to speedy attainment of our goal."

The Cocanada Congress was memorable for more than one feature. It was perhaps the grandest Congress ever held,—for the lay-out of roads, for the magnificent tent which was to be permanently the property of the Congress, for the close attention paid to the smallest detail in arrangements, for the equable weather, and for the housing of Presidents and leaders on the premises. Such a Congress made itself memorable too for the interpretation that Non-co-operation could be effected as much from inside the Councils as from outside. It was the unpleasant duty of Cocanada to record the Nation's sorrow over the demise of S. Kasturi Ranga Iyengar, whose Nationalism was an evergrowing culture and who, like Dadabhai, was on a level with his age, and of Aswini Kumar Datta who was loved all over Bengal and whose memory is revered all over the country. The continued incarceration of Damodar Vinayak Savarkar evoked condemnation by the Congress. The National Pact that was prepared was asked to be circulated along with the 'Bengal Pact' prepared by Deshbandhu Das. The Congress welcomed the movement for the formation of an all-India volunteer organisation into which was later merged the movement of Civic Guards.

A scheme of separate Congress Departments was called for, as also a scheme of a National Service of paid workers to work these various departments. Kenya aroused the whole-hearted—albeit powerless—sympathy of the Congress, and Srimathi Sarojini Devi and Mr. George Joseph were deputed as delegates to the Kenya Indian Congress.

The Civil Disobedience Committee appointed at Delhi and the Satyagraha Committee were absorbed in the Working Committee. An All-India Khaddar Board was formed with power to organise khaddar work. Emigration was advised to be stopped from India, and a Committee was appointed to examine Labour conditions of Indian emigrants to Ceylon. A number of amendments to the Constitution were carried, and finally the Congress took up Government's challenge to the right of free association of Indians for non-violent activities in attacking the Akali Dal of the S. G. P. Committee and resolved to stand by the Sikhs in their 'present' struggle and render all possible assistance, including assistance with men and money.

At this point, it is but meet to digress a while and give a succinct account of the birth of the Reform movement amongst the Sikhs. The Akali Sikhs with their black turbans and cries of 'Sat Sri Akal' and their

Langar Khanas had become an unfailing annexe to the Congress. When a foreign Government assumes control over the country, it is only to be expected that, octopus-like, they would extend their grasp over almost every institution in the land, economic, educational or even religious. The English annexed the Punjab in 1849, and when in the transition, the affairs of the Golden Temple at Amritsar, the centre and stronghold of Sikhism, were in confusion, a Committee of baptized Sikhs was appointed as Trustee with a Government-appointed Sarbrah or guardian. They had a manager handling lacs a year, and as often happens in such cases, the Committee was dropped in 1881, and the manager became all-powerful. Want of control bred irresponsibility and corruption, and after repeated clashes between managers and priests on one side and the Sikh public on the other, with a puzzled Government in the middle, a Committee was established towards the end of 1920 which became the Gurudwara Siromani Prabandhak Committee, whose first President was Sirdar Sundar Singh Majithia who became, shortly after, a Member of the Executive Council of the Punjab Government. The Reformists were known as Akalis who brought more historic Gurudwaras under their control. A collision occurred at Tara Taran in which several Sikhs were injured and two died. We have already described at length the tragedy of Nankana Sahib early in 1921, and the cold-blooded murders of innocent pilgrims in it. The Police looked upon the movement as one designed for the capture of power and wealth associated with the Gurudwaras. This view encouraged *mahants*—even those who had settled terms with the Akalis, to resile from them and Government also pursued a "policy of wholesale repression against the Reforming Sikhs." In May, 1921, hundreds of Sikhs were thrown into prison and the discredited *mahants* were restored to power.

The S.G.P.C., therefore, passed a resolution of N.C.O. with Government, so far as this Reform was concerned, in May, 1921.

The Gurudwara Bill contemplated by Government had to be dropped, being unacceptable to any shade of opinion, including moderates and co-operators. Sikhs were prosecuted for wearing *kripans* beyond certain length. The Punjab Provincial Congress Committee protested on 10th July, 1921, and the Sikhs imprisoned were released at the end of the month. Barbarous sentences of 18 years and 7 years R. I. were passed against Bhai Kartar Singh of Jhabbar and Bhai Raja Singh of Bhuchar. On the 28th August, 1921, the Sikh members of the Legislatures were called upon to resign. Sirdar Bahadur Sirdar Mehtab Singh, Barrister-at-Law, resigned his Government Advocateship and Deputy Presidentship of the Punjab Legislative Council, as a protest against the policy of Government regarding the Gurudwara movement. These two long-term prisoners and many others were released in the beginning of September, 1921. But Sirdar Sardul Singh Kaveeshar, General Secretary of the Punjab P.C.C., who had been sentenced to 5 years R. I. under S. 124-A I.P.C. in June, 1921, and other Gurudwara workers were not released. Suddenly on the 7th November, 1921, Government snatched away the keys of the *toshakhanas* of the Golden Temple. This prevented the decoration on the birthday of Sri Guru Nanak Dev. A certain manager was appointed temporarily by Government, but he was not allowed to assume charge by the S.G.P.C. and he resigned. Since then the 'keys' became the bone of contention and the subject of public meetings of protest. But Government applied the Seditious Meetings Act from the 26th November, 1921, and Sirdars Kharak Singh and Mehtab Singh were sentenced to R. I. Sri Guru Govind Singh's birthday was coming off on the 5th January, 1922, and Government offered the keys to the S. G. P. C. pending the final decision of the civil suit filed by Government. The S.G.P.C. refused. After 200 Sikh workers were arrested, Government stopped their course and released all prisoners unconditionally, and the keys were restored on 11-1-'22. Pandit Dina Nath's continued detention gave rise to renewed agitation and Civil Disobedience of the Seditious Meetings Act, the whole Executive Committee of the S.G.P.C. speaking at a public meeting on the 8th February, 1922. He was then released, as also Baba Gurudutt Singh of the *Komagatamaru* fame (1914). The S.G.P.C. was not a political body, but in a small community, politicians and Social or Religious Reformers easily get mixed up or even identified. Nor would Government allow this distinction to be maintained. The religious prestige of the Durbar Sahib was used to whitewash the crimes of General Dyer, when he was given Khila'at at the Golden Temple by the official manager, and Lord Finlay turned this event to the best account in the House of Lords when he said that the Sikhs had approved of General Dyer's action and even made him a Sikh. Again, it was in the Golden Temple that the official manager got it proclaimed that the Budge Budge martyrs were not Sikhs. Government obtained a war loan of Rs. 50,000 from the Temple funds during the Great War.

The Akalis wore black Turbans. From about the 2nd week of March, 1922, "by a well arranged *coup*, wholesale arrests of Akalis were carried simultaneously in 13 selected Districts of the Punjab and the Sikh States of Patiala and Kapurthala, and within a fortnight about 1,700 black-turbaned Sikhs were arrested." Sirdar Kharak Singh, President of the S.G.P.C. and the P.P.C.C. was given 4 years R. I. "Kripans," Government said, early in March, 1922, "were swords and their manufacture required licenses." People were directed to wear Kripans in the manner prescribed by Government. Some Military Sikhs were imprisoned for wearing them at all and received sentences ranging from 4 to 18 years, R. I. Baba Gurudutt Singh (of the *Komagatamaru*) was rearrested and sentenced to 5 years' transportation in July, 1922, and Master Mota Singh of the anti-Rowlatt Act agitation, for 8 years.

The Criminal Law Amendment Act was the supreme master of the day and the security sections were its assistants. "The Police were the masters of the situation and they had a jolly time of it," wrote a leader. Pandit Malaviya visited the Punjab and got a Committee appointed under the Presidency of Dewan Bahadur Raja Narendra Nath "to investigate the official excesses, illegalities and barbarities." The Punjab Government published a communique dated 14th May, 1922, warning the Religious Reformers against association with "the disorderly and Criminal conduct of men, who have no real connection with Reform." The reference was obviously to Congressmen. Altogether 1,900 to 2,000 Sikh workers were arrested by the 15th June, 1922.

Then occurred the Guruka Bagh affair which has been mentioned under the year 1922. Suffice it to say here that the Sikhs proved Gandhi's statement that "to face a bullet was easier than receive a *lathi* blow and those who endured it non-violently deserved their respect." The excesses committed in connection with this event were the subject of enquiry by an European of the Punjab Government. Men like Mr. Andrews bore testimony to their serious character. "It is one of the most moving and pathetic sights I ever have seen," said he, "the triumph of non-violence is so complete. It is to the men a real martyrdom. There was a blockade, as pointed out by Pandit Motilal Nehru, and not a particle of any foodstuff was allowed to pass the barbed wire fencing for several days and those who carried such stuff were severely beaten." "My car was searched," he added "at the entrance to the Gurudwaras, before it was allowed to pass through the small opening in the fencing."

One woman was wounded because she nursed some sufferers. One bore the marks of horse's hoofs. Two were killed and when Government launched a case against the alleged culprits, they were acquitted. Some of the spectators were harassed, there were allegations of theft and robbery and looting against the Police—in the Press. Mr. MacPherson, Superintendent of Police, was the author of a book on *lathi*-exercises and bore testimony as follows:—

> "It is quite possible that some injuries, such as fractures, may have occurred. The *jathas* did not resist the Police at any time, being quite non-violent. It is possible that some of the injured became unconscious. 953 cases of injuries had been tabulated as 269 above the trunk, 300 on the front of the body, 79 brain, 60 to genitals, 19 to perinaeum, 7 to teeth, and 158 contused wounds, 8 incised, 2 punctured, 40 urine trouble, 9 fractures and 2 dislocations."

There were 210 arrests in this connection. Fines to the tune of Rs. 1,27,000 were levied by a single Honorary Magistrate at 4 sittings. Swami Shraddhanand was sentenced to 18 months. On the 22nd October, a *jatha* solely composed of 101 Military pensioners, containing about 55 non-commissioned officers, the remaining being sepoys, started with Military band from Amritsar to Guruka Bagh and 50,000 men accompanied them. When the train carrying the Military prisoners after conviction was approaching Panja Saheb, a number of people were waiting with food for the prisoners and on hearing that the train would not stop at the station, squatted on the Railway line. The train was not stopped and the result was that two died and eleven were injured. After a time, the beating stopped and arrests took place. 'Ring-leaders' were severely punished. But the worst of it was not yet over. When in response to public pressure and to a resolution of the Punjab Council on the 8th March, '23; the Akalis were released in batches, one batch of 170 Akalis released at Rawalpindi were severely mauled and injured and dispersed by force on the ground that they did not take the stated route from the Railway station. Military, Police and Cavalry combined to effect the dispersal. 128 persons received serious injuries. Pindi observed a complete *hartal* from 3rd May in sympathy. When a Committee was suggested to go into the whole affair, in the Punjab Legislative Council, the Chief Secretary to the Punjab Government quietly asked the people to let by-gones be by-gones and let the memories of the unhappy events of Guruka Bagh die as speedily as possible and not to rake up old sores as the Hunter Committee had done. To knock down a fellow and ask him to forget it quickly is neither statesmanship nor sportsmanship. Yet the majority of the members of the Punjab Legislative Council were satisfied and did not press the Resolution moved by Mr. K. Rallia Ram. The troubles of the Akalis were not destined to be over yet, and we may as well give them now in a connected form, in spite of the fact that we are partly anticipating the events of the year 1924. The Maharaja of Nabha 'abdicated' in the middle of 1923, but this was interpreted by the S.G.P.C. as deposition and it began an agitation for his restoration, holding meetings at Jaito in the Nabha State, among other places. The speeches delivered were alleged to be seditious and the speakers, while engaged in reading the *Akhand Pant*, were arrested.

Trouble thus arose over the reading of the *Akhand Pant* at Jaito in the Nabha State and *jathas* of 25 continued to be sent daily for some time to Jaito to resume the reading. Later in February, a 'Shahidi' *jatha* of 500 was sent. Dr. Kitchlew and Acharya A. T. Gidwani accompanied this *jatha* as spectators. It was fired on near Jaito and there were some deaths. Kitchlew and Gidwani were both arrested by the Nabha authorities, on attempting to render aid to the injured, but the former was released after a few days while the latter continued to be in the Nabha jail till the year-end. 'Shahidi' *jathas* continued to march and met with arrests. Thousands of these Akalis were in jail and the treatment given to them was reported to be bad. Acharya Gidwani's place on the Akali Sahayak Bureau was taken by Mr. K. M. Panikkar. The Working Committee sent an Enquiry Sub-Committee to enquire into charges of ill-treatment of Akali prisoners and also rendered substantial financial aid to the families of Akali prisoners. The whole question was settled later when an Act was passed regarding the control of the Gurudwaras.

CHAPTER V

Congress at the Cross-roads (1924)

I

The year 1924 opened, in a sense, with absolute gloom in the atmosphere, Gandhi's sudden and serious illness in jail overshadowing every thing else. Most people associate particular years with particular outstanding events. So do we, and when we think of 1924, we call to mind Gandhi's serious illness, operation and release four years before it was due, the triumph of the Swaraj party in the Legislatures, then the Akali troubles to which we have already referred, the murder of Earnest Day in the streets of Calcutta and the Dinajpur resolution on Gopinath Saha, the Juhu conversations and their failure, the All-India Congress Committee meeting at Ahmedabad and the ever-memorable scenes and strifes that occurred at it, the renewed repression in Bengal followed by the arrest of Subash Chandra Bose and other eminent Congressmen, the communal riots, Gandhi's fast of 21 days and the Unity Conference at Delhi, the threat of arrest of C. R. Das, the All-Parties' Conference in Bombay and its infructuous deliberations, the death of Bi Amma, —the aged and venerable mother of the Ali Brothers,— the Belgaum Congress with Gandhi as President and the division of the Congress activities into two distinctive fronts,—the constructive front and the Council front.

Gandhi's sudden illness with appendicitis on the 12th January, 1924 and the radical operation for appendicitis at the hands of Colonel Maddock at dead of night caused widespread anxiety in the country, but it was soon relieved by Gandhi's fair recovery and his premature and unconditional release on the 5th February.

His release brought him, however, no rest or peace. The split that occurred at Cocanada was tending to become wider and wider. On the one hand the no-changers were hoping that Gandhi's return might reverse the engine of the Congress, back along the track of Civil Disobedience. On the other, the pro-changers were naturally anxious to consolidate their victories at Delhi and Cocanada and take away from them the taint that appeared still to be clinging to them. Earnest efforts were made to reconcile the conflicting issues and stand-points in the country. Gandhi spent some time in Juhu —a sea-side resort near Bombay, and what later came to be known as the Juhu conversations between Gandhi and Messrs. Das and Nehru went on for a time raising hopes of agreement. In the month of May, 1924, Gandhi published a statement which we make no apology for extracting in full, for its sympathetic tone is as clear as its prophetic character, and side by side with it we give the statement of Deshbandhu Das and Motilalji which were simultaneously published at the time.

Before we publish these historic statements, it is but right to state the developments in the Assembly and the powerful hold which the Swarajists had attained over the forces inside the Legislature.

The Swaraj Party having been organized, the elections to the various Legislative bodies were contested by the Swaraj Party, and the Legislative Assembly presented a compact and well-disciplined party of 45 Swarajists who were pledged to carry out their programme. They could easily command a working majority in the Legislature by securing the sympathy and support of the Nationalist Party—composed of equally patriotic citizens though they had not accepted the cult of Non-co-operation. With this accession of strength, the

Swarajists secured a series of victories,—the first being on Pandit Motilal Nehru's amendment in favour of "a Round Table Conference to recommend a Scheme of Full Responsible Government in India," to a proposition tabled by Mr. T. Rangachari pressing for an immediate change in the constitutional machinery. Panditji challenged the justice of the Preamble of the Government of India Act of 1919, and at the same time declared "that his party could not be dismissed as wreckers. He was not asking for Responsible Government, to be handed over as it were, tied up in a bundle. His party had come there to offer their co-operation. If the Government would receive this co-operation, they would find that the Swarajists were their men. If not, the Swarajists would stand on their rights and continue to be Non-co-operators."

Sir M. Hailey, the Home Member, stated that the demand for Dominion Status was entirely new and it was inconsistent with the specific provision of the Government of India Act, that advance towards Self-Government was to take the form of successive stages. Government had a series of defeats and amongst the most notable of these may be mentioned the passing of the resolutions calling for the release of certain political prisoners, for the repeal of Regulation III of 1818, for the imposition of a countervailing duty on South African coal imported into India and for the appointment of a Committee of enquiry into the Sikh situation. The defeats of Government were really victories to the Swaraj Party whose strength was reinforced by the strength of the Independents, the Nationalists, and even the Moderates from time to time. We say so because the Swaraj Party had laid down in its programme that its "demand should take the shape of an ultimatum calling for the release of all political prisoners, for the repeal of all repressive laws, and for the summoning of a National Convention to lay down the lines of the future Constitution for India."

Refusal of Supply:—The next great achievement for the Swarajists was the throwing out of the first four heads under the demand for grants. This "unprecedented course" was tantamount to the refusal of supplies. Pandit Motilal Nehru contended on the other hand "that his present motion has nothing to do with the wrecking or destroying policy of Non-co-operation, and was in effect a perfectly constitutional and legitimate means of drawing attention to the grievances of the country."

We now give the statements of Gandhi and of Das and Nehru which were issued as a result of the Juhu conversations, in order to present to the reader the developments that took place by the middle of summer, 1924.

Gandhi's Statement

A FUNDAMENTAL DIFFERENCE

After having discussed with Swarajist friends, the vexed question of entry into the Legislative Assembly and the Councils by Congressmen, I am sorry to have to say that I have not been able to see eye to eye with the Swarajists. I assure the public that there has been no lack of willingness or effort on my part to accept the Swarajist position. My task would be much simpler if I could identify myself with it. It can be no pleasure to me to oppose, even in thought, the most valued and respected leaders, some of whom have made great sacrifices in the cause of the country and who yield to no one in their love of freedom of the Motherland; but in spite of my effort and willingness, I have failed to be convinced by their argument. Nor is the difference between them and myself one of mere detail. There is an honest and fundamental difference. I retain the opinion that Council-entry is inconsistent with Non-co-operation, as I conceive it. Nor is this difference a mere matter of interpretation of the word 'Non-co-operation,' but relates to the essential mental attitude resulting in different treatment of vital problems. It is with reference to such mental attitude that the success or failure of the triple boycott is to be judged, and not merely by a reference to the actual results attained. It is from that point of view that I say that to be out of the legislative bodies is far more advantageous to the country than to be in them. I have, however, failed to convince my Swarajist friends, but I recognise, so long as they think otherwise, their place is undoubtedly in the Councils. It is the best for us all.

It was hardly to be expected that the Swarajists could be convinced by the arguments I advanced in the course of the conversations. There are many of them who are amongst the ablest, most experienced, and honest patriots. They have not entered the legislative bodies, without full deliberation, and they must not be expected to retire from the position until experience has convinced them of the futility of their method.

The question, therefore, before the country is not an examination and distribution of the merits of the Swarajist view and mine. The question is, what is to be done now regarding Council-entry as a settled fact? Are the Non-co-operators to keep up their hostility against the Swarajist method, or are they to remain neutral and even help wherever it is possible or consistent with their principles?

NO ANTI-SWARAJIST PROPAGANDA

The Delhi and Cocanada resolutions have permitted those Congressmen who have no conscientious scruples to enter the Councils and the Assembly if they wanted to. In my opinion, the Swarajists are, therefore, justified in entering the legislative bodies and expecting perfect neutrality on the part of the 'no-changers.' They are also justified in resorting to obstruction, because such was their policy, and the Congress laid down no condition as to their entry. If the work of the Swarajists prospers and the country benefits, such an ocular demonstration cannot but convince honest sceptics like me of our error, and I know the Swarajists to be patriotic enough to retrace their steps when experience has disillusioned them. I would therefore be no party to putting any obstacles in their way or to carrying on any propaganda against the Swarajists' entry into the Legislatures, though I cannot actively help them in a project in which I do not believe. The purpose of the Delhi and Cocanada resolutions was to allow the Swarajists a chance of trying the method of Council-entry and that purpose can be served only if the 'no-changers,' with scrupulous honesty, allow the Swarajists full liberty to pursue their programme in the Councils, unfettered by any obstruction from them.

POLICY WITHIN COUNCILS

With regard to the method of work in the Councils, I will say that I would enter a legislative body, if only I found that I could, at all, use it to advantage. If, therefore, I enter the Councils, I should, without following a general policy of obstruction, endeavour to give strength to the constructive programme of the Congress. I should, therefore, move resolutions requiring the Central and Provincial Governments, as the case may be,

(1) To make all their cloth purchases in hand-spun and hand-woven khaddar.

(2) To impose a prohibitive duty on foreign cloth.

(3) To abolish the drink and drug revenue, and at least correspondingly reduce the Army expenditure.

If the Government refuse to enforce such resolutions when carried in the Legislatures, I should invite them to dissolve them and take the vote of the electors on the specific points. If the Government would not dissolve, I should resign my seat and prepare the country for Civil Disobedience. When that stage is reached, the Swarajists will find me ready to work with and under them. My test of fitness for Civil Disobedience remains the same as before.

ADVICE TO NO-CHANGERS

During the state of probation, I should advise the 'no-changers' not to worry about what the Swarajists are doing or saying, and to prove their own faith by prosecuting the constructive programme with undivided energy and concentration. Khaddar and National Schools are enough to occupy every available worker who believes in quiet, honest and undemonstrative work. The Hindu-Muslim problem too will tax the best energy and faith of the workers. The 'no-changers' can justify their opposition to Council-entry, only by showing the results of their application to the constructive programme, even as the 'pro-changers' must justify their entry by results. The 'no-changers' are in one respect in an advantageous position, for they can secure the co-operation of the 'pro-changers.' The latter have declared their faith in the constructive programme, but their contention is that, by itself, the constructive programme cannot enable the country to reach the goal. In the prosecution, however, of the constructive programme outside the Legislatures, all,—'no-changers,' 'pro-changers' and others,—can, if they will, work in union through their respective organisations, if necessary.

The statement is incomplete without an examination of the working, of the Congress organisation. I hold drastic and definite views in the matter, but I must reserve their expression for a future, though early, occasion.

SWARAJIST STATEMENT

The following is the statement of Mr. C.R. Das and Pandit Motilal Nehru:—

We are obliged to Mahatma Gandhi for the trouble he has taken to discuss with us the various points involved in the question of Council-entry, and are indebted to his courtesy for the opportunity we have had of seeing an advance copy of the statement he has issued to the Press. The views expressed by him in the course of the conversation, and those embodied in the Press statement, have all been considered by us with the care and attention due to his great personality, but, with all the reverence we entertain for him and his opinions, we remain unconvinced by his reasoning.

COUNCIL ENTRY AND N. C. O

We regret that we have not been able to convince Mahatma Gandhi of the soundness of the Swarajist position regarding Council-entry. We fail to understand how such entry can be regarded as inconsistent with the Non-co-operation resolution of the Nagpur Congress. But if Non-co-operation is more a matter of mental attitude than of the application of a living principle to the existing facts of our national life, with special reference to the varying attitude of the bureaucratic Government which rules that life, we conceive it to be our duty to sacrifice even Non-co-operation to serve the real interests of the country. In our view, this principle includes self-reliance in all the activities which make for the healthy growth of the Nation and resistance to the bureaucracy as it impedes our progress towards Swaraj. We are, however, anxious to end this fruitless verbal discussion, making it clear that Council-entry is, and can be, thoroughly consistent with the principle of Non-co-operation as we understand that principle to be.

IMPLICATIONS OF OBSTRUCTION

We desire further to make it clear that we have not used in our programme the word 'obstruction' in the technical sense of English Parliamentary history. Obstruction in that sense is impossible in subordinate and limited legislative bodies, such as the Legislative Assembly and Provincial Legislatures under the Reforms Act undoubtedly are. Possibly another word should have been found to convey our meaning.

We may state, however, that our position is really not so much that of obstruction in the Parliamentary sense as that of resistance to the obstruction placed in our path to Swaraj by the bureaucratic Government. It is this resistance which we meant to imply when we used the word 'obstruction.' This was clearly indicated in the way we defined and described Non-co-operation in the preamble to the Constitution of the Swaraj Party. It is the removal of such bureaucratic obstruction which we feel we must emphasize. This is the policy which we have hitherto followed in the legislative bodies, and it is this policy which must in future be more and more effectively directed to the varying needs and problems of our national life.

Here again we are anxious to end all verbal discussion as to whether this can be aptly described as a policy of "uniform, continuous and consistent obstruction." We are content to detail our policy and then leave it to our friends to give it a more appropriate name, should they so desire.

FUTURE PROGRAMME OF WORK

In the light of this principle and policy, we would here state our future programme of action within and outside the legislative bodies.

Within the legislative bodies we must continue:—

(1). To throw out budgets unless and until the system of Government is altered in recognition of our rights, or as a matter of settlement between Parliament and the people of this country. In justification of this step, all that we need point out are a few salient facts connected with the Budget in the Central Government, which are more or less true of Provincial Budgets also. Out of a total of 131 crores (excluding railways) only 16 crores are votable. Further, out of the non-votable amount, as much as 67 crores, *i.e.*, more than half the amount of the Budget are for Military expenditure. It is thus clear that the people of this country have the right to vote only less than 1/7 of the total amount of the Budget, and even the exercise of this limited right is subject to the power of restoration vested in the Governor-General. It is, therefore, clear that the people have neither any voice in the framing of the Budget, nor any control over those who frame it. They have no power either over the raising of the revenue or its expenditure. On what principle then, may we ask, is it our duty to pass such a Budget and take the responsibility of being a party to it? We have no doubt of the support of many self-respecting men in the country in holding, as we do, that it is our clear duty to throw out such Budgets in all legislative bodies, unless and until this vicious system is changed.

REJECTION OF LEGISLATIVE PROPOSALS

2. To throw out all proposals for Legislative enactments by which the bureaucracy proposes to consolidate its power. It is conceivable that some good may incidentally result from a few of such measures; but we are clearly of opinion that in the larger interests of the country it is better to temporarily sacrifice such little benefits rather than add an iota to the powers of the bureaucracy, which are already irresistible.

THE CONSTRUCTIVE PROGRAMME

3. To introduce all resolutions, measures and bills which are necessary for the healthy growth of our National life and the consequent displacement of the bureaucracy. We heartily accept the suggestions made by Mahatma Gandhi in his statement, and we think that the resolutions mentioned by him in support of the constructive programme of the Congress should certainly be accepted by the Swaraj Party. The principle of self-reliance and resistance to bureaucratic obstruction, upon which we have hitherto acted, calls for their adoption, and if the constructive work of the Congress comes within the principle of Non-co-operation, no less do these resolutions, although they represent constructive activity within the legislative bodies.

4. To follow a definite economic policy, based on the same principles, so as to prevent the drain of public wealth from India by checking all activities leading to exploitation.

To make this policy effective, we should take and occupy every place which is open to the members of the Central and Provincial Legislatures by election. In our opinion, we should not only fill elective posts, but serve on every Committee where it is possible. We invite the attention of the members of our Party to this important question, and we call upon them to decide this matter as soon as possible.

POLICY OUTSIDE COUNCILS

Our policy outside the legislative bodies should be as follows:—

In the first place we should give our whole-hearted support to the constructive programme of Mahatma Gandhi and work that programme unitedly through the Congress organisations. We are decidedly of opinion that our Council work must necessarily lose much of its strength without the backing of the constructive work outside, for it is not inside but outside the Legislatures that we must look for that sanction without which the effective carrying out of our Council policy is impossible. Indeed, in the matter of constructive work, the mutual support of both inside and outside activity must, in our opinion, give strength to the very sanction upon which we rely. In this connection, we unhesitatingly accept the suggestion of Mahatma Gandhi regarding Civil Disobedience. We can assure him that the moment we find that it is impossible to meet the selfish obstinacy of the bureaucracy without Civil Disobedience, we will retire from the legislative bodies and help him to prepare the country for Civil Disobedience, if by that time the country has not already become prepared, and we will then unreservedly place ourselves under his guidance, and work through the

Congress organisation under his banner, in order that we may unitedly work out a substantial programme of Civil Disobedience.

LABOUR AND THE CONGRESS

In the second place, we must supplement the work of the Congress by helping the labour and peasant organisations throughout the country. The problem of labour is always a difficult problem to solve in every country, but in India the difficulties are greater. On the one hand, we must find out a way of organisation by which we can prevent exploitation of labour by capitalists or by landlords, but on the other hand, we must be on our guard to see that these very organisations may not themselves be the source of oppression by nursing extravagant and unreasonable demands. Labour, undoubtedly, requires protection, but so do industrial enterprises. Our organisation must protect both from exploitation, and the Trade Union Congress must be so organised as to be able to serve this useful purpose. We hold that in the long run the real interests of both and of the country at large are identical.

CONCLUSION

We feel happy that we have had this opportunity of putting our views before the country side by side with Mahatma Gandhi's opinion, for we feel certain that their persual will make it obvious that, notwithstanding some differences of view, there is an abiding and fundamental unity amongst both parties of the Indian National Congress. Both parties feel the necessity of working the constructive programme whether within or outside the legislative bodies. In this direction, we feel confident, lies the germ of a fruitful alliance between Mahatma Gandhi and the Swaraj Party. Our joint effort, in the same or different directions, will furnish a fitting answer to the bureaucracy, unwilling to recognise the rights and liberties of the Indian people, and we emphatically assert that, in our determination to work with the same object in the same or different spheres, is expressed the determination of the Indian Nation to bring the struggle for Swaraj to a successful issue.

The Juhu conversations paved the way for the decisions of the A.I.C.C. taken at Ahmedabad on June 27, 28, and 29th. All members of elected Congress organizations were required to send in 2,000 yards of even and well-twisted self-spun yarn every month, and a penalty clause was attached to it, by which any default in this behalf would automatically create a vacancy in the position of the defaulter. When this was being discussed, a number of members walked out of the Committee to mark their resentment of the penalty clause. Accordingly, although it was passed by 67 to 37 votes, still, in view of the possible reversal of voting "if the votes of the withdrawals had been given 'against,'" the penalty clause was withdrawn by Gandhi. The Committee recommended disciplinary action against defaulters in general.

Emphasis was laid next on the five boycotts,—of foreign cloth, Government Law Courts, schools and colleges, titles, and Legislatures, subject to the Cocanada resolution, and Congress voters were strictly enjoined not to elect to the various organizations subordinate to the Congress those who do not believe in the principle, and do not carry out in their own person, the said five boycotts. The opium policy of Government was condemned, the Rev. C. F. Andrews being requested to conduct an enquiry into the opium habits of the Assamese people. The Sikhs were congratulated on their bravery and cool courage exhibited at the time of unnecessary and cruel firing at Jaito.

The resolution of the sitting that excited much feeling was the one relating to the condemnation of the murder of Mr. Earnest Day by Gopi Nath Saha which the Committee regretted. It offered its condolence to the family of the deceased, and, though deeply sensible of the love, however misguided, of the country prompting the murder, the A.I.C.C. strongly condemned this and all such political murders and was emphatically of opinion that all such acts were inconsistent with the non-violent policy of the Congress, and was of opinion that such acts retard the progress towards Swaraj and interfere with the preparations for Civil Disobedience. There was a battle-royal over this resolution. There was no concealing the fact that it was not to the Deshbandhu's taste; not that he did not swear by non-violence, but that he would change the emphasis on the different clauses considerably. Gandhi was disappointed to find some of his dearest and closest followers voting against the resolution, and that was one of the few occasions on which he wept in public. The tension of the situation was due to the fact that at the Dinajpore (Bengal) Provincial Conference a much stronger resolution had been passed applauding Gopinath Saha's selflessness and sacrifice, and paying its respectful homage to his patriotism.

The Swarajists did not secure at this meeting all that they would have liked to, and they had to wait till November before they consolidated their hard-won success. So far as the no-changers were concerned, there was a wonderful response to the Yarn-membership. In August, there were 2,780, in September, 6,301, in October, 7,741, and in November, 7,905 members.

But the bane of the year was the outbreak of communal troubles in various places,—specially at Delhi,

Gulbarga, Nagpur, Lucknow, Shahjahanpur, Allahabad, Jubbulpore, and, worst of all, at Kohat. The Kohat riots really broke the backbone of India. A Committee was appointed to investigate the causes and conditions of the riot—composed of Gandhi and Shaukat Ali. The two produced a report, but unfortunately they differed in respect of the parties on which they fixed the blame for the disturbances. It is a decade since the events of the 9th and 10th September, 1924, occurred, but a perusal of the reports on the Kohat outrages, printed and published for the Kohat Refugees Working Committee, by Lala Nandlal, Head-Master, Bhratri School, Kohat, immediately after the riot, sends a thrill of horror through the reader. We cannot review the events beyond saying that after the shootings and carnage of the 9th and 10th September, a special train had to remove 4,000 Hindus, of whom 2,600 were living for two months after on the charity of Rawalpindi, and 1,400 of other places.

It is no wonder that Gandhi decided to go on a twenty-one days' fast. He held himself responsible for all this fury and murderousness and felt called upon to expiate his own guilt. The fast was a critical test to one who had just emerged from a sharp and nearly fatal attack of appendicitis. The fast was commenced in Maulana Mahomed Ali's house, Delhi, but later he was removed to a house outside the city. Advantage was taken of the fast to gather the leading Indians of all communities at a Unity Conference, which was attended also by the Metropolitan of Calcutta. The Conference had prolonged sittings from September 26th to October 2nd, 1924. The members of the Conference pledged themselves to use their utmost endeavours to enforce the principles (of freedom of conscience and religion) and condemn any deviation from them even under provocation. A central National Panchayat was appointed, composed of Gandhi, as Chairman and Convener, and Hakim Ajmal Khan, Lalaji, G. K. Nariman, Dr. S. K. Datta and Master Sunder Singh of Lyallpore. The Conference laid down certain fundamental rights relating to liberty of holding and expressing religious beliefs and following religious practice, sacredness of places of worship, cow-slaughter, and music before mosques, with a statement of the limitations they must be subject to. The Press was warned to be careful in its writings, and the people were requested to offer their prayers during the last week of Gandhi's fast. The 8th of October was marked out for mass meetings for thanksgiving.

Hardly had Gandhi emerged from this fast when he had to face an All-Parties' Conference in Bombey on the 21st and 22nd of November, and in continuation of it, a meeting of the A. I. C. C. on the 23rd and 24th of November, 1924. The object of the All-Parties' Conference was to consolidate opinion in India amongst all parties against the growing virulence of the repressive policy of Government in Bengal, which was directed obviously against the Swaraj Party as well as those conducting the Satyagraha at Tarakeswar. The Conference condemned the Criminal Law Amendment Ordinance promulgated by the Bengal Government, and urged its withdrawal, as well as the withdrawal of Reg. III of 1818. It put down the unrest to the withholding of Swaraj, and appointed a Committee of representatives of all political parties to prepare a scheme of Swaraj including a Communal Settlement,—to report not later than the 31st March, 1925. There was no doubt that the Conference was not expected to achieve much. But very likely, Deshbandhu Das's arrest was obviated by it. The event of the year was the surrender of Gandhi to Deshbandhu Das and Motilalji on the question of

Council-entry and the lifting of the boycott. The joint statement issued by those three eminent men was accepted by the A.I.C.C. Contrast this joint statement with the separate statements published in the month of May that very year. The substance of the statement was that, in order to secure the co-operation of all parties, the programme of N.C.O. should be suspended as a National programme, except in so far as it relates to the refusal to wear foreign cloth, and that, while different sections should devote themselves to different fields of constructive work, the Swaraj Party should work in the Councils. In exchange for this, Gandhi got a good price. In future, Congress members must give 2,000 yards of hand-spun yarn monthly, instead of the annual subscription of annas four. Let it be marked that it is not only the members of elected committees that should pay the yarn subscription, but every member of the Congress whom we ordinarily describe as the four-anna member. The year is drawing nigh. The Congress is to be held at Belgaum with Gandhi in the Chair. What an opportunity to preside over the Congress!

The Belgaum Congress (1924)

In the history of Non-co-operation, Belgaum is a landmark. The revolt against Gandhism was almost complete. The Congress stood at the parting of ways. Should Congressmen hereafter be in rival camps or cover up their differences by an agreement, and if the latter, who better than Gandhi, who other than Gandhi could achieve this formidable task of pacifying the no-changers while withdrawing Civil Disobedience, and assuaging the feelings of Swarajists while resisting Council-entry? If great programmes can be initiated only by great men, they can also be suspended by such great men and none others. It was, therefore, in the fitness of the times, though not in the fitness of things, that Gandhi should preside over the Belgaum Congress of 1924. At Belgaum he presented his marvellous Presidential Address, only a summary of which was delivered at the Congress. In it, he recapitulated the progress of events since September, 1920, and stated how the Congress had been principally an institution for developing strength from within. The boycotts were all taken up by the parties concerned. Though not a single boycott was anywhere near completion, every one of them tended to diminish the prestige of the institution boycotted. The greatest of all boycotts was the *boycott of violence*. Non-violence, however, did not quite develop from a passive form of helplessness to the enlightened form of resourcefulness. The intolerance against those who did not non-co-operate became a new violence of a subtler type. Nevertheless, non-violence, such as it was, kept violence under check. There was no mistaking the fact that the capacity for suffering for a cause must advance it. The time, however, came for a halt. People that had non-co-operated began to repent in many cases. The reaction made them worse than ever before they non-co-operated. So all the boycotts had to be lifted. The boycott of foreign cloth alone remained. That boycott was not merely a right but a duty—as much as it would be to boycott foreign water or foreign rice and wheat. Boycott is doubtless an exertion of pressure, but pressure coming from goodwill and gentleness, not anger and ill-will. The Lancashire trade was immoral, because it was raised and sustained on the ruin of millions of India's peasants, and one immorality led to another and many of the proved immoral acts of Britain were traceable to this one immoral traffic. Hence we had to take to hand-spinning and hand-weaving which brought us into direct touch with the villagers. Gandhi, however, did not mean that all British goods would harm us. But cloth, whether British or foreign, did harm us.

He was not fighting against machinery. He was not presenting all his views on machinery, any more than on non-violence. But the "wanton and wicked destruction of one cottage industry of India which kept the wolf from the doors of thousands" was what he resented. An agreement in difference was reached between the Swarajists and himself. They agreed to the spinning franchise. He agreed to their work in Councils. Then he deplored the Kohat riots, gave his sympathy to the Akalis, dwelt upon untouchability, and spoke of the Swaraj Scheme. It is the end; we do not know it. The spinning wheel, Hindu-Muslim unity and removal of untouchability were the means. "For me, it is enough to know the means; means and end are convertible terms in my philosophy of life." This summing up of Gandhi's philosophy was just what men of other persuasions resented. With this preface, Gandhi suggested some points as relating to a Swaraj Scheme:—

> Manual labour to be the qualification for franchise; the reduction of Military expenditure, the cheapening of justice, the abolition of intoxicating liquors and drugs and revenues therefrom, reduction of Civil and Military salaries, redistribution of Provinces on a linguistic basis, examination of monopolies of foreigners, guarantee of status to Chiefs without any hindrance from the Central Government, repeal of arbitrary powers, abolition of race distinction in services and religious freedom to various denominations, administration through vernacular languages, and Hindi to be the National language.

The subject of Independence naturally attracted his attention. His views had softened since Ahmedabad, for, then he was hoping for things. Now those hopes were all blasted so far as Government's position and attitude were concerned. "I would strive for Swaraj within the Empire, but would not hesitate to sever all connection, if severance became a necessity through Britain's own fault." He then referred to the Swaraj Party and the constructive programme and wound up with a statement of the position in Bengal and a reiteration of his faith in non-violence. In Bengal, Lord Reading had promulgated his Ordinance 1 of '24—establishing a summary procedure of arrest and trial, before Special Commissioners, of persons who, according to the Local Government, belonged to a revolutionary association. Gandhi accepted the view that the drive was being directed against Swarajists.

The Congress expressed its sorrow over the death of Bi Amma, Sir A. Chaudhuri, Sir A. Mukherji, Bhupendra Nath Basu, Dr. Subrahmania Aiyar, G. M. Bhurjie and several other Congress workers and leaders. The agreement between Gandhi, and Nehru and Das, which was passed by the A.I.C.C. in November, was ratified. Congress franchise was likewise altered. The exodus of Hindus from Kohat was deplored and the Muslim residents of Kohat were exhorted to assure their Hindu brethren of full protection of lives and property and the Hindu *Muhjarims* were advised not to return except upon an honourable invitation from the Kohat Muslims. Sympathy was likewise expressed for the sufferers in Gulbarga in the Nizam's State. Untouchability and Vaikom Satyagraha were dwelt upon. Paid National Service was declared to be perfectly honourable. The Akali movement, drink and opium traffic were all dealt with and some necessary changes in the Constitution were effected.

On the question of Indians Abroad, Mr. Vaze's and Benarsidas Chaturvedi's services in this behalf were appreciated, as also Shrimati Sarojini's. Nor was Government inactive. The Government of India put up a strong fight in the matter of Kenya, "warning the Secretary of State that, if the decision went against the Indians in Kenya, there would probably arise a strong agitation for the severance of India's connection with the British Commonwealth and for the adoption of retaliatory measures against the Colonies." Moreover, it will be remembered that as the result of the deliberations of the Imperial Conference of 1923, at which India was represented by Dr. Tej Bahadur Sapru and the Maharaja of Alwar, not only was the position of equality of rights to Indians conceded in the Conference of 1921 confirmed, but a Committee was to be set up by the Government of India which the Dominions agreed to consult, South Africa alone dissenting. The Colonies Committee consisting of Messrs. Hope Simpson, H.H. the Aga Khan, Sir Benjamin Robertson, Dewan Bahadur T. Rangachari and K. C. Roy, assembled in London early in 1924 and dispersed towards the end of July. Their deliberations covered the standing grievances of Indians in Kenya, Fiji, and Tanganyika. Mr. Thomas, Colonial Secretary, decided in August, 1924, that on the question of immigration, the Ordinance framed on the lines of restricting it should not be enacted. On the question of franchise, and of the Highlands, there was no change in the position. As regards Indian Colonization, it was proposed to set up an area in the Lowlands for agricultural immigrants from India. In June, 1924, an East African Committee was appointed under the Chairmanship of Lord Southborough by His Majesty's Government and it was agreed that the Indian point of view should be heard before it. In South Africa the Class Areas Bill lapsed owing to a change of Government, while the Natal Boroughs Ordinance, preventing further enrolment of Indians as burgesses, was passed.

CHAPTER VI

Partition, or Partnership ? (1925)

The politics of 1925 largely centre round Council work. The Swarajists were no longer harassed by the No-changers. Gandhi was there to keep the balance even between the two sections. Eminent men like Das and Nehru, Patel and Lalaji, did not require to live under the shadow of others. In two Provinces had Dyarchy been brought to an end—C.P. and Bengal. Das refused to form the Ministry in Bengal on Lord Lytton's invitation, nor would he allow others to form one. That was the wrecking he had all along been visualizing. Lord Reading's Ordinance No. 1 of 1924 having expired, a Bill was introduced into the Bengal Legislative Council which was rejected by and through the influence of the Swarajists, in January, 1925. It had to be certified by Lord Lytton, and remitted to London for the approval of His Majesty's Government. On the 17th February, the Bengal Legislative Council passed a resolution recommending to Government to make provision in the Budget for the salaries of Ministers. This was a set-back to the Swarajists, but soon the Party made up for its loss. On the 23rd March, in the course of the Budget discussion, the salaries of the two Ministers appointed were rejected by 69 votes to 63. While Bengal was upholding N.C.O. on these declared lines, in C.P. the question was openly canvassed as to why the party should not accept Ministries and "wreck from within." In the Central Legislature, the Party was merely filling the role of a constitutional Opposition, both in 1924 and in 1925. They sat on Select Committees and co-operated in the passage of useful legislation. They walked into the lobbies now with one party and now with another—and occasionally with Government.

When Mr. C. Doraiswami Iyengar moved a resolution urging the supersession of the Bengal Ordinance by an Act of the Legislature, it was passed by 58 against 45 votes. On February 3rd, 1925, Mr. V. J. Patel introduced a Bill to repeal the State Prisoners' Act of 1850, the Frontier Outrages Act of 1867, and the Prevention of Seditious Meetings Act of 1921, and it was passed except for the omission of the Frontier Outrages Act.

Mr. Neogy moved the consideration of his Bill to amend the Railway Act so as to abolish reservation of railway compartments for any particular community, and it was rejected. Dr. Gour moved a resolution for abolishing appeals to the Privy Council but it was rejected, the Swarajists voting with Government against the resolution. Pandit Motilal Nehru said on the occasion that, for a time, we must have appeals to the Privy Council in London. On Mr. Venkatapathi Raju's resolution urging the immediate establishment of a Military College in India, Government were defeated. The Swarajists and the Independents "turned their big guns upon each other, rather than upon the Treasury Bench," in the debate on the Railway Budget (25-2-'25). Eventually, Pandit Motilalji's resolution for rejecting the Railway Budget was defeated by 66 votes against 41. Thus the Budget and its items were dealt with on their intrinsic merits. There was no question of "constant, continuous, uniform obstruction," as was originally foreshadowed. Pandit Motilal's motion to reject the travelling allowances of Executive Councillors was passed by 65 votes against 48, each Party voting for its own reasons. The Kohat outrages, (non) Indianization of the Army, Muddiman

Report, Round Table Conference, repression—were all to the fore. A very queer situation arose in connection with a Bill in the Assembly to provide for appeals to the High Court in cases that came under the Bengal Criminal Law Amendment Act. But the Bill had three other provisions relating to the suspension of the Habeas Corpus and the detention of accused persons in custody outside Bengal. The Swarajists and Independents wanted to support the first clause and reject the last three. This would mutilate the Bill so far as Government were concerned, and Lord Reading had to certify it after it was passed by the Council of State.

It is clear that by this time Das carved out a high position for himself in the Halls of the Congress. Moreover, just on the eve of the Belgaum Congress, a statement had been published that Das had divested himself of almost all his property—which he left as a legacy to the Nation for some charitable purpose. And this fact had raised Das miles high in the estimation of the public. In the meantime, the National Convention of Dr. Besant published the draft of a Commonwealth of India Bill. The Committee appointed at the Unity Conference was racking its brains to find a solution of the communal tangle and Lalaji published a questionnaire in February, '25 on behalf of the Hindu Mahasabha. The Sub-Committee of the All-Parties' Conference held in Bombay the previous November, which was charged with the duty of preparing a Swaraj scheme did not succeed in producing any thing presentable and adjourned its sittings *sine die* in March. Gandhi visited South India and Kerala in March and April, 1925. The Vaikom Satyagraha was at its height and Gandhi's presence helped to bring about a settlement. The campaign was undertaken to effect the removal of the prohibition against certain untouchables or unapproachables passing along certain streets in Vaikom. The Travancore Government had put up certain barricades and posted certain pickets to prevent the entry of Satyagrahis. Government were made to realise that this act of theirs was lending itself to the view that they were supporting the conservatism of the Hindus of Travancore with their own physical force. And when Government removed both barricades and pickets, the only enemy remaining was public opinion and the *point di appui* for the Satyagraha disappeared for the time being. From the South, Gandhi was to visit Bengal. Das was then beginning to feel ill. Evening temperature was already causing anxiety. It was arranged that he should visit Europe for treatment.

At the same time, he was full of hope that he could effect a settlement with the British Government. Only a year previous to the time, when he was touring in South India, he had declared on the sands of the Madras Beach that Gandhi had 'bungled and mismanaged', referring to the Gandhi-Reading negotiations on the eve of the Ahmedabad Congress. He further declared that the terms came to him in the Alipore Jail then. This psychology of 'success' is commonly met with in public workers who have organised big movements. Mrs. Besant was overpowered by it when Montagu visited the country in 1917—after she had convulsed the British Empire in India. Here was Das who had organised in Bengal the Chittagong strike of 1921, whose Province organised an unprecedented boycott of the Prince, who captured the Legislative Councils of Bengal and made the formation of Ministries impossible and wrecked Dyarchy. Why should not a settlement be effected?

That was the position at the time of the Faridpur (Bengal Provincial) Conference. His offer of co-operation on certain conditions was made at Faridpur under this psychology. While Gandhi believed that there was not 'the change of heart' that was necessary for a composure of the prevailing unrest, Das believed there was. "I see signs of a real change of heart everywhere," said Das to a representative of *The Statesman*. "I see signs of reconciliation everywhere. The world is tired of conflicts and I think I see a real desire for construction and consolidation." This statement was made in Faridpur in the first week of May, 1925—and about the same time did Gandhi say to the same representative, "What, therefore, remains to me of non-co-operation is, as Mr. Das would put it, a matter of mental attitude. But it is an attitude that I personally prize because, claiming, as I do, to be a friend of the British, I want to tell them that I see no real trace yet, of any change of heart." Das said further, addressing the British statesmen, "You can have peace to-day on terms honourable both to you and to us." Gandhi had at this time declared Das to be his 'attorney' and always referred to the Swaraj Party as representing the Congress in the Councils. His self-obliteration was wonderful and at times went to the point of trying the patience, though not the loyalty, of his old-world orthodox adherents. At Faridpur, Das pronounced his terms of settlement. He declared violence was both immoral and inexpedient, and referring to Government's urge of co-operation by the Congress, Das said:—

> "Provided some real responsibility is transferred to the people, there is no reason why we should not co-operate with the Government. But two things are necessary—first, there should be a real change of heart, secondly, Swaraj in the fullest sense, must be guaranteed to us at once, to come automatically in the near future. I have always maintained that we should make a large sacrifice in order to have the opportunity to begin our constructive work at once and I think you will realise that a few years are nothing in the history of a Nation provided the foundation of Swaraj

is laid at once and there is real change of heart both in the rulers and in the subjects. You will tell me that 'change of heart' is a fine phrase and that some practical demonstration should be given of that change. I agree. But that demonstration must necessarily depend on the atmosphere created by any proposed settlement. An atmosphere of trust or distrust may be easily felt and in any matter of peaceful settlement a great deal more depends upon the spirit behind the terms than the actual terms themselves.

"A few suggestions may be made having regard to what is nearest to the hearts of the people of Bengal—(1) General amnesty of all political prisoners, (2) a guarantee of the fullest recognition of our right to the establishment of Swaraj within the Commonwealth in the near future, and in the meantime till Swaraj comes, a sure and sufficient foundation of such Swaraj should be laid at once, (3) we on our part should give some sort of understanding that we shall not, by word, deed or gesture, encourage revolutionary propaganda and that we shall make every effort to put an end to such a movement."

It will be seen that the proposed settlement was linked with a National effort to wipe out anarchy; not that the Faridpur Provincial Conference had ever identified itself with revolutionary propaganda, but that a change of heart would transform the revolutionary into an apostle of real service to the people.

At this time Lord Reading was in England on a short leave, and this fact, coupled with Lord Birkenhead's exhortation to the Swarajists to co-operate and not to wreck, was largely responsible for Das's expectations. Moreover, Colonel Wedgwood and Mr. Ramsay MacDonald were taking interest at the time in bringing about some settlement in India. Gandhi in one of his brief but significant revelations happened to say, after Das's death, that Das had great faith in Lord Birkenhead and that Das believed that he would do great things for India. Das was a great lawyer and so was 'F. E.' as Birkenhead was known before he was raised to Peerage. As Mr. F. E. Smith, he was along with Lord Carson,—really Sir Edward Carson of those days, the great enemy of the Irish Free State before the settlement was effected. Das would, therefore, have naturally thought that a formidable character like 'F.E.' who was helpful to Ireland would be equally reasonable with India. Das was supposed to have within him some such ideas.

In his last letter to Pandit Motilal, which the latter referred to as "Das's last political will and testament," he wrote: "The most critical time in our history is coming. There must be solid work done at the end of the year and the beginning of the next; all our resources will be taxed, and here we are both of us ill. God knows what will happen." Shortly after, it pleased the gods in heaven to take away Das from our midst and from his residence 'Step Aside,' Darjeeling, on the 16th June 1925. Das's life constitutes by itself a chapter of Indian history. Speaking of the death of Das, Gandhi spoke at Khulna with feeling and asked: "What shall we do to perpetuate his memory! It is easy to shed tears, but no tears can help us or his nearest and dearest. Only if every one of us, Hindus, Muslims, Parsees and Christians, all who call themselves Indians, pledge ourselves to do the work in which he lived, moved and had his being, shall we have done something. We are all believers in God. We should know that the body is ever perishing. The soul is imperishable. The body that held Mr. Das has perished, but his soul will never perish. Not only the soul; even the name of him who had served and sacrificed so much will remain immortal and every one, young and old, who follows his example to ever so little an extent will help to perpetuate his memory. We have none of his intellect, but we can imitate the spirit in which he loved the Motherland." Let us quote Government's opinion at the other end: "Mr. Das had an unerring instinct for the weak points in an adversary's position, and a tenacious resolution in the execution of his own plans which raised him far above the level of the ablest of his lieutenants." Like Gandhi he was honoured by his opponents even while they fought him, and amongst the numberless tributes paid to his memory are many sincerely felt and frankly worded, by Europeans, including high officers of Government. The Secretary of State and the Viceroy were among those who sent messages of regret, and one of the first acts of the Legislative Assembly, when it met in August, was to give fitting expression to the loss which the Nation had suffered in the deaths of Mr. Das and another veteran, Sir Surendra Nath Banerjea who died on 6th of August, 1925.

Gandhi was ever generous, forgiving, appreciative and affectionate towards Das. He stayed out in Bengal and built a great memorial in his honour. He collected ten lacs of rupees and Das's house—148, Russa Road—was saved for the Nation and was converted into a hospital for women and children in accordance with his wishes expressed in his Trust Scheme announced before the Belgaum Congress. Gandhi further put forth all his efforts in order to place the Swarajists in positions of power, and plant the Swaraj Party firmly in Bengal. Thus did he strive to make Mr. J. M. Sen-Gupta, the leader of the Swaraj Party in the Council, Mayor of the Corporation of Calcutta and President of the Bengal Provincial Congress Committee. The 'triple crown' that Das himself had been wearing was placed on Sen-Gupta's head.

While Gandhi was doing everything in his power to put the Swarajists at ease and even asked the 'waverers' to join and join at once the Swaraj Party, the response of the Swaraj Party to all these gestures was nothing commensurate with the spirit of self-abnegation shown by Gandhi. The general council of the Swaraj Party showed itself more and more hostile to the spinning franchise which had been conceded at Belgaum, and left it to the All-India Congress Committee, where the Swarajists had a majority, to scrap it if they chose. At the conclusion of the meeting of the Working Committee of the A. I. C. C. on the 15th July in Calcutta, it was understood that Gandhi sent a note to Pandit Motilal Nehru to the effect that since the Swarajists had a majority in the Congress, and since the Pandit was the President of the Swaraj Party, he should also assume the Presidentship of the Congress Working Committee. Gandhi made it clear that he did not like any longer to remain as the President of this Body. The note created a sensation in the Swarajist circles. It was however finally decided that, for at least the rest of that year, Gandhi would be continued to be the President of the A.I.C.C., but if the spinning franchise was dropped at the next meeting, he would resign and set up a separate spinning organisation. The Working Committee itself considered at some length the question of revision of the spinning franchise and ultimately decided to convene a meeting of the A.I.C.C. on the 1st of October to consider this question. In the meantime Gandhi did everything to support the Swaraj Party to the extent of giving his joint signature with Panditji to the resolutions of that Party, associating himself with the Party in threatening to obstruct in the Councils, in case certain conditions that were put forward were not agreed to. Those who were indignant with Gandhi over these happenings understood their meaning when they knew that he had offered his resignation. Things were developing rapidly. Soon after, the very resolution of the Congress of Belgaum and the pact between the two main wings of the Congress were to stand virtually annulled by one word of the mouth uttered by Gandhi. The spinning franchise must be cancelled and the Congress was to become a political body in answer to Lord Birkenhead's recent pronouncement. Slowly, then, Gandhi by a series of *obiter dicta* adopted Swarajists as his attorneys and political representatives, shortly after Das's demise and Lord Birkenhead's callous observations. Gandhi yielded more and more and, ultimately, so much more that he effaced himself and made a complete surrender. Gandhi wrote in August: "I must no longer stand in the way of the Congress being developed and guided by educated Indians rather than by one like myself who has thrown in his lot entirely with the masses, and who has fundamental differences with the mind of educated India as a body. I still want to act upon them but not leading the Congress. The best way in which I can help that activity is by removing myself out of the way, and by concentrating myself solely upon constructive work with the help of the Congress and in its name, and that too, only so far as educated Indians will permit me to do so." The fact is the Swarajists on the one hand denounced the principles of Gandhi and on the other demanded his leadership. They wanted his co-operation on their terms. His message is only one and that was growing stale, as Shrimati Sarojini put it at the time to many. About this time, Pandit Motilal had accepted a seat on the Skeen Committee. Panditji's acceptance of the seat, being himself a Swarajist, greatly irritated some of his own followers. He should really have accepted this place only on the vote of a three-fourths majority of the members of the Assembly belonging to the Party. This was seriously objected to. The objection was not merely technical; it went deeper, it attacked the change-of policy involved in such an acceptance, which was tantamount to positive co-operation. At the time it was said in reply that membership would afford rare opportunities of studying the Military problems of the country from inside, but the argument remained unconvincing to the critics.

It was shortly before the beginning of the Simla session of the Assembly (1925-1926) that Pandit Motilal Nehru had accepted this seat on the Indian Sandhurst Committee, popularly known as the Skeen Committee. The history of the Skeen Committee may shortly be told. For some years prior to 1925, a section of Indian opinion had been demanding the establishment of a Military College in India comparable with that at Sandhurst. The Military Budget of 1925 comprised nine lacs for Military education, and that account related chiefly to the Prince of Wales College at Dehra Dun and the King George's Military Schools, which were recently established at Jullunder and Jhelum in the Punjab. A resolution which was passed in the Delhi session of the Legislative Assembly in 1925 called upon the authorities to establish such an institution forthwith. The Government of India, accordingly, appointed a Committee consisting mainly of Indian members, including Pandit Motilal Nehru, Mr. Jinnah and Mr. M. Ramachandra Rao, under the Presidency of Lieut. General Sir Andrew Skeen, Chief of the General Staff, to consider the problem of how suitable Indian candidates for the King's Commission can be obtained in larger numbers and of how, when they are forthcoming, they can be trained most efficiently. That is to say, the Committee was asked to consider whether it is desirable and practicable to start a Military College in India then or at some later date, and if so, whether such a college should be self-contained or should be supplemented by further training in England. The

Committee held a number of sittings in India, and in the Spring of 1926 a Sub-Committee of its members went to Europe to investigate the systems of education by which officers are at present produced in England, France, Canada and America.

Attention must now be drawn to a debate of real importance. The Muddiman Committee was a committee appointed in 1924 to examine the working of the Montford Reforms. There was a majority and a minority Report. The former was of course the official Report. Government were not prepared to accept even its recommendations. A motion was tabled in September, 1925, that it should accept the principle of the Report. What was the principle broadly? It was this,—that the machinery, wherever it was creaking, must be oiled, that the bearings must be greased, that the gear must be smoothened. Thus would it be possible to appoint Ministers without their salaries being voted at the Budgets, to carry on Government in spite of obstruction. Such things had been visualized in the Montford Reforms, only as events distantly possible, but now they were actualities of a near past. The Swaraj Party had fully realized these reactionary potentialities lying embedded in the Montford Scheme soon after entering the Assembly, and had tabled a resolution in February, 1924, as follows:—

> "This Assembly recommends to the Governor-General-in-Council to take steps to have the Government of India Act revised with a view to establish full Responsible Government in India, and for the said purpose, (a) to summon at an early date a representative Round Table Conference to recommend, with due regard to the protection of the rights and interests of important minorities, a scheme of a Constitution for India; and (b) after dissolving the Central Legislature, to place the said scheme for approval before a newly elected Indian Legislature

for its approval and submit the same to the British Parliament to be embodied in a Statute."

It was as the result of this resolution that the Muddiman Committee was appointed and it sent up a majority and minority Report, which were considered on the 7th of September, 1925, by the Assembly in the form of a proposition moved by Sir Alexander Muddiman to which a long amendment was tabled by Pandit Motilal Nehru, the gist of which was that immediate steps be taken by His Majesty's Government (1) to make a declaration in Parliament embodying such fundamental changes in constitutional machinery and administration of India as would make the Government of the country fully responsible; further, (2) a Round Table Conference or other suitable agency adequately representative of all Indian, European and Anglo-Indian interests was to be summoned to frame, with due regard to the interests of the minorities, a detailed scheme based on the above principle and to place the said scheme for approval before the Assembly, after which it would be submitted to the British Parliament to be embodied in a Statute. This amendment was, after two days' discussion, carried against the Government by 72 votes to 45. It will be thus seen that the 'painfully tense atmosphere' of February, 1924, gave place to the far friendlier spirit of September, 1925, and the exclusive demand of an R.T.C. in February, 1924, was relaxed in the demand of September, 1925, for an R. T. C. or other suitable agency.

Birkenhead had spoken of the Swaraj Party as the "most highly organized political party in India." This was gratifying to a degree. But Lord Birkenhead only recognized the party that had recognized his Constitution and its organ. The Swaraj Party had not only entered the Councils and taken seats but passed budgets and sat on select committees. It had declined a seat on the Muddiman Committee but accepted one on the Skeen Committee. Lord Birkenhead himself was not without hope, nor were Das and, later, Nehru without hope that some kind of settlement could be effected. Sir Basil Blackett spoke explicitly in the Assembly of Pandit Motilal's co-operation. "What else is Panditji doing," he asked, "in passing the Steel Protection Bill, in passing last year's budget, in separating the Railway Finance?" "What else is Mr. Patel doing," he added, "in presiding over this House?" And then Sir Basil profusely complimented Mr. A. Rangaswami Iyengar for the valuable services rendered by him on the Public Accounts Committee. The fact was that Government were sparing no efforts to cajole the Swaraj Party into some kind of co-operation.

Before we proceed to narrate the events of September, 1925, at Patna, we must note some of the under-currents amongst the thoughts and programmes of the Swarajists themselves. Gandhi's willingness to place the whole machinery of the Congress at the disposal of Motilalji was deeply appreciated by the Swarajist leader who wrote to him:—"Lord Birkenhead seems to have spurned the honourable co-operation offered by Deshbandhu and to have made it clear that, in our struggle for freedom, we have still to face many unnecessary obstacles and many ill-informed opponents. Our plain duty at this stage is, therefore, to go ahead along lines chalked out for us and prepare the ground for an effective challenge to irresponsible and insolent authority." On July 25th, Lalaji wrote to the Press: "What is needed now is the chalking out of a middle course. We are not ready to co-operate, we must do what is best, practical and possible under the circumstances. For that, we require vigorous thinking, thorough discussion and honest consultation amongst all parties and determination to do what is decided upon." In Bengal, the hold of the Swarajists, who had made the acceptance of Ministries impossible, was fast weakening, an Independent having defeated a Swarajist candidate for the Presidentship of the Bengal Council by 6 votes. Things were doubtful enough even at the last test of strength when Das was carried on a stretcher to the Council Chamber. Dr. A. Suhrawardy resigned from the Swaraj Party. He had seen the Governor of Bengal and Gandhi took strong objection to this saying, first, that it was a most improper act on his part, and secondly that he had thereby "sold his country." On hearing this, the Doctor resigned, saying, "I deem political *harikari* more honourable than living under the new tyranny." The day after the report of Dr. Suhrawardy's interview appeared in the Press, Gandhi gave a full statement of his attitude to a representative of an Anglo-Indian newspaper in Calcutta and said: "I cannot, therefore, help saying that it is a healthy rule to prohibit members of the Swaraj Party from meeting or seeing officials without the permission of the Party." On the 22nd August, Vittalbhai was elected as the first non-official President of the Assembly.

It was at this juncture that the A.I.C.C. met at Patna on the 21st September, 1925. When we remember that it was at Patna in 1934 (May) that Civil Disobedience was withdrawn, this meeting of 1925 does not fail to strike us as particularly interesting, because at this meeting three outstanding changes were effected in the position of the Congress. Khaddar was divested of all political significance. Yarn franchise only became an alternative to four-anna membership of the Congress which was once again restored, and finally, political work was made over to the Swaraj Party. The Party was no longer a wing of the Congress,—a protestant wing,—a minority receiving concessions or a bare majority anxious to take the rest with it. It was the Congress itself. Thereafter elections would be run not by the Swaraj Party but by the Congress. The members of the Assembly of this persuasion would be not the 'Swarajists,' any longer, but the Congress members in the Councils. The Yarn franchise was to be no longer the sole franchise, not because the response was inadequate,—for there were 10,000 members on the rolls,—but because the Swaraj Party did not like it. Gandhi made up his mind to meet the Swarajists more than half way, as a reply to Lords Birkenhead and Reading. When the Serajgunj resolution on Gopinath Saha in 1924 jeopardised the position of Das and his liberty, and was followed up by the Bengal Ordinance Act, Gandhi decided to stand by Das. This year Das passed away and Birkenhead's bluster was in the air. Gandhi made up his mind to wind up the remnants of N.C.O. and render all assistance to the Council front. He had no answer to give to the Secretary of State and, therefore, clothed the Council Party with the full authority of the Congress to deal with the political situation. Thus was the country taken through a series of sudden and startling changes; the latter half (clause B) of the Patna resolution, making over the political work to the Swaraj Party, was not before the informal sitting of the A.I.C.C. on the 21st September, but was sprung upon the Working Committee itself on the morning of the 22nd September, and considered by it for a bare five minutes. Here is clause B of the resolution passed at Patna:—

"Whereas the Congress in the 39th session held at Belgaum endorsed an agreement entered into between Mahatma Gandhi on the one hand and Deshbandhu C. R. Das and Pandit Motilal Nehru acting on behalf of the Swaraj Party on the other, whereby the

Congress activity was restricted to the constructive programme mentioned therein and it was provided *inter alia* that the work in connection with the Central and Provincial Legislatures should be carried on by the Swaraj Party on behalf of the Congress organisation, and that for such work the Swaraj Party should make its own rules and administer its own funds; and whereas subsequent events have shown that this restriction should not continue under the altered circumstances that face the country and that the Congress should henceforth be a predominantly political body;

"It is resolved that the Congress do now take up and carry on all such political work as may be necessary in the interests of the country, and for this purpose do employ the whole of the machinery and funds of the Congress, save and except such funds and assets as are specially earmarked and belong to the All-India Khaddar Board and Provincial Khaddar Boards, which shall be handed over with all existing financial obligations to the All-India Spinners' Association started by Mahatma Gandhi as an integral part of the Congress organisation, but with independent existence and full powers to administer these and other funds for the fulfilment of its object.

"Provided that the work in connection with the Indian and Provincial Legislatures shall be carried on in accordance with the Policy and Programme laid down by the Swaraj Party under the constitution framed by the Party and the rules made thereunder, subject to such modifications made by the Congress as may be found necessary from time to time for the purpose of carrying out the said Policy."

When an amendment was tabled to the main resolution handing over the Congress to the Council Party, to the effect that clause B be replaced by a clause saying "Provided that the work in the Indian and Provincial Legislatures shall be carried on in accordance with such policy and programme laid down by the

Congress as may be found necessary from time to time for the purpose," instead of allowing the Council work to be done with the Swaraj Party as an intermediary, the very thought of an amendment to a resolution agreed upon, and a remark made in moving it that the Swaraj Party had 'betrayed its trust,' set Panditji ablaze and there was a general conflagration in the House. Gandhi assuaged the feelings by asking the mover of the amendment not to proceed with his diatribe against the Swaraj Party at such a juncture.

In the mood in which we found Gandhi at the time, all that Pandit Motilal had to do was to ask and it was given forthwith, and given wholesale. Gandhi as President of the A.I.C.C. would not allow the House even to examine the record of the Swaraj Party in the Assembly,—that would disturb the harmony of the situation and deprive the gift of its grace as well as its value. When Rajendra Babu asked Gandhi whether there was a pact between him, and Nehru and Das; Gandhi replied in the negative and added that with him, personally, *it was a point of honour to concede what the other side demanded.* It was a point of honour too with his following to concede to Gandhi what he demanded of them, for they trusted to his judgment as the instinctive judgment of a pure-hearted person in all times of doubt or difficulty.

The question at and after Patna was whether it was a partition or partnership that the Patna decisions had brought about. The Congress changes had been kaleidoscopic in character. Each shift of the panes and pieces in the tube had brought about during the previous two years new dispositions, a new play of colours, new scenes and sights. At Juhu, affairs were amorphous. When we met at Ahmedabad in June, 1924, Gandhi was still trying to hold on to the fundamentals of his position. He was in a mood to assert himself. He had tightened the rigor of khaddar and compelled the Executive to spin everywhere. The threats of the bureaucracy against Das, following the Serajgunj resolutions, impelled him to close up the ranks of the Congress. When an inch was given, usually an ell would be taken. So was it here. The equities of Belgaum were set at nought at Patna, for at Patna, the Council wing took the whole prestige of the Congress and took away the spinning franchise as well. It was, therefore, a partition of the Congress between the apostles of the Councils and those of khaddar. Whatever show of unity there was externally, people could not fail to perceive the discontent of the latter wing. For one thing, the demand of the Swaraj Party "for a Round Table Conference or *other suitable agency*" was considered inadequate. People began to feel that the Attorney went beyond or below the instructions of the Principal, but Gandhi would not countenance such arithmetical calculations. When he gives, he gives unreservedly, wholly, and without regret in himself, or generating regret in his recipient. That is what Bhishma of old prescribed in respect of all gifts. Accordingly, at Cawnpore, we had only to register what at Patna he had decreed.

The Cawnpore Congress (1925) was ahead. We are in the month of October. Shrimati Sarojini Devi was elected President according to the Constitution. Gandhi had said at Belgaum that he was stepping in where really Shrimati Sarojini should have been. Early in October the President-elect published her message for the new year:—

"Mine, as becomes a woman, is a most modest, domestic programme merely to restore to India her true position as the supreme mistress in her own home, the sole guardian of her own vast resources, and the sole dispenser of her own hospitality. As a loyal daughter of Bharata Mata, therefore, it will be my lovely though difficult task, through the coming year, to set my mother's house in order, to reconcile the tragic quarrels that threaten the integrity of her old joint-family life of diverse communities and creeds, and to find an adequate place and purpose and recognition alike for the lowest and the mightiest of her children, and foster-children, the guests and the strangers within her gates."

That was a fine ideal, especially for a lady to lay down. What should the no-changers do to bring about such a harmony? Gandhi exhorted them to fall in with the Patna resolution or to resign from the Congress. They had to hibernate or extinguish themselves. Gandhi's position was that he recanted his programme for the time being, while reiterating his principles.

The people are there, the mass that may develop momentum at any time as once they did, but they can develop that momentum only on the impact of a dynamic force, a living idea, a convulsing programme which must be carried to them by a body of 'educated' people. But these have failed. While, therefore, the material remained, the momentum has disappeared. The sparks from the centre would not explode the air in the chamber.

The passage for the jet of petrol is occluded somewhere, and in the absence of petrol, more air and electricity cannot cause the first explosion that starts the motor. When a motor does not start by the ordinary process, an ingenious method resorted to is to push it from behind. Within a few yards, the engine begins to work until the next halt necessitates a repetition of the process. Even so, when the dynamic force of Civil

Disobedience was for the time being held in suspense, all sorts of devices began to push themselves to the fore. The capture of Local Bodies became more and more attractive. Though the elders of the Congress might have enough legitimate preoccupations and public activities, it was a problem how to divert the energies and the enthusiasm of the younger folks. With the wine of elections before them, with the consciousness and confidence of success in their own minds and hearts, they could not be easily restrained. And too, the Mayoralty of Calcutta held with such lustre by Das and later by Sen-Gupta was captivating to a degree. Already four big corporations were captured by Congressmen. Vallabhbhai J. Patel had for sometime been President of the Ahmedabad Municipality and was the only person who would occupy that position till 1928. Vittalbhai was adorning the Mayoralty of Bombay, and when interviewed on the subject as to how he would discharge his duties if he became the President of the Assembly, said in reply, with his wonted wink in the eye and mischievous smile on the lips, "just as I have done the duties of the President of the Bombay Corporation." Jawaharlal had become the President of the Allahabad Municipality but did not take long to discover that he was a round man in a square hole, and that Local Bodies were not for Congressmen. Babu Rajendra Prasad became Chairman of the Patna Municipality and was not overpleased with his experiences and cleared out after about 15 months. But the alphabet of life, like that of letters, should be learnt by every one and will not be taken on trust. Most people would learn by their own experience, not by others'. And the lessons of Local Bodies must be learnt by Madras too. It was at this time, *i.e.*, about May, 1925, that the Madras Congress Committee began to take interest in the capture of seats in the Madras Corporation, and after an arduous campaign in which neither energy nor expense was spared, it succeeded in capturing 7 seats out of 10. The object of one and all in thus capturing Local Bodies, was to get power with which to push the constructive programme through those bodies. It was a laudable idea and, throughout the campaign, we had the advantage of conceiving our ideas and planning their execution much in advance of Governmental preparations to resist our plans or rebut our ideas. The wheels of Government grind slow, but grind steady. Within a short time Government made it impossible for the Local Bodies to engage the services, as teachers or otherwise, of those who had gone to jail, to buy khaddar, to teach Hindi, to introduce the charkha into schools, to give addresses of welcome to national leaders or to raise the national flag over the corporation schools or offices. Anyway, there was reason for interest in Local Bodies, and the same reason brought out Mr. Srinivasa Iyengar in Madras from his comparative quiet into the *maelstrom* of politics. He assumed command in the city, spent lavishly out of his purse, being never a niggard in public or private life, and in a moment installed himself as the head of the Congress Party. New programmes bring new leaders, and must bring them, when old leaders cannot trim their sails to the new winds or disappear altogether from the winds and the boat alike.

Altogether, the year 1925 was a stormy year. When from this distance of time we survey the incidents and summarise the history, we cannot fail to be impressed by the conflicts that arose between party and party in the Congress, and between section and section in a party. If even the no-changers with their residual legacy of khaddar, removal of untouchability and communal unity, could present schisms and fissions, it is no wonder that the pro-changers with a positively new programme, a dynamic programme as it was also believed to be, exhibited differences, too, among themselves. The revolt against the tenets of the Swaraj Party took origin in C. P. and Maharashtra, which were the worthy colleagues of Bengal, and which had kept pace with Bengal only so long as the great Deshbandhu was alive. Deshbandhu's was not the temper to 'stand any nonsense'; he would put it down with a heavy hand. He who had wrung concessions from Gandhi would not readily yield to rebels or renegades in his party. But the moment he passed away, unexpected happenings took place in Maharashtra. Mr. Tambe, the Swarajist President of the C. P. Council, accepted an Executive Councillorship under the C. P. Government. This was the subject of fierce warfare between the leaders in C.P. and Berar, in Maharashtra and Bombay. Pandit Motilal resented Tambe's conduct and the extenuation of it by men like Kelkar and Jayakar, and threatened to take disciplinary action against these two offenders apparently for being "accessories after the event." They in turn wanted the whole Swaraj Party of Bombay to repeat their sentiments. Kelkar's slogan was "Back to Amritsar: Back to the Lokamanya." Pandit Motilal Nehru was equally unbending. Speaking at Nagpur in November, 1925, he declared that Mr. Tambe's acceptance of office was not an isolated act but the culmination of a series of attempts to take office, commencing with the intrigue to form a Ministry. The retort came at once that Panditji himself showed the way by accepting membership of the Skeen Committee. Of course, the two were quite different things. When the Swarajists held a conference in C. P., animated and heated discussions took place between Abhyankar and Khare on one side and Dr. Moonje on the other. The latter was suspected to be encouraging the acceptance of Ministries. Mr. E. Raghavendra Rao and Mr. B. G. Khaparde were for acceptance. Dr. Moonje vehemently denied the charge and was confronted with a certain letter, after which he admitted that, personally, he was for acceptance but he was loyal to the Party to which he belonged and to Pandit Motilalji, its leader.

Mr. N. C. Kelkar wrote to the Press, criticising the rigid discipline of the Swaraj Party which gave no play to the aspirations of the different sections of its members. He traced the steady deviation of the Swaraj Party away from its original programme of 'consistent and uniform obstruction' in the Central Legislature, and asked whether it would not be logical at the present stage to allow the acceptance of office. "There was a time," he said, "when in the Assembly we could make no constructive proposal, say, a motion even to refer a Bill to a select committee. Then came a time when we were allowed to make such motions, but not to take a seat on any of the committees. Then came a time when we could accept only elective seats on committees. And then came a time when we could accept nominated seats on committees under a special dispensation of executive authority. Now I grant that all these developments were natural and were symptoms of a definite new policy, that is to say, a policy of revolt from hidebound obstruction." On the 1st November, the Executive of the All-India Swaraj Party met at Nagpur and strongly condemned the action of Mr. Sreepad Balwant Tambe as being a flagrant breach of discipline and treachery to the Party. Now we come to Bombay where Motilalji hastened from Nagpur to crush the revolt of Jayakar and Kelkar. They had raised the cry of Responsive Co-operation already. Both these scholar-politicians, so well-known in India for their erudition and keen political sense, resigned their seats on the Executive of the All-India Swaraj

Party and issued, in that connection, the following statement:—

"We find that Pandit Motilal is violating the understanding arrived at at Nagpur, by openly preaching a crusade against Responsive Co-operation while insisting on our remaining silent. We wish to exercise our right to reply to his criticisms which are causing great misunderstanding and prejudice in the public mind. We recognize the desirability of our ceasing to be members of the Swaraj Party Executive Council while we reply to the Pandit's criticism. We are, therefore, tendering our resignation of our membership of the Council so as not to embarrass our colleagues thereon, and in order to be able to exercise our right of reply to the Pandit with freedom and frankness."

That was not all. Moonje, Jayakar and Kelkar subsequently resigned their membership of the Legislature, to which they had been elected on the Swarajist ticket.

Thus they disinfected themselves of Swarajist taint, —body, soul and clothing. Panditji, replying on the 9th November, said that "the Swaraj Party stood for its own programme which included co-operation, Non-co-operation, construction, destruction, as occasion and national interests demanded." Jayakar resented the Pandit's 'hectoring tone.' In the end, on the 4th of December, it was agreed that "all public controversy on the question of the Swarajist Party's policy should cease until the Congress meets."

One other event of 1925 must be referred to here. It is not directly connected with the Congress. But Government themselves attributed the rebellion in the Gudem Agency,—Godavari and Vizagapatam Districts of

Andhra,—under the leadership of Sitarama Raju, to the subversive influence of the Civil Disobedience movement. They had made a similar mistake in regard to the Moplah rebellion. The Gudem rebellion also started some time in 1922,—but later than the Moplah revolt,—but had nothing of the communal tension which characterised its predecessor. Here too, semi-military operations were necessitated and not much progress had been made by the end of the year 1923. In 1924, the Assam Rifles were sent for, consisting of about 250 officers and other ranks. The rebellion was ultimately put down after nearly three years of Guerilla warfare between the mighty and puissant forces of the British Government and Sitarama Raju with a following of two hundred. But the saddest event was the shooting of Raju, on his alleged attempt to flee from arrest. The Government were challenged on many occasions to publish details and to produce the inquest report, but they would not accept the challenge.

Now we pass on to the Cawnpore Congress. There were difficulties ahead. The Cawnpore Session was to confirm what Patna had decreed. It was a moot point even at Patna whether such cataclysmal changes as Patna had affected in franchise,—contrary to Belgaum's decree,—in partition of properties, and in division of functions could be done by an All-India Congress Committee. Then there was the larger question whether the Congress should endorse the Demand of the Swaraj Party in the Assembly which was embodied in their amendment to the resolution on the Muddiman Report. All these complex questions were before the session at Cawnpore presided over by the Poetess of India. A novel feature of the Congress was the handing over of the charge by Gandhi, the outgoing President, to Sarojini Devi, the incoming one. Gandhi spoke for but five minutes and declared that on reviewing his five years' work, he had not one item to retrace or one statement to take back. The more he saw life, he said, the more he was convinced that he was right in every step he had taken. "To-day I would commence Civil Disobedience," he added, "if I thought that the fire and fervour are there in the people. But alas! they are not. The South African question is considered by many to be a suitable question, but I shall be overpowered by numbers that I may not care for." Sarojini Devi took charge with a few choice words. Her Presidential Address was perhaps the shortest address delivered from the Congress rostrum, while of course it was the sweetest ever delivered. She emphasised unity,—unity between the parties and unity between India and the Indians abroad. She referred to the National Demand as put forth from the Assembly, and pleaded for the obliteration of fear. "In the battle for liberty fear is the one unforgivable treachery, and despair the one unforgivable sin." Her Address, therefore, was an expression of courage and hope. With this gentle hand to exercise discipline as well as forbearance, the Cawnpore Congress had an easy time, except for certain labour demonstrations and small troubles from certain delegates which were brought under control by sturdier men like Jawaharlal.

The Cawnpore Congress naturally began with the expression of deep sorrow over the deaths of Deshbandhu Chittaranjan Das, Sir Surendra Nath Banerjea, Dr. Sir Ramakrishna Gopal Bhandarkar and other leaders. There was a South African Deputation in India at the time to which the Congress extended its welcome. and the Congress declared the Area-Reservation and Immigration Registration (Further Provision) Bill to be a breach of the Smuts-Gandhi Agreement of 1914, and urged an arbitration to settle the interpretation of the latter. The Congress endorsed the idea of the R.T.C. to settle the question and urged that the Imperial Government should withhold its assent to the Bill if passed. The Bengal Ordinance Act and the Gurudwara prisoners were the subjects of suitable resolutions, and the Expulsion of Non-Burman Offenders Bill, and Tax on Sea-Passengers Bill of Burma were regarded as new attacks on the liberty of the citizen. Then came the resolution of the Congress dealing with franchise, which confirmed Part B. of the resolution of Patna dated 22-9-'25 calling upon the Congress to take up such political work as was necessary in the interests of the country, and for this purpose employ the whole of the machinery and funds of the Congress except those made over to the A.I.S.A. The Congress of course reiterated its faith in C.D. and urged that self-reliance should be the guiding principle in carrying on all political work. Then the Congress adopted a detailed programme:

(i) The work in the country shall be directed to the education of the people in their political rights and training them to acquire the necessary strength and power of resistance to win those rights by carrying out the constructive programme of the Congress, with special reference to popularising the spinning wheel and khaddar, promoting inter-communal unity, the removal of untouchability, ameliorating the conditions of the suppressed classes and the removal of the drink and drug evil, and shall include the capture of Local Bodies, the organisation of villages, the promotion of education on National lines, the organisation of Labour, both industrial and agricultural, the adjustment of relations between employers and workmen and between landlords and tenants, and the general advancement of the national, economical, industrial and commercial interests of the country.

(ii) The work outside the country shall be directed to the dissemination of accurate information in foreign countries.

(iii) The Congress adopts on behalf of the country the terms of the settlement offered to the Government by the Independent and Swaraj Parties of the Assembly by the resolution passed on the 18th February, 1924, and having regard to the fact that the Government have so far not made any response to the said offer, resolves that the following action shall be taken:

1. The Swaraj Party in the Assembly shall, at the earliest opportunity, invite the Government to give their final decision on the said terms, and in case no decision is announced before the end of February, or the decision announced is held not to be satisfactory by a Special Committee consisting of the Working Committee of the Congress and such other members as may be appointed by the All-India Congress Committee, the Party shall, by adopting the proper procedure, intimate to the Government on the floor of the House that the Party will no longer continue to remain and work in the present Legislatures as heretofore. The Swarajist members of the Legislative Assembly and the Council of State, shall vote for the rejection of the Finance Bill and, immediately after, leave their seats. The Swarajist members of such Provincial Councils as may be in session at the time shall also leave their seats and all members of such Councils as are not in session at the time shall not attend further meetings of the said Councils and shall likewise report themselves to the Special Committee.

2. No member of the Swaraj Party in the Council of State, in the Legislative Assembly, or in any of the Provincial Councils shall thereafter attend any meeting of any of the said Legislatures, or any of their Committees, except for the purpose of preventing his seat from being declared vacant and of throwing out the Provincial Budget or other measure involving fresh taxation.

Provided that, prior to their being called upon to leave their seats, it shall be open to Swarajist members of the various Legislatures to engage themselves in such activities in their Legislatures as are permissible to them under the existing rules of the Party.

Provided also that it shall be open to the Special Committee to allow the Swarajist members of any Legislature to attend the said Legislature when such attendance is in its opinion essential for some special or unforeseen purpose.

3. The Special Committee shall, immediately on receipt of the reports mentioned in sub-clause (i), call a meeting of the All-India Congress Committee to frame a programme of work which shall be carried out by the Congress and Swaraj Party organisation in co-operation with each other throughout the country.

4. The said programme of work shall include selected heads of the general work mentioned in clauses I and II above, as also the education of the electorates in the policy herein laid down, and shall indicate the lines on which the next general election is to be run by and in the name of the Congress and state clearly the issues on which Congressmen shall seek election.

Provided that the policy of non-acceptance of offices in the gift of the Government shall continue to be followed until, in the opinion of the Congress, a satisfactory response to the terms of settlement aforesaid is made by the Government.

5. This Congress hereby authorises the Executive of the several Provincial Congress Committees to select candidates for the Provincial Legislative Councils and the Indian Legislative Assembly in their provincial areas for the general elections next year as early as possible.

6. In the event of the final decision of the Government on the terms of settlement offered in the resolution of the Assembly aforesaid being found satisfactory and acceptable by the aforesaid Special Committee, a meeting of the All-India Congress Committee shall forthwith be held to confirm or reject the decision of the Special Committee and to determine the future course of action.

7. Until the Swarajists leave the Legislatures as herein provided, the Constitution of the Swaraj Party

and the rules made thereunder shall be followed in the Legislatures, subject to such changes as may be made by the Congress or the All-India Congress Committee from time to time.

8. For the purpose of starting the work referred to in Sub-clauses (3) and (4), the All-India Congress Committee shall allot such funds as it may consider sufficient for the initial expenses of the necessary propaganda in this behalf, but any further funds required for the said purpose shall be raised by the Working Committee or under its directions by contributions from the public."

It was not without some bickering that the main resolution of Cawnpore was passed. Pandit Madan Mohan Malaviya, whose very fight against Non-co-operation from inside the Congress endeared him to friends and opponents alike, moved an amendment which was seconded by Mr. Jayakar, to the effect:

> "That the work in the Legislatures shall be so carried on as to utilize them to the best possible advantage for the early establishment of full Responsible Government, co-operation being resorted to when it may be necessary to advance the National cause, and obstruction when that may be necessary for the advancement of the same cause."

It was while seconding that Jayakar announced his own and Kelkar's and Moonje's resignations from the Legislatures. In the course of the discussion, Motilalji was fiercely attacked for accepting a membership of the Indian Sandhurst or Skeen Committee. "The Assembly," he said, "had asked for an Indian Sandhurst and the Government had said, 'show the way.' What they wanted was negotiation to show the Government the way to meet their demands, and if in the same way, the Government asked them to show the way to reforms, they would certainly co-operate."

Finally, Hindustani was prescribed as the language in which the proceedings of the Congress and the A.I.C.C. should ordinarily be conducted, and the A.I.C.C. was authorised to open a Foreign Department under it to look after the interests of the Indians abroad. The next Congress was to meet in Assam. Dr. M. A. Ansari and Syts. A. Rangaswami Iyengar and K. Santanam were appointed Secretaries. Shortly after the Cawnpore Congress, Mr. B. G. Horniman returned to India in the 2nd week of January, 1926.

One pleasant feature of the Cawnpore Congress was the presence of the Rev. J. H. Holmes of America, dressed in American clothes, but wearing a Gandhi cap. He rose in the midst of cheers and said:

> "Yesterday, I heard Dr. Abdur Rahman claiming Gandhiji as a South African. May I not claim him to-day for the whole world? May I not say that the Society of Friends which I represent regard him with the same reverence and believe in his work as you do? I ought to say that we have gone very far wrong in our Western Civilization. We have gone too far in the pursuit of wealth and power. It is a deep evil in our whole Western Civilization. Our love of wealth has resulted in its concentration, our longing for power has brought on war after war and will likely plunge us in further wars until civilization is destroyed. So we gladly turn to you who are indicating another and better way, and we hope that while keeping the good things in nature and inventions, we should follow the brotherly spirit which is represented by the great prophet among you."

Before closing the year, we must make reference to the unfortunate Hindu-Muslim riots which occurred from time to time throughout 1925, and, as we shall see later, 1926 also. Speaking of Hindu-Muslim unity Gandhi said, addressing a meeting at Mirzapore Park in Calcutta on May 1st:

> "I have admitted my incompetence. I have admitted that I have been found wanting as a physician prescribing a cure for this malady. I do not find that either Hindus or Muslims are ready to accept my cure, and therefore I simply nowadays confine myself to a passing mention of this problem and content myself by saying that some day or other we Hindus and Muslims will have to come together, if we want the deliverance of our country. And if it is to be our lot that, before we can come together, we must shed one another's blood, then I say, the sooner we do so, the better it is for us. If we propose to break one another's heads, let us do so in a manly way. Let us not then shed crocodile tears, let us not ask for sympathy from any quarter, if you do not propose to give any quarter."

There was tension throughout July, 1925, the principal places affected being Delhi, Calcutta and Allahabad. Another riot took place during the Bakr Id celebrations at Humnabad in the Nizam's Dominions, about 40 miles from Gulbarga where like riots had occurred the previous year. Before closing the year 1925, we have also to refer to the Sikh question which received a sort of quietus in the year 1925. A Gurudwara Bill was introduced and passed, and it was stated by Sir Malcolm Hailey that the Gurudwara prisoners would be released if they signed a condition accepting the Act and undertaking not to engage themselves in campaigns similar to previous ones. This was deeply resented by many. But in course of time feelings were assuaged. Many prisoners gave the undertaking to abide by the Act. Even the G. S. P. C. was split on the question. While most prisoners were released, a few remained in jails to serve out their terms.

CHAPTER VII

THE COUNCIL FRONT (1926)

The year opened somewhat inauspiciously for the Council programme. The charm of novelty of the year 1923 had worn off.

A perpetual fight for the sake of fight was somewhat tiresome and signs of fatigue as well as reaction were visible early in the year.

The cult of Responsive Co-operation was indeed definitely in the air by the end of 1925. Before the opening of the Assembly on January 20th, 1926, the Bombay Council of the Swaraj Party definitely decided to extend its full support to Responsive Co-operation in their propaganda.

Let us turn once again to the activities of the Swaraj Party. Pandit Motilal Nehru had crossed the threshold of the Viceregal Lodge in the 2nd week of January (1926) with, of course, the permission of the Executive of the Party. With him were five other leaders including Lalaji, and the purpose of the visit was to discuss the South African question. Though this news raised hopes for a time, it was soon discovered that there was no ray of light brightening the clouds that began to lower on the skies What really had kindled hope in the public breast for a time was the exceedingly conciliatory speech made by Lord Reading in opening the Assembly on the 20th January, 1926, and an extract he gave from Birkenhead's speech of July 7th, 1925: "We desire and request good will; nor shall we be niggardly bargainers if we met with that generous friendship which is near and dear to our hearts." In the month of March, the A.I.C.C. met on the 6th and 7th at Raisina, Delhi, and confirmed the Cawnpore decision. Delhi declared once again in favour of "determined resistance and obstruction to every activity, Governmental or other, that may impede the Nation's progress towards Swaraj. In particular, Congressmen in the Legislatures shall refuse to accept offices in the gift of the Government, until, in the opinion of the Congress, a satisfactory response is made by the Government." It is necessary, while we are on the subject of the A.I.C.C., to state that the Working Committee which met on March 5, voted Rs. 2,000 to the Hindustani Seva Dal and Rs. 5,000 for foreign propaganda. The Dal was the body of volunteers organised under the resolution of the Cocanada Congress. It had held two annual sessions—one under Maulana Shaukat Ali's Presidentship at Belgaum, and the second under Mr. T. C. Goswami's at Cawnpore. Foreign propaganda, hitherto only talked of, became a subject of practical importance, and we shall have occasion to trace the development of both these as years roll by. The departure of Jawaharlal Nehru for Switzerland about the time for the treatment of his wife, Kamala Nehru, as well as the expected departure of Pandit Motilal to England for the sittings of the Skeen Committee, must doubtless have given a fillip to this question of foreign propaganda which had hitherto been only in a moribund stage. In the Assembly, when the Budget was taken up, Pandit Motilal announced that he and his supporters would abstain from a division. The public galleries were crowded with visitors eager to witness the Swarajists' withdrawal which was widely known beforehand. Pandit Motilal showed how Government had spurned Deshbandhu Das's terms for honourable co-operation. He warned the Government that, unless it took great care, it would find the whole country honeycombed with secret societies. With these words, he walked out of the Chamber accompanied by all the members of his party.

The walk-out created a little incident which may be briefly described. President Patel referred to the walk-out and declared that, as the strongest Party had vacated the Chamber, the Assembly ceased to retain the representative character required by the Government of India Act. It was, therefore, for Government to consider whether the Assembly should continue to function. He asked Government not to introduce any controversial legislation as, otherwise, he might be forced to use the extraordinary powers accorded under the Act of adjourning the House *sine die*. The next day, he gracefully took back these words and, in particular, he said: "I might add further that I felt on reflection that the Chair should not have made reference to its own powers or have used language which might perhaps be construed as a threat to the Government, but should have awaited further developments before deciding any course of action." This relieved the feelings of the Government.

The stone that began to glide down the hill of Non-co-operation from the heights of Gaya, nearly reached the bottom at Sabarmati early in 1926. We have seen how the Responsivists came near being absorbed into the fold of the Independents and Nationalists. Accordingly, they held a conference with the leaders of other parties on the 3rd April in Bombay, and the result was the formation of an 'Indian National Party' to prepare for and accelerate the establishment of Swaraj of the Dominion type, by all peaceful and legitimate means (excluding Mass Disobedience and non-payment of taxes) with liberty to resort inside the Legislature to Responsive

Co-operation. Pandit Motilal regarded the formation of the new Nationalist Party as a challenge to the Swarajists and described it as a "conglomerate in the first stage of geological formation." After some negotiations, it was decided to hold a meeting of the two wings of the Swaraj Party at Sabarmati on April 21st, to see if reunion were possible. Amongst others present at the meeting were Sarojini Devi, Lala Lajpat Rai, Syts. Kelkar, Jayakar and Aney, and Dr. Moonje. Subject to the confirmation of the A.I.C.C., it was agreed amongst the signatories to the agreement arrived at at Sabarmati, that "the response made by Government to the Swarajist Demand of February, 1924 in the Assembly should be considered satisfactory if, in the Provinces, the power, responsibility and initiative necessary for the effective discharge of their duties are secured to Ministers." The Congress members in the Legislative Councils of the Provinces were to decide the question of sufficiency of such power, but their decision was to be "subject to confirmation by a Committee consisting of Pandit Motilal Nehru and Mr. M. R. Jayakar." "The ink on the Pact was, however, barely dry," says 'India, 1925-26,' "when Mr. Prakasam, President of the Andhra Provincial Congress Committee expressed dissent and said that the position of the Congress had been compromised even more at Sabarmati than at Cawnpore." Numerous other prominent Congressmen expressed dissatisfaction likewise. It was generally thought, though for a while, that Swarajists would soon 'walk in' and form Ministries, but Panditji cleared the atmosphere by declaring that three conditions had to be satisfied before Office could be accepted, namely,

1. that the Ministers should be made fully responsible to the Legislature, free from all control of Government;

2. that an adequate proportion of the revenues be allotted for the development of 'nation-building' departments;
3. and that Ministers be given full control of the Services in the transferred departments.

Things were once more thrown into the melting pot. Jayakar characterised the draft placed before the Committee as a travesty of the Pact and a complete repudiation of the terms of the same, under the guise and in the name of clearing doubts and differences about the interpretation of the Pact. From this moment, the relations between the Swarajists and the Responsivists became more and more strained. The Sabarmati Pact, however, was yet to be disposed of by the A.I.C.C. which met on the 5th May at Ahmedabad. At this meeting, Pandit Motilal announced that, owing to irreconcilable differences between the signatories of the Pact regarding the interpretation of its terms, the negotiations that he had, for the past few days, been carrying on with the Responsivists had broken down and the Pact, therefore, had fallen through and was non-existent. A letter from the Responsivists was read which confirmed, in the main, Motilalji's statement. That Mr. S. Srinivasa Iyengar should have moved a vote of thanks to Panditji at this meeting was significant. The fact was that S. India was against the Sabarmati Pact. Motilalji was not perhaps quite wise in not having consulted them from the outset. Very often in such matters, the confidence that you can command from others is in proportion to the confidence you give to them, and when the latter is not forthcoming, the former is withheld. At this meeting, Pandit Motilal proposed a Committee to go into and report on Dr. Besant's Commonwealth of India Bill but this was turned down. When Sir Moropant Joshi, who attended the meeting on behalf of the Responsivists, thanked the

President for the invitation and urged that the Sabarmati Pact be considered, Pandit Motilal explained the different view-points of the two wings. Whereas the Responsivists held that the Reforms should be worked for all they were worth, his own section thought that the Faridpur conditions of the late Deshbandhu Das should be fulfilled before any response by Government could be considered satisfactory. At the end of this controversy, it cannot be said that Pandit Motilal came out altogether unscathed. He wanted to go to England and took two months' leave. Mr. S. Srinivasa Iyengar took his place. For the time being, and all too suddenly, Mr. Iyengar's star shot up into the high heavens.

While this was so in respect of leadership, the following everywhere began to show fissiparous tendencies. In Bengal, there was a revolt at Krishnagar in the middle of 1926, and although J. M. Sen-Gupta had a sort of victory, still, rumblings of revolt were not altogether subdued. There were really four sections of Swarajists at the time in Bengal: Hindu Swarajists and Swarajist Hindus, Muslim Swarajists and Swarajist Muslims, the difference being the emphasis based on the adjective or the substantive. There were secessions from the ranks of the B.P.C.C of men like Babu Amarendra Nath Chatterjee and Nirmal Chander Chander. The issue centred around the pact that was being observed in Bengal for sometime between the Hindus and the Muslims. Sen-Gupta's triple demand was (1) observe the pact, (1) ignore the Krishnagar Conference, and (3) do not accept office. The split between the two wings soon became a wide chasm. Sen-Gupta was charged with being given to cavalier methods, with neglecting village reconstruction and indifference to the fund collected for the purpose, with his rupture with the very men who had raised him aloft, and with taking powers to nominate

30 members to the Executive in addition to 30 elected ones. The Karmis took up the revolt under the leadership of Babu Nirmal Chander Chander and Sarat Chandra Bose. We have dwelt upon this at length because this rift in the lute continues to this day in Bengal.

In the middle of the year 1926, we can pause for a while to take a retrospect and prospect of the political picture. Lord Irwin stepped into India on April 6th, 1926. Almost simultaneously, there were communal riots in the streets of Calcutta of the fiercest kind ever known, only equalled if not excelled by those of Bombay in a later year. For six weeks the streets of Calcutta were the scenes of carnage and confusion. It was in May, 1925 that Gandhi, speaking at Mirzapore Park had said in solemn tones that if bloodshed was inevitable, let blood be shed in a manly spirit without any mockery of sympathy or sentiment. As if to make this statement prophetic, disturbances started in an affray between Muslims and Arya Samajists outside a mosque, and on the 5th April fire had to be opened. Sporadic street-fighting, incendiarism to the extent of 110 fires, attacks on temples and mosques,—all these destroyed the fair name of Calcutta. 44 deaths and 584 persons injured in the first bout, and 66 deaths and 391 injured in the second, represent the official figures. After 6 weeks of vandalism and massacre, the riots died down. Lord Irwin was greatly upset by these unfortunate happenings. He put all his faith and fervour, all his religious devotion and humanitarian instinct into his speeches, meant to exhort people "in the name of Indian national life and of Religion, to rescue the good name of India from the hurt which the present discords inflict upon it."

In the month of August, the Hilton Young Commission published its report on currency and exchange, and following it Government hurriedly introduced legislation in favour of the 18d. ratio. Government's hurry was adversely commented upon and they agreed to wait till February, 1927, in order to enable people and publicists to judge whether prices were stabilizing themselves at the 1s. 6d. ratio.

In September, differences again arose between Lala Lajpat Rai and Pandit Motilal Nehru about the work in the Assembly. Lalaji considered the Swarajist policy of walk-out as distinctly harmful to the interests of the Hindus. He was also in favour of confirming the Sabarmati Pact on the question of the acceptance of office. The controversy that ensued between him and Motilalji was vehement and very often personal. Lalaji resigned from the Congress party in the Assembly. The Assembly term was to be shortly over. New elections were ahead. President Patel was profusely complimented by Dewan Bahadur T. Rangachariar, Sir P. S. Sivaswamy Aiyer, Baptista, Neogy, Muhammad Yakub, Malaviya and Muddiman. It was all praise, admiration, well-wishing—all prophecy of a sure return in the coming elections—all expressing an ardent wish that the Speaker's seat should not be contested by any one else. In the new elections, Government were not a little intrigued to know whether the Swarajists would come in in large numbers. Col. Wedgwood was in communication with Lalaji, and his influence was visible in Lalaji's plumping for Responsive Co-operation.

At this very time, Sir Abdur Rahim was employing his good offices to secure the appointment of a Muslim on the Government of India Executive. Lord Irwin gave a smart reply: "The Governor-General must hold himself free to make whatever appointment seems to him most in accordance with public interests." Lord Irwin was fast infecting everybody with the virtues of communal unity, and even the Raja of Panagal in Madras echoed the sentiment of communal concord. It was at this time that the Imperial Conference was sitting in London, at which the now-famous definition of Dominion was evolved, and by the third week of October, a South African Deputation which was invited by the Government of India toured from Madras to Peshawar under the leadership of Mr. Bayers in order to study Indian conditions and culture first-hand within the space of three weeks.

General elections took place in November, 1926. In Madras the Congress candidates, no longer 'Swarajists,' came out with flying colours. Lord Birkenhead was waiting to see if, at Gauhati, the Congress would show any inclination to co-operate. Mr. S. Srinivasa Iyengar had been elected President of the Gauhati Congress. And he had an individuality all his own. That individuality brought him later into sharp conflict with Pandit Motilal Nehru. In fact, the germs of such a conflict had shown themselves earlier even at the Delhi meeting of the A.I.C.C. Two eminent lawyers—when, in addition, they are also two eminent politicians—are bound to come into conflict with each other. Panditji and Jayakar, Panditji and Lalaji; Panditji and Iyengar,—it was all a series of conflicts for the learned Pandit with Bombay, Punjab and Madras. A masterful personality like the Pandit could not be all things to all men, nor could he be the same to himself all along. Lesser men surely could feel quite at ease over their quarrels.

Gauhati Congress

The Gauhati Session then naturally met under a certain tension of feeling. The tension was caused by the warfare between Co-operation and Non-co-operation. It will be remembered that Non-co-operation stood for continuous, constant and uniform obstruction. Later, it became a statement of policy to be pursued only if the Swarajists came in a majority. Gradually, it came perilously near co-operation, what with acceptance of elected seats on Legislative Committees and of nominated seats on Government of India Committees. Finally, it hovered on the borderland of co-operation at Sabarmati where it was just fighting shy of it. The Council Party was willing to negotiate but afraid to accept. Then there was the spirit of co-operation in the Swaraj Party itself which would not straightway take up the position, say of the Nationalists, the Independents, or the Liberals, but coquet with the idea, speaking of Responsive Co-operation, honourable co-operation, co-operation if possible and obstruction if necessary, and co-operation for all that the Reforms were worth. It was these subtle but thoroughly practical questions that created the tension of feeling at *Pragjyotishapura* (Gauhati). Added to this, there was Government throwing out baits in the form of open praises and veiled invitations, and indulging in all those blandishments and arts by which wavering minds and timid hearts are won over.

This tension, sufficiently trying in itself but by no means tragic, was aggravated at Gauhati by the sudden news that Swami Shraddhananda had been shot in his sick bed by a certain Muslim who had sought and obtained an interview with him. The news was received at Gauhati on the day of the elephant procession of the President. Assam, the land of elephants, was anxious to give a remarkable and unprecedented ovation to the President of the Congress, but the procession had necessarily to be abandoned. Gloom overhung the session. Hindus and Muslims felt the deepest grief over the tragedy. The usual formalities initiated the sittings of the Congress session. The unsophisticated music of the tribal men of Assam added a romantic note to the natural romance of the country known to our *Ithihasas* as Kamarupa. Gandhi was given quarters in a small hut on the banks of the Brahmaputra, the camp and Mandap being a bit removed from his lodging.

When Mr. Srinivasa Iyengar delivered his Address, there was none of the unexpected element in his pronouncement, his views having been well-known before-hand. After paying a well-merited tribute to the memory of Swami Shraddhananda and referring in suitable terms to the melancholy death of Omar Sobhani, some time Congress treasurer, he dealt with the Elections, and stated how the results had justified the policy of the Swaraj Party in the Legislatures. The Provinces of Madras, Bengal, Bihar and Orissa in a striking degree, and the other Provinces including the Punjab to a lesser extent, he said, had responded to the Congress mandate and come under the Congress discipline. Dyarchy was then dissected and anatomized, the dry bones of the Central Government were exposed in the valley of the shadow of despotism. Deshbandhu's offer was recalled, India's status was examined, Army and Navy were dealt with, the Council programme was discussed. "Resistance to every activity, governmental or other, that may impede the Nation's progress towards Swaraj" was the basic principle laid down at Cawnpore on which the particular duties of Congressmen in Councils were to be framed. He condemned acceptance of office in unequivocal terms and with a logic that was unassailable. But at the same time he valued the position of the Swaraj Party as forming the "opposition whose power, though indirect, is very real and much more effective than the power of Ministers and if we are disciplined and energetic and in sufficient numbers in any Council, we can carry out our policy and programme more easily than the Ministers." There is a veiled sarcasm in the statement which implied that the Ministers have no power whatever. Then he dealt with the burning topics of the day, namely, currency and communalism, and the cold topics of the hour such as khaddar, untouchability and prohibition, and put in a strong plea for tolerance and unity and closed with the following peroration:—

> "Swaraj is not an intellectual but an emotional proposition. We must cherish it in our hearts with unquenchable faith. Neither genial humour nor mordant sarcasm, neither the persuasion of friends nor the wrath of foes, neither appreciation nor calumny, should make our patriotism tepid or the singleness of our purpose qualified."

The resolutions of Gauhati are of the usual type. The resolution on the late Swami Shraddhananda was moved, as was to be expected, by Gandhi and seconded by Mahomed Ali. Gandhi expounded what true religion was and explained the causes that led to the murder. "Now you will perhaps understand why I have called Abdul Rashid a brother and I repeat it. I do not even regard him as guilty of Swami's murder. Guilty indeed are those who excited feelings of hatred against one another." Kenya figured next on the list of resolutions. There, restrictive legislation against the Indian settlers became more and more progressive, the original poll-tax of 20s. which by currency manipulation was raised to 30s. had been raised to 50s. by legislation, thus conserving European interests against Indian interests, liberty and aspirations. On the question of work in Councils, it was definitely laid down that Congressmen shall:—

> (a) refuse to accept Ministerships or other offices in the gift of the Government and oppose the formation of a Ministry by other parties until, in the opinion of

the Congress or the All-India Congress Committee, a satisfactory response is made by the Government to the National Demand;

(b) subject to clause (d), refuse supplies and throw out budgets until such response is made by the Government or unless otherwise directed by the All-India Congress Committee;

(c) throw out all proposals for legislative enactments by which the bureaucracy proposes to consolidate its powers;

(d) move resolutions and introduce and support measures and Bills which are necessary for the healthy growth of National life and the advancement of the economic, agricultural, industrial and commercial interests of the country, and for the protection of the freedom of person, speech, association and of the Press, and the consequent displacement of the bureaucracy;

(e) take steps to improve the condition of agricultural tenants by introducing and supporting measures to secure fixity of tenure and other advantages with a view to ensure a speedy amelioration of the condition of the tenants; and

(f) generally, protect the rights of Labour, agricultural and industrial, and adjust on an equitable basis the relations between landlords and tenants, capitalists and workmen.

The policy of invoking emergency legislation for dealing with the Bengal detenus was condemned; work in and outside the country, Hindu-Muslim unity, Gurudwara prisoners, and currency were the subjects of suitable resolutions. The venue of the next session of the Congress was left to be decided by the A.I.C.C.

A few interesting points relating to the Congress have to be noted here. Two professors of Zurich were there, deeply interested in an old Coat of Arms that formed one of the exhibits in the Exhibition. They had a smattering of English, and when asked how they happened to pick it up, said, "Oh, we learn it; we have to learn much as you."

Mr. and Mrs. Pethwick Lawrence were there. The former was a bit hard of hearing; the latter was perhaps the more intelligent of the two. To them, it was a discovery to be told that India's slavery was not merely political, but economic and commercial as well. Gandhi was there too; he was not a passive spectator. He took an active part in the deliberations, so much so that two resolutions actually passed by the Subjects Committee had to be reversed the next day. One of them related to Nabha and the other to currency. Gandhi has never sympathised with Nabha's lot to the extent of committing the Congress to a particular position on it. A third resolution—on Independence—was simply smothered and scorched under the fire of Gandhi's eloquence.

Motilal made a statement on the subject of Nabha. He said at that particular moment he had been briefed by the Maharajah and could not, therefore, commit himself to a speech at a public meeting on a matter in which he was briefed. Narottam Morarji and certain economists were there at Gauhati, for the obvious reason that the question of currency and exchange was to be dealt with. Neither Mr. Jayakar nor Mr. Kelkar was present. For one thing, both were ill at the time. For another, the Responsivists by this time definitely cut themselves off from the Congress. Gauhati laid emphasis on work in the villages and made the habitual wear of khaddar compulsory, to enable Congressmen "to vote at the election of representatives or delegates or any Committee or Sub-Committee of any Congress organization whatsoever, or to be elected as such, or to take part in any meeting of the Congress or Congress organization or any Committee or Sub-Committee thereof." We take leave of the Gauhati Congress and the charming country of Kamarupa, which, despite the Mongoloid features of the people that inhabit it, worships the same gods and goddesses as the Hindus in the rest of India, and observes the same manners and customs and cherishes the same culture. We were shown the Kamakhya temple, the Unananda that is enthroned on the height of a rock in the midst of the Brahmaputra, and the Vasishta Ashram about 13 miles from Gauhati.

From the meditation of these gods and goddesses, let us descend to matters of the earth, earthy. The President of the Gauhati Congress had made a casual reference to the election of the Swarajists at the elections of 1926. Their election programme had been carefully drawn up Madras gave a glorious account of itself and Government acknowledged it. U. P. fared badly and, to use Pandit Motilalji's language,

> "There has been a veritable rout of the Swarajists. 'Defeat' is no word for it. But this was not because they were Swarajists, but because they were Nationalists. The political programmes of the various parties had nothing to do with the elections. It was a fight between the forces of Nationalism and those of a low order of Communalism reinforced by wealth, wholesale corruption, terrorism and falsehood. 'Religion in danger', was the cry of the opponents of the Congress, both Hindu and Muslim. I have been freely denounced as a beef-eater and destroyer of cows, the supporter of the prohibition of music before mosques, and the one man responsible for the stoppage of Ramlila processions in Allahabad. I could only contradict these lies in public meetings, but they penetrated hamlets and villages which I could not reach. Staying in Dak and Inspection bungalows, and eating food cooked in European style, was taken to confirm the lying propaganda."

The history of the Congress has by this time become a monotonous tale of pious resolutions at the annual sessions and perpetual strifes in the Councils. There was, however, one redeeming feature brought into greater prominence than ever before. Since the formation of the

A.I.S.A. khaddar had a pure atmosphere of village uplift and economics. Men and women wedded to it were strenuously labouring in its cause without the excitement of votes and the sensations of lobbies. The annual exhibitions showed how splendid was the development of the craft. At Gauhati, the comparative progress of six or seven years which Bihar had been able to effect in the production of khaddar was an object lesson to the whole of India. 'Khokti' of Bihar and Chicacole muslin of Andhra were glorious, but the glory is not of modern revival. The ancient craft has been there in all its splendour. Even so were the 'endi' and 'muga' silks of Assam which were being greatly helped by the Assam Government. The points of progress did not merely concern the fineness of the counts, but the tension of the yarn and its twist on which the durability of cloth depends. But the most remarkable feature was that, in each Province, the hidden talents of the artisans and craftsmen of the collateral crafts came to be revived once again, and the skilled workmen who were driven out of their homes and hearths and became common, mechanical labourers, were restored to their traditional professions. They have brought art and beauty to khaddar. Old blocks have been recovered, new designs are being invented. The printing and dyeing industry is really the right hand of the textile industry, and when the spinner and the weaver have been resuscitated, they have brought to life, with them, the printer and the dyer, the dhobie, the bleacher, the engraver and the petty trader. The exhibitions which have become adjuncts of the Congress and which, except in one or two years, are exclusively of khaddar,—so far as the textile industry is concerned,—have helped to concentrate interest upon the economic rehabilitation of the country, side by side with the political, social and cultural, and have convinced the people that Swaraj means food and raiment to the poor.

CHAPTER VIII

THE COUNCIL FRONT (1927) A STALEMATE

We now pass on to a study of the position and work of the Congress Party in the various Legislatures. It will be remembered that Dyarchy was destroyed in Bengal and C. P. during the three previous years. In both Provinces, it was restored in the year 1927. In Bengal, the demand for the Ministers' salaries was carried by 94 to 88 votes, and in C. P. by 55 to 16. Let us recall a few facts of the year 1926 relating to the Assembly. In March, 1926, the Swaraj Party walked out of the Council Chamber with no intention of re-entering it before the general election. But Government's strategy in introducing legislation on the question of equating the rupee to 18d. instead of 16d. drew the Swaraj Party barely for a minute, so to put it, to the Assembly just to secure the adjournment of its consideration till the next session (*i.e.* till the elections were over). Therefore when the new Assembly met, every one was agitated by the thought of the 18d. ratio. Other sensational questions arose in the opening session which set the tune for the main song of the drama. Panditji opened his first attack on the policy of Government with a motion for adjournment of the House to discuss the non-attendance of Satyendra Chandra Mitra who had been in prison and who was elected to the Assembly while in prison. The importance of the debate lay in the development of parliamentary practice in the country. To anticipate events, let us point out that a similar motion was made and passed in the Assembly in 1935 on the question of the non-attendance of Mr. Sarat Chandra Bose who was a State prisoner at the time and had been elected whilst in prison. Panditji's position was that Mitra's detention was an encroachment on the privileges of the Legislative Assembly and on the rights of the constituency which had elected him. Sir Alexander Muddiman showed that the Indian Legislatures had no such complete code of powers, privileges and immunities as Legislatures as other parts of the British Empire enjoyed, by virtue, generally, of a provision in their Acts of Constitution, whereby they were enabled to define their own privileges, subject only to the restriction that they should not exceed those for the time being enjoyed by the British House of Commons. In the end, the division went against the Government by 18. But all the same, Mr. Mitra was not released to attend the Assembly meeting. The question of Bengal detenus was taken up. Panditji's demand, stated in the form of an amendment to the original resolution, was that they should be released or brought to trial.

Lalaji, then a member of the Nationalist Party, said that he would prefer the Government to try to justify its imprisonment of these men without trial, on grounds of necessity rather than of Law. Panditji's amendment was passed by a majority of 13 votes. A number of motions for the adjournment of the House followed that relating to S. C. Mitra. Despatch of troops to China, non-publication of the Report of the Indian Delegation to Fiji (disallowed), the adjournment of the discussion of the currency legislation till after the disposal of the Railway Budget and the presentation of the General Budget. This last one was passed by a majority of 7 votes. The last of the series was the strike situation at Kharagpur and other places on the Bengal-Nagpur Railway. Then a series of clashes took place between Government and non-officials. The first was on the Steel Protection Bill. A few words would not be out of place on the subject. About the year 1923, the question of protection to the Indian Steel and Iron Industry was raised. The Tariff Board had recommended certain bounties and a revision of the question in three years. The interval passed. The question was taken up by the Board and the recommendation this time was in favour of an increase of import duties,—with a basic duty on British goods and differential rates on other goods. This raised the question of Imperial Preference and the popular view was against it, but after a keen discussion Government proposals were upheld by the House. Mr. Jayakar, Deputy Leader of the Nationalist Party, moved for the refusal of the entire grant of the Budget. And the discussion resulted in a victory for the popular opposition by 8 or 9 votes. Then came the question of questions,—the question of the 18d. ratio. This affected not merely the millowners and the merchants but the people of India,—notably the exporters of raw produce and food material. The pound which was in the pre-war and the war days worth Rs. 15/- is now made equivalent to Rs. 13-5-4. In other words, the importer is encouraged to import more foreign goods, because they have become cheaper by 2d. a rupee or 2d. out of 16d., *i.e.*, by an eighth or 12½ p.c. Applying the reverse reasoning to exports of the ryots' produce, if a pound worth of cloth which is imported into India and which formerly cost, at the 16d. ratio, Rs. 15/- now cost only Rs. 13-5-4, a pound worth of produce which formerly fetched the cultivator Rs. 15/- would now yield him only Rs. 13-5-4. Thus computing the total exports, say for 1925, at 316 crores, one eighth of 316 crores or nearly 40 crores would be lost to the ryot year after year. If the imports of the year were 249 crores, the statement that the importer gained 31 crores thereby would not be a solace to the cultivator, and granting that it were so, the country would still be losing 40—31, or 9 crores annually, and a recurring loss is inevitable with a country like India having a favourable trade balance, *i.e.*, whose exports are greater than her imports. This is the reason why a battle-royal raged over the question, but the popular view was defeated and Government won by 68 to 65 votes. With the Steel Protection, Finance and Currency problems disposed of, the most important work of the Congress at the Delhi Session of 1927 came to an end.

We pause for a moment to record a few happenings of abiding interest. We have referred to the valedictory scenes of the Assembly and the warm *au revoir* extended to President Patel. It need hardly be said that he was once again elected President, but what is of particular interest is that he promised to make over to Gandhi Rs. 1,656 a month from out of his pay, keeping to himself Rs. 2,000 for his personal expenses and so as to be able to comfort himself with befitting dignity. Gandhi himself did not want to take the entire responsibility for administering the trust and invited suggestions and had other trustees associated with him. On the 31st May, 1935, Gandhi stated in opening a girls' High School at Ras in Gujarat, that this fund amounting to Rs. 40,000 was still with him, only Rs. 1,000 out of the interest on it having been spent.

After a year's vow of voluntary silence and immobility taken at Cawnpore, Gandhi released himself from both. To those of us who are only acquainted with his recent retirement from politics, this vow at Cawnpore in December, 1925, comes as a key that explains what otherwise might appear quaint or cranky. Whenever the Congress has ignored his advice, he has cleared the way for it to march along its chosen path. He began his work by a tour in Bihar making collections for the

Deshbandhu Memorial, only the proceeds so collected were to go in aid of khaddar. Council programme had no charm for him,—had no charm even for men like Lala Lajpat Rai who condemned work in the Assembly as infructuous and as a weary waste of National effort and energy. Lalaji's pronouncement was followed by S. Srinivasa Iyengar's that "the Assembly is not the place, much less the Councils, to which you can look for a policy of obstruction by the Nation."

We have already referred to Sarojini Devi's visit to South Africa. It was in 1924, when things in S. Africa were at their worst and General Smuts was on the point of carrying through a Segregation Bill, that Mrs. Sarojini Naidu went on from East Africa to South Africa at the request of the Indian National Congress and had a very remarkable reception. The Bill, which was very nearly passed, had to be abandoned owing to the downfall of General Smuts's Government on other issues. General Hertzog came into power, and in 1925, an even more drastic Segregation Bill, called the Class Areas Bill was drawn up, which would have immediately gained the consent of Government and Opposition alike, if it had been brought before the Union Parliament. Mr. Andrews was asked by Gandhi and the Congress leaders to go out, and he raised at once the issue of a breach of the Gandhi-Smuts Agreement, if such a Bill was passed. Later on, the Government of India sent out the Paddison Deputation which had a very cold reception from the Union Government. But gradually the proposal took shape that the Bill should be held over until a Deputation from the Government of India, with powers of entering into a formal agreement with the Union Government, should have been sent and the whole Indian position in South Africa should have been discussed. This led to the first Cape Town Conference. Mr. Andrews was asked again to go out in order to act as adviser to the South Africa Indian Congress delegates. Though this Conference brought little immediate gains, it had the effect of bringing a pause to any legislation of a segregating character. It also led to the establishment of an Agent-General in South Africa whose duty it was to protect Indian interests.

Now a word regarding the South African agreement. It will be remembered that a South African Congress Delegation had toured India in 1925-1926, and on the 16th October, 1926, an Indian Delegation to South Africa was announced with Sir Muhammad Habibullah as the Leader. A Conference was summoned which was opened by the Premier of South Africa, General Hertzog, on December 17th, 1926. The session lasted till January 13th, 1927, and a provisional agreement was arrived at between the two Delegations on the following lines:—

> Both Governments reaffirm the recognition of the right of South Africa to use all just and legitimate means for the maintenance of Western standards of life.
>
> The Union Government recognises that Indians domiciled in the Union who are prepared to conform to Western standards of life should be enabled to do so.
>
> For those Indians in the Union who may desire to avail themselves of it, the Union Government will organise a scheme of assisted emigration to India or other countries where Western standards are not required. Union domicile will be lost after three years' continuous absence from the Union, in consonance with the proposed revision of the law relating to domicile which will be of general application. Emigrants under the assisted emigration scheme, who desire to return to the Union within three years, will only be allowed to do so on refund to the Union Government of the cost of assistance received by them. The

Government of India recognise their obligation to look after such emigrants on their arrival in India. Admission into the Union of wives and minor children of Indians permanently domiciled in the Union will be regulated by paragraph 3 of Resolution XXI of the Imperial Conference of 1918, which lays down that Indians already permanently domiciled in the other British countries should be allowed to bring in their wives and minor children on condition, (a) that not more than one wife and her children shall be admitted for each such Indian, and (b) that each individual so admitted shall be certified by the Government of India as being the lawful wife or child of such Indian.

In the expectation that the difficulties with which the Union has been confronted will be materially lessened by the agreement now happily reached between the two Governments, and in order that the agreement may come into operation under most favourable auspices and have a fair trial, the Union Government of South Africa have decided not to proceed further with the Arch Reservation and Immigration and Registration (further Provision) Bill.

The two Governments have agreed to watch the working of the agreement now reached and to exchange views from time to time concerning any changes that experience may suggest.

The Union Government of South Africa have requested the Government of India to appoint an Agent in order to secure continuous and effective co-operation between the two Governments.

At the end of the first Cape Town Round Table Conference, Gandhi, who had been in favour of an Agent being sent to South Africa, put forward in the public Press of India the name of the Rt. Hon. V. S. S. Sastri. This immediately gained consent from the Government and the people of India and his appointment proved a very great success, as we shall have occasion to say later on.

The results of the Conference were acclaimed with joy on every side. Gandhi himself had characterized the settlement as an honourable compromise. He, however, saw some danger to assisted immigration to other parts of the Empire than India. The details of the settlement may be obtained from 'India, 1926-27.'

The formal omission of all reference to Civil Disobedience in the Gauhati resolution created a new atmosphere in the year 1927. Government, it is true, were disappointed to find that Gauhati did not plump for co-operation, but in actual fact, the Provinces were all forming Ministries and working Dyarchy. When Gandhi began his tour, the Maharajahs were no longer afraid of him. He began to be invited by some of them. They no longer looked upon khaddar as a National uniform for a semi-military band of volunteers of the Congress, but as an innocent factor in the economic regeneration of the country. They also saw in Gandhi a truthful and honest man, somewhat misguided in his political methods and cranky in his political beliefs. After a short tour, Gandhi fell ill. The A.I.C.C. that met on the 15th and 16th May, wished him a speedy recovery. At this time, Lalaji also sailed for Europe and his departure was adversely commented upon. The previous year also, he had left India and occasioned adverse criticism. To his credit, however, it must be noted that when Shraddhananda was murdered, he was in Calcutta on his way to Gauhati but returned to the Punjab without attending the Congress. We mention these things in order to show that the political atmosphere was full of bickerings. When the A.I.C.C. met in Bombay on the 15th and 16th May, there was a formula evolved by the Working Committee placed before it and approved of by it, which dealt with the Hindu-Muslim problem. Read at this distance of time and with a knowledge of the numerous transformations the question has since undergone, the formula of Bombay cannot fail to strike us as academic. Mr. S. Srinivasa Iyengar was anxious to settle this problem, but he had not a grip of issues in all their seriousness. It is not the evolution of a formula that was required, but the approximation of the hearts, a clearing of the minds, of the two great communities. So we shall not pause to give the details of this formula at length but content ourselves with saying that it contemplated joint electorates, with reservation of seats on the basis of population in the Provinces, and, in the Central Legislature, provided reciprocal concessions in favour of minorities, including Sikhs in the Punjab, by mutual agreement so as to give them weighted representation and maintain the same proportions in the Central Legislature as well.

Other subjects dealt with at the meeting of the A.I.C.C. in Bombay were the International Congress Against Imperialism and Colonial Oppression, and National Independence. Jawaharlal at this time was in Europe and he represented India at the Congress and sent up a report from Brussels where it was held, and the A.I.C.C. expressed its high appreciation of his services. It appreciated the efforts that were being made by the League against Imperialism and for National Independence, and resolved to recommend to the Congress (I.N.C.) to give support to the League as an Associate organization.

This is a rather important move, for we shall hear later something of foreign propaganda started a year previously, and continued for a couple of years. Another resolution assured the Chinese people of India's fullest sympathy in their struggle for freedom, condemned the action of the Government of India in despatching troops to China and demanded their immediate withdrawal. The A.I.C.C. appreciated the resolve of the Hindusthani Seva Dal to send an ambulance corps to China. Then the British Trade Union Bill, Bengal Congress disputes, organization of Labour, Nagpur Satyagraha, and the Boycott of British goods were the subjects of suitable resolutions. The last was to be seriously taken up. The Congress Party in the Madras Council came up for severe comments and even a motion of censure was threatened. The fact was that when the Congress Party was returned in good strength,—45 out of 104 elected members, or according to Government's admission, 38 out of 104,—the Leader was sent for by the Governor and asked to form a Ministry, but he declined. He himself became the President of the Council, and it was an open secret at the time that, with the private offer of support from the Congress Party, the Independents formed a Ministry. This was naturally objected to on strict principle. The A.I.C.C., though there was no programme of Civil Disobedience, was animated by a non-co-operative spirit and outlook. Vigorous canvassing went on in favour of a censure motion against the Madras Council members of the Congress Party moved by Mr. Gopala Menon. It was expected that Kelkar would oppose the motion. Only, he took the opportunity to describe in choice language,—previously prepared and committed to writing,—the infatuation, as he said, of Pandit Motilal Nehru for power and position, authority and wealth. He contented himself with this piece of verbal vengeance. The South Indians, therefore, made the best of a bad position by accepting an amendment to refer the matter, as to why the Congress Party did not vote down the salaries of Ministers and refuse supplies, to the Working Committee for enquiry and report. Mr. Srinivasa Iyengar was not against the Independent Ministry in Madras; so, he had to oppose the orthodox Congress members of the Council

Party by whose co-operation he had risen to be the head of the political movement. The fact was that the members of the Working Committee were tired. Statutory enquiry, Royal Commission, Deputation to England, were all in the air and they were hard realities which could not be ignored. Even Motilalji, whose repugnance to Ministry formation was pronounced and uncompromising, did not expose or attack the South Indian procedure. Bombay marked once again a notable change in the outlook of the Congress,—a realignment from the highways of N.C.O. to the much trodden rut of a Royal Commission.

One piece of good news at the time in the fourth week of May was the release of Subash Chandra Bose after four years of imprisonment. Lord Lytton had all along been nervous and it was left to Sir Stanley Jackson to give relief to the Bengal Detenus. Subash completely broke down in health in his internment and this became a source of general anxiety.

The summer of 1927, like other summers, was barren of Legislative labours; but the country was ablaze with Hindu-Muslim riots. The most serious riot took place in Lahore between the 3rd and 7th May, 1927, the toll being 27 killed and 272 injured. In Bihar, in Multan (Punjab), Bareilly (U.P.) and in Nagpur (C.P.) similar riots occurred. The Nagpur riots were easily the worst of these, coming only next to those of Lahore, with 19 persons killed and 123 injured. A few details may be given here of the circumstances which led to some at any rate of these outbreaks. Three years previously, a pamphlet had been published, named *Rangila Rasul,* the title itself showing how objectionable the contents would be. This was the subject of a criminal prosecution which had dragged on for over two years, and which after resulting in conviction, upheld in the court of appeal, finally ended in acquittal in the High Court. There was another case called the *Risala Vartaman* case which however ended in conviction. The law being considered on the whole uncertain, a Bill was introduced into the Assembly, in August, 1927, the operative clause of which was as follows:—

> "Whoever with deliberate and malicious intention of outraging the religious feelings of any class of His Majesty's subjects, by words, either spoken or written, or by visible representations, insults or attempts to insult religion or religious beliefs of that class, shall be punished with 2 years' imprisonment, or with fine, or with both."

The Bill was passed after 2 days' discussion. Altogether 25 riots had broken out. Of them, 10 were in U.P., 6 in Bombay, 2 each in Punjab, C.P., Bengal, Bihar, and Delhi. In less than 18 months, the toll taken was stated by Lord Irwin in his Address to the Indian Legislature on August 29th, 1927, to be between 250 killed and over 2,500 injured. The Viceroy's exhortation to unity was followed by a Unity Conference which, however, did not achieve much. A similar Unity Conference was organized by the A.I.C.C. on the 27th October, 1927, and it was opened by Mr. Srinivasa Iyengar, whose one ambition in life, as he repeatedly said,—an ambition which rested in a fund of self-confidence,—was to evolve a formula for Hindu-Muslim unity. After a long discussion the Conference accepted the following resolution:—

> "Whereas no community in India should impose or seek to impose its religious obligations or religious views upon any other community, but free profession and practice of religion should, subject to public order and morality, be guaranteed to every community

and person, Hindus are at liberty to take processions and play music before mosques at any time for religious or social purposes, but there should be no stoppage nor special demonstration in front of the mosque, nor shall songs or music, played in front of such mosques, be such as is calculated to cause annoyance, special disturbance, or offence to worshippers in the mosques. Muslims shall be at liberty to sacrifice or slaughter cows in exercise of their rights in any town or village in any place, not being a thoroughfare, nor one in the vicinity of a temple, nor one exposed to the gaze of Hindus. Cows should not be led in procession or in demonstration for sacrifice or slaughter. Having regard to the deep-rooted sentiment of the Hindu community in the matter of cow-killing, the Muslim community is earnestly appealed to to so conduct cow-sacrifice as not to cause any annoyance to Hindus of the town or village concerned."

The Conference also condemned certain recent murderous assaults and appealed to Hindu and Muslim leaders to create an atmosphere of non-violence in the country, and it empowered the All-India Congress Committee to appoint a Committee in each Province for propaganda work in connection with Hindu-Muslim unity.

The All-India Congress Committee met immediately after the Unity Conference, *i.e.*, on the 28th, 29th, and 30th October, 1927, in Calcutta. The resolutions of the Unity Conference on the communal relations were passed bodily. The Bengal Detenus, naturally, were the next to attract attention. Some of them had been in prison for over four years. Accordingly, a Committee was appointed to devise means of effecting their early release. As soon as these two subjects were done with, there was a thinning of attendance, the President himself being absent on account of break-down of health. A resolution, moved by Mr. T. Viswanatham (Andhra), saying that according to the Gauhati resolution it was mandatory on Congressmen to refuse offices within the gift of Government and to prevent the formation of Ministries, was disallowed and this caused a measure of discontent. The Secretary, on behalf of the President, informed that the Resolution was out of place, since the Committee had at the outset resolved to postpone the consideration of the question till the Madras Session. As a protest against this, some Bengal members moved an adjournment *sine die* and it was carried.

Other subjects dealt with and disposed of by suitable resolutions at the Calcutta meeting were 'Indians in America' and expression of gratitude to Senator Copeland for his support of the Indian cause, refusal of passports to Saklatwalla, and Nabha 'abdication' which was dropped at Gauhati but revived in Calcutta. The last subject was taken up by Mr. B. G. Horniman and the Committee passed a resolution demanding justice to the Maharajah.

The first week of November was rather a sensational week. The Viceroy had cancelled his tour programme and gone back to Delhi. Invitations were issued to the leading politicians in India to see the Viceroy on the 5th November and succeeding days at their convenience. It was evident that there was something important, though not urgent, to be communicated to them. Gandhi was at this time in Mangalore, a thousand miles away from Delhi. He too got an invitation and had to cancel his tour programme and proceed to Delhi. When he saw the Viceroy, the interview was a cold affair. Lord Irwin placed in his hands the Secretary of State's announcement regarding the Simon Commission, and when asked whether that was all the business, Lord Irwin said 'Yes.'

Gandhi felt that a one-anna envelope would have reached it to him. Lord Irwin was, however, helpless and was only doing a duty somewhat timidly and, therefore, canvassing the sympathies of politicians beforehand. The announcement itself was made in the country on the 8th November, 1927. The Viceroy was trying to secure friendly co-operation. "But what was behind this sudden rush into hurried action?" asked Dr. Besant. It was the fear of the General Election in 1929 in Great Britain. The Simon Commission was not 'wanted' by any party —be the reasons as they might. The omission of any Indian from its personnel supplied the common basis of resentment for all the political parties in India, except the Congress. The Congress naturally felt that the idea came nowhere near its Demand, which itself was a kind of patchwork. Dr. Besant felt it added insult to injury. She quoted the Maharajah of Burdwan's warning to Lord Birkenhead and the latter's sneer on lines such as this:— "You dare not reject anything that we offer you, and if you dare do it, we shall see." "Quite so," said Dr. Besant, "all the world will see, and the world will remember that Lord Birkenhead was one of those who entered into a treasonable conspiracy, drilling an army and filling a treasury to fight His Majesty's troops in Northern Ireland. And now that a Commission is appointed in which India's immediate destiny is to be fixed, and from which Indians are boycotted, he loses his temper over a suggestion that Indians may copy his own policy of boycott. Surely, imitation would be the sincerest flattery."

Pandit Motilal Nehru who was just then in England looked upon the Commission as an eyewash. "The only honest course is to declare what Government wants to do and then to appoint a Commission to draft a scheme giving effect to that declaration." A manifesto was published against the Commission over the signatures of all-India leaders like D. E. Wacha and others. The signatories were of all political parties outside the Congress. Miss Wilkinson stated that since the Amritsar tragedy, there was not such a universal condemnation of any act of the British as attended the appointment of the Simon Commission. The Labour Party appointed Lansbury, MacDonald and Snowden to see Lord Birkenhead on the matter. There was a suspicion of the Labour Party in India, for it was Lord Olivier who, as Secretary of State in the last Labour Government, had put his signature to the Bengal Ordinances under which thousands had been interned. The President of the Congress condemned the Commission and quoted Colonel Wedgwood's view that the cause of India would not be prejudiced by the Boycott of the Commission.

What was this Commission to do which was being condemned from every quarter? The Commission was charged with the duty of "inquiring into the working of the system of Government, the growth of education and the development of representative institutions in British India and matters connected therewith, and reporting whether and to what extent it is desirable to establish the principle of Responsible Government or to extend, modify or restrict the degree of Responsible Government then existing therein, including the question whether the establishment of Second Chambers of the Local Legislatures is or is not desirable."

> "When the Commission has reported and its Report has been examined by the Government of India and His Majesty's Government, it will be the duty of the latter to present proposals to Parliament. But it is not the intention of His Majesty's Government to ask Parliament to adopt these proposals without first giving a full opportunity for Indian

opinion of different schools to contribute its view upon them. And to this end, it is intended to invite Parliament to refer these proposals for consideration by a Joint Committee of both Houses, and to facilitate the presentation to that Committee both of the views of the Indian Central Legislature by delegations who will be invited to attend and confer with the Joint Committee, and also of any other bodies whom the J.P.C. may desire to consult.

"The method chosen by His Majesty's Government will also assure to Indians a better opportunity, than they would have enjoyed in any other way, of influencing the passage of these great events. For not only will they, through representatives of the Indian Legislatures, be enabled to express themselves freely to the Commission itself, but it will also be within their power to challenge in detail or principle any of the propoosals made by His Majesty's Government before the Joint Select Committee of Parliament and to advocate their own solutions."

The plan outlined is a single comprehensive one and should be so regarded.

"Above all, friends will strive to correct differences by appeal to the many things on which they are agreed, rather than lightly imperil friendship by insistence on points in regard to which they take conflicting views."

We now pass on to the Congress of the year 1927. It was to be held in the city of Madras. Even at Gauhati, people did not like the idea of the annual session being held in some district town, as the Royal Commission would be coming in 1927. What exactly the Congress would be called upon to do in relation to the Commission, no one knew. The choice of the venue was left at Gauhati to the A.I.C.C. It is now clear that in the year 1927 Hindu-Muslim unity was in the air, while Hindu-Muslim riots were on the *terra firma*. Two Unity Conferences had been held and the A.I.C.C. endorsed the resolutions of one of them. Who was better fitted to preside over the Congress of such an year than a Muslim, and among the Muslims, than Dr. Ansari? Ansari was a student of the Madras Medical College in 1896 or '99. He had gone to the Balkans in 1912 along with the Red Cross Mission. In his profession, he had a highly distinguished career. Outside it, his culture and catholicity were well-known. Dr. Ansari accordingly presided over the Madras Session and naturally devoted the bulk of his Address to the question of communal concord. He summarised the Congress policy as one of co-operation for 35 years, Non-co-operation for an year and a half, and obstruction within the Councils and constitutional dead-locks for four years. "Non-co-operation did not fail us," he remarked, "we failed Non-co-operation." Then came the subject of the Statutory Commission, the Detenus, India and Asia, and National Health. Amongst those present at the Congress were Mr. Mardy Jones, Labour M. P., Mr. Purcell and Mr. Spratt. There was nothing very striking about the resolutions of the year on subjects other than the Statutory Commission. Condolences, League against Imperialism, China, refusal of passports were all familiar or usual subjects. The note of 'war danger' was sounded in one of the resolutions and the Congress declared it would be the duty of the people of India to refuse to take any part in such a war or to co-operate with them (Government) in any way whatsoever. General Avari's hunger-strike had reached the 75th day. He had carried on an Arms Act Satyagraha which consisted in leading processions carrying prohibited weapons. The General received, *in absentia*, a vote of congratulations and of sympathy. The proposed separation of Burma from India was condemned. It will be remembered that its annexation with India was condemned at the very first Congress (1885), and that that Congress held that if Burma should be annexed, it must be made a Crown Colony. And the State prisoners received their due attention from the Congress which demanded their immediate release. Indians in South Africa and East Africa had two resolutions for themselves. Their exact position was dealt with earlier in this chapter. Hindu-Muslim unity, both in respect of religious and political rights, was the subject of a resolution on the lines already adopted at the A.I.C.C. Boycott of British goods had come to be a new feature in recent years. A Swaraj Constitution having been asked to be drawn up, several drafts were before the House and the Working Committee was given power to co-opt and to confer with other bodies and draft a constitution and place it before a Special Convention for approval. A change was introduced in the Congress Constitution. But the resolution of the year was the one dealing with the Statutory Commission which we give in full:—

BOYCOTT OF THE STATUTORY COMMISSION

"Whereas the British Government have appointed the Statutory Commission in utter disregard of India's right of self-determination;

"This Congress resolves that the only self-respecting course for India to adopt is to boycott the Commission at every stage and in every form. In particular,

(a) this Congress calls upon the people of India and all Congress organisations in the country:

(i) to organise mass demonstrations on the day of the arrival of the Commission in India, cities of India which the Commission may visit;

(ii) to organise public opinion by vigorous and similar demonstrations in the various propaganda so as to persuade Indians of all shades of political opinion effectively to boycott the Commission.

(b) This Congress calls upon non-official members of the Indian Legislatures and leaders of political parties and communities of India and all others not to give evidence before the Commission nor co-operate with it in any manner, public or private, nor attend or participate in any social functions given to them.

(c) This Congress calls upon the non-official members of the Indian Legislatures;

(i) neither to vote for nor serve on Select Committees that may be set up in connection with this Commission;

(ii) to throw out every other proposal, motion or demand for grant that may be moved in connection with the work of the Commission.

(d) This Congress also calls upon the non-official members of the Legislatures not to attend meetings of the Legislatures except for the purpose of preventing their seats being declared vacant, or for the purpose of making the boycott effective and successful, or for the purpose of throwing out a Ministry, or opposing any important measure which, in the opinion of the Working Committee of the Congress, is detrimental to the interests of India.

(e) This Congress authorises the Working Committee to confer with and secure the co-operation, wherever possible, of other organisations and parties with a view to make the boycott effective and complete."

This resolution speaks for itself and needs no commentary. A special resolution was passed deploring the callousness of Government in not commuting the brutal sentences passed in the Kakori case, in spite of the powerful public indignation aroused by the vindictive sentences, and offering the heartfelt sympathy of the Congress to the families of the victims.

Finally, the creed of the Congress was defined in a separate resolution to the effect that "This Congress declares the goal of the Indian people to be complete National Independence." This resolution had for some time become a hardy annual. It received an added impetus by the arrival of Jawaharlal Nehru from Europe and the espousal of the cause by him. Even Mrs. Besant did not see much to object to in it. She said in the Subjects Committee that it was a dignified and clear statement of India's goal. Gandhi was absent from the Committee at the time and heard of it after it had been passed.

CHAPTER IX

The Rendition of the Congress (1928)

In the beginning of the year 1928 the political atmosphere of India was charged with feelings of resentment against Government over the appointment of the Simon Commission. The boycott of that Commission was the one pre-occupation of the country. In making the announcement of the Commission, Lord Irwin had said: "His Majesty's Government whilst not dictating to the Commission what procedure it should follow, were of opinion that its task in taking evidence will be greatly facilitated if it were to invite a Joint Select Committee of the Central Legislature chosen from amongst its non-official members, to convey its views to the Commission in any manner decided upon by the latter." This arrangement made the Indian Committee assessors or appraisers and not Jurors,—a position which was regarded as an affront to India. But Lord Irwin took pains to show that it was not true that any deliberate affront to Indian honour and to Indian pride was meant by His Majesty's Government. At the same time, he declared that whether Indian assistance was forthcoming or not the inquiry would proceed and a report would be presented to Parliament, on which the latter would take whatever action it deemed appropriate. It was on the 2nd of February that the Viceroy made this speech and threw out his challenge. On February 3rd, the Statutory Commission landed in Bombay. The boycott began by an All-India *hartal* observed on the day of their arrival. The day was otherwise uneventful. In Madras, however, the attitude of the crowds was considered threatening at the High Court and in the end, unfortunately and perhaps avoidably, the Police opened fire injuring a number of people of whom one fell dead on the spot and two died later. In Calcutta also there was a conflict between the students and the Police. In Delhi, which was the first place to be visited, the landing of the Commission was marked by hostile demonstrations with placards and banners bearing the words, "Go back, Simon." Except for the South Indian Liberal Federation in South India (popularly known as the Justice Party) and some Muslim organisations, it may be said that the boycott was complete.

The great success of the boycott of the Simon Commission induced the Government to try methods of coercion and terrorism. In Lahore a vast gathering of people headed by Lala Lajpat Rai, to demonstrate against the Commission, was assaulted by policemen and many respected leaders were treated to baton and *lathi* blows. Lalaji was one of the sufferers, and it is believed that his death was hastened by this cowardly assault. But in spite of this charge being made openly, an impartial enquiry was denied by Government.

Lucknow experienced several wanton and unprovoked Police charges on unarmed and peaceful gatherings on the occasion of the visit of the Commission. Even Jawaharlal was not spared by the U.P. Police. Mounted and foot Police displayed their skill with the baton and the *lathi* on the heads and backs of well-known public workers of all parties and injured scores of people.

Lucknow was converted into an armed camp with thousands of mounted and foot Police and for four days there were brutal attacks by the Police. Private houses were invaded by the Police and respected national workers were beaten and arrested for daring to call out,

"Simon, go back." The citizens of Lucknow, however, refused to be cowed down by these brutalities and increased their demonstrations. They even added a touch of humour to them and set the whole city laughing at the discomfiture of the authorities. During a party given by some Talukdars to the Simon Commission, the Kaiserbagh was surrounded by thousands of Police and none who was suspected of being a boycotter was allowed to approach even the public roads near the Bagh. In spite of these precautions the harmony of the party was marred by the arrival from the skies of numerous black kites and balloons bearing the legends "Simon, go back," "India for Indians," etc.

In Patna a mammoth gathering of 50,000 people gathered to make a hostile demonstration against the Commission on its arrival to the city, while there were but a few hundred people who waited to give a welcome, composed mostly of *Chaprasis* and Government servants. Lorries of tenants whom Government had imported from the neighbourhood walked into the boycott camp, and not the welcome camp. The spectacle presented at the Railway Station, of monster crowds without a trace of violence, and the study in contrast presented by the two wings was an eye-opener to Government.

The Madras Congress, in pursuance of the boycott of the Simon Commission, had restricted the work inside the Legislative Councils to a minimum. Difficulties, however, were experienced in carrying out this direction and it was regretted that it was more honoured in the breach than in the observance. Ultimately, the Working Committee recommended to the A.I.C.C. to give greater freedom to members of the Assembly and the Provincial Councils. The A.I.C.C. accepted the recommendation of the Working Committee.

The Commission left Bombay on the 31st March after establishing, as Sir John Simon said, "personal contact with all communities and classes in various parts of India." Of course, this was a piece of what people call 'terminological inexactitude,' for, the official report itself admits that the leaders of the Assembly were "pledged to the boycott of the Commission not only officially but also to the length of boycotting it socially," and, therefore, Sir John and his colleagues were unable to come in contact with them.

Soon after the arrival of the Commission in India, Sir John addressed a letter to the Viceroy dated 6th February, and published on the 7th, proposing that the Commission would take the form of a Joint Free Conference between the English seven and an Indian seven,—to be chosen by the Central Legislature. All materials would be available to the whole Conference, the Indians sitting on it on free and equal terms.

The Provincial Councils were also to be asked to constitute a similar body. The Indian part of the Conference would consist, when the central subjects were being discussed, of the Joint Committee of the Central Legislature and when provincial subjects were discussed, of the Committee of Provincial Council concerned The British Commissioners were, however, to send up their report separately to His Majesty's Government, and the Joint Committee to the Central Legislature. This announcement evoked no response. Within two or three hours of its issue, the political leaders met at Delhi and declared that their objection to the Commission remained unaffected and that they could not have anything to do with the Commission, at any stage or in any form. The Assembly did not care to elect their representatives to the Central Committee. Lala Lajpat Rai moved a resolution on February 16th in the Assembly, "that the constitution and scheme of the Commission were wholly unacceptable to the Assembly which should have nothing to do with it, at any stage or in any form." Pandit Motilal Nehru declared that "the resolution was not negative but was a positive assertion that an equal number of Indians must be appointed to the Commission by His Majesty the King before Indians would co-operate." The resolution was carried by 68 to 62 votes. The Government had, therefore, to nominate members from the Assembly to the Central Committee. It may be mentioned here that when the Commission visited Bombay, not one of the 22 belted knights of the city cared to meet the Commission.

This was a fact which was more eloquent of the spirit of boycott in the country than either the votes of councils or the co-operation of communities. Incidentally, let us note that, while the Simon Commission was engaged in its own legitimate labours, the shrewder members of it who were more interested in trade than in politics were busy with a study of the Indian market. Punjab, thought Lord Burnham, offered the best possibilities of Indo-British trade. Then Lord Burnham emphasized the scope for export into India of British cars, tractors and lorries. "The Indian market must be studied in India not only by the agent," said he, "but by the principals who should examine the problem in the broad light of national predilections and prejudices."

The running events of the year 1928 are the marches of the Simon Commission, the sittings of the All-Parties' Conference and the movement in Bardoli. In accordance with the resolution of the Congress, an All-Parties' Conference was summoned at Delhi in February and

March, 1928, and it was agreed between the Congress and other organizations present that the question of a Constitution for India should be discussed on the basis of "Full Responsible Government." The second question was the question of communal relations and proportions. Altogether 25 sittings had been held in those two months and three-fourths of the issues were settled amicably. The third Conference of the year met on the 19th of May, Dr. Ansari presiding, and a resolution was passed appointing a Committee with Pandit Motilal Nehru as President, to draft the principles of a Constitution before the 1st July, 1928, the draft to be circulated amongst the various associations in the country. 29 political organizations voted in favour of the resolution. We shall revert to it later.

In the middle of June, three events occurred which must arrest our attention. The ensuing Congress was to be held in Calcutta and Pandit Motilal Nehru was freely talked of as its President. In order to make that easy, he had also resigned his seat on the Empire Parliamentary Delegation to which he had been elected in the March previous by the Legislative Assembly as one of the four representatives. The Pandit put down his resignation to political developments. Gandhi himself said: "Bengal wants the elder Nehru. He is a man for honourable compromise. The country is in need of it and is in the mood for it. Therefore have him." The second event was the controversy in Calcutta over the character of the exhibition to be held in connection with the Congress. Mr. N. R. Sircar, the Secretary of the Exhibition Committee, stated that the exhibition would be open to all articles manufactured or produced in India, prominence being given to khaddar. As regards Indian mill-made cloth, and cloth made from Indian mill-yarn, the question was for the time being left open. No foreign goods or articles would be exhibited except tools, machinery and appliances, such as were calculated to help the development of our national resources. Swadeshi goods made by the provincial Departments of Industries would be permitted. No pecuniary help would be taken from Government. This raised a hue and cry from orthodox Non-co-operators like Babu Satish Chandra Das-Gupta of 'Khadi Pratishtan,' (Sodepur, Calcutta), and his spirited brother Khitish Babu. It was fortunate that the protests came forth in good time to save the situation.

The third event was one of abiding interest. Its magnitude was only equalled by its magnificence. The ryots of Bardoli are a splendid lot of citizens. Bardoli was the Tehsil where Gandhi wanted to experiment Mass Civil Disobedience. That was, after two or three postponements, ultimately given up in February, 1922, and the Bardoli resolutions of the Working Committee of February 11th and 12th have associated the name of the place with the withdrawal of the struggle, not always appreciated. But that stigma, if stigma it was, was destined to be wiped out. Bardoli was to have one of the periodical re-settlements of land which occurs once in a stated period of years, say 20 or 30, and the result of which is generally to raise Land Revenue by about 25 per cent. The people of Bardoli felt that they did not deserve any enhancement, as any larger or better produce they had from their land was due to the improvements they had effected at great cost of money and labour. They did not say that the taxes should not be raised, but only prayed that an impartial Committee should be appointed to investigate the conditions of the labour, roads, prices, economic outlook and taxation, to see whether an enhancement was to be effected, and if so how much. The usual procedure of Government is arbitrary, secret and one-sided. They do not take the public into confidence when they conduct economic enquiries. They do not publish the preliminary reports of the settlement officers to the Board of Revenue, or the latter's recommendations to Government, and if at all anything is published, the publication is in English and not the provincial languages of the area concerned. In this particular case, the Bardoli ryots were to pay an enhanced revenue of 25 per cent. All the customary and constitutional methods for any inquiry were tried but in vain. Then an ultimatum was issued and a No-tax campaign was organised,—not for Swaraj, nor as part of a Civil Disobedience campaign,—but for the purpose of obtaining redress of an agrarian grievance. Government were adamant, so were the people.

Congress did not interfere in the earlier stages. The people had resolved not to pay taxes at their Taluka Conference and invited Vallabhbhai J. Patel to help them,—virtually to lead them. It was then that he organised the campaign,—not in anger, not with any impetuosity or impulsiveness, but reluctantly, with premeditation, and with grave and solid deliberation. Government embarked upon their attachments of cattle and began with a Vaisya who, they thought, would be timid. The man was unbending. Then they pitched upon a Muslim, but he was equally unrelenting. Neither threats nor efforts to divide the communities succeeded. So there was a promiscuous campaign of attachments helped by imported Pathans. The employment of Pathans was uncalled for. People did not resist attachments, and Government had enough of man-power under them and had no need to import men of a furious temper and habits who, once they are employed, could not be restrained. It was complained that there were 40 of these. Sir Leslie Wilson, the Governor, stated they were only 25. It was not a question of numbers, but it was a question of the Pathans.

Pathans to the right of them
Pathans to the left of them
Pathans to the front of them
Police at the tail of them
Marched the Buffalo Brigade.

That was how boys were singing the events of the day at public meetings. Very soon, some of the elected members of the Legislative Council of the Bombay Presidency resigned their seats in protest and took interest in the campaign.

Vittalbhai J. Patel—the President of the Assembly—wrote a letter to the Viceroy threatening to resign and take up the work if Government did not relent. At last, a formula was evolved by which the excess assessment was deposited by an intermediary. Prisoners were to be released, property was to be restored, and the movement was to be called off. A Court was established of which Mr. Bloomfield, who had convicted Gandhi in 1922, was the Judicial representative, the other being an Executive Officer, Mr. Maxwell. The Court went into the matter and declared that not more than 6¼ per cent. should be the measure of enhancement. This was agreed to in August, and the benefit of it was extended to Chorasai Tehsil which had not joined the movement and had paid the enhanced taxes, and whose good example had been commended by Government to Bardoli saying, "If Chorasai can pay why not Bardoli?" Bardoli did not pay, and its fight benefited Chorasai as well in the end.

It may be of interest to note that in a speech delivered at Poona in the Legislative Council, the Governor of Bombay declared that all the resources of the

Empire would be used to crush the No-tax campaign of Bardoli. Shortly after, the settlement took place. There was really no provision anywhere in the law or in the Land Revenue Code, for the appointment of the kind of Court which was constituted. It must be noted that although they recommended the increment by only 6¼ per cent. yet when the several factors which were urged by the ryots and which the Court expressed itself as not competent to go into at the time, were given due consideration, there was virtually no enhancement of Land Revenue in the Bardoli Tehsil, and at the end of the settlement it stood at its former level. The credit of the settlement lay in the restoration of the sold out lands to their owners, and the Patels and the Talatis to their jobs.

Once again the All-Parties' Conference met at Lucknow on the 28th, 29th, and 30th of August, 1928, to consider the Report of the Nehru Committee. Congratulations were offered to the Nehru Committee on its labours, and without restricting the liberty of action of those political parties, whose goal is Complete Independence, the Conference declared in favour of Dominion Self-Government. Those for Complete Independence, and not for Dominion Status, issued a statement which was read out at the Conference and which made it clear that the Constitution of India should only be based on Complete Independence. The signatories wanted to take full advantage of the Preamble which gave freedom to those who would plump for Complete Independence. They had decided accordingly not to support the resolution, but not to obstruct the work of the Conference either. They would accordingly dissociate themselves from the resolution and abstain from taking part in the discussion or moving amendments to it. Other questions dealt with related to Sindh, redistribution of Provinces, and joint electorates. There was some agitation over a remark let fall by Jawaharlal saying that the gentlemen on the platform (referring to the Talukdars like the Maharajah of Mahmudabad and Raja Rampal Singh) were unnecessary men in society. The result of the remark which was deeply resented by those against whom it was directed, was that a resolution was passed the next day that "All titles to private and personal property lawfully acquired and enjoyed at the establishment of the Commonwealth are hereby guaranteed."

Amongst those present at Lucknow were, besides the two amiable Zamindars referred to, Dr. Sapru, Sir Ali Imam, Sir C. Sankaran Nair, Mr. Sachchidananda Sinha, Sir. C. P. Ramaswami,—all ex-Members of the Central or Provincial Executive Councils. It must be owned that the Lucknow scheme contemplated Dyarchy in Military matters. The portion of the scheme relating to Defence is embodied in clauses 75 to 78 of Chapter VII and also in the last two paragraphs of Chapter VI. "The Governor-General-in-Council shall appoint a Committee of Defence consisting of the Prime-Minister, the Minister for Defence, the Commander-in-chief, the Commanders of Air forces and Naval forces, the Chief of the General Staff and two other experts. This Committee shall advise the Government and the various departments concerned with questions of Defence and upon general questions of policy. The estimates shall be framed according to the recommendations of the Committee."

Again, "No measure affecting the discipline or maintenance of any part of the Military, Naval and Air forces of the Commonwealth shall be introduced in Parliament except on the recommendation of the Committee of Defence appointed under the Constitution." The functions of the Committee which has a clear official majority are to control expenditure and estimates as well as measures. What else is this but Dyarchy at the Centre? Now let us complete this story of the All-Parties' Conference. Its Report was taken up by the All-India Congress Committee at its sitting in Delhi in the 1st week of November, (4th and 5th). It reiterated the goal of Complete Independence, endorsed the communal solution of the Nehru Committee, and gave the opinion that the proposals of the Nehru Committee were "a great step towards political advance," and generally approved them, without committing itself to every detail.

Let us now turn to the Council front. We had really a Council front, where the cult of resistance was gradually melting away, and a 'Simon' front where boycott was getting stronger and stronger. In the Assembly, a controversy was raging regarding the organization of the President's Office and its separation from the Legislative Department of the Government. Evidently, some responsible members were talking at random in the lobbies about the President. *The Pioneer* had brought forward a charge that the Home Department of the Government of Simla was openly abetting a plot to disparage the work and decisions of President Patel. Leaders of Parties strengthened those charges by bearing personal testimony to having heard the charges themselves in the lobbies. Disrespect shown to the President is disrespect to Parliament, by tradition, and therefore Lord Irwin, when the matter was brought to his notice, had no hesitation in making the Government of India tender an apology to the people of India. The Home Member tendered the apology and Pandit Motilal Nehru accepted it.

The other big items on the agenda of the Assembly were the Reserve Bank Bill, and the Public Safety Bill. The Gold Standard and Reserve Bank of India Bill battle was one of the biggest but fruitless battles fought by the

Congress against Government. It was the Government's contention that that Bill, intended as it was to constitute another step towards autonomy in India's progress, and shifting as it would do the control of the currency policy from the Secretary of State to an indigenous banking institution in the country, would really be a sort of financial and currency counterpart to the Government of India Act, 1919. It was difficult to believe in the purity of motive from this high constitutional standpoint. A Government of India which had done havoc in working the scheme of Dyarchy, such as it was, would not *suo moto* divest themselves of control over currency and Banking. So the people's representatives smelt something adverse to public interests in it. When the combatants came to grips with the problem, the issues came to be centred round several questions,—the chief of which was whether the Bank should be a shareholders' bank as Government desired, or a State Bank as the people suggested. Then the next issue was what was to be the electorate for the Directorate and how many of the Directors were to be nominated and how many elected and how? Once the structure of the Bank was settled, the rest of the development would naturally follow. If it was a shareholders' Bank, these would constitute the electorate, but if it was a State Bank, then semi-public Institutions would elect the Directors such as the Federated Chambers, Associated Chambers, Provincial Co-operative Banks and the Central and Provincial Legislatures. We need not go into figures of representation. But let us only say that Government had offered at first 9 elected Directors out of sixteen. To-day the Reserve Bank Act provides for 8 only out of 16,—the same coming to be elected in four years. Various were the transformations that the Bill had undergone from stage to stage. At last, on the motion of Mr. Srinivasa Iyengar, Government agreed to have a stockholders' Bank—the maximum stock that could be held by any one being Rs. 10,000, and each stock-holder having but one vote irrespective of the stock he held. It looked as though everything was well. When almost every one was satisfied, Government felt apprehensive of the result, and in view of the divergence in certain important particulars, decided not to proceed any further but bring forward a new Bill. But the President would not allow its introduction, on a principle laid down by the Speaker of the House of Commons that, when essential alterations were to be made in any Bill which had come before the House, the proper course was to ask leave to withdraw the original Bill and re-submit it as altered. In the circumstances, the Government decided to proceed with the old Bill, but lost an important clause in a snap division, as it was said. So it was decided to adjourn the Bill *sine die*.

The Public Safety Bill was another measure which had occasioned acute controversy and provoked the hostility of the Congress Party. Though ostensibly it was directed against Foreigners, yet, no doubt was left in the minds of the people that it would be used against Indians, as was the case with the D. O. R. A. of India. Speaking in the Assembly on the Bill, Lala Lajpat Rai said:

> "I will break no bones by stating to this House that this is not a measure really intended against foreign Communists only. It is only the thin end of the wedge. It is really directed against the Indians themselves, Nationalists as well as Labourites. The foreign Communist will go away, will be turned out at the cost of the Indian tax-payer, and will be taken to the British Isles or anywhere else, being comfortably berthed in the P. and O. steamer, but if this House accepts the principle of this Bill, and accepts Clause 2, that acceptance could at any time be utilized for the purpose of prosecuting Nationalists

> and others who want Indian economic and political freedom. This is really the motive behind this legislation. The clause is wide. It is not Communist action that is proposed to be punished or dealt with. It is the advocacy, directly or indirectly, of the doctrine stated in the clause. The words are 'directly or indirectly advocates the overthrow by force or violence the Government established by Law in British India.' Messrs. Jawaharlal and Srinivasa Iyengar who advocate Complete Independence come under the Law".

The Bill was voted upon and there was a tie. The President voted against and it was dropped.

The Calcutta Congress was one of the important sessions of the National gathering, in that it was destined to show the way to future progress. It was this importance that led to the election of Pandit Motilal Nehru as the President. There was the additional circumstance of a full Convention of the All-Parties' Conference being tacked on to the Congress. The Simon Commission's second visit to India had taken place and the Commission was actually touring the country while the Congress was sitting. Pandit Motilal Nehru's Address gives some details of the intensity of the boycott of the Commission particularly at Cawnpore, Lahore and Lucknow, and the reaction it had on the Anglo-Indian mind and outlook. English newspapers of Calcutta were suggesting "twenty years of resolute Government," and threatening a resistance of the Indian demand for freedom to the "last ounce of ammunition." Lord Irwin himself declared that it was the plain duty of the Government to take whatever steps it deemed necessary to prevent the recurrence of these discreditable incidents. But what did Government do in their own turn? Motilalji asked how any Englishman would like his house to be broken into, his guests treated to a sound thrashing and then arrested and imprisoned for the night for making a peaceful demonstration from his own terrace. It was a fact that the Maharajah of Mahmudabad and his palace were surrounded with a cordon of Police while the Commission was being entertained in a neighbouring park. When the Commission was touring Lahore, men like Dr. Alam and Dr. Satyapal, under the leadership of Lala Lajpat Rai, conducted processions against the Commission. Lajpat Rai was beaten on the chest and hardly recovered from the effects of the injuries. Shortly after, he passed away. Panditji declared in emphatic terms that our destination is freedom, the form and extent of which would depend upon the time when, and the circumstances under which, it came. Then he dwelt upon the All-Parties' Conference and asserted that Government must "begin at the point at which the All-Parties' Conference have now arrived and push forward with them as far as they would go." Panditji continued: "Let us then pause and take stock of our equipment and finally throw the strength of our whole being into one great effort to reach the goal." A special feature of the Calcutta Congress (1928) was the large number of messages of sympathy and congratulations from individuals and institutions abroad, ranging from Mrs. Sarojini Naidu in New York, Mrs. Sun Yat Sen and M. Romain Rolland, to the Persian Socialist Party, the Communist Party of New Zealand, and the League of the Rights of Man.

The resolutions dealt with were of the usual type, except that an ultimatum was given to the Government, in regard to the destiny of India. The greetings of the friends in foreign countries were heartily reciprocated, and the A.I.C.C. was called upon to establish a contact by opening a Foreign Department in this behalf. A pan-Asiatic Federation was contemplated. Congratulations were sent to China on having attained full freedom and greetings to Syria, Palestine, Egypt and Iraq. The second World Congress of the League against Imperialism was welcomed. The Madras resolution against war-danger was reiterated. British goods were asked to be boycotted.

Congratulations were offered to Mr. Vallabhbhai Patel on the success of the Bardoli struggle. Congressmen were asked to abstain from attending Government parties, Darbars, and all other official and non-official functions held by Government officials, or in their honour. There was a demand put forward for Responsible Government in the Indian States. The Calcutta resolution on the question of Indian States has since become classical, and the volume of agitation that has grown in the country has largely centred round it. Accordingly we quote it in full:

> "XVII. The Congress urges (on) the Ruling Princes of the Indian States to introduce Responsible Government based on representative institutions in the States, and to issue immediately Proclamations or enact Laws guaranteeing elementary and fundamental rights of citizenship, such as rights of association, free speech, free Press and security of person and property."

The Congress once again passed a resolution expressing sympathy with the ex-Maharajah of Nabha and also with the families of five Bengalis who died in incarceration. Certain Police raids and searches in Lahore were condemned. A tribute was paid to the memory of Lala Lajpat Rai, Hakim Ajmal Khan, Andhra Ratna Gopala Krishnayya, Maganlal Gandhi, Gopabandhu Das and Lord Sinha. Regarding the ultimatum referred to already, the Congress passed the following resolution:—

"This Congress having considered the Constitution recommended by the All-Parties' Committee Report welcomes it as a great contribution towards the solution of India's political and communal problems and congratulates the Committee on the virtual unanimity of its recommendations, and, whilst adhering to the resolution relating to Complete Independence passed at the Madras Congress, approves of the Constitution drawn up by the Committee as a great step in political advance, specially as it represents the largest measure of agreement attained among the important parties in the country.

"Subject to the exigencies of the political situation, this Congress will adopt the Constitution if it is accepted in its entirety by the British Parliament on or before the 31st December, 1929, but in the event of its non-acceptance by the date or its earlier rejection, the Congress will organise a campaign of non-violent Non-co-operation by advising the country to refuse taxation and in such other manner as may be decided upon.

"Consistently with the above, nothing in this resolution shall interfere with the carrying on in the name of the Congress of the propaganda for Complete Independence."

This was the form in which the main resolution of the session was passed. But it had a sad and controversial history behind it. The resolution as it was originally introduced by Gandhi in the Subjects Committee stood thus:—

"This Congress having considered the Constitution recommended by the All-Parties' Committee Report welcomes it as a great contribution towards the solution of India's political and communal problems and congratulates the Committee on the virtual unanimity of its recommendations, and, whilst adhering to the resolution relating to Complete Independence passed at the Madras Congress, adopts the Constitution drawn up by the Committee as a great step in political advance, specially as it represents the largest measure of agreement attained among the important parties in the country.

"Provided however that the Congress shall not be bound by the Constitution if it is not accepted on or before the 31st December, 1930, and provided further that in the event of non-acceptance by the British Parliament of the Constitution by that date, the Congress will revive non-violent Non-co-operation by advising the country to refuse taxation and every aid to Government.

"The President is hereby authorised to send the text of this resolution together with a copy of the said Report to His Excellency the Viceroy for such action as he may be pleased to take.

"Nothing in the resolution shall interfere with the propaganda for familiarising the people with the goal of Independence, in so far as it does not conflict with the prosecution of the campaign for the adoption of the said Report."

To this, amendments were moved by Jawaharlal Nehru and Subash Chandra Bose of an identical nature. Their aim was to put no time-limit, nor, even by implication, to accept for India Dominion Status as contemplated in the Constitution drawn up by the All-Parties' Conference. Pandit Jawaharlal's amendment ran thus:—

"i. This Congress adheres to the decision of the Madras Congress declaring Complete Independence to be the goal of the Indian people and is of opinion that there can be no true freedom till the British connection is severed.

"ii. The Congress accepts the recommendations of the Nehru Committee as agreed to by the Lucknow All-Parties' Conference for the settlement of communal differences.

"iii. The Congress cordially congratulates the Nehru Committee for their labours, patriotism and foresightedness, and, without prejudice to the resolution of the Congress relating to Complete Independence, is of opinion that the recommendations of the

Nehru Committee are a great step towards political advance, and without committing itself to every detail, generally approves of them."

Gandhi, who was the sponsor of the resolution, deprecated the omission of the clause, "the President is hereby authorised to send the text of this resolution together with a copy of the said Report to His Excellency the Viceroy for such action as he may be pleased to take." Gandhi held that the sending of the resolution to the Viceroy was only an act of necessary courtesy, and if we were not suffering from a needless superiority complex and a sense of diffidence, we would not insist upon this clause being dropped. On the rest of the resolution, after a great deal of discussion a compromise was arrived at between the members of the Independence League and others in the Subjects Committee. This compromise was however not respected in the open Congress where an amendment was moved by Subash Chandra Bose and seconded by Jawaharlal,—and both of them parties to the compromise. The repudiation of a solemn promise deeply hurt Gandhi and others. Gandhi gave expression to his feelings in very strong terms, when he moved the compromise resolution in the open session which was carried by a majority.

> "You may take the name of Independence on your lips, as the Muslims utter the name of Allah or the pious Hindu utters the name of Krishna or Ram, but all that muttering will be an empty formula if there is no honour behind it. If you are not prepared to stand by your own words, where will Independence be? Independence is a thing, after all, made of sterner stuff. It is not made by the juggling of words."

The Congress also laid down the future programme in the following Resolution:—

"XIV. Meanwhile the Congress shall engage in the following activities: —

(1) In the Legislatures and outside, every attempt will be made to bring about total prohibition of intoxicating drugs and drinks; picketing of liquor and drug shops shall be organised wherever desirable and possible;

(2) Inside and outside the Legislatures, methods suited to respective environments shall be immediately adopted to bring about boycott of foreign cloth by advocating and stimulating production and adoption of hand-spun and hand-woven khaddar;

(3) Specific grievances wherever discovered and where people are ready shall be sought to be redressed by non-violent action as was done recently at Bardoli;

(4) Members of Legislatures returned on the Congress ticket shall devote the bulk of their time to the constructive work settled from time to time by the Congress Committee;

(5) The Congress organisation shall be perfected by enlisting members and enforcing stricter discipline;

(6) Measures shall be taken to remove the disabilities of women and they will be invited and encouraged to take their due share in national upbuilding;

(7) Measures shall be taken to rid the country of social abuses;

(8) It will be the duty of all Congressmen, being Hindus, to do all they can to remove untouchability and help the so-called untouchables in every possible way in their attempt to remove their disabilities and better their condition;

(9) Volunteers shall be enlisted to take up work among the city labourers and village reconstruction, in addition to what is being done through the spinning wheel and khaddar;

(10) Such other work as may be deemed advisable in order to advance nation-building in all its departments and in order to enable the Congress to secure the co-operation in the national effort of the people engaged in different pursuits.

In order to finance the activities mentioned in the foregoing programme, the Congress expects every Congressman to contribute to the Congress coffers a certain percentage of his or her income according to his or her ability."

Amongst the more important resolutions of Calcutta was one "condemning the action of Government in arresting and deporting without trial of Mr. W. J. Johnstone, the fraternal delegate to the Congress from the League Against Imperialism, and considers this as a deliberate attempt to prevent Congress from developing international contacts."

The Calcutta Session will be remembered for a demonstration in which the labourers numbering over 50,000 men from neighbouring mill areas marched in an orderly fashion and saluted the National Flag hoisted in the Congress grounds, occupied the Pandal for nearly two hours, and passed their resolution deciding for Independence for India and then walked out.

An outstanding feature of the year was the rise of the Youth movement in the country. Youth Leagues and students' organisations had been formed all over the country and were specially strong in Bombay and Bengal. Delegates were sent by some of these organisations to the World Youth Congress held at Eerde in Holland in the previous August. Young men had also taken a very prominent part in the Simon Boycott demonstrations. In Lucknow they were the chief sufferers from police *lathis* and baton blows.

The Working Committee earlier in the year had decided to appoint research scholars to carry on research work on behalf of the Congress. This was an important decision which should have been of great help in bringing together useful information on public questions and at the same time in training competent young men for national service. But research work could only be done properly in a permanent office with a good library attached to it and in an atmosphere free from political excitement.

The Hindustani Seva Dal had started a physical culture institution at Bagalkot in the Karnatak. They had held several training camps in various parts of the country and they had added to their reputation for doing rough work.

We must now tell the reader how Gandhi was drawn to Calcutta from his comparative retirement. It may be remembered that he was imprisoned soon after the Ahmedabad Congress in March, 1922, and was absent from the Congress at Gaya, 1922, the Special Session at Delhi (September, 1923,) and the Annual Session at Cocanada, 1923. He was released on the 5th of February, 1924 and presided over the Belgaum Congress. He attended the Cawnpore Congress only to ratify the Patna decisions of partition, or partnership,—whatever you may call it,—with the Swaraj Party. Then he took a vow of a year's political silence which he broke at Gauhati. At Gauhati his participation in the Congress deliberations was active. But in Madras he was absolutely unconcerned and did not even attend the sittings of the Subjects Committee. It was doubtful whether he would have taken any interest in the Calcutta Session. For some years previously he had been spending a month at the Wardha Ashram on the eve of the annual sessions of the Congress. This year too when the Calcutta Session was about to meet in December, 1928, he was at Wardha, and Pandit Motilal Nehru, who was given a grand reception in a carriage drawn by 36 horses, found himself in the midst of a somewhat intricate situation. The protestants who had signed a letter at Lucknow (All-Parties' Conference) advocating Independence as against the Dominion Status on which the Conference had framed a Constitution were there, (Jawaharlal being one of them) having formed an Independence League. The Bengal friends had a league of their own. Subash Chandra Bose was at its head.

A word now requires to be said about the All-Parties' Conference itself. It became a sad failure; except the Muslims, the other minorities, one after another, deprecated communal representation. On the other hand, Mr. Jinnah who had just come from England and who had, ever since he arrived, been falling foul of the Nehru Report, began to oppose it. Some Muslims had even earlier evinced hostility to it.

From the supplementary Report of the Committee of the All-Parties' Conference, we learn that the Report published by the Conference had been subject to various kinds of criticisms. Says the supplementary Report:—

> "The ranks of our critics have been joined recently, we regret to say, by the Aga Khan. He tells us that the British people could never honourably agree to leave an armed force, or even civil administrators, in a country for the good government of which it was no longer responsible . . . if the British did this in a fit of madness, of which there has been no parallel in history, they would go down not only in the estimation of the whole world, but in history for all time, for supplying armed force to a country wherein their responsibility had come to an end, to be administered at the beck and call of other people."

The Aga Khan advocated independence for each Indian Province and said, that the position of each

Province must be akin to that of Bavaria in the former German Confederation,—rather than that of an American State or a Swiss Canton. The Committee combated both these positions in their supplementary Report. At the Convention itself in Calcutta, Mahomed Ali moved a number of amendments which, however, were rejected.

Jinnah summarily adjourned the Muslim League for want of a quorum. The All-Parties' Convention was really lying in Calcutta on its sick bed, one might say, its death bed. The longer it lived, the more numerous became the demands of the poor relations that gathered round it. Like the calf at Sabarmati, it could not live but would not die. It was therefore necessary to smoothen its way to heaven. Who else could have the courage to do this last act of service to the dying friend than Gandhi? His shoulders are broad enough to bear the obloquy of doing to death the Convention. He moved that the Convention do adjourn *sine die* and the motion was passed. At this time the Congress was definitely coming back to Gandhi; but it came back burdened with its own new loads. Gandhi was yet to see what the Congress Party in the Council would do to shake itself off from the charm of the Councils. Already the A.I.C.C. had passed in Delhi, in October, 1928, the following resolution on Councils:—

> "The Committee notes with regret that various Congress Council Parties have not been following the instructions contained in the Madras Congress resolution on Council work. While giving therefore greater latitude to the Congress Parties in view of the difficult situation, the Committee hopes that the spirit of the Congress resolution would be adhered to."

Four contradictory positions were delineated there. First a condemnation, then a condonation, next the urge for a certain latitude and finally the demand for not abandoning the longitude.

Gandhi having gone to Calcutta, remained there to take active part in the Congress deliberations, shaped the resolution of the session and sponsored it. The political situation was very dark at the time. The rumour of the impending prosecutions of the advocates of Independence, the provoking speech of the Viceroy in Calcutta, the conviction of the Editor of *Forward*, and the orgy of prosecutions in Madras, made a deep impression upon his mind. Disquieting as all these happenings were, Gandhi was greatly disturbed by all that he had seen in Calcutta,—a compromise deliberately entered into and the breaking of it first by Bengal, then by U.P., and finally by Madras. As against these two sets of conditions, he had an invitation from Europe and, circumstances permitting, he had fully intended to undertake the European tour early in 1929. Strangely enough, he had Pandit Motilal Nehru's permission for it. But after the most careful consideration and, consultation with friends, he had come to the conclusion that circumstances compelled him to give up the tour, for that year at any rate. "I dare not think of next year," wrote he. "A Danish friend writes to me saying that I could usefully go to Europe only as a representative of Free India. I feel the truth of the remark." Gandhi instictively came to the right decision and wrote:

> "I have no voice from within prompting me to go. On the contrary, having put a constructive resolution before the Congress and having received universal support, I feel that I will be guilty of desertion if I now went away to Europe. It may be that those who voted for the resolution never meant to carry it out. It may be that I shall have nothing to do during the year in respect of the programme,

> but I feel that it is not for me to reason thus. I must not lose faith in the workers. A voice from within tells me that I must not only hold myself in readiness to do what comes my way, but I must even think out and suggest means for working out what, to me, is a great programme. Above all, I must prepare myself for the next year's struggle whatever shape it may take."

This was uttered in the 1st week of February, 1929. We shall presently see what remained in store for the country in February, 1930.

Sir Henry Cotton
1904 : Bombay

G. K. Gokhale
1905 : Benares

Rash Behari Ghose
1907 : Surat
1908 : Madras

Madan Mohan Malaviya
1909 : Lahore
1918 : Delhi

Part IV

SYNOPSIS

CHAPTER I

THE PREPARATION (1929)

Early situation—Public Safety Bill re-introduced—Auxiliary Committees—Legislative Front—President Patel's Statement—Working Committee's resolution—Reports of Sub-Committee of Volunteers—Foreign cloth—Prohibition—Untouchability—Congress organization—Repression—Gandhi's Burma tour—A. I. C. C. meets in Bombay—Working Committee's instructions—Rs. 1,500 voted in aid of the Meerut prisoners on their Trial—Working Committee meets in Delhi—Adjourned—Advises Council Party to resign seats till A. I. C. C. meets—Congressmen to pay a quota to Congress—Repression again—Jatindra Nath Das's hunger-strike—Hunger Strikers' Bill—Lahore Congress Presidentship—The National train—Phongy Wizaya and Jatindas succumb—A. I. C. C. meets at Lucknow—African situation—Lord Irwin's Announcement re: Reforms—Leaders' Manifesto—The terms—Gandhi's Reply—Uproar in Parliament—Change of policy—All-Parties' Conference—Pandit Motilal unrelenting—Interview with the Viceroy arranged for Leaders—Bomb under the Viceregal train—The interview—Embassy leaves Viceregal lodge empty-handed—The Lahore Congress—Intense cold—The Congress in a Cauldron—Issues—Presidential Address—Independence and the Congress Creed—The main Resolution—Congress dates altered—Other resolutions—East Africa—The States—Communal question—Financial Burdens—Gandhi fails to carry Decentralization of the three Committees and reduction of delegates—Labour Strikes—Foreign Propaganda—Foreign Department—Pan-Asiatic Federation—Labour Research Department—Volunteers—One year's time passes—Flag of Complete Independence hoisted—General observations—The formation of the new Working Committee—Congress Democratic Party formed—A rough voyage—But a safe haven.

CHAPTER II

A Fight to the Finish (1930)

The year of action—The key to the situation—Declaration re: Independence—The Purna Swaraj Day—The celebrations—The object of the London Conference—Viceroy speaks before the Assembly—Gandhi's reply—His eleven points—Textile Industry Bill—Civil Disobedience—The resignations—Working Committee meets at Sabarmati—Its resolution on C. D.—C. D., how begun—Fears re: C. D.—Story of Salt—History of Salt Duties—The Philosophy of the Satyagraha Campaign—Theodore Parker's example—Gandhi sees by instinct—Gandhi's Letter to the Viceroy—Viceroy's reply—Gandhi's rejoinder—Preparation for Gandhi's March—Vallabhbhai's arrest—The Sabarmati Meeting—The given vow—Some speeches of Vallabhbhai—Dandi March begins—New expressions—Satyagrahi's pledge—"When I am arrested"—Swarajya Bhavan—Truly a royal gift—Progress of Movement—The Birth of Purna Swaraj—India's miracles—The March begins—A.I.C.C. confirms the Satyagraha movement—Gandhi reaches Dandi—Gandhi's Statement—What women should do—Salt Satyagraha begun on 6th April—Firing at Karachi—Bengal Ordinance—Press Ordinance—'Navajivan' Press to be forfeited—Gandhi's second letter to the Viceroy—Certain barbarous acts—Gandhi's arrest—Gandhi's Message—Sarojini Devi's Statement—A voluntary and complete 'hartal'—World-wide interest in Gandhi's Arrest—Viceroy prepares for the 1st R. T. C—Working Committee . resolutions—Tyabji arrested—Sarojini Devi leads—Effect of Boycott—Salt Raids—Wadala Raids—Some details—Lathi Charge—An European eye-witness—Slocombe's Despatch—Philosophy of Non-violence—Power behind the bars—Viceroy tightens the screw—Government on .treatment of prisoners—Dr. Besant on Gandhi—Movement generalized—Boycott of foreign cloth—The Working Commitee meets in June—Urges Boycott of foreign cloth and British goods—Control of Mills—Mr. Brailsford's testimony—Interpellations in the Assembly—Sholapur—In Peshawar on 23rd April—On Ganga Singh's family—The Working Committee meets in July in Bombay—Lokamanya Tilak's Anniversary—Some members of the W. C. arrested—Also a hundred ladies—Lathi Charge—And yet more severe lathi charges—A novel type of Unlawful Assembly—Vallabhbhai and Gujarat—No-tax campaign in Gujarat—Lathi Charges all over—Another testimony by Mr. Brailsford—A strange migration—The Gharwali soldiers—The heroism of Borsad women—Early peace negotiations—The Conference in Yeravada fails—The First R. T. C.—The Premier's Announcement—Privileged Resolution of the Working Committee—Cablegram from Sapru and Sastri—The Viceroy's orders of release of Members of the Working Committee.

Part IV

CHAPTER I

The Preparation (1929)

Early in 1929, the situation in India was really of a trying character. It will be remembered that the Public Safety Bill introduced in the Assembly in September, 1928, was rejected by the casting vote of the President. The Bill was again introduced in January, 1929, and became the centre of a minor storm. The Central Committee, composed of four members of the Council of State elected to it and of five members of the Assembly nominated by Government, was touring the country along with the Simon Commission. There were auxiliary committees also at work. The Indian States' Committee presided over by Sir Harcourt Butler presented its Report to Parliament in April, 1929. The Education Committee under the Chairmanship of Sir Philip Hortogg was touring up and down the country to review the growth of education in British India and was to publish its Report in September, 1929. The Simon Commission itself concluded its labours in India on the 14th April, 1929. Hardly did they reach England when the Conservative Government was defeated in the general election in May, 1929, yielding place to a Labour Ministry with Mr. MacDonald as Premier and Mr. Wedgwood Benn as Secretary of State for India. Lord Irwin had taken four months' leave and gone to England at the end of June "to devise some means whereby the constitutional question might be clarified, and a greater degree of co-operation obtained from all sections of Indian political opinion before Parliament was asked to pronounce upon whatever scheme of Reforms might be laid before it as a result of the Statutory enquiry."

We shall in due course study the statement of policy made by him on his return. In the meantime, let us study the developments on the Legislative front of the Congress.

The Public Safety Bill which was reintroduced in January, 1929, was taken up in April, but was disallowed by the President on the 11th April. On the 2nd of April, the President made the following statement:—

> "Before I ask the House to resume the debate on the motion that the Public Safety Bill, as reported by the Select Committee, be taken into consideration, I should like to make a few observations. Since we met last, I have been at pains to examine the speeches made by the Leader of the House from time to time on the Public Safety Bill on the one hand, and the complaint lodged by the Crown against the 31 persons in the Meerut Court. As a result of my labours, I have found that the fundamental basis of the Public Safety Bill is virtually identical with that of the case against the 31 accused. Honourable members are aware that the rules of business of this House provide that no question shall be asked nor any resolution moved in regard to any matter which is under adjudication by a Court of Law having jurisdiction in any part of His Majesty's Dominions. The question therefore arises, whether it is possible for this House to discuss the motion that the Public Safety Bill be taken into consideration without referring to any of the matters which are *sub judice* in the Meerut trial. I think there can be no two opinions that real debate on the Bill is not possible. Besides, acceptance of the Bill would mean practically the acceptance of the fundamental basis of the case for it, and rejection of the

Bill would mean the rejection of that basis, and in either case such a course is bound to effect prejudicially the case for the prosecution or for the defence in the Meerut trial as the case may be. I do not see how in these circumstances I can legitimately allow the Government to proceed further with this Bill at this stage. I have decided, instead of giving any Ruling, to advise the Government themselves in the first instance to consider the observations I have made and postpone the Bill pending the Meerut trial, or, if they attach greater importance to the passing of the Bill at this juncture, to withdraw the Meerut Case and then proceed with the Bill."

Government expressed themselves as unable to accept either of the two alternative suggestions put before them and the President finally gave his verdict, ruling out the motion on the ground that it "involved an abuse of the forms and procedure of this House." The next day the Viceroy addressed the two Houses and declared that it was imperative for Government to obtain the powers proposed in the Public Safety Bill without further delay. Accordingly he issued an Ordinance giving to the Executive the arbitrary power they needed. Mr. Patel thereupon wrote a letter to the Viceroy protesting against what he considered to have been the criticisms passed on his Ruling in the Viceroy's Address. But the Viceroy's Private Secretary answered stating that "His Excellency desires me to say that it was no part of his intention either to criticise the Ruling you had given or pass censure upon you for it, and that he fully shares your anxiety to maintain the dignity of the House and the authority of the Chair."

We have referred to the Trades Disputes Bill. It only remains to state that the Bill was passed on the 8th of April and its passage was rendered memorable by the fact that, at the moment when the House was reassembling after the division and while the President was announcing his intention of proceeding to other business, two bombs flung from the visitors' gallery burst amongst the benches occupied by the official members and some persons were slightly injured.

Immediately after the Congress session in Calcutta, the Working Committee appointed a number of sub-committees to give effect to the Congress programme. Committees were formed for the boycott of foreign cloth, prohibition, removal of untouchability, Congress organisation, volunteers, and the removal of disabilities of women. The last named sub-committee has apparently done no work and has submitted no report.

The Volunteers Sub-Committee made various recommendations, in particular recommending that the Hindustani Seva Dal be strengthened and should be fully utilized for training volunteers for national work.

The Foreign Cloth Boycott Committee under the chairmanship of Gandhi and with Mr. Jairamdas Doulatram as its able and effective Secretary, functioned throughout the year and carried on ceaseless activity in favour of the boycott. Mr. Jairamdas resigned his membership of the Bombay Council in order to devote himself wholly to the work of the boycott and fixed the head-quarters of his committee in Bombay. The Committee developed direct contacts with Provincial and District Congress Committees and issued numerous pamphlets and leaflets. Early in the year, numerous bonfires of foreign cloth took place. One of these in Calcutta resulted in the prosecution by Government of Gandhi as already referred to.

The Prohibition Committee had been in the charge of Syt. C. Rajagopalachari, who made the subject of prohibition his very own and had brought his great abilities to bear on the furtherance of this campaign. Work was carried on largely in South India and in Gujarat and the results achieved have been considerable. The campaign had attracted international attention. The Madras Government had been induced to allot four lakhs of rupees for carrying on an official propaganda against the drink and drug evil. The U.P. Government appeared likely to take a similar step. Mr. Rajagopalachari became the Secretary of the Prohibition League of India and was editing their quarterly magazine, *Prohibition.*

The Campaign for the removal of untouchability was in the charge of Syt. Jamnalal Bajaj who had worked strenuously in its behalf. Public opinion was everywhere being roused in favour of the removal of the disabilities of the classes which have for long been suppressed. Many well-known temples, which would not admit these classes, were thrown open to them. The Committee has also succeeded in opening numerous wells and schools to these suppressed classes. Many Municipalities are co-operating in this work. The Secretary of the Committee, Syt. Jamnalal Bajaj, toured extensively in Madras, Central Provinces, Rajputana, Sindh, Kashmir, Punjab and the N.-W. Frontier Province.

The effect of the propaganda for the removal of untouchability was two-fold. The so-called higher castes have been induced in some measure to give up the exclusiveness which they had for long jealously kept, and the suppressed classes have become self-conscious and assertive of their rights. In some places, where the demand from the latter for a removal of their disabilities has not met with an adequate response, friction has arisen and 'Satyagraha' or some kind of Passive Resistance has been threatened. The tension that prevailed for some time during the year has eased a little now. It is clear that untouchability and other social disabilities which certain classes have suffered from are doomed and cannot last much longer.

The Committee for Congress re-organisation submitted its Report early in the year. In view of the action contemplated next year, great importance was attached to the question of organisation and the subject was fully considered by the Working Committee and the A.I.C.C.

Before we continue the story of Legislative activity in the September session, we must describe one or two events connected with Gandhi. Gandhi was making a tour in India and passed Calcutta on his way to Burma. There a bonfire of foreign cloth took place and in that connection he was charged in the second week of March, 1929, with committing nuisance, in that he chose to disobey or abetted disobeying an order designed to prohibit the burning in public of straw and such other articles. Sir Charles Tegart, the Police Commissioner of Calcutta, had exhumed Section 66 (2) of the Calcultta Police Act. It is said that a drowning man catches at a straw. But it is not known why this living bureaucracy should have clutched at this 'straw' section of the City Police Act. To make a long story short, the Police tried to shunt the engine off the main line of F.C.B. (Foreign Cloth Boycott) to the side track of the C.D. (Civil Disobedience). But this proved a failure. Gandhi proceeded to Burma and returned shortly after. He was tried and fined Re. 1. Thereafter he made his memorable tour in Andhra Desa in which he collected for khaddar two lacs and seventy thousand rupees in six weeks. Soon after, the All-India Congress Committee met in the month of May, 1929, in Bombay.

The Bombay meeting was rather an important one. Government had announced that the life of the Assembly would be extended. This alone called for action from the Congress. The large number of arrests all over the country including that of Mr. Sambamurti, a member of the Working Committee, the ruthless repression going on in the Punjab lending itself to the suspicion that it was being done with the view *inter alia* of interfering with preparations for the forthcoming session of the Congress in Lahore,—these called for vigorous action from the Congress organisations in every Province. It was decided at Bombay that Provincial Congress Committees should have not less than a quarter per cent. of the total population of the Province as original members, and should have not less than 50 per cent. of the districts represented on the Province. District and Tehsil organisations should have not less than 3/4 per cent. of the population as original members and so on. A village organisation was to have not less than 1 per cent. of its population as original members. It would be open to the Working Committee to disaffiliate any organisation that did not carry out the instructions. Power was given to the Working Committee to adopt such measures as it might consider fit in the interests of the country as regards the action to be taken by the members of the Congress Parties in the Assembly and the Provincial Councils. East Africa was the subject of a resolution that it should receive the full support of the Congress in its struggle for political and economic equality. The Committee further resolved that a *Congress Manual* be prepared, embodying authoritative chapters on the various political, administrative, economic and cultural problems comprised by the Swaraj movement, and that the A.I.C.C. office do incur the necessary expenditure therefor.

The Working Committee confirmed the deputation, by the President, of the Rev. Ottama to represent the Congress at the State funeral of Dr. Sun Yat Sen, and Mr. Shiva Prasad Gupta was elected to represent India at the Congress of the League Against Imperialism. In regard to the Council Party in the Legislatures, the Working Committee resolved that "all Congress members of the Central Legislature or of any of the Provincial Councils, excepting Bengal and Assam, shall abstain from attending any meeting of the said Legislatures or Councils or any of the Committees appointed by them or by the Government till such time as the A.I.C.C. or the Working Committee decides otherwise, and that the Congress members shall henceforth devote all their available time to the carrying out of the Congress programme, provided that the Congress members of Bengal and Assam Councils shall, after being elected, attend only one meeting for the sole purpose of registering their names." It was in the sitting of the A.I.C.C. held in May that the Committee resolved it to be essential to make revolutionary changes in the present economic and social structure of society and to remove the gross inequalities in order to remove poverty and misery and to ameliorate the condition of the Indian masses. A sum of Rs. 1,500 was voted in aid of the Meerut prisoners.

On March 20th, 1929, in Bombay, Punjab and the United Provinces, under Sec. 121 A of the Indian Penal Code, hundreds of houses were searched. Those arrested included eight members of the All-India Congress Committee. All the arrested persons were brought to Meerut where their trial began in what has come to be known as the Meerut Conspiracy Case, the charge being that they were spreading Communistic propaganda. Mr. H. L. Hutchinson, Editor of *New Spark*, was later added to the accused. A Central Defence Committee, chiefly consisting of prominent Congressmen, was formed to help the accused. As already stated, the Working Committee, contrary to its usual practice, made a grant of Rs. 1,500 towards the defence. The preliminary enquiry in the Case dragged on for many months and was concluded a few days prior to the close of the year. The trial attracted great attention in India and England. The Director of Government Publicity was present at the trial to supervise personally the publicity and propaganda arrangements in the Case.

The Working Committee met soon after once again, on July 15th, in Delhi and was of opinion that it would be in the interest of the Swaraj movement to advise the members of the various Legislatures to resign their seats. In view, however, of the importance of the question, the Committee considered that the final decision should be taken by the A.I.C.C. It therefore resolved that a special meeting of the A.I.C.C. be convened for the purpose at Allahabad on Friday, the 26th July, 1929. It will be remembered that the last clause of the main resolution of Calcutta called upon the people to finance the Congress movement by paying a particular percentage of their income to the national cause. At first 5 per cent. was proposed, later 2½ per cent., but it was considered wise, judging from the timidity and nervousness exhibited at the meeting by some of the richer members of the Congress, to leave the matter to their discretion. A list was published in the July *Bulletin* showing some of the collections so made. Altogether the response was poor.

The period was one of much repression in the country. At this time Government had banned

Dr. Sunderland's book, *India in Bondage,* and Babu Ramananda Chatterjee, Editor of *The Modern Review,* was arrested for publishing the book.

Bhagat Singh and Dutt who had been arrested in connection with the Delhi (Assembly) Bomb Case were sentenced to transportation for life. They had declared that they had thrown the bomb for demonstrative purposes.

We have already dwelt at length upon the hunger-strike in the Lahore Conspiracy Case.

Another group Case was going on in Calcutta in which Syt. Subash Chandra Bose, a member of the Working Committee, and several other prominent Congressmen were being tried.

Arrests of Indians for political reasons were also reported from Shanghai and the Malay States.

Apart from numerous trials and convictions of political and labour workers, methods of repression were used by the Police which were described by the A.I.C.C. as 'barbarous.' On one occasion seven young men collecting funds for the defence of the Lahore under-trial prisoners were beaten by the Police, in the presence of the District Magistrate, till some of them were senseless and all had received severe injuries. Their offence was their crying "Down with Imperialism!" and "Long Live Revolution!" Even more barbarous treatment was resorted to in Lahore in the case of the under-trial prisoners in the Conspiracy Case. They were beaten in the open court in the presence of the trying Magistrate and, it was stated, they were ill-treated in a variety of ways, outside the court-house.

Apart from them and the later trials and convictions, it should be remembered that there were a large number of long-term political prisoners in various jails in India and the Andaman Islands. These included detenus under Regulation III of 1818, and Martial Law prisoners who were sentenced by special tribunals during the Martial Law regime in the Punjab in 1919. Besides these, there were twenty-seven political prisoners in jails who were sentenced to transportation for life in 1914-15 during war time. They were tried and sentenced by special commissions and not by the ordinary Law Courts. They had been in prison for 15 years by this time.

Labour troubles and strikes continued during the year and came to a head. There was a big general strike in the Bombay textile mills involving 150,000 workers. The strike demonstrated that Indian Labour was developing a new outlook. The strike was a great success to begin with, and showed that there was considerable organising ability behind it. But after six months or more it failed. Another general strike took place in the Jute areas in Bengal, involving about 25,000 workers. The Jute workers were badly organised but they succeeded. Sporadic strikes however continued and partly undid the work of the general strike.

Still another strike which had attracted widespread attention and sympathy was the strike of the tin-plate workers in Golmuri near Jamshedpur. This strike involved 3,000 workers, mostly skilled, and it continued for eight and a half months. The demands of the strikers were very moderate but the empoyers and the Bihar Government persistently refused even an enquiry. The Legislative Assembly censured the attitude of Government and passed a resolution for the withdrawal of the protection given to the tin-plate industry. But, as often happens with the resolutions of the Assembly, this resolution also was ignored by Government. No enquiry took place and the strike continued. Sympathetic strikes took place in Budge Budge and elsewhere.

The South Indian Raiway strike of 1928 was followed by the arrest and trial for conspiracy of many persons. The Judge of Trichinopoly sentenced fifteen of these to ten years' rigorous imprisonment in April.

Two of the members of our Working Committee were absent in foreign countries for the greater part of the year. Shrimati Sarojini Naidu returned from America after a very successful tour in August. In November, she went to East Africa to preside over the East African Indian Congress. One of the Congress Treasurers, Syt. Shiva Prasad Gupta, had been in Europe for many months.

Mr. Shiva Prasad Gupta attended the second World Congress of the League Against Imperialism at Frankfurt in July on behalf of the National Congress. His report of this Congress was placed before the Working Committee.

Immediately aftre the Calcutta Congress, the Working Committee made a grant of £30 per month for the establishment of a Students' Information Bureau in Berlin. This Bureau was opened soon after under the supervision of A. C. Nambiar, and it fully justified itself by the help it gave to numerous Indian students and visitors. Mr. Shiva Prasad Gupta inspected it during his European tour and he wrote in terms of high appreciation of its work. On his recommendation the Working Committee increased the grant by £2 per month for a reading room. The Bureau was run efficiently and sent full reports and accounts monthly. Its success was largely due to the honorary service of Mr. Nambiar.

The Calcutta Congress directed the A.I.C.C. to open a Foreign Department and the Working Committee authorised the working Secretary to take the necessary steps in this behalf. The Secretary had been in personal charge of the foreign work of the A.I.C.C. and had endeavoured to develop contacts with organisations and individuals in other countries. This was not particularly easy, as numerous difficulties were placed in the way of foreign correspondence by the Government censorship.

The Calcutta Congress also directed the Working Commitee to take steps to summon a meeting of a Pan-Asiatic Federation in 1930 in India. The Committee called upon Mr. S. Satyamurti and the Secretary to take the necessary steps and to report. In this report it was pointed out that, if the meeting was to be held in 1930, it should take place at the time of the Congress in December 1930. Further, various difficulties in the way of holding such a Pan-Asiatic Conference were pointed out.

In compliance with the decision of the A. I. C. C., a Labour Research Department was opened, as a branch of the A. I. C. C. Office.

The Hindustani Seva Dal carried on their work of training volunteers in various parts of the country. Most of this work was done in Karnataka, a Province where the Head Office of the Dal and their Academy of Physical Culture were situated. But many camps were held in other parts of the country, and the demand for trainers had been greater than the supply. The Dal helped greatly in enrolling members for the Congress and in the boycott of foreign cloth. They fully co-operated in organising an efficient volunteer corps for the Lahore Congress.

The Hindustani Seva Dal succeeded beyond expectation in organising a National Flag Day every month. At Calcutta they decided that the National Flag be hoisted all over the country at 8 A.M. on the last sunday of every month. This monthly Flag unfurling became very popular. Buildings and many Municipalities had it unfurled with solemn ceremony. The H. S. Dal was reorganized and a Constitution was framed.

The month of August was no better than the previous months. Leading men were being arrested everywhere. Sirdar Mangal Singh, Maulana Zafar Ali Khan, Master Mota Singh who had served out his 7 years' term, and Dr. Satyapal, in the Punjab, Mr. Annapoornayya in Andhra, were all placed under arrest. Dr. Satyapal was sentenced to two years' R. I. Repression in the Punjab was particularly ruthless. While free men were thus being arrested, those inside the jails were being treated with undue severity. Bhagat Singh and Dutt and several other prisoners had been by this time for 6 weeks on hunger-strike. Bhagat Singh and Dutt were just then sentenced to transportation for life, in the Assembly Bomb Case. But Bhagat Singh and Dutt were also among the accused in the case known as the Lahore Conspiracy Case, although Dutt was later discharged in that Case. That Case arose out of the murder at 4 p.m. on the 17th September, 1928, of the Superintendent of Police of Lahore, named Mr. Saunders. The prisoners went on hunger-strike to secure redress of their grievances, notably to secure humane treatment to prisoners in jails, and the famous Jatindra Nath Das was one of the batch. Jatin's contention was that the treatment accorded to Indians was different to that of Europeans. He did not care for special facilities accorded to them. And he was the solitary individual who, like Mac Swiney, continued his hunger-strike to death on the 64th day, as we shall see later on.

During this year contact was established with various nationl and international organisations, in England and the Continent. A Congress Muslim Party was formed in Bombay, and an All-India Nationalist Muslim Party was organised on the occasion of the A. I. C. C. meeting at Allahabad. At this meeting, the Committee endorsed the opinion of the Working Committee that Congress members of Councils should resign their seats, but deemed it proper, in view of the letters received on the subject, to hold over the matter till after the Lahore Congress. But that did not mean that those who were willing to resign earlier should not do so.

We have, in passing, referred to the hunger-strike in the Punjab. Government felt embarrassed by these strikes. They thought that the strikes were particularly designed to embarrass the Police in its prosecution of the Lahore Conspiracy Case. They therefore brought up a Bill before the Assembly on the 12th September, 1929, to enable the magistracy to go on with cases in spite of the absence of the accused, when such absence is due to the fact of their having by their own acts disabled themselves. On the 16th of September, however, Government agreed, in view of the controversial character of the Bill, to circulate it for further opinion, but reserved to themselves the right to take such action in the future as lay within their powers, should urgent necessity arise. As a matter of fact, the Governor-General did pass an Ordinance in this behalf shortly after, known as the Lahore Conspiracy Trial Ordinance.

Great events were ahead. The Lahore Congress, which has since become a historic session, required a President like any other. In the provincial voting, ten Provinces voted for Gandhi, five for Vallabhbhai J. Patel, and three for Jawaharlal Nehru. Gandhi was declared duly elected, but he resigned and it became necessary under the Constitution to elect a substitute. Accordingly, a meeting of the A.I.C.C. was held in Lucknow, on the 28th September, 1929. The Presidentship of the Congress was a source of concern to the Nation.

All eyes had turned to Gandhi as the man who would rescue the Congress once again and lead it on to the path of victory. The disgust felt with Councils and some Council members, by men like Motilalji, was hardly concealed. The clear indication was given that Council members should resign. What next? Nothing but Civil Disobedience would be the logical consequence of such a course. And who could lead the Nation to victory along this untrodden path?—who else than Gandhi? That was why he was thought of. Gandhi was pressed hard at Lucknow, even as he had been pressed earlier, to reconsider his refusal. But he saw the wisdom of installing on the Gadi of the Congress a younger man who would inspire confidence in the younger folk of the country. This national train had to run from one station to another, from Ahmedabad, *via* Gaya, Delhi, Cocanada, Belgaum, Cawnpore, Gauhati, Madras and Calcutta, to Lahore. It carried all grades of men,—the older elements who held the flag aloft, the middle-aged who were willing to work along under the leadership of the old, and the younger elements who kicked against the pricks and resented certain methods as too slow, but were not able to formulate quicker methods themselves. If the train should move in time, free from dangers, and if it should carry all its passengers, it is better that the engine should be in the charge of a young man full of enthusiasm, daring and confidence, though the brakes should be in the charge of older and more seasoned and sedate politicians. It was, doubtless, this line of reasoning that made Gandhi adhere to his decision. Vallabhbhai did not choose to intervene between Gandhi and Jawaharlal. The attendance at Lucknow was not large and the majority of friends present voted for Jawaharlal, who was to be one of the youngest Presidents of the Congress. Bengal, strangely enough, had plumped for Gandhi, and even sent circulars to sister Provinces to vote for him.

The next subject that engaged the Congress Committee at Lucknow was the death of Jatindra Nath Das after 64 days' starvation in a Punjab jail and the Rev. Wizaya after 164 days in Burma. Both laid their lives at the feet of the Mother. The latter had not attracted much attention, but the former did. A word is due on Phongy Wizaya's death. The Rev. Wizaya was a Buddhist monk who was released from jail on February 28, 1929, after serving 21 months' R.I. for sedition. He was re-arrested for a seditious speech on April 4, just 5 weeks after his release, and sentenced to 6 years' transportation which was later reduced to three years. Soon after his arrest, he started a hunger-strike, demanding better treatment and the right to wear his yellow monk's robe on special days, and continued it till his death on the 164th day on 19-9-1929.

Jatindra Nath Das's death had occurred just 6 days earlier, *i.e.*, on the 13th September, 1929. Thus in two successive weeks did these two patriots lay down their lives voluntarily and wholeheartedly to preserve national self-respect. The death of Das evoked the deep distress and deeper admiration of his countrymen in India, occasioning big demonstrations and a vast procession in Calcutta. But that was not all; messages of sympathy came forth from several foreign countries, and amongst these was one from the family of Terence Mac Swiney of Ireland.

Before we pass on, let us add that the All-India Congress Committee that met at Lucknow on September 28th passed a resolution on hunger-strikes in jails which, while deeply appreciating the motive of the prisoners, expressed the opinion that a hunger-strike should not be undertaken except upon the gravest emergencies. The Committee advised those who had imposed the sacrifice on themselves to end their strike, specially in view of the self-immolation of Das and Wizaya and the fact that Government had at the eleventh hour yielded to most of the demands of the hunger-strikers and an effort was being made to secure full redress.

The situation in East Africa and the Government of India's confession that they were only advocates and not high contracting parties, were the subject of a resolution. Just then a Deputation from East Africa was touring India and the A.I.C.C. had the advantage of hearing Mr. J. B. Pandya at Lucknow. While this was so, the South African Government imposed unfair restrictions upon the Ali Brothers who wanted to visit the Union, and the Committee passed a suitable resolution on the subject.

The month of October was an eventful month. Lord Irwin who had gone to England returned on the 25th October and made an announcement to the country. In view of the announcement, Pandit Motilal Nehru summoned an emergent meeting of the Working Committee to Delhi on the 1st November, and besides the members of the Committee there were leaders of other schools of thought at the Metropolis to receive the expected announcement and concert measures for common action thereupon. On the eve of Lord Irwin's departure for England at the end of June, 1929, he had said: "When I go to England I shall seek opportunities of discussion with His Majesty's Government on these grave matters. It will be my duty, as I have said elsewhere, to represent to His Majesty's Government the different standpoints of those who can speak for Indian political opinion." Then he had referred to the two governing pronouncements of August, 1917 and his own Instrument of Instructions from the King-Emperor wherein His Majesty affirms that, "Above all things it is our will and pleasure that the plans laid by our Parliament for the progressive realisation of Responsible Government in British India, as an integral part of our Empire, may come to fruition, to the end that British India may attain its due place among our Dominions."

In the statement Lord Irwin made on the 31st October, His Excellency said:—

"The Chairman of the Commission has pointed out in his correspondence with the Prime-Minister, which, I understand, is being published in England, that as their investigation has proceeded, he and his colleagues have been greatly impressed, in considering the direction which the future constitutional development of India is likely to take, with *the importance of bearing in mind the relations which may, at some future time, develop between British India and Indian States.* In his judgment it is essential that the methods, by which this future relationship between these two constituent parts of Greater India may be adjusted, should be fully examined. He has further expressed the opinion that if the Commission's Report and the proposals subsequently to be framed by the Government take this wider range, it would *appear necessary for the Government to revise the scheme of procedure as at present proposed.* He suggested that what might be required, after the Reports of the Statutory Commission and the Indian Central Committee have been made, considered and published, but before the stage is reached of the Joint Parliamentary Committee, would be the setting up of a Conference in which His Majesty's Government should meet representatives both of British India and of the States, for the *purpose of seeking the greatest possible measure of agreement for the final proposals which it would later be the duty of His Majesty's Government to submit to Parliament.* The procedure by Joint Parliamentary Committee conferring with delegations from the Indian Legislature and other bodies, which was previously contemplated and is referred to in Sir John Simon's letter to myself of 6th February, 1928, would *still be appropriate for the examination* of the Bill when it is subsequently placed before Parliament, but would, in the opinion of the Commission, obviously have to be preceded by some such Conference as they have suggested.

"With these views I understand that His Majesty's Government are in complete accord. For, while they will greatly desire, when the time comes, to be able to deal with the question of British Indian political development under conditions the most favourable to its successful treatment, they are, with the Commission, deeply sensible of the importance of bringing under comprehensive review the whole problem of the relations of British India, in their view essential for the complete fulfilment of what they consider to be the underlying purpose of British policy, whatever may be the method for its furtherance which Parliament may decide to adopt.

"The goal of British policy was stated in the declaration of August, 1917 to be that of providing for the gradual development of self-governing institutions, with a view to the progressive realisation of Responsible Government in India as an integral part of the British Empire. As I recently pointed out, my own Instrument of Instructions from the King-Emperor expressly states that it is His Majesty's will and pleasure that the plans laid by Parliament in 1919 should be the means by which British India may attain *its due place among his Dominions.* Ministers of the Crown, moreover, have more than once publicly declared that it is the desire of the British Government that India should, in the fullness of time, take her place in the Empire in equal partnership with the Dominions. But in view of the doubts which have been expressed both in Great Britain and India regarding the interpretation to be placed on the intentions of the British Government in enacting the Statute of 1919, *I am authorised on behalf of His Majesty's Government to state clearly that in their judgment it is implicit in the declaration of 1917 that the natural issue of India's constitutional progress, as there contemplated, is the attainment of Dominion Status.*"

This announcement was made on the 31st of October, and in less than 24 hours, the leading personages were in Delhi, including Pandit Malaviya, Sir T. B. Sapru and Dr. Besant. The Working Committee of the Congress was of course there. After deep consideration, the mixed gathering came to conclusions which were embodied in a Manifesto, in which the signatories expressed their appreciation of the sincerity underlying the declaration, as also the desire of the British Government to placate Indian opinion. They proceeded:—

"We hope to be able to tender our co-operation to His Majesty's Government in their effort to evolve a scheme of Dominion Constitution suitable to India's needs, but we deem it necessary that certain acts should be done and that certain points should be cleared so as to inspire trust and to ensure the co-operation of the principal political organisations in the country.

"We consider it vital for the success of the proposed Conference that,

(a) a policy of general conciliation should be adopted to induce a calmer atmosphere,

(b) political prisoners should be granted an amnesty,

(c) the representation of progressive political organisations should be effectively secured, and the Indian National Congress, as the largest amongst them, should have a predominant representation.

"Some doubt has been expressed about the interpretation of the paragraph in the statement made by the Viceroy on behalf of His Majesty's Government regarding Dominion Status. We understand, however, that the Conference is to meet not to discuss when Dominion Status is to be established, but to frame a scheme of Dominion Constitution for India. We hope we are not mistaken in thus interpreting the import and implications of the weighty pronouncement of His Excellency the Viceroy. Until the new Constitution comes into existence, we think it necessary that a more liberal spirit should be infused in the Government of the country, that the relations of the Executive and the Legislature should be brought more in harmony with the object of the proposed Conference and that greater regard should be paid to constitutional methods and practices. We hold it to be absolutely essential that the public should be made to feel that a new era has commenced even from to-day, and that the new Constitution is to be but a register of that fact.

"Lastly, we deem it as an essential factor for the success of the Conference that it should be convened as expeditiously as possible."

There is no doubt that it was the wider outlook of the Labour Party that was responsible for the new alignment. Sir John Simon had written a letter to the Premier, to which reference had been made in the Viceroy's statement, and in which he advocated some sort of Conference after his Report had been published, "for the purpose of seeking the greatest possible measure of agreement for the final proposals which it would be later the duty of His Majesty's Government to submit to Parliament." When we remember that these words were written on the 16th of October, 1929, and how the Viceroy repeated those words not only in his statement but time after time in his subsequent important pronouncements, we shall be able to understand that it was not the G.C.M. of Indian opinion that was ultimately accepted but the least common measure which had formed the basis of the proposals made by the Cabinet to Parliament. When, therefore, the leaders demanded that the public should be made to feel that a new era had commenced even from that day and that the new Constitution was to be but a register of that fact, the leaders' Manifesto was only giving expression to their inner apprehensions. The Congress members present at the meeting did not expect the minimum straightway from the Conference. Nothing was done really regarding the release of the prisoners. The release of the Martial Law prisoners of 1919 had been recommended by the Punjab Jails Committee, as also the Lahore Conspiracy prisoners of 1915. Mr. Fenner Brockway had raised the question of the release of Mr. Sambamurti in the House of Commons, but nothing was done. In the meantime, English friends had been sending cables to Gandhi to reciprocate the efforts of the Labour Government to help India. In answer, Gandhi stated that he was 'dying for co-operation':—

> "I have, therefore, responded on the very first opportunity that offered itself, but I have meant every word of the joint Manifesto, as I have of the now-famous Calcutta resolution of the Congress. The two are in no sense contradictory. The letter of a document is nothing, if the spirit of it is preserved in effect. I can wait for a Dominion Constitution if I

can get real Dominion Status in action. That is to say, if there is a real change of heart, a real desire on the part of the British people to see India a free and self-respecting Nation, and on the part of the officials in India a true spirit of service. But this means substitution of the steel bayonet by the goodwill of the people. Are Englishmen and Englishwomen prepared to rely for the safety of their lives and property upon the goodwill of the people rather than upon the gun-mounted forts? If they are not yet ready, there is no Dominion Status that would satisfy me. My conception of Dominion Status implies present ability to sever the British connection if I wish to. Therefore, there can be no such thing as compulsion in the regulation of the relations between Britain and India.

"If I choose to remain in the Empire it is to make a partnership of power for promoting peace and goodwill in the world, never to promote exploitation or what is known as Britain's imperialistic creed.

"It is likely that the Labour Government has never meant all the implications mentioned by me. In my opinion, I have not stretched the meaning of the Manifesto in stating the implications, but whether the Manifesto can bear the weight of these implications or not, it is due to the friends in England and in India that they should clearly realise my own fundamental position.

"I am fully aware that India has not developed strength enough to assert the position here adumbrated. If, therefore, it is realised now, it will be largely through the good grace of the British people. It will be nothing strange, if they exhibit it at the present juncture and it will be some reparation for past wrongs done to India.

"But if the time is not yet ripe for India to come to her own, I have patience enough to wait. I can work and live for no other goal. I recognise that mine is but the voice of an individual. How far it is representative of India's millions, no one can say. I certainly cannot."

Small as the offer made to the Indian people in the Viceroy's statement was, there was nevertheless an uproar in Parliament. The House of Commons was on the defensive. Baldwin took the responsibility on himself for agreeing to what Mr. Benn and Lord Irwin had suggested. Sir John Simon was hard put to it to defend himself and his Commission. Captain Benn spared no pains to defend himself and his Government. The Premier took up the task of defending the whole policy of conciliating India and pacifying those amongst the Indians who had till then been stroked the wrong way. The Lords were on the offensive. Lord Birkenhead unrolled the map of despotism. But as Captain Benn had pointed out in the Commons, he held no official position in the Empire and had desired that he should be divorced from politics. "He is engaged in some kind of trade or commerce, though I have no personal knowledge of it,"—added Benn. The reference was to Lord Birkenhead having taken up the Managing Directorship of the Greater London and Country Trust Limited, on £15,000 a year, soon after he had laid down the reigns of office as Secretary of State on account of the change of Government. Lord Reading was the Chairman of a South African mining syndicate on £15,000 a year. It may be remembered here that it was elicited in 1934-35 that he became the Chairman of the Imperial Chemicals,—a company secretly formed in England to explore the mineral wealth of India without a single Indian knowing aught about its formation. This is only by the way. Captain Benn announced that there was a change of Policy, that is to say, a change of spirit, and the Conference was to meet next. Mr. Lloyd George asked whether Captain Benn accepted the interpretation of the joint Manifesto. Mr. Lansbury exhorted people to accept the Viceroy's statement at its face value. Of course the Indians would take it at its market value and found it to be a transaction under discount. The Liberals in India were only keen on the Conference which they chose to term as the Round Table Conference, but which, as we shall see, was always described by Lord Irwin as the London Conference. The Congressmen interpreted the joint Manifesto in the light of the four conditions embodied in it. Captain Benn was announcing to the Indians a change of policy and allaying the alarms of members of Parliament by saying that the Policy is not changed, because it is in the Preamble, the Preamble is in the Act and the Act is in the Laws of England. This kind of feeling discouraged the younger Congressmen. A fresh meeting of all Parties was summoned in Allahabad on the 16th November, and the Working Committee met simultaneously. Every effort was made to maintain unity of spirit. We had to 'confound our enemies' and consolidate our friends. We had to leaven the Moderates and temper the Extremists. Jawaharlal and Subash Babu had tendered their resignations of the membership of the Working Committee even before the Committee itself had given any considered verdict. Pandit Motilal Nehru was more unrelenting than even his younger colleagues. It required much cajoling and coaxing to keep the Pandit to the lines of the All-Parties' gathering. He was fulminating over the artifice and duplicity practised in the Commons, the double-faced Janus that we saw in Captain Benn, the picture that the Cabinet was painting, which made it look like Swaraj to India but British Raj to England. Yet patience had to be exercised. We had formed a train at Delhi, with Independence as the engine and the Moderates as the brake, and the Congress with its several shades of opinion forming the several bogey carriages of the train. Gandhi was there in a saloon. The train had travelled from Delhi to Allahabad, and should it be derailed before it returned to Delhi?

Mr. Wilson, formerly of *The Pioneer*, was writing a series of letters to the Press and urging Lord Irwin to make a gesture before the Lahore Congress, so that the leaders of Indian politics might not have to go to Lahore empty-handed. Lord Irwin had sent an invitation through Dr. Sapru to Pandit Motilal Nehru to meet him "on the 15th inst." But Panditji could not extricate himself from his professional engagement in Lucknow by the 15th. Mr. Wilson wrote to the Press that the Viceroy would shortly be meeting Gandhi, Pandit Nehru and Pandit Malaviya. The Viceroy himself was leaving for South India on the 15th and therefore he wrote to Dr. Sapru that he would see Gandhi and Nehru on the 23rd December at Delhi, if not earlier at Hyderabad (Deccan),—and in any case before the Christmas. Lord Irwin returned to Delhi in time on the 23rd December, and his train met with a bomb accident within a mile of New Delhi at the site of the old fort, the bomb being worked by a fuse connected with a clock-work mechanism. He narrowly escaped, but his dining saloon was damaged and one of his servants was hurt. The accident should really have told upon Lord Irwin deeply. The 23rd December, 1929, was the day on which the 'Viceroy's House' was occupied. On that day Gandhi and Motilalji were to see the Viceroy on behalf of the Congress. There were also Jinnah and Sapru and Vittalbhai Patel to represent other views. What was expected to be a heart-to-heart talk among friends became a formal deputation. Yet Lord Irwin was jovial, unperturbed by the accident of the morning. His equipoise was only excelled by his cordiality towards the guests. There was nothing of the coldness that was noticed when in November, 1927, the Simon Commission was announced to Gandhi. For 45 minutes the bomb and its effects occupied their time. Then Lord Irwin took up the subject on hand. "Where shall we begin?"

enquired he. "Here is your Manifesto. Shall we begin with the political prisoners?" He was anxious to make a good beginning and 'political prisoners' would easily lend itself to a tangible proof of goodwill. But Gandhi wanted to take the Viceroy through the question of Dominion Status. Gandhi wanted an assurance on this point, that the Round Table Conference would proceed on the basis of full Dominion Status. The Viceroy's answer was that the Government view was explained in their Communique and he could make no further promise. He was not in a position to extend an invitation to the R.T.C. with any definite promise of Dominion Status.

We had the news on our way to Lahore, both of the bomb that burst under the Viceroy's train and the hopes that burst in the Viceregal lodge. "Every one to his place, and all for their life," we thought. Thus began the determination for a grim struggle in the near future. The Lahore Congress was the last session that met in the midst of the bleak winds of Northern India in mid-winter. The arrangements at Lahore did not include any house accommodation for those unaccustomed to North Indian cold. The lodging in the tents made life hard. In the Working Committee we had to warm our feet every now and then. It was intolerably cold outside, but the warmth of feeling, the heat of passion and excitement, the resentment at the failure of negotiation, the flushing of face on hearing the beat of the war drums, —oh, it was all in marked contrast with the conditions of the weather. Pandit Jawaharlal was undoubtedly the most popular young politician of the hour, even as he was the youngest statesman of the day. His speech poured forth his soul to his countrymen,—his wrath and indignation over the insults heaped on India, his plans of emancipation, his distinct socialistic ideals and his determination to win.

The Congress was in a cauldron in Lahore. Ideas and ideals were boiling on the fires of national patriotism kindled by the ever increasing arrests. Mr. Benn's statement in the 3rd week of December, that "the freest expression of opinion in India is not only desirable but at the present time is a most helpful thing," neither helped to assuage public feeling in India nor abate the policy of repression. As for Dominion Status, he had been assuring the world that Dominion Status was already in action for a decade. India's signature to the Treaty of Versailles, the appointment of an Indian High Commissioner, an Indian at the head of the Indian delegation at the League, a separate vote at the International Navigation Commission, participation in the Conference of Dominion Legislatures, and in the Five-Power Naval Conference, a seat for India on the Governing Body of the International Labour Conference, —all these were cited as proofs of the millennium of Dominion Status, already in action.

But people were not deceived by such a toy show. They had to face hard realities, and settle issues of an immediate present.

The points of dispute at Lahore centred round these questions: Shall we endorse the Delhi Manifesto? Shall we appreciate the good intentions of the Viceroy? Shall we retain the words *'under the existing circumstances'* in the resolution? Shall we not alter the 'Creed' instead of merely saying that 'Swaraj' in the Creed means this or that? Shall we boycott the Legislatures? If so, shall we not also add University bodies, Port Trusts, Schools, Colleges and Courts? Shall we include Local Bodies at all? Shall we draw up a Republican Constitution? Shall we attend the Round Table Conference on the material before us, or shall we wait for two months before we declare Independence as the Creed of the Congress?

Pandit Jawaharlal Nehru in his Presidential Address thanked the country for putting him in charge of the glorious heritage which we had all received,—and which he had described at some length,—and he spoke of the rapidly changing world, a world which is in labour and out of her travail will give birth to a new order.' India to-day, he said, is a part of a world-movement alongside of other Eastern nations, but suffers because she is unable to effect that social adjustment based on equality which stability and permanence always demand. Her religious liberty was her redeeming feature, though to-day it has yielded place to fear, distrust and mutual suspicion. Attempts are being made to readjust the communal and political relations between the Hindus, Muslims and Sikhs, but the scheme evolved at the All-Parties' Conference has not satisfied the Parties concerned. The Viceroy's announcement is a seeming offer of peace. The Viceroy meant well and his language was the language of peace, but courteous phrases are a poor substitute for the hard facts around us. We have not precipitated a terrible national struggle No,—the door of negotiation is all kept open. 'Dominion Status in action' of Captain Wedgwood Benn has been a snare for us For us the Calcutta resolution holds and we have but one goal to-day; that of Independence. The President spoke of British Imperialism and frankly stated that he was a socialist and a republican and was no believer in Kings and Princes. Then he described the three major problems before us,—the Minorities, the Indian States, and Labour and Peasantry. Then he dealt with the question of non-violence.

"Violence too often brings reaction and demoralization in its train, and in our country especially it may lead to disruption. It is perfectly true that organised violence rules the world to-day and it may be that we could profit by its use. But we have not the material or the training for organised violence, and individual or sporadic violence is a confession of despair. The great majority of us, I take it, judge the issue not on moral but on practical grounds and if we reject the way of violence, it is because it promises no substantial results. Any great movement for liberation must necessarily be a mass movement, and a mass movement must essentially be peaceful, except in times of organised revolt." After this lucid exposition of non-violence by 'policy' as opposed to 'creed' or 'faith,' the President spoke of the boycott of Legislatures, the question of debts and the necessity to overhaul the machinery of the Congress and make it really efficient, by making it a compact and disciplined body. Finally he concluded with a plea for a supreme endeavour in these words: "None of us can say what and when we can achieve. We cannot command success. But success often comes to those who dare and act; it seldom goes to the timid who are ever afraid of the consequences. We play for high stakes; and if we seek to achieve great things, it can only be through great dangers."

The question before the Lahore Congress was whether the resolution passed at the Madras Congress (1927) relating to Independence should be incorporated as part of our Creed in Art. I of the Constitution or only as an explanation to it. On this subject the Presidential speech has some interesting observations: "Independence for us means complete freedom from British domination and British Imperialism. Having attained our freedom, I have no doubt that India will welcome all attempts at world co-operation and federation, and will even agree to give up part of her own independence to a larger group of which she is an equal member." The President proceeded to observe: "India could never be an equal member of the Commonwealth, unless Imperialism and all that it implies is discarded." Other excerpts from the Presidential speech which may be helpful in understanding the real position, may be quoted here:—

> "The real thing is the conquest of power, by whatever name it may be called. I do not think that any form of Dominion Status applicable to India will give us real power. A test of this power would be the entire withdrawal of the alien Army of occupation and Economic control. Let us therefore concentrate on these and the rest will follow."

In these views Gandhi and Jawaharlal Nehru, the leader of India and the President of the year, agreed. There was therefore no difficulty whatever in conducting the transactions of the Lahore Congress. After an expression of appreciation of the supreme self-sacrifice of Jatindas and Phongy U. Wizaya, and of condolences in connection with the death of Pandit Gokarnath Misra, Prof. S. M. Paranjpe, Syts. Bhaktavatsala Naidu, Rohini Kanta Hatibarua, B. K. Lahiri and Byomakesh Chakravarti, the following resolution was passed about the recent bomb outrage:—

> "This Congress deplores the bomb outrage perpetrated on the Viceroy's train, and reiterates its conviction that such action is not only contrary to the Creed of the Congress but results in harm being done to the national cause. It congratulates the Viceroy and Lady Irwin and their party, including the poor servants, on their fortunate and narrow escape."

The main resolution of the Congress was about Independence.

COMPLETE INDEPENDENCE

"This Congress endorses the action of the Working Committee in connection with the Manifesto signed by party leaders, including Congressmen, on the Viceregal pronouncement of the 31st October relating to Dominion Status, and *appreciates the efforts of the Viceroy towards* a settlement of the national movement for Swaraj. The Congress, however, having considered all that has since happened and the result of the meeting between Mahatma Gandhi, Pandit Motilal Nehru and other leaders, and the Viceroy, is of opinion that nothing is to be gained in the existing circumstances by the Congress being represented at the proposed Round Table Conference. This Congress, therefore, in pursuance of the resolution passed at its session at Calcutta last year, declares that the word 'Swaraj' in Art. I of the Congress Constitution shall mean Complete Independence, and further declares the entire scheme of the Nehru Committee's Report to have lapsed, and hopes that all Congressmen will henceforth devote their exclusive attention to the attainment of Complete Independence for India. As a preliminary step towards organising a campaign for Independence, and in order to make the Congress policy as consistent as possible with the change of Creed, this Congress calls upon Congressmen and others taking part in the national movement to abstain from participating directly or indirectly in future elections, and directs the present Congress members of the Legislatures and Committees to resign their seats. This Congress appeals to the Nation zealously to prosecute the constructive programme of the Congress, and authorises the All-India Congress Committee, whenever it deems fit, to launch upon a programme of Civil Disobedience including non-payment of taxes, whether in selected areas or otherwise, and under such safeguards as it may consider necessary."

Next the season for the holding of the annual Session of the Congress was altered:

> "Inasmuch as the Congress is intended to be representative of the poor masses, and inasmuch as the holding of the Congress at the end of December involves very considerable expense to the poor people in providing for extra clothing for themselves and is otherwise inconvenient to them, the date of holding the Congress session is hereby altered to some date in February or March, to be fixed by the Working Committee in consultation with the Provincial Committee of the Province concerned."

The Congress authorised the Working Committee to make all necessary consequential changes in the Constitution.

East Africa had a resolution as usual. The Congress congratulated Shrimati Sarojini Devi who went to East Africa at considerable inconvenience to herself, and also the Indians in East Africa on the national stand they took upon the Indian problem in that sub-continent. No solution of the question, it was said, that accepts communal electorates and is based on a discriminate franchise, or that imposes disqualification on Indians holding property, could satisfy the Nation.

An important subject taken up was the Indian States, and the Congress thought it was time the Ruling Princes of India granted Responsible Government to their people and enacted laws or issued proclamations safeguarding the elementary and fundamental rights of the people such as freedom of movement, freedom of speech, freedom to hold public meetings, and security of person and property.

The communal question had to be taken up afresh in view of the lapse of the Nehru Report. It was felt necessary to declare the policy of the Congress regarding communal questions. The Congress believed that in an Independent India communal questions can only be solved on strictly National lines. But as the Sikhs in particular, and the Muslims and the other Minorities in general, had expressed dissatisfaction over the solution of communal questions proposed in the Nehru Report, this Congress assured the Sikhs, the Muslims and other Minorities, that "no solution thereof in any future Constitution would be acceptable to the Congress that did not give full satisfaction to the parties concerned." On the question of the refusal of passports, the Congress condemned the refusal of these for return to India, to Syt. Shapurji J. Saklatwalla ex-M. P. and others who were living in England and other foreign countries.

The subject of Financial burdens and their repudiation was taken up after a long interval since Gaya (1922):—

> "This Congress is of opinion that the financial burdens directly or indirectly imposed on India by the foreign administration were such as a Free India cannot bear and cannot be expected to bear. The Congress whilst re-affirming the resolution passed at the Gaya Congress in 1922, therefore, records its opinion for the information of all concerned that every obligation and concession to be inherited by Independent India would be strictly subject to investigation by an independent tribunal, and every obligation, every concession, no matter how incurred or given, would be repudiated, if it is not found by such tribunal to be just and justifiable."

It was not without some difficulty that the resolution on the bomb outrage was passed. The resolution was stoutly opposed by a certain section of the delegates and it was only by a narrow majority that it could be passed. On the cardinal resolution also, there was considerable objection to the incorporation of the idea of "appreciating the efforts of the Viceroy towards a settlement of the national movement for Swaraj." Again, when the Congress said that "nothing is to be gained under the existing circumstances by the Congress being represented at the Round Table Conference," serious objection was taken to the words "under the existing circumstances." The fear was that the Round Table Conference, like King Charles's head, might turn up every now and then under the pretext of circumstances having changed. But it was obvious, as Gandhi had repeatedly explained, that all his Non-co-operation was for co-operation and all his fight was for a settlement. Finally Gandhi was not able to carry the House with him when he wanted to decentralize the work of the Congress by making the Foreign Cloth Boycott Committee, the Prohibition Committee, and the Committee for the Removal of Untouchability somewhat autonomous, and also when he wanted to reduce the strength of the Congress and render the organisation less cumbersome.

It is necessary to state that these several Committees had been brought into existence after the Calcutta Congress, since the month of February, 1929. Work was entrusted to experts. The organisation of volunteers had been entrusted to Jawaharlal and Subash Bose. For the first time, Congress work was divided into departments and entrusted to particular members of the Working Committee. But Gandhi wanted to place these Committees on a par with the All-India Spinners' Association, so that they might be functioning independently. His proposals were however viewed with suspicion, for a leader is always in advance of his following and his proposals of yesterday are only accepted by them to-day. This was what happened. To-day (1935) the work of untouchability is being conducted apart from the dust and din of high politics by an independent organisation unaffected by the political vicissitudes of the Nation. To-day again, the strength of the Congress delegates stands cut down to a third of its former strength in Bombay, and what Gandhi could not achieve at Lahore he achieved partly while he was in jail and partly after his release.

In Calcutta a year's time was given to Government to comply with the National Demand, and it was at 12, mid-night, on the 31st December that the poll on the most controversial clause was finished. The whole Congress proceeded at that hour to unfurl the flag of Complete Independence.

Altogether the Lahore Session was as strenuous a session as it was critical. The alternative resolutions put forward against Gandhi were either academic or destructive. Men who wanted to stick to "Independence and no damned nonsense," were keen on not resigning from Councils. Their attempt was to behead the main resolution or amputate its limbs and thus truncate it altogether. Amongst the ranks of the opposition some were opposed to Independence itself, and were plumping for the Round Table Conference, while others would have Independence, but would not tolerate the conventional courtesies of the Working Committee on the one hand or the Viceroy on the other, and under cover of this iconoclasm, would serve the country through Legislatures. The debates, therefore, round the main resolution ceased to be single-pointed or well-meaning. Each opponent had his own issue and his own object in combating the cardinal proposition of the House. But in the open session, there were only 15 hands raised against the main proposition. A really close division took place on the question of appreciating the Viceroy's efforts. Even on this issue, the difference in voting was 180, while on the question of condemning the bomb outrage the majority was only 84 in favour of the condemnation. In all these differences the common bond was common antipathies, not community of sympathies, convictions, or programmes.

The internal differences in Bengal which had led to long-standing election disputes, became the cause of an exchange of hot words between Subash Babu and Motilalji, and exhibited themselves markedly in the Congress week at Lahore. The leadership of the Province being the bone of contention between Syts. J. M. Sen-Gupta and Subash Chandra Bose, the differences came to a head on the issue of Council-entry on which there were sharp divergences of views. Again, while considered and thoughtful opinion asked for an examination of the financial commitments of the Nation by an Independent tribunal, an extremist view did not fail to express itself that all debts should be repudiated outright. Gandhi earnestly endeavoured to secure the change of "peaceful and legitimate means" in the Creed into "truthful and non-violent means" but did not succeed.

That question is still hanging fire, being adjourned at the last Bombay Congress (1934 October). In any case, the success of Gandhi and Jawaharlal at the Lahore Session was undeniable, in spite of the fact that almost immediately after the conclusion of the plenary session, Mr. Srinivasa Iyengar and Mr. Subash Chandra Bose announced the formation of a new organisation known as the Congress Democratic Party, which was supposed by Government at the time to indicate that the attempt to placate the left wing had not really succeeded and that a split was, after all, imminent. These friends had desired that the Working Committee should be formed by a process of election, and when it was defeated, they walked out along with certain South Indian friends. Gandhi's practice was to ask the retiring members of the Working Committee as to who would cut himself or herself out from it. In Lahore, the Working Committee for the next year was formed by preparing two independent lists, one by Pandit Motilalji in consultation with Gandhi, and one by Seth Jamnalal Bajaj. There was only one name which did not coincide in the two lists. That difference was adjusted, and the W. C. was formed. But these friends wanted election. That was thrown out, with the result that there was a dramatic exit. In less than ten minutes, the news was broadcast that a new Party was formed, and as soon as this new Party, which was known as the Congress Democratic Party, was organised in Lahore, Syt. Subash Chandra Bose sent the following telegram to Mrs. C. R. Das: "Circumstances and tyranny of majority forced us to form separate Party, as at Gaya, named Congress Democratic Party. Pray spirit of Deshbandhu may guide us and your blessings may inspire us."

In the official declaration of its policy, the Secretaries stated that:—

> "The new Party will, without prejudice to the Party's objective of Complete Independence for India, endeavour to the best of its ability to co-operate as far as possible with the other Parties in the country in such programmes, policies and activities as the Party may accept for the purpose of attaining its objective."

The opponents of the cardinal resolution, doubtless, endorsed Council resignations, but supported a contest and a re-entry. At Lahore, we witnessed strange combinations and a fear in some, at any rate, of Gandhiji's firm hand. We knew we had a rough voyage ahead, the bark was frail, the seas were boisterous, the clouds were overhanging, there was fog all round, and the sailors were undisciplined and new to their work. Our safety, however, lay in but one circumstance, namely, *the pilot knew his course.* He was a seasoned captain and had his chart and his compass. If the crew obeyed him, success was in sight. Else, we had a Court Martial by the Nation looming before us.

Bishan Narayan Dhar
1911 : Calcutta

R. N. Mudholkar
1912 : Bankipore

Nawab Syed Md. Bahadur
1913 : Karachi

Bhupendra Nath Basu
1914 ; Madras

CHAPTER II

A Fight to the Finish (1930)

The year of waiting was over, the year of action began for Congressmen; but before three weeks passed, there appeared a revolt in Maharashtra. We have seen how in the early years of N.C.O., Maharashtra paired with Bengal in resisting the new movement. Now the Maharashtra P.C.C. asked the Working Committee of the Congress not to urge Council boycott and asked the country to hasten to the R.T.C. on the Delhi conditions and on the basis of Independence. These questions had been settled really once for all. What were the Delhi conditions if they did not mean the change of heart indicated by the release of prisoners and the Dominion Status at work even from that day? Gandhi had refused to discuss the release of prisoners in his interview with the Viceroy on the 23rd December, 1929. The prisoners could afford to wait a while in the jails, said he; he had concentrated on the question of Dominion Status. On this the Viceroy refused to give his (Viceregal) assurances. It may be advantageous to know why Gandhi insisted on getting such assurances from the Viceroy. In 1925 Earl Winterton (Under-Secretary for India) replying to an enquiry by Mr. Lansbury as to whether Lord Birkenhead (Secretary of State) intended to invite Das and Gandhi and others to London for a negotiation of the conditions of co-operation, answered the question in the negative and stated his reasons thus:—

> "Firstly, the direct conduct of the policy and the administration in India was entrusted to the Government of India and the Local Governments.

> Therefore it was with these authorities that such discussions must take place and no useful purpose would be served by the Government's intervention and participation at this stage in matters which must ultimately come before them for decision, and for the decision of which they were responsible to Parliament. Secondly, though the Viceroy was about to visit this country for the purpose *inter alia* of discussing the political situation in India, it would be placing him and the Government of India entirely in a false position if his presence here was made the occasion for negotiations with Indian political parties."

The Viceroy held the key to the situation and Gandhi wanted to get possession of that key in Delhi on the 23rd December, 1929.

The new Working Committee met on the 2nd January, 1930. The old Committee had disposed of all outstanding questions including the appointment of a permanent Secretary to the Congress. When the new Committee met, the first thing it did was to take steps to implement the Congress resolution on the boycott of Councils urging the registered voters to compel the resignation of those who may not respond to the Congress appeal for resignation, as well as to refrain from participating in the ensuing elections to the Legislatures. As the result of this, 27 members of the Assembly resigned. It was decided to observe a day all over India as the Purna Swarajya Day and the 26th January, 1930, was fixed for the purpose.

A declaration to be issued was to be read to the people in the villages and towns all over the country, and the assent of the audience was to be taken by a show of hands. A Committee was appointed to enquire into certain obnoxious measures and laws in force in the

N. W. F. Province. The several Sub-Committees were asked to prosecute their work vigorously, and an equally vigorous enrolment of the Congress members was urged on the Nation. The declaration to be read on the 26th January, was as follows:—

The following resolution has been issued on behalf of the Working Committee for adoption by public meetings all over the country on Purna Swarajya Day, Sunday, January 26th, 1930:

"We believe that it is the inalienable right of the Indian people, as of any other people, to have freedom and to enjoy the fruits of their toil and have necessities of life, so that they may have full opportunities of growth. We believe also that if any Government deprives a people of these rights and oppresses them, the people have a further right to alter it or to abolish it. The British Government in India has not only deprived the Indian people of their freedom but has based itself on the exploitation of the masses, and has ruined India economically, politically, culturally and spiritually. We believe therefore that India must sever the British connection and attain Purna Swaraj or Complete Independence.

"India has been ruined economically. The revenue derived from our people is out of all proportion to our income. Our average income is seven pice (less than two pence) per day, and of the heavy taxes we pay 20% are raised from the Land Revenue derived from the peasantry, and 3% from the Salt Tax, which falls most heavily on the poor.

"Village industries, such as hand-spinning, have been destroyed, leaving the peasantry idle for at least four months in the year, and dulling their intellect for want of handicrafts, and nothing has been substituted, as in other countries, for the crafts thus destroyed.

"Customs and currency have been so manipulated as to heap further burdens on the peasantry. British manufactured goods constitute the bulk of our imports. Customs duties betray clear partiality for British manufactures, and revenue from them is used not to lessen the burden on the masses but for sustaining a highly extravagant administration. Still more arbitrary has been the manipulation of exchange ratio which has resulted in millions being drained away from the country.

"Politically, India's status has never been so reduced as under the British regime. No reforms have given real political power to the people. The tallest of us have to bend before foreign authority. The rights of free expression of opinion and free association have been denied to us, and many of our countrymen are compelled to live in exile abroad and cannot return to their homes. All administrative talent is killed and the masses have to be satisfied with petty village offices and clerkships.

"Culturally, the system of education has torn us from our moorings and our training has made us hug the very chains that bind us.

"Spiritually, compulsory disarmament has made us unmanly and the presence of an alien army of occupation, employed with deadly effect to crush in us the spirit of resistance, has made us think that we cannot look after ourselves or put up a defence against foreign aggression, or even defend our homes and families from the attacks of thieves, robbers and miscreants.

"We hold it to be a crime against man and God to submit any longer to a rule that has caused this four-fold disaster to our country. We recognise, however, that the most effective way of gaining our freedom is not through violence. We will, therefore, prepare ourselves by withdrawing, so far as we can, all voluntary association from the British Government, and will prepare for Civil Disobedience, including non-payment of taxes. We are convinced that if we can but withdraw our voluntary help and stop payment of taxes without doing violence, even under provocation, the end of this inhuman rule is assured. We, therefore, hereby solemnly resolve to carry out the Congress instructions issued from time to time for the purpose of establishing Purna Swaraj."

The Independence Day celebrations revealed what a fund of pent-up feeling, enthusiasm and readiness of sacrifice there lay beneath the seeming torpor and despair of the people. The fires of patriotism and sacrifice were covered by the embers of loyalty or submission to Law and Order. All that had to be done was to blow off the ashes covering the red-hot cinders of emotion and fervour, Hardly had the celebrations been concluded when the Viceroy's speech before the Legislature on the 25th January became available to the country. It blasted whatever little hope might be lingering in the minds of the optimistic or credulous section of the Indian politicians. We have already seen how Sir John Simon in his letter, Ramsay MacDonald in his reply, Lord Irwin in his statement, and Wedgwood Benn in his debates, had been studiously using the same language in describing the object as being "to explore means by which the greatest possible measure of agreement or the widest measure of general assent amongst the various classes and communities and from all parties and interests concerned may be secured in India for the proposals, which it will later be the duty of the Cabinet to place before Parliament." The Viceroy denied that he had ever "sought to delude Indian opinion into the belief that a definition of the purpose, however plainly stated, would of itself, by the enunciation of a phrase, have provided a solution for the problems which have to be solved before that purpose is fully realised." It was up to the Viceroy when the leaders raised an issue within 24 hours of his statement, and up to the Secretary of State when Lloyd George heckled Mr. Benn in the Commons, to say that the Round Table Conference was meant only to elucidate the definition of Dominion Status and not to offer a solution of the problems that lay on the way to its attainment, and India would have felt highly grateful. The Viceroy, in one word, stated that the assertion of a goal, however precise its terms, is of necessity a different thing from the goal's attainment. "No sensible traveller would," he added, "feel that a clear definition of his destination was the same thing as the completion of his journey, but it is an assurance of direction." Thus he contrasted *definition* with *solution*, *assertion* with *attainment*, and *direction* with *destination*. Then he disillusioned India about Benn's statement regarding Dominion Status being at work for ten years. Lord Irwin said:—

> "Although it is true that, in her external relations with the other parts of the Empire, India exhibits already several of the attributes of a Self-Governing Dominion, it is also true that Indian political opinion is not at present disposed to attach full value to these attributes of status, for the reason that their practical exercise is, for the most part, subject to the control or concurrence of His Majesty's Government."

* * * *

> "The Conference which His Majesty's Government will convene is not indeed the Conference that those have demanded who claimed that its duty should be to proceed by way of a majority vote to the fashioning of the Indian Constitution which should thereafter be accepted unchanged by Parliament."

* * * *

> "The Conference will be convened for the purpose of elucidating and harmonizing opinion and so affording guidance to His Majesty's Government on whom the responsibility must subsequently devolve of drafting proposals for the consideration of Parliament."

Thus did the Viceroy make it clear that self-determination was out of the question, that joint deliberation or determination was only to enable Government to perform their duty. Altogether, it was evident that what India should expect was neither self-determination noı joint determination, but 'other determination.'

In answer to this speech, Gandhi wrote in *Young India* as follows:—

> "His Excellency the Viceroy deserves thanks from every Congressman for having cleared the atmosphere and let us know exactly where he and we stand.
>
> "The Viceroy would not mind waiting for the grant of Dominion Status till every millionaire was reduced to the level of a wage-earner getting seven pice per day. The Congress will to-day, if it had power, raise every starving peasant to the state in which he at least will get a living, even equal to the millionaire's. And when the peasant is fully awakened to a sense of his plight and knows that it is not the 'kismet' that brought him to the helpless state but the existing rule, unaided, he will in his impatience abolish all distinctions between the constitutional and the unconstitutional, even the violent and non-violent means. The Congress expects to guide the peasants in the right direction."

Proceeding, Gandhi made the following offer to Lord Irwin:—

(1) Total prohibition.
(2) Reduction of ratio to 1s. 4d.
(3) Reduction of Land Revenue at least by 50 per cent. and making it subject to Legislative control.
(4) Abolition of the Salt Tax.
(5) Reduction of Military expenditure at least by 50 per cent. to begin with.

(6) Reduction of salaries of the highest grade services by half or less, so as to suit the reduced revenue.
(7) Protective tariff on foreign cloth.
(8) Passage of the Coastal Traffic Reservation Bill.
(9) Discharge of all political prisoners, save those condemned for murder or attempt to murder, or trial by ordinary judicial tribunals, withdrawal of all political prosecutions, abrogation of Sec. 124-A and Regulation III of 1818, and giving permission to all Indian exiles to return.
(10) Abolition of the C.I.D., or its popular control.
(11) To issue licenses to use fire-arms for self-defence, subject to popular control.

In fact, these were the terms, we are told, which Mr. Gandhi communicated to Mr. Bomanji who undertook to negotiate with Mr. Ramsay MacDonald, the Prime-Minister, as early as January, 1930.

"This is by no means an exhaustive list of the pressing needs," wrote Mahatma Gandhi, "but let the Viceroy satisfy us with regard to these very simple but vital needs of India. He will then hear no talk of Civil Disobedience; and the Congress will heartily participate in any Conference where there is a perfect freedom of expression and demand." That is to say, non-compliance with these simple and vital demands would mean Civil Disobedience.

"Other nations," said Mr. Gandhi, "might have different and other means for getting their country's freedom, but for India there is no way but non-violent Non-co-operation. May you be the exponents of this *mantra* of Swaraj, and may God give you strength and courage enough to give all that you have in India's fight for Independence, a fight which is drawing very near."

The Legislative Assembly before which the Viceroy's speech was delivered was in its spring session. The atmosphere of the time was by no means genial, on account of the passing of the Textile Industry (Protection) Bill which was believed by many of its opponents to represent the enforcement upon India of Imperial Preference, in violation of the spirit of the Fiscal Convention. This led to the resignation of Pandit Madan Mohan Malaviya and some members of his Nationalist group. Really it was providential that help should have come to the Congress movement from unexpected quarters, and so often it was Government and its unimaginativeness that brought this help. Malaviyaji was no non-co-operator. At this time, however, his position was that he would not resile even from Civil Disobedience, but that he did not endorse Independence. At this juncture, when he was still continuing as a member of the Assembly whose term had been extended, the Textile Industry Bill forced his hands.

It is necessary to state what this Bill was, and, for that, to state the history of the Excise and import duties on cotton textiles. By the time the war ended, the position was that there was an Excise duty of 3½% on cotton yarn and cloth of above 19 counts, manufactured by Indian mills, payable to Government for the very manufacture, not on sales or profits. The import duties which were purely Revenue duties stood at 7% *ad valorem*. The mill-owners, merchants and Moderates recited their services to Government in the war and pointed out that the import of foreign cloth after the war hit the Indian mills badly. In 1925, Government agreed to raise the import duties from 7 to 11%, thus making foreign cloth 4% dearer and to abolish the Excise duties, thus making Indian cloth 3½% cheaper than the former. While the Indian public were thus rejoicing over the gains to the Indian mill-cloth, Government introduced and carried the Ratio Bill early in 1927, making the foreign cloth—always sold to India in prices reckoned in pounds and shillings—cheaper by 12½% by raising the exchange from 16d. (pre-war ratio) to 18d., that is, by 2d. out of 16d., *i.e.*, by 1/8 or 12½%, so that a packet of cloth (Lancashire) costing £1 formerly cost the Indian importer Rs. 15/- at 16d. ratio but now only Rs. 13-5-4. at 18d. ratio. So that the gains of 7½% to the Indian mill-owner, of 1925, were more than counter-balanced two years later by a gain to the foreigner of 12½%. Now the Indians were agitated over the problem and demanded a revision of the Tariff. Government agreed to raise the import duties by the Textile Protection Bill to 20% on cotton textiles imported from all countries except England, which was to be charged only 15%. This was objected to by Pandit Malaviya as a violation of the Fiscal Convention. To anticipate events, Japan, whose competition with Lancashire this enhancement was designed to check, gave a rebate of 5% in the shipping rates on all cotton textiles brought to India and thus combated successfully the Indian tariffs, the Japanese Government in turn giving a 5% bounty to the shipping companies. Later on, a surcharge of 5 p.c. was made on these rates by the Government of India, but the extra five per cent. charged on Lancashire goods was virtually annulled by levying an import duty of ½ anna per lb. on cotton imported into India. Such cotton as is generally imported from Egypt and America is intended for the manufacture of cloth of higher counts which compete with Lancashire cloth. Thus what Lancashire had lost in a five per cent. surcharge in India on Import duties, has been made up for by the Indian Government for her, by making dearer by 5 per cent. or ½ anna on the pound the cotton imported by Indian mills for manufacturing cloth which competes with Lancashire cloth. This is only by the way. When the Cotton Textiles Protection Bill was before the Assembly and two amendments were put forward, one being Pandit Malaviya's which proposed a flat rate for all countries without any preference for England, President Patel, on the 31st March, the last day of the session, urged that "the Government should reconsider its position and tell the House if it had not finally decided to drop the Bill in the event of the House amending its proposals." The Government, however, was of opinion that such action on its part would amount to an abdication of its responsibilities, and at the conclusion of the debate the House rejected Malaviyaji's amendment and accepted Mr. Chetty's amendment. But before the Bill, as amended, was finally voted upon, Pandit Malaviya and his followers and then Diwan Chamanlal and other members of the new Swaraj Party rose and left the House. At the end of the day, before adjourning the House, the President asked each member to shake hands with him, saying, "we do not know how many of us will be here." Really, these events since February, 1930, of the Assembly do not concern the fight. But we have given this small episode in order to give completion to the events of the season and to explain how Pandit Malaviya and others resigned their seats in the wake of the Congress Party.

Now we pass on to a study of the great movement inaugurated in 1930. We have already stated that the Independence Day celebrations were a great success, being held all over the country. Arrests were going on briskly in India for one reason or another. In the Meerut Case, of the 32 accused, all but one were committed to trial in the sessions. In Calcutta, Subash

Chandra Bose and eleven others were convicted and sentenced to a year's rigorous imprisonment. In obedience to the Congress mandate, 172 members of the Legislatures had resigned by February, 1930, the Assembly contributing 21 and the Council of State 9 Among the Provincial Councils, Bengal led with 34, Bihar and Orissa coming next with 31, C. P. 20, Madras 20, U. P. 16, Assam 12, Bombay 6, Punjab 2, Burma 1.

The Working Committee met at Sabarmati on the 14th, 15th and 16th February. Members of Legislatures who had not resigned, or who resigned and immediately sought re-election, were asked to resign their membership of any elective Congress Committee that they might hold, on pain of disciplinary action being taken against them. Regret was expressed that the assurances given by Government for the better treatment of political prisoners which induced the A.I.C.C. to pass a resolution on the 28th September, 1929, in Lucknow, advising those who were imposing the sacrifice on themselves to give up the hunger-strike, had not been fulfilled and that the Lahore prisoners had felt impelled in protest to resort to hunger-strike in jail. But the cardinal resolution of the sitting was the one relating to Civil Disobedience which ran as follows :—

> "In the opinion of the Working Committee, Civil Disobedience should be initiated and controlled by those who believe in non-violence for the purpose of achieving Purna Swaraj, as an article of faith, and as the Congress contains in its organisation not merely such men and women but also those who accept non-violence as a policy essential in the existing circumstances in the country, the Working Committee welcomes the proposal of Mahatma Gandhi and authorises him and those working with him who believe in non-violence as an article of faith to the extent above indicated, to start Civil Disobe-

dience as and when they desire and in the manner and to the extent they decide. The Working Committee trusts that when the campaign is actually in action, all Congressmen and others will extend to the civil resisters their full co-operation in every way possible and that they will observe and preserve complete non-violence notwithstanding any provocation that may be offered. The Working Committee further hopes that, in the event of a mass movement taking place, all those who are rendering voluntary co-operation to the Government, such as lawyers, and those who are receiving so-called benefits from it, such as students, will withdraw their co-operation or renounce benefits as the case may be and throw themselves into the final struggle for freedom.

"The Working Committee trusts that in the event of the leaders being arrested and imprisoned, those who are left behind and have the spirit of sacrifice and service in them will carry on the Congress organisation and guide the movement to the best of their ability."

The resolution authorised Gandhi and his followers in faith, to start Civil Disobedience. This was generalized later by the All-India Congress Committee that met shortly after at Ahmedabad, into a campaign of Civil Disobedience. We mention this point in particular to show how, when in May, 1934, the movement was withdrawn, an exception was still made in favour of Gandhi, so that the Civil Disobedience campaign that started with permission to Gandhi was suspended with that permission intact. More important than the formal resolution passed by the Working Committee at Sabarmati, were the informal talks given at the time by Gandhi to a number of friends who had been invited for the occasion. They centred round salt, how to break the salt laws, by manufacturing salt, by collecting it from deposits and by raiding salt depots.

At this meeting, fears were expressed by some that the country was not prepared for Mass Civil Disobedience. The question of preparedness and preparation lay in the answer to the question whether they would be civil in their disobedience, invite suffering, not inflict, bear sorrows and strife in a spirit of composure and cheerfulness. Amongst those who expressed such fears were candid friends, who had a decade's notice of Mass Civil Disobedience. But if they were carping critics, they needed no answer. By postponing Mass Civil Disobedience, would they prepare themselves for action on a day to be fixed by themselves? Really the best preparation for swimming is to swim, even as the best test of a country's fitness for Self-Government was, according to Lord Ripon, to give it Self-Government. Learning by doing applies to this moral discipline equally with the physical training of the hand and the eye.

If Civil Disobedience was to be embarked upon, what should we do? Gandhi had already indicated what he intended to do. The news had travelled to Bombay that he would raid salt depots, even before the Sabarmati meeting of the Working Committee began its sittings. Propaganda was started then and there in Bombay before the 14th February. The genesis of salt duties was unearthed. It was pointed out that a Salt Commission had sat in 1836 and recommended that Indian salt should be taxed in order to enable English salt to sell in India. The ships in Liverpool were lying idle in the dockyard for want of cargo, and without cargo to the extent of supplying at least the keel ballast, they could not sail safely on the high seas. So they had to carry some cargo, some load, some weight. For some time they had brought earth to India, from the Strand in London, with which the Chowringee Road in Calcutta, which was once a canal running from the Hughli to the

Kalighat Temple, was filled up. The fact is that the exports of India have always been greater than her imports. In 1925, the exports were 316 crores and the imports were 249 crores. That was not all. The exports are more voluminous, being largely food products and raw materials. Thus the volume of shipping to take the Indian exports abroad would, all things considered, be at least four to five times greater than the volume required for the import of the manufactured articles resulting from those imports. Therefore, the in-coming ships to India must be much more numerous than is justified by the imports only, as they have to take the exports on their way back. That is, they must come empty. British shipping takes 72 per cent. or roughly three-fourths of the total shipping of the Indian trade and, therefore, some British products must be carried to India by the in-coming ships to serve as keel ballast. What else could be thought of than Cheshire salt? Of course, there are other articles being brought to India such as old newspaper bales and broken porcelain chips. The Italian ships would bring Italian marbles and Italian potatoes under similar conditions as keel ballast. That is why they are able to beat the Indian articles in prices.

Shortly after the Sabarmati meeting, the atmosphere was surcharged with salt. People asked whether it would be paying to manufacture salt. Government officers went the length of computing the cost of manufacturing salt from sea water, the cost of fuel and labour, and showing that the manufactured salt would be thrice as much expensive as duty salt. The pity of it all was that they did not see that the struggle was a moral, not a material one.

Those gathered at Sabarmati inquired of Gandhi about his plans. It was but right that they should do so, although nobody would have asked Lord Kitchener or Marshal Foch or Von Hindenberg to unfold their plans on the eve of the Great War. Plans they had, but they might not reveal them. It was not so with Satyagraha. There was no privacy about our plans. But they were not clear-cut either. They would unfold themselves, much as the path on a misty morning reveals itself to a fast-moving motor, almost from yard to yard. The Satyagrahi carries a searchlight on his forehead. It shows the way for the next step.

The present Salt Satyagraha was to evolve thus. Gandhi would go and pick up salt in some salt area. Others should not. If they asked him whether they should remain idle, the answer was 'yes,' but 'idle for action.' He expected an immediate reaction. Even Vallabhbhai was not to march with him. Gandhi would confine himself to the members of the Ashram as his companions. Even the Wardha Ashram might only make preparations, but must wait till he was arrested. Then there will be simultaneous reaction all over India. After his arrest he would leave people to their own counsel and do what they might think proper. After him, he expected the movement to spread to all places and in all directions and in the intensest form. We must conquer or be wiped off. But it was impossible for the opponents to wipe out a Nation which has never wished ill to Englishmen. If they are wiped out, that very act would shake the Empire. That is the logical and relentless working out of non-violence. If people ask what should happen if the Government should shower bombs, the answer was, if innocent men, women and children should be thus reduced to ashes, from out of those very ashes would rise a fire which would react on the Empire.

They committed Civil Disobedience in South Africa, and when they were arrested support came from all quarters, food, provisions and what not. In South Africa there was a general strike,—labourers downed tools, factory hands did not work, markets closed down.

That is the kind of response that they had in South Africa. South Africa might be a limited compact country, while ours was extensive. Therefore the task would be harder.

There might not be manufacture of salt everywhere, but there were depots. We could take possession of the depots. "But is this not loot?" people might ask. No. Because you did not want a grain for yourselves. Salt is necessary for life. Our duty was not to egg on mass action. If it came, we should control it and regulate it. We need not invite it, but were to provide for it if it came. In the event of mass action, the lawyers were to give up their courts and the students to give up their studies. Gandhi was no longer a spent bullet that he felt himself to be, the previous year.

Gandhi held that we were getting mixed up with violence all round. It was growing up because of want of resistance. Therefore, our duty was to offer resistance to violence by practising non-violence. It was some such line of thought that inspired the Congress in 1930.

History is indeed replete with many stories of heroism. Theodore Parker was a great American Theist who became a world character in the emancipation of slavery in America. The Theologians of the time challenged Parker to a public debate.. His friends advised him to absent himself from the proposed meeting. He was locked up in his place. His enemies threatened to kill him if he was there, and charged him with cowardice. Suddenly, Parker appeared on the scene, rose like a rocket and leaped to the platform and cried: "Kill me if you can! From every drop of blood that you draw, a thousand Parkers will rise and emancipate the slaves." The accusers were paralysed and the convocation was dissolved.

Gandhi's plans have all along been revealed to him by his own instinct, not evolved by the cold, calculating logic of the mind. His inner voice is his mentor and monitor, his friend, philosopher and guide. It was thus that he condensed the progress of centuries in a decade, as Lloyd George would say. In India, one might have said, the progress of a thousand years was encompassed within the events of a year. The purity of Gandhi's vision and view was universally conceded, and even the Moderates who held the Salt Satyagraha to be fantastic or dangerous, would not deny the exalted character of his motives. Gandhi lost no time in appraising the Viceroy of his pans. As is usual with him, he sent a letter to Lord Irwin, the full text of which is given below:—

Satyagraha Ashram,
Sabarmati, March 2nd, 1930

"Dear Friend,

"Before embarking on Civil Disobedience, and taking the risk I have dreaded to take all these years, I would fain approach you and find a way out.

"My personal faith is absolutely clear. I cannot intentionally hurt anything that lives, much less fellow human beings, even though they may do the greatest wrong to me and mine. Whilst, therefore, I hold the British rule to be a curse, I do not intend harm to a single Englishman or to any legitimate interest he may have in India.

"I must not be misunderstood. Though I hold the British rule in India to be a curse, I do not, therefore, consider Englishmen in general to be worse than any other people on earth. I have the privilege of claiming many Englishmen as dearest friends. Indeed much that I have learnt of the evil of British rule is due to the writings of frank and courageous Englishmen who have not hesitated to tell the unpalatable truth about that rule.

"And why do I regard the British rule as a curse?

"It has impoverished the dumb millions by a system of progressive exploitation and by a ruinously expensive military and civil administration which the country can never afford.

"It has reduced us politically to serfdom. It has sapped the foundations of our culture. And, by the policy of disarmament, it has degraded us spiritually. Lacking the inward strength, we have been reduced, by all but universal disarmament, to a state bordering on cowardly helplessness.

"In common with many of my countrymen, I had hugged the fond hope that the proposed Round Table Conference might furnish a solution. But, when you said plainly that you could not give any assurance that you or the British Cabinet would pledge yourselves to support a scheme of full Dominion Status, the Round Table Conference could not possibly furnish the solution for which vocal India is consciously, and the dumb millions are unconsciously, thirsting. Needless to say there never was any question of Parliament's verdict being anticipated. Instances are not wanting of the British Cabinet, in anticipation of the Parliamentary verdict, having pledged itself to a particular policy.

"The Delhi interview having miscarried, there was no option for Pandit Motilal Nehru and me but to take steps to carry out the solemn resolution of the Congress arrived at in Calcutta, at its session in 1928.

"But the resolution of Independence should cause no alarm, if the word Dominion Status mentioned in your announcement had been used in its accepted sense. For, has it not been admitted by responsible British statesmen that Dominion Status is virtual Independence? What, however, I fear is that there never has been any intention of granting such Dominion Status to India in the immediate future.

"But this is all past history. Since the announcement, many events have happened which show unmistakably the trend of British policy.

"It seems as clear as daylight that responsible British statesmen do not contemplate any alteration in British policy that might adversely affect Britain's commerce with India or require an impartial and close scrutiny of Britain's transactions with India. If nothing is done to end the process of exploitation, India must be bled with an ever increasing speed. The Finance Member regards as a settled fact the 1s. 6d. ratio which, by a stroke of the pen, drains India of a few crores. And when a serious attempt is being made, through a civil form of direct action, to unsettle this fact, among many others, even you cannot help appealing to the wealthy landed classes to help you to crush that attempt in the name of an order that grinds India to atoms.

"Unless those who work in the name of the Nation understand, and keep before all concerned, the motive that lies behind the craving for Independence, there is every danger of Independence itself coming to us so changed as to be of no value to those toiling, voiceless millions for whom it is sought and for whom it is worth taking. It is for that I have been recently telling the public what Independence should really mean.

"Let me put before you some of the salient points.

"The terrific pressure of Land Revenue, which furnishes a large part of the total, must undergo considerable modification in an Independent India. Even the much vaunted Permanent Settlement benefits the few rich Zamindars, not the ryots. The ryot has remained as helpless as ever. He is a mere tenant-at-will.

"Not only, then, has the Land Revenue to be considerably reduced, but the whole revenue system has to be so revised as to make the ryot's good its primary concern. But the British system seems to be designed to crush the very life out of him. Even the salt he must use to live is so taxed as to make the burden fall heaviest on him, if only because of the heartless impartiality of its incidence. The tax shows itself still more burdensome on the poor man, when it is remembered that salt is the one thing he must eat more than the rich man, both individually and collectively. The drink and drug revenue, too, is derived from the poor. It saps the foundations both of their health and morals. It is defended under the false plea of individual freedom, but, in reality, is maintained for its own sake. The ingenuity of the authors of the Reforms of 1919 transferred this revenue to the so-called responsible part of Dyarchy, so as to throw the burden of prohibition on it, thus, from the very beginning, rendering it powerless for good. If the unhappy Minister wipes out this revenue, he must starve education, since in the existing circumstances he has no new source of replacing that revenue. If the weight of taxation has crushed the poor from above, the destruction of the central supplementary industry, *i.e.*, hand-spinning, has undermined their capacity for producing wealth.

"The tale of India's ruination is not complete without reference to the liabilities incurred in her name. Sufficient has been recently said about these in the public Press. It must be the duty of a Free India to subject all the liabilities to the strictest investigation, and repudiate those that may be adjudged by an impartial tribunal to be unjust and unfair.

"The inequities sampled above are maintained in order to carry on a foreign administration, demonstrably the most expensive in the world. Take your own salary. It is over Rs. 21,000 per month, besides many other indirect additions. The British Prime-Minister gets £ 5,000 per year, i.e., over Rs. 5,400 per month at the present rate of exchange. You are getting over Rs. 700 per day, against India's average income of less than 2 annas per day. The Prime-Minister gets Rs. 180 per day against Great Britain's average income of nearly Rs. 2 per day. Thus, you are getting much over five thousand times India's average income. The British Prime-Minister is getting only ninety times Britain's average income. On bended knee, I ask you to ponder over this phenomenon. I have taken a personal illustration to drive home a painful truth. I have too great a regard for you as a man to wish to hurt your feelings. I know that you do not need the salary you get. Probably the whole of your salary goes for charity. But a system that provides for such an arrangement deserves to be summarily scrapped. What is true of the Viceregal salary is true generally of the whole administration.

"A radical cutting down of the revenue, therefore, depends upon an equally radical reduction in the expenses of the administration. This means a transformation of the scheme of government. This transformation is impossible without Independence. Hence, in my opinion, the spontaneous demonstration of 26th January, in which hundreds of thousands of villagers instinctively participated. To them Independence means deliverance from the killing weight.

"Not one of the great British political Parties, it seems to me, is prepared to give up the Indian spoils to which Great Britain helps herself from day to day, often, in spite of the unanimous opposition of Indian opinion.

"Nevertheless, if India is to live as a Nation, if the slow death by starvation of her people is to stop, some remedy must be found for immediate relief. The proposed Conference is certainly not the remedy. It is not a matter of carrying conviction by argument. The matter resolves itself into one of matching forces. Conviction or no conviction,

Great Britain would defend her Indian commerce and interests by all the forces at her command. India must consequently evolve force enough to free herself from that embrace of death.

"It is common cause that, however disorganised, and, for the time being, insignificant it may be, the party of violence is gaining ground and making itself felt. Its end is the same as mine. But I am convinced that it cannot bring the desired relief to the dumb millions. And the conviction is growing deeper and deeper in me that nothing but unadulterated non-violence can check the organised violence of the British Government. My experience, limited though it undoubtedly is, shows that non-violence can be an intensely active force. It is my purpose to set in motion that force, as well against the organised violent force of the British rule as the unorganised violent force of the growing party of violence. To sit still would be to give reign to both the forces above-mentioned. Having an unquestioning and immovable faith in the efficacy of non-violence, as I know it, it would be sinful on my part to wait any longer.

"The non-violence will be expressed through Civil Disobedience, for the moment confined to the inmates of the Satyagraha Ashram, but ultimately designed to cover all those who choose to join the movement with its obvious limitations.

"I know that in embarking on non-violence, I shall be running what might fairly be termed a mad risk. But the victories of Truth have never been won without risks, often of the bravest character. Conversion of a Nation that has consciously or unconsciously preyed upon another far more numerous, far more ancient and no less cultured than itself, is worth any amount of risk.

"I have deliberately used the word 'conversion'. For my ambition is no less than to convert the British people, through non-violence, and thus make them see the wrong they have done to India. I do not seek to harm your people. I want to serve them, even as I want to serve my own. I believe that I have always served them. I served them up to 1919 blindly. But when my eyes were opened and I conceived Non-co-operation, the object still was to serve them. I employed the same weapon that I have, in all humility, successfully used against the dearest members of my family. If I have equal love for your people with mine, it will not long remain hidden. It will be acknowledged by them, even as the members of my family acknowledged it after they had tried me for several years. If the people join me, as I expect they will, the sufferings they will undergo, unless the British Nation sooner retraces its steps, will be enough to melt the stoniest hearts.

"The plan through Civil Disobedience will be to combat such evils as I have sampled out. If we want to sever the British connection, it is because of such evils. When they are removed, the path becomes easy. Then the way to friendly negotiation will be open. If the British commerce with India is purified of greed, you will have no difficulty in recognising our Independence. I respectfully invite you then to pave the way for an immediate removal of those evils, and thus open a way for a real conference between equals, interested only in promoting the common good of mankind through voluntary fellowship and in arranging terms of mutual help and commerce equally suited to both. You have unnecessarily laid stress upon the communal problems that unhappily affect this land. Important though they undoubtedly are for the consideration of any scheme of government, they have little bearing on the greater problems which are above communities and which affect them all equally. But if you cannot see your way to deal with these evils and my letter makes no appeal to your heart, on the 11th day of this month, I shall proceed, with such co-workers of the Ashram as I can take, to disregard the provisions of the Salt Laws. I regard this tax to be the most iniquitous of all from the poor man's standpoint. As the Independence movement is essentially for the poorest in the land, the beginning will be made with this evil. The wonder is that we have submitted to the cruel monopoly for so long. It is, I know, open to you to frustrate my design by arresting me. I hope that there will be tens of thousands ready, in a disciplined manner, to take up the work after me, and, in the act of disobeying the Salt Act, to lay themselves open to the penalties of a Law that should never have disfigured the Statute Book.

"I have no desire to cause you unnecessary embarrassment, or any at all, so far as I can help. If you think that there is any substance in my letter, and if you will care to discuss matters with me, and if to that end you would like me to postpone publication of this letter, I shall gladly refrain, on receipt of a telegram to that effect soon after this reaches you. You will, however, do me the favour not to deflect me from my course, unless you can see your way to conform to the substance of this letter.

"This letter is not in any way intended as a threat but is a simple and sacred duty peremptory on a civil resister. Therefore, I am having it specially delivered by a young English friend who believes in the Indian cause and is a full believer in non-violence, and whom Providence seems to have sent to me, as it were, for the very purpose.

I remain,
Your sincere friend,
M. K. Gandhi"

To
H. E. Lord Irwin,
Viceroy's House,
New Delhi.

This letter was taken to Delhi by Mr. Reginald Reynolds, a young Englishman, who had been in the Ashram for some time. Lord Irwin's answer to this letter of Gandhi,—which people and the Press described as an ultimatum,—came back quick and was unequivocal. His Excellency expressed his regret that Mr. Gandhi should have been "contemplating a course of action which was clearly bound to involve violation of the Law and danger to the public peace." Gandhi's rejoinder to this was characteristic of him and was abounding in that spirit of humility and courage which make up the equipment of every honest Satyagrahi.

"On bended knees," he wrote, "I asked for bread and received a stone instead. The English Nation responds only to force, and I am not surprised by the Viceregal reply. The only public peace the Nation knows is the peace of the public prison. India is a vast prison-house. I repudiate this (British) Law and regard it as my sacred duty to break the mournful monotony of compulsory peace that is choking the heart of the Nation for want of free vent."

Gandhi's march had thus become inevitable. All necessary preparations had been already made, nor did they need to be elaborate. His seventy-one followers who were picked and chosen from among the members of the Ashram and the students of the Vidya Pith who had offered themselves as volunteers, were soldiers who had been steeled to the disciplines and hardships which a two hundred miles' march on foot would necessarily entail on them. Villages on the way to Dandi, a seaside village which was Gandhi's destination, were strictly warned not to give any rich fare to the pilgrims in their progress. While yet Gandhi was making these preparations, which were purely of a moral nature, Vallabhbhai went before his master, to prime up the villagers for the coming ordeals. It did not take long for Government to strike the first blow. When Vallabhbhai was moving in advance as Gandhi's forerunner, Government saw in him John the Baptist that was the forerunner of Jesus, nineteen hundred years ago, and forthwith they laid hands on him in the first week of March at Ras and sentenced him to three months' imprisonment. With his arrest and conviction, the whole of Gujarat rose to a man against Government. 75,000 people gathered on the sands of Sabarmati and passed the following resolution:—

> "We the citizens of Ahmedabad, determine hereby that we shall go the same path where Vallabhbhai has gone, and we shall attain full Independence while attempting to do so. Without achieving freedom for our country, we shall not rest in peace, nor will we give Government peace. We solemnly declare that India's emancipation lies in truth and non-violence."

Gandhiji then asked the gathering to raise their hands if they meant to take the vow, and the whole of that throng raised their hands. Vallabhbhai's speeches to the people of Gujarat had been soul-stirring. He warned them about the seizure of their dear cattle before their very eyes.

> "Give up your wedding festivities," said he, "a people at war with a mighty Government cannot afford to indulge in these pastimes. From tomorrow, you might have to keep your doors closed and locked, and betake to the fields, only to return home in the evening. You have earned a reputation that you have yet to do much to deserve. Now the die is cast, and there is no turning back; you have to vindicate Gandhi's choice of your Taluka as the scene of his first experiment in Mass Civil Disobedience. ....I know some of you are afraid of your lands being confiscated. What is confiscation? Will they take away the lands to England? Rest assured, when you allow all your lands to be confiscated, the whole of your Gujarat will be at your back.

> "Organise your village and set an example to others. Every village must now be an armed camp. Discipline and organisation mean half the battle. Government at least have one Patel and one Talati to every village; for us, every adult in the village must be a volunteer.
>
> "I see that these fifteen days have taught you to cast off your fear. But two annas in the rupee are still there. Shake it off. It is Government that has cause to fear. This is not a reign of peace but a reign of fear. I want to inoculate you with fearlessness. I want to galvanise you into life. I miss in your eyes the flash of indignation against wrong. Non-violence excludes anger. The defection of two unfortunate brethren should serve to stiffen your resolve and to warn you for the future. You must not be angry with two friends who fell a prey to official machinations. If those who sign the pledge break it with eyes open, how long can you stop them? Let Mahalkari chuckle over his precious gains. He will soon find his occupation gone."

Gandhi began his march on 12-3-1930 to Dandi, accompanied by his seventy-nine 'padacharees.' It was a historic scene, nay an epic scene, calling back to our minds like scenes of old coupled with the names of Sree Rama and of the Pandavas. But here it is a march of revolt, not a mere submission to the decree of a father or the ukase of an uncle. As the march was progressing, three hundred village officers tendered their resignations. Gandhi had said during his informal talks at Ahmedabad, "Wait till I begin. Once I march to the place, the idea will be released. You will know what to do." It was, in effect, a warning against an intellectual analysis of a scheme of resistance, which even the best of adherents could not visualise in its full proportions at the time. It was also prophetic visualisation of what was to come to pass. Perhaps Gandhi himself had no full conception of what was to follow. He saw things as if by a flash and framed his conduct by impulse. To the righteous man, these two are the supreme guides of life, not reason nor intellect. Once the march began, people caught the spirit of his teaching and the plan of his campaign. They gathered round his banner. The idea was released, and the released idea coursed along different channels, seeking various forms of expression. People soon realised that Non-co-operation and non-violence were not a mere negation, but a scheme of resistance. They had their own strategy too; Truth was that strategy. Non-violence was the resistance. The liberation of ideas and emotions brought with it a liberation of energies as well. The march was ridiculed at first, watched with attention later, and finally was admired. Where the towns feared, the villages followed. The unsophisticated had full faith in his unerring judgment. His salt campaign was not a depredatory march against a depot well-guarded, or against the limitless ocean. It was symbolical of the revolt of thirty-one crores of Indians against the authority of the British,—British laws and British regulations, based neither on the consent of the people nor even upon the unimpeachable principles of ethics or humanity. People were expecting the first blow to be a stupendous blow, a stunning blow, a spectacular blow. The rapid march of the Germans, from the Rhineland on to the Marne, within gun-shot range from the fort of Paris, was such a spectacular achievement. Satyagraha was not a spectacular process. Yet there was enough of the unexpected and dramatic in it.

The first blow was, it is true, not dealt either by the dynamite or nitro-glycerine with all its din of explosion, nor with picric acid or potassium-chlorate with their booms and bursts, but with sodium-chloride or common salt, a salt which is bland and free from all pungency. Yet, the momentum that gathered round this elementary need of life is wonderful. The reaction in Government to this tame and semi-comic campaign is amazing to a degree. As for the response which the civilised world has shown, we lack words to describe its intensity and its promptness. The one idea released by Gandhi's march is that India is in revolt, in bloodless revolt, against the British Government; and India is bound to triumph, if, in the supreme wisdom of providence, Truth should triumph over untruth, light over darkness, and life eternal over death.

While this mighty scene in the drama of Indian emancipation was being enacted, new expressions came into existence. We had already learnt what it was to 'Bardolise' the country. Now the 'spirit of Borsad' had come in as a companion phrase and had come to stay. During the march, the A.I.C.C. met at Ahmedabad on 21st March, 1930, and approved of and endorsed the resolution of the Working Committee already quoted, and urged concentration on the salt laws, and warned against Civil Disobedience anywhere in the country being started before Gandhi had actually reached his destination and committed a breach of the salt law himself. Sirdar Vallabhbhai and Sen-Gupta were congratulated on their arrests, as also the village officials of Gujarat who had resigned from Government service. A Satyagrahi pledge of a uniform kind was considered desirable and, with Gandhi's approval, the following pledge was drawn up:—

1. I desire to join the civil resistance campaign for the Independence of India undertaken by the National Congress.

2. I accept the Creed of the National Congress, that is, "the attainment of Purna Swaraj (Complete Independence) by the people of India by all peaceful and legitimate means."

3. I am ready and willing to go to jail and undergo all other sufferings and penalties that may be inflicted on me in this campaign.

4. In case I am sent to jail, I shall not seek any monetary help for my family from the Congress funds.

5. I shall implicitly obey the orders of those who are in charge of the campaign.

It was usual for Gandhi to give instructions to the public regarding their duties and behaviour on his arrest. On the eve of the March, and the expected arrest which would soon follow, Gandhi wrote the following article on 27th February.

WHEN I AM ARRESTED:

"It must be taken for granted that when Civil Disobedience is started, my arrest is a certainty. It is, therefore, necessary to consider what should be done when the event takes place.

"On the eve of my arrest in 1922, I had warned co-workers against any demonstration of any kind save that of mute, complete non-violence, and had insisted that constructive work, which alone could organise the country for Civil Disobedience, should be prosecuted with the utmost zeal. The first part of the instructions was, thanks be given to God, literally and completely carried out, so completely that it has enabled an English noble contemptuously to say, "Not a dog barked." For me, when I learnt in the jail that the country had remained absolutely non-violent, it was a demonstration that the preaching of non-violence had had its effect and that the Bardoli decision was the wisest thing to do. It would be foolish to speculate what might have happened if 'dogs' had barked and violence had been let loose on my arrest. One thing, however, I can say, that in that event there would have been no Independence Resolution at Lahore, and no Gandhi, with his confidence in the power of non-violence, left to contemplate taking the boldest risks imaginable.

"Let us, however, think of the immediate future. This time, on my arrest, there is to be no mute, passive non-violence, but non-violence of the activest type should be set in motion, so that not a single believer in non-violence as an article of faith for the purpose of achieving India's goal should find himself free or alive at the end of the effort, to submit any longer to the existing slavery. It would be, therefore, the duty of every one to take up such Civil Disobedience or civil resistance as may be advised and conducted by my successor, or as might be taken up by the Congress. I must confess that, at the present moment, I have no all-India successor in view. But I have sufficient faith in the co-workers, and in the mission itself, to know that circumstance will give the successor. This peremptory condition must be patent to all, that he must be an out-and-out believer in the efficacy of non-violence for the purpose intended. For, without that living faith in it, he will not be able at the crucial moment to discover a non-violent method.

"It must be parenthetically understood that what is being said here in no way fetters the discretion and full authority of the Congress. The Congress will adopt only such things said here that may commend themselves to Congressmen in general, if the nature or organic value of the charter of full liberty given to me by the Working Committee should be adequately appreciated. Non-violence, if it does not submit to any restrictions upon its liberty, subjects no one and no institution to any restriction whatsoever, save what may be self-imposed or voluntarily adopted. So long as the vast body of Congressmen continue to believe in non-violence as the only policy in the existing circumstances, and have confidence not only in the *bona fides* of my successor and those who claim to believe in non-violence as an article of faith to the extent indicated but also in the ability of the successor wisely to guide the movement, the Congress will give him and them its blessings and even give effect to these instructions and his.

"So far as I am concerned, my intention is to start the movement only through the inmates of the Ashram and those who have submitted to its discipline and assimilated the spirit of its methods. Those, therefore, who will offer battle at the very commencement will be unknown to fame. Hitherto the Ashram has been deliberately kept in reserve in order that, by a fairly long course of discipline, it might acquire stability. I feel that if the Satyagraha Ashram is to deserve the great confidence that has been reposed in it and the affection lavished upon it by friends, the time has arrived for it to demonstrate the qualities implied in the word Satyagraha. I feel that our self-imposed restraints have become subtle indulgences, and the prestige acquired has provided us with privileges and conveniences of which we may be utterly unworthy. These have been thankfully accepted in the hope that some day we would be able to give a good account of ourselves in terms of Satyagraha. And if at the end of nearly 15 years of its existence, the Ashram cannot give such a demonstration, it and I should disappear, and it would be well for the Nation, the Ashram, and me.

"When the beginning is well and truly made, I expect the response from all over the country. It will be the duty then of every one who wants to make the movement a success to keep it non-violent and under discipline. Every one will be expected to stand at his post except when called by his chief. If there is a spontaneous mass response, as I hope there will be, and if previous experience is any guide, it will largely be self-regulated. But every one who accepts non-violence whether as an article of faith or policy would assist the mass movement. Mass movements have, all over the world, thrown up unexpected leaders. This should be no exception to the rule. Whilst, therefore, every effort imaginable and possible should be made to restrain the forces of violence, Civil Disobedience, once begun this time, cannot be stopped and must not be stopped so long as there is a single civil resister left free or alive.

A votary of Satyagraha should find himself in one of the following states:

1. In prison or in an analogous state, or
2. Engaged in Civil Disobedience, or
3. Under orders at the spinning wheel, or at some constructive work advancing Swaraj.

M. K. Gandhi."

It was about this time that the princely gift of 'Anand Bhawan' was made by Pandit Motilal Nehru.

When Pandit Jawaharlal was speaking with great fervour on Socialism at the All-Parties' Conference at Lucknow in 1920, a certain Thakur of U. P. got up and ejaculated, "What about Anand Bhawan? It is not yet demolished!" No, a work of art like 'Anand Bhawan' cannot be destroyed. It can only change hands and change purposes. Even the Soviets have not destroyed or demolished the Kremlin Palace which was the residence of the Czar. It is now converted into a kind of museum, a sort of educational centre for social culture. Even so, the 'Anand Bhawan' has changed hands, names and purposes. It is to be known hereafter as 'Swaraj Bhawan' and being situated in the holy place of Prayag, stands to the Nation as the centre and symbol of India's Independence. How fast is Indian history making? The palace now presented by Pandit Motilal Nehru to President Jawaharlal Nehru is easily worth several lacs of rupees. Doubtless does it require a few thousands to set it in perfect order, but we have no time for gardens, floral fountains, and various other luxuries. Let the 'Swaraj Bhawan' be the rallying place for the Congressmen. Bless the name alike of the father who is the donor and of the son who is the donee, as the representative of the Nation. Between the donor and the donee, they have completed the title-deeds of the Nation and we congratulate both on their great gift to it.

While the march was progressing, India was in a state of tense expectancy. It is often as difficult to control impatience as it is to dispel inertia. But discipline is the essence of organisation and India showed its discipline at this trying hour. The movement inaugurated by Gandhi was gaining strength in number, in wealth, and in influence. Gandhi having released the idea in the form of a *sutra,* his apostles explained it to the public and the missionaries carried the gospel far and wide. The prophet is one, the apostles are only a few, the missionaries are a legion. Thus did the new cult spread from door to door throughout the country. Only Dr. Besant was describing the combat as a mock-fight. The criticism came with little grace from a leader whose release was secured by planning out Passive Resistance. Much water had flown in the rivers of national life since Passive Resistance was talked of. Passive Resistance gave place to Non-co-operation and Civil Disobedience, and these in turn to Satyagraha. The movement easily rose in its level from the physical to the intellectual, and from the intellectual to the moral plane. Hardly had a week passed since Gandhi began his march when, seemingly unruffled, the Civil Government of the country suddenly lost balance. Vallabhbhai's arrest in the first week of March, even before Gandhi's 'Mahaprasthan' began, was an illegal act and his punishment of 4 months still more illegal. Soon after the march, came the order that the cinema film representing the march of Gandhi armed with a sliver and spindle and wearing a loin cloth should not be exhibited, and the order was repeated in Province after Province,—Bombay, U. P., Punjab, Madras. The Police were virtually relieved of their normal duties. All attention was directed towards the Non-co-operator. It is no wonder that a Government not based on Truth and non-violence would not readily give credit to the votaries of the two eternal principles for sincerity or honestly.

In the midst of all this travail and suffering, we had the satisfaction of witnessing the birth of Purna Swaraj. It required no instrumental aid. It is the product of normal labour. There is a show of pain about it, but all the suffering is of Mother India that reproduces herself in a purer, stronger, and more glorified form. Let no one imagine that we were out to give trouble to Government, other than moral trouble involved in the loss of its prestige, and political trouble involved in the impending loss of its despotic powers. This fight between Government and the people is a clean fight. It is Government that is making it unclean by sending for landed proprietors, house-owners, sowcars and merchants, and threatening them with displeasure if they assist the Satyagrahis. To the extent people yield to these threats, to that extent they become demoralized. But to the extent to which they resist, to that extent they hasten the advent of Swaraj. We know that men with a touch of English education and town life are easily brought under; not so, however, men who are unsophisticated and patriotic. It is real pleasure to notice that the villages abound in patriots; and not merely in patriotism but also in leadership. When once leadership has been taken possession of in the villages, the success of the movement now in progress is assured.

Every age and every clime has its miracles and India was to produce its own. It was to witness this miracle of the twentieth century in their own Motherland that thousands of people gathered round the banner of Gandhi at the Sabarmati Ashram on the 6th March, 1930, and accompanied him as far as their legs could carry their bodies, or their enthusiasm could sustain their energies. Amongst those that accompanied Gandhi and his pilgrim-fighters were newspaper correspondents from various parts of India and from abroad, photographers, cinemamen, and of course the vast concourse of village people from round about, with batches of leading men from different Provinces. Gandhi had all along said that Gujarat would bear the brunt of the fight for Indian emancipation, and if Gujarat did it and was allowed to do it, the rest of India need not pass through the agonies and anguish inevitable in the struggle. People who know Gandhi know how fast he walks. Here is a description by a correspondent who was with the party:—

> "Early on the morning of the 12th March, Gandhi left the Ashram on a campaign of Civil Disobedience, with his 75 volunteers picked and chosen, for Dandi, a sea-side village 200 miles distant, for the manufacture of salt."

In the words of *The Bombay Chronicle*, "The scenes that preceded, accompanied and followed this great national event, were so enthusiastic, magnificent and soul-stirring that indeed they beggar description. Never was the wave of patriotism so powerful in the hearts of mankind, as it was on this great occasion which is bound to go down to the chapters of the history of India's national freedom as a great beginning of a great movement."

He was carrying a long stick in hand, obviously for support. The whole army was marching in a perfectly disciplined manner. The agile General in front was indeed a source of inspiration to all. The army passed all along the distance of ten miles up to Aslali between the densely packed rows of people who were standing in their places for hours together, eager for the 'darshan' of

India's great General. Ahmedabad had had on the occasion one of its hugest processions during living memory. With the possible exceptions of children and decrepits, every resident of the city must have watched the great procession which was at least two miles in length. Those who could not find a standing place in the streets through which the army marched had made use of house tops and galleries, open walls and trees and every conceivable place they could get hold of. The whole city seemed to be *en fete* on this historic occasion. The cries of 'Gandhi-ki-jai' were rending the skies all along the march.

Crowds gathered everywhere to witness the march and pay homage to the great deliverer. A new salvation was in sight; but it was the old gospel that was preached. Khaddar, abstinence from drink, and removal of untouchability were the three favourite themes, but the new demand was that all should join the Satyagrahis. In the march he declared that he would either die on the way or else keep away from the Ashram until Swaraj was won, and that he "had no intention of returning to the Ashram until he succeeded in getting the Salt Tax abolished. Spinning and sanitation of the villages were emphasised by him. Volunteers came in their hundreds joining the campaign. The arrest of Gandhi was imminent. His place should be taken up by Abbas Tyabji. P. C. Ray said, "Mahatma Gandhi's historic march was like the exodus of the Israelites under Moses. Until the Seer seized the promised land, he won't turn his back."

Gandhi said: "The British rule in India has brought about moral, material, cultural and spiritual ruination of this great country. I regard this rule as a curse. I am out to destroy this system of Government. I have sung the tune of 'God Save the King' and have taught others to sing it. I was a believer in the politics of petitions, deputations, and friendly negotiations. But all these have gone to dogs. I know that these are not the ways to bring this Government round. Sedition has become my religion. Ours is a non-violent battle. We are not out to kill any body but it is our *dharma* to see that the curse of this Government is blotted out."

Speaking at a place called Jambusar, Gandhi denounced the enforcement of social boycott against sub-inspectors of Police. It was not religion to starve Government officials, said Gandhi, and he would suck the poison out of a dying enemy of his if he was bitten by a snake, in order to save his life.

As already stated, the All-India Congress Committee met at Ahmedabad on the 21st March, 1930, and endorsed the resolution about Salt Satyagraha passed by the Working Committee on the 14th of February. The All-India Congress Committee resolution ran as follows:—

"This meeting of the A.I.C.C. approves of and endorses the resolution of the Working Committee dated February 16th, authorising Mahatma Gandhi to initiate and control Civil Disobedience, and congratulates him and his companions and the country on the march begun by him on the 12th instant in pursuit of his plan for Civil Disobedience. The Committee hopes that the whole country will respond to the action taken by Gandhiji so as to bring the campaign for Purna Swaraj to a speedy and successful issue.

"The A.I.C.C. hereby authorises the Provincial Congress Committees, subject to any directions that the Working Committee might issue from time to time, to organise and undertake such Civil Disobedience as to them may seem proper and in the

> manner that may appear to them to be most suitable. The Committee, however, hopes that the Provinces, so far as is possible, will concentrate on a civil breach of the Salt Laws. The Committee trusts that while full preparation will be carried on in spite of any Government interference, Civil Disobedience will not be started till Gandhiji has reached his destination and has actually committed a breach of the Salt Laws and given the word. In the event, however, of Gandhiji's earlier arrest, the Provinces shall have full liberty to start Civil Disobedience."

Gandhiji's march lasted 24 days, and all along he was emphasising how the march was a pilgrimage the merit of which lay in keeping the body and soul together and not in feting and feasting. He was constantly turning the torch inward. At Surat he said:—

> "Only this morning at prayer time, I was telling my companions that as we had entered the district in which we were to offer Civil Disobedience, we should insist on greater purification and intenser dedication, and warned them that as the district was more organised and contained many intimate co-workers, there was every likelihood of our being pampered. I warned them against succumbing to their pampering. We are not Angels. We are very weak, easily tempted. There are many lapses to our debit. Even to-day, some were discovered. One defaulter confessed his lapse himself whilst I was brooding over the lapse of the pilgrims. I discovered that my warning was given none too soon. The local workers had ordered milk from Surat to be brought in a motor lorry, and they had incurred other expenses which they could not justify. I, therefore, spoke strongly about them. But that did not allay my grief. On the contrary it increases with the contemplation of the wrong done.
>
> "In the light of these discoveries, what right had I to write to the Viceroy the letter in which I have severely criticised his salary which is more than 5,000 times our average income? How could he possibly

do justice to that salary? And how can we tolerate his getting a salary out of all proportion to our income? But he is individually not to be blamed for it. He has no need for it. God has made him a wealthy man. I have suggested in my letter that probably the whole of his salary is spent in charity. I have since learnt that my guess is largely likely to be true. Even so, of course, I should resist the giving of such a large salary. I could not vote Rs. 21,000 per month, not perhaps even Rs. 2,100 per month. But when could I offer such resistance? Certainly not, if I was myself taking from the people an unconscionable toll.

"I could resist only if my living bore some correspondence with the average income of the people. We are marching in the name of God. We profess to act on behalf of the hungry, the naked, and the unemployed. I have no right to criticise the Viceregal salary, if we are costing the country, say fifty times seven pice, the average daily income of our people. I have asked the workers to furnish me with an account of the expenses and the way things are going. I should not be surprised if each of us is costing something near fifty times seven pice. What else can be the result if they will fetch for me, from whatever source possible, the choicest oranges and grapes, if they will bring 120 when I should want 12 oranges, if, when I need one pound of milk, they will produce three? What else can be the result if we would take all the dainties you may place before us under the excuse that we would hurt your feelings, if we did not take them? You give us guavas and grapes and we eat them because they are free gift from a princely farmer. And then imagine me with an easy conscience writing the Viceregal letter on costly glazed paper with a fountain pen, a free gift from some accommodating friend. Will this behove you and me? Can a letter so written produce the slightest effect?

"To live thus would be to illustrate the immortal verse of Akhobhagat who says, 'stolen food is like eating unprocessed mercury,' and to live above the means befitting a poor country is to live on stolen food. This battle can never be won by living on stolen food. Nor did I bargain to set out on this march for living above our means. We expect thousands of volunteers to respond to the call.

"It will be impossible to keep them on extravagant terms. My life has become so busy that I get little time to come in close touch even with the eighty companions so as to be able to identify them individually. There was, therefore, no course open to me but to unburden my soul in public. I expect you to understand the central point of my message. If you have not, there is no hope of Swaraj through the present effort. We must become real trustees of the dumb millions."

Needless to say the speech produced a tremendous impression on the audience and 200 Patels had already resigned. Addressing the Parsees at Navasari, Gandhi appealed to them to give up drink and the liquor trade: "If they are successful in doing away with the Salt Tax and the liquor traffic from India, there is the victory for *ahimsa*. And what power on earth is there then, that would prevent Indians from getting Swaraj? If there be any such power, I shall like to see it. Either I shall return with what I want, or else my dead body will float in the Ocean."

Gandhi reached Dandi on the morning of the 5th April. Shrimati Sarojini Devi had also gone there to see him. In an interview to the Associated Press at Dandi, Gandhi said:—

"God be thanked for what may be termed the happy ending of the first stage in this, for me at least, the final struggle for freedom. I cannot withhold my compliments from the Government for the policy of complete non-interference adopted by them throughout the march. After the graceless and childish performance in the matter of Mr. Vallabhbhai's arrest and imprisonment and equally unprovoked arrest and imprisonment of Mr. Sen-Gupta, I was wholly unprepared for this exemplary non-interference. I am not so foolish as to imagine that the Government has suddenly lost their proved capacity for provoking popular resentment and then punishing with frightfulness. I wish I could believe this non-interference was due to any real change of heart or policy. The wanton disregard shown by them to popular feeling in the Legislative Assembly and their high-handed action leave no room for doubt that the policy of heartless exploitation of India is to be persisted in at any cost, and so the only interpretation I can put upon this non-interference is that the British Government, powerful though it is, is sensitive to world opinion which will not tolerate repression of extreme political agitation which Civil Disobedience undoubtedly is, so long as disobedience remains civil and, therefore, necessarily non-violent.

"It remains to be seen whether the Government will tolerate, as they have tolerated the march, the actual breach of the Salt Laws by countless people from to-morrow. I expect extensive popular response to the resolution of the W.C. I have seen nothing to warrant the cancellation of the notice I have already issued that all committees and organisations throughout the length and breadth of the land are free, if they are prepared, to commence from to-morrow Civil Disobedience in respect of the Salt Laws. God willing, I expect with my companions (volunteers) to commence actual Civil Disobedience at 6-30 to-morrow morning. The 6th April has been to us, since its culmination in Jallianwala massacre, a day for penance and purification. We, therefore, commence it with prayer and fasting. I hope the whole of India will observe the National Week commencing from to-morrow in the spirit in which it was conceived. I am positive that the greater the dedication to the country's cause and the greater the purification, the speedier will be the glorious end for which the millions of India consciously or unconsciously are striving."

Soon after the morning prayers, Gandhi and his volunteers proceeded to break the Salt Law by picking up the salt lying on the sea-shore. Immediately after breaking the Salt Law, Gandhi issued the following Press statement:—

"Now that the technical or ceremonial breach of the Salt Law has been committed, it is now open to any one who would take the risk of prosecution under the Salt Law to manufacture salt wherever he wishes, and wherever it is convenient. My advice is that workers should everywhere manufacture salt, and where they know how to prepare clean salt, make use of it and instruct the villagers likewise, telling the villagers at the same time that they run the risk of being prosecuted. In other words, the villagers should be fully instructed as to the incidence of the Salt Tax, and the manner of breaking the laws and regulations connected with it so as to have the Salt Tax repealed.

"It should be made absolutely clear to the villagers that the breach is open. and in no way stealthy. This salt being manufactured by Nature in creeks and pits near sea-shore, let them use it for themselves and their cattle, and sell it to those who will buy it, it being well understood that all such people are committing a breach of the Salt Law and running the same risk of a prosecution. or even without a prosecution are to be subject by so-called salt officers to harassment.

"This war against the Salt Tax should be continued during the National Week, that is, up to the 13th April. Those who are not engaged in this sacred work should themselves do vigorous propaganda for the boycott of foreign cloth and the use of khaddar. They should also endeavour to manufacture as much khaddar as possible. As to this and the prohibition of liquor, I am preparing a message for the women of India who. I am becoming more and more convinced, can make a larger contribution than men towards the attainment of Independence. I feel that they will be worthier interpreters of non-violence than men, not because they are weak, as men, in their arrogance, believe them to be, but because they have greater courage of the right type, and immeasurably greater spirit of self-sacrifice."

In a statement, Gandhi said:—

"From information available up to now, I gather that the striking manifestation of Mass Civil Disobedience in Gujarat has had its effect on the Government, who have lost no time in arresting the chief men. But I know that similar attention must have been bestowed by the Government on the workers in the other Provinces. This is a matter for congratulation.

"It would have been surprising if the Government had allowed civil resisters to have their own way. It would have been barbarous if they had violated the persons and property of civil resisters without judicial process.

"No exception can be taken to orderly prosecutions and penalties thereunder. After all, this is the logical outcome of civil resistance.

"Imprisonment and the like is the test through which the civil resister has to pass. He gains his end when he himself is found not to flinch, and those whom he represents do not betray any nervousness when the leader is put away. Now is the time for every one to be both chief and follower.

"It would pain me if even after these imprisonments students who are in Government or Government-controlled schools and colleges do not respond by giving up their schools and colleges."

When one of the volunteers was slightly injured by the Police on the wrist, Gandhi wrote:—

"This laying hand on the people for the purpose of seizing the salt they were carrying was morally wrong, and even wrong, I fancy, according to the English Common Law. But I do not know what powers are given by the Statute. The legal procedure may be a cumbersome business for the Government, but since they have begun well, let them not end ill. If they resort to terrorism, they will find the people prepared. Let the people defend the salt in their possession till they break in the attempt, but they should do so without an angry word. The Police have the easiest way open to them for taking possession of the salt. Let them arrest the civil resisters and they can take possession of the salt, because they have possession of their persons; but it can become forfeit only after conviction, not before."

Regarding women, Gandhi said at Navasari:—

"Women ought not to take part alongside of men in defence of salt pans. I still give credit to the Government that it will not make war upon our women. It will be wrong on our part to provoke them into so doing. This is men's fight, so long as the Government will confine their attention to men. There will be time enough for women to court assaults when the Government has crossed the limit. Let it not be said of us that men sought shelter behind women, well knowing they will be safe if they took women with them in what may be called, for want of a better name, aggressive non-violence. Women have, in the progamme I ventured to place before them, enough work and to spare, and all adventure and risk they may be capable of undertaking."

The country was ablaze from end to end, being permitted to start Salt Satyagraha as from the 6th April. Huge public meetings were held in all big cities, the audience running up to six figures. The events at Karachi, Shiroda, Ratnagiri, Patna, Peshawar, Calcutta, Madras and Sholapur, constituted a new experience and bore witness to the violence that lay behind this civilized Government. In Peshawar, the military firing resulted in many deaths. In Madras there was firing too.

Referring to the Karachi tragedy Gandhi wrote:—

> "Brave young Dattatraya who is said to have known nothing of Satyagraha and, being an athlete, had merely gone to assist in keeping order, received a fatal bullet wound. Meghraj Revachand, 18 years old, has also succumbed to a bullet wound. Thus did seven men, including Jairamdas, receive bullet wounds."

Writing under the title 'Black Regime,' Gandhi reviewed the events and said: "If Government neither arrest nor declare salt free, they will find people marching to be shot rather than be tortured."[1]

The Bengal Ordinance was renewed on April 23rd, and the Viceroy promulgated on the 27th April another Ordinance reviving the powers of the Press Act of 1910, with certain amendments.

Gandhi's *Young India* began to be issued in cyclostyle. Gandhi in a Press Statement declared:—

> "Revival, in the form of an Ordinance, of the Press Act that was supposed to be dead was only to be expected, and, in its new form, the Act contains

---

[1] The reference was to a firing which had taken place at an early stage in Karachi, where the movement was quite strong. Mr. Jairamdas Daulatram, the leader of Sindh, had resigned his membership of the Bombay Legislative Council, and was a member of the original Working Committee of the year. He was striving his best to maintain order among the crowds who gathered at the Magistrate's court during a trial of certain C. D. prisoners, and was shot in the thigh along with others by the Police. Mr. Jairamdas was only wounded and soon recovered, and continues to be a member of the Working Committee.

additional provisions making the whole piece deadlier than before.

"Whether we realise it or not, for some days past, we have been living under a veiled form of Martial Law. After all, what is Martial Law, if it is not the will of the commanding officer? For the time being, the Viceroy is that officer and wherever he considers it desirable, he supersedes the whole of the Law; both Common and Statute, and imposes Ordinances on a people too submissive to resent or resist them. I hope, however, the time for tame submission to dictation from the British rulers is gone for ever.

"I hope that the people will not be frightened by this Ordinance. Press-men, if they are worthy representatives of public opinion, will not be frightened by the Ordinance. Let us realise the wise dictum of Thoreau that it is difficult, under tyrannical rule, for honest men to be wealthy, and if we have decided to hand over our bodies without murmur to the authorities, let us also be equally ready to hand over our property to them and not sell our souls.

"I would, therefore, urge Press-men and publishers to refuse to furnish security, and if they are called upon to do so, either to cease publication or challenge the authorities to confiscate whatever they like. When freedom is actually knocking at our doors, and when, for the sake of wooing it, thousands have suffered tortures, let it not be said of Press representatives that they were weighed and found wanting. They may confiscate the type and machinery. They will not confiscate the pen and still less the speech, but I recognise they can succeed in stifling, what is after all the thing that matters, the thought of the Nation."

Gandhi subsequently asked the manager of his Navajivan Press to allow it to be forfeited rather than deposit security, if security was demanded by the Government under the Press Ordinance. The Navjivan fell, and with it the journals issued by that Press

Most journalists in the country paid the securities demanded of them.

It was at this time that Gandhi asked people to cut off all the palm trees in the village, himself inaugurating the ceremony of destruction. Addressing a meeting of women in Surat on May 4, he said that they should not attend his meetings in future without their *taklis*. They could spin the finest counts on the *taklis*. Women of Surat had to atone for the admission of foreign cloth through the port of Surat. At the same place, he called upon the caste Panchayats to observe their pledge to abstain from drink. At Navasari, however, he warned the people against the social boycott of Government officials. Kaira District became the theatre of war in Gujarat and Gandhi, in an article in *Navajivan*, wrote:—

> "People have preserved peace but there are anger and malice and, therefore, violence in their intensive social boycott. They censure and harass Government officers in small matters. They will not succeed in this manner. We should expose the evils of the offices of Mamlatdar and Fozdars. There should be sweetness and respect in our intense boycott. Otherwise there will be riots some day. Mamlatdar and Fozdar etc., will cross the limit. Fozdar is already said to have crossed the limit. What wonder if the people crossed the limit? Similarly if some abuse, how can they blame those who resort to blows?
>
> "People of Kaira District should take a warning and enforce boycott within limits. I have indicated, for instance, boycott of village officers should be with regard to their office only. Their order should not be obeyed but their food supplies should not be stopped. They should not be ejected from their houses. If we are not capable of doing this we should give up the boycott."

Gandhi then drafted his second letter to the Viceroy and had also announced his intention of raiding the salt works of Dharsana and Chharsada. Then came the time for the arrest of Gandhi, and it was not until Gandhi was actually removed to Yeravada on the morning of the 5th, that it was known that his arrest had taken place.

The depot selected for the first attack was situated at Dharsana in the Surat District. It was argued that the natural salt, like air and water, was the property of the public. Government had no right to create a monopoly of it against the interests of the people who had every right to the so-called Government Stores. If the Government wanted the people to keep back from these stores, it could do so only at the point of the bayonet. Accordingly, Gandhi decided to seize, rather demand and take possession of the Dharsana Depot, and as usual wrote the following letter to the Viceroy:—

"Dear Friend,

God willing, it is my intention to set out for Dharsana and reach there with my companions and demand possession of the Salt Works. The public have been told that Dharsana is private property. This is mere camouflage. It is as effectively under Government control as the Viceroy's House. Not a pinch of salt can be removed without the previous sanction of the authorities.

"It is possible for you to prevent this raid, as it has been playfully and mischievously called, in three ways:

1. by removing the Salt Tax;

2. by arresting me and my party, unless the country can, as I hope it will, replace every one taken away;

3. by sheer goondaism, unless every head broken is replaced, as I hope it will.

"It is not without hesitation that the step has been decided upon. I had hoped that the Government would fight the civil resisters in a civilised manner. I could have had nothing to say if, in dealing with the civil resisters, the Government had satisfied itself with applying the ordinary processes of law. Instead, whilst the known leaders have been dealt with more or less according to the legal formality, the rank and file have been often savagely, and in some cases even indecently, assaulted. Had these been isolated cases, they might have been overlooked. But accounts have come to me from Bengal, Bihar, Utkal, U.P., Delhi, and Bombay, confirming the experiences of Gujarat of which I have ample evidence at my disposal. In Karachi, Peshawar, and Madras, the firing would appear to have been unprovoked and unnecessary. Bones have been broken, private parts have been squeezed for the purpose of making volunteers give up, to the Government valueless, to the volunteers precious, salt. At Mathura an Assistant Magistrate is said to have snatched the national flag from a ten year old boy. The crowd that demanded restoration of the flag thus illegally seized, is reported to have been mercilessly beaten back. That the flag was subsequently restored betrayed a guilty conscience. In Bengal there seem to have been only a few prosecutions and assaults about salt, but unthinkable cruelties are said to have been practised in the act of snatching flags from volunteers. Paddy fields are reported to have been burnt, eatables forcibly taken. A vegetable market in Gujarat has been raided because the dealers would not sell vegetables to officials. These acts have taken place in front of crowds who, for the sake of the Congress mandate, have submitted without retaliation. I ask you to believe the accounts given by men pledged to truth. Repudiation even by high officials has, as in the Bardoli case, often proved false. The officials, I regret to have to say, have not hesitated to publish falsehood to the people even during the last five weeks. I take the following samples from Government notices issued from Collectors' offices in Gujarat:

1. 'Adults use five pounds of salt per year, therefore, pay three annas per head as tax. If Government removed the monopoly, people will have to pay higher prices and, in addition, make good to the Government the loss sustained by the removal of

the monopoly. The salt you take from the sea-shore is not eatable, therefore the Government destroys it.'

2. 'Mr. Gandhi says that Government has destroyed hand-spinning in this country, whereas everybody knows that this is not true, because throughout the country, there is not a village where hand-spinning of cotton is not going on. Moreover, in every Province cotton spinners are shown superior methods and are provided with better instruments at less price and are thus helped by Government.'

3. 'Out of every five rupees of the debt that the Government has incurred, rupees four have been beneficially spent.'

"I have taken these three sets of statements from three different leaflets. I venture to suggest that every one of these statements is demonstrably false. The daily consumption of salt by an adult is three times the amount stated and, therefore, the poll tax that the Salt Tax undoubtedly is, is at least 9 as. per head per year. And this tax is levied from man, woman, child and domestic cattle, irrespective of age and health.

"It is a wicked falsehood to say that every village has a spinning wheel, and that the spinning movement is in any shape or form encouraged or supported by the Government. Financiers can better dispose of the falsehood that four out of every five rupees of the public debt is used for the benefit of the public. But these falsehoods are mere samples of what people know is going on in everyday contact with the Government. Only the other day a Gujarati poet, a brave man, was convicted on perjured official evidence, in spite of his emphatic statement that at the time mentioned he was sleeping soundly in another place.

"Now for instances of official inactivities. Liquor dealers have assaulted pickets admitted by officials to have been peaceful, and sold liquor in contravention of regulations. The officials have taken no notice either of the assaults or the illegal sales of liquor. As to the assaults, though they are known.

to everybody, they may take shelter under the plea that they have received no complaints.

"And now you have sprung upon the country a Press Ordinance surpassing any hitherto known in India. You have found a short cut through the Law's delay in the matter of the trial of Bhagat Singh and others by doing away with the ordinary procedure. Is it any wonder if I call all these official activities and inactivities a veiled form of Martial Law? Yet this is only the fifth week of the struggle.

"Before then the reign of terrorism that has just begun overwhelms India, I feel that I must take a bolder step, and if possible divert your wrath in a cleaner, if more drastic, channel. You may not know the things that I have described. You may not even now believe in them. I can but invite your serious attention to them.

"Anyway I feel that it would be cowardly on my part not to invite you to disclose to the full the leonine paws of authority, so that the people who are suffering tortures and destructions of their property inspiring them to action that has brought to light the Government in its true colours, had not left any stone unturned to work out the Satyagraha programme as fully as it was possible under given circumstances.

"For according to the science of Satyagraha, the greater the repression and lawlessness on the part of authority, the greater should be the suffering courted by the victims. Success is the certain result of suffering of the extremest character, voluntarily undergone.

"I know the danger attendant upon the methods adopted by me. But the country is not likely to mistake my meaning. I say what I mean and think. And I have been saying for the last fifteen years in India, and outside for twenty years more, and repeat now that the only way to conquer violence is through non-violence, pure and undefiled. I have said also that every violent act, word, and even thought, interferes with the progress of non-violent action. If, in spite of such repeated warnings people will resort to violence, I must disown responsibility save such as inevitably attaches to every human being for the acts of every other human being. But the question of responsibility apart, I dare not postpone action on any cause whatsoever, if non-violence is the force the seers of the world have claimed it to be, and if I am not to belie my own extensive experience of its working.

"But I would fain avoid the further step. I would, therefore, ask you to remove the tax which many of your illustrious countrymen have condemned in unmeasured terms and which, as you could not have failed to observe, has evoked universal protest and resentment expressed in Civil Disobedience. You may condemn Civil Disobedience as much as you like. Will you prefer violent revolt to Civil Disobedience? If you say, as you have said, that the Civil Disobedience must end in violence, history will pronounce the verdict that the British Government, not heeding because not understanding non-violence, goaded human nature to violence which it could understand, and deal with. But in spite of the goading, I shall hope that God will give the people of India wisdom and strength to withstand every temptation and provocation to violence.

"If, therefore, you cannot see your way to remove the Salt Tax, and remove the prohibition on private salt-making, I must reluctantly commence the march adumbrated in the opening paragraph of my letter.

I am,
Your sincere friend,
M. K. Gandhi."

It was ten minutes past one in the night when Gandhi was placed in a motor lorry accompanied by policemen. He was then taken to Borivli near Bombay by train and thence by motor car to Yeravada prison. Ashmead-Bartlett of the *London Telegraph* wrote:—

"There was something intensely dramatic in the atmosphere while we were waiting for the train, for we all felt we were sole eye-witnesses of a scene which may become historical,—this arrest of a prophet, false or true, for, false or true, Gandhi is now regarded as a holy man and saint by millions of Indians. Who knows whether, one hundred years from now, he may be worshipped as a supreme being by 300 million people. We could not shake off these thoughts, and it seemed incongruous to be at a level-crossing at dawn to take the prophet into custody."

Before the arrest, however, Gandhi had dictated at Dandi his last message which we give below:—

"If such an auspicious beginning is carried to its full conclusion, complete Swaraj is a certainty, and India will have set to the whole world an example worthy of her. Swaraj obtained without sacrifice, never endures. People have, therefore, to make endless sacrifice. In real sacrifice there is only one-sided suffering, that is, without killing others one has to die. May India accomplish this ideal. At present the self-respect and everything of India are concealed in a handful of salt. The fist may be broken, but it should never be opened.

"After I am arrested, neither the people nor my colleagues should be daunted. The conductor of this fight is God and not I. He dwells in the heart of all. If we have faith in us, God will certainly lead us. Our path is fixed. Whole villages should come forward to pick or manufacture salt. Women should picket liquor and opium shops and foreign cloth shops. In every house young and old should begin spinning on *takli* and heaps of yarn should be daily woven. There should be bonfires of foreign cloth. Hindus should regard none as untouchables. Hindus, Muslims, Parsees and Christians, all should heartily embrace one another. The major communities should be satisfied with what remains after satisfaction of minor communities. Students should leave Government schools, and Government servants should resign and be employed in the service of the people, like the brave Patels and Talatis who have resigned. Thus shall we easily complete Swaraj."

Sarojini Devi in a statement to the Press on Mahatma Gandhi's arrest said:—

> "A powerful Government could have paid no more splendid tribute to the far-reaching power of Gandhi than by the manner of his arrest and incarceration without trial, under the most arbitrary law on their Statute Book. It is really immaterial that the fragile and ailing body of the Mahatma is imprisoned behind stone walls and steel bars. It is the least essential part of it. The man and his message are identical, and his message is the living heritage of the Nation to-day and will continue to influence the thought and action of the world, unfettered and unchallenged by the mandate of the most autocratic Government of the earth."

Gandhi's arrest was followed by spontaneous demonstrations of sympathy from one end of the country to the other. It was the signal for a voluntary and complete *hartal* in Bombay, Calcutta and several other places. The day after the arrest the *hartal* was even more widespread. In Bombay, a huge procession was taken out, and a public meeting in the evening had to be addressed from several different platforms. About 40 out of the 80 mills had to be inactive, because over 50,000 men had come out in protest. The workmen of the G. I. P. and the B. B. and C. I. Workshops also came out and joined the *hartal*. The cloth merchants decided on a six days' *hartal* to indicate their disapproval of the arrest. In Poona, where Gandhiji was interned, the *hartal* was complete. Resignations from honorary offices and from the services were announced at frequent intervals. Troubles were brewing at one or two places, though on the whole the country had imbibed Gandhi's teachings rather astonishingly. The disturbances in Sholapur resulting in the burning of six Police Chaukis led to Police firing in which 25 were killed and about a hundred wounded. In Calcutta though the *hartal* was peaceful in the city, there were disturbances at Howrah where the Police opened fire at Panchanantala to disperse a crowd. Under Section 144, all assemblies of more than five were prohibited.

But Gandhi's arrest had a world-wide interest. Indians engaged in business in Panama called a 24-hour sympathetic *hartal.* A similar step was taken by Indians on the east coast of Sumatra, who wired to the Viceroy and the Congress regretting Gandhi's arrest. French papers were full of Gandhi and his doings. The boycott movement had a repercussion in Germany also, where textile exporters were advised by their agents in India to suspend exports. Reuter reported that Saxon manufacturers of cheap printed cotton goods were particularly hard-hit. The Indian community of Nairobi declared a *hartal* in consequence of the arrest.

Meanwhile, an influentially signed message was cabled to Mr. Ramsay MacDonald by 102 American clergymen of various denominations, urging him to seek an amicable settlement with Mr. Gandhi and the Indian people. Signatures were collected by Dr. John Haynes Holmes, New York, and the message appealed to the Prime-Minister in the interests of Britain, India, and the world to avoid the tragedy of a conflict which would mean catastrophe for all mankind.

The signatories refused to believe that Mr. MacDonald, representing the principles of freedom, democracy and brotherhood, could find it impossible to negotiate with Mr. Gandhi and make peace with the spiritual ideals he so sublimely embodies.

The Government of India was no doubt keenly alive to the seriousness of the situation. H. E. the Viceroy interviewed the Liberal leaders, Sir Tej Bahadur Sapru and Sir Chimanlal Setalvad, at great length. The Council of the Liberal Federation met at Bombay to consider the political situation, and leading Liberals gave expression to the urgent need for another announcement from the Viceroy fixing the early date of the Round Table Conference. But the day before the meeting of the All-Parties' Conference and the Council of the Liberal Federation, H. E. made another important announcement and released for publication his correspondence with the Prime-Minister. The Council of the Federation also issued a statement on the situation. The Council, while unequivocally condemning the Civil Disobedience movement, urged the Viceroy to speed up the preparations for the Round Table Conference for the discussion of Dominion Status. It stressed the importance of the Government indicating the terms of reference and the scope of the R.T.C., "in order that even at this stage those who keep aloof may join hands with the Liberals and other Parties who are proceeding to the Conference."

It further laid stress on the simultaneous cessation of Civil Disobedience and the initiation of active conciliation on the part of the Government, to be manifested by "the release of those whose freedom has been restrained for political reasons, and the taking of all political Parties into Government's full confidence."

Mr. Abbas Tyabji who took up Gandhi's place as leader of the Salt Satyagrahis was arrested on the 12th April. Arrests, *lathi*-charges and repression went on as usual. Batches of volunteers raided the salt depot and used to be beaten with *lathis* by the Police and many of them suffered severe injuries.

After Gandhi's arrest, the Working Committee met in May at Allahabad and expanded the scope of Civil Disobedience and passed resolutions which we give below:—

"1. The Working Committee congratulates the Satyagrahi volunteers who accompanied Mahatma Gandhi at Karadi and trusts that fresh batches would take up raids, and decides that Dharsana should henceforth be treated as an all-India centre for salt raids.

"2. The Working Committee records its appreciation of the lead given by Gandhiji for the conduct of the great campaign, reiterates its abiding faith in Civil Disobedience and resolves to carry on the struggle during the incarceration of Mahatmaji with redoubled vigour.

"3. In the opinion of the Committee the moment has arrived when the entire Nation should make a supreme effort to achieve the goal, and it calls upon students, lawyers, and other professional men, workers and peasants, merchants, industrialists and Government servants and all others to contribute to the success of the fight for freedom, making all sacrifices they are capable of.

"4. The Committee holds that in the interests of the country it is essential to carry out a complete boycott of foreign cloth throughout the country without delay, and for that purpose to take effective steps to prevent sales of existing stock, to secure the cancellation of orders already placed and to prevent the placing of future orders. The Committee calls upon all Congress bodies to carry on an intensive propaganda of the boycott of foreign cloth and to picket shops dealing in foreign cloth.

"5. The Committee while appreciating the efforts of Pandit Madan Mohan Malaviya to help the boycott movement, regrets that it cannot endorse any agreement or understanding that the sale of the existing stock is to be permitted in return for the promises by the dealers, not to import or order foreign cloth for a specified period. The Committee directs all Congress organisations to be no party to any such or similar agreements or understandings with the dealers and importers of foreign cloth.

"6. The Committee decides to promote the increase of the production of hand-spun and hand-woven cloth, in order to meet the growing demand and to set up organisations to introduce the system of exchanging khaddar cloth for hand-spun yarn in addition to selling it for money, and calls upon Congress organisations generally to encourage hand-spinning. The Committee appeals to every individual to devote some part of his or her time to spinning.

"7. The Committee is of opinion that the time has arrived for the inauguration of No-tax campaign by non-payment of special taxes in certain Provinces, and that a beginning should be made by non-payment of the land tax in the Provinces where the ryotwari system prevails, such as Gujarat, Maharashtra, Karnatak, Andhra, Tamil Nadu and the Punjab, and the non-payment of the Chowkidari tax in Provinces like Bengal, Bihar and Orissa. It calls upon such Provinces to organise campaigns of non-payment of the land tax or Chowkidari tax in areas selected by the Provincial Congress Committees.

"8. It calls upon the Provincial Congress Committees to continue and extend the manufacture of contraband salt and directs that technical breaches of the Salt Law shall be continued with redoubled energy at places where it is sought to be prevented by the Government by arrests or otherwise. The Committee resolves that as a mark of the country's disapproval of the Salt Law, Congress organisations should organise public breaches of those laws on every Sunday.

"9. The Committee approves and confirms the action of the Acting President in permitting the breach of Forest Laws in the C.P. and resolves that in other Provinces similar laws in force may be breached after the sanction of the Provincial Congress Committees.

"10. The Committee authorises the Acting President to enter into negotiations with Indian mill-owners with a view to devising means to prevent an unfair increase in the prices of Swadeshi mill cloth and the manufacture of spurious khaddar, and generally to take steps to promote the boycott of foreign cloth.

"11. Regarding the boycott of British goods, it urges the people to make earnest attempts to bring about an effective boycott thereof at an early date.

"12. The Committee further appeals strongly to the public to boycott all British banking, insurance, shipping and similar other institutions.

"13. The Committee once again emphasises the necessity of carrying on an intensive propaganda in favour of total prohibition and calls upon the Provincial Congress Committee to picket liquor or toddy shops.

"14. The Committee regrets the outbreak of mob-violence in certain places and cannot too strongly condemn such violence. The Committee desires to emphasise the necessity of a strict observance of non-violence.

"15. The Committee strongly condemns the Press Ordinance and appreciates the action of those newspapers which have refused to submit to it. It calls upon Indian newspapers which have not yet ceased publication, or having ceased publication have re-appeared, to stop further issues. The Committee calls upon the people to boycott all Anglo-Indian and Indian papers which continue publication hereafter."

Shrimati Sarojini Devi had proceeded to Allahabad to attend the W. C. meeting. On hearing of Mr. Tyabji's arrest she hurried to Dharsana, in fulfilment of her promise to Gandhi, and continued to direct the raid. She and her batch of volunteers were formally arrested on 16th morning, taken out of the Police cordon and then released. Batches of volunteers rushed later towards the salt depot. They were beaten and chased out. The same evening over 220 volunteers were arrested by the Police on a charge of being members of an unlawful assembly and were detained in the segregation camp at Dharsana.

Later, a large number of volunteers congregated on the Wadala Salt Works (19th morning). The 'raid' was frustrated by the prompt action of the Police, who, armed with revolvers, arrested over 400 of the Satyagrahis.

The Free Press Correspondent, writing of the effect of the boycott movement, observed:—

> "Since the attack seems to be concentrated on the textile goods, it is here that the effectiveness of the movement is most visibly felt. But what worries manufacturers is not so much the feeling that they would ultimately lose the Indian market as the fear that the existing contracts would either not be fulfilled or would be cancelled. The tendency to cancel the present orders seems to be on the increase, and the Manchester correspondent of *The Daily Mail* says, 'The latest news from India is likely to bring Lancashire's Indian trade to a complete standstill. Already spinning mills and weaving sheds are closing down indefinitely and thousands of operatives are joining the ranks of the unemployed.' "

More salt raids took place and we take the following account from *Gandhi—the Man and his Mission* p. 133 onwards:—

> "Meanwhile successive meetings of the Working Committee decided to continue the programme and the raids were to go on. A mass raid at Dharsana took place on the 21st of May, when 2,500 volunteers from all parts of Gujarat took part in it. They were led by Imam Saheb, the 62 year old colleague of Gandhiji in South Africa. The volunteers commenced the raid early in the morning and as they attacked the salt heaps at different places the Police charged

them with *lathis* (bamboo sticks) and beat them back.

"Thousands witnessed the spectacle. After this had gone on for two hours, the leaders, Messrs. Imam Saheb, Pyarelal and Manilal Gandhi were arrested, and later Mrs. Sarojini Naidu also. The total number of injured volunteers on that day was 290. One injured volunteer, Mr. Bhailalbhai Dajabhai, died, as also Babu Hule from Maharashtra, from the effects of the injuries. The Police with the help of the Military, then practically isolated Dharsana and Untadi by blocking the main road leading to these places and preventing any car or pedestrian from going along it. All the volunteers who were camping at Untadi were taken to some unknown destination and later released.

"Two batches of volunteers numbering about 200 were led on the 3rd June from Untadi camp to raid the Dharsana Salt Depots. Both were held up by the Police who, when the crowd entered the prohibited area, charged them with *lathis*. The injured men were taken to the camp hospital.

"Wadala Raids:—a succession of raids were also made on the Wadala Salt Depot. On the 22nd, 188 volunteers were arrested and taken to Worli. On the 25th, 100 volunteers were accompanied by a huge crowd of 2,000 spectators. The Police charged them with *lathis* injuring 17, and later arrested 115. The rest with the crowd got off with the salt. An official afternoon when 18 more were injured. On the 26th, 65 volunteers were afield and 43 of them were arrested. The rest with the crowd got off with salt. An official Press Note stated that the disturbances that had so far taken place, had been caused largely by the sight-seers who were, unlike the volunteers, not disciplined. The Note warned the public to keep away from Wadala while the raids were in progress.

"But the most demonstrative raid was to come off on the 1st June for which the War Council was diligently preparing. On the morning of the 1st nearly 15,000 volunteers and non-volunteers participated in the great mass action at Wadala.

"Successive batches marched up to the Port Trust level-crossing and the swelled crowd were held up there by the Police cordon. Soon the raiders, among whom were women and children, broke through the cordon, splashed through slime and mud, and ran over the pans. Congress raiders numbering about 150 were slightly injured. The raiders were repulsed by the Police who were acting under the immediate supervision of the Home Member.

"Serious troubles ending in two Police charges and the calling out of the Military to cope with the situation occurred at the Worli Detention Camp on the 3rd June, when about four thousand under-trial Wadala 'Raiders' were involved in a brush with the Police, resulting in about ninety casualties, twenty-five of them being serious."

But the way in which the raiders were dealt with by the Police caused considerable public indignation and protest. On-lookers were aghast at the gruesome spectacle. Mr. Hussain, ex-Judge, Small Causes Court, Bombay, Mr. K. Natarajan, and Mr. G. K. Devadhar, President, Servants of India Society, who personally watched the Dharsana raid, issued a statement in which they said:—

"They saw with their own eyes that after Satyagrahis were driven out of the Salt boundary, mounted European Sowars rode at full gallop with *lathis* in their hands beating people between the spot where Satyagrahis had reached for raid and the village itself. They actually galloped full speed through the streets of the village, scattering men, women and children. Villagers ran into bye-lanes and closed themselves in houses. But if, by accident, they were unable to escape, they were beaten with *lathis*."

Mr. Webb Miller, writing to the *New Freeman* expressed abhorrence of the sights at Dharsana:—

"In eighteen years of reporting in twenty-two countries, during which I have witnessed innumerable civil disturbances, riots, street fights and rebellions, I have never witnessed such harrowing scenes as at Dharsana. Sometimes the scenes were so painful that I had to turn away momentarily. One surprising feature was the discipline of the volunteers. It seemed they were thoroughly imbued with Gandhi's non-violence creed."

Both in 1930 and 1932 the Sanikatta salt stores in Karnataka under Government Guard were raided by a mass consisting of 10,000 to 15,000 people, and the quantity of salt taken away on each occasion amounted to thousands of maunds.

Mr. George Slocombe, the representative of *The Daily Herald*, London, was also an eye-witness to some of the Salt raids:—

"I watched the events from an observation-post on one of the rocky hills which ring in Wadala. It was humiliating for an Englishman to stand among the ardent, friendly, but deeply moved crowd of volunteers and sympathisers and watch the representatives of the country's administration engaged in this ludicrous, embarrassing business."

The scenes that he witnessed burnt themselves into his mind, and like a true evangel he was groping for a way out of the *impasse*. It was now that he achieved a journalistic coup more impressive and certainly more fruitful than Mr. Bartlett's interview at the railway level-crossing. On May 20, Mr. Slocombe saw Gandhi in Yeravada Jail and wrote a masterly despatch to his paper a despatch which disturbed the slumbers of the House of Commons and threw the Tory Press into a paroxysm of chagrin and fury. It was in that despatch that Mr. Slocombe announced that "even at this critical hour, a settlement is possible and Mr. Gandhi is prepared to recommend to the Congress a suspension of the Civil Disobedience movement and co-operation with the R. T. C." on the following terms:—

> "(1) The terms of reference of the R. T. C. to include the framing of a Constitution giving India the substance of Independence.
>
> (2) Satisfaction to be granted to Mr. Gandhi's demand for the repeal of the Salt Tax, prohibition of liquor and the ban on foreign cloth.
>
> (3) An amnesty for prisoners convicted of political offences, to coincide with the end of the Civil Disobedience campaign.
>
> (4) The remaining seven points raised in Mr. Gandhi's letter to the Viceroy to be left for future discussion."

Mr. Slocombe enquired whether the Government was prepared to make honourable peace with him. "Negotiation is still possible," said he, "and after my two meetings with Mr. Gandhi in prison, I am convinced that conciliation will be met with conciliation, but that violence on either side will not compel surrender of the other. Incalculable disaster may yet be avoided by the frank recognition that the imprisoned Mahatma now incarnates the very soul of India."

A war of non-violent resistance has its own philosophy by which it is inspired, its own time, place and circumstance which it can select, its rules and regulations to which every soldier should conform. Gandhi repeatedly explained that his objective was democracy attained by the method of Truth and non-violence, as opposed to the alternative method of fraud and force. Force always includes fraud, he said; non-violence excludes it. Non-violence need not always be in acts. If ill-will is harboured in the breast, that is violence, to be sure, and that is why it happens that apparently peaceful people are fraudulent. Non-violence and hatred are incompatible with each other. Some people say that a large-scale boycott of foreign cloth would be more potent than mere Civil Disobedience. No, the former requires the co-operation of 300 millions,—the latter requires the sacrifice of say ten thousand. They will have to hang these ten thousand before they could dismiss them from their mind. If these men are trusty and true, their presence will *worry Government to death.* Other people say that the movement may lead to violence. It is really to subdue violence that this movement was inaugurated. At that moment then, there was greater risk of violence in the absence of any safety-valve in the shape of a movement of non-violence. As a matter of fact, the party of violence gave an assurance to Gandhi, at the time, of their full co-operation in this experiment and gave him time till the middle of 1931. Still others thought that the time was not opportune, as there were numerous obstacles and obstructions. Just so. Non-violence when exercised in the most effective way must act, in spite of the most fatal outward obstructions. In fact, non-violence by its very nature, would neutralize all of them. On the contrary, inward obstacles in the shape of fraud, hatred and ill-will, would be fatal to the movement. Gandhi was always saying to them, "let me get control over the forces of violence." It was growing upon him, that the forces of violence were in motion and that he could get those elements of violence under control. The fear that people entertained that the movement would get out of control on Gandhi's arrest was groundless, for in South Africa, it gained considerable momentum without any action on his part. He was in jail and that was enough.

So often, a man behind the bars is a greater power than one that is 'free.' Thousands joined the movement in South Africa. They saw in the twinkling of an eye that the movement was for their liberation. They knew that there was a man prepared to fight the £ 3 tax and they took the plunge,—and against what odds? They knew that there would be hell let loose upon them. And yet they did not waver or falter. It was a perfect miracle. A doubt was oppressing some that the time was not ripe. Gandhi's answer is perfect. "Nothing has happened externally since Calcutta, but the internal conflict in me, which was the only barrier, has ceased. I am absolutely certain now that the campaign is long overdue. I might have started it long before this." Gandhi had not a shadow of doubt that the salt campaign would lead him to jail. "I expected a crisis to be soon reached which would lead to a proper Conference,—not R. T. C. but a square-table one, where everybody attending it would know his bearings. The exact lineaments of that Conference I cannot at present depict, but it will be a Conference between equals, met to lay their heads together to devise ways and means for the establishment of an Independent Constitution in India."

The time is past when the progress of events could be described in any circumstantial detail. Lord Irwin began to tighten the screw. At first he would not allow Gandhi to be arrested. Gandhi's march infected the whole Nation. There were marches everywhere. His call to the women of the country brought them into the arena by thousands. They proved a huge big complication to Government. Picketing liquor shops and foreign cloth shops was taken charge of by them, and the Police became powerless until their chivalry succumbed to their despotism. Not to arrest Gandhi was to leave him free to tap hidden and unthought of resources.

He had a magic wand in his hands, one waving of which brought men and money. He had to be arrested but the time was not yet, for Gandhi arrested would mean the whole Nation arrested. On the 14th of April, Jawaharlal[1] had been arrested and convicted, and that meant the arrest of the Congress. It was only a transference from the larger jail to a smaller jail. Ordinances were passed prohibiting picketing, preaching of non-payment of taxes, and social boycott. Numerous skirmishes were waged round the hoisting of the national flag. Punishments soon became severe. Fines were added to imprisonment. Then came the *lathi* charges. People could hardly believe that the Police were being drilled with *lathis* and all the exercises *cap-a-pie* were being practised to charge the Satyagrahis. It was not a threat or a suspicion. It was a grim reality—this *lathi* charge. Meetings were ordered to be dispersed under the ruling Law of the land, and the dispersal was effected under the inexorable blows of the *lathis*. Salt sections were coupled with the Penal Code and sentences were made as long as possible. A G.O. had been published in the middle of February, 1930, framing rules for the classification of political prisoners. Of course, the word 'political' was sedulously omitted, despite the fact that for ten years previously, Government had been freely using this expression though within inverted commas in their annual publication of *India*. The G. O. is published in Appendix IV.

The 'A' class was there only nominally. The 'B' class was given in a niggardly spirit. Men with large

---

1 He was released on the 11th October, 1930, and was re-arrested on the 19th October, and convicted on the 20th, being sentenced to 23 months' imprisonment. His wife—Mrs. Kamala Nehru—was arrested on the 1st January, 1931, under the Instigation Ordinance. A few days after Jawaharlal's arrest his 41st birthday fell on the 14th November, and was celebrated as the Jawahar Day all over the country, particularly in U. P.

property and refined standards of life, and fulfilling the conditions set by Government themselves, would get 'C' class and set to stone-breaking, oil-grinding and pump work in jails. The treatment of Satyagrahis soon revealed that the G. O. of February, 1930, was an eyewash. But the volunteers never complained or grudged this treatment. They poured into the movement. Many were not arrested but only *lathi*-charged, and if by a fortunate chance they found their way into jails, there they had sometimes another *lathi* charge awaiting them. Early in the movement, the audience that assembled in a public park in Calcutta was locked up there and barbarously beaten. The gates of exit were barred and guarded. At first, in U. P. and Bengal, the treatment given was brutal. Very soon the scene shifted to South India which experienced the worst phases of repression in the latter half of the movement.

There the policy of arresting and heavy fines was tried at first but it was readily replaced by beating. Men wearing khaddar or Gandhi cap were beaten while they were shopping in the bazaars. The Malabar Military Police were sent to Andhra and they visited places from Berhampore to Ellore, visiting Cocanada and Rajahmundry (Rajamahendravaram) on the way for the mere pleasure of marching along the bazaar and beating every khaddar-wearer that they met on the way. Their exploits were only stopped by the resistance they met with at Ellore, which ended in firing by the Police and death of 2 or 3 people and injuries to 5 or 6.

It is really difficult to describe the various aspects of repression. Like the Civil Disobedience movement itself, which it was designed to subdue, it assumed protean shapes. We would, therefore, describe some outstanding events in the history of 1930 and 1931.

Previously we adverted to certain attempts at compromise and settlement with which those events were interspersed. Bombay soon became the storm centre. The boycott of foreign cloth was the item round which all interest gathered. The mill-owners had an obvious though indirect interest in the movement. Fortunately at that time Pandit Motilal Nehru was free, and he visited Bombay and negotiated with the Mills of Bombay and Ahmedabad. The latter were easy to deal with, but the former were partly owned by Europeans. To make these accept the conditions of the Congress for certification proved a Herculean task for Panditji. Yet he was able to achieve what appeared to be impossible. The fact was that the spirit of boycott was in the air. People were permeated with it. Hundreds of bales of foreign cloth were lying in the dockyard uncleared by merchants. The importers, gathered together, resolved that they should not take delivery of them. There was, therefore, a shortage of cloth in the country.

It was at this time that the Working Committee met at Allahabad on the 27th June and passed the following resolutions:—

"1. The W. C. notes with satisfaction the progress made in the boycott of foreign cloth in a very large number of cities, towns and villages, and appreciates the patriotic spirit of the dealers who have, in pursuance of the resolutions of the Committee, not only stopped the sale of such cloth but also have agreed to cancel orders already placed and refrained from placing fresh orders, thereby causing a very considerable fall in the imports of all foreign textile goods. The Committee calls upon the dealers in foreign cloth in places where they have not yet stopped the sale of such cloth to stop such sale forthwith, and on their failure to do so directs the Congress organisations concerned to enforce strict and vigorous picketing of the shops of such dealers. The

Committee expects the sales of foreign cloth will be stopped everywhere in India before the 15th July, 1930, and calls upon the Provincial Congress Committees to make a full report on that day.

"2. The Committee calls upon all Congress organisations and the country at large to take more vigorous steps to bring about a complete boycott of British goods generally than have so far been taken, by giving preference to goods of non-British manufacture wherever similar Swadeshi goods are not available.

"3. This Committee calls upon the people to organise and enforce a strict social boycott of all Government officials and others known to have participated directly in the atrocities committed upon the people to stifle the national movement.

"4. The Working Committee calls attention to the resolution of the Indian National Congress passed at Gaya in 1922 and at Lahore in 1929, whereby the Congress repudiated the financial burdens and obligations directly or indirectly imposed on India by the foreign administration, except such burdens and obligations as are adjudged to be just by an independent tribunal, and advises the Indian public not to buy or accept any fresh bonds of the Government of India whether as new investment or in conversion of their existing holdings of the same or similar bonds.

"5. Whereas the present legal tender value in exchange of the silver rupee in India has been fixed arbitrarily by the British Government in the teeth of strong public opposition, while the intrinsic value of the rupee is not even a third of the legal tender value so fixed, and whereas there is imminent likelihood of further depreciation of the value of the rupee, the W.C. strongly advises the people of India not to accept rupees or currency notes in payment of any claims against the Government but to insist on payment in gold wherever possible. The Committee further advises the people to take the earliest opportunity to convert all their currency holdings of rupees or notes into gold, and particularly to insist on all payments for their exports to be made in gold only.

"6. In the opinion of this Committee the time has arrived when students of Indian Colleges should take their full share in the movement of national freedom and directs all Provincial Committees to call upon such students within their respective jurisdictions to place their services at the disposal of the Congress, in such manner and to such extent, including complete suspension of their studies, as the exigencies of the national movement may require. The Committee trusts that all students will readily respond to such call.

"7. Whereas in pursuance of the policy of repression the Government has declared a certain number of Provincial and District Congress Committees and other subordinate and allied organisations as unlawful Associations, and whereas it is likely that other Congress Committees and organisations may be similarly declared unlawful Associations in the near future, this Committee directs the Committees and organisations affected by those declarations, and those that may hereafter be similarly affected, to continue to function as before, and carry out the Congress programme notwithstanding such declaration.

"8. The Committee notes the amazing declaration of the U. P. Governor-in-Council, forfeiting copies of Resolution No. 5 of this Committee about the duty of Military and Police forces passed at its meeting held on the 7th June. The Committee maintains that the use of the Military and the Police by the Government as their tools for perpetrating shocking atrocities on the people would have fully justified it in passing a much stronger resolution, but that for the present it was considered sufficient to pass the resolution as it stands containing as it does merely an accurate statement of the existing law on the subject. The Committee calls upon all Congress organisations to give the widest publicity to the said resolution in spite of the said declaration.

"9. Whereas the Government has since the last meeting of the Committee continued its headlong career of relentless repression to stifle the Satyagraha movement and has to that end permitted acts of increasing cruelty and brutality to be committed by its servants and agents, this Committee congratulates the country on the splendid stand made by the people against the atrocities committed by the officials and reiterates its warning to the Government that the people of India will continue their fight for freedom to the bitter end in spite of all conceivable tortures inflicted on them.

"10. The Committee notes with grateful appreciation that the women of India are continuing to take an increasing part in the national movement and bravely suffering assaults, ill-treatment and imprisonment."

The boycott of foreign cloth was becoming more and more effective. Khaddar under no circumstances would be able to cope with the demand. Mill-yarn and hand-woven cloth was the next best commodity for patriotic citizens. Therefore it was that the mills had to be distinguished one from the other,—those that would help the national cause and those that would hinder it. Accordingly the mills had to be certified and virtually brought under the control of the Congress, to the point of agreeing to certain conditions, the chief of which were that they would not place orders with the British Companies for their machinery, that they would throw no obstacles in the way of their staff helping the national movement, and finally that they would not abuse the privileged position they thus obtained by raising prices of commodities to the detriment of the consumers. Mill after mill accepted the pledge which is given in full in Appendix V. Only a few remained unbending, and these soon discovered what a mighty power the Congress was at the moment.

It was at this stage that the All-India Working Committee of the Congress was declared unlawful and Pandit Motilal Nehru was arrested on the 30th June, 1930, and sentenced to 6 months' imprisonment. To continue the story of repression, we have only to state that its intensity grew with the intensity of the boycott movement. The volunteer organisation in Bombay was thoroughgoing. Women came into the movement, and with their orange robes and delicate frames, won the hearts of the people by the very gentleness of their picketing. When a shop-keeper would not seal his goods, his wife would be brought as a picket. In Bombay, public meetings were prohibited as elsewhere in the country and the people would not obey the orders. We have the testimony of Mr. Brailsford, who had toured the country during the movement, to the brutality of the treatment accorded to the people. He wrote in the course of an article in the *Manchester Guardian* on 12th January, 1931:—

"The charges which responsible Indian leaders make against the Police range in space and time over vast areas which defy investigation. Everywhere one heard complaints about the brutality of the Police in dispersing prohibited meetings. I heard much to this effect from an English eye-witness and from Indian doctors who attended the injured. I also questioned Police officers. My conclusion was that in most of these cases the mistake lay with the higher officials who prohibited the meetings. I saw two which were tolerated. Though the speeches, quietly spoken, were seditious, they always condemned violence, and the immense crowds, squatting silent on the ground, often spinning as they listened, with a big proportion of women among them, were gentle and passive as only Indians can be. If such meetings had always or usually been tolerated, there would have been no disorder, and the audiences would soon have grown bored. As it was, especially in Bombay, the policy of rough dispersal moved the whole city to anger; to face the *lathi*-charges became a point of honour, and in a spirit of martyrdom, volunteers went out in hundreds to be beaten. They gave a display of disciplined, passive courage. Again and again, I heard descriptions by Europeans of the beating of slight and perfectly passive youths by burly constables which made one almost physically sick. I should not care to repeat the comments of a French lady who saw one of these scenes.

"That the Police, even under English officers, often meant to inflict physical punishment for disaffection, I could not doubt. At Calcutta some students, witnessing from a balcony of the University the brutal beating of participants in a peaceful procession shouted 'cowards.' Two hours later, the Police returned, rushed into the University under an English officer, invaded the class-room, and beat the students indiscriminately as they sat at their desks, till the walls were spattered with blood. The University made an official protest, but no punishment followed. I heard details of this affair from professors whose repute in the European scientific world stands high. An Indian Judge of the High Court whose student-son had been beaten spoke with a vehemence which I wish some members of the Government could have heard. A similar affair occurred at Lahore where the Police, again under an English officer, invaded a college and beat not only students in the class but the professor also. The excuse in this case was that some students belonging, I was assured, to another college had been 'peaceful pickets' in the street. At Contai, in Bengal, five villagers were pushed into a tank and drowned during the dispersal of a crowd which seems to have been harmless. At Meerut, I met a leading lawyer who was the chief speaker at a dispersed meeting. While under arrest he was beaten, and in this position, a policeman shot him at close range, so that his arm had to be amputated. The importance of such affairs (and I might mention many more) was psychological. They helped to discredit the Government during the critical time when the masses were hesitating whether they should unreservedly support Congress. The privations (of which I saw something) suffered by the main body ('C' class) of the political prisoners in jail had the same effect.

"Of Police brutality in the villages of Gujarat, I had ample evidence, for I spent five days touring them. The legal repression, to begin with, was sufficiently harsh. The peasants, almost to a man, in the Bardoli and Kaira districts were refusing,—from a mixture of motives, personal devotion to Gandhi, desire for Swaraj, and economic distress due to the terrific fall in agricultural prices—to pay the land tax. The reply is to confiscate their fields, buffaloes, irrigation pumps, etc. and these are sold at nominal prices, so that for a tax of Rs. 40 or so, a man may lose his all. Further, the usual date of collection was anticipated by three months so that peasants who had already paid the two instalments due for 1930 were required last October to pay the instalment normally due in January, 1931. All this may have been just legal, but it was provocatively severe. On top of it came physical terrorism. The Police, armed with rifles and *lathis*, made a practice of surrounding the disaffected villages and beating the peasants indiscriminately with the *lathi* or the butt-end of a rifle. I have forty-five narratives given to me personally by the victims, and in all but two cases, I saw their wounds and bruises (one girl was too modest to show them). Some of these cases were serious; one man had a broken arm, another a thumb-joint cut to the bone, while others had their whole bodies covered with marks. Other cases which I could not verify were in a distant hospital. The motive was sometimes to extort the tax,—and occasionally it was paid after a beating and the seizure of a buffalo,—though, by the normal reckoning, it was not yet due. I have the statements of several men who themselves were not tax-payers, but were compelled after a beating, to pay an absent neighbour's tax. In other numerous instances, the motive was apparently simply to terrorise a 'disaffected' village, for no attempt was made to get the tax. The national flags in one village were torn down from trees and houses, together with the Congress placards, and eight peasants beaten, apparently because their houses were near these symbols. In two cases, a man was beaten till he removed his Gandhi cap. In another instance, a man was beaten (twelve *lathi* blows) till he saluted the Police seven times. A frequent Police joke was to say, "Do you want Swaraj? Then, here it is," and down would come the *ldthi.* Worst of all, the Indian officials (both civilian and Police officers) were engaged in an effort to rouse the Barias, classed in the census as a 'criminal tribe' against the yeoman class (Pattidars). There was direct incitement to beat them, to refuse to pay debts, even to burn their houses. For this, I had the evidence of five Barias in different villages. To these people the lands of the small owners were offered at one or two rupees an acre. This was much what the worse type of Russian Communist official did when the party was stirring up class war in the villages.

"'This,' you may say, 'is *ex parte* evidence.' But I took such precautions as I could. I gave all my evidence to the higher officials. The Commissioner went with me to one 'sample' village, saw the peasants' injuries, and questioned them. I have not the right to anticipate his mature conclusion, but on the spot he expressed doubts only about one case out of nine (the modest girl). Moreover, I met two of the local Indian officials, and had a chance of observing their ways; one of them in my presence perpetrated an act of wanton physical brutality. Finally, I saw the cage in which he kept his untried prisoners at Borsad. It was an open den, of the zoo type, with iron bars, and measured about thirty feet square. In it, day and night, lived eighteen politicals, and one of them had spent six weeks in it, without books or work. From this crowded cage, the prisoners were let out only once a day, and only for three-quarters of an hour, to wash and visit the latrines. Ought I to have been sceptical, when one of them told me that he and two others had been beaten in gaol? Beating belonged to the same medieval century as this prison.

"May I, in conclusion, touch on the bearing that all this has on the good work of the R.T.C.? English public opinion, carefully screened by Censors and Editors from any perception of what is happening in India, forgets that the great mass of the population is not in a normal state of mind. It has been roused to a high pitch of sustained exaltation, it has been goaded, gentle though it is, to anger, it doubts our sincerity, and, above all, it is passionately devoted to its imprisoned leaders. I gravely fear that in this mood it may not study the proposed Constitution with the favourable attention it deserves. So long, indeed, as Gandhi is in prison, I doubt whether the main body of his movement will abandon, or even slacken, its resistance. The one chance lies in an act of generosity which will proclaim a new era. May one hope that the completion of the sketch of the Constitution, and its acceptance at Westminster will be heralded by a general amnesty? Failing the most tactful handling during the next six months, India may have to start her career of freedom with the repression of Indians by Indians. We ought to know more of the history of this painful year; she should be helped to forget it."

The question of firings in the country—notably in Peshawar, was raised on the 15th July, 1930, in the Assembly and we give below the question and answer:—

Moulvi Abdul Matin Chowdhary (on behalf of Mr. S. C. Mitra).

(a) Is it a fact that while Sirdar Ganga Singh, Supervisor, Military Dairy Farm, Peshawar, was coming on a tonga with the members of his family to attend the Gurudwara on a religious ceremony, a British soldier fired upon him near the Kabli Gate, Peshawar city, killing his son, a boy of 15 months and a daughter aged 9 years, and seriously wounding his wife?

(b) Is it a fact that neither the Police nor the Military took any steps to take the wounded lady to the hospital and it was left to the public to render first aid and to take the poor family to the hospital?

(c) Is it a fact that while the dead bodies of the children were being taken in a procession to the funeral ground through the bazaar, with the permission of the Deputy Commissioner, some British soldiers without giving any warning fired at the procession and killed and wounded several persons? Will Government please state how many were killed and wounded on this occasion?

(d) Is it a fact that Government thought of starting an inquiry into this matter by a Sessions Judge but had to give up the idea because of the opposition of the Military authorities?

The Honourable Mr. H. G. Haig. (a) The facts are stated in the judgment of the Additional District Magistrate, Peshawar, dated the 3rd June, 1930, a copy of which is placed in the Library. This most regrettable incident was the result of a pure accident.

(b) omitted.

(c) My information is that the procession met a detachment of British troops, that the crowd was very excited and attempted to seize the rifles of the soldiers and that it refused to disperse and that the order to fire had to be given. The casualties were 9 persons killed and 18 wounded.

(d) The answer is in the negative.

In answer to a question by S. C. Mitra regarding the number of cases of firing, the Hon. Mr. H. G. Haig furnished a table (See Page 237—Legislative Assembly debate—Monday 14th July 1930. Vol. 4—No. 6) which shows as under:—

CASUALTIES AMONGST THE PUBLIC

Province	Date	Killed	Wounded	Remarks
Madras City ...	April 27th ...	2	6	1 died subsequently.
Karachi ...	„ 16th ...	1	6	„
Bengal, Calcutta ...	„ 1st ...	7	59	„
	„ 15th ...	—	3	
24 Parganas ...	„ 24th ...	1	3	
Chittagong ...	„ 18, 19 and 20th ...	10	2	Both died subsequently
N. W. F. Province Peshawar ...	„ 23rd ...	30	33	
Chittagong ...	„ 24th ...	1	—	

Province	Date	Killed	Wounded	Remarks
Madras ...	May 30th 1930.		2	
Bombay, Sholapur.	" 8th ...	12	28	
Wadala Salt Pans.	" 24th ...		1	
Bhendy Bazaar ...	" 26th, 27th	5	67	
Bengal-Howrah ...	" 6th ...		5	
Chittagong ...	" 7th ...	4	6	3 died subsequently.
Mymensingh ...	" 14th ...	1	Between 30 to 40	
Midnapur (Pratapdighi) ...	" 31st ...	2	2	
United Provinces . Lucknow ...	" 26th ...	1	42	2 died subsequently.
Punjab Kalu-Jhelum Dts.	" 18th ...		1	
Burma-Rangoon ...	" Last Week ...	5	37	
		17	37	
N,W.F. Province Delhi ...	" 6th ...	4	40	

"The District Magistrate of Sholapur, for the reasons given in the Communique of the Bombay Government issued on the 19th May, handed over the control of the situation to the Military authorities at 8-30 P. M. on the 12th of May. He had informed the Bombay Government that afternoon of his intention and the latter, on the same evening, approved of his action. The Government of India received information the next morning and the Sholapur Martial Law Ordinance was promulgated on the 15th May. The casualties at Sholapur on the 8th May were 12 killed and 28 wounded. Firing took place on six separate occasions." (See page 272 and 238—Legislative Assembly debates, 14th July, 1930. Vol. IV, No. 6).

The facts of the matter relating to this extract are as follows: We had an ugly development in Sholapur. The volunteers were maintaining order and regulating the traffic in the streets. This went on day after day. The Police were virtually replaced. The sight was not an enviable one altogether to the authorities. A situation like this was only too likely to develop points of contact and conflict between the volunteers and the Police. There was a clash, and four or five policemen were done to death. This led to the proclamation of Martial Law as in the Punjab in 1919, and with all its ugly accompaniments. Four men including a rich Seth were hanged and a number of prisoners were sentenced under the Martial Law to long terms of imprisonment. The release of these prisoners became one of the bones of contention in the peace negotiations of July and August which ultimately failed, and to which we shall presently make reference.

The events of the 23rd April, 1930, at Peshawar may be briefly narrated. As in the rest of India, the C. D. movement was in operation in the N.W.F. Province as well. Congress notified in the city of Peshawar that liquor picketing would commence on the 23rd April. The setting for the event, however, proved inauspicious. On the 22nd April, a deputation of the A.I.C.C. proceeding to Peshawar to enquire into the working of the N.W.F. regulations was stopped at Attock and not allowed to enter the Province. The news led to a procession at Peshawar and a public meeting at Shah-i-Bagh. Nine leaders were arrested early morning next day. Two other leaders were arrested at 9 A.M. but as the lorry on which they were being taken broke down, they undertook to appear at the Thana office themselves and were allowed to do so. Accordingly a procession of the people with the leaders started and reached the Kabuli Gate Thana but the Thana was closed. A Police officer arrived on horseback, when the people shouted and sang national songs. He went away and all of a sudden two or three armoured cars came and drove into the crowd. At this time an Englishman came dashing on a motor cycle which collided with the armoured car and he fell down and was crushed. Fire was opened by some one in the car and one of the cars also caught fire accidentally. The Deputy Commissioner came out of his armoured car, and he, when on his way into the Thana, fell down on the staircase, lost consciousness and regained it quickly. Fire was then opened by the armoured cars. People tried to remove the dead bodies. The troops and the cars were removed. A second firing began and, off and on, lasted for about 3 hours. The casualties are described in the reply by Government, as per the statement published, as 30 killed and 33 wounded. The popular version put it at nearly seven to ten times the figures. In the evening, the Military raided the Congress office and removed the badges and the Congress flag. On the 25th, the Military and even the usual Police were suddenly removed. On the 28th the Police reappeared and took charge of the city from the Congress and the Khilaphat volunteers who had, in the short interval, been guarding the gates of the city on the 4th May. The city was occupied by the Military. It is but fair to give the Government version of the events as they gave it on the 6th May. The two leaders who are represented by the people as having undertaken to present themselves at the Thana are described as having been rescued by the mob from Police custody. The Police officer who heard the shouts and national songs and returned from the Police Thana is reported to have informed the Deputy Commissioner that he had been injured by a brickbat, that there was a violent crowd at the Police Station and the situation was such that the Police were unable to deal with it. When the Deputy Commissioner himself passed the gate, his car was pelted with brickbats and stones. He turned behind and saw a second armoured car stranded with a despatch-rider under the wheels. The latter, it was alleged, was knocked off his bicycle by a blow on the head dealt by a member of the crowd and was then run over by the armoured car. The Deputy Commissioner, while endeavouring to argue with the crowd, was assaulted with stones and brickbats. The Military officer in the armoured car was also attacked and his revolver was sought to be removed. The Deputy Commissioner was knocked down senseless and had to be taken into the Police Station. The armoured car was also set fire to by the crowd.

Then the Deputy Commissioner gave orders to fire and the mob dispersed. The casualties were 20 killed and 30 wounded. On the 29th April, the Peshawar Congress Committee issued posters and bulletins stating that they were in correspondence with the Haji of Turangzai who, being invited by them, was raising a *lashkar* (army) with the intention of entering Peshawar district. The Congress and Naujawan Bharat Sabha were then engaged in fomenting rebellion.

On 31st May, 1930, during the C.D. movement, a gentleman who was a Government servant employed in a Military Dairy, Ganga Singh Kamboj by name, was passing in a tonga in Peshawar city through the Kabul Gate along with his children, when a British Lance Corporal of K.O.Y.L.I. fired at the carriage. Two of the children,—Bibi Herpal Kaur, daughter aged 9½ years, and Kaka Bachitar Singh, son, 16 months,—dropped dead like birds from a tree and the mother Shrimati Tejkaur was severely wounded on arm and breast, the breast being completely blown. The dead bodies of the children were taken in procession by several thousand persons which was allowed by the Deputy Commissioner. Yet, the carriers of the bier and the funeral processionists were shot at by the Military,—without giving any previous warning to disperse,—from a distance of two yards only.

The dead bodies of the children were dropped on the ground, but they were carried again and again by others. Thus 9 men were killed and 18 wounded, as per Government reply in the Legislative Assembly, from firing 17 rounds.

Another statement was furnished by Government in July, 1930, which showed that under the Press Ordinance No. 11, securities aggregating to Rs. two lacs and forty thousand were by that time demanded and taken from 131 newspapers and that nine newspapers declined to pay and suspended publication.

(*Vide* Answer to Q. 116—P—541 I—A.D. Vol. IV, No. 8 dated 15-7-'30)

On the 31st July, 1930, Lokamanya Tilak's anniversary was celebrated in Bombay and a procession was led by Shrimati Hansa Mehta, who was the Congress dictator for the city at the time. The Working Committee of the Congress was assembled in the city, holding their meeting on three successive days. It was not as yet under ban, for Government was extending the ban on the Working Committee from Province to Province. Some of the members of the Committee joined the evening procession, and while they were marching, a notice was served on them under Sec. 144, Cr. P. C., prohibiting the procession, which had swelled by that time to thousands. When the order was served, the mammoth gathering squatted on the road and would not budge an inch, in spite of the heavy rain pouring all the night. People literally sat in pools of water. It was expected that the procession would be allowed to proceed after midnight, as was the case on a previous occasion. But that was not to be. Mr. Healy was the Commissioner of Police,—an officer who, later, was considered not good enough or equal to executing Government policy. The Chief Presidency Magistrate wired about the situation to the Home Member in Poona. Mr. Hotson replied that nothing should be done till he came. He appeared on the scene in the early hours of the morning and began to watch the crowds from the gallery on a terrace of the Victoria Terminus Buildings. A few picked men were arrested in the morning, and with them a hundred ladies, and a *lathi*-charge was ordered to disperse the crowd. Among the members of the Working Committee present and arrested were Pandit Madan Mohan Malaviya, Vallabhbhai J. Patel, Jairamdas Daulatram, and Mrs. Kamala Nehru. Shrimati Mani Ben, the daughter of Vallabhbhai, whose fame was widespread in the salt campaigns of Gujarat and the No-tax campaign of Borsad, was in the procession and was arrested. A hundred other ladies were arrested, including Shrimati Amrit Kaur of the Punjab, and the dictator, Mrs. Hansa Mehta.

The scenes and sights in Bombay were blood-curdling, whenever a public meeting was convened against the prohibitory orders. The old Commissioner of Police was transferred, apparently because he was not sufficiently stern. A new one was brought—Mr. Wilson—who hoped to be able to disperse the crowds instantly. On the very first occasion after his taking over charge, the *lathi* hitherto flourished on the body was applied to the head, and when blood began to flow and volunteers fell reeling and rolling on the ground, the spectacle of suffering was so harrowing, and at the same time so infecting, that thousands gathered from the crowds of sight-seers in the neighbourhood and the audience swelled from five to twenty-five thousands. When the end of the movement came rather unexpectedly, this failure to control non-violence by violence, and more violence, undoubtedly played its part in determining the termination. Almost the last big collision took place on the occasion of celebrating the anniversary of the passing of the Independence Resolution. A lac of people gathered at midnight, which was the time fixed for the demonstrations, and the event was marked by firing by the Police.

The Azad Maidan in Bombay was the scene of battle. Throughout the campaign, the fourth of every month was observed as the Gandhi Day,—the day of his arrest in May, 1930; then the last Sunday of each month was being observed as the Flag-hoisting Day. These demonstrations were attended by thousands who could only be dispersed by severe *lathi*-charges. But as people dispersed at one place, they gathered at another on the Maidan, and it was a job altogether for the Police to disperse the crowds. In Bombay, the beating of the volunteers was witnessed by a Prince, who thereupon remarked that Martial Law was much better than the *lathi*-charge and that a Nation which had withstood the *lathi*-charges would be much better able to stand Martial Law. The Prince was the Maharajah of Bikaner who went out to see a procession which was to be led in Bombay while Pandit Motilal was there, and before his arrest on the 30th June, 1930. The strange part of the occurrences was that while fathers and uncles were at the Round Table Conference, their daughters and nieces were shedding their blood in India.

In Madras, the beating was so indiscriminate that on one occasion a Missionary, the Rev. F. Paton, was severely beaten in the neighbourhood of a Police Station when he was watching the picketing and *lathi*-charges from near, one evening, dressed in khaddar robes and wearing a hat. This was the subject of a severe attack on the methods of the Police, but neither the Government nor the Police would make reparation or even acknowledge their indiscretion. In the South, a Missionary named Mr. Khaitan was served with an order to leave India and he had to depart forthwith.

The Police made a new departure in prosecuting people as forming an unlawful assembly, by gathering together a number of picketers from various centres, putting them in a lorry, taking them a long distance from the city, and leaving them there to find their way back as well as they could without any money. In Bombay, picketing and the sealing of foreign cloth in the shops of merchants was so rigidly carried out that, when foreign cloth was being surreptitiously removed in lorries, a boy named Babu Ganno stood across the lorry on the Kalbadevi Road to prevent its progress, but whoever may have driven the car, it was driven over the boy and he succumbed. Ever since this event occurred, Babu Ganno Day was being celebrated every month, and it added to the list of sacred days observed by the Congress.

Patel (Vallabhbhai J.) was released after serving out his first term of imprisonment of 3 months and was appointed Acting President of the Congress by Pandit Motilal Nehru. He began organizing work in Bombay and Gujarat and stiffened the movement. His speeches gave a new tone and temper to the workers. On July 13th, he was referring to the Ordinance which had declared as illegal almost all the Congress organisations in the country and the seizure of the Congress offices, and remarked that every home must thereafter be a Congress office, and every soul a Congress organisation. This was the fitting reply that Vallabhbhai gave to Lord Irwin's reactionary speech delivered in the Legislative Assembly on the 9th, flourishing the big stick against the Civil Disobedience movement. The great event, one had almost said, the central event of the whole movement was the No-tax campaign successfully carried out in Gujarat, in the Bardoli and Borsad and Jambusar Talukas. The oppression by the authorities was so great that 80,000 people migrated from the British territory to the villages in the neighbourhood in the Baroda State.

Mr. Vallabhbhai's own mother aged over 80 was cooking her food, and the boiling pot was knocked down by the Police. Stones and sand and kerosene oil were mixed with rice,—all this in addition to the other physical sufferings inflicted upon the poor villagers. Their organisation was, however, wonderful, but more wonderful was their adherence to the cult of non-violence in letter and spirit.[1]

To make a long story short, it only requires to be mentioned that every Province and part of India bore its share of sufferings in the national struggle.

Local variations did exist, which were based upon differences of degree and kind,—due to environment, the personal equation of the officers concerned, the conditions of tenure of land and various other matters. South India had in one sense seen the worst of it. The *lathi*-charges as well as heavy fines and long-term sentences were an early feature, not a late development, of the movement. Bengal yielded the largest number of prisoners in the country. The measure of boycott of British cloth was highest in Bengal, and Bihar and

1 Early in the movement, there was a raid on a Military camp in Chittagong, in which young Indians dressed in Military uniform shot down some officers. This was followed by terrible reprisals calling back to mind the pogroms of the Black and Tans in Ireland in 1921—1922.

Orissa, where the figures of import in November, 1930, fell by 95 per cent. as compared with those for November, 1929. We have already referred to Gujarat's unique part and performance in the drama of national emancipation. U. P. was the only Province where a general No-tax campaign was inaugurated, both the Zamindars and the tenants being called upon to withhold, in October, 1930, payments of rent and revenue. The Punjab pulled its weight along with the rest. The whole-hearted adoption of non-violence by the N. W. F. Province was no less a moral than a political gain. In Bihar, the Chowkidari tax was withheld in large areas, and the Province suffered to the full from the imposition of Punitive Police and confiscation of large properties in lieu of petty sums. In the C.P., Forest Satyagraha was successfully launched and continued, in spite of heavy fines and Police excesses. Karnataka organised a No-tax campaign which was highly creditable to the Province. Three lacs of palm and date trees were cut down, 96 out of 130 Patels resigned in the Sirsi Taluka, 25 in the Siddapur Taluka, and 43 out of 63 in the Ankola Taluka, all in North Kanara.

In the No-tax Campaign in Karnataka, "More than 800 families participated in the No-tax campaign in the Kanara District. In the Siddapur and Ankola Talukas which suffered the worst, there were about 800 convictions including those of 100 ladies. The losses by reason of forfeiture of lands and homes, attachments of movable property and loss of crops amount to about 15 lacs of rupees. The table below gives statistics only of those who have lost lands and homes and does not include those whose losses involved only movable property."

In Ankola and Siddapur, 330 families had their lands forfeited. The population involved was nearly 2,000.

The lands forfeited were over 2,000 acres in extent, valued at over 8 lacs of rupees. 166 houses were also forfeited, valued at a lac and a half. The convictions were 218 and the movable property attached was valued at Rs. 20,000.

Many farmers were ejected from their homes, some of which were used as camps by the Police. Hired labour from outside the Taluka had to be employed for reaping the crops from forfeited lands. There were 37 lady Satyagrahis in Siddapur, who fasted at the door of the persons who had bought the properties of the No-taxers. The longest fast was for 31 days at Mavinagundi. There were 110 special police posted in Siddapur and punitive police in Ankola. Rs. 37,000 was realised on account of these punitive police. The special Ordinance relating to the non-payment of Revenue was applied to Kanara from January, 1932 to the end of the Campaign, though it was not applied in the later period to Gujarat.

In his message to Gujarat peasants Sirdar Vallabhbhai made the following special reference to the peasants of Kanara:—

"The brave peasants of Karnataka have vied with you in their sacrifices, in their loss of lands and property, in their privations and their suffering. They have courted attachments, confiscations, imprisonments and worse. Both men and women have shown utter disregard to sufferings and privations and they are to-day as ruined and resourceless as can be imagined. The tales of their bravery and their sacrifices have filled me with admiration and pride and the news of their sufferings at times unhinged me."

In Ankola the No-tax campaign was political in character and origin, while in Sirsi and Siddapur Talukas it was undertaken for reasons of économic and agrarian distress as well. In Kerala, the smallest of the Provinces, the banner of Civil Disobedience was kept steadily flying till the last day of the movement, while, at the other end, Assam including Kachar and Sylhet responded splendidly to the call of the Congress.

Attention may now be drawn to a few outstanding events in some of these Provinces. To all of them certain factors were common,—the closing of the Congress offices, the taking away of Congress papers, books, accounts and flags, *lathi*-charges, dispersal by force of public meetings, promulgation of Section 144 over whole areas, serving notices on individuals under Section 108, raids on houses, searches, seizure of printing presses, securities demanded of newspapers and presses alike. But what struck the on-looker most was that the Government of the country was being run in the interests of foreign cloth and the liquor shops. In Bengal, Midnapur was specially unfortunate in the extent of repression. Householders were imprisoned both in Bengal and in Andhra for giving shelter, food, or water to Congress volunteers, or volunteers who had been beaten and were lying helpless. Orders to fire were issued in Bengal—in Khersai notably, on the slightest pretext. When, in Khersai, a crowd collected round a house where distraint of property was being made, order to fire was given and one man was killed and several were injured. In Chechna firing on a retreating crowd resulted in 6 persons being killed and 18 wounded. In Contai, a crowd watching preparation of salt was fired upon in June, 1930, and 25 persons were wounded. In Khersai again, a crowd that gathered at the arrest of a person and would not disperse on warning, was fired upon with the result that eleven persons were killed. The celebration of the death anniversary of Deshbandhu Das was prohibited by the Police in Calcutta on the 22nd June, and, when the men in the procession were mercilessly beaten, the women who had come out of their seclusion flung themselves into the front in order to save the wounded from being trampled under horses' hoofs.

The Police entered college buildings and belaboured the students sitting in class-rooms. In Barisal, 500 persons were injured in a *lathi*-charge on one day. In Tamluk, the Police were said to have set fire to the property of Satyagrahis and their sympathisers. Reports of indecent assaults were received from many quarters. In Gopinathpur, Congress volunteers were mercilessly beaten, and amongst those beaten there was a Mussalman boy. The village became infuriated and arrested the Police, and after locking them up in the local school, set fire to it. Two Congress Volunteers broke the door open and rescued the Police from the flames at the risk of their own lives. On the 31st December, 1931, the anniversary of the passing of the Independence resolution at Lahore, Subash Babu while marching in a procession was severely beaten. He had returned from jail shortly before, after serving his term of a year for sedition. In Lahore the authorities were so nervous as to proscribe the picture of a Non-co-operation tree. A veiled Mussalman lady-picketer was arrested at Ludhiana. Siapa[1] was practised at the houses of those who would sell foreign cloth! In Rawalpindi prisoners were prosecuted for refusing to take bad food. In Montgomery, one hunger-striker, Lala Lakhi Ram, died after many days of fasting. In Tam Tam a lady was roughly handled. The firing on the Governor of the Punjab at the Senate-

1 Wailing at funerals.

Hall gave the Police an opportunity to carry on indiscriminate searches. In Bihar the movement made a quiet progress. In Samastipur Sub-division, there is a small bazaar called Shahpur Patoria. Four days after the celebration of the Jawahar Week, 125 policemen under the leadership of the Superintendent of Police surrounded it, made 46 arrests, and took away the property of some of those who were not at their houses, on 12 bullock carts. Similar reports were received from other districts. Monghyr and Bhagalpur were in the forefront of the movement. Picketing of liquor shops caused a loss of 40 lacs to the Government. Military Police and Gurkhas were taken through the paddy fields of Phulwaria in Motihari, crushing the same, and overawing people round about by arresting numerous villagers. Non-payment of Chowkidari Tax was organised in Champaran, Saran, Muzaffarpur, Monghyr, Patna and Shahabad districts. In C.P. liquor bids went down by 60 per cent. At Amraoti, there was a *lathi*-charge for celebrating the Garhwali Day. In Andhra the worst achievement of the Police was the beating of about 80 friends that met at a picnic at Peddapur on 21st December, 1930. Serious injuries were inflicted upon the people including two or three ladies. The incident has given rise to civil litigation which is still going on. In Kerala, toddy sales had gone down by 70%. In Tamil Nadu, stoppage of toddy sales was the scene of firing and several *lathi*-charges. In Delhi, a Rai Saheb was the wine merchant who had attained notoriety by being responsible for the arrest of 80 ladies and hundreds of male vounteers. In Gujarat, the exodus of the peasants is the historic event whose description by Mr. Brailsford is given below:—

"And then began one of the strangest migrations in history. One after another, acting with a unanimity of which only Indians with their tight caste organisations are capable, these villagers packed their belongings into their bullock carts and drove them across the border into Baroda. A few even burned the rich crop which they were too late to remove. I visited one of their camps. They have built temporary shelters with matting for walls and palm leaves on sacking for a roof. The rains are over; they will suffer no grave hardship till May. But they are crowded together with their beloved cattle, and packed in the narrow space are all their household goods, the great jars in which they store their rice, cloths and churns, chests and beds, shining pots of brass, here a plough, there a picture of the gods, and everywhere, at intervals, the presiding genius of this camp, a photograph of Mahatma Gandhi. I asked a big group of them why they had left their homes. The women gave the promptest and simplest answer,—"Because Mahatmaji is in prison." The men were still conscious of an economic grievance; "farming does not pay, and the tax is unjust." One or two said "To win Swaraj" or Self-Government.

"I spent two memorable days touring the deserted villages in company with the Chairman of the Congress organisation of Surat. One passed row after row of the padlocked cottages, and through the bars of the windows one could see only empty rooms. The streets were silent lakes of sunlight. Nothing moved until a monkey swung himself over a roof.

"To some of these villages, however, a few of the men returned to work in the fields, while their families and goods remained in Baroda. Some of them complained of the terrorism of the Police.

"It was not hard to believe, for I had seen something of their ways myself. As our car was leaving one of these abandoned villages, a policeman armed with rifle, with a fixed bayonet, ordered us to stop. We might leave the village, he said, only with written permit from the Police. The man collapsed promptly when he saw my European clothes and presently began babbling in broken English 'me nice policeman,' but it interested me particularly to discover that nowhere on his uniform did he carry a number. When I demanded a number, he assured me that 'every man had a secret number.' He belonged to an emergency force which is carrying for itself reputation that unpleasantly resembles that of the Black and Tans in Ireland. It can hardly have been an oversight on the part of the organisers of this force, that their uniforms show no number.

"One cannot blame a Government confronted by open, if passive, rebellion, if it retaliates within the law. It has proclaimed Congress an illegal organisation. It has confiscated the fine 'Ashram' in the Bardoli district. It arrested my host the Chairman of Surat on the day after we parted. It 'attacked' the properties of the Bardoli refugees and will sell their fields to recover the tax, if it can find a purchaser, a risk which leaves the peasants calm.

"All this is within the rules of the game. Terrorism is outside them, and terrorism is being used. My note-book is full of the complaints of the peasants with whom we talked on this tour. I could seldom verify their stories, but I questioned them carefully and do not doubt their word. These notes with names and dates shall go to the superior officials. One village was haunted every night by a gang of ruffians, who fired guns, tore veils, and on one occasion murdered an old peasant with an axe. When the villagers asked for protection, a high Police official is said to have answered: 'You have it when you pay your tax.' Most of the complaints were of unprovoked beating by the Police with their formidable *lathis*.

"One scene I managed, after much questioning, to reconstruct. It happened in the abandoned village of Afwa. Here some peasants who own no land had remained behind, and with them were some who had returned from Baroda to cultivate their fields. On October 21st, about 3 A.M., a car arrived with ten policemen under a certain Sub-Inspector. The Police found these men sleeping in the fields. They beat them and then demanded the tax. They were then brought before this Sub-Inspector, who beat some of them with his own hands and kicked others. One was still limping and another showed a painful swelling. The heads of two brothers he knocked together. They were then taken in the lorry to the lock-up in Bardoli. There the Sub-Inspector threatened, with unprintable details, to 'make them useless to their wives.' That threat told and the younger brother, though not himself a landowner, paid the tax for his father's farm. In another case, a passer-by from another village was seized and beaten, and the money in his pocket picked. A receipt was given in the name of a local tax-payer, and the stranger was told to recover it from him. This Sub-Inspector was a person who combined ingenuity with brutality. Finding in the village another stranger, a man from Surat, he appropriated his gold ornaments and tried to force some of the villagers to buy,—a species of summary distraint. But I might continue this narrative indefinitely and still it would record only one morning of this officer's activity. I might have hesitated to believe these peasants, had I not happened to meet this person in the flesh, and caught him out in a ludicrous and palpable lie. By such hands, in brief, far from the heights of Simla and the security of Whitehall, is law and order dispensed to the 'silent millions'."

Now in closing this tale of woe, we have to mention a word finally regarding Peshawar and its Pathans. These men, whose name is a by-word for cruelty and violence, became veritable lambs and real embodiments of non-violence. Khan Abdul Gaffar Khan had organised his Khudai Khidmatgars in such a disciplined and devoted manner that the most feared part of India became the safest centre of the working of the non-violent Non-co-operation movement. The atrocities of the Frontier Province were not allowed to see the light of day, and Vittalbhai's report on the happening there was proscribed by Government. But a few instances are well-known and are undeniable. Some of these have already been described.

An incident of importance took place in the Frontier Province which deserves to be described here. In the course of the repression adopted in the Province, some Garhwali soldiers were asked to fire upon a meeting. They refused to board the lorry brought to take them, in order to fire upon a peaceful and unarmed crowd. These soldiers were, therefore, court-martialled and given long sentences, ranging from 10 to 14 years. The release of these prisoners became the bone of contention between Congress and Government in the final negotiations of March, 1931.

To anticipate events, let us note that these prisoners were not released as the result of the Gandhi-Irwin agreement, but their sentences were revised some years after, and some of them were released in batches. Others are still in prison.

We shall conclude this harrowing tale of woes with an account relating to the heroism of the women of Borsad, on the 21st January, 1931, to celebrate one of those periodical events which sprung up in the movement. The Police were determined to counter the demonstration. The women had placed large pots of water to quench their thirst, at different places. The first thing done by the Police was to break these pots. The women were dispersed by force and the specific allegation was made that, when the ladies were thrown down, the police-men trod upon their chests with their boots. This was almost the last act of Police hooliganism. On the 26th January, a notification was issued releasing unconditionally Gandhi and 26 of his colleagues, in order to make it possible for them to conduct negotiations for a truce. Efforts had been made indeed earlier to bring about similar negotiations in July and August 1930, but they had proved abortive. We shall give a detailed account of these endeavours presently. They deservedly failed, because they were premature. The organisation of India had not been developed to the fullest measure as yet. The volunteers were still steeling themselves to fight. The Prabhat Pheris and Vanara-senas of Bombay were yet to become a historic institution. The roads of Bombay had not as yet been converted into public notice-boards. The Congress *Bulletin* and its daily publication running up to five figures did not as yet prove the mystery that later it turned out to be, both in regard to the origin of its printing and the man-power behind. The patriotism and self-sacrifice of the Bombay and Ahmedabad merchants had not as yet developed those resources which later came over so profusely to help the cause of the Congress.

We now take the reader back to the months of June, July and August. On the 20th of June, 1930, while yet Pandit Motilalji was free, he gave an interview to Mr. Slocombe, the correspondent of the *Daily Herald*, and shortly after, Mr. Slocombe had a conversation with Panditji in Bombay on the terms and conditions on which Congress might be willing to participate in the R. T. C. Certain terms drafted by Mr. Slocombe were discussed and approved of at a meeting, at which Panditji, Mr. Jayakar and he were alone present. Mr. Slocombe also addressed a letter to Dr. Sapru, and in the result, Dr. Sapru and Mr. Jayakar became the intermediaries for approaching the Viceroy on the basis of these terms. Pandit Motilal Nehru had agreed to approach Jawaharlal Nehru, the President of the Congress, and Gandhi, with proposals for a settlement, if in the first place the British Government and the Government of India would be willing to give a private assurance that, apart from any recommendations that may be made by the R. T. C. or from the attitude which Parliament may maintain towards them, they would support the demand for full Responsible Government for India, subject to certain adjustments and terms of transfer to be decided by the R. T. C. On this basis, the intermediaries wrote to the Viceroy and requested permission to interview Gandhi, Motilalji and Jawaharlal in Prison. This was on the 13th of July, and by that time Motilalji had been convicted. The Viceroy in his reply still further toned down the nature of the Self-Government to be given to Indians, and promised, "to assist the people of India to as large a degree of management of their own affairs as can be shown to be consistent with the making of provision for those matters in regard to which they are not in a position to assume responsibility." With these two documents, Sapru and Jayakar interviewed Gandhi in Yeravada jail on the 23rd and 24th July, on which Gandhi gave them a note and a letter to be handed over to the Nehrus in the Naini Jail, Allahabad. Gandhi wanted the discussions of the R. T. C. to be restricted to a discussion of the Safeguards during the transitional period. The question of Independence should not be ruled out. The composition of the Conference should be satisfactory. Peaceful picketing of foreign cloth and liquor would be continued in spite of the withdrawl of Civil Disobedience, unless Government themselves would enforce prohibition of liquor and foreign cloth. The manufacture of salt would have to be continued with impunity.

Then he referred to the release of prisoners, restoration of properties, fines and securities, and reinstalling of officers who had resigned, and the repeal of Ordinances. He cautioned the emissaries that he was a prisoner and therefore had no right to pronounce opinions on political activities, that these suggestions were purely his own, and that he reserved to himself the right of testing every-

Swaraj scheme by his eleven points. In his letter to the Nehrus, Gandhi doubted if the time was ripe for negotiations. With these papers, the emissaries saw the Nehrus on the 27th and 28th July, and had a thorough discussion with them. The Nehrus in a letter dated 28th July, 1930, expressed their opinion that at any Conference they would not be able to achieve anything unless an agreement on all vital matters was reached. Jawaharlal in a separate note stated that Gandhi's point regarding the constitutional issue did not appeal to him or to his father, for it did not fit in with the position and the pledges of the Congress or the realities of the day. On the 31st July, and 1st and 2nd August, Mr. Jayakar saw Gandhi, when Gandhi stated clearly that no constitutional scheme would be acceptable to him, which did not contain a clause allowing India to secede from the Empire at her desire, and another clause which gave the right and power to India to deal satisfactorily with his eleven points. He would also have an independent tribunal to examine all the British claims, and concessions given to the Britishers in the past. Gandhi desired that the Viceroy should be made aware of this position of his, lest he should say later that with these views of his (Gandhi's) he had taken him by surprise. Shortly after, the Nehrus along with Doctor Syed Mahmud were taken over to Yeravada to have an opportunity of meeting Gandhi and other friends in the Yeravada Jail.

There was thus a conference on the 14th of August between the emissaries on the one hand, and on the other Gandhi, the Nehrus, Vallabhbhai Patel, Dr. Syed Mahmud, Mr. Jairamdas Doulatram and Mrs. Naidu, and the result of this conference was embodied in a letter dated 15th of August in which the signatories, all the Congressmen present, categorically restated the conditions, already referred to, which they would demand for a settlement and in which they included the right of India to secede and the tribunal for examining British claims and concessions. In concluding the negotiations, Gandhi, Mrs. Sarojini, Vallabhbhai Patel and Jairamdas thanked the emissaries for the pains they had taken to bring about peace and suggested, "It would naturally be open to those in charge of the Congress organisations to see any of us. In that case, and when the Government itself is equally desirous for peace, they should have no difficulty in having access to us."

The Viceroy wrote a letter dated 28th August, stating that he could only move the Local Governments to consider the release of prisoners on a generous scale, but that they would consider the cases on their merits. The Nehrus were taken back to Naini, wrote to Gandhi on the 31st that Lord Irwin in his letter considered even a discussion of the preliminaries as impossible, and the tone of the letter indicated that Government had no desire for peace. Correspondence went on for some time longer and, to make a long story short, the peace negotiations failed.

The full details of these negotiations and their failure are published in Appendix VIII-A. The failure of the Jayakar-Sapru negotiations did not fill India's well-wishers with despair. They were followed up by the earnest efforts of Mr. Horace G. Alexander, Professor of International Relations at Selly Oak College, who sought interviews with the Viceroy, as well as Gandhi in jail. He was struck by the clarity of Gandhi's demands, which did not wrangle about high-sounding names but sought to wrestle with the simple problems of Indian poverty. By this time, Lord Irwin had promulgated about a dozen Ordinances—including the Unlawful Instigation Ordinance, the Press Ordinance and the

Unlawful Association Ordinance. Lord Irwin was faithfully following the 'dual policy.' In the same breath, he was blowing the hot necessity for Ordinances and a cold appreciation of Indian Nationalism. "However emphatically we may condemn the Civil Disobedience movement, we should, I am satisfied," said he, to the European Association, Calcutta, "make a profound mistake if we underestimated the genuine and powerful meaning of Nationalism that is to-day animating much of Indian thought." In pursuance of this ever-recurring dual policy, it was the Secretary of State's function to arrange the R.T.C. in England, and the Governor-General's to flourish the big stick in India.

The Round Table Conference met on the 12th November, 1930. It was opened with stately splendour in the Royal Gallery of the Upper House, with 86 delegates in all, of whom 16 were from the States and 57 from British India. The remaining 13 were the spokesmen of the different political parties in England. The Conference met at intervals at St. James' Palace, and in the gala speeches with which such conferences begin, almost everybody spoke of Dominion Status. The Princes, represented by Patiala, Bikaner, Alwar and Bhopal, were for Federation. Sastriar who pleaded eloquently for India's freedom, demurred at first to Federation, but later became a sincere convert to it. The Premier put forward the two fundamental requirements necessary for the success of the Constitution.

First, it must work; second, it must evolve. He contrasted the latter—a Constitution that evolves—with a static Constitution which will be treated by posterity as a sacred inheritance. Various sub-committees were then appointed and they duly reported on Defence, Franchise,

Frontier, Minorities, Burma, Public Services, and Provincial, and last, Federal structure. The Conference was in a hurry to close its session. The plenary session was, therefore, held on the 19th January, when it was resolved that the reports and the notes afforded material of the highest value in framing a Constitution for India and that the work be continued.

It was made clear by the Prime-Minister that in the Legislature constituted on a Federal basis, with the States and the Provinces represented thereon, the Government would be prepared to recognise the principle of responsibility of the Executive to the Legislature. Only Defence and External Affairs would be reserved. Special powers would be vested in the Governor-General to discharge his special responsibilities, to maintain the tranquillity of the State and secure its financial stability. Various other details were described. The Premier then announced the policy and intentions of His Majesty's Government in regard to the future Constitution of India:—

> "The view of His Majesty's Government is that responsibility for the Government of India should be placed upon the Legislatures, Central and Provincial, with such provision as may be necessary to guarantee, during a period of transition, the observance of certain obligations and to meet other special circumstances, and also with such guarantees as are required by the minorities to protect their political liberties and rights.
>
> "In such statutory safeguards as may be made for meeting the needs of the transitional period, it will be the primary concern of His Majesty's Government to see that the reserved powers are so framed and exercised as not to prejudice the advance of India through the new Constitution to full responsibility for her own Government."

The Premier added that "if in the meantime there is response to the Viceroy's appeal from those engaged at present in Civil Disobedience, steps will be taken to enlist their services."

Now, the justification for giving a rapid summary of the proceedings of the first R.T.C., which did not in any way concern the Congress, is supplied by this last sentence which we have quoted from the Premier's announcement. Within less than a week of the termination of the Conference, an important development occurred in India, as the result of which Gandhi and 19 of his colleagues were released unconditionally. The number was added to by the release of seven others later. The statement issued by the Viceroy ordering this release was exquisite both in language and sentiment and we give it in full below. But before giving it, we must give here a certain resolution passed by the Working Committee marked 'privileged.'

WORKING COMMITTEE'S RESOLUTION

Privileged resolution passed by the Working Committee which was held at Swaraj Bhawan, Allahabad, at 4 p.m. on the 21st January, 1931:—

> "The Working Committee of the Indian National Congress is not prepared to give any recognition to the proceedings of the so-called R.T.C. between certain members of the British Parliament, the Indian Princes, and individual Indians selected by the Government from among its supporters and not elected as their representatives by any section of the Indian people. The Committee holds that the British Government stands self-condemned by the methods it has employed of making a show of consulting representatives of India, while as a matter of fact it has been smothering her true voice, by the incarceration of the real leaders of the Nation like

Mahatma Gandhi and Pandit Jawaharlal Nehru, by Ordinances and imprisonments and by *lathi*-charges and firing on thousands of peaceful, unarmed and unresisting citizens engaged in the patriotic pursuit of winning freedom for their country by resorting to Civil Disobedience which, the Committee maintains, is a legitimate weapon in the hands of all oppressed nations.

"The Committee has carefully considered the declaration of the policy of the British Government made by Mr. Ramsay MacDonald, the Prime-Minister of England, on behalf of the Cabinet on the 19th January, 1931, and is of opinion that it is too vague and general to justify any change in the policy of the Congress.

"While adhering to the resolution of Independence passed at the Lahore Congress, this Committee endorses the view taken by Mahatma Gandhi, Pandit Motilal Nehru, Pandit Jawaharlal Nehru and others in their letter of the 15th August, 1930, from the Yeravada Central Prison and is unable to see in the pronouncement of the policy made by the Premier an adequate response to the position taken by the signatories to the said letter. The Committee considers that in the absence of such response, and while thousands of men and women including almost all the original members of the Working Committee and a great majority of the members of the All-India Congress Committee are locked in jail, and while the Government repression is in full swing, no general enunciation of policy can be helpful in bringing to a satisfactory issue the struggle which the Nation has entered upon or justifying the suspension of Civil Disobedience. The Committee can, therefore, only advise the country to carry on the struggle with unabated vigour along the lines already laid down and trusts that it will maintain the high spirit it has shown so far.

"The Committee takes this opportunity to record its high appreciation of the courage and firmness with which the men and women and even the children of the country have faced Government persecution that is accountable for the imprisonment of about 75 thousand innocent men and women, numerous indiscriminate and brutal *lathi*-charges, various forms of torture even of those in custody, firing resulting in the maiming and deaths of hundreds of people, looting of property, burning of houses and marching of moving columns of armed Police and *sowars* and British soldiers in several rural parts, depriving people of the right of public speech and association by prohibiting meetings and processions and declaring Congress and allied asociations unlawful, forfeiting their movables and occupying their houses and offices.

"The Committee calls upon the country to observe the anniversary of the Independence Day which falls on the 26th January, by carrying out the programme already issued as a mark of its determination to persevere in the fight for freedom, undaunted and undismayed."

When this resolution was taken up by the Working Committee, Rajendra Babu was the President. He had been delegated the duties by Vallabhbhai who had been arrested for the third time in eleven months. Pandit Motilal Nehru had also been released, a few days earlier than the due time on account of his severe illness which, shortly after, was to prove fatal. The meeting of the Working Committee and its object were openly advertised in the Press and the members met at Allahabad for the occasion. The resolution in question was after some discussion accepted. Pandit Madan Mohan Malaviya was present at this meeting in spite of his illness. The question was whether the resolution was to be published or not. There was a difference of opinion. Ultimately it was decided not to publish it till the next day. But an unexpected event happened the next day which justified the decision not to publish it. A cablegram was received from Dr. Sapru and Mr. Sastri, who were in London and who were about to leave for India after the Round Table Conference, asking the Working Committee not to arrive at any decision on the Premier's speech, until their arrival and without hearing them. Accordingly the resolution was not published, but, as happens in all such cases, information found its way to Government right enough and almost immediately after it had been passed.

The following statement was issued by His Excellency the Governor-General on the 25th January, 1931.

> "In order to provide opportunity for consideration of the statement made by the Prime-Minister on the 19th January, my Government, in consultation with Local Governments, have thought it right that members of the Working Committee of the All-India Congress should enjoy full liberty of discussion between themselves and with those who have acted as members of the Committee since 1st January, 1930.
>
> "In accordance with this decision and with this object, and in order that there may be no legal bar to any meeting they may wish to hold, the notification declaring the Committee to be an unlawful Association under the Criminal Law Amendment Act will be withdrawn by all Local Governments and action will be taken for the release of Mr. Gandhi and others who are now members of the Committee, or who have acted as such, since 1st January, 1930.
>
> "My Government will impose no conditions on these releases, because we feel that the best hope of restoration of peaceful conditions lies in discussions being conducted by those concerned under terms of unconditional liberty. Our action has been taken in pursuance of a sincere desire to assist the creation of such peaceful conditions as would enable the Government to implement the undertaking given by the Prime-Minister that if civil quiet were proclaimed and assured the Government would not be backward in response.
>
> "I am content to trust those who will be affected by our decision to act in the same spirit as inspires it. And I am confident that they will recognise the importance of securing for those grave issues calm and dispassionate examination."

Part V

SYNOPSIS

CHAPTER I

The Gandhi-Irwin Agreement (1931)

Gandhi's Message—Pandit Motilal's last illness—Pandit Motilal passes away—Gandhi on the Pandit's death—Interview fixed up with the Viceroy—The famous interview—Victory to both—Appeal to Englishmen—The Karachi Congress—Presidential Address—Resolution on Bhagat Singh—Black flags to Gandhi—The gloom over Karachi—Ganesh Shankar Vidyarthi's murder—The main Resolution—Indians Abroad—Sastriar's achievements—East Africa—Power to A.I.C.C. to revise the Fundamental Rights—The Flag Committee—Bhagat Singh Cremation Committee—Fundamental Rights Committee—Public Debts Committee—Deputation re:communal unity—Gandhi alone to attend the R. T. C.

CHAPTER II

The Breach of the Settlement

Arms down—Picketing Committee—The agreement resented by high officials—Working Committee confirms participation in the R. T. C.—Other resolutions of the Working Committee—Gandhi warns country against aggressive campaign—Lord Willingdon's sympathetic attitude—Peace not Truce—Breaches of settlement—Gandhi's letters to Mr. Emerson and his replies—Government release correspondence—Gandhi refuses to attend the R. T. C.—Working Committee on Communal problems—A solution suggested—Exclusion of foreign cloth—Residual powers—An explanation—A. I. C. C. meets—National Flag design altered—Working Committee confirms Gandhi's view not to attend R. T. C.—Gandhi leaves Bombay for Ahmedabad—Sir P. Pattani alone cancels his voyage—Disturbing factor—Sir E. Hotson fired at—Mr. Emerson's clinching letter—Should Congress have the last word in Revenue Collection!—Dr. Ansari not nominated as Delegate—Threat of outbreak of hostilities—Pandit Malaviya and Sarojini Devi cancel their passages—Door not banged against peace—Gandhi's letter to the Viceroy—No scope for peace till Civilians are converted—The Conference at Simla—Gandhi to proceed to London—Official Communique—Inquiry ordered into Bardoli Collections affair—Defensive Direct Action reserved to Congress on other matters—But Gandhi-Irwin Pact Continues—Gandhi sets sail for London—Working Committee ratifies—Gandhi's Voyage —Welcome at Aden—The sale of the shawl—Egypt's greetings—"Balance your relations with India"—Welcome at Marseilles—Gandhi prefers East End to West End—Gandhi at the R. T. C.—Gandhi on the Congress—Gandhi at the Minorities Committee—Cabinet fed up with R. T. C.—Gandhi on the Army question—Was the Congress one of many parties?—Congress has a universal platform and an exalted Creed—'Whilst there is yet a little sand left in the glass'—Partnership for Mutual Benefit—India only needs a will of its own—'For Heaven's sake give me a little bit of chance'—Gandhi proposes vote of thanks—The Situation in India: (1) *Gujarat,* (2) *U. P.,* (3) *Bengal.*

Sir S. P. Sinha
1915 : Bombay

Ambika Charan Mazumdar
1916 : Lucknow

Annie Besant
1917 ; Calcutta

Hasan Imam
1918 : Bombay (Special)

Part V

CHAPTER I

The Gandhi-Irwin Agreement (1931)

The releases were meant to take place before the midnight of the 26th, and instructions were issued to release the wives of the members of the Working Committee if they happened to be in jail. The number rose to 26, because the instructions of release covered also those who were *interim* members. As soon as Gandhi was released, he gave a message to the Indian people which is characteristic of him, for he knows no pride in success as indeed he knows no depression in defeat:–

"I have come out of jail with absolutely open mind unfettered by enmity, unbiassed in argument, and prepared to study the whole situation from every point of view and discuss the Premier's statement with Sir Tej Bahadur Sapru and others on their return. I make this statement in deference to the urgent wish expressed in a cable sent to me from London by some of the delegates."

The fact is that the delegates in London put themselves in touch with Government and with the Congress towards the end of the sittings of the Round Table Conference. Pandit Motilal Nehru had been released a little earlier than his time, on account of his serious illness, and the Working Committee, mostly composed of *interim* members, having met on the 21st of January, 1931, in Allahabad expressed their inability to take any action in the absence of a duly constituted meeting of the original Working Committee. The resolution was marked 'privileged' as we have seen and was not meant for publication. As it always happens, such resolutions have the knack of forcing their way to the

Press and, more than the Press, to the very quarter from which they are sought to be withheld. Thus the resolution was forthwith wired out to Delhi, and it is believed that it virtually determined the action taken by the Viceroy. Gandhi, however, felt that the release of the members of the Working Committee alone made a difficult situation infinitely more difficult, and made any action on the part of the members almost, if not altogether, impossible. The authorities, he said, had not evidently perceived that the movement had so much affected the mass mind that leaders, however prominent, would be utterly unable to dictate to them a particular course of action. He hinted to Press representatives what his conditions would be for a settlement, but he lost no time in declaring "that the right of picketing could not be given up, nor the right of the starving millions to manufacture salt." "The manufacture of salt," he added, "and the boycott of foreign cloth and liquor which had occasioned most of the Ordinances, were not intended to register the resistance of the Nation to existing misrule but intended to achieve these ends for all time." He was hankering after peace, he said, if it could be had with honour, but even if he stood alone, he would be no party to any peace which did not satisfactorily solve the three questions he had mentioned. "I should, therefore, judge the R.T.C. tree by its fruit."

Gandhi hastened to Allahabad to see Pandit Nehru in his sick-bed. All the released members of the Working Committee were accordingly summoned and met at Swaraj Bhawan, Allahabad, and the following Resolution was passed by the W.C. held on the 31st January, and 1st February, 1931:—

"The Working Committee having, out of regard for the wishes of Syts. Sastri, Sapru and Jayakar, suspended publication of its resolution passed on 21-1-31, an impression has got abroad that the movement of Civil Disobedience has been suspended. It is, therefore, necessary to reiterate the decision of the Committee that the movement is to continue unabated until explicit instructions are issued to the contrary. This meeting reminds the public that picketing of foreign cloth and drink and drug shops in itself is no part of the Civil Disobedience campaign, but that it is the exercise of the ordinary right of a citizen, so long as it remains strictly peaceful and causes no obstruction to the public.

"This meeting further reminds the sellers of foreign cloth, including foreign yarn, and Congress workers that the boycott of foreign cloth being a vital necessity in the interest of the masses, is a permanent feature of national activity and will remain so till the Nation has acquired the power to exclude foreign cloth and foreign yarn from India, whether by total prohibition or by prohibitive tariff.

"Whilst appreciating the response made by dealers in foreign cloth and foreign yarn to the appeal of the Congress to bring about a boycott of foreign cloth, this meeting reminds them that it is not open to any Congress organisation to hold out hopes of their being able to dispose of their existing stock in India."

The members of the Working Committee, original and *interim*, remained at Allahabad till the 3rd of February. Panditji was getting worse day by day and it was considered necessary to take him to Lucknow for an X-ray examination. Almost all the visitors were dispersed temporarily except a few, including Gandhi, who continued to stay there. Gandhi accompanied Motilalji to Lucknow. But the Pandit was rapidly sinking and the party returned to Allahabad where he passed away after a hard struggle, with these last words on his lips. "Decide India's fate in the Swaraj Bhawan, decide it in my presence; let me be a party to the final honourable settlement of the fate of my Motherland. Let me die, if die I must, in the lap of a Free India. Let me sleep my last sleep, not in a subject country but in a free one." Thus passed away the great Pandit who was truly an aristocrat in every sense,—aristocrat of intellect no less than of wealth, of culture no less than of character. His loss at this juncture, when his keen vision and quick wit would have helped the Nation to reach clear decisions on the complicated issues before it, was truly irreparable, for he was not only able to think in broad curves and wide sweeps, but he could take his mind through the intricate details of the political problems confronting us and arrive at his decisions both quickly and correctly.

Though he was an aristocrat of wealth, yet he recognised, under the inspiration of Gandhi, the need to chasten life and character by passing through the disciplines of poverty and self-abnegation. Nor did he enjoy his wealth alone. He is one of the few plutocrats that helped the Nation share his wealth. His gift to the Congress of the Anand Bhawan was as magnanimous as patriotic. This gift in brick and mortar is not, however, his greatest legacy to the Nation, for the gift of his son to it,—a gift truly in flesh and blood,—is incomparably greater. Few are the fathers that would not like to see their sons as Judges or Ministers, as Ambassadors or Agents-General. But Motilalji had chosen otherwise. Motilalji has passed away but his spirit hovers over the Congress and shapes its counsels and guides its destiny.

The following statement was sent out by Gandhiji from Allahabad on February 7th, on Panditji's death: "Motilal's death should be the envy of every patriot. He died after having surrendered his all for the country and up to the very last thinking only of the country. Let us deserve this hero's sacrifice by each sacrificing, if not all, at least enough to attain freedom which he was yearning after and which is within easy grasp now."

The message that Gandhi gave to *Liberty* is even more pathetic. "My position is worse than a widow's. By a faithful life she can appropriate the merit of her husband; I can appropriate nothing. What I have lost through Motilalji's death is a loss for ever. 'Rock of Ages cleft for me, let me hide myself in Thee'."

What really was distressing in the political situation at the time, and what worried Gandhi in particular, was the absence of any reaction in official India to the much advertised offer of freedom to her from England. "It was black repression continuing unabated on all sides," wrote Gandhi in his cable to the *News-Chronicle*, "'unprovoked assaults on innocent persons still continue, respectable people are summarily and without apparent reason deprived of their movable and immovable property by mere executive action. A procession of women was forcibly dispersed. They were seized by the hair and kicked with boots. The continuance of such repression will make the Congress co-operation impossible even if other difficulties were got over."

Private instructions were issued that, while the movement must go on, no new campaigns be organised or new situations developed. Just at this time, *i.e.*, on the 6th February, 1931, 26 R.T.C. delegates made an appeal to the Congress in the following terms, immediately on their landing in India:—

> "The scheme represents a bare outline; the details—some of which are of a substantial and far-

> reaching character—have yet to be worked out. We earnestly hope that the leaders of the Congress and of other parties will now come forward to make solid contribution to the completion of the scheme. It is our hope that an atmosphere of complete peace will be created for the consideration of these questions of high import and that the release of other political prisoners who have suffered incarceration for their convictions will follow."

So late as in February, 1931, 136 arrests were made in the city of Cawnpore on a charge of picketing, and the treatment of prisoners in jail both in regard to food and clothing, medical aid and punishments, continued to be as bad as ever before. The Working Committee formally met again on the 13th February at Allahabad. By this time Doctor Sapru and Mr. Sastri returned to India and they hastened to Allahabad to meet Gandhi and the Working Committee. Long discussions were held, and both of them laid themselves open to the severest cross-examination by the members of the Committee who were not altogether gentle in handling the two eminent men, for the public mind was not only agitated, but even embittered, by some remarks which Sastriar had let fall from his lips in England. Be this as it may, Gandhi wrote a letter to Lord Irwin inviting his attention to the Police excesses in the country and particularly to the assault on women at Borsad on the 21st January, and asked for an enquiry into the conduct of the Police. This was summarily turned down, and it seemed for the moment as if it was all over with the Peace negotiations. It was felt, however, that if the Congress and the Government were to meet, they could not meet unless one or the other party took the initiative in the matter. On Government's part, they had unconditionally released the members of the Working Committee. Why not, on its part, the Committee, or

Gandhi on its behalf, address the Viceroy and ask for an interview instead of relying on formal correspondence? The Satyagrahi has no hesitation in exploring such an avenue to peace. Accordingly, Gandhi wrote to Lord Irwin a short letter seeking an interview and expressed the desire to talk to him as man to man. The letter was sent on the 14th and the reply came by telegram on the 16th, in the early hours of the morning. Gandhi left for Delhi on the 16th February, and, shortly after, the other members of the old Working Committee were in Delhi too. The Working Committee had formally passed a resolution investing him with the powers of a plenipotentiary to negotiate a settlement in the name of the Congress. Gandhi saw the Viceroy for the first time on February 17th and had a talk with him for about four hours. For three days together the conversations continued.

In the course of these conversations, Gandhi emphasised his demand for an enquiry into Police excesses and the right to picket, in addition to the usual conditions of a settlement which must include a general amnesty, repeal of Ordinances, restitution of confiscated property, and reinstatement of all officials and servants who had resigned or were removed. The points raised, especially the first two, were of so controversial a character that no ready agreement could be expected of them, and the Government Communique published from the Viceroy's House on the 19th February, stated that various matters emerging from the discussion were under examination and it was possible that some days might elapse before a further stage of discussions was reached.

On the first day Gandhi returned to his camp, which was at Doctor Ansari's house, in high spirits. The first day's conversations were characterised by a note of almost certain hope. On the second day it was evident that the Viceroy was *understanding*, not *accepting*, Gandhi's position. A temporary break was predicted, as a cable would be expected shortly from England and the Viceroy himself proposed to invite Gandhi back on Saturday the 21st, but a sudden call came on the 19th, Thursday. A small conference of twelve was proposed, and the number grew to twenty, to discuss the various matters on hand, between the Government and the Congress. A cable was expected from London by the Viceroy on the matter, and the conference was intended to be delayed till the 24th.

The 20th, 21st, 22nd, 23rd, and 24th were days of waiting, the Committee expecting a call and the proposed conference on Tuesday the 24th. Gandhi broke his usual fast and silence on Monday the 23rd at 3 P.M. so as to be prepared for the expected call. But no call having reached the Committee, there was a feeling of impatience shown by some members. Gandhi counselled patience. The 25th, and 26th were again days of weary waiting. The interval was spent in planning certain arrangements for the next Congress, as there would be difficulties in regard to the election of delegates on account of the dislocation of the regular Congress organisation during the previous ten months. On the 26th, the long-expected call at last came. On the 27th, Gandhi visited the Viceroy. He had a three-and-half hour conversation with him, which was free, frank and friendly. Not one harsh word was thrown out, and the Viceroy was anxious that Gandhi should not break the negotiations.

On the 28th, Gandhi sent a note on picketing as desired, and the Viceroy sent notes of the proposed settlement.

The Viceroy wanted the definite conclusions of Gandhi on each of the points raised and invited him, as previously arranged, to the Viceregal Lodge on the 1st March at 2-30 P.M. On the 1st March, the situation appeared desperate. Renewal of hostilities appeared inevitable. "Break the negotiations," was the one cry on the lips of every member of the Working Committee; there was no exception. The news got wind quickly. There was alarm all round, consternation in every quarter.

Pandit Malaviya alone did not lose hope and was predicting a favourable turn. The Press, however, predicted the several plans that were being hatched by Government. The Working Committee, it was expected, would be deported *en bloc* to Kuriamuria, a nice little island in the Arabian Sea. The situation was altogether depressing. Gandhi saw the Viceroy at the appointed hour and returned at 6 P.M. from the Viceregal Lodge. His short stay appeared at first to spell disaster, but it did not take long to discover that hopes of settlement were to be revived. On the afternoon of the 1st of March, when Gandhi met the Viceroy, the Viceroy's attitude was quite friendly. Mr. Emerson, the Home Secretary, was equally cordial. The Viceroy called upon Gandhi to evolve a formula on picketing in consultation with Mr. Emerson. In fact Gandhi had been asked, it will be remembered, to submit such a formula earlier and a draft was sent the previous day; only, the Viceregal note and Gandhi's draft on picketing had crossed each other between the Viceregal Lodge and Dr. Ansari's place.

The atmosphere was thus wholly changed on the 1st of March. It was one of friendliness. At this distance of time, we may almost say that the sense of duty predominated over the consciousness of right, but for which the agreement would not have materialised at all. One point at issue in regard to picketing was whether it should be directed against 'foreign goods' or 'British goods.' Another point related to the methods to be employed. It was obvious that the boycott of British goods which was not on the Congress programme from the outset, and found a place in later years and notably during the war period, was meant undoubtedly as an act of hostility and as a political weapon to exert pressure for political ends. Accordingly, picketing was to be contemplated against 'foreign' commodities. The language of the agreement, as we shall see later on, was thus made unequivocal. The Viceroy objected to the use of the word 'boycott.' Picketing and boycott were, to him, convertible terms. Of course, during a truce, foreign goods and British goods must be distinguished one from the other. After a general discussion on the subject, Lord Irwin asked Gandhi and Emerson to evolve a formula on picketing and a formula was evolved.

The conversations turned on the subject of Punitive Police and were satisfactory. No collections of fines would be made thereafter, but there was to be no refund either of collections already made.

As regards release of prisoners, the Viceroy promised free and liberal treatment. Jail offences, rioting, mischief, theft,—all these came up for discussion on the night of the 1st March. It is necessary to state by the way that the conversations were continued till late in the night, Gandhi having gone back to the Viceregal Lodge after his evening meal and resumed the conversations. Gandhi raised the question of internees and the Viceroy definitely promised to examine their cases individually.

Regarding properties confiscated, sold properties could not be given. Gandhi was asked to see the Provincial Governments, as the Government of India refused to negotiate with them. A definite note was, however, promised by the Viceroy to be given to Gandhi for the Bombay Government about the confiscated lands. Mr. Vallabhbhai Patel, on hearing the report of the conversations as narrated by Gandhi, wanted the question of the two Deputy Collectors who had resigned in Gujarat to be raised. The position in regard to Salt was very much advanced in favour of the popular claim. The Viceroy promised to allow free collection of salt from deposits,—a concession which was very satisfactory to Gandhi.

On the issue of Police excesses, there was an attitude of *non-possumus*. Gandhi offered to make himself only the agent of the Working Committee on the question and said he would carry out its wishes cheerfully. "If you break," said he, "I go to the Viceroy's House only to break." He went to the Viceregal Lodge and returned at 1 A.M. and addressed the Working Committee and friends till 2-15 A.M. The Viceroy and Emerson were both very good. A formula on picketing was reached that night, but further consideration was reserved to Tuesday, 3rd March, as the next day—the 2nd March—happened to be Monday, the day of Gandhi's silence. A formula was also to be evolved between Gandhi and Sir George Schuster on Salt. That had taken the bulk of the time that night, but no formula could be evolved. Certain misunderstandings which had occurred were cleared.

With regard to the restoration of properties, it appeared as though the intervention of some outsider would become necessary in order to negotiate it, and

Sir Ibrahim Rahimtoola and Sir Purushothamdas Thakurdas offered their services in this behalf.

In regard to the two Deputy Collectors of Gujarat, the Viceroy could not promise restoration but offered to arrange for the payment of gratuity or pension to them. It was 2-15. A.M. by the time Gandhi narrated in full the discussions of the night. On the 3rd March, an interview was fixed up with Sir George Schuster at 11 A.M. to evolve the Salt formula, as the interview with the Viceroy was to take place at 2 P.M. There was a little commotion over this engagement with the Finance Member. Mr. Shiror, the representative of the *Chicago Tribune,* was asking a member of the Working Committee whether Gandhi was well posted with facts so as to be able to face the Finance Member. The idea was that Gandhi was to discuss with Sir George the question of Debts. They did not know that he was only going to fix up the Salt formula; nor was it a difficult task for Gandhi, even if he was faced with facts and figures on the question of Debts, to rise equal to the occasion. His resources were unlimited, but his security lay in his truthfulness, for, if he had not studied a subject or did not understand an issue, he frankly owned his ignorance,—which has been exploited by his opponents as indicating his permanent limitations.

On the 3rd March, another formidable difficulty arose in the way of the expected settlement. The restitution of the lands of the Bardoli peasants had been discussed earlier and was again taken up. Any formula that might be evolved in the matter must be acceptable to Vallabhbhai. So, in the course of the day, Gandhi had told the Viceroy that he would return in the night with a formula acceptable to Vallabhbhai and, therefore, asked the Viceroy not to discuss the matter any further.

The fact is that the Viceroy had his own difficulties. He had passed a letter, it was believed, to the Government of Bombay, when the Bardoli No-tax campaign was at its height, that he would not ask for the restitution of properties to the peasants under any circumstances. Therefore, he would naturally be most unwilling to address them now in a directly opposite manner. He wanted Gandhi to ask Sir Purushothamdas Thakurdas and Sir Ibrahim Rahimtoola to intervene, and he hoped everything would be all right. Gandhi wanted the Viceroy to do it. At last, the Viceroy agreed to give a letter to the Government of Bombay to help the two gentlemen in recovering the lands. As a matter of fact, the Revenue Member of Bombay had gone over to Delhi during the *pourparlers*, apparently to talk over the matter. Sapru and Jayakar as well as Sastriar had done great service in smoothening matters whenever there was difficulty. Clause 17 (c) of the Gandhi-Irwin agreement was the subject of a heated debate between Government and the Congress. The clause runs as follows:—

> "Where immovable property has been sold to third parties the transaction must be regarded as final, so far as Government are concerned."
>
> "Note:—Mr. Gandhi has represented to Government that, according to his information and belief, some at least of these sales have been unlawful and unjust. Government, on the information before them, cannot accept this contention."

After prolonged controversy, which threatened to break up the negotiations altogether once again on the 3rd evening, the formula embodied in the note quoted above was evolved, and besides this, in the body of clause (c) the expression 'so far as Government are concerned' was intended to leave a margin for the intervention of men like Sir Purushotham Das Thakurdas and Sir Ibrahim Rahimtoola, and negotiate the return of the lands if possible to the peasants.

Gandhi returned on the 3rd night from the Viceregal Lodge at 2-30. A.M. (4-3-34). Everybody was keeping vigil. Gandhi came back very enthusiastic.

Gandhi, as usual, narrated all that had happened in the night to the members of the Working Committee. Even in the evening, there was a heated debate among the members of the W.C. on the formula for picketing which, as originally drafted, embodied a clause of exemption of Mussalman shop-keepers. The Government wanted it. But it was finally abandoned.

In each of the items of settlement there was a lacuna. (1) The release of prisoners expressly included only the Satyagraha prisoners. The internees' cases would only be examined in detail. The Sholapur prisoners and Garhwali prisoners were not in the picture. (2) Picketing did not permit the distinction in favour of 'British' goods. (3) The restoration of lands confiscated or sold constituted a problem by itself, and clause 17 (c) was there staring the Congress in the face. Finally, Gandhi had settled a matter of supreme importance in the last sitting by himself, of course subject to the approval of the W.C., and that related to the constitutional question in respect of which Gandhi agreed to further consideration of "the scheme for the constitutional Government of India discussed at the R.T.C. Of the scheme there outlined, Federation is an essential part. So also are Indian responsibility and reservations or safeguards in the interests of India, for such matters as, for instance, Defence. External Affairs, the position of Minorities, the financial credit of India, and the discharge of obligations" (clause 2 of the Gandhi-Irwin agreement).

Now this tentative settlement was formulated by Gandhi and the Viceroy and was brought back to the Working Committee for its acceptance or rejection. 'In the interests of India,' was considered to be the real protection for the Congress in this part of the settlement. It was the antidote to the safeguards. The members of the W. C. were not without doubt that this expression might not only be perversely interpreted but be made positively to turn against Indian interests. It is not, however, in Gandhi's nature to take the market value of things. He takes only the face value of the words and statements of others, even as he would like his own words and statements to be taken at their face value by others. This was disarming altogether. Vallabhbhai was not satisfied on the question of land settlement. Jawaharlal was not satisfied on the constitutional question. Nobody was satisfied with the question of prisoners. If everybody were satisfied on every question, it would not be a settlement, but a victory to the Congress. When the Congress was on a settlement or a compromise, it could not have its own way. But it was open to the W.C., to reject any or all of the items of the proposed settlement. Gandhi put it to member after member of the W.C., individually, and asked whether he should break on prisoners, on picketing, on lands, on anything, on everything, or the whole. Regarding the final clause of the agreement in which Government reserved to themselves, "in the event of Congress failing to give full effect to the obligations of this settlement," the right "to take such action as may in consequence become necessary for the protection of the public and individuals, and the due observance of law and order," there was a controversy as to why such a reservation of rights was unilateral and not bilateral. In other words, the objectors would ask for another clause reserving to the Congress the right to declare Civil Disobedience in the event of Government failing to give full effect to the obligations of this settlement. But a little imagination was necessary to see that the Congress had not inaugurated Civil Disobedience with the permission of the Government, nor would require it for its renewal.

Thus was the agreement hammered out after 15 days of strenuous discussion between Government and Congress. It was the result of the full play of some of the noblest qualities in man, both in Gandhi and in Irwin.

The full text of the agreement is published below:—

S. 481/31-POLITICAL

GOVERNMENT OF INDIA

HOME DEPARTMENT

New Delhi, the 5th March, 1931

NOTIFICATION

The following statement by the Governor-General-in-Council is published for general information:

(1) Consequent on the conversations that have taken place between His Excellency the Viceroy and Mr. Gandhi, it has been arranged that the Civil Disobedience movement be discontinued, and that, with the approval of His Majesty's Government, certain action be taken by the Government of India and Local Governments.

(2) As regards constitutional questions, the scope of future discussion is stated, with the assent of His Majesty's Government, to be with the object

of considering further the scheme for the constitutional Government of India discussed at the Round Table Conference. Of the scheme there outlined, Federation is an essential part. So also are Indian responsibility and reservations or safeguards in the interests of India, for such matters as, for instance, Defence, External Affairs, the position of Minorities, the financial credit of India, and the discharge of obligations.

(3) In pursuance of the statement made by the Prime-Minister in his announcement of the 19th of January, 1931, steps will be taken for the participation of the representatives of the Congress in the further discussions that are to take place on the scheme of constitutional reform.

(4) The settlement relates to activities directly connected with the Civil Disobedience movement.

(5) Civil Disobedience will be effectively discontinued and reciprocal action will be taken by Government. The effective discontinuance of the Civil Disobedience movement means the effective discontinuance of all activities in furtherance thereof, by whatever methods pursued, and in particular the following:—

(1) The organised defiance of the provisions of any law.

(2) The movement for the non-payment of Land Revenue and other legal dues.

(3) The publication of news-sheets in support of the Civil Disobedience movement.

(4) Attempts to influence Civil and Military servants or village officials against Government or to persuade them to resign their posts.

(6) As regards the boycott of foreign goods, there are two issues involved; firstly, the character of the boycott, and secondly, the methods employed in giving effect to it. The position of Government is as follows. They approve of the encouragement of Indian industries as part of the economic and industrial movement designed to improve the material condition of India, and they have no desire to discourage methods of propaganda,

persuasion or advertisement pursued with this object in view, which do not interfere with the freedom of action of individuals, or are not prejudicial to the maintenance of law and order. But the boycott of non-Indian goods, (except of cloth, which has been applied to all foreign cloth) has been directed during the Civil Disobedience movement chiefly, if not exclusively, against British goods, and in regard to these it has been admittedly employed in order to exert pressure for political ends.

It is accepted that a boycott of this character and organised for this purpose will not be consistent with the participation of representatives of the Congress in a frank and friendly discussion of constitutional questions between representatives of British India, of the Indian States, and of His Majesty's Government and political parties in England, which the settlement is intended to secure. It is, therefore, agreed that the discontinuance of the Civil Disobedience movement connotes the definite discontinuance of the employment of the boycott of British commodities as a political weapon and that, in consequence, those who have given up, during a time of political excitement, the sale or purchase of British goods must be left free without any form of restraint to change their attitude if they so desire.

(7) In regard to the methods employed in furtherance of the replacement of non-Indian by Indian goods or against the consumption of intoxicating liquor and drugs, resort will not be had to methods coming within the category of picketing, except within the limits permitted by the ordinary law. Such picketing shall be unaggressive and it shall not involve coercion, intimidation, restraint, hostile demonstration, obstruction to the public, or any offence under the ordinary law. If and when any of these methods is employed in any place, the practice of picketing in that place will be suspended.

(8) Mr. Gandhi has drawn the attention of Government to specific allegations against the conduct of the Police, and represented the desirability of a public enquiry into them. In the present circumstances, Government see great difficulty in this

course and feel that it must inevitably lead to charges and counter-charges, and so militate against the re-establishment of peace. Having regard to these considerations, Mr. Gandhi agreed not to press the matter.

(9) The action that Government will take on the discontinuance of the Civil Disobedience movement is stated in the following paragraphs:—

(10) Ordinances promulgated in connection with the Civil Disobedience movement will be withdrawn.

Ordinance No. 1 of 1931 relating to the terrorist movement does not come within the scope of the provision.

(11) Notifications declaring associations unlawful under the Criminal Law Amendment Act of 1908 will be withdrawn, provided that the Notifications were made in connection with the Civil Disobedience movement.

The notifications recently issued by the Burma Government under the Criminal Law Amendment Act do not come within the scope of the provision.

(12) (i) Pending prosecutions will be withdrawn if they have been filed in connection with the Civil Disobedience movement and relate to offences which do not involve violence other than technical violence, or incitement to such violence.

(ii) The same principles will apply to proceedings under the security provisions of the Criminal Procedure Code.

(iii) Where a Local Government has moved any High Court or has initiated proceedings under the Legal Practitioners' Act in regard to the conduct of Legal Practitioners in connection with the Civil Disobedience movement, it will make application to the Court concerned for permission to withdraw such proceedings, provided that the alleged conduct of the person concerned does not relate to violence or incitement to violence.

(iv) Prosecutions, if any, against soldiers and Police involving disobedience of orders will not come within the scope of this provision.

(13) (i) Those prisoners will be released who are undergoing imprisonment in connection with the Civil Disobedience movement for offences which did not involve violence, other than technical violence, or incitement to such violence.

(ii) If any prisoner who comes within the scope of (i) above has been also sentenced for a jail offence, not involving violence, other than technical violence, or incitement to such violence, the latter sentence also will be remitted, or if a prosecution relating to an offence of this character is pending against such a prisoner, it will be withdrawn.

(iii) Soldiers and Police convicted of offences involving disobedience of orders—in the very few cases that have occurred—will not come within the scope of the amnesty.

(14). Fines which have not been realised will be remitted. Where an order for the forfeiture of security has been made under the security provisions of the Criminal Procedure Code, and the security has not been realised, it will be similarly remitted.

Fines which have been realised and securities forfeited and realised under any law will not be returned.

(15) Additional Police imposed in connection with the Civil Disobedience movement at the expense of the inhabitants of a particular area will be withdrawn at the discretion of Local Governments. Local Governments will not refund any money, not in excess of the actual cost, that has been realised, but they will remit any sum that has not been realised.

(16) (a) Moveable property, which is not an illegal possession and which has been seized in connection with the Civil Disobedience movement under the Ordinances or the provisions of the Criminal Law, will be returned, if it is still in the possession of Government.

(b) Moveable property forfeited or attached in connection with the realization of Land Revenue or other dues will be returned, unless the Collector of the District has reason to believe that the defaulter will contumaciously refuse to pay the dues recoverable from him within a reasonable period. In deciding what is a reasonable period, special regard will be paid to cases in which the defaulters, while willing to pay, genuinely require time for the purpose, and if necessary, the revenue will be suspended in accordance with the ordinary principles of Land Revenue administration.

(c) Compensation will not be given for deterioration.

(d) Where moveable property has been sold or otherwise finally disposed of by Government, compensation will not be given and the sale proceeds will not be returned, except in so far as they are in excess of the legal dues for which the property may have been sold.

(e) It will be open to any person to seek any legal remedy he may have on the ground that the attachment or seizure of property was not in accordance with the law.

(17) (a) Immoveable property of which possession has been taken under Ordinance IX of 1930 will be returned in accordance with the provisions of the Ordinance.

(b) Land and other immoveable property in the possession of Government, which has been forfeited or attached in connection with the realization of Land Revenue or other dues, will be returned unless the Collector of the District has reason to believe that the defaulter will contumaciously refuse to pay the dues recoverable from him within a reasonable period. In deciding what is a reasonable period special regard will be paid to cases in which the defaulter, while willing to pay, genuinely requires time for the purpose, and if necessary the revenue will be suspended in accordance with the ordinary principles of Land Revenue administration.

(c) Where immoveable property has been sold to third parties, the transaction must be regarded as final, so far as Government are concerned.

Note:—Mr. Gandhi has represented to Government that according to his information and belief some at least of these sales have been unlawful and unjust. Government, on the information before them, cannot accept this contention.

(d) It will be open to any person to seek any legal remedy on the ground that the seizure or attachment of property was not in accordance with the law.

(18) Government believe that there have been very few cases in which the realization of dues has not been made in accordance with the provisions of the law. In order to meet such cases, if any, Local Governments will issue instructions to District Officers to have prompt enquiry made into any specific complaint of this nature, and to give redress without delay if illegality is established.

(19) Where the posts rendered vacant by resignations have been permanently filled, Government will not be able to reinstate the late incumbents. Other cases of resignation will be considered on their merits by Local Governments who will pursue a liberal policy in regard to the re-appointment of Government servants and village officials who apply for reinstatement.

(20) Government are unable to condone breaches of the existing law relating to the Salt administration, nor are they able in the present financial conditions of the country to make substantial modifications in the Salt Acts.

For the sake, however, of giving relief to certain of the poorer classes, they are prepared to extend their administrative provisions, on lines already prevailing in certain places, in order to permit local residents in villages immediately adjoining areas where salt can be collected or made, to such villages, but not for sale to, or trading with, individuals living outside them.

(21) In the event of Congress failing to give full effect to the obligations of this settlement, Government will take such action as may in consequence become necessary for the protection of the public and individuals and the due observance of law and order.

(Sd) H. W. Emerson,
Secretary to the Government of India.

While these negotiations were going on, Gandhi and the Viceroy had prolonged and repeated talks on the commutation of death sentence on Bhagat Singh and his comrades, Raja Guru and Sukhadev, who were sentenced to be hanged for the murder of Mr. Saunders on the 13th September, 1928, in the Lahore Conspiracy Case. The country was greatly agitated over the impending executions. Congressmen themselves were anxious to explore the good-will prevalent all round for securing this commutation. The Viceroy spoke with reserve. He had never made any promise in the matter beyond assuring Gandhi that he would employ his good offices with the Punjab Government in this behalf. He himself had the right to commute the sentences, but that is a right that could not be invoked or exercised for political reasons. On the contrary, it was the political reasons themselves that would stand in the way of the Punjab Government yielding in the matter.

Stand they did, as a matter of fact. Anyway Lord Irwin was unable to help in the matter, but undertook to secure a postponement of the execution till after the Karachi Congress. The Karachi Session was to meet in the last week of March, but Gandhi himself definitely stated to the Viceroy that if the boys should be hanged, they had better be hanged before the Congress, than after. The position of affairs in the country would be clear. There would be no false hopes lingering in the breasts of the people. The Gandhi-Irwin Pact would stand or fall on its own merits at the Congress, and on the added fact that the three boys had been executed. The agreement was signed on the 5th March, 1931, and was followed up by a splendid letter to Gandhi from Mr. Emerson who described himself as the man responsible for the administration of the previous ten months. He added that he would be happy to serve

India under Swaraj. Lord Irwin wrote a fine letter to Gandhiji hoping to be able to see him in England shortly.

One great feature of the negotiations was the perfect secrecy that was maintained about the progress of events from day to day and hour to hour. The fact becomes all the more noteworthy when we remember that the secrets of the Gandhi-Irwin negotiations were confined not merely to the members of the W. C. in Delhi, but to at least a dozen other friends. It was amusing, even as it was distressing, to see distorted versions of the events being published day after day with ornate details as if the writers were eye or ear-witnesses of the transactions. A perusal of these reports at once served as a warning to the public against accepting all that is in the Press as gospel truth. But equally is it a warning to responsible bodies that authoritative reports should be furnished of important events to the Press whose contribution to the public life of a country is immeasurable, even as it is invaluable. It is singularly gratifying to note that the date of the signing of the agreement was exactly identical with the date on which the so-called ultimatum of Gandhi was delivered to the Viceroy. It may be noted that it was on the 4th of March, 1930, that Gandhi's letter to the Viceroy was delivered to him by Mr. Reginald Reynolds. Exactly one year after the delivery of this letter and the declaration of hostilities, the agreement was signed between Gandhi and the Viceroy on the 5th March, 1931.

Gandhi's Statement to Pressmen

On the conclusion of the agreement, almost the first thing that Gandhi did was to make an epoch-making statement before a gathering of American, English and Indian journalists and pressmen on the evening of the 5th

March. It took over an hour and a half for him to dictate his full statement without the aid of a single note, and without the need to make a single correction. In this statement, he paid a well-deserved tribute to Lord Irwin and made a suitable appeal to the Police, to the Civil Service and the Revolutionaries. We give below the full text of the statement, as it constitutes permanent literature on the subject of Indian Swaraj:—

VICEROY'S COURTESY

"In the first place I would like to state that this settlement, such as it is, would have been impossible without the Viceroy's inexhaustible patience and equally inexhaustible industry and unfailing courtesy. I am aware that I must have, though quite unconsciously, given him causes for irritation. I must have also tried his patience, but I cannot recall an occasion when he allowed himself to be betrayed into irritation or impatience. I must add that he was frank throughout these very delicate negotiations and I believe he was determined, if it was at all possible, to have a settlement. I must confess that I approached the negotiations in fear and trembling. I was also filled with distrust, but at the very outset he disarmed my suspicions and put me at ease. For myself, I can say without fear of contradiction that when I wrote my letter inviting the invitation to see him, I was determined not to be outdone in the race of reaching an honourable settlement, if it could be reached at all. I am, therefore, thankful to the Almighty that the settlement was reached and the country has been spared, at least for the time, the sufferings which in the event of a break-down would have been intensified a hundredfold.

VICTORY TO BOTH

"For a settlement of this character, it is not possible nor wise to say which is the victorious party. If there is any victory, I should say it belongs to both. The Congress has never made any bid for victory.

"In the very nature of things the Congress has a definite goal to reach, and there can be no question of victory without reaching the goal. I would, therefore, urge all my countrymen and all my sisters, instead of feeling elated, if they find in the terms any cause for elation, to humble themselves before God and ask Him to give them strength and wisdom to pursue the course that their mission demands for the time being, whether it is by way of suffering or by way of patient negotiation, consultation, and conference.

HEROIC PERIOD

"I hope, therefore, that the millions who have taken part in this struggle of suffering during the past twelve months will now during the period of conference and construction show the same willingness, the same cohesion, the same effort and the same wisdom that they have, in an eminent degree, shown during what I would describe as a heroic period in the modern history of India.

"But I know that if there would be men and women who will feel elated by the settlement, there are also those who will be, and are, keenly disappointed.

"Heroic suffering is like the breath of their nostrils. They rejoice in it as in nothing else. They will endure unendurable sufferings, be they ever so prolonged, but when sufferings cease they feel their occupation gone and feel also that the goal has receded from the view. To them I would only say, 'Wait, watch, pray, and hope.'

"Suffering has its well-defined limits. Suffering can be both wise and unwise, and, when the limit is reached, to prolong it would be not wise but the height of folly.

REAL OPENING

"It would be folly to go on suffering when the opponent makes it easy for you to enter into a discussion with him upon your longings. If a real opening is made it is one's duty to take advantage of it, and in my humble opinion, the settlement has made a real opening. Such a settlement has necessarily to be provisional, as this is. The peace arrived at is conditional upon many other things happening. The largest part of the written word is taken up with what may be called, 'terms of truce.' This had to be naturally so. Many things had to happen before the Congress could participate in the deliberations of the Conference. A recital of these was absolutely necessary. But the goal of the Congress is not to get a redress of past wrongs, important though they are. Its goal is Purna Swaraj which, indifferently rendered in English, has been described as Complete Independence.

"It is India's birthright, as it is of any other nation worthy of that name, and India cannot be satisfied with anything less, and throughout the settlement one misses that enchanting word. The clause which carefully hides that word is capable of a double meaning.

"Of the 'three girders,' Federation may be a mirage or it may mean a vital organic State in which the two limbs might work so as to strengthen the whole.

"Responsibility, which is the second girder, may be a mere shadow or it may be a tall, majestic, unbending and unbendable oak. 'Safeguards in the interests of India' may be purely illusory, and so many ropes tying the country hand and foot and strangling her by the neck, or they may be like so many fences protecting a tender plant requiring delicate care and attention.

"One party may give one meaning and another may give the three girders the other meaning. It is open under that clause to either party to work along its own lines, and if the Congress has shown readiness to take part in the deliberations of the Conference, it is because it seeks to make Federation, Responsibility, Safeguards, Reservations, or whatever other names that may be known by, such as would promote the real growth of the country along political, social, economic and moral lines.

"If the Congress succeeds in making its position acceptable to the Conference, then I claim that the fruit of that effort will be Complete Independence. But I know that the way to it is weary. There are many rocks, many pitfalls to be found across the way. But if Congressmen will approach the new task to which they are called with confidence and courage, I have no misgivings about the result. It is, therefore, in their hands either to make something noble and worth looking at out of the new opportunity that has come to them, or, by lack of self-confidence and want of courage, to fritter away the opportunity.

HELP OF OTHERS

"But I know that in this task Congressmen will require the aid of the other parties, the aid of the great Princes of India, and last, but by no means the least, the aid of Englishmen. I need not make any appeal at the present juncture to the different parties. I have little doubt that they are no less eager than Congressmen for the real freedom of their country.

FEDERATION IDEAL

"But the Princes are a different proposition. Their acceptance of the idea of Federation was certainly for me a surprise, but if they will become equal partners in a Federated India, I venture to suggest that of their own free will they should advance towards the position that what is called British India has been all these long years seeking to occupy.

"An undiluted autocracy, however benevolent it may be, and an undiluted democracy are an incompatible mixture bound to result in an explosion. It is, therefore, I think, necessary for them not to take up an uncompromising attitude and impatiently refuse to listen to an appeal from, or on behalf of, the would-be partner. If they refused any such appeal, they would make the position of the Congress untenable and indeed most awkward. The Congress represents or endeavours to represent the whole of the people of India. It recognises no distinction between those who reside in British India or in Indian States.

"The Congress has with great wisdom, and equally great restraint, refrained from interfering with the doings and affairs of the States and it has done so in order not to unnecessarily wound the susceptibilities of the States, but also by reason of the self-imposed restraint to make its voice heard by the States on a suitable occasion. I think that that occasion has now arrived. May then I hope that the great Princes will not shut their ears to the Congress appeal on behalf of the people of the States?

A WORD TO ENGLISHMEN

"I would like to make a similar appeal to the English. If India is to come to her own through conference and consultation, the good-will and active help of Englishmen are absolutely necessary. I must confess that what seems to have been yielded by them at the Conference in London is not even half enough, no approach to the goal that India has in view. If they will render real help, they must be prepared to let India feel the same glow of freedom which they themselves would die in order to possess. Their English sentiment would have to dare to let India wander away into the woods through errors. Freedom is not worth having if it does not connote freedom to err and even to sin. If God Almighty has given the humblest of His creature the freedom to err, it passes my comprehension how human beings, be they ever so experienced and able, can delight in depriving other human beings of that precious right.

"Anyway, the implication of inviting the Congress to join the Conference is most decidedly that the Congress may not be deterred, from any consideration save that of incapacity, from pressing for the fullest freedom. And the Congress does not consider India to be a sickly child requiring nursing, outside help, and other props.

TO OTHER NATIONS

"I would like also to register my appeal to the people of the great American Republic and the other nations of the earth. I know that this struggle, based as it is on truth and non-violence from which, alas! we, the votaries, have on occasions undoubtedly strayed, has fired their imagination and excited their curiosity. From curiosity they, and specially America, have progressed to tangible help in the way of sympathy. And I can say on behalf of the Congress and myself that we are all truly grateful for all that sympathy. I hope that in the difficult mission on which the Congress is now about to embark, we shall not only retain their sympathy but that it will grow from day to day. I venture to suggest, in all humility, that if India reaches her destiny through truth and non-violence, she will have made no small contribution to the world peace for which all the nations of the earth are thirsting, and she would also have, in that case, made some slight return for the help that those nations have been freely giving to her.

APPEAL TO POLICE

"My last appeal is to the Police and the Civil Service departments. The settlement contains a clause which indicates that I had asked for an inquiry into some of the Police excesses which are alleged to have taken place. The reason for waiving that inquiry is stated in the settlement itself. The Civil Service is an integral part of the machinery which is kept going by the Police Department. If they really feel that India is soon to become mistress in her own household and they are to serve her loyally and faithfully as her servants, it behoves them even now to make the people feel that when they have to deal with the members of the Civil Service and the Police Department, they are really dealing with their servants, honoured and wise undoubtedly, but nevertheless servants and not masters.

NON-SATYAGRAHI PRISONERS

"I owe a word to hundreds, if not thousands, of my erstwhile fellow prisoners on whose behalf I have been receiving wires, and who will still be languishing in jails when Satyagrahi prisoners who were jailed during the past 12 months will have been discharged. Personally I do not believe in imprisoning, by way of punishment, even those who commit violence. I know that those who have done violence through political motives, are entitled to claim, if not the same wisdom, certainly the same spirit of love and self-sacrifice that I would claim for myself. And, therefore, if I could have justly secured their liberty in preference to my own or that of fellow Satyagrahis, I should truthfully have secured it.

"But I trust they will realize that I could not in justice ask for their discharge. But that does not mean that I or the members of the Working Committee have not them in mind.

"The Congress has embarked deliberately, though provisionally, on a career of co-operation. If Congressmen honourably and fully implement the conditions applicable to them of the settlement, the Congress will obtain an irresistible prestige and would have inspired Government with confidence in its ability to ensure peace as, I think, it has proved its ability to conduct disobedience.

"And if the people in general will clothe the Congress with that power and prestige, I promise that it will not be long before every one of these political prisoners is discharged, including the detenus, the Meerut prisoners, and all the rest.

VIOLENT ORGANISATIONS

"There is, no doubt, a small but active organisation in India which would secure India's liberty through violent action. I appeal to that organisation, as I have done before, to desist from its activities, if not yet out of conviction, then out of expedience. They have perhaps somewhat realized what great power non-violence has. They will not deny that the almost miraculous mass awakening was possible only because of the mysterious and yet unfailing effect of non-violence. I want them to be patient and give the Congress, or, if they will, give me, a chance to work out the plan of truth and non-violence. After all, it is hardly yet a full year since the Dandi march. One year in the life of an experiment affecting 300 millions of human beings is but a second in the cycle of time. Let them preserve their precious lives for the service of the Motherland to which all will be presently called, and let them give to the Congress an opportunity of securing the release of all the other political prisoners and, maybe, even rescuing from the gallows those who are condemned to them as being guilty of murder.

"But I want to raise no false hopes. I can only state publicly what is my own and the Congress aspiration. It is for us to make the effort. The result is always in God's hands.

A PERSONAL NOTE

"One personal note and I have done. I believe that I put my whole soul into the effort to secure an honourable settlement. I have pledged my word to Lord Irwin that in making good the terms of the settlement, in so far as they bind the Congress, I should devote myself heart and soul to the task. I worked for the settlement, not in order to break it to pieces at the very first opportunity, but in order to strain every nerve to make absolutely final what to-day is provisional, and to make it a precursor of the goal to attain which the Congress exists.

"Lastly, I tender my thanks to all those who have been unceasing in their efforts in making the settlement possible."

AN EPOCH-MAKING INTERVIEW

Another epoch-making interview was granted the next day (the 6th of March, 1931) at 11-30 to the various journalists present in Delhi, Indian and foreign, in answer to their questions. Among those present on the occasion were Mr. James Mills, of the Associated Press of America, Mr. Peterson of the *London Times*, Mr. Shirer of the *Chicago Tribune*, Mr. Holton James of *The Boston Evening Transcript*, Mr. Ingles of *The Christian Science Monitor* (U. S.), Mr. J. N. Sahani of *The Hindustan Times* and Mr. Needham of *The Pioneer* and *The Civil and Military Gazette*. Here are the questions and answers in full:—

'PURNA SWARAJ'

Q. You used the expression 'Purna Swaraj' in your yesterday's statement, which you say can be indifferently translated into 'Complete Independence.' What is your correct interpretation of 'Purna Swaraj'?

A. I cannot give you a proper answer as there is nothing in the English language to give the exact equivalent of 'Purna Swaraj.' 'Swaraj.' in its original meaning, means 'self-rule.' Independence has no such meaning about it. 'Swaraj means 'disciplined rule from within.' 'Purna' means 'complete.' Not finding any equivalent, we have loosely adopted the word 'Complete Independence,' which every body understands. 'Purna Swaraj' does not exclude association with any nation, much less with England. But it can only mean association for mutual benefit, and at will.

INDEPENDENCE RESOLUTION

Q. In view of the second paragraph of the agreement, would it be consistent for the Congress to reaffirm its resolution relating to full Independence, passed at the Madras, Calcutta and Lahore Sessions?

A. Yes; decidedly. Because there is nothing to prevent the Congress at Karachi passing a similar resolution, and. what is more, pressing that at the forthcoming R. T. C. I am betraying no secret by telling you that I took good care to ascertain that position and to make my own position clear before agreeing to the settlement.

THE IMMEDIATE PROGRAMME

Q. What is your immediate programme?

A. I am going on Sunday to Ahmedabad, will stay there for two days, and then go to Kaira for two days and to Surat for another two days. I will reach Bombay on the 16th and then return to Delhi on the 19th.

SECOND R. T. C.

Q. Do you favour the second Round Table Conference to be held in India or England?

A. It all depends. I have no views for the present. Thinking audibly, however, I would prefer the first part of the Conference to be held in India, to be wound up later in London.

Q. Will you participate formally in the Conference?

A. I hope to. In fact, it is highly likely. (Laughter)

Q. Will you press for 'Purna Swaraj' at the Conference?

A. We shall deny our very existence if we do not press for it.

CONGRESS AND 'SAFEGUARDS'

Q. Will you accept the present safeguards and reservations?

A. Not the present safeguards and reservations. Truly, in this respect the Congress position has been made clear to the world, and whoever invites the Congress to a political conference is expected to know what the Congress stands for. I have taken as much precaution as my being is capable of to make the Congress position clear, and knowing that it is even now open to His Majesty's Government not to invite the Congress to participate in the Conference. There is nothing in the settlement, as I read it, to compel that participation.

Q. What will be the agenda before the Karachi Congress?

A. I cannot say. It will depend on the W. C. which will meet before the Karachi Session.

SENTENCE ON BHAGAT SINGH

Q. Would it be fair to ask, if I may do so, whether the sentences on Bhagat Singh and others will be commuted to transportation for life?

A. It would be better not to ask me that question. Regarding this there is sufficient material in the newspapers to allow journalists to draw their own inferences. Beyond that I would not like to go.

'YOUNG INDIA'

Q. Do you intend bringing out *Young India* again?

A. As soon as I can. It all depends on the putting into effect the settlement, which implies the return of machinery, etc., which was confiscated under the Press Ordinance. I would certainly be eager to resume the printing of *Young India*. Of course, *Young India* has continued to be published on a cyclostyle. We have suspended the publication of this week's issue to fulfil the terms of settlement, which includes the discontinuance of unauthorised news-sheets.

MUTUAL 'GOODNESS'

Q. What was that which turned the tide of negotiations when things became hopeless on Saturday?

A. (Mahatmaji smilingly retorted) Goodness on the part of Lord Irwin and, perhaps, (added he, still more smilingly,) equal goodness on my part as well. (Laughter).

Q. Do you regard the present agreement to be the greatest achievement of your life, to your credit, so far?

A. (Mahatmaji laughed and remarked) I do not know what great achievements there are to my credit so far, and if this is one of them.

Q. If you could attain 'Purna Swaraj' would you consider that such an achievement?

A. I think, if that comes, I should certainly consider it as such.

Q. Do you expect to achieve 'Purna Swaraj' in your life time?

A YOUNG MAN OF 62

A. I do look for it most decidedly. (And then Mahatmaji added smilingly) I still consider myself a young man of 62 according to Western notions.

SAFEGUARDS

Q. Would you be prepared to admit any safeguards in the future Constitution?

A. Yes. Those that are reasonable and wise. Take, for example, the question of Minorities. I can understand that we cannot achieve our purpose as a great Nation, if we do not regard the rights of Minorities as a sacred trust. I should regard that as a legitimate safeguard.

ARMY AND FINANCE

Q. What about Army and Finance?

A. Finance, yes. That is to say, if we have a Public Debt, as we have, so much as falls to our lot will have to be secured. To that extent I would be bound in honour to entertain safeguards for the country's credit and her consequent expansion. With reference to the Army, so far as my intelligence takes me, I cannot think of any safeguards except this, that we should guarantee the pay and the fulfilment of any other condition we might have undertaken to fulfil in connection with British soldiers required for the sake of India. That I can well understand.

DEBTS REPUDIATION

Q. Will you repudiate India's debts?

A. I will not repudiate one single farthing that can be legitimately debited to us. But unfortunately there has been a great deal of confusion about this talk of repudiation. The Congress has never sought to repudiate a single rupee of the national obligation. But what the Congress has asked for, and will insist upon, is the justness of the obligation that might be sought to be imposed on a future Government, even as a buyer would like to know what obligation is undertaken when entering on a new purchase. The Congress has suggested that in case there can be no adjustments, an independent Tribunal may be appointed.

QUESTION OF TRIBUNAL

Q. Do you think the League of Nations a proper Tribunal?

A. So far as I can say off-hand, the League of Nations is a proper Tribunal. But the League of Nations may not undertake such a responsibility. Besides, England may not like such a Tribunal. Any Tribunal agreeable, therefore, to England and India would be acceptable to me.

Q. Will you press this question at the Round Table Conference?

A. It will be necessary to do so when the question of examination and acceptance of national obligations came up. You may say, in other words, that these obligations will be taken up subject to national audit.

'SERMON ON THE MOUNT'

Q. Does this provisional settlement represent the practical application of the Sermon on the Mount suggested by *The Hindustan Times* this morning? (asked a foreign journalist).

A. I do not think I can judge. It is for the critics to judge how far this has been done.

BOYCOTT OF FOREIGN CLOTH

Q. Do you think boycott of foreign cloth should be relaxed as a result of the settlement?

A. On the contrary, no. The boycott of foreign cloth is not a political weapon, but is intended for the promotion of the universal supplementary industry of India—Charkha. Its activity is wholly in connection with importation of foreign cloth. If I had the reigns of Government, I would certainly resort to high protective tariff. I consider such protective tariff possible even by the present Government. The present duties that have been imposed are, however, not prohibitive but merely revenue duties for economic purposes.

COMPLETE EQUALITY

Q. What is your idea of 'Purna Swaraj'?

A. I am a visionary and, therefore, picture to myself all kinds of things that have no reality about them. 'Purna Swaraj' is not incompatible with, but is based upon, complete equality. The popular mind cannot conceive of that equality. By equality I mean that instead of Downing Street being the centre of Imperial activity, Delhi should be the centre. Friends suggest that England may not accommodate herself to that position. The British are a practical people and as they love liberty for themselves, it is only a step further to have liberty for others. I know, if the time comes to concede the equality I want for India, they will say that that is what they have all along desired. The British people have a faculty of self-delusion as no other people have. Yes, to my mind equality means the right to secede.

NOTHING TO CHOOSE

Q. Do you prefer the English people as a governing race to other races?

A. I have no choice to make. I do not want to be governed but by myself.

Q. Would you like to have 'Purna Swaraj' under the British flag?

A. Not under this flag. Under a common flag, if possible; under a separate national flag, if necessary.

Q. Do you expect to solve the Hindu-Muslim question before you go to the Conference?

A. That is my desire, but I do not know how far I can realise it. At present, I do not think it will be worth while our going to the

Conference without solving this question. I do not think unity can be brought about at the Conference.

Q. Will it take years to bring about Hindu-Muslim unity?

A. I do not think so. There is no disunity among the Hindu and Muslim masses. The disunity is at the surface, and this counts so much, since those who are at the surface are the people who represent the political mind of India.

NATIONAL ARMY

Q. Do you envisage the possibility of doing away with a National Army when 'Purna Swaraj' is obtained?

A. As a visionary, yes. But I do not think it is possible for me to see it during my life time. It may take ages before the Indian Nation may accommodate itself to having no Army at all. It is possible my want of faith may account for this pessimism on my part. But I do not exclude such a possibility. No one was prepared for the present mass awakening and the strict adherence to non-violence—aberrations notwithstanding—on the part of the people, and that certainly fills me with some hope that Indian leaders will be courageous enough in the near future, when they will be able to say that they do not need to have any Army. For civil purposes, the Police may be considered sufficient.

BOLHEVIK INVASION

Q. Do you not fear a Bolshevik invasion in the near future?

A. I have no such fear.

Q. Are you not afraid of Bolshevik propaganda spreading into India?

A. I do not think the Indian people are so gullible.

Q. What good do you see in Bolshevism?
A. (Mahatmaji laughed and remarked) I have not really studied Bolshevism to that extent. If there is anything good in it, India should have no hesitation to take it and adopt it as its own.

INDIA'S PREMIER

Q. Would you agree to become the Prime-Minister of the future Government?
A. No. It will be reserved for younger minds and stouter hands.
Q. Supposing the people want you and insist?
A. I will seek shelter behind journalists like you. (laughter).
Q. Will you abolish all machinery if Purna Swaraj is achieved? (asked an American Journalist).
A. Not a bit. Far from abolishing it, I am likely to order much more from America (laughter), and who knows I may give preference to British machinery instead? (further laughter).
Q. Will you return to the Ashram before Swaraj is attained?
A. No; I propose to see the Ashram but will not live at the Ashram till my vow of Purna Swaraj is fulfilled.

'AN EFFECTIVE WEAPON'

Q. From your answer regarding Military for India, is it to be concluded that you do not envisage the possibility of non-violence becoming an effective weapon in solving international complications?
A. I consider that non-violence will become such a weapon, supposing that the Army is in India, as there may be in other nations in the world. First, there is a change in ideas. Action is a slow process. Nations will rely more and more on consultation and arbitration, and progressively less and less on armies. Armies may gradually be reduced to spectacular things, just as toys, remnants of something that is past and not as instruments of protection of the Nation.

High tributes were paid by Lord Irwin to Gandhi, even as Gandhi himself had showered them on Lord Irwin. At a banquet given to the Viceroy, His Excellency paid an eloquent tribute to the honesty, sincerity, and lofty patriotism of Mahatma Gandhi, with whom, he said, it was a pleasure and privilege to work. Mahatma Gandhi, he added, was on his side doing everything possible to convince his countrymen and to bring about an atmosphere congenial to peace, and he on his part hoped to do every thing to make it possible for England and India to arrive at a peaceful settlement. Lord Irwin, speaking at a luncheon of the British Indian Union at the Hyde Park Hotel, London, on the 15th May, said: "I believe, from my knowledge of India, that if Mr. Gandhi comes to London, he will strain every nerve to secure an agreement, on these safeguards and other matters which will form the subject of discussion."

Now that hostilities had ceased, the Congress organisations were once more revived, the ban upon them being lifted. The Congress organisation is like a hibernating animal which lies seemingly dormant for a season and develops tremendous activity with the change of seasons. No sooner had the Pact been signed than the General Secretary of the A.I.C.C. issued instructions to Congressmen regarding the conduct of election of delegates to the next Congress. The W.C. divided the quota of delegates allotted to each district into two halves, one-half being elected by those who have suffered imprisonment in the campaign and the other half in the usual manner. Various detailed instructions to implement this new method were also issued. The ex-prisoners were to be elected at a meeting. Mr. Aney was appointed referee for the election of delegates from Bengal. Instructions were also issued on the same day to Congressmen, to discontinue Civil Disobedience and No-tax campaigns, as well as boycott of British goods as such. But the boycott of intoxicating drinks and drugs and of all foreign cloth and liquor shops was permitted, and directed to be continued. Picketing should be unaggressive and should not involve coercion, intimidation, hostile demonstration or obstruction to the public, or any offence under the ordinary law. Unauthorised news-sheets should be stopped. In fact, the instructions covered every item in the agreement. Gandhi himself added to these instructions the following set of conditions to be observed by the volunteers while picketing liquor and foreign cloth shops:—

1. The seller or the purchaser cannot be treated discourteously.
2. Volunteers cannot prostrate themselves before the shops or before the vehicles.
3. They cannot raise shouts as raised at the time of mourning. (Cries of 'Hai! Hai!')
4. Effigies cannot be burnt or buried.
5. Even if he is boycotted, one cannot stop a shop-keeper or a purchaser purchasing his provision or other necessaries. But one cannot go to his place for dinners or accept any services from him.
6. Fasts and hunger-strikes cannot be resorted to under any circumstances. Fasts could only be resorted to in case of a breach of contract, and when the parties respect and love each other.

Continuing, Gandhi writes:—

"If anybody contends that under the above restricted conditions the boycott of foreign cloth or liquor could not be successful, then, I would say: 'let the boycott be unsuccessful.' Such sceptics have apparently no faith in the efficacy of non-violence. My object in placing ladies in charge of this function was to get complete observance thereof and create an atmosphere of complete non-violence.

"If the non-violence atmosphere could be observed in every respect, I trust both boycotts could be carried out. If, on the contrary, we cross the limits, then, however good the immediate result may seem to be, poison will permeate among us and a fight may ensue. And if we fall a prey to a family-war, boycott is doomed and Swaraj would only be a dream. I, therefore, trust that my advice, considering it to be that of an experienced physician, will be observed by all. If the boycott is not successful by the observance of my conditions, I know that the responsibility for the failure of boycott will rest upon me. I am prepared to take that responsibility."

(*Free Press of India*).

The Working Committee also elected Vallabhbhai the President of the Karachi Congress, as the normal procedure for election of President was not possible under the abnormal conditions that had prevailed for about a year.

There was no small difficulty in making the necessary arrangements for the Karachi Congress, for, although the session was contemplated ever since the release of the members of the W.C. on the 1st of March, the uncertainty about the fate of the truce made the position of the Karachi friends most unenviable. But there was one adavantage in that the Karachi Session was the first to be held after the severe winter had passed. At Lahore, the decision had been made that the Congress should meet not in December, but late in February, or early in March, and by a strange coincidence it became possible for the Congress to hold its annual session in the month of March as the truce had just then materialised. The change of season made a pavilion unnecessary, for the Congress would meet in the open air. All that was required was a rostrum and a platform with grounds enclosed.

The success of the arrangements for the Karachi Session was mainly due to the co-operation of the local Municipality under the inspiration and guidance of Jamshed N. R. Mehta. Before the open session of the Congress began, an open air meeting preliminary to the regular session of the Congress was arranged at Karachi on the 25th March, where persons paying an admission fee of four annas would be allowed to see and hear Gandhi. The collection thus made alone amounted to Rs. 10,000 in Karachi. It was at this meeting that Gandhi coined the now-famous expression, "Gandhi may die, but Gandhism will live for ever."

Sirdar Vallabhbhai J. Patel who presided over the Congress, acknowledged in his short Presidential Address the tribute paid, in his election as President, not to him, a mere peasant, but to Gujarat which had taken a large share in the fight for freedom. He pointed out that if the Congress had not entered into the Gandhi-Irwin Pact, it would have put itself in the wrong and he proceeded to explain the significance of the Pact and the duty of Congressmen in the light of the Pact.

The Karachi Congress which should have met under the radiance of universal joy met really under the gloom cast by the news of the execution of the three youths, Bhagat Singh, Raja Guru and Sukha Dev. The ghosts of these three departed young men were casting a shadow over the assembly. It is no exaggeration to say that at that moment Bhagat Singh's name was as widely known all over India and was as popular as Gandhi's. Gandhi, in spite of his best efforts, had not been able to get the sentences of these three youths commuted.

That was not all. They who were praising Gandhi for his strenuous efforts to save their lives began to pour forth volleys of wrath over the language to be adopted in regard to the resolution to be moved for the three martyrs. It is really a point of doubt, even at this distance of time, as to which resolution was the more arresting one at Karachi—that relating to Bhagat Singh or that relating to the ratification of the Gandhi-Irwin agreement. The resolution relating to Bhagat Singh was taken virtually as the first on the agenda, after the usual condolences were offered in respect of the demise of Pandit Motilal Nehru, Maulana Mahomed Ali,—who passed away while in London for the R.T.C. and whose body was buried in Jerusalem,—Maulvi Mazar-ul-Haq, Sjt. Revashanker J. Jhaveri, Shah Muhammad Zubair and Gurunadha Mudaliar. The point at issue on the Bhagat Singh resolution was, whether the phrase "while dissociating itself from and disapproving of political violence in any shape or form," should be incorporated in recording the admiration of the bravery and sacrifice of himself and his comrades. We give the resolution below:—

II. SIRDAR BHAGAT SINGH AND HIS COMRADES

"This Congress, while dissociating itself from and disapproving of political violence in any shape or form, places on record its admiration of the bravery and sacrifice of the late Sirdar Bhagat Singh and his comrades Syts. Sukha Dev and Raja Guru, and mourns with the bereaved families the loss of these lives. The Congress is of opinion that this triple execution is an act of wanton vengeance and is a deliberate flouting of the unanimous demand of the Nation of commutation. This Congress is further of opinion that Government have lost the golden opportunity of promoting good-will between the two nations, admittedly held to be essential at this juncture, and of winning over to the method of peace the party which, being driven to despair, resorts to political violence."

The reservation made by the Congress was but the minimum that Congress could have made consistently with its cult of non-violence, but it must be remarked that the phrase gave occasion for the younger section, inclined unfavourably to Gandhism, to move amendments for its omission. The Volunteers' Conference passed the resolution with the phrase omitted, and the phrase became the bone of contention subsequently at Provincial Conferences. While the proceedings were going on, there was tumult and uproar outside the enclosure from young friends who had, the previous morning, organised a black flag demonstration at the station when Gandhi and Vallabhbhai had left the train, 12 miles from Karachi. Gandhi with his good humour greeted the band of young men and gracefully received the black flowers from their hands. And the band who came to 'attack' remained to 'protect.' It escorted Gandhi and his party to a little distance from the station.

The next resolution considered by the Congress was the one relating to the release of prisoners. By that time it had become evident that Government were pursuing not merely a niggardly policy, but proving untrue to the promises made and even the terms agreed upon in regard to the release of prisoners. Therefore, the Congress expressed its emphatic opinion that, "if the object of the settlement between the Government and the Congress is the promotion of good-will between Great Britain and India and if the settlement is an earnest of Great Britain's determination to part with power, the Government should release all political prisoners, detenus and under-trials not covered by the settlement, and remove all political disabilities imposed by the Government on Indians, whether in India or abroad, on account of their political opinions or acts," and added that "this Congress reminds the Government that if they will respond to this resolution, they will somewhat allay the strong public resentment that has been roused by the recent executions."

There was yet another cause which cast a gloom over the Karachi Congress. While the Congress was in session, serious Hindu-Muslim riots started in Cawnpore resulting in the murder of Ganesh Shankar Vidyarthi in his attempt to promote peace and good-will and save the Muslims from the fury of the Hindus. It was an event that drowned the country and the Congress in the same immeasurable sorrow as the murder of Swami Shraddhananda had done on the eve of the Gauhati Congress (1926). It is but appropriate to say a word about the Cawnpore riots. Cawnpore was not a place notorious for its communal outbursts There was a sporadic outbreak in 1907, and again in 1928 and 1929. Cawnpore is populated mainly by the Hindus who form 5/6 of the population while the Muslims and other minorities form a sixth. Bhagat Singh and his two comrades had been executed on the 23rd March in Lahore. There were *hartals* all over the country, and those in Bombay, Karachi, Lahore, Calcutta, Madras and Delhi passed off quietly. A partial *hartal* was observed in Cawnpore and a large mourning procession was taken out with the pictures of the three martyrs and with black flags. The Hindus had closed the shops but the Muslims did not do it. Shortly before, when Mahomed Ali died, the Hindus had not participated in the *hartal* oragnised by the Muslims. Well, a situation like this needs no further elaboration. The match as well as the gunpowder are there. On the 24th March, began the plunder of Hindu shops. Even on the night of the 23rd March, some fifty were wounded. On the 25th, there was a blaze. Shops and temples were set fire to and burnt to cinders. The Police did not render any assistance; disorder, arson, loot, murder, spread like wild fire. Five hundred families abandoned their houses and took shelter in villages. Dr. Ramachandra was one of the worst sufferers. All the members of his family, including his wife and aged parents, were killed and their bodies were thrust into gutters. According to the official estimates, 166 were killed and 480 were injured. Babu Purushottam Das Tandon and a few other friends were immediately sent to the scene at Cawnpore by the Congress, but little could be done to restore peace. Ganesh Shankar was missing from the 25th and it was only on the 29th that his body was recovered, being identified by his pure khaddar, that being the only corpse having khaddar, and by the tattoo mark—Gajendra—on his arm, and from certain papers including an article on the Karachi Congress recovered from his pocket. He had saved many Muslim families that day and appears to have been decoyed into a quarter which he entered unhesitatingly and where he bowed his head before the furious mob like a true Satyagrahi. If his blood could effect unity and quench their thirst, they were most welcome to stab him to death. The Congress passed the following resolution on this tragic event:—

"The Congress notes with deep grief the news of the death, during the strife, of Ganesh Shankar Vidyarthi, President, UP. P.C.C., who was one of the most selfless among national workers and who, by his freedom from communal bias, had endeared himself to all parties and communities. While tendering condolence to the family of the deceased, the Congress notes with pride that a prominent worker of the first rank was found sacrificing his precious life in the attempt to rescue those in danger and restore peace and sanity in the midst of strife and insanity. The Congress asks all concerned to utilize this noble sacrifice for promoting peace and never for vengeance, and appoints a Committee to discover the cause of the tension and to take such measures as may be necessary to heal the breach and to prevent the poison from spreading to the adjoining areas and districts."

The Committee that was appointed consisted of six members with Dr. Bhagavandas as Chairman. We may here anticipate events and point out that a bulky volume was produced and presented to the Working Committee. It was ultimately printed after a long time, but its circulation has been stopped by the Government.

Then comes the resolution on the provisional settlement.

The cardinal resolution of the Congress is a consummate draft embodying in it the standpoint of the Congress and striving to secure through it, for the Congress, what might be considered ambiguous or even dubious in the Gandhi-Irwin agreement. The 'safeguards' of the latter are the 'adjustments' of the former and the "safeguards in the interests of India" of the agreement are "the adjustments that may be demonstrably necessary in the interests of India." Again what the agreement might be interpreted to deduct, the Karachi resolution has expressly sought to add, namely, "so as to give the Nation control over the Defence forces, External Affairs, finance, and fiscal and economic policy." Here, in a sentence, is the objective of the Congress. The Congress next proceeded to congratulate all those that

C. R. Das
1922 : Gaya

Mohamed Ali
1923 : Cocanada

Abdul Kalam Azad
1923 : Delhi (Special)

Mahatma Gandhi
1924 : Belgaum

underwent great sufferings in the late Civil Disobedience campaign, especially the women, and resolved that no discrimination against the sex in the matter of franchise would be accepted by the Congress. The rest of the resolutions speak for themselves. They relate to the constructive programme and are given hereunder:—

THE GANDHI-IRWIN AGREEMENT

"The Congress, having considered the provisional settlement between the W. C. and the Government of India, endorses it, and desires to make it clear that the Congress goal of Purna Swaraj (Complete Independence) remains intact. In the event of the way being otherwise open to the Congress to be represented at any Conference with the representatives of the British Government, the Congress delegation will work for this objective and, in particulâr, so as to give the Nation *control over the Defence forces*, External Affairs, finance, fiscal and economic policy, and to have a scrutiny, by an impartial Tribunal, of the financial transactions of the British Government in India and to examine and assess the obligations to be undertaken by India or England, and the right of either party to end the partnership at will and to make India free to accept such adjustments as may be demonstrably necessary in its interests.

"The Congress appoints and authorises Mahatma Gandhi to represent it at the Conference with the addition of such other delegates as the W. C. may appoint to act under his leadership."

VI. CIVIL DISOBEDIENCE SUFFERERS

"This Congress congratulates all those who underwent great sufferings during the late Civil Disobedience campaign, whether through imprisonment, shooting, bayonet or *lathi*-charges, emigration from their homes and loss of property by repression. The Congress more especially congratulates the women of India who rose in their thousands and assisted the Nation in its struggle for freedom, and respectfully assures them that no Constitution will be acceptable to the Congress that discriminates against the sex in the matter of franchise."

VII. COMMUNAL RIOTS

"This Congress regards the communal riots of Benares, Mirzapur, Agra, Cawnpore and other places as highly injurious to the movement for India's freedom and strongly condemns those who are responsible for causing or provoking such riots, or disseminating false rumours which promote such riots and considers their peace-destroying activities deserving of the strongest censure. This Congress also deeply deplores the murders of citizens, especially of women and children, and sincerely sympathises with the living victims of the savagery and with the families of the dead."

VIII. PROHIBITION

"The Congress notes with satisfaction the visible progress of the Nation towards total prohibition during the past twelve months and calls upon all Congress organisations to continue the anti-drink and drugs campaign with renovated vigour and hopes that the women of the country will redouble their efforts in weaning the drink and drug addict from a habit that ruins both body and soul and desolates happy homes."

IX. KHADDAR

"Experience gained during the past ten years through work in hundreds of villages has made it abundantly clear that the deepening poverty of the masses is due, among other things, to forced unemployment for want of a supplementary industry during leisure hours, and that only the spinning-wheels supply that want on a universal scale. It has been further observed that the people having given up the wheel, and consequently khaddar, buy foreign cloth or cloth made in indigenous mills, thus causing a double drain from the villages,—the drain in the shape of loss of fruits of labour and price of cloth. This double drain can be avoided only by the exclusion of foreign cloth, and Indian mills supplementing khaddar only so far as it may be necessary. This Congress, therefore, appeals to the public to refrain from the purchase of foreign cloth and to the dealers in foreign cloth and yarn to give up a trade that seriously injures the interests of the millions of villagers.

"This Congress further calls upon all Congress organisations and allied bodies to intensify the foreign cloth boycott by increasing khaddar territories.

"This Congress appeals to the States to associate themselves with this constructive effort and prevent the entry of foreign cloth and foreign yarn into their territories.

"This Congress also appeals to the owners of indigenous mills to assist the great constructive and economic movement by

1. giving their moral support to the supplementary village industry of hand-spinning by themselves using hand-spun.
2. by ceasing to manufacture cloth that may in any way compete with khaddar and to that end co-operating with the effort of the All-India Spinners' Association.
3. by keeping down the prices of their manufactures to the lowest possible limit.
4. by refraining from using foreign yarn, silk, or artificial silk in their manufacture.
5. by exchanging the existing stock of the foreign piecegoods merchants for swadeshi cloth and thus helping them to convert their business into swadeshi and by re-exporting the former; and
6. by raising the status of the mill workers and making them fell that they are

co-sharers with them as well in prosperity as in adversity.

"This Congress suggests to the great foreign houses that they will help international brotherhood and revolutionise commercial ethics if they will take the first step by recognising the soundness and necessity of the economic boycott by India of foreign cloth, and denying themselves a foreign trade that has admittedly hurt the economic well-being of India's masses, and diverting their attention to enterprises more in keeping with the wants of the nations other than their own."

X. PEACEFUL PICKETING

"This Congress notes with gratification the great success that has so far attended the boycott of foreign cloth and the sales of intoxicating drugs and drinks, and calls upon the Congress organisations not to relax their efforts in the matter of peaceful picketing, provided that the picketing shall be in strict accord with the terms of the settlement in this behalf between the Government and the Congress."

XI. FRONTIER PEOPLE

"This Congress declares that the people of India have no quarrel with the countries and peoples bordering on India and desires to establish and maintain friendly relations with them. The Congress disapproves of the so-called 'forward' policy of the British Government in India in the North-West Frontier and of all imperialist attempts to destroy the freedom of the people of the frontier. The Congress is strongly of opinion that the Military and financial resources of India should not be employed in the furtherance of this policy and the Military occupation of the tribesmen's territory should be terminated."

XII—N. W. F. PROVINCE

"Inasmuch as propaganda is said to be going on in the Frontier Province that the Congress does not mean well by them and it is desirable that the Congress should take steps to dispel this suspicion, this Congress hereby places on record its opinion that in any constitutional scheme the N. W. F. Province shall have the same form of Government as the other Provinces in India."

XIII—BURMA

"This Congress recognises the right of the people of Burma to claim separation from India to establish an independent Burma State or to remain an autonomous partner in a Free India with a right of separation at any time they may desire to exercise it. The Congress, however, condemns the endeavour of the British Government to force the separation of Burma without giving adequate opportunity to the Burmese people to express their views and against the declared wishes of their national political organisations. This endeavour seems to be deliberately engineered to perpetuate British domination there so as to make Burma, together with Singapore, by reason of the presence of oil and their strategic position, strongholds of Imperialism in Eastern Asia. The Congress is strongly opposed to any policy which would result in Burma being kept as a British dependency and her resources exploited for British Imperialism and would also be a menace to a Free India as well as to the other nations of the East. The Congress urges that the extraordinary powers given to the Government of Burma be withdrawn and the declaration by the Government that representative and important organisations of Burmese national opinion are illegal be also withdrawn, so that normal conditions be restored and the future of Burma may be discussed by her people without hindrance in a peaceful atmosphere and the will of the Burmese people may prevail."

XIV. INDIANS IN SOUTH AND EAST AFRICA

"The Congress views with alarm the trend of events in South Africa and East Africa regarding the position of Indian settlers in those countries. The contemplated legislation in South Africa is in contravention of promises and in some respects constitutes an attack even on legal rights. This Congress appeals to the Governments concerned to mete out to the Indian settlers the same measure of justice that they would claim for their nationals in a Free India. This Congress renders its thanks to Dinabandhu Andrews and Pandit Hridaynath Kunzru for their selfless labours on behalf of the settlers overseas."

It only remains to be remarked that the resolution on the Fundamental Rights and economic changes was somewhat sudden in its appearance before the W. C. The fact is that the atmosphere of the country determines the resolutions of the Congress. The question of Fundamental Rights was originally handled by Mr. C. Vijiaraghavachariar at the Amritsar Congress at dead of night in the bleak cold of the Punjab. Then it gained importance when he himself presided over the Nagpur Session. At Karachi, there was a certain cleavage between the younger and the older sections. People were not wanting who began to doubt whether, after all, the Congress was not drifting with the old current of Dominion Status, British Imperialism and a Brown Bureaucracy, and whether Labour problems,—of the peasants and the workers—and socialistic ideals were not going by the board. It was necessary to reassure the country on this subject. Gandhi was game for any issue provided it was an issue based on Truth and Non-violence, and it was an issue too of the village and the poor man.

Subject to these conditions, he had nothing to fear from socialistic ideals, or economic reform or Fundamental Rights. Jawaharlal Nehru was rather keen on these matters, not because of the rival groups bent on criticising the Congress but because these were matters on which the Nation should be clear in its own mind and should carry on education and propaganda among the masses. This was the genesis of the resolution. But it was also felt that a resolution of such far-reaching importance should be considered at greater leisure and should be studied and pondered over by the members of the W. C. as well as by the A.I.C.C. This view was accepted and accordingly power was given to the A.I.C.C. to revise, amend or add to the main resolution without injuring the principles and policy underlying it. The resolution, as amended by the A.I.C.C. in August, 1931 at Bombay, was as follows:—

> "This Congress is of opinion that to enable the masses to appreciate what 'Swaraj,' as conceived by the Congress, will mean to them, it is desirable to state the position of the Congress in a manner easily understood by them. In order to end the exploitation of the masses, political freedom must include real economic freedom of the starving millions. The Congress, therefore, declares that any Constitution which may be agreed to on its behalf should provide, or enable the Swaraj Government to provide, for the following:

FUNDAMENTAL RIGHTS AND DUTIES

1. (1) Every citizen of India has the right of free expression of opinion, the rights of free association and combination, and the right to assemble peacefully and without arms, for purposes not opposed to law or morality.

(2) Every citizen shall enjoy freedom of conscience and the right freely to profess

and practise his religion, subject to public order and morality.

(3) The culture, language and script of the minorities and of the different linguistic areas shall be protected.

(4) All citizens are equal before the law, irrespective of caste, creed or sex.

(5) No disability attaches to any citizen, by reason of his or her religion, caste, creed or sex, in regard to public employment, office of power or honour, and in the exercise of any trade or calling.

(6) All citizens have equal rights and duties in regard to wells, tanks, roads, schools and places of public resort, maintained out of State or local funds, or dedicated by private persons for the use of the general public.

(7) Every citizen has the right to keep and bear arms, in accordance with regulations and reservations made in that behalf.

(8) No person shall be deprived of his liberty nor shall his dwelling or property be entered, sequestered or confiscated, save in accordance with law.

(9) The State shall observe neutrality in regard to all religions.

(10) The franchise shall be on the basis of universal adult suffrage.

(11) The State shall provide for free and compulsory primary education.

(12) The State shall confer no titles.

(13) There shall be no capital punishment.

(14) Every citizen is free to move throughout India and to stay and settle in any part thereof, to acquire property and to follow any trade or calling, and to be treated equally with regard to legal prosecution or protection in all parts of India.

LABOUR

2. (a) The organisation of economic life must conform to the principle of justice, to the end that it may secure a decent standard of living.

(b) The State shall safeguard the interests of industrial workers and shall secure for them, by suitable legislation and in other ways, a living wage, healthy conditions of work, limited hours of labour, suitable machinery for the settlement of disputes between employers and workmen, and protection against the economic consequences of old age, sickness and unemployment.

3. Labour to be freed from serfdom and conditions bordering on serfdom.

4. Protection of women workers, and specially, adequate provision for leave during maternity period.

5. Children of school going age shall not be employed in mines and factories.

6. Peasants and workers shall have the right to form unions to protect their interests.

TAXATION AND EXPENDITURE

7. The system of land tenure and revenue and rent shall be reformed and an equitable adjustment made of the burden on agricultural land, immediately giving relief to the small peasantry by a substantial reduction of agricultural rent and revenue now paid by them, and in case of uneconomic holdings, exempting them from rent, so long as necessary, with such relief as may be just and necessary, to holders of small estates affected by such exemption or reduction in rent, and to the same end, imposing a graded tax on net income from land above a reasonable minimum.

8. Death duties on a graduated scale shall be levied on property above a fixed minimum.

9. There shall be a drastic reduction of Military expenditure so as to bring it down to at least one-half of the present scale.

10. Expenditure and salaries in civil departments shall be largely reduced. No servant of the State, other than specially employed experts and the like,

shall be paid above a certain fixed figure, which should not ordinarily exceed Rs. 500 per month.

11. No duty shall be levied on salt manufactured in India.

ECONOMIC AND SOCIAL PROGRAMME

12. The State shall protect indigenous cloth; and for this purpose pursue the policy of exclusion of foreign cloth and foreign yarn from the country and adopt such other measures as may be found necessary. The State shall also protect other indigenous industries, when necessary, against foreign competition.

13. Intoxicating drinks and drugs shall be totally prohibited, except for medicinal purposes.

14. Currency and exchange shall be regulated in the national interest.

15. The State shall own or control key industries and services, mineral resources, railways, waterways, shipping and other means of public transport.

16. Relief of agricultural indebtedness, and control of usury—direct and indirect.

17. The State shall provide for the Military training of citizens so as to organise a means of national defence apart from the regular Military forces.

The success of the Gandhi-Irwin Pact and the still greater success of the Karachi resolutions only added load after load to the already heavy burdens of Gandhi and the Congress. At the Karachi Congress one or two important matters were left over to be attended to or completed by the W. C. and the All-India Congress Committee. The Sikhs had raised the question of the flag and the incorporation into it of a colour acceptable to them. This matter had been moved even earlier at Lahore, and at Karachi it only gained an added importance demanding the attention of the Executive, as the general Congress could not possibly address itself off-hand to changes of a detailed nature, such as were involved in the Sikh demand. Accordingly, the new W. C. meeting on the 1st and 2nd April at Harchandnagar, Karachi, resolved to appoint a Committee for examining the objections taken to the existing colours as having been conceived on a communal basis and recommending a flag for the acceptance of the Congress. The Committee was authorised to take evidence and send up its report before July, 1931. Another subject which had greatly agitated the Congressmen at Karachi was the wild and vague report that the remains of the late Sirdar Bhagat Singh and Sriyuts Raja Guru and Sukhadev were mutilated and were not properly cremated, and were otherwise dealt with in an insulting manner. Accordingly the W. C. appointed a Committee to examine the allegations forthwith and to report to the W. C. on or before the 30th April. We may at once state that Bhagat Singh's father, who was largely responsible for the step taken was not able to produce any evidence in that behalf nor did he appear before the Committee to help it in any manner. Accordingly, nothing resulted. Thirdly, we have already referred to the manner in which the resolution on Fundamental Rights and economic programme was passed at the open Congress, and therefore a Committee was appointed to invite opinions and suggestions from Provincial Congress Committees and other bodies and persons and to report and to recommend to the W. C., on or before the 31st of May, such revision or amendment or addition as in its opinion may be necessary to make the resolution fuller and more exhaustive. Fourthly, we have seen that the Congress had all along been insisting upon an independent examination of the financial transactions of the British in India by an impartial tribunal and it was necessary to get our powder and shot ready for the battle that would necessarily rage over the subject. Accordingly a Committee was appointed to carry out a scrutiny into the financial transactions of the East India Company and the British Government in India and the so-called Public Debt of India and to report upon the obligations which should in future be borne by India or England. The Committee was requested to present its report by the end of May. Then again another Committee was appointed—it was not merely a Committee, but a deputation consisting of Gandhi, Vallabhbhai and Seth Jamnalalji—to meet the Muslim leaders to settle the communal question. There remained the political prisoners who were to be released under resolution No. III of the Congress, and Mr. Nariman was appointed to collect from all the Provinces details regarding such prisoners, and others covered by the resolution. The last question disposed of before the W. C. dispersed related to the resolution concerning the Congress delegation to the R. T. C. Most of the members of the W. C. were of the opinion that the deputation should consist not of a single individual but of about 15 members. Government were quite willing to accommodate up to 20. To them, it was undoubtedly a strategic advantage to have 15 or 20, not one. In the discussions that took place, the point was cleared that Gandhi was going to London, not to hammer out the details of a Constitution but to negotiate the fundamentals of a treaty. When this point was clarified, there were no two views on the subject, and opinion was unanimous that Gandhi alone should represent India. It was not only unanimous but ungrudging. One man would represent India better than many. It would be a moral asset to the Congress, as signifying unity of leadership in negotiating peace, as it doubtless connoted unity of command in conducting war. The representation of Congress by a single person with no axe to grind, and with no worldly desires beyond peace and goodwill and the happiness of the human kind, was in itself an achievement in the domain of the moral world which it would be difficult to appraise. Thus did it happen that the prestige of Britain was destined to be compromised by the exertion of the 'half-naked *fakir*' of India not only walking up and down the steps of the Viceregal Lodge in Delhi, but also negotiating peace on terms of equality in the halls of St. James' Palace.

CHAPTER II

The Breach of the Settlement

The period of strife and struggle was over. Arms were laid down but peace was not in sight. The victories of peace, it is true, are greater than those of war and in a sense the Congress was able to gain these victories and conserve them. But the very success of the Congress was destined to prove its disaster. In the first place, Congress attained a moral victory the multiple aspects of which began to unfold themselves rapidly with the march of time. Here are Congress Committees which were non-existent till yesterday, once more rising up in all their bloom, like the trees in the spring which had appeared almost withered up and dying. Here is the Congress flag, once again flying full-mast high on Congress offices and Congressmen's houses. Here are Congress officers, claiming as of right the return by the Police of every scrap of paper and every rag of cloth that had once been seized and taken away from them. Here are processions of volunteers marching in their semi-military uniforms or their national costumes with stars and stripes, batons and belts, singing national songs which were prohibited till only a moment ago, and carrying flags and festoons.

Above all here are the Congress folks, little girls and boys, grown-up men and women, picketing at liquor shops and foreign cloth shops and exhorting people not to drink and not to dress in 'videshi' fabrics. All these things are going on with impunity under the eye of the very policeman who was till yesterday jumping upon these people like a wolf on a fold. The underlings in the Police were not reconciled to such a surrender. The magistracy would not look upon it with favour. The Civilians felt crest-fallen. The bureaucracy thought they had lost everything. There was a feeling of disappointment and defeat in the myrmidons of Law and Order. The prisoners were being released every day and were being taken out in procession and garlanded and were making speeches, not always discreet, never perhaps humble, speeches which smacked of a tone of derision and a spirit of defiance, and every day the Congress was a factor to reckon with. Congress office-bearers would demand the release of a prisoner here or the return of the property there or the restoration of a public servant elsewhere. On the 18th of April, Lord Irwin left India and Gandhi bade him good-bye in Bombay. The personnel in the Viceregal Lodge changed. Old friendships and old promises were factors unknown to the new Viceroy. What if Lord Irwin had promised to secure the release of the Sholapur prisoners? What if he had offered to examine the cases of the internees individually? What if the Viceroy had promised to secure the pensions and the provident fund of the two Deputy Collectors who had resigned in Gujarat? What if he had promised to write to the Local Government for the restoration of properties sold to third parties in Bardoli? What if Lord Irwin undertook to include in the terms of their sentences the under-trial periods spent by the Meerut prisoners in prison?

Lord Irwin left India on the 18th April. Lord Willingdon had taken charge on the 17th—the previous day. Viceroys come and go but the Secretariat remains for ever. The Civilians that rule over the Districts are the real Viceroys. It was the democratization of the Indian Government and relief from the autocracy of the Civilian Collectors that were in the minds of the signatories of the Delhi Manifesto of November 2nd, 1929, when they wrote that the spirit of administration must change from that very day. No, it did not change after a year's fight; it did not change even after the signing of the Gandhi-Irwin agreement. The officialdom in the country felt the agreement to be an affront to their *Izzat* (prestige). There was virtually a revolt everywhere. Day in, day out, complaints poured into the Congress offices that the terms of the agreement were not duly implemented. The Congress on its part was most anxious to observe the conditions imposed upon it by the Pact. Those conditions chiefly related to the picketing and the avoidance of the mention of British goods in preaching boycott. If there were lapses here and there, the watchdogs of Government were there to call Congressmen to order. Congressmen did not mind even the *lathi*-charges that continued to be practised here, there and elsewhere. In Guntur, even after the Pact was signed, the Police indulged in this pastime. In East Godavari, a most tragic firing took place at Vadapalli resulting in four persons killed and several wounded, simply because the people put up Gandhi's portrait on a car and the Police objected. A situation developed erelong resulting in this unfortunate and unjustifiable firing. *Lathi*-charges and firing had become the second nature of the Police. They simply could not help doing it. Not that such oddities were at all a common feature, but that even the few cases that occurred were under utterly inexcusable conditions.

When the Congress concluded the truce, it was in high hopes that an agreement could be reached between the various communities in India, and also that Government would lend a helping hand to that end. But all such hopes failed. Gandhi knew quite well that instead of going to London without a Hindu-Muslim agreement in hand, he had much rather sit at home. Nevertheless, the W. C. met on the 9th, 10th, and 11th of June, 1931 in Bombay, and at the instance of Muslim friends and much against the inclinations of Gandhi, it passed a resolution to the effect that

> "The Committee is of opinion that, even should these efforts unfortunately fail, in order to avoid any possibility of the Congress attitude being misunderstood in any shape or form, other conditions being favourable, Mahatma Gandhi should represent the Congress at the R. T. C., if thereto required, for the presentation of the Congress position."

The W. C. was not without hopes that an agreement would be possible in England, if not earlier.

We shall presently revert to the subject of the observance of the conditions of the truce, but before doing so give a summary of the transactions of the meeting of the Working Committee in the month of June. Time was extended for the submission of the Reports of the Fundamental Rights' Committee and the Public Debt Committee. The Committee discountenanced the practice that had recently sprung up of Congress organizations issuing certificates to shops and handlooms dealing in cloth made of other than hand-spun yarn. Some Congress organizations were permitting the sale of existing stocks of foreign cloth. This was deprecated. A list of the prisoners not covered by the truce, which was prepared by Mr. Nariman, was asked to be submitted to Gandhi. A Swadeshi Board was to be formed to certify goods other than cloth. Some election disputes (Bengal and Delhi) were attended to. A grant of Rs. 250 was voted for the translation of Congress resolutions since 1885—in Hindi.

Now we resume the story of the truce and how far its conditions were being observed. The policy of the Congress was entirely one of a defensive nature. Gandhi had strictly warned the Congressmen in the country not to initiate any aggressive campaign, but not to suffer lying any insults to national self-respect. Demoralization was the great demon that Gandhi was seeking to avoid. Fear and a sense of helplessness were the things he insisted on conquering. The following is a summary of his instructions:—

"If they make the working of the settlement honourably impossible, if those things permitted us, Satyagrahis, are denied, it is the clearest warning that we are entitled to take defensive measures. But we go further. They say in Madras, 'you shall not put more than 5 pickets.' I have said previously, 'for the time being submit,' but hereafter we shall not submit; we shall put 5 at each entrance. But you may be sure that this will be a nine days' show; either they will have to recant or go ahead. We do not create a situation but we must act on the defensive. If, for instance, a flag demonstration is prohibited, we cannot put up with it, we must assert ourselves. If a procession is forbidden, we may even apply for a license, and if the license is not given, we break the prohibitory order. But where the monthly Flag demonstrations and usual public meetings are concerned, we need not wait and shall not wait for such permission nor apply for any. We must avoid helplessness and the demoralization arising therefrom.

"Regarding No-tax campaign, you can only permit it, you cannot place it as a programme; they must take it up themselves and bring their comrades into the movement. When that comes about, it becomes an economic issue. And where it becomes an economic issue, the masses will be drawn into the movement."

From the side of Government, there was abundant sympathy, and sweet words were poured forth by Lord

Willingdon. There was no reason to doubt the sincerity of his professions and faith. But it did not take long to discover that the high hopes engendered by the Viceroy's airy speeches were not to be realised. By the first week of July, Gandhi's mind was overcome with doubt as to whether all was not crumbling.

U. P.

In Sultanpur 90 persons had been prosecuted under Sec. 107 Cr. P. C. In another place—Bhavan Shahpur—the tenants were called upon to remove the national flags, by the Talukdar, and were taken into custody on their refusal. All the prominent members of the District Congress Committee were served with notices under Sec. 144 Criminal P. C. In Muttra a public meeting was forcibly dispersed by a Sub-Inspector. A Press message from Lucknow stated that 700 prosecutions were taking place at the time. All over the country, teachers and other employees who were suspended or had resigned from service for political propaganda sought to be restored, but in many cases in vain. Undertakings were demanded of students seeking admission into colleges that they would not take part in any future campaign. In Bichari lorry loads of policemen raided the houses of Congress workers, insulted women and burnt the national flags. In Bara Banki general orders under Sec. 144 applicable to areas, and blank orders signed by the District Magistrate, were given to Police Inspectors. Gandhi caps were removed by the Deputy Commissioner, and people were warned against their use, as also against going to the Congress. The same story repeats itself in the different districts of U. P. Some Talukdars, assured of Government support, reverted to their barbarous methods. Armed Police were terrorizing the villagers. One man died by beating administered by an Estate Zilladar and his men. Practice of making tenants 'murga', *i.e.*, making them stand like a cock, became common. The Punitive Police at Nowshara in the Chowtala in Hissar (Punjab) were not removed. A retired military sepoy's pension was forfeited. Inoffensive processions at Tarutan were *lathi*-charged. Political meetings were forbidden in cantonments.

BOMBAY.

Peaceful picketing against liquor was not allowed at unlicensed places and unlicensed hours in Ahmedabad, Ankaleswar and in Ratnagiri Districts. Prisoners were not released. In Bulsar five people were asked to pay fine for having allowed volunteer camps on their lands during the campaign and the lands were not restored unless the fines were paid. A boat sold by mistake by the Salt Collector long after the truce, was not restored, nor was the owner compensated. The Navajivan Press was not yet returned. *Watan* lands in Karnatak were not restored, except on an understanding not to take part in any future movement. Several Patels and Tallatis were not restored. The two Deputy Collectors that had resigned were not given their pension as Lord Irwin had promised. Two doctors and a supervisor were not restored. Eight girls and eleven boys were rusticated from Government schools for all time. Likewise four studied in Ankola. In Sirsi and Siddapur Talukas coercive processes were started against the cultivators, only partial relief being given in respect of their agrarian distress.

BENGAL

In Bengal one new circumstance was the demand of undertaking from legal practitioners. An Ashram seized under Ordinance IX was not restored. In Gauhati, students were asked a security of Rs. 50. In Jorhat, Prabhat Pheri boys were assaulted on the 19th June under orders of Superintendent Bartly.

DELHI

Undertakings were demanded of students.

AJMER-MERWARA

Certain teachers were debarred from service in aided schools.

MADRAS

On 13th July a Press Communique was published and officers were circularized that the peaceful picketing of the truce did not include picketing at *Slikari sals*. Members of the Tanjore Bar were served notices under Sec. 144 for picketing liquor shops. Volunteers were not permitted to stand nearer than 100 yards from toddy shops, while picketing and faked charges were brought against them. They were assaulted at different places and ordered not to hold umbrellas or flags and the public were warned against giving them water. At Ellore the number of picketers at each cloth shop was restricted to one or two. At Koilpatti, where the number was restricted to 5, pickets were prosecuted in May. At Coimbatore the number was restricted to 6. The fact is that the authorities were hostile to picketing. In Guntur an honorary assistant opthalmic surgeon was not restored to his office unless he would express regret for anti-Government propaganda.

Guns and gun-licenses forfeited for participation in the movement were not being returned in numerous cases. Prisoners who were convicted in groups on common evidence were not all released, though the evidence was the same against all. The Sholapur Martial Law prisoners in respect of whose release Lord Irwin had made a definite promise were not released.

But all these paled into insignificance before the flagrant breach of the truce committed by Government in Bardoli. In this Taluka, it will be remembered, there was a No-tax campaign. The current revenues payable were 22 lakhs of rupees, out of which 21 lakhs were paid. We give below an extract giving Gandhi's complaint and Government's reply:—

GANDHI'S COMPLAINT

"(1) In Bardoli Rs. 21,00,000 out of Rs. 22,00,000 have been paid out of the current dues. It is claimed that Congress workers are responsible for these payments. When they began collections, it is common knowledge that they told the peasants that they were to pay all they could both of the current dues and arrears. The majority declared themselves to be hardly able to pay even the current dues. The authorities after hesitation, and even flat refusal for some time in some cases, accepted payments and gave receipts on account of current dues. Now to demand arrears or current dues from those who plead inability is a breach of faith with the workers and the people. So far as the arrears are concerned, it is contended that if the authorised arrears are suspended because of the fall in prices, as they are, the unauthorised arrears deserve the same treatement with greater force, because the men having been civil resisters have in addition to the losses due to low prices, suffered severe losses through migration. These losses have been estimated and presented to the authorities. Nevertheless Congress workers have offered to re-examine cases suspected by the authorities. What they resent is coercive processes, fines and display of the Police who surrounded people's houses."

Reply of Bombay Government

"(1) It cannot be admitted that to demand arrears or current year's dues from those who plead inability is a breach of faith with the workers and the people; inability must be proved and not merely pleaded. The suggestion that unauthorised arrears deserve at least the same treatment as authorised arrears this year has no force. Authorised arrears only exist when the crops on account of which they are due were whole or partial failures and the cultivators could not afford to pay their dues at the usual season. Unauthorised arrears in Bardoli exist not because the crops failed but because the cultivators refused to pay their land revenue as part of the Civil Disobedience campaign. The question whether any particular individual can or cannot pay owing to losses of any kind is a matter for investigation in each case. In Bardoli there has only been one attachment of property in connection with the realisation of revenue. The fact that the Collector has had regard to deserving cases is shown by the circumstances that he has suspended land revenue collections to the extent of about Rs. 18,000 and granted remissions to the extent of about Rs. 1,900. Police were not used directly for the collection of land revenue, but they were taken only to a few villages which the revenue officers were afraid to visit for the purpose of collecting land revenue without the support of the Police, in case of a disturbance. Their duties were confined to protecting the person of the Mamlatdar or the principal revenue officer at the village, to guarding a house in case attachment proceedings were undertaken, and in some cases to accompanying the inferior village servants when sent to call a defaulter."

All these complaints were handed to the Government of India when Gandhi went to Simla about the middle of July. The developments that took place within the next ten days were indeed most unexpected. Gandhi wrote straight to the Collector of Surat from Bardoli what he felt on the subject, and forwarded a copy of the letter to the Government of Bombay.

The reply of the Governor of Bombay was altogether disappointing. The Simla authorities supported the Government of Bombay.

Arbitration Board

Then there was the question of arbitration which had been raised by Gandhi. The correspondence that ensued in this connection is given below:—

Extract from the letter of M. K. Gandhi Esq, to the Hon'ble Mr. H. W. Emerson. C.S.I., C.I.E., C.B.E., Home Secretary to the Government of India, dated Borsad, the 14th June, 1931:—

"You might be unable to interfere with the working or not working of the settlement by Local Governments, or your interference may not go far enough according to my view of the settlement. The time has, therefore, perhaps arrived for the appointment of a permanent board of arbitration to decide questions of interpretation of the settlement and as to the full carrying out of terms by the one party or the other. I would, therefore, like you to consider this suggestion."

PROPOSAL FOR ENQUIRY

Copy of a letter from M. K. Gandhi Esq., to the Hon'ble Mr. H. W. Emerson, C. S. I., C. I. E., C. B. E., Home Secretary to the Government of India, dated Borsad, the 20th June, 1931:—

"I have your letter of the 16th June enclosing extract from an account received from the Madras Government regarding picketing. It does make a bad reading if the report is true. But what I am receiving almost daily from Madras from the workers who are thoroughly reliable eye-witnesses makes me to distrust the reports that you are receiving. But I know that this takes us no further. So far as the Congress is concerned, I want it to implement the settlement to the fullest extent. I, therefore, make an offer. Will you advise Local Governments to appoint a board of enquiry, consisting of a nominee on their behalf, and a nominee on behalf of the Congress, to conduct a summary enquiry into the allegations on either side, and wherever it is found that the rule of peaceful picketing has been at all violated, picketing should be entirely suspended, the Government undertaking on its part to stop prosecutions whenever it is found that they have been undertaken in spite of peaceful picketing, and if my suggestion does not commend itself to you, you will perhaps suggest something better and more acceptable. Meanwhile, I am enquiring into the specific charge mentioned in your letter."

(14) Copy of a letter from the Hon'ble Mr. H. W. Emerson, C. S. I., C. I. E., C. B. E., Home Secretary to the Government of India, to M. K. Gandhi Esq., No. F. 33|1|31 Poll. dated Simla, the 4th July, 1931:—

"In your letter of June 14th, you have suggested that the time had perhaps arrived for the appointment of a permanent board of arbitration to decide questions of interpretation of the order. Again in your letter of June 20th, you made the further suggestion that in regard to picketing the Government of India should advise Local Governments to appoint a board of enquiry, consisting of a nominee on their behalf and a nominee on behalf of the Congress to conduct a summary enquiry into the allegations on either side, and wherever it is found that the rule of peaceful picketing has been violated picketing should be entirely suspended, the Government undertaking on its part to stop prosecutions wherever it is found that they have been undertaken in spite of peaceful picketing. I much appreciate your offer of removing the possible causes of dispute arising out of the settlement, accepting this proposal. To take the lesser one first, as I understand it, it is mainly limited to cases in which it is alleged that the methods of picketing have contravened the ordinary law and that the Police have, therefore, prosecuted or proposes to prosecute the picketer. One effect of your proposal would be that before bringing the law into operation there should be a summary enquiry carried out by a nominee of the Government and a nominee of the Congress and that further proceedings would depend on their decision. In other words, the duty of maintaining law in this particular respect would be transferred from the Police, who have statutory duties, to a board of enquiry the members of which might well arrive at a different conclusion, while the Police, of course, must act only in accordance with the law. It is not practicable nor was it intended by the settlement that their duty in this respect should in any way be abrogated.

"In cases of this kind a practical test as to whether the law has or has not been contravened is the decision of the Court which tries the cases, and unless its decision is reversed on appeal the finding of the Court that picketing has contravened the law, and consequently the terms of the settlement, should *prima facie* be followed automatically by a suspension of picketing. The above illustrates one of the difficulties that would also arise in the case of standing boards of arbitration. The obligation imposed on the Congress by the settlement relates largely to matters affecting law and order, the freedom of action of the individual, and the carrying on the administration. That is to say, any serious breach of it has important reactions on one or other of these matters. So far as individual breaches contravened the ordinary law, the position would be the same as for picketing. If general breaches of it raised questions of policy affecting law and order, or the effective working of the administration, it would be clearly impossible for the Government to restrict their freedom of action by reference to a board of arbitration. This was not contemplated when the last clause of it was drafted, nor would it be consonant with the discharge by the Government of fundamental responsibilities. It seems to me that the working of this settlement must depend primarily on the faith of the parties to it. So far as the Government are concerned, they desire to adhere strictly to its terms and our information shows that Local Governments have been scrupulous in carrying out the obligations imposed on them. Doubtful cases are, of course, inevitable, but the Local Governments are prepared to give them most careful examination and the Government of India will continue to bring to the notice of the Local Governments any cases that are reported to them, and if necessary, satisfy themselves in regard to the facts."

(15) Copy of a letter from M. K. Gandhi, Esq., to the Hon'ble Mr. H. W. Emerson, C.S.I., C.I.E., C.B.E., Home Secretary to the Government of India, dated Simla, the 21st July, 1931:—

"In accordance with my promise made at the Viceregal Lodge this evening I reduce to writing my request for an impartial tribunal to decide upon matters of interpretation of the settlement between the Government and the Congress that might be submitted to it from time to time, whether on behalf of the Government or the Congress. The following are the matters that require immediate adjudication unless there is an agreement between the Government and the Congress as to the interpretation:

(1) Whether picketing includes the picketing of liquor shops and auction sales.

(2) Whether it is competent for Provincial Governments to prescribe the distance at which picketing can be done so as to render it impossible for the picketers to be within the sight of the shop picketed.

(3) Whether it is competent for a Government to limit the number of picketers so as to make it impossible to picket all the entrances of a particular shop.

(4) Whether it is competent for a Government to defeat peaceful picketing by permitting the sale of liquor by the picketed shop-keeper at places other than licensed and during odd hours.

(5) Interpretation of Clauses 13 and 14 in the application of particular cases, which Provincial

Governments have regarded were not coming under those clauses and the Congress has held otherwise.

(6) Interpretation of the word 'return' in Clause 16 (A).

(7) Whether a return of guns forfeited after the cancellation of licenses for participation in Civil Disobedience is covered by the settlement.

(8) Whether the restoration of certain property seized under Ordinance 9 and of *watan* lands in the Karnatak is covered by the settlement, and if it is competent for a Government to impose any condition upon such restoration.

(9) The meaning of the word 'permanent' in Clause 19.

(10) Whether it is competent for the Education Department to impose conditions upon students who took part in the Civil Disobedience campaign before admitting them or, in virtue of perpetual restriction imposed during the Civil Disobedience campaign, to debar the admission of students under the ban.

(11) Whether it is competent for a Government to punish a person or corporation by reason of his or its having taken part in the Civil Disobedience campaign, *e.g.*, forfeiture of pension, or grants and the like to Municipalities.

"These are not to be treated as the only matters to be submitted to the tribunal. It is possible that unforeseen cases may arise in future, which may be claimed to come under the settlement. The procedure to be adopted would be written statements and would be submitted both on behalf of the Government and the Congress, and the points would be argued by counsel. The decision of the tribunal would be binding on both the parties. As I told you in the course of our conversation, whilst I say nothing at the present moment as to a tribunal for the examination of questions of facts in the event of differences between the Government and the Congress, I have not waived the demand. Occasion may arise when the difference may be so vital as to make it obligatory on my part to press for a tribunal for the examination of such cases also. I should, however, hope that we might be able to settle all points of difference without reference to any tribunal."

GOVERNMENT OF INDIA'S REPLY

Copy of a letter from the Hon'ble Mr. H. W. Emerson, C.S.I., C.I.E., C.B.E., Home Secretary to the Government of India, to M. K. Gandhi, Esq., No. D-4980 (A) Poll. dated Simla, the 30th July, 1931:

"I write to thank you for your letter of July 21st in which (a) you request an impartial tribunal be appointed for the decision of matters of interpretation of the settlement of March 5th, and (b) you state specific points which you desire to be referred to the tribunal if appointed, on the failure of an agreement between the Government and the Congress as to their interpretation. In your previous letter of the 14th of June, you made a suggestion for the appointment of a permanent board of arbitration to decide questions of interpretation of the settlement, and as to the full carrying out of the terms by the one party or the other. In a demi-official letter No. F. 33-1-31 Poll. of the 4th of July, 1931, the reasons were given why the Government were not able to accept the suggestion. In your interview with His Excellency the Viceroy on July 21st, you expressed the view that while it might not be possible for the Government to accept the general proposition made in your letter of June 14, it would be unreasonable for them to refuse to accept a more narrow proposal relating to arbitration on questions of interpretation of the settlement. After some discussion, His Excellency suggested that you could communicate the specific points which you consider suitable for submission to arbitration, and he undertook that on their receipt the Government of India would examine the proposal. . . .

"3. The Government of India have given the matter their most careful consideration. They observe that while you do not wish to press at the moment for a tribunal to examine questions of fact in the event of difference between the Government and the Congress, you do not waive this demand and you suggest that occasions may arise when it may be necessary to press it. You will doubtless agree that the only distinction between this request and the suggestions made in your letter of the 14th of June is that you now desire to hold in suspense the broader question, while asking for the immediate agreement of the Government to arbitration on questions of interpretation. For the reasons stated in my letter of the 4th July, the Government of India regret that they are unable to alter the views already expressed on the former questions.

"4. They have given further consideration to the more restricted proposals, namely, the reference to arbitration of questions relating to interpretation for reaching a decision. They have given particular attention to the eleven points stated in your letter which you regard as coming within this category and to the implications which acceptance of arbitration on these points would necessarily involve, with special regard to the responsibilities and functions inherent in the Government. You will no doubt recognise that it would not be possible for the Government to agree to any arrangement which involved the suspension of the ordinary law or of the regular machinery of administration, or which included the appointment of an external authority to whom the Government would delegate the responsibility for reaching decisions in matters closely affecting the administration or of which the effect, direct or indirect, would be to provide a special procedure, to the benefits of which members of the Congress could lay claim and from which other members of the public would be excluded and which would trench upon the jurisdiction and discretion of the court of law. The settlement of March 5th did not, of course, contemplate any provisions of this kind.

"5. I am now to examine some of the points stated in your letter with reference to the above principles. The first three relate to picketing, and are of a general character. The action that it may be necessary to take in particular cases of picketing is obviously dependent on the nature of the particular circumstance, and the Government can clearly not agree to any decision of a general character which might have the effect of prejudicing the discharge by the executive or judicial authorities of their responsibility for the maintenance of law and order or of interfering with the liberty of individuals. General references of the nature you suggest are precluded by these considerations, nor can the Government agree to the reference of particular cases, for, apart from the reasons given in my letter of July 4th, the effect would often be to give to the individuals concerned in them a position not enjoyed by members of the public in similar circumstances. With regard to the fourth point, the Government of India have no information which suggests that Local Governments are condoning breaches of the Excise Law in the manner suggested. In so far as the matter relates to the administration of Excise matters within the law, you will no doubt realise that it is not practicable to set up a tribunal with power to decide in effect how the Local Government should conduct the administration of Excise which, it may be observed, is a provincial transferred subject. Points (10) and (12) raise a different issue, but one of great importance. The questions mentioned in them were not discussed during the conversations leading to the settlement regarding them. The reference of these matters to a tribunal would, therefore, involve acceptance of a principle which would clearly be capable of unlimited extension, that the tribunal should be competent to extend the operation of the settlement beyond its original scope and intention and without the concurrence of the Government.

"6. These instances appear to the Government sufficiently to indicate that there are insuperable difficulties in the way of arbitration even although references be ostensibly confined to matters of interpretation. There would be constant disputes as to whether the matter was one of interpretation or not, and the arrangement would create new difficulties rather than remove old ones.

"7. Several of the points have in their aspect already received the careful consideration of the

Government and in this connection I would refer you to my letter No. 4291, Poll. dated the 2nd of July, 1931, which related to students, and to my letter No. D 3801—31, Poll. dated the 28th of June, 1931, which related to arms licenses. The list of alleged breaches of particular provisions of the settlement which you gave to me at Simla contained specific instances coming within most of the points. This list was referred within a few days of its receipt to the Local Governments for communication of the facts, and the Government will satisfy themselves as to whether any breach of the settlement is involved. They are similarly prepared to satisfy themselves in regard to future cases of alleged breaches of specific provisions, for it is a matter of honour with the Government to observe the settlement and they have no doubt that this is equally held by you. It is by approaching the matter in this spirit and not by resort to arbitration that the Government believe that difficulties can best be surmounted."

In U. P., coercive measures in connection with tenants continued. The position of the evicted tenants caused anxiety to the U.P. leaders including Pandit Madan Mohan Malaviya. Gandhi sent a telegram to Sir Malcolm Hailey, the Governor of U.P. But the reply was disappointing in the extreme. It was under these depressing circumstances, with complaints pouring in from all quarters, that Gandhi was obliged to send the following telegram to the Viceroy on 11th August, 1931:—

GANDHI'S TELEGRAM (11th August, 1931)

"Exceedingly regret to inform you that a letter from the Bombay Government just received renders impossible my departure for London. The letter raises issues of first magnitude, as well of facts as of law, and contends that the Government must be the final judges on both. In naked terms, this means that the Government should be both the prosecutor and the judge with reference to matters arising out of a contract to which they and the complainants are parties. This is impossible for the Congress to accept. When I read the Bombay Government's letter together with Sir Malcolm Hailey's telegram received in answer to my enquiry, and the reports of continuing harassment in the U. P., Frontier Province, and other Provinces, they seem to me complete indication that I must not sail as I promised. To communicate with you before coming to a final decision, I have brought the foregoing facts to your notice. I shall await reply before making an announcement."

VICEROY'S REPLY (13th August, 1931).

"I should regret extremely if, for reasons you have given, the Congress were to be unwilling to carry out the arrangement which provided for their representation at the Conference. I am unable to accept these reasons as valid, and I cannot but feel that your misgivings arise from a misunderstanding of the policy of the Government and the grounds on which it rests. In particular, I should have thought that any misgivings as regards the United Provinces would have been removed by Sir Malcolm Hailey's telegram to you of the 6th August, and as regards Gujarat by Para 4 of the letter of the Private Secretary to Sir Earnest Hotson to you of August 10th. I would remind you of my personal letter to you of July 31st, in which I gave you the fullest assurances of my personal interest in everything that has to do with the settlement and could, therefore, have hoped that you would not allow disputes over the present details to prevent your serving India by participating in the momentous discussion of the future Constitution, which may determine the destiny of the country beyond your time or mine. If, however, your telegram represents the final word, I will at once inform the Prime-Minister of your inability to attend the Conference."

GANDHI'S FINAL 'NO' (13th August, 1931)

"Thank you for your wire of assurance. I must read in the light of the present happenings, and if you can see in them nothing inconsistent with the settlement, it shows fundamental differences in our respective outlooks upon the settlement. In the circumstances, I regret to say that there is no way left open to me but to confirm the decision already conveyed. I can only add that I tried my utmost best to go to London but failed. Please inform the Prime-Minister accordingly. I presume I may release the correspondence and wires for publication."

Telegram from His Excellency the Viceroy to M. K. Gandhi, Esq., dated Simla, the 14th August, 1931:—

"I have informed the Prime-Minister of your decision. I am releasing the relevant correspondence to the Press at 4 o'clock this afternoon. You are, of course, free to do the same."

Although it was being apprehended even from the month of June that there might be trouble in the matter of the Congress participating in the Round Table Conference, still everybody was hoping till the last moment that things might right themselves. It is not untrue to say that they were even hoping against hope, but the Congress could not sit idle on the off-chance of miscarriage of negotiations. They had to be fully prepared for the contingency of the agreement working itself out in all its fulness. Thus while Gandhi was carrying on his correspondence with the Viceroy and the Governments of Bombay and U. P., the Congress Executive was carrying on its normal work to which we must now turn for a moment. The Working Committee met on July 20th, and authorised the publication of the Report prepared on Indo-British financial obligations. The Fundamental Rights' Committee had held its sittings at Masulipatam and prepared its Report, which the Working

Committee resolved to place before the A.I.C.C. The Hindustani Seva Dal was the cause of certain misapprehensions in regard to its relations to the Congress, and, therefore, the Dal was recognized as the Central Volunteer Organisation of the Congress, working directly under the authority of the Working Committee or such person as it might appoint in this behalf. Its functions were categorically mentioned. Provincial Congress Commitees were authorised and required to form duly recognised volunteer corps, all the members of which are required to be members of the Congress, and must conform to the disciplines of the Central Volunteer Organization. The Seva Dal, which had held its first All-India Conference at Cocanada and was doing splendid work ever since under the guidance and leadership of Dr. Hardiker, was made an affiliated body of the Congress, pledged to its Creed of legitimate and peaceful means for attaining Swaraj. Then came the *magnum opus* of the Congress. It was a scheme of agreement in regard to the communal question, which we give *in extenso* here.

W. C.'s Statement on Communal Question

The following statement was issued by the Working Committee:—

"However much it may have failed in the realisation, the Congress has, from its very inception, set up pure nationalism as its ideal. It has endeavoured to break down communal barriers. The following Lahore resolution was the culminating point in its advance towards nationalism:

'In view of the lapse of the Nehru Report, it is unnecessary to declare the policy of the Congress regarding communal question, the Congress believing that in an Independent India communal questions can only be solved on strictly national lines. But as the Sikhs in particular, and the Muslims and the other minorities in general, had expressed dissatisfaction over the solution of communal questions proposed in the Nehru Report, this Congress assures the Sikhs, the Muslims and other minorities that no solution thereof in any future Constitution will be acceptable to the Congress that does not give full satisfaction to the parties concerned.'

"Hence the Congress is precluded from setting forth any communal solution of the communal problem. But at this critical juncture in the history of the Nation, it is felt that the Working Committee should suggest for adoption by the country a solution, though communal in appearance, yet as nearly national as possible and generaly acceptable to the communities concerned. The Working Committee has therefore after full and free discussion passed the following scheme:—

'1. (a) The article in the Constitution relating to Fundamenal Rights shall include a guarantee to the communities concerned of their cultures, languages, scripts, education, profession and practice of religion, and religious endowments.

(b) Personal laws shall be protected by specific provisions to be embodied in the Constitution.

(c) Protection of political and other rights of minority communities in the various Provinces shall be the concern and be within the jurisdiction of the Federal Government.

'2. The franchise shall be extended to all adult men and women. (Note:—The Working Committee is committed to Adult Franchise by the Karachi resolution of the Congress and cannot entertain any alternative franchise. In view, however, of misapprehensions in some quarters, the Committee wishes to make it clear that in any event the franchise shall be uniform and so extensive as to reflect in the electoral roll the proportion in the population of every community).

'3. (a) Joint electorates shall form the basis of representation in the future Constitution of India.

(b) For the Hindus in Sindh, the Muslims in Assam and the Sikhs in the Punjab and the North-West-Frontier Province, and for Hindus and Muslims in any Province where they are less than 25 per cent. of the population, seats shall be reserved in the Federal and Provincial Legislatures on the basis of population with the right to contest additional seats.

'4. Appointments shall be made by non-party Public Service Commissions which shall prescribe the minimum qualifications, and which shall have due regard to efficiency of the public service as well as to the principle of equal opportunity to all communities for a fair share in the public services of the country.

'5. In the formation of Federal and Provincial cabinets, the interests of minority communities should be recognised by convention.

'6. The North-West-Frontier Province and Baluchistan shall have the same form of government and administration as other Provinces.

'7. Sindh shall be constituted into a separate Province, provided that the people of Sindh are prepared to bear the financial burden of the separated Province.

'8. The future Constitution of the country shall be federal. The residuary powers shall vest in the federating units, unless, on further examination, it is found to be against the best interests of India.'

"The Working Committee has adopted the foregoing scheme as a compromise between the proposals based on undiluted communalism and undiluted nationalism. Whilst on the one hand the Working Committee hopes that the whole Nation will endorse the scheme, on the other it assures those who take extreme views and cannot adopt it that the Committee will gladly, as it is bound to, by the Lahore Resolution, accept without reservation any other scheme if it commends the acceptance of all the parties concerned."

The pledge for exclusion of foreign cloth and yarn was drawn up and it was resolved that any pledge in connection with the exclusion of foreign cloth and yarn, inconsistent with the following pledge, shall be held to be invalid:—

> "We pledge ourselves that we shall observe the following conditions so long as the Working Committee of the Congress does not give express permission by resolution to do otherwise:—
>
> '1. We undertake not to purchase or sell any foreign yarn made from cotton, wool or silk, or cloth manufactured from such yarn.
>
> '2. We undertake not to purchase or sell any yarn or cloth manufactured by mills that have not accepted the Congress conditions.
>
> '3. We undertake not to sell in this country any foreign yarn made of cotton, wool or silk, or cloth manufactured from such yarn or silk that may be lying with us.' "

Then it was resolved that the Anti-Untouchability Committee, which had merged in the campaign of last year, should be revived and, therefore, instructed Syt. Jamnalal Bajaj to take the necessary steps for the purpose. The Committee would have such powers of co-operation and the like that may be required.

On the question of the Textile Mills Exemption Committeee and Labour conditions, the Working Committee was of opinion that "the Textile Mills Exemption Committee should endeavour, wherever possible and necessary, to prevent by amicable arrangement any penalisation or victimization of Labour in the mills which have signed the Congress declaration, and to help in the bettering of Labour conditions in these mills."

It will be seen that in regard to the communal settlement, the residual powers were left in the hands of the federating units. It is a fashion to speak of these residuary powers. They are an academic perfection but in practice no one has been able to define them. The question may arise in regard to Provinces which are strangers to one another, federating anew with one another, but in a country like India where central and provincial subjects have for long been carefully demarcated, such a discussion is a purely theoretical pastime. Be that as it may, the final solution itself was the suggestion of Gandhi who, with his usual resourcefulness, added the subjunctive clause, "unless, on further examination, it is found to be against the best interests of India." The fact is that the Muslims wanted to have a reserve power in their hands,—in the hands of the Provinces,—so as to be able to deal effectively with Provinces having a majority of Hindus which might ill-treat the Muslims. Where a partner is suspicious, the best thing is to allow him a safeguard. But provision was left in the scheme for a future re-examination, and this satisfied all parties.

The All-India Congress Committee met once again on August 6th, 7th and 8th, 1931, and passed very important resolutions, the first of which related to the attempted assassination of His Excellency the Acting Governor of Bombay and the assassination of Judge Garlic in Bengal. In deploring as well as condemning these outrages, the Committee pointed out the heinousness involved in the attempt on the life of the Governor who was invited by the Fergusson College as its honoured guest.

The report of the National Flag Committee was considered and it was resolved that "the National Flag shall be three coloured, horizontally arranged as before, but the colours shall be Saffron, White and Green, in the order stated here from top to bottom, with the spinning-wheel in dark blue in the centre of the white stripe, the colours standing for qualities, not communities. The saffron shall represent courage and sacrifice, while peace and truth, and green shall represent faith and chivalry and the spinning-wheel the hope of the masses. The proportions of the flag should be as three to two." The new national flag was required to be hoisted on August 30th, the last Sunday of the month, which was to be celebrated as the Flag Day. The Fundamental Rights Committee's Report was considered and the rights and duties already mentioned were adopted.

The Fundamental Rights resolution, as it stood in its final shape, was also adopted at this meeting.

The Working Committee, meeting about the same time in Bombay, dealt with the question of Bhagat Singh's cremation and came to the conclusion, as we have already mentioned, that "there is no warrant for the serious allegations that were made." An important decision was taken in respect of the North-West Frontier Provincial Congress Committee and the Afghan Jirga and the Khudai Khidmatgars. The Committee having conferred with the representatives of the N. W. F. Province, resolved on the re-constitution of the Frontier P. C. C. and the incorporation of the Afghan Jirga in it. It was further resolved that Khudai Khidmatgars should become a part of the Congress Volunteer Organisation. The following statement, embodying the decisions of the Working Committee was issued on behalf of the Committee:—

> "Some misunderstandings having arisen in regard to Congress work in the North-West Frontier Province and the relations between the Provincial

Congress Organisation and the Afghan Jirga and Khudai Khidmatgars, the Working Committee met Khan Abdul Gaffar Khan and Khan Aligul Khan, Hakim Abdul Jalil, Mr. Peer Baksh, Khan Amir Mohammad Khan and Shrimati Nikho Devi and discussed future work in the N. W. F. Province. As a result of these discussions, misunderstandings were removed and the Frontier leaders agreed to work together in accordance with certain decisions arrived at. It was pointed out that the Afghan Jirga was working the Congress programme and the Khudai Khidmatgars were acting as volunteers for giving effect to this programme. But as the Afghan Jirga had a separate constitution of its own, it was no part of the Congress organisation. Confusion had also arisen owing to the use of a variety of flags by the Jirga.

"It was agreed by the Frontier leaders that the present P. C. C. and the Afghan Jirga should coalesce and the new provincial organisation, formed in accordance with the Congress Constitution, should represent the Congress in the Province. This newly elected Committee will be the Frontier P. C. C. In the language of the Province, it may be described as the Frontier Province Jirga. Similarly the district and the local Congress Committees may be described as local Jirgas, the fact that they are Congress Committees being also clearly stated. The Khudai Khidmatgars, it was agreed, should become Congress volunteer organisations in accordance with the Working Committee's recent resolution. The name Khudai Khidmatgars may however be retained. The whole organisation should be conducted in accordance with the Constitution, rules and programme of the Congress. The flag to be used henceforth will of course be the National Flag.

"At the request of the Working Committee, the Frontier Leader, Khan Abdul Gaffar Khan, has undertaken to shoulder the burden of leading the Congress movement in the Province."

The Working Committee also passed a resolution to the effect that it had reluctantly come to the conclusion that, consistently with the terms of the settlement and the national interest, the Congress could not and should not be represented at the Round Table Conference. But the Committee declared that the Delhi Settlement was still in force as indicated by the following proposition:—

> "In view of the resolution relating to the Congress non-participation in the Round Table Conference passed by the Working Committee on August 13, the Committee desires to make it clear that the resolution should not be construed as ending the Delhi Settlement. The Committee therefore advises the Congress organisations and all Congressmen to continue to comply, until further instructions, with the terms of the settlement, in so far as they are applicable to the Congress."

Emergency powers were, however, given to the President, in the event of emergency arising, so as to leave no time for calling the Working Committee. "The President is hereby authorised to act in the name of and on behalf of the Working Committee."

Mani Bhuvan was thick with rumours, the whole day, of expectations and hopes that eleventh hour peace efforts on the part of Sir T. B. Sapru and Mr. Jayakar might enable Gandhi to proceed to London, but towards sunset important Congress leaders, coming out of Mani Bhuvan, began to tell the expectant Press correspondents that there was absolutely no chance of eleventh hour negotiations fructifying and Gandhi's changing his decision. Hopes were still entertained by some optimists that, after all, things might take a better turn but all doubts were finally set at nought when Gandhi left Mani Bhuvan at 8-45 P.M. and finally boarded a third class compartment of the Gujarat Mail at the Bombay Central Station.

Sir Prabhasankar Pattani had half an hour's interview with Gandhi that afternoon. Interviewed by the Associated Press, Sir Prabhasankar Pattani (who had cancelled his passage to England by the S. S. *Mooltan*) was unwilling to say anything more than that he had cancelled his passage for many reasons.

Thus ended the first scene in the Act of the Round Table Conference. By the 15th of August, Dr. Sapru, Mr. Jayakar and Mr. A. Rangaswami Iyengar left Bombay after paying a visit or two to Gandhi. A perusal of the correspondence published on the subject reveals the mentality of the Government officials. The Secretariat threw the Pact overboard; possibly it was disturbed by the tragic incident at Poona. Every now and then the Congress activities were disturbed by some act of violence at the psychological moment. The firing at the Acting Governor of Bombay, Sir E. Hotson, in the Fergusson College in Poona, by a young student, about this time was unfortunate. But Sir E. Hotson himself maintained the same equanimity as Lord Irwin had maintained on the 23rd of December, 1929. Gandhi expressed his sorrow at the Poona incident and congratulated the Acting Governor on his escape. The Working Committee as well as the A. I. C. C. passed suitable resolutions condemning the outrage. But this is only an interlude. There were deeper causes for the virtual breaches of the Gandhi-Irwin Agreement. The concrete breaches have already been categorised. Government published answers to each of Gandhi's charges on the 24th of August, and the Congress published, in October, a detailed rejoinder to these replies. These breaches were undoubtedly one cause for Gandhi refusing to attend the Round Table Conference and communicating his decision, endorsed by the Working Committee, in a telegram addressed to the Viceroy on the 13th of August. It was Mr. Emerson's letter dated July 30th (*vide supra*) which really had clinched the situation. Not less decisive was the letter from the Governor of Bombay dated 10th August. Sir Malcolm Hailey's telegram, though couched in polite and polished language, was an equally determining factor. But the greatest of these was the adoption of coercive processes in the collection of taxes in Bardoli. 21 lakhs out of 22 lakhs was paid and the Congress contended that the defaulters were in distress and wanted time. There was a sum of about 2 lakhs due to Government by way of arrears of previous years, most of which was 'authorised' on account of the distress in Gujarat. Government set about collecting the current dues as well as arrears at the point of Police threats and Police 'zoolum.' It was their contention that the Congress should not be the body at whose bidding Government revenues should be paid or withheld. They distinctly wrote in their correspondence that such an implication was not contained in the Agreement, much less could it be tolerated by Government. Congress was prepared to prove that Police were requisitioned to overawe the people and in several cases to exercise undue influence in order to collect the extra revenue. After all, the extra revenue so collected did not amount even to a lakh of Rupees. Government's point was that the last word in the payment of taxes should not rest with the Congress, but that Government and its authority, Pax Britannica and British rule, still were there. They wanted to assert and prove these. Moneys collected were only token collections. They did not care for the revenue as such. They cared for prestige, that very prestige which was apostrophised by Montagu in 1912.

There was a second and a very important reason why Gandhi would not go to England. This was the failure of the Government of India to nominate Doctor Ansari as a delegate to the Round Table Conference. Of course, the Congress would have taken him. Besides being a Congressman, he represented a great Party in India, the Nationalist Mussalman Party. The mussalmans were not all reactionary. There was a distinct group which was nationalistic in mind and plumped for *Purna Swaraj—Mukammal Azadi*. But it is an open secret that Lord Irwin had made a distinct promise at the instance of Gandhi to nominate three individuals, namely, Pandit Madan Mohan Malaviya, Mrs. Sarojini Naidu and Doctor Ansari. While the two former were nominated, Doctor Ansari was cut out. Lord Willingdon was in a pitiable position. It was not as if he did not know what Lord Irwin had committed himself to. But it suited Britain's interests to make it appear at the Round Table Conference that Mussalman India was against Swaraj. In answer to the demand for the fulfilment of Lord Irwin's promise, Lord Willingdon pleaded that the Mussalman delegates were opposed to Doctor Ansari's delegation. Of Course, they would be. If they were not they would not be Mussalman delegates, they would be Indian delegates. How could they tolerate the selection of Doctor Ansari with his unchallengable position in the country and a vast following and nationalistic ideals, and with outspoken and vehement resistance to communalism? The Congress had prepared a formula on the communal question and it must be vouched for at the Round Table Conference by a Hindu and a Mussalman. Government knew it, and apparently Government wanted to paralyse the Congress by cutting the Mussalman limb. Gandhi took, under the circumstances, the only course open to the Congress consistent with national honour and declined to go to London for the R. T. C.

Once again preparations were made for the outbreak of hostilities. All that a Satyagrahi wants to this end is intimation. There are no material preparations necessary—such as *lathis* and man-power as on the side of Government. On the popular side, volunteers would be coming as need presented itself. Of course we must realise that there is a limit to human endurance and even in the Satyagrahic struggle, it is the last man and the last rupee that tells. Of this, we shall have occasion to speak later once again. But on the 15th August, it was all a story of war mentality. No doubt Lord Willingdon had been adopting an attitude of perfect politeness, asking Gandhi not to break, advising Gandhi to approach him, whenever he had any difficulty. But Gandhi's approaches were of no avail. The country was plunged into gloom. Pandit Madan Mohan Malaviya and Sarojini Devi cancelled their passages by the *Mooltan* by which Sapru, Jayakar and Iyengar left. Gandhiji could only explain his position in a simple formula:—

> "If there was a contract between the Government and the Congress, and if there was a dispute as to the interpretation of the contract, or if there was a breach on either side, surely the rules governing all contracts must be applicable to this contract and, in my opinion, the more so because it is a contract between a great Government and a great organisation claiming to represent the whole Nation. That the contract is not legally enforceable imposes a double obligation upon the Government to submit to an impartial tribunal questions in dispute between the contracting parties, if they cannot agree. The Government, in their wisdom, have rejected a very simple and a very natural suggestion of the Congress, that such matters in dispute should be referred to an impartial tribunal."

Indeed Gandhi never banged the door against peace. He said he would "dash to London the moment the way is clear" if only the local authorities implemented the settlement. He publicly expressed what had all along been lurking in the minds of every political thinker, "the great Civilians here do not want me to attend the Conference, or if they do, they do so under circumstances which a national organisation like the Congress can never tolerate." The Civilian element in the country was sedulously fostering the view that Gandhi wanted to set up a parallel Government in the shape of the Congress and that such a subversive institution should not be tolerated. Accordingly, Gandhi wrote a private letter to Lord Willingdon as he was leaving Bombay for Ahmedabad, that it was far from his intention to set up a parallel Government with himself as its head, that he had never insisted upon a Board of Arbitration, though he claimed it as a matter of right and that all that he wanted was simple justice. Here is the full text of the letter:—

> "Events have moved so fast that I have not had the time to acknowledge your very kind personal letter of July 31.
>
> "I recognise the sincerity running through the communication, but the latest developments have made that letter past history and, as I said in my wire of August 13, the sum-total of all circumstances betrays a fundamental difference of outlook between us.
>
> "I can only give you my assurance that it was not without the greatest and most anxious deliberation that I came to the conclusion that, in view of your decision, I could not, consistently with my obligation here, attend the Round Table Conference.
>
> "I was grieved when I heard that your decision was affected by the opinion, ascribed to you, that I had insisted upon a Board of Arbitration and that I

was trying to set myself up as the head of a parallel Government.

"As for a Board of Arbitration, it is true that I have claimed it as a matter of right, but, if you recall our conversations, I never insisted upon it. On the contrary, I told you that so long as I got the justice to which I was entitled I would be quite satisfied. You will agree that this is wholly different from insisting on a Board of Arbitration.

"As to the alleged parallel Government, I thought I had dispelled the illusion when, in reply to a jocular remark by you, I had told you that I did not claim to be a district officer, but that my co-workers and I had acted as voluntary Patels or village headmen, and that too, with the consent and knowledge of the district officers. I should, therefore, be sorry if these two opinions, which I submit were erroneous, had affected your decision.

"The purpose, however, of writing this letter is to inquire whether you regard the Delhi Settlement as now at an end, or whether it is to still continue in spite of the abstention of the Congress from participation in the Round Table Conference. The Congress Working Committee arrived at the following decision this morning:

'In view of the resolution relating to Congress non-participation in the Round Table Conference passed by the Working Committee on August 13, the Committee desires to make it clear that this resolution should not be construed as ending the Delhi Settlement. The Committee, therefore, advises the Congress organisations and all Congressmen to continue to comply, until further instructions, with the terms of the Delhi Settlement in so far as they are applicable to the Congress.'

"From this you will observe that the Working Committee has no desire to embarrass the Government at the present juncture, and that, therefore, it is prepared to continue honourably to work the settlement; but such working must depend upon a reciprocal attitude on the part of the Provincial Governments.

"As I have told you so often, through correspondence and in conversations, this reciprocity has been found to be progressively missing. Information continues to be received at the office of the Working Committee of Government activity which can be only interpreted to be a token of a design to crush the Congress workers and normal Congress activities."

Gandhi concluded the letter with a request for an early reply and for early relief in the matter of complaints if the settlement was to abide, as otherwise his co-workers were anxious to have permission at least to adopt defensive measures. Gandhi did not mind if the Congress was not accepted by Government as the intermediary between it and the people. He did not want to embarrass or humiliate the Government, but the fact remained that it was Government, not the Congress, that was terminating the truce, through the determined antagonism of the Civil Services. Gandhi was not failing to distinguish essentials from non-essentials. He was convinced that the Civil Service was not ready to recognize the right of India to full freedom. "Therefore, till all the members of that Service are converted," said Gandhi, "there is no scope for the Congress to enter upon negotiations for full freedom. It must go through further suffering, however costly the process may be. Bardoli, therefore, was for me an acid test. It was designed to gauge the Civilian temper. Looked at in that light, it was not a small thing."

The publication by Gandhi of the charge-sheet, which was really authorised by the telegram of the 14th August from Simla, was regarded by some as a challenge to Government. Dr. Sapru and Mr. Jayakar wirelessed from S. S. *Mooltan* to that effect and added that it embarrassed them in their negotiations for peace with the Viceroy and the S. of S. Gandhi was prepared even for a unilateral enquiry by an impartial tribunal into the allegations made against the Congress. The Viceroy's reply to Gandhi's letter was nothing reassuring. He referred to "the activities of the Congress during the past five months" and said they were contrary both to the letter and the spirit of the Delhi Settlement and had involved a constant menace to the maintenance of peace, particularly in U. P. and N. W. F. Province. His Excellency held the failure of the Congress to attend the R. T. C. involved the failure of one of the main objects of the settlement, but added that "Government would continue to avoid resort to special measures so far as possible restricting action to the requirements of the specific situation." Gandhi warmly reciprocated the Viceroy's desire to observe the settlement and issued instructions to Congressmen for its meticulous observance. He also wired to the Viceroy for an interview to talk over matters. This was agreed to, whereupon Gandhi, Vallabhbhai J. Patel, Jawaharlal and Sir Prabhasankar Pattani,—the solitary friend who had not rushed up to London in the *Mooltan* on the 15th August, —met the Viceroy. The Viceroy held a meeting of the Executive Council. Ultimately, after several hitches, matters were squared up and Gandhi left Simla by a special train so as to catch the train on the line which would enable him to sail on the 29th August.

Thus, as a result of conversations between Gandhi and representatives of the Government of India at Simla, it was agreed that Gandhi should proceed to London in order to attend the Round Table Conference, on behalf of the Congress, and Gandhi sailed accordingly on August 29th from Bombay.

*   *   *   *

The agreement was published by the Government of India in an official Communique to which were attached letters from Gandhi to Mr. Emerson, Secretary, Home Deparment, Government of India, and from Mr. Emerson to Gandhi. The letters were integral parts of the agreement. The text of the Communique and the letters is given below:

Official Communique

1. As a result of conversation between His Excellency the Viceroy and Mr. Gandhi, the Congress will now be represented by Mr. Gandhi at the Round Table Conference.

2. The settlement of March 5, 1931, remains operative. The Government of India and the Local Governments will secure the observance of the specific provisions of the settlement in those cases, if any, in which a breach is established and will give their careful consideration to any presentation that may be made in this respect. The Congress will fulfil their obligations under the settlement.

3. In regard to collections of Land Revenue in the Surat District, the point in issue is whether in those villages of Bardoli Taluka and Valod Mahal, which were visited by Revenue officials, accompanied by a party of Police, during the month of July, 1931, more severe demands, having regard to their material circumstances, were made from revenue payers and enforced by coercion exercised through the Police, than were made from and met by revenue payers of other villages of the Bardoli Taluka. The Government of India, in consultation and full agreement with the Government of Bombay, have decided that an inquiry shall be held into this issue in accordance with the following terms of reference:—

"To inquire into the allegations that *khetedars* in the villages in question were compelled by means of coercion exercised through the Police, to pay revenue in excess of what would have been demanded if the standard had been applied, which was adopted in other villages of the Bardoli Taluka, where collections were effected after March 5, 1931, without the assistance of the Police, and to ascertain what sum, if any, was so paid."

Within the terms of reference, evidence may be produced on any matter in dispute. The Government of Bombay have appointed Mr. R. C. Gordon, I.C.S., Collector, Nasik, to hold the inquiry.

4. In regard to other matters hitherto raised by Congress, the Government of India and the Local Governments concerned are not prepared to order an inquiry.

5. In regard to any further matters of complaint by the Congress, not coming within the specific provisions of the settlement, such complaints will be dealt with in accordance with the ordinary administrative procedure and practice, and if any question of an enquiry arises, the decision as to whether an inquiry shall be held and, if so, the form it shall take, will be made by the Local Government concerned, in accordance with such procedure and practice.

Letter from Mr. Gandhi to Mr. Emerson: Simla, August 27, 1931:—

"Dear Mr. Emerson,

I have to acknowledge with thanks your letter of even date, enclosing a new draft. Sir Cowasji has kindly also communicated to me the amendments suggested by you. My colleagues and I have very carefully considered the amended draft, which we are prepared to accept, subject to the following remarks:

"In paragraph 4, it is not possible for me, on behalf of the Congress, to subscribe to the position taken up by the Government. For, we feel that where, in the opinion of the Congress, a grievance arising out of the working of the settlement is not redressed, an inquiry is a necessity of the case, because of the fact that Civil Disobedience remains under suspension during the pendency of the Delhi Pact. But if the Government of India and Local Governments are not prepared to grant an inquiry, my colleagues and I have no objection to the clause remaining. The result will be, that whilst the Congress will not press for inquiry in regard to "the other matters hitherto raised," on its behalf, if unfortunately any grievance is so acutely felt that it becomes a paramount duty of the Congress to seek some method of relief, in the absence of an inquiry, in the shape of defensive direct action, the Congress should be held free to adopt such remedy, notwithstanding the suspension of Civil Disobedience.

"I need hardly assure the Government that it would be the constant endeavour of the Congress to avoid direct action and to gain relief by discussion, persuasion, and the like. The statement of the Congress position given here has become necessary in order to avoid any possible misunderstanding in the future or a charge of breach of faith on the part of Congress. In the event of a successful issue to the present discussions, I assume that the Communique, this letter and your reply would be simultaneously published.

Yours Sincerely,
M. K. Gandhi."

Government of India, Home Department, Simla, August 27, 1931:—

"Dear Mr. Gandhi,

I write to thank you for your letter of to-day's date, in which you accept the draft Communique subject to the observations contained in your letter. The Governor-General-in-Council has noted that it is not the intention of the Congress to press for any inquiry into those matters hitherto raised by them, but that while you give an assurance that it will be the constant endeavour of the Congress to avoid direct action, and to gain relief by discussion, persuasion, and the like, you wish to make clear the position of the Congress in regard to any future action that they may decide to take. I am to say that the Governor-General-in-Council shares your hope that no resort to direct action will be taken. In regard to the general position of Government, I am to refer you to the letter of His Excellency the Viceroy, dated August 19, to your address. I am to say that the Communique, your letter of to-day's date and this reply will be published simultaneously by Government.

Yours sincerely,
H. W. Emerson."

It will be observed that an enquiry was to take place in Bardoli. Regarding all other existing grievances where relief was not forthcoming, the Congress had reaffirmed its right to resort to defensive direct action, notwithstanding the continuance of the Delhi Agreement. In regard to future grievances, there might or might not be an enquiry. Where there was no enquiry and relief was not given, the Congress might also, if it so chose, commence direct action in defence of the people's rights.

Congress Committees and Congressmen were, however, to bear in mind that the Delhi Agreement continued and there should be no breach of it on their part, without reference to the President. Wherever there was a grievance against the Government or its officials, every effort should be made to get it remedied by methods of peaceful persuasion. Where these efforts failed, the matter must be referred to the President for his advice and directions.

Some of the existing grievances were mentioned by Gandhi in a charge-sheet he drew up against Government and to this the Government replied. All Congress Committees concerned were asked to consider carefully the charge and the reply and send their rejoinder to the latter, to the All-India Congress Committee, Ahmedabad. All additional and further instances of breaches, as well as other grievances, were also to be sent immediately to him.

Gandhi did set sail for London but he had no hopes of success in spite of his general optimism. He hoped, however, that Provincial Governments, the Civil Service and the English mercantile houses would help the Congress to realise its mission. The action of Gandhi and of the President in entering into a fresh agreement with

Government in Simla dated 27th August, was duly ratified by the Congress Working Committee at its next meeting held at Ahmedabad on September 11, 1931. One other important matter disposed of at this meeting of the Working Committee was relating to Indian collieries which were to be recommended to all Industrial concerns in this country particularly to Textile Mills, provided these collieries signed a pledge, much on the lines of the Textile Mills, sympathising with the aspirations of the people, and had no less than 75 per cent. of their share capital as well as directorate held by Indians. There should be no foreign interest in the Managing Agent's Firm. They should assist the propagation of Swadeshi by regulating their prices and quality aright. The management should not engage itself in propaganda hostile to the national movement. Indians should be exclusively employed, except where special reasons exist. Insurance, Banking and Shipping business should be passed only to Indian Companies. Likewise, auditors, solicitors, shipping agents, brokers and contractors should all be Indians. All purchases for business should as far as possible be of articles of Indian manufacture. Persons connected with the management should wear Swadeshi cloth and a satisfactory scale of wages and conditions of work and life should be secured to the operatives of the mines. Audited Balance-sheets of mines should be supplied to the Congress every year.

Before we proceed to the stirring events of October and November, both in India and in England, let us make a reference to the voyage of Gandhi and his party. Gandhi was accompanied by Mahadev Desai, Devadas Gandhi, Pyarelal and Mira Ben. Mrs. Sarojini was with him. The kit that they were allowed to take was of the meagrest description; it was sufficiently meagre on account of the shortness of notice and of the uncertainty of the voyage, but made more so on account of the stern looks of Gandhi. They had a hearty welcome at Aden, where the Arabs and the Indians together presented an address after some difficulty. The Resident would not allow the national flag to be hoisted at the meeting and the poor people could not assert themselves until Gandhiji himself cut the Gordian knot by suggesting to Mr. Framroz Cowasji Dinshaw, the President of the Reception Committee, that he should phone to the Resident, tell him that he could not think of receiving an address under those conditions, that there was a truce between the Government of India and the Congress, and the Government must not resent the flag, if only under the truce. The argument went home, and the Resident saved an ugly situation by consenting to the Indian National Flag flying at the place where Gandhiji received the citizens' address.

Replying to the address, and thanking them for the purse of 328 guineas that was presented to him, Gandhiji said:—

> "I thank you for the honour you have done me. I know that the honour is not meant for me personally or for my friends. It is an honour done to the Congress whom I hope to be able to represent at the Round Table Conference. I came to know that there was a hitch in your proceedings on account of the national flag. Now it is inconceivable for me to find a meeting of Indians, especially where national leaders are invited, without the national flag flying there. You know that many people sustained *lathi* blows and some have lost their lives in defending the honour of the flag, and you cannot honour an Indian leader without honouring the Indian national flag. Again there is a settlement between the Government and the Congress, which is no longer a hostile party but a friendly party. It is not enough, therefore, to tolerate or permit the Congress flag, but it must be given the place of honour where Congress representatives are invited."

On board the ship, Gandhi was leading his normal life as in the Ashram, with prayers, his spinning-wheel and his amusements with children. Gandhi is nothing if he is not a business man as well, and he created a flutter of surprise one evening when he announced to the friends gathered that he had sold a shawl worth Rs. 700 for a sum of Rs. 7,000 to a friend on board. Gandhiji received greetings from Madame Zaghul Pasha and Nahas Pasha, President of the Wafd Party. The former's was naturally a very touching message, while the warmth of the latter can be judged from the text which is published below:—

"The Great Leader Al Mahatma Gandhi"
'Rajputana.'

"In the name of Egypt who is now fighting for its liberties and its independence, I welcome in you the foremost leader of that India who is also struggling to attain the same end, and I convey to you my hearty wishes for a safe journey and a happy return. I also ask God to grant to you success in your quest,—a success equal to the greatness of your determination. I hope to have the pleasure of meeting you on your homeward journey, and trust that the land of the Pharoahs will then be favoured by your visit, thus enabling the Wafd and the Egyptian Nation at large to express to you, whatever be the result of your journey, both their appreciation of your noble achievements to promote the welfare of your country, and their reverence for the greatness of the sacrifice made by you in support of your principles. May God prolong your life, and crown your endeavours with a victory far-reaching and abiding. Our representatives, both at Suez and at Port Said, will have the honour of conveying to you by word of mouth our welcome and our best wishes

Mustafa El Nahas Pasha,
President of the Wafd."

The Egyptian deputations were not accorded permission to see Gandhi at Port Said, but the Indian deputation was permitted to see him at Cairo. It was with great difficulty that a single representative of Nahas Pasha could get permission to see him. It was when he was approaching Marseilles that he made his budget, "not for one but for many."

When Gandhi reached Marseilles, a warm welcome was awaiting him at the hands of Mademoiselle Madeleine Rolland, the sister of Romain Rolland who was unable to be present in person on account of ill-health. She was accompanied by Monsieur Privat and his good wife. M. Privat is the Swiss professor who has become famous by the Government of India describing him later in the 1932-33 movement, as "an obscure and unknown member of the teaching profession." He was also greeted by a number of French students. Gandhi stayed in London in Kingsley Hall in East End with Miss Muriel Lester "in the midst of noisy public houses and destitute and squalid private houses." Numerous invitations were awaiting him in London and still more numerous were the invitations to spend a quiet week-end in country places. One friend enclosed a cheque for 50 pounds on reading in *The Times* that morning a report of the address delivered by Gandhi at the Friends' Meeting House in Euston Road, and the message broadcast to New York from Kingsley Hall.

Gandhi preferred in London the East End to the West End, the hospitality of Miss Muriel Lester against that of the British Government, the company of the poor in opposition to that of the wealthy. 'Uncle Gandhi,' bare of foot except for his Indian sandals, bare of shirt except for his *chadar*, was the popular figure round whom gathered the children of East End every morning. Gandhi and his evening prayers, Gandhi the guest alike of Lancashire labourers, and of Bishops and Archbishops, Gandhi and his famous visit in his usual dress to His Majesty the King—all these are aspects which do not directly concern this work, but which are of perennial interest to the Indians to whom life is one and indivisible, and is incapable of being vivisected into the various compartments which have now become almost traditional.

Gandhi at the R. T. C. is the figure that must arrest our attention now. His speech at the Federal Structure Committee is a fitting introduction to the rest of his speeches in London at the Conference table. He gave a terse but comprehensive summary of the Congress, its history, its composition, its outlook, its methods and its object, which we have made virtually the Introduction to this humble book. He paid a tribute to Mr. A. O. Hume who had assisted at the birth of the Congress and nursed it. He pointed out the fundamental differences between the Government and the Congress, between the Congress and other parties; he read out the Karachi resolution and explained it briefly. He pointed out how the Premier's statement fell short of the Indian ideal pictured by the three beams of Central Responsibility, Federation, and Safeguards in Indian interests. He dwelt upon the supreme need of the hour, which was not merely a political constitution but a scheme of partnership between two equal nations, and contrasted his former position of a British subject with his 'present' position of a 'Rebel'—contrasted really the Empire Ideal with that of the Commonwealth. He quoted the parallel of business changing hands and spoke of stock-taking between the out-going and the in-coming partners, and finally assured that we were not interlopers in the domestic crisis of England, for it was only if England held India not by force but by the silken cord of love, that India herself could help England in balancing her budget.

Speaking at the Minorities Committee, Gandhi gave expression to some home truths. He cleared the situation of much of its fog by declaring in unambiguous language that the different Communities were encouraged to press, with all the vehemence at their command, their own respective views, and pointed out that this question was not the fulcrum, but the central fact was constitution-building. He asked whether it was to settle the communal question that the delegates were brought 6,000 miles from their homes. They were invited to London to have the satisfaction, before they went away, of having built up an honourable and practicable framework for the freedom of India, which would await only the imprimatur of the approval of Parliament. He twitted Sir Hubert Carr in respect of his Minorities' Scheme saying that he would not deprive him and his associates of the feeling of satisfaction that evidently actuated them, but, in his opinion, what they had done was to dissect a carcase. Apparently Government's scheme was only a scheme for Indians sharing power with the bureaucracy, not one designed to achieve Responsible Government. "I wish them well and the Congress is entirely out of it. The Congress will wander," said he, "no matter how many years, in the wilderness, rather than bend itself to a proposal under which the hardy tree of freedom and Responsible Government can never grow." Finally he concluded with that mighty vow which nearly cost his life a little while later. "One word more as to the so-called 'untouchables'" said he, "I can understand the claims advanced on behalf of other communities, but the claims advanced on behalf of the 'untouchables' are to me the unkindest cut of all. It means a perpetual bar sinister. We do not want the 'untouchables' to be classified as a separate class. Sikhs may remain *such in perpetuity*, so may Muslims and Christians. Will the untouchables remain untouchables in perpetuity? I would far rather that Hinduism died than that untouchability lived. Those who speak of the political rights of untouchables do not know India and do not know how Indian society is constructed. Therefore, I want to say with all the emphasis I can command that if I was the only person to resist this thing, I will resist it with my life." On the suggested arbitration by the Premier, Gandhi was not unwilling to such a course provided it related only to the Muslims and Sikhs. He would not be a party to the separate representation of other communities. The Premier asked a plain question on this subject: "Will you, each of you, every member of the Committee, sign a request to me, to settle the community question and pledge yourself to accept my decision? That, I think, is a very fair offer." It will be remembered that when the decision of the Premier was finally published sometime in June, 1932, the question arose whether it was a Governmental decision on a par with the rest of the proposals of the White Paper, or whether it was the Premier's Award. The members of the Round Table Conference not having all signed such a request, there could be no award and, therefore, the decision was only a proposal and could not be regarded as sacrosanct.

By the 18th of November, 1931, the Cabinet was fed up with the Round Table Conference. Lord Sankey brought a fresh surprise from the Premier that day in announcing the latter's intention to wind up the Committee after the speeches, and summoning the plenary session next week. Mr. Benn speaking for the Opposition protested, pointing out that Government were killing the Conference. Sir Samuel Hoare suggested that they had better face the facts and realise that in the circumstances it would be better to bring the chapter to a close and await the Premier's Statement regarding the machinery to be set up anew. The Army question was being debated and Gandhi made some more plain statements on the subject. Before doing so, he declared his intention to wait in England if necessary, as he had gone to London to explore every possible avenue to achieve an honourable settlement. The Congress, he asserted, was capable of shouldering all responsibilites that flow from Responsible Government, *i.e.*, from a complete control of Defence and External Affairs with of course necessary adjustments. The Army, he pointed out, was really an army of occupation and its members, no matter to what race they belonged, were all foreigners, because he could not speak to them, they could not approach him openly, and they were taught to regard Congressmen as other than their own countrymen. "There is an absolute wall between them and us," said Gandhi. "The British Army," he said "was there for the defence of the British interests, for resisting foreign aggression and putting down internal revolt." In fact, these were the purposes of the whole Army. But the British Army was there to hold the balance evenly. The whole Army must pass under Indian control in its entirety. "But the Army would not accept my command," said Gandhi, "nor the Commander-in-Chief, nor the Sikhs nor the Rajputs. But I expect even so to exercise that command with the good will of the British people. The British troops may also be told that they are there to protect, not British interests but India against foreign aggression." All this, Gandhi said, was only his dream. He knew that he could not infect the British statesmen or public with the idea or with the ideal that this dream should be their cherished mission, and until that is realized he would wait till eternity, if he could not get control of the Defence. India knew how to defend herself. Mussalmans and Gurkhas, Sikhs and

Rajputs can defend India. The Rajputs are responsible for a thousand victories, not one.

The fact is that Gandhi had faith in Englishmen some day doing their duty, and said, "we must infect the British with that love for India. If the British people think that we shall require a century before that can be done, then for that century the Congress will wander through that terrible fiery ordeal; it must go through that storm of distress, of misrepresentation and,—if it becomes necessary and if it is God's will,—a shower of bullets." He spoke of the safeguards and said that although they were stated to be in the interests of India, yet he would reciprocate Lord Irwin's statement who used Gandhi's name and said that Gandhi also admitted that they must be in the mutual interests of India and England. "I endorse," said Gandhi, "that I do not conceive of a single safeguard that will be only in the interests of India, not a single safeguard that will not be also in the interests of Britain, provided that we contemplate a partnership, a partnership at will and a partnership on absolutely equal terms." Speaking at the plenary session of the Conference, Gandhi made plain to the people assembled, that he was under no delusion that liberty could be obtained by argumentation or even by negotiation. But he felt called upon to point out how, after having declared that no decisions would be taken by the test of majority at the Conference or at the Committee, the conveners jotted down opinions of a large majority in report after report of such committees, and did not even mention the name of the 'one' dissenting. Who was that 'one'? Was the Congress one of the many parties there? He had already claimed that it represented 85 per cent. of the population. Now he would claim by right of service, it claimed to represent even the Princes, the landed gentry and the educated classes. All other delegates represented sectional interests. The Congress was the one body which had no communalism about it. It had its platform as a universal one, recognising no distinction of race, colour or religion. It had an exalted creed to which it may be that people could not come up, but the Congress was a daily growing organisation reaching the remotest villages. Yet it was being treated as one of the parties, but let it be remembered that it was the only body that could deliver the goods, being bereft of all communal bias. Some people were feeling that it was trying to run a parallel Government. Well would he endorse the charge, if it could be run by non-violence, eschewing the dagger of the assassin, the poison bowl, the bullet and the spear. A damaging reference had been made to the Calcutta Corporation, but it was only fair to the Mayor, who, when called upon by the Congress to explain, owned up the mistake and made handsome reparation in regard to the policy of violence. The Congress stood not for violence but for non-violence. Hence its Civil Disobedience movement. Even this was not tolerated. But no one could resist it. General Smuts himself could not. What was resisted in 1908, had to be yielded in 1914 Civil Disobedience succeeded in Borsad and Bardoli. Lord Chelmsford had recognised it. There were a few men in England like Professor Gilbert Murray who would ask Gandhi not to think that Englishmen did not suffer when Indians suffered. Lord Irwin tried to govern India by his Ordinances. He failed. "Whilst there is yet a little sand left in the glass," said Gandhi, "I want you to understand what the Congress stands for. It stands for liberty, call it by whatever name you will." The difficulty that Gandhi felt was that there was not one mind and one definition of any idea recognized by the Conference. When words have different meanings and different implications to different people, no agreement could be possible.

A friend had drawn his attention to the Statute of Westminster and asked whether he had noted the definition of the word 'Dominion.' 'Yes,' he did. The Dominions were enumerated but not defined. They could not adopt even the earlier definition of 1926 which was to the effect that "Dominions are autonomous communities within the British Empire equal in Status, in no way subordinate one to another in any aspect of their domestic or external affairs, though united by a common allegiance to the Crown and freely associated as members of the British Commonwealth of Nations." Egypt was not there. Gandhi felt relieved because he was out of it. He wanted Complete Independence. An English statesman had told him that he did not know what Gandhi meant by Complete Independence. Partnership with England? Yes; partnership for mutual benefit. Gandhi only craved for friendship. A Nation of 350 million people does not need the dagger of the assassin, the poison bowl, the sword, the spear or the bullet. It needs simply a will of its own, an ability to say 'no' and the Nation is to-day learning to say 'no.'

He then dwelt upon safeguards and pointed out how he had been informed by three experts that no responsible Minister could carry on administration when 80 per cent. of the resources are irretrievably mortgaged. He was not asking for the protection of the illegitimate interests of India. He would not allow the safeguards in Indian interests to be prejudicial to English interests. Even Mr. Jayakar and he did not agree on these safeguards; much less could Sir Samuel Hoare and himself. "India," he added, "survived many problems, the problems of plague and malaria, of snakes and scorpions and tigers. It will not be baffled. For heaven's sake, give me, a frail man 62 years gone, a little bit of chance. Find a little corner for him and the organisation that he represents. You distrust that organisation, though you may seemingly trust me. Do not for one moment differentiate me from the organisation of which I am but a drop in the ocean. I am no greater than the organisation to which I belong. I am infinitely smaller than that organisation, and if you find me a place, if you trust me, I invite you to trust the Congress also. Your trust in me otherwise is a broken reed. I have no authority save what I derive from the Congress. If you will work the Congress for all it is worth, then you will say, good-bye to terrorism, then you will not need terrorism. To-day you have to fight the school of terrorists which is there, with your disciplined and organised terrorism, because you will be blind to the facts or the writing on the wall. Will you not see the writing that these terrorists are writing with their blood, will you not see that we do not want bread made of wheat, but we want the bread of liberty, and without that liberty, there are thousands to-day who are sworn not to give themselves peace or to give the country peace."

When the Conference concluded on the 1st of December, Gandhi proposed a vote of thanks to the Chair and pointed out that they had come to the parting of ways and their ways would take different directions,—the dignity of human nature, he said, required that we must face the storms of life. "I do not know in what directions my path would lie, but it does not matter to me. Even though I may have to go in an exactly opposite direction, you are still entitled to a vote of thanks from the bottom of my heart." With these ominous words did he bid good-bye to the Round Table Conference. The position then was that one of the conditions on which the Congress agreed to participate in the R. T. C., the abandonment of stark repression, was altogether broken. Gandhi was greatly worried by the ugly situation developing in Bengal and U.P., as he considered that the sanctioning of the repressive policy in India was wholly inconsistent with the desire expressed in London to part with power and give India freedom.

When Gandhi had left for the Round Table Conference, there was the understanding that an enquiry should be held into the allegations of Police excesses in connection with the collection of Revenue in Bardoli. Mr. R. G. Gordon, I.C.S., was appointed special officer, with powers under the Land Revenue Code, within the District of Surat for the purpose of the Bardoli inquiry, which commenced on the 5th of October '31. Mr. Bhulabhai Desai and Sirdar Vallabhbhai Patel, the Congress President, were present, the former of whom represented the Congress. At the very outset, the Government Pleader objected saying that Mr. Desai's appearance was unauthorised and irregular, and argued that the Congress by its Constitution could only appoint a legal representative at a special session of the Congress, by a resolution duly passed. The objection was overruled. It was agreed by both sides that the people should pay Revenue to the utmost of their capacity. They must even borrow and pay if they were not amongst the Satyagrahis that had suffered substantially. Mr. Desai quoted various letters, articles and telegrams, amongst which there was a telegram from Bardoli that 'Rayam' village was raided by the Collector accompanied by 15 policemen. Also the villages of Timberva, Rajapure, Lambha, Managpore, Navafaly, of Valod Godhe, Alghod and Jamania. The inquiry proceeded some length. Then the Congress asked for all orders of the

Government of India and the Government of Bombay which had been issued between March 5th and August 28th, because they "would and must throw considerable light on the question of standard which is referred to in the agreement." Mr. Gordon was unable to see why Government should be asked to produce evidence to prove things for them. "Presumably before the Congress made these allegations," he said, "they were in full possession of the material upon which they were based, and it was for them to produce their materials and to prove their case." The inquiry officer said that if there was any definite order of Government to which Congress desired to refer, that was a different matter. Thereupon the Congress stated the reasons for asking for the papers desired by them and they indicated the nature of the documents in the possession of the opponents. Mr. Gordon passed the order on 12-11-31: "It is impossible to agree to the vague and unreasonable demands made in the reference now in question." Mr. Desai objected to this order which presumed that the decision of the Congress to ask for the production of Government records was made at that late stage in order to fill up a large hiatus discovered in their own evidence, and felt that it was a clear indication to the Congress as to the spirit in which the opponents intend to co-operate in an inquiry intended for ascertainment of essential facts, and also an indication as to their desire to act for 'public good.' "And having regard to that spirit, I am the more fortified in the conclusion to which I have regretfully come." "The trend of the enquiry has appeared to be hostile and one-sided," wrote Vallabhbhai in his Manifesto to the farmers, "but I was prepared to go to the end until our Counsel was satisfied that further prosecution of the enquiry was futile." In fact, the refusal to produce papers in the possession of the Government removed the one salutary check on the cross-examination of Government witnesses, and it was realised that "such mutilated inquiry was worse than useless." Accordingly, Vallabhbhai withdrew from the inquiry and sent the following Cable to London to Gandhi on 13th November, '31:—

> "Examined 62 Khatedars and 71 witnesses belonging to the seven out of the eleven villages allowed. Five villages disallowed as not falling within the terms of reference. After important admissions in part cross-examination of the Mamlatdar, first Government witness, inquiry officer held we were not entitled to production and inspection of Government documents of any kind relating to the issues in the inquiry. Trend of inquiry distinctly hostile and one-sided. In agreement with Bhulabhai, withdrew from inquiry to-day. Vallabhbhai."

In the U.P., a situation of first class importance was developing, which ultimately shaped the destiny, it may be said, of Indian politics for the next few years. The agrarian conditions of the tenants in the U.P., mostly of those under Talukdars and Zamindars, was anything but enviable. Their distress was appalling. There was no relaxation shown in the methods of collecting rents. The intermediaries had neither the sense of responsibility that animates a Government, nor did they understand the pinch of depression which was oppressing the poor cultivators. They were middlemen, happily situated, secure in the protection afforded by a benevolent Government, free from the cares and worries of labour, and always invoking the interference of the authorities on grounds of sedition, Non-co-operation, lawlessness and anarchy, of any friends of the ryot and public men who chose to plead his cause. It is one of the tragedies of life in India that whatever service is rendered to the dumb millions, especially in administrative and political matters, should be through the agency of Congressmen, for, other schools of thought, while they argue for the ryot and sincerely sympathise with his causes, do not descend to the plane of action. Accordingly the Congressmen in the U.P., were all marked and made the victims of the wrath of the Zamindars and Talukdars, with the active support of Government. The correspondence about the agrarian crisis in the United Provinces relating to the months of October, November and December 1931 has been published and is very interesting, but too big to be published here. A short but sufficiently detailed summary, however, is included in the publication by way of 'Foreward' to an official publication.

Immediately after the Delhi Settlement, the United Provinces Provincial Congress Committee put themselves in touch with the Provincial Government. A large number of letters were exchanged. Pandit Govind Ballabh Pant was specially appointed by the Provincial Congress Committee to bring to the notice of Government the various grievances of the people and to put before them the view-point of the Congress. The continuing agrarian crisis particularly occupied the attention of the Provincial Congress Committee, and the correspondence largely dealt with this. Pandit Jawaharlal Nehru also wrote frequently to the Local Government. Both Pandit Govind Ballabh Pant and Pandit Jawaharlal Nehru had several interviews with the Chief Secretary and other officials. Pandit Jawaharlal Nehru also sought an interview on two occasions with His Excellency Sir Malcolm Hailey but this could not be arranged. Gandhi interested himself in the United Provinces agrarian crisis, and besides writing to the officials of the Government of India and the Local Government, interviewed Sir Malcolm Hailey.

The condition of the United Provinces peasantry became progressively worse during the months that followed the Delhi Settlement. Inadequacy of remissions, in spite of the heavy fall in prices, resulted in great distress and this was intensified by large numbers of ejectments and coercive processes. In many rural areas the tenantry were subjected to a reign of terror and atrocities were perpetrated on them. The United Provinces Provincial Congress Committee appointed several Enquiry Committees to visit the affected districts and to report on the prevailing agrarian conditions and the distress. These reports, supported by evidence taken on the spot, were then considered by a special Provincial Agrarian Enquiry Committee. The reports of this Special Committee, known as the Pant Committee, was published in September 1931.

Meanwhile attempts continued to be made by Gandhi and the United Provinces Provincial Congress Committee to obtain relief for the unhappy and suffering peasants. In the Simla conversations between Gandhiji and the Government of India in August, 1931, the United Provinces agrarian crisis was specially considered and it was pointed out by Gandhiji that failing relief the peasantry would be entitled to defensive direct action or Satyagraha. In the letter dated August 27, 1931, addressed by Gandhi to Mr. Emerson, Home Secretary to the Government of India, which formed an integral part of the Simla Agreement, it was expressly mentioned that "if unfortunately any grievance is so acutely felt that it becomes a paramount duty of the Congress to seek some method of relief, in the absence of an enquiry, in the shape of defensive direct action, the Congress should be held free to adopt such remedy, notwithstanding the suspension of Civil Disobedience."

This statement of the position of the Congress was noted in the reply of Mr. Emerson to Gandhi, dated August 27.

It may be added that the President of the Congress, Sirdar Vallabhbhai Patel, addressed the Government of India on several occasions on the United Provinces agrarian crisis.

It will thus be seen that the Congress in the United Provinces did everything in their power to co-operate with the Government in finding a solution of the agrarian problem. Repeated letters were sent after the Simla Agreement but no relief was forthcoming for the ejected tenants and others, and coercive processes and enforced collections, often accompanied by physical violence, continued long after the usual period for collections.

Before any satisfactory solution was found for the last season's difficulties and ejectments, a new situation arose with the beginning of the new Fasli year 1339 when the question of fresh collections had to be considered. The peasantry, exhausted and worn out by a continuous struggle against heavy odds, had to face a repetition of this. The remissions announced by the Local Government were considered wholly inadequate and no arrangements were made for the ejected tenants or for the arrears or for local calamities. On the top of this came the official announcement in many districts that if the full rent as demanded was not paid within a month, even the remissions sanctioned might be withdrawn. Further, it was stated that the tenants could only raise any objections after they had paid up the rent demanded. These announcements brought about an immediate crisis. It has to be borne in mind that in fixing the remissions neither the Congress nor any other representative of the tenants was consulted.

The Allahabad District Congress Committee raised the issue immediately after the official announcements were made, and pointed out that it was not possible for the peasantry to pay the amounts demanded. Most other districts were in the same or in a worse position. The Local Government was again approached and it was pointed out how unfairly the tenants were being treated in regard to remissions, ejectments, arrears and local calamities. A Conference was arranged between some local officials and the Settlement Commissioner on the one hand and Congress representatives on the other, in order to discuss specially the case of Allahabad District as exemplifying most districts in the United Provinces. This Conference proved ineffective, as it was stated on behalf of Government that they were not prepared to discuss any of the vital matters in issue. They could only discuss the application of the rules already laid down by them. The crux of the problem was thus not touched.

During the last months repeated attempts were made on behalf of the United Provinces Provincial Congress Committee to arrange a Conference with representatives of the Local Government who would be in a position to discuss all the aspects of the problem. The Provincial Congress Committee appointed a special committee with full powers to negotiate with Government. These attempts did not succeed either.

In the course of the correspondence it was made clear on behalf of the Congress that they were prepared to accept any solution, however arrived at, provided it gave sufficient relief to the peasantry. When the time for collections came, advice was repeatedly sought by the tenants as to what they should do. The United Provinces Congress Committee wished to take no steps to put an end to negotiations which might result in a settlement. At the same time, they could not remain silent when advice was sought and they could not advise payment of a demand which, they were convinced, was grossly unfair and likely to ruin the peasantry whom they represented. The Congress thereupon, after obtaining permission therefor from the President of the All-India Congress Committee, advised the peasantry to withhold payment of rent and revenue temporarily, pending negotiations. They made it clear, however, that they were ready and willing to negotiate and, as soon as relief was given, to vary their advice. They further suggested to the Government that they would withdraw their advice as to withholding payment if Government would suspend collections while negotiations were going on. The suggestion was not accepted by Government who wanted the advice to be withdrawn first. The United Provinces Provincial Congress Committee had no alternative left but to repeat its advice to the peasantry to withhold payment. In spite of these developments, the Provincial Congress Committee adhered to the position that it was prepared to explore all avenues leading to a settlement and to withdraw its advice regarding non-payment as soon as sufficient relief was in sight or collections were suspended. Government's view was to meet popular representatives at a Conference only if, as they called it, the No-tax campaign was suspended. But on their own part they had put into prison hundreds of Congressmen 'sharp shooting,' so to speak, all tall poppies and all earnest workers—a policy which culminated in the arrest of Jawaharlal and Sherwani and Purshottamdas Tandon 5 days before the arrival of Gandhi from England. As a matter of fact, Jawaharlal and Sherwani had been served notices that they should not leave their places. Jawaharlal soon after had attended a meeting of the Working Committee on the eve of Gandhi's return to Bombay. He could not possibly obey this order as against the imperious, public calls on his time and personal presence at various important meetings, and when he broke the order, he was arrested and so was Sherwani and both were subsequently sentenced for breach of Internment orders.

Then there was the third centre of strife in Bengal. During the period of truce, atrocious scenes were enacted. They were probably meant as reprisals against the terrorist outrages in the district. A non-official Committee of Enquiry was appointed on the happenings in the town and district of Chittagong on August 31, 1931, and the three subsequent days. Certain non-official Europeans and hooligans broke at night into the premises of a Printing Press and with huge hammers and iron rods broke the machinery and belaboured the manager and others connected with the Press. The Working Committee having considered the report on the 27th, 28th and 29th November 1931 at Delhi, recorded "its severe condemnation of the local Police and Magistracy who, with the assistance of certain non-official Europeans and hooligans, inflicted terrible losses and indignities on innocent people in pursuance of a policy of terrorization." The Committee noted with satisfaction that there was no communal strife in Chittagong in spite of deliberate efforts to create one by the employment of hooligans whose activities were intended to give the occurrence a communal colour. The Committee was of opinion that "the least that the Government of Bengal should do was to compensate those who had suffered and to punish all those whose responsibility for the incidents was established." While the people outside the Jails were being thus victimized by the 'Black and Tan' methods of Bengal, those inside jails and detention camps were being subjected to even more severe treatment. The tragedy which had occurred in the Hijli detention camp for detenus resulted in the death of two and in injury to 20 detenus. The Working Committee "while awaiting the report of the commission of enquiry appointed by the Government," felt that "the Government were specially responsible for the lives and well-being of unarmed men detained in custody by Government without trial. against whose detention the Nation had for long protested; and the callous disregard of this fundamental duty must be met with punishment of those who were guilty." It was at this same meeting that the U.P. situation was considered and the Working Committee expressed the opinion that the question of defensive action should first be considered by the U.P. P.C.C., before permission could be granted, as asked for by the Allahabad District Congress Committee, "to offer Satyagraha as against the present agrarian policy of the U.P. Government, and in particular the oppressive collection of rent and revenue at a time when the agriculturists were unable to pay on account of acute economic depression." The Committee accordingly referred the application to the U.P.P.C.C. and in the event of its being of opinion that the case was a fit one for defensive Satyagraha on the part of the agriculturists in terms of the Simla Agreement dated August 27th, 1931, the Committee authorised the President of the Congress to consider the application and to give such decision on it as he may consider necessary.

Incidentally we may add that the Working Committee at this very meeting protested against the proposal to impose an additional duty on Salt as a breach of faith by the Government of India re. the implications of the Delhi Settlement. It passed another resolution regarding Currency and Exchange policy. It will be remembered that on September 21, the Bank of England took a three-day holiday in view of the shortage of its gold, and England went off the Gold Standard. The problem at issue was whether the Indian rupee was to be tied down to the coat tails of the pound sterling or whether it should be left to find its own level in terms of gold. The former course which was adopted by Government was conceived solely in the interests of England so as to provide *inter alia* a back-door preference for Britain's imports into India, and deplete the gold resources of the Indians. A resolution was passed to this effect.

There was a fourth fire kindled by Government at the Northern gateway of India. The Khudai Khidmatgars have figured already in the history of India as well as in these pages. They are a splendid lot,—these Frontier men who had been brought together and drilled and disciplined for national Non-co-operation. There were over a lakh of these who were working under the guidance and inspiration of Khan Abdul Gaffar Khan Saheb. These Khudai Khidmatgars were till the month of August unattached to the Congress. Gandhi had, ever since the truce, been striving to obtain permission to go to the Frontier and study the organisation which had given such a wonderful account of itself. He had asked Lord Irwin for permission in this behalf but they said 'not yet.' The same answer was being repeated throughout the year and so he had sent Davadas Gandhi to the Frontier Province, and this young friend produced a marvellous Report which was considered by the Working Committee, and a great achievement was wrought when the Khudai Khidmatgars were made a part of the

Congress organisation. With this culminating act, the organisation should have been above all suspicion but Government were not willing to allow a seemingly semi-military organisation—albeit they were Congress volunteers—with band and bugle, dressed *cap-a-pie* in red robes and owning allegiance to a towering personality who, by his character, humanity, sacrifices and services, had already earned the title of Frontier Gandhi and been fast becoming the observed of all observers, the cynosure of all eyes. Who knows, beneath his meek countenance and Satyagrahi looks, there might not be a deep design to set up a buffer State on the Frontier, to contract an alliance with the Amir, to befriend the Tribes on the Frontier, and to lead an expedition into India? A lakh of red robed army—Pathans all. They were not to be trusted. And so, on the pretext that Khan Abdul Gaffar Khan did not co-operate with Government because he did not care to attend a Durbar held by the Chief Commissioner of the N. W. F. Province and preached Complete Independence, the innocent Khan Saheb and his devoted and equally innocent brother, Dr. Khan Saheb, were put into prison just a few days before Gandhi's return to India in 1931. Thus, by the time Gandhi returned to India, a pretty mess was created. In Gujarat the enquiry into excesses which was promised to Gandhi and on the promise of which he had left for London, proved abortive on the 13th November. Let it be noted that it was not an impetuous and explosive Vallabhbhai that resiled from the enquiry in a fit of disgust, but it was the sober and sedate Bhulabhai that withdrew after due deliberation. In U.P. the partial relief that was given by the landlords through the influence and intervention of Government was inadequate and unsatisfactory and Government would not meet popular representatives unless they ate the humble pie and withdrew their injunction advising suspension of rent. The situation that was thus developed led to the arrest, as already mentioned, of Jawaharlal and Sherwani, five days before Gandhi's return, and although the news was wirelessed to the steamer on which Gandhi was sailing home, it was withheld from him. Gaffar Khan and his brother and son were detained as State prisoners from the N.W.F. Province. The Bengal situation did not consist of one occurrence or one event, although the happenings at Chittagong and Hijli constituted two such, but one festering sore that had been left open for long and appeared to be destined to remain open and raw for an unlimited length of time.

It was in the midst of such a situation that Gandhi returned to Bombay on the morning of the 28th December, 1931.

Sarojini Naidu
1925 : Cawnpore

S. Srinivasa Iyengar
1926 : Gauhati

Dr. Ansari
1927 : Madras

Jawharlal Nehru
1929 : Lahore

Part VI

SYNOPSIS

CHAPTER I

Back to the Wilderness

Meeting at Azad Maidan—Gandhi's Vow repeated—Gandhi studying the Situation—Telegrams between Gandhi and the Viceroy—Working Committee Resolutions—Benthall's Circular—Government preparations for renewed hostilities—Emergency Powers Ordinance—Intensive fight—Political Conferences—Fate of Ashrams—In Bihar—In Andhra—In Bengal—In Bombay—In C. P.—In Delhi—In Gujarat—In Karnataka—In Kerala—In N. W. F.—In Sindh—In Tamil Nadu—Events in Bengal, Gujarat and Karnataka in 1933.

CHAPTER II.

From the Fast to the Loose Pulley

Gandhi's fast to death—The Poona Pact—Poona Pact accepted—The Message of Freedom—Meaning of Fasting—Gandhi applies the reins—Wide response to Gandhi's call for Harijan uplift—Gandhi once more a prisoner—Gandhi allowed to carry on Untouchability Propaganda—Gandhi's Vow at the Minorities Committee—Gandhi's Letter to Sir Samuel Hoare—Separate Electorates harmful—"Shall fast unto death"—Government Terrorism—An article of faith—Sir S. Hoare's reply—Terrorism necessary—Gandhiji's Letter to Prime-Minister—Decision to Fast—"Not to compass release"—

Premier's Reply—Government decision explained— Safeguards temporary—Reservation minimum—Government decision stands—Final reply to Gandhi—Decision unchanged—Gandhi's Letter to Bombay Government—"The dream of my life"—A cry for justice—Fight for humanity—Issue suppressing Swaraj—The Yeravada Pact—Other Fasts—The Poet's Verdict—The Poet's change of view—Rajendra Babu issues Statement—The Calcutta Session held under ban—Resolutions—Gandhi's 21 days' fast—Gandhi contemplates march to Ras—Arrest and release—Re-arrest—The Bihar Earthquake—Jawaharlal's arrest and imprisonment—Council-entry programme.

CHAPTER III

Marking Time

Suspension of Civil Resistance—The Patna Decision—The Working Committee at Patna—The Socialist Party—Government ban and Congress reorganisation—Wardha and Bombay decision—Sirdar Vallabhbhai's release—Benares meeting of the Working Committee—Jawaharlal's release and Re-arrest—The Nationalist Party—Release of Khan Abdul Gaffar Khan—Last meeting of Working Committee—Gandhi's withdrawal from Congress—Details regarding 21 days' fast—Self-purification—"There must be will behind fast"—A pleasant surprise—Gandhi's Statement—Interrupted thread—"I shall not abuse release"—Vallabhbhai Patel's care for Gandhi—No room for smallness—"Not a party to cat and mouse game"—Referendum at Guruvayoor—Gandhi's Letter to Dr. Ansari—Gandhi's Statement—Congress reorganisation—Reply to critics—A substitute for Violence—Constitutional by instinct—An optimist—Authority of General in Non-violent Warfare—Spirituality in Politics—Bardoli Decision—Congratulations to

Pathans—Suspension of Civil Disobedience, act of wise Statesmanship—Need of severe discipline—Woes of Bengal—Incarceration of masses—Nehru, Gaffar and Vallabhbhai—Bigger jail outside—Previous History—Council work of little value—Different conditions—Advice to Socialists—Confidence in Pandit Malaviya—Government's good-will—Gandhi's Statement after retirement—Difference in outlook—Terrible oppression—Social group—Question of States—Untouchability—Non-violence—Failure of Non-violence—Satyagrdha—Purna Swaraj—Means and end, convertible terms—Differences sterilised Congress Programme—Corruption in our ranks—Congress to be tested—Khaddar Franchise—Habitual wearer of Khaddar—Delegates to be restricted to 1,000—Conclusion—A. I. V. I. A.—Gandhi's exit—New Congress—Bombay Session—Rajendra Babu's Address—Bombay Resolutions—Exhibitions and demonstration—Congress Parliamentary Board—Election Campaign—Assembly verdict on J. P. C. Report—Jinnah's Amendment—Working Committee on withdrawal of C. D.—Disciplinary rules—Famine in Andhra—All-India Protest Day re. J. P. C. Report—Unity talks—Government's repressive policy continued—The Congress Museum—The Detenu Fund—Bengal's prohibition—Bengal Government's Communique—Congress President's Rejoinder—Congress reorganisation in the N. W. Frontier—Frontier will fight Communalism—The Quetta Earthquake—The Working Committee's Resolution—Acceptance of Office—The Congress and the States—Resolution on office acceptance—50 years' Anniversary of the Congress—A. I. C. C. meets in Madras—The Government of India Act—The Congress President's growing responsibility.

CHAPTER IV

CONCLUSION

I

The Presidents—The Religion of Politics—Prof. Gilbert Murray on Gandhi—Success and Failure—The Programme of the Congress—The three planes of Constructive Work—Village Leadership.

II

The new Technique, Satyagraha—Its Contribution to Life and Politics—The Evolution of Satyagraha—The Principle of Non-violence—'Tapasya'—Lingering doubts.

III

The Manhood of Nation on Trial—A Graph of our Progress—Swaraj a Process—Conclusion.

Part VI

CHAPTER I

Back to the Wilderness

There were gathered in Bombay representatives of all parts and Provinces of India to accord a fitting welcome to the Tribune of the People. Gandhi greeted the friends that went on board the steamer to welcome him, patting many, thumping a few and pulling the venerable Abbas Tyabji by his beard. There was a formal welcome in one of the Halls of Customs House and then a procession in the streets of Bombay which kings might envy in their own country, but which political leaders and ambitious statesmen always get from an admiring populace. How much more then should the people of India have felt when they were welcoming not an adventurer carving out a kingdom, not a statesman wringing out concessions from an unwilling monarch, not a warrior decorated with marks of honour for deeds of prowess on the battle-field, but a Saint and Satyagrahi who had renounced the world but yet was of it and in it, who had no axe to grind but was himself being ground down between the mill-stones of an active legalized terrorism above and a passive impotent thraldom below, whose only purpose in life was the emancipation of his Motherland and the evolution of a feeling of fellowship, friendliness, and fraternity amongst the nations of the world. That day the menfolk of Bombay were on the roads and the womenfolk were gathered on the balconies of the sky-scrapers of the city. Almost the first thing that Gandhi did was to address the public of Bombay,—indeed the people were assembled on the Azad Maidan—and in grave and solemn tones, Gandhi poured out his heart to the vast concourse of men and women before him, saying that he would strive his best and strain every nerve to work for peace.

In this speech, he again repeated his terrific vow that he would not have the dismemberment of the 'untouchables' from the Hindu fold and would resist any attempts that way, with his very life. Let it be confessed that neither on this occasion, nor when he had spoken at the Minorities Committee in London, did it occur to any one that Gandhi would on this issue declare a fast unto death. Either the vow escaped attention altogether or made no further impression upon the hearers' and the readers' minds than as a piece of the usual rhetoric. But everyone knows that Gandhi indulges in no exaggeration and never allows himself to make any wild statement. His 'yea' is 'yea' and his 'no' is 'no.' They must be taken at their value and do not admit of any 'bear' and 'bull' transactions.

For three days together, Gandhi was acquainting himself with the woes of the different Provinces. What was he to do? Here was Subash Babu with four companions from Bengal, who, though they chose to meet Gandhi independently and severally, still gave the same account of Repression following on the Bengal Ordinance. The U. P. friends had their Ordinance, and the N. W. F. had its Ordinance. During the truce period, these Ordinances were holding the field. Gandhi playfully called these Ordinances his New Year gifts from Lord Willingdon. But he was not the man to plunge the country into the depths of suffering without exploring like a true Satyagrahi every avenue to peace. Deputations were waiting on him from morning to evening and repeating the same tale of official excesses in Province after Province. The country was passing through dire distress and depression. Yet Karnataka got no relief in spite of the long struggle it was engaged in. In Andhra, the taxes were to be raised in periodical revisions of settlement by 18¾ p.c. and the Governor of Madras was threatening the promulgation of an Ordinance if the people should talk of the suspension of payment of taxes.

These were the woes of the country narrated to Gandhi by his friends. He himself had a tale of woe to tell his friends, which he brought from London. He was never willing to go to the R.T.C. The shadows of the coming Conference were cast even in the months of July and August. But the Working Committee had insisted on his going. He had an opportunity later, on the ground of breach of the truce, of avoiding the London visit. But the Labour Government was anxious that he should be bundled into the steamer somehow. He went to London and saw things for himself. The first thing he told his colleagues was that the realization of a thing was quite different from its visualization. He knew the Moderate mentality in India but he was not prepared for the scenes enacted in London. He knew the temperament of the Muslims and their reactionary bent of mind, but he was not prepared for the vivisection that was practised at the R.T.C. He had made up his mind that the Congress should not lend its support thereafter to any kind of communalism. Its cult must be one of pure and unadulterated Nationalism. He said that India had no chance if she went on dallying with the communal problem in the same old fashion. He wanted an assurance from his Mussalman and Sikh friends that they would agree to any future Constitution of India being fashioned, only on the basis of Indian Nationalism untainted by any communal considerations. He was really tormented by these thoughts and experiences and had to face the situation in front of him with calmness and equanimity—qualities that have never failed him. He had abundant confidence in himself and in his countrymen. They had trusted him and he returned the trust. He saw a huge chasm before him. Could he bridge it, or should he make a bridge of men, living and dead, on which to cross the yawning gulf? With these conflicts surging in his breast, with this storm raging in his bosom, he set about his business. The Working Committee was with him. It was not a Committee of fourteen colleagues that he was counting upon. The country was his Working Committee. Accordingly he gave a telegram to Lord Willingdon which got a reply—long, detailed, and minatory. Gandhi sent a rejoinder without any avail. We give below the telegram *in extenso*:—

1. Telegram from Mr. Gandhi, to His Excellency the Viceroy, dated the 29th December, 1931.

"I was unprepared on landing yesterday to find Frontier and U.P. Ordinances, shootings in Frontier and arrests of valued comrades in both, on top of Bengal Ordinance, awaiting me. I do not know whether I am to regard these as indication that friendly relations between us are closed or whether you expect me still to see you and receive guidance from you as to course I am to pursue in advising Congress. I would esteem wire in reply."

2. Telegram from the Private Secretary to the Viceroy, to Mr. Gandhi, dated the 31st December, 1931, No. 306 C.

"His Excellency desires me to thank you for your telegram of the 29th instant in which you refer to Bengal and United Provinces and N.W.F.P. Ordinances. In regard to Bengal it has been and is necessary for Government to take all possible measures to prevent dastardly assassination of their officers and private citizens.

"2. His Excellency wishes me to say that he and his Government desire to have friendly relations with all political parties and with all sections of the public and, in particular, to securing co-operation of all in great work of constitutional reforms which they are determined to push forward with minimum delay. Co-operation, however, must be mutual. His Excellency and his Government cannot reconcile activities of Congress in the United Provinces and N.W.F.P. with spirit of friendly co-operation which good of India demands.

"3. As regards United Provinces, you are doubtless aware that while the Local Government were engaged in devising means to give all possible relief in the existing situation, the Provincial Congress Committee authorised a No-rent campaign which is now being vigorously pursued by Congress organisations in that Province. This action on the part of the Congress bodies has compelled Government to take measures to prevent a general state of disorder and spreading of class and communal hatred which the campaign, if continued unchecked, would inevitably involve.

"4. In North-West Frontier Province, Abdul Gaffar Khan and bodies he controlled have continuously engaged in activities against Government and in fomenting racial hatred. He and his friends have persistently refused all overtures by the Chief Commissioner to secure their co-operation, and, rejecting the declaration of the Prime-Minister, have declared in favour of Complete Independence. Abdul Gaffar Khan has delivered numerous speeches open to no other construction than an incitement to revolution, and his adherents have attempted to stir trouble in tribal area. The Chief Commissioner, with the approval of His Excellency's Government, has shown utmost forbearance and to the last moment continued his efforts to secure assistance of Abdul Gaffar in carrying into effect, with the least possible delay, the intentions of His Majesty's Government regarding constitutional reforms in the Province. The Government refrained from taking special measures until activities of Abdul Gaffar Khan and his associates and, in particular, open and intensive preparation for an early conflict with Government, created a situation of such grave menace to peace of Province and of tribal areas as to make it impossible further to delay action. His Excellency understands that Abdul Gaffar Khan was in August last made responsible for leading Congress movement in Province; and that volunteers' organisations he controlled were specially recognised by All-India Congress Committee as Congress organisations. His Excellency desires me to make it clear that his responsibilities for peace and order make it impossible for him to have any dealing with persons or organisations upon whom rests the responsibility for activities above outlined. You have yourself been absent from India on the business of Round Table Conference, and in the light of the attitude which you have observed there, His Excellency is unwilling to believe that you have personally any share in responsibility for, or that you approve of, recent activities of Congress in the United Provinces and North-West Frontier Province. If this is so, he is willing to see you and to give you his views as to the way in which you can best exert your influence to maintain a spirit of co-operation which animated proceedings of Round Table Conference, but His Excellency feels bound to emphasise that he will not be prepared to discuss with you measures which Government of India, with the full approval of His Majesty's Government, have found it necessary to adopt in Bengal, United Provinces and North-West Frontier Province. These measures must in any case be kept in force until they have served the purpose for which they were imposed, namely, preservation of law and order essential to good Government. On receipt of your reply, His Excellency proposes to publish this correspondence."

3. Telegram from Mr. Gandhi, to the Private Secretary to His Excellency the Viceroy, dated the 1st January, 1932.

"I thank His Excellency for wire in reply to mine of 29th instant. It grieves me, for, His Excellency has rejected, in a manner hardly befitting his high position, an advance made in friendliest spirit. I had approached as seeker wanting light on questions, while I desired to understand Government version of very serious and extraordinary measures to which I made reference. Instead of appreciating my advance,

His Excellency has rejected it by asking me to repudiate my valued colleagues in advance and telling me that, even if I become guilty of such dishonourable conduct and sought an interview, I could not even discuss these matters of vital importance to the Nation.

"In my opinion, constitutional issue dwindles into insignificance in face of Ordinances and acts which must, if not met with stubborn resistance, end in utter demoralisation of Nation. I hope no self-respecting Indian will run the risk of killing national spirit for a doubtful contingency of securing a Constitution, to work which no Nation with a stamina may be left. Let me also point out that, as to the Frontier Province, your telegram contains a narration of facts which, on face of them, furnish no warrant for arrests of popular leaders, passing of extra-legal Ordinance, making life and property utterly insecure, and shooting unarmed peaceful crowds for daring to hold demonstrations against arrests of their trusted leaders. If Khan Saheb Abdul Gaffar asserted the right of Complete Independence, it was a natural claim and the claim made with impunity by the Congress at Lahore in 1929, and by me with energy put before the British Government in London. Moreover let me remind the Viceroy that despite knowledge on Government's part that Congress mandate contained such claim, I was invited to attend London Conference as Congress delegate. Nor am I able to detect in a mere refusal to attend Durbar an offence warranting summary imprisonment. If Khan Saheb was fomenting racial hatred, it was undoubtedly regrettable. I have his own declarations to the contrary made to me, but assuming that he did foment racial hatred, he was entitled to open trial, where he could have defended himself against accusation. Regarding United Provinces, His Excellency is surely misinformed, because there was no 'No-rent' campaign authorised by Congress, but whilst negotiations were proceeding between Government and Congress representatives, the time for collection of rents actually arrived and rents began to be demanded. Congressmen were, therefore, obliged to advise tenants to suspend payment pending the result of the negotiations, and Mr. Sherwani had offered on behalf of the Congress to withdraw this advice if the authorities suspended collections pending negotiations. I venture to suggest that this is not a matter which can be so summarily dismissed as your wire has done. Controversy in the United Provinces is of long standing and involved well-being of millions of peasantry known to be economically ground down. Any Government jealous of the welfare of the masses in its charge would welcome voluntary co-operation of a body like the Congress, which admittedly exercises great influence over the masses and whose one ambition is to serve them faithfully; and let me add that I regard the withholding of payment of taxes as an inalienable ancient and natural right of a people who have exhausted all other means of seeking freedom from an unbearable economic burden. I must repudiate suggestion that the Congress has slightest desire to promote disorder in any shape or form.

"As to Bengal, the Congress is at one with the Government in condemning assassination and should heartily co-operate with the Government in measures that may be found necessary to stamp out such crimes. But whilst the Congress would condemn in unmeasured terms the methods of terrorism, it can in no way associate itself with Government terrorism as is betrayed by the Bengal Ordinance and acts done thereunder, but must resist, within the limits of its prescribed creed of non-violence, such measures of legalised Government terrorism. I heartily assent to the proposition laid down in your telegram that co-operation must be mutual, but your telegram leads me irresistibly to the conclusion that His Excellency demands co-operation from the Congress without returning any on behalf of Government. I can read in no other way his peremptory refusal to discuss these matters which, as I have endeavoured to show, have at least two sides. Popular side I have put, as I understand it, but before committing myself to definite judgment, I was anxious to understand the other side, *i.e.*, the Government side, and then tender my advice to the Congress.

"With reference to the last paragraph of your telegram, I may not repudiate moral liability for the actions of my colleagues, whether in the Frontier Province or in the United Provinces, but I confess that I was ignorant of the detailed actions and activities of my colleagues whilst I was absent from India, and it was because it was necessary for me to advise and guide the Working Committee of the Congress and in order to complete my knowledge, I sought with an open mind and with the best of intentions an interview with His Excellency and deliberately asked for his guidance. I cannot conceal from His Excellency my opinion that the reply he has condescended to send was hardly a return for my friendly and well-meant approach, and if it is not yet too late, I would ask His Excellency to reconsider his decision and see me as a friend without imposing any conditions whatsoever as to the scope or subject of discussion, and I, on my part, can promise that I would study with an open mind all the facts that he might put before me. I would unhesitatingly and willingly go to the respective Provinces and, with the aid of the authorities, study both sides of the question and if I came to the conclusion after such a study that the people were in the wrong and the Working Committee including myself were misled as to the correct position and that the Government was right, I should have no hesitation whatsoever in making that open confession and guiding the Congress accordingly.

"Along with my desire and willingness to co-operate with Government, I must place my limitations before His Excellency. Non-violence is my absolute creed. I believe that Civil Disobedience is not only the natural right of people, especially when they have no effective voice in their own Government, but that it also is an effective substitute for violence or armed rebellion. I can never, therefore, deny my creed. In pursuance thereof and on the strength of uncontradicted reports, supported by recent activities of the Government of India, to the effect that there may be no other opportunity for me to guide the public, the Working Committee has accepted my advice and passed resolutions tentatively sketching a plan of Civil Disobedience. I am sending herewith text of the resolution. If His Excellency thinks it worth while to see me, operation of the resolution will be suspended pending our discussion, in the hope that it may result in the resolution being finally given up. I admit that correspondence between His Excellency and myself is of such grave importance as not to brook delay in publication. I am, therefore, sending my telegram, your reply, this rejoinder and the Working Committee's resolution for publication."

Resolution of the Working Committee.

"The Working Committee has heard Mahatma Gandhi's account of his visit to the West and considered the situation created by the extraordinary Ordinances promulgated in Bengal, United Provinces and the Frontier Province and by the actions of the authorities, including the numerous arrests made, among those of Khan Abdul Gaffar Khan, Mr. Sherwani and Pandit Jawaharlal Nehru, and by the shootings in the Frontier Province of innocent men resulting in many deaths and many more being injured. The Working Committee has also seen the telegram from His Excellency the Viceroy in reply to the telegram sent by Mahatma Gandhi to him.

"The Working Committee is of opinion that these several acts, and others of lesser gravity, that have taken place in some other Provinces, and the telegram from His Excellency, seem to make further co-operation with the Government on the part of the Congress utterly impossible unless the Government policy is radically changed. These acts and the telegram betray no intention on the part of the bureaucracy to hand over power to the people and are calculated to demoralise the Nation. They also betray a want of faith in the Congress from which co-operation is expected by the Government.

"The Working Committee yields to no one in its abhorrence of terrorism, on any account whatsoever, resorted to by individuals, such as was recently witnessed in Bengal, but it condemns with equal force terrorism practised by Government as shown by its recent acts and Ordinances. The Working Committee marks the deep national humiliation over the assassination committed by two girls in Comilla and is firmly convinced that such crime does great harm to the Nation, especially when through its greatest political mouth-piece—the Congress—it is pledged to non-violence for achieving Swaraj. But the Working Committee can see no justification whatsoever for the Bengal Ordinance which seeks to punish a whole people for the crime of a few. The real remedy lies in dealing with the known cause that prompts such crime.

"If the Bengal Ordinance has no justification for its existence, the Ordinances in the United Provinces and the Frontier Province have still less. The Working Committee is of opinion that the measures taken by the Congress in the U.P. for obtaining agrarian relief are and can be shown to be justified. The Working Committee holds that it is the unquestionable right of all people suffering from grave economic distress, as the tenantry of the United Provinces is admittedly suffering, to withhold payment of taxes if they fail, as in the United Provinces they have failed, to obtain redress by other constitutional methods.

"In the arrest and imprisonment of Mr. Sherwani, the President of the United Provinces Congress Committee, and Pandit Jawaharlal Nehru, the Working General Secretary of the Congress, who were proceeding to Bombay to confer with Mahatma Gandhi and to take part in the meeting of the Working Committee, the Government have gone even beyond the limits contemplated by their Ordinance, in that there was no question whatsoever of these gentlemen taking part, in Bombay, in a No-tax campaign in the United Provinces.

"So far as the Frontier Province is concerned, on the Government's own showing, there appears to be no warrant for either the promulgation of the Ordinance or the arrest and imprisonment without trial of Khan Abdul Gaffar Khan and his co-workers. The Working Committee regards the shooting in that Province of innocent and unarmed men to be wanton and inhuman, and congratulates the brave men of the

Frontier Province upon their courage and endurance and the Working Committee has no doubts that, if the brave people of the Frontier Province retain their non-violent spirit in spite of the gravest provocations, cause of India's Independence.

"The Working Committee calls upon the Government of India to institute a public and impartial enquiry into the events that have led up to the passing of these Ordinances, the necessity of superseding the Ordinary Courts of Law and Legislative machinery and the necessity of several acts committed thereunder. And thereafter, if a proper enquiry is set up and all facilities are given to the Working Committee for the production of evidence, it will be prepared to assist the enquiry by leading evidence before it.

"The Working Committee has considered the declaration of the Prime-Minister made before the Round Table Conference and the debates in the Houses of Parliament, and regards the declaration as wholly unsatisfactory and inadequate in terms of the Congress Demand and places on record its opinion that nothing short of Complete Independence carrying full control over the Defence and External Affairs and Finance, with such Safeguards as may be demonstrably necessary in the interests of the Nation can be regarded by the Congress as satisfactory.

"The Working Committee notes that the British Government was not prepared at the Round Table Conference to regard the Congress as representing and entitled to speak and act on behalf of the Nation as a whole, without distinction of caste, creed or colour. At the same time the Committee recognises with sorrow that communal harmony could not be attained at the said Conference. The Working Committee invites the Nation, therefore, to make ceaseless effort to demonstrate the capacity of the Congress to represent the Nation as a whole and promote an atmosphere that would make a Constitution framed on a purely national basis acceptable to the various communities composing the Nation. Meanwhile, the Working Committee is prepared to tender co-operation to the Government, provided His Excellency the

Viceroy reconsiders his telegram and adequate relief is granted in respect of the Ordinances and its recent acts, free scope is left to the Congress in any future further negotiations to prosecute the Congress claim for Complete Independence, and the administration of the country is carried on in consultation with popular representatives, pending the attainment of such Independence.

"In the absence of any satisfactory response from the Government in terms of the foregoing paragraph, the Working Committee will regard it as an indication on the part of the Government that it has reduced to nullity the Delhi Pact. In the event of a satisfactory response not forthcoming, the Working Committee calls upon the Nation to resume Civil Disobedience including non-payment of taxes under the following conditions and illustrative heads:—

(1) No Province or district or tahsil or village is bound to take up Civil Disobedience unless the people thereof understand the non-violent nature of the struggle with all its implications, and are ready to undergo sufferings involving loss of life and property.

(2) Non-violence must be observed in thought, word and deed in the face of the gravest provocation, it being understood that the campaign is not one of seeking revenge or inflicting injuries on the oppressor but it is one of converting him through self-suffering and self-purification.

(3) Social boycott with the intention of inflicting injury on Government officers, Police or anti-nationalists should not be undertaken and is wholly inconsistent with the spirit of non-violence.

(4) It should be borne in mind that non-violent campaigns are independent of pecuniary assistance; therefore, there should be no hired volunteers but their bare maintenance and maintenance of the dependents of poor men and women who might have been imprisoned or killed is permissible wherever it is possible. The Working Committee, however, expects workers in the cause to continue the struggle even though they might have to suffer privations.

(5) Boycott of all foreign cloth, whether British or of other countries, is obligatory under all circumstances.

(6) All Congress men and women are expected to use hand-spun and hand-woven khaddar to the exclusion of even cloth manufactured in the indigenous mills.

(7) Picketing of liquor shops and foreign cloth shops should be vigorously conducted chiefly by women but always so as to ensure perfect non-violence.

(8) Unlicensed manufacture and collection of salt should be resumed.

(9) If processions and demonstrations are organised, only those should join them who will stand *lathi*-charges or bullets without moving from their respective places.

(10) Even in non-violent war boycott of goods manufactured by the oppressors is perfectly lawful, inasmuch as it is never the duty of the victim to promote or retain commercial relations with the oppressor. Therefore, boycott of British goods and concerns should be resumed and vigorously prosecuted.

(11) Civil breach of non-moral laws and of laws and orders injurious to the people wherever it is considered possible and advisable may be practised.

(12) All unjust orders issued under the Ordinances may be civilly disobeyed."

VICEROY'S 'NO.'

4. Telegram from the Private Secretary to His Excellency the Viceroy, to Mr. Gandhi, dated the 2nd January, 1932.

No. 3-S.—"His Excellency desires me to acknowledge receipt of your telegram of 1st January which has been considered by him and his Government.

"They much regret to observe that under your which are stated in your telegram and the resolution.

"They regard this attitude as the more deplorable in view of the declared intentions of His advice the Congress Working Committee has passed a resolution which involves general revival of Civil Disobedience unless certain conditions are satisfied

Majesty's Government and the Government of India to expedite the policy of constitutional reform contained in the Premier's statement.

"No Government, consistent with the discharge of their responsibility, can be subject to conditions sought to be imposed under the menace of unlawful action by any political organisation, nor can the Government of India accept the position implied in your telegram that their policy should be dependent on the judgment of yourself as to necessity of measures which Government have taken after the most careful and thorough consideration of the facts, and after all other possible remedies had been exhausted.

"His Excellency and his Government can hardly believe that you or the Working Committee contemplate that His Excellency can invite you, with the hope of any advantage, to an interview held under the threat of resumption of Civil Disobedience.

"They must hold you and the Congress responsible for all the consequences that may ensue from the action which the Congress have announced their intention of taking, and to meet which, Government will take all necessary measures."

GANDHI'S FINAL TELEGRAM

5. Telegram from Mr. M. K. Gandhi, to the Private Secretary to His Excellency the Viceroy, dated the 3rd January, 1932.

"Thanks your wire even date. I cannot help expressing deep regret for decision of His Excellency and his Government. Surely it is wrong to describe honest expression of opinion as threat. May I remind Government that Delhi negotiations were opened and carried on whilst Civil Disobedience was on, and that when Pact was made Civil Disobedience was not given up but only discontinued? This position was re-asserted and accepted by His Excellency and his Government in Simla in September last, prior to my departure for London. Although I had made it clear that under certain circumstances Congress might have to resume Civil Disobedience, Government did not break off negotiations. That it was made clear by Government that Civil Disobedience carried with it penalty for disobedience, merely proves what civil resisters bargain for, but does not in any way affect my argument. Had Government resented attitude, it was open to them not to send me to London. On the contrary, my departure had His Excellency's blessings. Nor is it fair or correct to suggest that I have ever advanced the claim that any policy of Government should be dependent on my judgment. But I do submit that any popular and constitutional Government would always welcome and sympathetically consider suggestions made by public bodies and their representatives and assist them with all available information about their acts or Ordinances of which public opinion may disapprove. I claim that my messages have no other meaning than what is suggested in last paragraph. Time alone will show whose position was justified. Meanwhile I wish to assure Government that every endeavour will be made on the part of Congress to carry on struggle without malice and in strictly non-violent manner. It was hardly necessary to remind me that Congress and I, its humble representative, are responsible for all the consequences of our actions."

For the sake of convenience all the telegrams are given together but they cover a range of six days. On the 30th of December, Mr. Benthall who was commercial representative for India on the R.T.C. had seen Gandhi and had a long talk. There was no doubt that Gandhi's attitude was alarming to the commercial community, and well might that be, for later events and experiences proved what a mighty weapon boycott was in the hands of the Nation. Yes, but this same Mr. Benthall and his fellow loyalists expressed their view in language which, at this distance of time, has lost none of its poignancy. We give some extracts from the 'confidential' circular issued by them:—

"We went to London determined to achieve some settlement if we could, but our determination in that regard was tempered with an equal determination that there should be no giving way on any essential part of the policy agreed to by the (European) Associated Chambers of Commerce in regard to financial and commercial Safeguards, and by the European Association on general policy. It was obvious to us, and we had it in mind throughout the Conference, that the united forces of the Congress, the Hindu Sabha and the (Indian) Federated Chambers of Commerce would be directed towards whittling down the Safeguards already proposed."

"If you look at the results of this last session, you will see that Gandhi and the (Indian) Federated Chambers are unable to point to a single concession wrung from the British Government as the result of their visit to St. James' Palace. He landed in India with empty hands."

"There was another incident, too, which did him no good. He undertook to settle the communal problem and failed before all the world."

"The Muslims were a solid and enthusiastic team: Ali Imam, the Nationalist Muslim, caused no division. They played their cards with great skill throughout; they promised us support and they gave it in full measure. In return they asked us that we should not forget their economic plight in Bengal and we should 'without pampering them' do what we can to find places for them in European firms so that they may have a chance to improve their material position and the general standing of their community."

"On the whole, there was one policy of the British Nation and the British Community in India, and that was to make up our minds on a national policy and to stick to it. *But after the general elections, the right wing of the Government made up its mind to break up the Conference and to fight the Conference and to fight the Congress.* The Muslims, who do not want responsibility at the Centre, were delighted. Government undoubtedly changed their policy and tried to get away with Provincial Automony, with a promise of Central reforms. We had made up our minds that the fight with the Congress was inevitable; we felt and said that the sooner it came the better, but we made up our minds that for a crushing success we should have all possible friends on our side. The Muslims were alright; the Minorities Pact and Government's general attitude ensured that. So were the Princes and the Minorities."

"The imporant thing to us seemed to be to carry the Hindu in the street as represented by such people as Sapru, Jayakar, Patro and others. If we could not get them to fight the Congress, we could at least ensure that they would not back the Congress, and that, by one simple method of leaving no doubt in their minds that there was to be no going back on the Federal Scheme which broadly was also the accepted policy of the European Community, and we acted accordingly. We pressed upon the Government that the one substantial earnest of good faith which would satisfy these people was to bring in the Provincial and Central Constitutions in one place. Provincial Autonomy could not be forced upon India; the Muslims alone could not work it. Congress Provinces facing a bitter Centre present grave political difficulties; each Province would be a Calcutta Corporation on its own. So we joined with strange companions; Government saw the arguments, and the Conference, instead of breaking up in disorder with 100 per cent. of Hindu political India against us, ended in promises of co-operation by 99 per cent. of the Conference, including even such people as Malaviya, while Gandhi himself was indisposed to join the Standing Committee."

"The Muslims have become firm allies of the Europeans. They are very satisfied with their own position and are prepared to work with us."

"It must not, however, be supposed that when we agree that Reforms are necessary, we advocate democratic reform in every Province. All that we mean is such change in the system of Government as will improve its efficiency."

These extracts sufficiently show how the Tory Government and its allies worked to defeat the object of the declaration that the Labour Government had made promising to concede to India her due. But it would be wrong to believe that the pact between the Muslim reactionaries who were prepared to sell their country for a mess of pottage,[1] and the British reactionaries who wanted to keep Indians down for ever, was an impromptu performance. The foundations for it were laid in India and England long before the second session of the Conference. In fact when Gandhiji and Lord Irwin came to an understanding between themselves, those of the reactionary element in India which did not like this alliance immediately gathered forces and organized themselves into a united force to defeat the Indian Nationalists. It was in Simla, at the headquarters of the Indian Government, that a part of this conspiracy was hatched.

The Working Committee having picked up the gauntlet thrown by Mr. Emerson and Lord Willingdon, the members departed to their places and found on return home that they had not much or anything to do. Government really took up the fight where it had been left on the 4th March, 1931. They had ordered thousands of new *lathis* during the truce period. In fact the truce period was the period of preparation on the part of Government for renewed hostilities, the outbreak of which was imminent almost any month during the truce and inevitably on Gandhi's return. Three Ordinances had already been promulgated and three more were in the pocket of the Viceroy, to be released the moment they were called for. The Govenment offensive commenced on the 4th January, 1932. Every Congress organization and every allied organization was banned, and Congressmen, whether they

---

1 The recent revelations in the Indian Legislative Assembly about the demand of H. H. The Aga Khan to be made a Ruling Prince of some territory in India, as a reward for his services at the Round Table Conference, throw much lurid light on these transactions.

did any overt act or not in defiance of the Law or the Ordinances, which came to be spoken of as the Lawless Law, were got hold of, arrested and sentenced. We had no reason to complain either. The truce was at an end and the drill-master cried, "As you were." In fact, if only the Congressmen had been so desired, they would have found their way to their old jails and taken their lodgings in their old quarters. But Government had apparently not the courage required for such an unusual and 'illegal' course. Nor would they like the dramatic settings which it would give to the Civil Disobedience movement.

While Government began where they had left, the Congress had to begin it all over again. The *lathi*-charge of Government was a later development in the first movement (1930). In 1932, it was the first friend that greeted the Satyagrahis. Lord Willingdon, it was widely believed, hoped to be able to put down this outbreak in six weeks, but six weeks are such a short time and Satyagraha is such a long drawn struggle that his hopes could not be realised. Gandhi was intending to go to the Talukas in Gujarat which had borne the brunt of the struggle in 1930, but before he could do so, he and his trusty lieutenant Vallabhbhai were both arrested and spirited away as State prisoners in the small hours of the 4th of January, 1932. Khan Saheb and Jawaharlal had already led the van. The rest of the Indian politicians led the rear. The Satyagrahis came forward in their thousands. In 1921 they were thirty thousand in number and that was considered a big number. In 1930-31, within a short interval of 10 months, ninety thousand men, women and children were convicted and sentenced. No one knows how many were beaten, but the number cannot be less than 3 or 4 times the number imprisoned. People were either beaten down into paralysis of all activity, or simply tired down by a 'cat and mouse' policy. The old game of beating prisoners was renewed. Office secrets were asked to be divulged. "Where are your papers, your books, and your lists of subscriptions and volunteers?" That was the demand of Government and young men were harassed and unutterable things were said, unspeakable punishments were planned and executed. Imagine an advocate of the High Court being subjected to the torture of his hair being plucked out one by one as a mark of Police displeasure at his not giving out his name and address.

New occasions called for new Ordinances. Though they were promulgated from time to time, it would be convenient to refer to them together. Reference has already been made to an Ordinance which was issued in Bengal while Gandhiji was still in London. It was said to be for the purpose of suppressing the terrorist movement in Bengal and for speedier trial of offences in connection therewith. It gave power to any officer of Government authorised by the Local Government to require any person whom he suspected to give his identity and movements and to arrest and detain him for a day for verifying his statements; and in making his arrest the officer might use any means that might be necessary. The Local Government might require the occupier or owner of any building to place it at the disposal of Government for any time with all its furniture etc., with or without compensation. Similarly a District Magistrate could call upon the owner or possessor of any article or thing to place it at his disposal, with or without compensation. The District Magistrate could prohibit or limit access to any building or place including Railways etc. He could also regulate traffic, require a person to submit a return of vehicles or other means of transit owned or possessed by him or commandeer the same. He could prohibit or regulate sale of arms and ammunition or take possession of the same. He might require a land-holder or a teacher or any other person to assist in the restoration of Law and Order. He could issue search warrants. The Local Government could impose collective fines on the inhabitants of a particular area, could exempt a particular person or class from any liability, and the amount of fine apportioned to any individual could be recovered as a fine or arrears of Government Revenue. Any disobedience would entail imprisonment of six months, or fine, or both. The Local Government was authorised to make rules to prevent communication with absconders and secure information of their movements, to prevent attacks on persons or property of the King's subjects, to secure the safety of His Majesty's forces and Police and provide for the custody of prisoners. No action taken under the Ordinance could be challenged in Civil Courts. New Courts of Criminal jurisdiction known as Special Tribunals or Special Magistrates might be constituted for trying cases which the Local Government might determine for their trial. Special rules of procedure were laid down for these Special Tribunals. The Special Courts might proceed under certain conditions with the trial, in the absence of the accused.

The United Provinces Emergency Powers Ordinance which was issued on the 14th December, 1931, authorised the Local Government to declare any dues paid to Government, local authority or landlord, to be a notified liability which was made recoverable as arrears of Land Revenue. The Local Government could direct any person, believed to be acting prejudically to public safety, not to reside in a particular area, to remove himself from a particular area, to conduct himself in a particular way. This order was to remain in force for a month. The Local Government may require the owner of a particular land or building to place it at the disposal of the Government with all its fixtures and furniture, with or without compensation. The District Magistrate might prohibit or limit access to any building or place, require any person to take such order as he might be directed with any vehicle or means of transport in his possession. Any authorised officer of Government might require any landholder, local authority, or teacher to assist in the maintenance of Law and Order. Any person suspected of instigating non-payment of a notified liability was punishable with imprisonment of two years, or fine, or both. Any person inducing a public servant to disregard his duty or dissuading any person from entering Police or Military service was punishable with imprisonment for a year or fine.

A Local Government could impose collective fines on the inhabitants of a particular area which could be recovered as Land Revenue. Any person repeating the contents of any proscribed document was punishable with six months' imprisonment or fine. A fine imposed upon a young person under 16 years could be realised from his parent or guardian, who could be convicted to imprisonment in default as if he himself had committed the offence. Such order could not be challenged in a Civil Court.

The three Ordinances relating to the North-West Frontier Province were issued on the 24th of December, 1931. One of them ran on the lines of the U. P. Ordinance and provided against non-payment of liabilities. The other two were known as N. W. F. P. Emergency Powers Ordinance and the N. W. F. P. Unlawful Association Ordinance. Under the former any authorised officer could arrest or detain any suspected person for a day without warrant, for a period of two months which could be extended by the Local Government. The Local Government could direct any person to enter or remain or not in any area to remove himself from such area, and generally to conduct himself in a particular way for a period of one month. A failure to comply with such orders was made punishable with imprisonment for two years. The Local Government could take possession of any private building. The District Magistrate might regulate, prohibit or limit access to any building, and traffic by any road or waterway. The Local Government might control the supply and sale of any commodity, requiring traders and manufactures to submit returns of their dealings in such commodity or to place the whole or a portion of their stocks at the disposal of the Government. Similarly it might require the owner of any article or thing to place it at the disposal of the Government. The District Magistrate could require a return of vehicles or any means of transport or their possession to be delivered. The District Magistrate could regulate the sale of arms and ammunition. The Local Government may appoint anybody as Special Police Officer or require a landholder or teacher or a local authority to assist in the maintenance of Law and Order. The Local Government might require the owner or person in charge of an utility service to take any specified action in respect thereof, and on failure of compliance assume control of such service. The District Magistrate could control operation of the post, telegraph, telephone and the wireless, intercept articles or messages, require accommodation in any Railway train or vessel, order any specified person or goods not to be carried to any destination, or exclude or eject any passenger from a train, stop any train at a particular station, and require special conveyance of troops and Police. He might depute a Police officer to attend any public meeting even though the meeting was held in a private place and the admission was by tickets. Special powers were conferred regarding searches. Any person inducing a public servant to disregard his duties or dissuading a person from entering the Police or Military service, or propagating any statement or rumour likely to create hatred or contempt towards a public servant or to cause alarm to the public was liable to imprisonment for a year, or fine, or both. The Local Government could impose a collective fine on the inhabitants of an area which was realisable like Land Revenue. Any person repeating the contents of a confidential document was liable to imprisonment for six months and fine. Parents or guardians of young men under 16 years were liable to pay fines imposed on their wards and in default to imprisonment. Special Courts under Special Judges, Special Magistrates and Summary Courts were constituted and their jurisdictions defined and special procedure laid down for trial and appeal.

Under the other Ordinance, the Local Government might notify any place as a place which is used for an unlawful association and the Magistrate could take possession of such a notified place, ejecting therefrom any person found therein. The Magistrate could also take possession of moveables and the Local Government might declare them forfeited. Any person entering or remaining on a notified place committed criminal trespass. The Local Government could forfeit moneys etc., belonging to an unlawful association and seize the same and prohibit any person in possession of moneys believed to be for an unlawful association from dealing with such money except under Government orders. The Local Government could authorise the examination of books of such persons or enquiries touching the origin and dealings in such moneys.

On the 4th of January, four new Ordinances were issued known as (1) the Emergency Powers Ordinance, (2) Unlawful Instigation Ordinance, (3) Unlawful Association Ordinance, and (4) Prevention of Molestation and Boycott Ordinance. Under the first Ordinance, powers similar to those already detailed above were taken relating to arrest and detention of persons, restricting their movements, commandeering of buildings, restricting access to buildings and Railways, controlling traffic, controlling supply and sale of any commodity of general use or its seizure, relating to control of means of transport, control of sale of arms and ammunition, appointment of Special Police Officers, obligation on landlords and teachers etc., to assist in the maintenance of Law and Order, control of Public Utility Services, withholding and interception of articles and messages transmitted by post, wire or air, commandeering accommodation on Railways and vessels, control of traffic thereon, and attendance of Police officers at meetings. Similarly Special Courts, special procedure, new offences and special punishments, were provided as in the case of the Frontier Regulation. The Indian Press Emergency Act was made more stringent by a Special Section of the Ordinance.

Under the Unlawful Instigation Ordinance the Government could notify any liability as a notified liability and any person instigating non-payment of a notified liability could be imprisoned for six months and also fined. A person to whom a notified liability was due could ask the Collector and the Collector could realise it as arrears of Land Revenue.

Under the Unlawful Association Ordinance the Local Government could seize, as in the case of the North-West Frontier Province Ordinance referred to above, and take possession of any buildings, moveable property and funds belonging to an unlawful association. The Local Government could also forfeit such funds and require any person in custody of such funds not to deal with them except with Government permission, and order examination of books etc., relating to such funds. Any association could be declared unlawful which, in the opinion of the Governor-General-in-Council, interfered with the administration of Law and Order and constituted a danger to the public peace.

Under the Prevention of Molestation and Boycott Ordinance, whoever molested and boycotted or abetted the molestation or boycott of another person was liable to six months' imprisonment or fine. A person was said to molest another when he obstructed or used violence or intimidated another or any one in whom such other person was interested, or loitered at or near a house of such other person, or persistently followed him from place to place, or interfered with his property, or dissuaded any person from entering, approaching or dealing at such place, with a view to cause such other person to abstain from doing, or to force him to do, a thing or to cause loss to him. Boycott was defined as refusal to deal or do business with, or supply goods to, or to let a house or land to, or to render any customary service to, any person or to any one in whom such person is interested, or refusal to do any of the above things on ordinary terms and in ordinary course, or abstention from professional or business relations. The performance of a mock ceremony resembling a funeral ceremony done with intent to annoy a person was declared to be an offence punishable with imprisonment for six months or with fine.

It would thus appear that under these Ordinances very wide powers were taken and they were extended to practically the whole country.

When the Ordinance period expired, they were renewed in a consolidated form for another term, and in November, 1932, they were validated by regular legislation. Unlawful associations, molestation and boycotting, and the Press were all brought under the operation of these Ordinances.

So early as on the 26th of March, 1932, Sir Samuel Hoare in the House of Commons admitted that the Ordinances were very drastic and severe. They covered almost every activity of Indian life. They were drawn up in that comprehensive form because "the Government, with the full knowledge at their disposal, sincerely believed that they were threatened with an attack on the whole basis of Government and that the Ordinances were essential if India was to be prevented from drifting into anarchy." Pandit Madan Mohan Malaviya had sent a 1,100 word telegram to England but the Postal authorities refused to send it at the prescribed rates. It will be remembered that the Press Law (Act XXIII of 1931) passed during the truce period expired on October 9th, 1931. The Criminal Law Amendment Bill of 1932 contained provisions to place the Press Law (Act of XXIII of 1932) permanently on the Statute Book. The provisions of this Press Law resemble those of the Press Act of 1910. Besides the Government of India Ordinances and Ordinance Bills or Acts, the Bombay Government brought forward, in November, 1932, a Provincial Ordinance Bill in which adequate safeguards were provided against a No-tax campaign as well. Wilful refusal to pay the arrears of a notified liability involved a punishment of one year's imprisonment, with or without fine. In prosecutions under this section, unless the contrary was proved, it was to be presumed that failure or refusal to pay arrears of a notified liability was wilful. All these Ordinances and repressive measures were in fact under contemplation even in year of truce (1931). The fact is that the Secretary of the Bombay Branch of the European Association wrote a letter, in 1931, to the Secretary, Home Department, Government of Bombay, after the presentation of an address to him on the 15th October, 1931, by the Europeans of Poona. The delegation then suggested to Government to take firm and immediate action in the event of a recrudescence of the Civil Disobedience movement,—all this when the R.T.C. was sitting in London, with a view ostensibly to conciliate the Congress school of thought,—and made specific suggestions that the Congress flag should be forbidden and likewise all parading or drilling of volunteers, that all ex-Civil Disobedience men should forthwith be brought under restraint, treated as enemy subjects in war and interned, that Congress funds should be stopped at the source and unearthed by a special Ordinance, that mills which agreed to Congress conditions should be made to withdraw their pledges on pain of being denied Rail transit of their goods, that no one should be permitted to benefit financially from political agitation and boycott.

The events of 1932-33 ran on much the same lines as those of 1930-31. Only, the fight was more intensive and more determined. The repression was ever so much more ruthless and the suffering was ever so much more deep.

The Government offensive started with the arrest of Gandhi and the President of the Congress, Sirdar Vallabhbhai Patel, in the early hours of the 4th of January. The above mentioned Ordinances of 1932 were issued the same morning and extended to several Provinces. Within the next few days, they were applied to practically the whole country. Many Provincial and subordinate Committees, Ashrams, National Schools and other National institutions were declared unlawful, and their houses, furniture and funds and other moveables seized. Most of the leading Congressmen in the country were suddenly clapped into jails. The Congress organisation was thus apparently left without leaders, without funds, and even without any local habitation. The Congressmen who had been left behind were not, in spite of this sudden and determined swoop, without resources. Every one took up the work wherever he happened to be. The Working Committee had decided that vacancies on it, unlike in 1930, be not filled up and Sirdar Vallabhbhai, anticipating his own arrest, had made out a list of several persons who would act in his place during his absence, one after another. The Working Committee had transferred all its powers to the President, and the President in his turn transferred them to his successors who, in their turn, could nominate their own successors with similar powers. In the Provinces also, wherever it was possible, the whole power of the organisation was delegated to one person and similarly these powers percolated to a series of individuals exercising the rights of a Congress Committee in Districts, Thanas, Talukas and even villages. It was these individuals who came to be popularly known as 'Dictators.'

One of the difficulties which faced the organisers of any Civil Disobedience campaign related to the laws which could be selected for disobedience. It is evident that any law and every law may not be disobeyed. The Ordinances with their wide ramifications solved this difficulty for the Congress. In the different Provinces different items were selected, while there were certain items prescribed from time to time by the Acting President of the Congress. Thus, picketing of liquor shops and foreign cloth shops and of British goods was an item common to all Provinces. In the United Provinces on a pretty large scale, and in a portion of Bengal, non-payment of rent was an important item. In places in Bihar and Bengal, payment of Chaukidari tax was withheld. In the Central Provinces and the Berars, Karnatak and some places in U. P., the Madras Presidency and Bihar, Forest Laws were disobeyed. Salt Laws were defied in many places by manufacture, collection, or sale of illicit salt. Meetings and processions were of course prohibited and were held in spite of such prohibition. At an early stage of the struggle, a favourite item of the programme was the observance of what came to be known as special days. These were in connection with special events or individuals, or for special purposes, *e.g.*, Gandhi Day, Motilal Day, Frontier Day, Martyrs Day, Flag Day and a number of other days.

As already stated, the Government had taken possession of Congress offices and Ashrams. Attempts were made in many places to get back symbolical possession of these places in Government hands, thus disobeying the Ordinance which made entry into those places a trespass. These attempts came to be known as 'raids.' Under the Ordinances the service of any Press was not available to the Congress. This deficiency was made up by the issue of unauthorised bulletins, leaflets, news-sheets, reports, etc., which were typed, cyclostyled, duplicated, or even printed, but without the names of the Press or the printers as required by law, sometimes under the names of non-existent Presses and persons. It is remarkable that in spite of Police vigilance these news-sheets and bulletins were issued regularly and continued to furnish information to the country, as a whole, of all that was happening. The service of the Post-Office and the Telegraph was denied to the Congress, and it established its own system of carrying its post not only from place to place in a Province but also from the All-India Office to the Provinces. Sometimes the volunteers carrying these postal articles were detected and naturally arrested or otherwise dealt with. This system which had really been started towards the latter part of the movement of 1930 was almost perfected in 1932. The Government were unable to locate even the offices of the A.I.C.C. or the Provincial Committees, from whence not only the bulletins but also instructions for the carrying on of the movement emanated, and when once either an office or an individual conducting it was located and put out of action, another sprang up and carried on the work. Another item which created much enthusiasm among the people and caused not a little embarrassment to the Police, was the holding of a session of the Congress followed by a series of Conferences in the Provinces and the Districts all over the country. In some places an attempt was made to interfere with the regular working of the Railways by volunteers pulling the alarm signal in Railway trains and bringing them to a stop. An attempt was even made to make the Railway working difficult by large numbers of people boarding trains without tickets, simply to cause loss to the managements, but these found no encouragement from responsible quarters and were stopped.

The Boycott took a most intensive form and special items were selected for concentrated work. Thus in some places separate weeks were devoted to intensive propaganda for boycott of foreign cloth, of British medicines, British Banks, Insurance Companies, foreign sugar, kerosine oil, and British goods generally.

It is not to be supposed that Government after arresting the leaders would become quiet and mild. All the powers referred to in the Ordinances were used. But there were certain other forms of repression which even the Ordinances, drastic as they were, did not sanction or contemplate. Needless to say that arrests were made in large numbers but they were made with discrimination, the total number of convictions being anything not less than a lakh. It soon became apparent that, in spite of camp jails and temporary jails being opened, the numbers that offered themselves for arrest could not all be accommodated. It was therefore necessary to make a selection, and only those who were supposed to possess some organising capacity or were prominently associated with the Congress organisation were ordinarily imprisoned. Nor was it an easy matter to deal with them in prison. More than ninety-five per cent of the persons convicted were placed in the 'C' class. There was a very small sprinkling of Congressmen placed in the 'B' class, while the 'A' class was maintained only in name in several places, and very sparingly granted in others. It will be recalled that early in 1930 this classification had been introduced, and while Government had resolutely refused to recognise political prisoners as a class by themselves, their statements had led people to believe that most of the Civil Disobedience prisoners would, by reason of their education, social status, and mode of living, fall in class 'B' at least. Graduates, Professors, Lawyers, Editors, well-to-do traders and businessmen, rich Zamindars, high grade agriculturists, philanthropic workers,—men whom the Government themselves recognised as well-to-do by imposing heavy fines running often into four figures,—were all thrown pell-mell into the last class, with the food and clothing of ordinary convicts. No wonder that, apart from other considerations, men and women who had sought imprisonment for the sake of their convictions and, as they felt, for the noble cause of gaining freedom for their country, were not likely to submit to humiliating conditions such as sitting in a particular posture in a row or lifting their hands on order and so on. The conditions of prison life were also not such as to be easily tolerated by a class of persons well brought up and having their own ideas about them. All this very often brought them into conflict with prison authorities, which resulted in the imposition of various kinds of jail penalties sanctioned by the rules and not unoften in beatings and other kinds of torture which can easily be practised within prison walls where there is no fear of detection. One particularly atrocious case of assault and beating for refusal to submit to the humiliating condition of sitting in a particular posture led to the prosecution and conviction of a jailor and his assistant and some others in Nasik Jail, but *lathi*-charges on Civil Disobedience prisoners were not uncommon. The conditions of life in the temporary jails, with their tin sheds which gave protection neither against the heat of May and June nor the cold of December and January, with their over-crowding and consequent insanitary conditions, were quite intolerable. There were, no doubt, some jails where the treatment was tolerably fair but that was rather the exception than the rule. Some of the permanent jails also were no better. It was reported that the health of the political prisoners in many of the jails, particularly in camp jails, was far from satisfactory. Dysentery was common in all the seasons, while the rains and cold weather brought pneumonia and serious lung trouble to not a few. Many died as prisoners. The conditions in the permanent jails in some places were not much better. The treatment depended naturally on the character and temper of the immediate jail officials, and these, with some notable exceptions here and there, were neither considerate nor even fair.

The Police had early taken to the device of dispersing crowds and processions by *lathi*-charges. There was hardly an important place in any Province where the movement showed signs of life which did not experience these *lathi*-charges. In many places, the injuries caused were serious and the number of those injured large. It was a practice with the crowds to collect together to see what was happening where some Satyagrahis were marching in procession, holding a meeting, carrying on what is called a 'raid' or engaged in picketing, and when the *lathi*-charge was made, no discrimination was made between those who had assembled as sight-seers and those who had gone with the set purpose of disobeying the law. It was not unoften that the sight-seers were the victims of these *lathi*-charges and the Satyagrahis were arrested and otherwise dealt with. The Satyagrahis, too, had their share of these assaults, not only in a crowd where they were mixed up with other people but within the quieter and less exciting environments of a Police lock-up or a prison cell. It was commonly reported that in many places unmentionable atrocities and tortures were perpetrated, the variety and the cruelty of which varied with the intelligence, resourcefulness and callousness of the particular officers concerned. Even women and boys and children were not spared. The Government had discovered that while the Satyagrahis were prepared for prison, beating and torture, and many of them even to be shot, there were many who would succumb if an attack was made on their property. Accordingly heavy fines were imposed on conviction. Sometimes they rose to five figures. Three and four figures were common enough. Where non-payment of Revenue, rent or taxes was resorted to, for realisation of such dues and taxes and for realisation of fines, the properties of not only the defaulters and the convicts but also the property of joint families and sometimes of relatives were attached and sold. This by itself would be nothing if, as a result of such attachment and sale, properties of much value were not sold off virtually for a song. Besides the legally correct form of distress and attachment, what really mattered even more was the extra-legal and the illegal harassment and loss amounting in not a few cases to wanton loot and waste. Not only were moveables like furniture, household utensils, jewellery and even cattle and standing crop attached and sold and sometimes destroyed, but the very lands and homesteads were not spared. There are many in Gujarat, the U.P. and Karnatak who are landless even to-day and whose suffering was entirely voluntary, in the sense that they refused to pay what they could easily have paid if they cared to save themselves and their property. These sufferings were none-the-less imposed upon them, because, if the object was the realisation of the dues only, they need not have been deprived of all that they lost. The agriculturists of Gujarat who joined in the non-payment of Revenue and rent campaign, went through sufferings which it is impossible to describe, but they did not bend. There were many places where extra Police were posted as a punitive measure and their cost realised from the inhabitants. From four or five places only in Bihar where such extra Police were posted in the Province, no less than four lakhs and seventy thousand was realised as Punitive tax. The terror and havoc created by the posting of additional force was so great in parts of the district of Midnapore in Bengal that the bulk of the Hindu population of two Thanas in the district actually evacuated their homes and shifted to the neighbouring areas in the midst of indescribable suffering resulting in the death of women.

Besides such Punitive tax, collective fines were also imposed on many localities and the inhabitants made to pay them. In several places in the country, firing was resorted to and many persons killed and many more injured. In this respect the N.W.F.P. suffered the severest losses in killed and injured.

It is unnecessary to burden this description with details. It would be invidious to mention names of persons or places. If we attempted anything like an adequate account of all the acts of defiance on the part of Congressmen and women, and all the legal, illegal and extra-legal measures adopted by the Government and its officials and all that the people had to suffer in consequence, it would cover a volume by itself. The movement was country-wide and the Provinces vied with one another in putting forth their best effort. It was not confined to British India alone. Some of the Indian States as, for example, Baghelkhand contributed their mite to it and workers and people belonging to many of the States joined in the fray and suffered

The Ashrams and Congress offices which had been taken possession of were demolished or even set fire to.

The newspaper Press was hard hit. Many of the newspapers were called upon to furnish securities. The securities of many of them were forfeited and many had to stop publication on account of failure to deposit security or seizure of press or fear of action by Government.

In the midst of all this havoc and terror, one thing stands out most prominently. Never did the people resort to any serious acts of violence and the lesson of non-violence had gone deep down and enabled the movement to be continued for months and months, when the Government had expected to finish it in a few weeks. Nor would it be an exaggeration to say that it would have been even more difficult to control it than it actually was, had it not been for the extra-legal and the extra-Ordinance methods which were employed in dealing with it and which in themselves constituted the very negation of all law and civilised Government. All open avenues of communication having been closed, the Congress workers, many of them, almost unconsciously slided into methods of secrecy and in this too they proved themselves quite resourceful and quite a match to the widespread ramifications of the Police—ordinary, secret and special. We have already referred to the maintenance of Congress offices, regular publication of bulletins, timely promulgation of instructions to Congressmen and the public in respect of programmes to be observed. Although Satyagraha does not need much money, a campaign on such an extensive scale could not be conducted without it. At no stage did the work come to a standstill for want of funds. They came, nobody knew from where. The anonymous donor paid without knowing to whom he paid. It is remarkable how under such conditions the moneys received were scrupulously used for the purposes of the campaign, and how strict accounts were maintained even in those exciting times when the whole office was carried about in people's pockets. The secrecy enabled the movement to be guided and conducted by a Head, but at the same time it reduced what ought to have been an open battle of defiance regardless of consequences, and carrying its own appeal to the nobler instincts of our people, to a mere battle of wits which only evoked admiration of cleverness.

We may not close this description without referring to two sessions of the Congress which were held in the month of April 1932 and 1933 in Delhi and Calcutta respectively. The session at Delhi was held in spite of Police vigilance which succeeded in spotting and arresting large numbers of delegates on their way to Delhi.

The Congress session was held under the clock tower in Chandni Chowk. In spite of Police vigilance, about 500 delegates found their way to the meeting place. The Police, suspecting the announcement regarding the place of meeting as a mere ruse, were looking for the delegates somewhere in New Delhi, and others were busy dealing with a procession of Akalis elsewhere, and before they could arrive at the Chandni Chowk in sufficient numbers, the delegates had assembled and commenced business. It is said Seth Ranchhod Das Amritlal of Ahmedabad presided. The Annual Report was presented and four resolutions were passed,—the first reiterating Complete Independence as the goal of the Congress, the second whole-heartedly endorsing the revival of Civil Disobedience, the third congratulating the Nation on its splendid response to Mahatma Gandhi's call and expressing complete faith in his leadership, and the fourth re-affirming deep faith in non-violence and congratulating the country, particularly the brave Pathans of the Frontier Province, upon their non-violence in face of acts of gravest provocation from the authorities.

Pandit Madan Mohan Malaviya was the President-elect of the Delhi Congress but he was arrested *en route*. During the whole of this period he was the only leader of note amongst Congressmen who was out, and ever since the date he landed after his return from the Round Table Conference, in spite of growing years and frail health, he never spared himself and was ever busy issuing statements exposing the high-handed action of the authorities, ever encouraging and inspiring Congress workers by his indomitable will and phenomenal energy. In all moments of doubt and difficulty, it was to him that the Congress workers turned and were never disappointed.

CHAPTER II

From the Fast to the Loose Pulley

It will be remembered that at the second Round Table Conference Mr. MacDonald, the Premier, offered to arbitrate on the communal question if every one present put his signature to that agreement in that behalf, and that that arbitration never materialised. The Premier took an unusual course, for it is considered improper for any one to offer his own arbitration instead of leaving the parties to invite him to arbitrate, and therefore he naturally failed. Accordingly the decision that the Government gave upon the Minorities question was a proposal on a par with the rest of the proposals embodied in the White Paper, and not an Award. It will be remembered further how Gandhi indicated his determination at the second R.T.C. to resist the dismemberment of the 'untouchables' from the Hindu community with his life. Now came the time for testing Gandhi's fateful vow. He had written so early as in March 1932 a letter to the Secretary of State on the subject which we extract here (*vide infra*) and which speaks for itself. The Lothian Committee had arrived in India on January 17th, to determine franchise and electoral seats. Time was flying, their Report would be ready and the British have the knack of doing things while we are cogitating. So, after furious thinking and after anxious meditation, Gandhi drafted his letter to Sir Samuel Hoare on the 11th March, 1932, conveying his decision to 'fast unto death' in case Government decided to carve out separate electorates for the untouchables or depressed classes. Sir Samuel sent his reply on the 13th April, 1932. It was a piece of petrified routine. He must await the Lothian recommendations. Of course, Gandhi's views would be taken into account at the proper time.

It was on the 17th of August that Mr. MacDonald's decision—which has wrongly come to be spoken of as an Award—was announced. (*See* Appendix VI). It was a wanton attempt on the Premier's part to put Gandhi in the wrong if he should oppose it. The depressed classes were not only to have separate electorates, but additional votes and the right to contest seats in the general electorate. This was a bounty with a vengeance. On August 18th, Gandhi decided his course of action and intimated the same to the Prime-Minister, adding that the fast would begin on September 20th noon (1932). Mr. MacDonald replied on the 8th September—somewhat at leisure—and the whole correspondence was published on the 12th September. That the Premier should have thought fit to impute to Gandhi inimical intention in respect of the depressed classes has to be referred to here, only to be condemned. We shall not discuss here the merits of the communal decision. Part of it has been scrapped and replaced by the Poona Pact, and the other part remains yet to be scrapped. Now we are on the question as to how the Poona Pact was hammered out. That was the direct result of Gandhi's fast to death.

That fast was to begin on the 20th September, 1932. The interval of one week between the publication of correspondence and the commencement of the fast was a period of utter stress and strain to the Nation,—yea, to the whole world,—a period of tension, in which people, institutions and nations tried to do whatever immediately occurred to them. Interviews were sought and rejected. Cables flew from the ends of the earth to Poona. Exhortations and argumentation were resorted to, to dissuade Gandhi from his determination. While friends were anxious to save his life, enemies were watching the process with a derisive interest. While the great Russian Church was on fire, people were rushing to hear the tintinabulary crash from near. When storm breaks and floods uproot trees, submerge houses, demolish buildings, and sweep away roads and bridges, when conflagrations rage and destroy life and property, when natural cataclysms occur, they rouse the idle interest of the curious and the greedy interest of the wicked. Some such outbreak of emotions was witnessed when Gandhi, in reply to the Premier, declared that his fast would begin. It threw the country into a state of alarm, consternation and confusion. All of us have witnessed death-bed scenes in our life. People gather round the dying person, and when the doctor arrives, he is almost to feel like one of them,—not like the physician that must send people out, each about a business improvised for the occasion. When a series of remedial measures are suggested, hot water fomentations, smelling salt, medicine, turpentine, brandy, this, that and the other, people disperse each to do his bit for the dying patient or the living physician, and the latter gets some little peace of mind to think and act. Here was Gandhi, not accidentally struck by appendicitis as he was 8 years previously in the same jail, but deliberately taking to his death-bed and entering upon a fast. No wonder then that the country should have been thrown into a state of paralysis, from which, however, the patient himself raised it to life and activity.

The Premier's decision was to be scrapped. He would not do it himself. It must therefore be done by agreement amongst the Hindus themselves. A Conference was therefore a desideratum. Was it to be on the 19th or the 20th? That was the question. Gandhi's life must be saved. It was creditable that a leader of the depressed classes should have made the first move in the matter.

M. C. Rajah, Rao Bahadur, condemned the separate electorates. Sapru demanded the release of Gandhi. Congressmen naturally strove to mobilize thought and arrange a settlement. But Pandit Malaviya, always on a level with his age, immediately thought of organising a Conference of leaders. In England, Mr. Andrews, Mr. Polak and Mr. Lansbury began to invite the attention of the English people to the serious character of the issues involved and an appeal was made, which was influentially signed, for a special prayer throughout the country. In India the 20th of September was observed as a day of fasting and prayer and Shantiniketan participated in the observance. It did not take long for the movement inaugurated to secure an amendment of the Premier's decision, and to sublimate itself into a wider movement for the removal of untouchability. Temples were being thrown open to the untouchables in Calcutta, Delhi and other places. It was hoped that Gandhi would be released as soon as he began his fast, but as it was discovered that Gandhi's so-called release would take the shape of an internment at some suitable place of private residence under certain restrictions of movement, Gandhi wrote to Government sparing them the expense and the trouble of such a change and expressing his inability "to conform to any conditions." Government readily agreed and refrained from forcing any arrangements upon Gandhi which were distasteful to him.

It is not possible for us to take the reader through a detailed history of the developments which resulted in the Poona Pact. The Conference convened by Pandit Malaviya met first in Bombay but it shifted its scene of labour soon to Poona. We would refer those interested in these details to the magnificent publication entitled 'The Epic Fast' by Pyarelal, Gandhi's Private Secretary, but suffice it to say that Dr. Ambedkar was soon drawn into the negotiations, and with the aid of men like Syt. Amritlal Thakkar, Syt. Rajagopalachari, Sir Chunilal Mehta, Pandit Malaviya, Birla, Sirdar Patel, Mrs. Naidu, Mr. Jayakar, Dr. Ambedkar, M. C. Rajah, Rajendra Prasad, Hridaynath Kunzru and others, a scheme was formulated which met with the acceptance of all parties by the fifth day of the fast. The depressed classes were to forego their separate electorates and content themselves solely with the general Hindu electorates (in which, of course, they were already included, as well, by the terms of the British Award), subject to important safeguards which the caste Hindus are to concede to them. In the first place, they are to have a specific number of reserved seats (148) out of those assigned by the British Award to the general constituencies in the various Legislatures. In the second place, they are to elect by themselves, four candidates for each reserved seat, the general electorate being confined, in its subsequent choice, to one of these four. The settlement as a whole is to last until altered by common agreement. The depressed classes primary elections are to last for a maximum period of ten years.

The Poona agreement was accepted by the British Government in so far as it would modify the Premier's decision, subject to reservation of judgment on points in the Poona agreement that fell outside the scope of the Award. The depressed class leaders had reason to be grateful because the Poona Pact secured them double the number of the seats granted in the Prime-Minister's decision, and a measure of representation somewhat in excess of the proportion of their population. The question of a referendum at the end of ten years became the subject of a last moment controversy but Gandhi fixed five years instead of ten if there should be a referendum; postponing it to ten years, people would suspect hat Ambedkar wanted was not to "test the *bona fides* of the caste Hindus but time to organize the depressed classes for an adverse referendum." "Five years, or my life" was the ultimate reply of Gandhi. Ultimately it was decided to leave the whole question to be decided by mutual agreement in the future—a formula evolved by Syt. Rajagopalachari and approved of as 'excellent' by Gandhi. On the 26th. Syt. Rabindranath Tagore visited Gandhi just when the news of the Cabinet having accepted the agreement was received. Simultaneous statements were issued in England and India on the morning of the 26th announcing the acceptance of the Poona agreement. Mr. Haig made a statement in the Assembly embodying the following points :—

(1) It accepted for recommendation to Parliament the scheme of representation of the depressed classes in the Provincial Legislatures, adopted under the Yeravada agreement, in place of the scheme of separate electorates in that behalf that had been adumbrated in the Premier's decision.

(2) It accepted the number of seats in the Provincial Legislatures assigned to the depressed classes under the Yeravada agreement.

(3) As regards the clauses in the Yeravada agreement, referring to the guarantees for the welfare of the depressed classes, it recognised them as a definite pledge of the intentions of the caste Hindus to the depressed classes.

(4) As regards the method of electing depressed class representatives to the Central Legislature and the level of franchise, it stated that whilst the Government could not definitely commit itself to the terms of the agreement, as the whole question of representation in Central Legislature and the franchise was under consideration, the Government was not against it.

(5) It recognised the figure of 18 per cent. of the British general seats at the Centre to be reserved for the depressed classes as a matter of arrangement between them and the other Hindus.

Gandhi felt a little difficulty in accepting the wording of Government. He felt that the depressed class leaders should be satisfied as well. The issue to him was not the saving of his own physical life but the saving of the moral lives of the millions for whom he was fasting. In the end, however, Pandit Hridaynath Kunzru and C. Rajagolachariar satisfied Gandhi who then decided to break his fast on the 26th at 5-15 p.m. after prayer and the singing of religious hymns. It was true that Gandhi's life was saved for the moment, but almost in the same breath in which he had agreed to break the fast, he foreshadowed the certainty of its resumption if the reform of the removal of untouchability was not faithfully achieved within a measurable period. He had thought of laying down a period but he had no definite call from within. "The message of freedom," said Gandhi, "shall penetrate every untouchable home, and that can only happen if reforms will cover every village." It was Gandhi's hope, we are told, that the almost ideal solution reached on the question would pave the way for the larger unity between the various communities.

People had doubted the efficacy or appropriateness of a fast. Gandhi had something to say, and this he said in statements issued on the 15th and the 20th September. Gandhi's position is this: "Fasting for light and penance is a hoary institution. It can be observed commonly in Christianity and Islam, while Hinduism is replete with instances of fasting for purification. Having made a serious attempt to attain self-purification, I have developed some little capacity to hear correctly and clearly the 'still small voice within.' My present penance I have undertaken in obedience to this voice." Some would hold the view that the fast is a coercion. To them Gandhi's reply is that "love compels, it does not coerce," even as Truth and right do. "My fast I want to throw in the scale of justice. This may look childish to the on-lookers but not so to me. If I had anything more to give, I would throw that also to remove this curse. But I have nothing more than my life." "The impending fast is against those who have faith in me—whether Indians or foreigners—and for those who have it not." Thus did he show that his fast was not against the English official world nor against his opponents in India, whether Hindus or Muslims, but against countless Indians who believed that he represented a just cause. Above all, Gandhi said: "It is intended to sting the Hindu conscience into right religious action." Gandhi was all the while searching his heart to see if malice and anger were still lurking in his breast. At any rate he felt that he was not conscious of any feelings of hatred or anger in him and that his penance was undertaken from the purest of motives and with goodwill towards all.

Immediately after the Pact was accepted by the Premier, and Gandhi had broken his fast, the Conference met again in Bombay and passed a resolution practically pledging the Hindu community to the removal of untouchability. What has developed into the Harijan Sevak Sangh was founded as a result of this resolution with Syt. Ghansyamdas Birla as President and Syt. Amritlal Thakkar of the Servants of India Society as Secretary.

We give below the resolution unanimously passed by the meeting held at Bombay on 25th September, 1932,—Pandit Malaviya being in the chair,—which has been adopted as the motto of the *Harijan*:—

> "The Conference resolves that, henceforth, amongst Hindus no one shall be regarded as an untouchable by reason of his birth and that those who have been so regarded hitherto will have the same

right as other Hindus in regard to the use of public wells, public schools, public roads and all other public institutions. This right shall have statutory recognition at the first opportunity and shall be one of the earliest Acts of the Swaraj Parliament, if it shall not have received such recognition before that time.

"It is further agreed that it shall be the duty of all Hindu leaders to secure, by every legitimate and peaceful means, an early removal of all social disabilities now imposed by custom upon the so-called untouchable classes, including the bar in respect of admission to temples."

A penance so pure naturally bore its full result. There was widespread response in the country for the cause of the removal of untouchability, so much so that this new field of work,—rather this new interest in an old field of work—came in as a means of satisfaction to those that did not seek imprisonment in the Civil Disobedience movement and as an excuse to those that would or could not go back to jail for a second or third time. People doubted whether a note of warning should not be administered to Congressmen that they should not be deflected from Congress work on account of untouchability work. The country was big enough to produce the required number of workers for the removal of untouchability without encroaching upon the claims of the Congress. Gandhi made it clear in so many words and the very fact that he entrusted the organization of untouchability work to men like Birla and Thakkar showed that he was inclined to pick and choose his untouchability workers from non-Congress workers. Anyway, the loss to the Congress work is a gain to the untouchability work and this field of work received a great impetus by Gandhi's fast. The danger lay in young men going too fast. Gandhi had to apply his reins. A fast unto death was undertaken by more than one person in the country in order to secure the entry into temples of untouchables or 'Harijans' as they were soon called. Just as in the Non-co-operation movement people were anxious to precipitate Civil Disobedience, so too in the Harijan movement did young enthusiasts want to precipitate Satyagraha, little caring for the conditions around or the competence of themselves to undertake such austere penance. Gandhi's restraining influence which had saved many a situation in 1921-22 was once again at work.

The response to the call of Gandhi both to men and women to interest themselves in the Harijan movement was so quick and so ample that the complexion of affairs began to be transformed almost every hour and every minute. Here was the Nawab of Bhopal offering a 5,000 rupee donation to the Hindu Reform movement. There was Father Winslow issuing an appeal with fellow Christian signatories condemning separate electorates for the Indian Christian community. Elsewhere was Shaukat Ali asking for the release of Gandhi and urging the settlement of the Hindu-Muslim question as well. The atmosphere was surcharged with a feeling of, and a cry for, unity everywhere and communal unity would doubtless have been achieved had it not been for the sudden reversal of the Government's policy and the withdrawal, on the 29th September, of all the new privileges regarding visitors etc., conceded to Gandhi during his fast. Mr. Jayakar who wanted to see him was not permitted to see him. Mrs. Sarojini Naidu was sent back to her own Ladies' Jail. Mrs. Gandhi was taken away from Gandhi's presence. Visitors were cut off. Gandhi was once more a prisoner, as he was before the 13th of September. But it must be said to the credit of the Government that Mrs. Gandhi alone was allowed to be with him from the next day as she had been released five days before her time. Gandhi protested against the sudden deprivation of the opportunities for serving the Harijan cause. It was opposed to the terms of Poona Pact itself.

After protracted correspondence Government at last allowed Gandhi to carry on his 'untouchability' propaganda, removed the restrictions regarding visitors, correspondence and publicity lately imposed, and on 7th November, Mr. Haig, the Home Member, made the following statement in the Assembly:—

> "Recently Mr. Gandhi represented that if he was to carry out a programme which he has set before himself in regard to the removal of untouchability, it is necessary that he should be given greater freedom in regard to visitors and correspondence on matters strictly limited to this question. The Government does not wish to interpose obstacles in Mr. Gandhi's efforts in connection with the problem of untouchability which, as Mr. Gandhi pointed out, is a moral and religious reform having nothing to do with the Civil Disobedience movement. The Government have, therefore, removed all restrictions regarding visitors, correspondence and publicity relating to matters which are strictly limited to the removal of untouchability. However, the restrictions in regard to interviews specifically on political questions, stand totally on a different footing and the position in regard to this remains unchanged, as is clear from the reply given by the Private Secretary to the Viceroy to Maulana Shaukat Ali."

We now publish below the correspondence on the subject of the Fast and the text of the Poona Pact, in full.

The following is the relevant portion of Gandhi's speech at the Minorities Committee of the 2nd R. T. C. delivered on 13-11-'31 in London:—

"I WILL RESIST IT WITH MY LIFE"

"I can understand the claims advanced by other minorities, but the claim advanced on behalf of the 'untouchables' is to me the unkindest cut of all. It means a perpetual bar sinister.

"I would not sell the vital interests of the 'untouchables' even for the sake of winning the freedom of India. I claim myself, in my own person. to represent the vast masses of the 'untouchables.' Here I speak not merely on behalf of the Congress. but I speak on my own behalf, and I claim that I would get, if there was a referendum of the 'untouchables,' their vote and that I would top the poll. And I would work from one end of India to the other to tell the 'untouchables' that separate electorates and separate reservation is not the way to remove this bar sinister.

"Let this Committee and let the whole world know that to-day there is a body of Hindu reformers who feel that this is a shame, not of the 'untouchables' but of orthodox Hinduism, and they are, therefore, pledged to remove this blot of untouchability. We do not want on our rolls and on our census 'untouchables' classified as a separate class. Sikhs may remain as such in perpetuity, so may Muslims, so may Europeans. Would 'untouchables' remain untouchables in perpetuity? I would far rather that Hinduism died than that untouchability lived.

"Therefore, with all my regard for Dr. Ambedkar and for his desire to see the 'untouchables' uplifted, with all my regard for his ability, I must say that here is a great error under which he has laboured and, perhaps, the bitter experiences he has undergone have for the moment warped his judgment. It hurts me to have to say this, but I would be untrue to the cause of the 'untouchables' which is as dear to me as life itself, if I did not say it. I will not bargain away their rights for the kingdom of the whole world. I am speaking with a due sense of responsibility when I say it is not a proper claim which is registered by Dr. Ambedkar, when he seeks to speak for the whole of the 'untouchables' in India. It will create a division in Hinduism which I cannot possibly look forward to with any satisfaction whatsoever.

"I do not mind the 'untouchables' being converted to Islam or Christianity. I should tolerate that, but I cannot possibly tolerate what is in store for Hinduism if there are these two divisions set up in every village. Those who speak of political rights of 'untouchables' do not know India and do not know how Indian society is to-day constructed. Therefore, I want to say with all the emphasis that I can command that if I was the only person to resist this thing, I will resist it with my life."

Gandhi-Hoare-MacDonald Correspondence

Gandhi's Letter to Sir Samuel Hoare

Yeravada Central Prison,
March 11, 1932.

"Dear Sir Samuel,

You will perhaps recollect that at the end of my speech at the Round Table Conference when the minorities' claim was presented, I had said that I should resist with my life the grant of separate electorate to the depressed classes. This was not said in the heat of the moment nor by way of rhetoric. It was meant to be a serious statement. In pursuance of that statement I had hoped on my return to India to mobilize public opinion against separate electorate, at any rate for depressed classes. But it was not to be.

"From the newspapers I am permitted to read, I observe that any moment His Majesty's Government may declare their decision. At first I had thought, if the decision was found to create separate electorate for the depressed classes, I should take such steps as I might then consider necessary to give effect to my vow. But I feel it would be unfair to the British Government for me to act without giving previous notice. Naturally, they could not attach the significance I give to my statement.

SEPARATE ELECTORATES HARMFUL

"I need hardly reiterate all the objections I have to the creation of separate electorates for the depressed classes. I feel as if I was one of them. Their case stands on a wholly different footing from that of others. I am not against their representation in the Legislatures. I should favour every one of their adults, male and female, being registered as voters irrespective of education or property qualification, even though the franchise may be stricter for others. But I hold that separate electorate is harmful for them and for Hinduism, whatever it may be from the purely political standpoint. To appreciate the harm that separate electorates would do them, one has to know how they are distributed amongst the so-called caste Hindus and how dependent they are on the latter. So far as Hinduism is concerned, separate electorates would simply vivisect and disrupt it.

"For me the question of these classes is predominantly moral and religious. The political aspect, important though it is, dwindles into insignificance compared to the moral and religious issue.

"You will have to appreciate my feelings in this matter by remembering that I have been interested in the condition of these classes from my boyhood and have more than once staked my all for their sake. I say this not to pride myself in any way. Now I feel that no penance that the Hindu may do can in any way compensate for the calculated degradation to which they have consigned the depressed classes for centuries.

'SHALL FAST UNTO DEATH'

"But I know that separate electorate is neither a penance nor any remedy for the crushing degradation they have groaned under. I, therefore, respectfully inform His Majesty's Government that in the event of their decision creating separate electorate for the depressed classes, I must fast unto death.

"I am painfully conscious of the fact that such a step, whilst I am a prisoner, must cause grave embarrassment to His Majesty's Government, and it will be regarded by many as highly improper on the part of one holding my position to introduce into the political field methods which they would describe as hysterical if not much worse. All I can urge in defence is that for me the contemplated step is not a method, it is part of my being. It is the call of conscience which I dare not disobey, even though it may cost whatever reputation for sanity I may possess. So far as I can see now, my discharge from imprisonment would not make the duty of fasting any the less imperative. I am hoping, however, all my fears are wholly unjustified and the British Government have no intention whatever of creating separate electorate for the depressed classes.

GOVERNMENT TERRORISM

"It is, perhaps, as well for me to refer to another matter that is agitating me and may also enforce a similar fast. It is the way that repression is going. I have no notion when I may receive a shock that would compel the sacrifice. Repression appears to me to be crossing what might be called legitimate bounds. A governmental terrorism is spreading through the land. Both English and Indian officials are being brutalized. The latter, high and low, are becoming demoralized by reason of Government regarding as meritorious disloyalty to the people and inhuman conduct towards their own kith and kin. The latter are becoming cowed down. Free speech has been stifled. Goondaism is being practised in the name of Law and Order. Women, who have come out for public service, stand in fear of their honour being insulted.

"And all this, as it seems to me, is being done in order to crush the spirit of freedom which the Congress represents. Repression is not confined to punishing civil breaches of common law. It goads people to break newly made orders of autocracy designed for the most part to humiliate them.

"In all these doings, as I read them, I see no spirit of democracy. Indeed, my recent visit to England has confirmed my opinion that your democracy is a superficial, circumscribed thing. In the weightiest matters decisions are taken by individuals or groups without any reference to Parliament, and these have been ratified by members having but a vague notion of what they were doing. Such was the case with Egypt, the war of 1914, and such is the case with India. My whole being rebels against the idea that, in a system called democratic, one man should have unfettered power of affecting the destiny of an ancient people numbering over three hundred millions and that his decisions can be enforced by mobilizing the most terrible forces of destruction. To me this is a negation of democracy.

AN ARTICLE OF FAITH

"And this repression cannot be prolonged without further embittering the already bitter relations between the two peoples. In so far as I am responsible and can help it, how am I to arrest the process? Not by stopping Civil Disobedience. For me it is an article of faith. I regard myself by nature a democrat. The democracy of my conception is wholly inconsistent with the use of physical force for enforcing its will. Civil resistance, therefore, has been conceived to be a proper substitute for physical force, to be used wherever generally the latter is held to be necessary or justifiable. It is a process of self-suffering, and part of the plan is that in given circumstances a civil resister must sacrifice himself even by fasting to a finish. That moment has not yet arrived for me. I have no undeniable call from within for such a step. But events happening outside are alarming enough to agitate my fundamental being. Therefore, in writing to you about the possibility of a fast regarding the depressed classes, I felt I would be untrue to you if I did not tell you that there was another possibility, not remote, of such a fast.

"Needless to say, from my side absolute secrecy has been maintained about all the correspondence I have carried on with you. Of course, Sirdar Vallabhbhai Patel and Mahadev Desai, who have just been sent to join us, know all about it. But you will no doubt make whatever use you wish of this letter.

Yours sincerly,
(Sd.) M. K. Gandhi."

SIR S. HOARE'S REPLY.

India Office, Whitehall,
April 13, 1932.

'Dear Mr. Gandhi,

I write this in answer to your letter of 11th March, and I say at once I realize fully the strength of your feeling upon the question of separate electorates for the depressed classes. I can only say that we intend to give any decision that may be necessary solely and only upon the merits of the case. As you are aware, Lord Lothian's Committee has not yet completed its tour and it must be some weeks before we can receive any conclusions at which it may have arrived. When we receive that report we shall have to give most careful consideration to its recommendations, and we shall not give a decision until we have taken into account, in addition to the view expressed by the Committee, the views that you and those who think with you have so forcibly expressed. I feel sure if you were in our position you would be taking exactly the same action we intend to take. You would await the Committee's report, you would then give it your fullest consideration, and before arriving at a final decision you would take into account the views that have been expressed on both sides of the controversy. More than this I cannot say. Indeed I do not imagine you would expect me to say more.

TERRORISM NECESSARY

"As to the Ordinances, I can only repeat what I have already said both publicly and privately. I am convinced that it was essential to impose them in the face of the deliberate attack upon the very foundations of ordered Government. I am also convinced that both the Government of India and the Local Governments are not abusing their extensive powers and are doing everything possible to prevent excessive or vindictive action. We shall not keep the emergency measures in force any longer than we are obliged to, for the purpose of maintaining the essentials of Law and Order and protecting our officials and other classes of the community against terrorist outrages.

Yours truly,
(Sd.) Samuel Hoare."

GANDHI'S LETTER TO PRIME-MINISTER

Yeravada Central Prison.
August 18, 1932.

"Dear Friend,

There can be no doubt that Sir Samuel Hoare has showed you and the Cabinet my letter to him of 11th March on the question of the representation of the depressed classes. That letter should be treated as part of this letter and be read together with this.

DECISION TO FAST

"I have read the British Government's decision on the representation of minorities and have slept over it. In pursuance of my letter to Sir Samuel Hoare and my declaration at the meeting of the Minorities Committee of the Round Table Conference on 13th November, 1931, at St. James' Palace, I have to resist your decision with my life. The only way I can do so is by declaring a perpetual fast unto death from food of any kind, save water with or without salt and soda. This fast will cease if during its progress the British Government, of its own motion or under pressure of public opinion, revise their decision and withdraw their scheme of communal electorates for the depressed classes, whose representatives should be elected by the general electorate under the common franchise, no matter how wide it is.

"The proposed fast will come into operation in the ordinary course from the noon of 20th September next, unless the said decision is meanwhile revised in the manner suggested above.

"I am asking the authorities here to cable the text of this letter to you so as to give you ample notice. But in any case, I am leaving sufficient time for this letter to reach you in time by the slowest route.

"I also ask that this letter and my letter to Sir Samuel Hoare, already referred to, be published at the earliest possible moment. On my part, I have scrupulously observed the rules of the jail and have communicated my desire or the contents of the two letters to no one, save my two companions, Sirdar Vallabhbhai Patel and Mr. Mahadev Desai. But I want, if you make it possible, public opinion to be affected by my letters. Hence my request for their early publication.

"NOT TO COMPASS RELEASE"

"I regret the decision I have taken. But as a man of religion that I hold myself to be, I have no other course left open to me. As I have said in my letter to Sir Samuel Hoare, even if His Majesty's Government decided to release me in order to save themselves embarrassment, my fast will have to continue. For, I cannot now hope to resist the decision by any other means. And I have no desire whatsoever to compass my release by any means other than honourable.

"It may be that my judgment is warped and that I am wholly in error regarding separate electorates for the depressed classes as harmful to them or to Hinduism. If so, I am not likely to be in the right with reference to other parts of my philosophy of life. In that case my death by fasting will be at once a penance for my error and a lifting of a weight from off those numberless men and women who have children's faith in my wisdom. Whereas, if my judgment is right, as I have little doubt it is, the contemplated step is but due to the fulfilment of the scheme of life which I have tried for more than a quarter of a century, apparently not without considerable success.

I remain,
Your faithful friend,
(Sd.) M. K. Gandhi."

PREMIER'S REPLY

10, Downing Street,
September 8th, 1932.

"Dear Mr. Gandhi,

I have received your letter with much surprise and, let me add, with very sincere regret. Moreover, I cannot help thinking that you have written it under a misunderstanding as to what the decision of His Majesty's Government as regards the depressed classes really implies. We have always understood you were irrevocably opposed to the permanent segregation of the depressed classes from the Hindu community. You made your position very clear in the Minorities Committee of the Round Table Conference and you expressed it again in the letter you wrote to Sir Samuel Hoare on 11th March. We also know your view was shared by the great body of Hindu opinion, and we, therefore, took it into most careful account when we were considering the question of representation of the depressed classes.

'GOVERNMENT DECISION EXPLAINED'

"Whilst, in view of the numerous appeals we have received from depressed class organisations and the generally admitted social disabilities under which they labour and which you have often recognised, we feel it our duty to safeguard what we believed to be the right of the depressed classes to a fair proportion of representation in the Legislatures, we were equally careful to do nothing that would split off their community from the Hindu world. You yourself stated in your letter of March 11, that you were not against their representation in the Legislatures.

"Under the Government scheme the depressed classes will remain part of the Hindu community and will vote with the Hindu electorate on an equal footing, but for the first twenty years, while still remaining electorally part of the Hindu community, they will receive, through a limited number of special constituencies, means of safeguarding their rights and interests that, we are convinced, is necessary under present conditions.

"Where these constituencies are created, members of the depressed classes will not be deprived of their votes in the general Hindu constituencies, but will have two votes in order that their membership of the Hindu community should remain unimpaired.

"We have deliberately decided against the creation of what you describe as a communal electorate for the depressed classes and included all depressed class voters in the general or Hindu constituencies so that the higher caste candidates should have to solicit their votes and they of the higher castes at elections. Thus in every way was the unity of Hindu society preserved.

'SAFEGUARDS TEMPORARY'

"We felt, however, that during the early period of Responsible Government when power in the Provinces would pass to whoever possessed a majority in the Legislatures, it was essential that the depressed classes, whom you have yourself described in your letter to Sir Samuel Hoare as having been consigned by caste Hindus to calculated degradation, for centuries, should return a certain number of members of their own choosing to Legislatures of seven of the nine Provinces, to voice their grievances and their ideals and prevent decisions going against them without the Legislature and the Government listening to their case, in a word, to place them in a position to speak for themselves, which every fair-minded person must agree to be necessary. We did not consider the method of electing special representatives, by reservation of seats in the existing conditions under any system of franchise which is practicable, of members who could genuinely represent them and be responsible for them, because, in practically all cases, such members would be elected by a majority consisting of higher caste Hindus.

"The special advantage initially given under our scheme to the depressed classes, by means of a limited number of special constituencies in addition to their normal electoral rights in the general Hindu constituencies, is wholly different in conception and effect from the method of representation adopted for a minority such as the Muslims by means of separate communal electorates. For example, a Muslim cannot vote or be a candidate in a general constituency, whereas any electorally qualified member of the depressed classes can vote in and stand for the general constituency.

'RESERVATION MINIMUM'

"The number of territorial seats allotted to Muslims is naturally conditioned by the fact that it is impossible for them to gain any further territorial seats, and in most Provinces they enjoy weightage in excess of their population ratio; the number of special seats to be filled from special depresssed class constituencies will be seen to be small, and has been fixed not to provide a quota numerically appropriate for the total representation of the whole of the depressed class population, but solely to secure a minimum number of spokesmen for the depressed classes in the Legislature who are chosen exclusively by the depressed classes. The proportion of their special seats is everywhere much below the population percentage of the depressed classes.

"As I understand your attitude, you propose to adopt the extreme course of starving yourself to death not in order to secure that the depressed classes should have joint electorates with other Hindus, because that is already provided, nor to maintain the unity of Hindus, which is also provided, but solely to prevent the depressed classes, who admittedly suffer from terrible disabilities to-day, from being able to secure a limited number of representatives of their own choosing to speak on their behalf in the

Legislatures which will have a dominating influence over their future.

"In the light of these very fair and cautious proposals, I am quite unable to understand the reason of the decision you have taken and can only think you have made it under a misapprehension of the actual facts.

'GOVERNMENT DECISION STANDS'

"In response to a very general request from Indians, after they had failed to produce a settlement themselves, the Government, much against its will, undertook to give a decision on the minorities question. They have now given it, and they cannot be expected to alter it except on the conditions they have stated. I am afraid, therefore, that my answer to you must be that the Government's decision stands and that only agreement of the communities themselves can substitute other electoral arrangements for those that Government have devised in a sincere endeavour to weigh the conflicting claims on their just merits.

"You ask that this correspondence, including your letter to Sir Samuel Hoare of March 11th, should be published. As it would seem to be unfair if your present internment were to deprive you of the opportunity of explaining to the public the reason why you intend to fast, I readily accede to the request if, on reconsideration, you repeat it. Let me, however, once again urge you to consider the actual details of Government's decision and ask yourself seriously the question whether it really justifies you in taking the action you contemplate.

I am,
Yours very sincerely,
(Sd.) J. Ramsay MacDonald."

FINAL REPLY OF GANDHIJI

Yeravada Central Prison,
September 9th, 1932.

"Dear Friend,

I have to thank you for your frank and full letter telegraphed and received this day. I am sorry, however, that you put upon the contemplated step an interpretation that never crossed my mind. I have claimed to speak on behalf of the very class, to sacrifice whose interests you impute to me a desire to fast myself to death. I had hoped that the extreme step itself would effectively prevent any such selfish interpretation. Without arguing, I affirm that for me this matter is one of pure religion. The mere fact of the depressed classes having double votes does not protect them or Hindu society in general from being disrupted. In the establishment of the separate electorate at all for the depressed classes, I sense the injection of a poison that is calculated to destroy Hinduism and do no good whatever to the depressed classes. You will please permit me to say that, no matter how sympathetic you may be, you cannot come to a correct decision on a matter of such vital and religious importance to the parties concerned.

"I should not be against even over-representation of the depressed classes. What I am against is their statutory separation, even in a limited form, from the Hindu fold, so long as they choose to belong to it. Do you realise that if your decision stands and the Constitution comes into being, you arrest the marvellous growth of the work of Hindu reformers who have dedicated themselves to the uplift of their suppressed brethern in every walk of life?

'DECISION UNCHANGED'

"I have, therefore, been compelled reluctantly to adhere to the decision conveyed to you.

"As your letter may give rise to a misunderstanding, I wish to state that the fact of my having isolated for special treatment the depressed classes question from other parts of your decision does not in any way mean that I approve of or am reconciled to other parts of the decision. In my opinion, many other parts are open to very grave objection. Only, I do not consider them to be any warrant for calling from me such self-immolation as my conscience has prompted me to in the matter of the depressed classes.

I remain,
Your faithful friend,
(Sd.) M. K. Gandhi."

GANDHI'S LETTER TO BOMBAY GOVERNMENT

The following is the statement that Gandhiji sent to the Bombay Government on September 15th regarding his decision to fast in connection with the depressed classes problem. The statement was released to the Press on September 21:—

"The fast which I am approaching was resolved upon in the name of God, for His work, and, as I believe in all humility, at His call. Friends have urged me to postpone the date for the sake of giving the public a chance to organise itself. I am sorry it is not open to me to change even the hour except for the reason stated in my letter to the Prime-Minister.

"The impending fast is against those who have faith in me, whether Indians or foreigners, and for those who have it not. Therefore, it is not against the English official world, but it is against those Englishmen and women, who, in spite of the contrary teaching of the official world, believe in me and the justice of the cause I represent. Nor is it against those of my countrymen who have no faith in me, whether they be Hindus or others, but it is against those countless Indians (no matter to what persuasion they belong) who believe that I represent a just cause. Above all, it is intended to sting Hindu conscience into right religious action.

"The contemplated fast is no appeal to mere emotion. By the fast I want to throw the whole of my weight (such as it is) in the scales of justice pure and simple. Therefore there need be no undue haste in the feverish anxiety to save my life. I implicitly believe in the truth of the saying that not a blade of grass moves but by His will. He will save it if He needs it for further service in this body. None can save it against His will. Humanly speaking, I believe it will stand the strain for some time.

"The separate electorate is merely the last straw. No patched-up agreement between the caste Hindu leaders and rival depressed class leaders will answer the purpose. The agreement, to be valid, is to be real. If the Hindu mass mind is not yet prepared to banish untouchability, root and branch, it must sacrifice me without the slightest hesitation.

"There should be no coercion of those who are opposed to joint electorates. I have no difficulty in understanding their bitter opposition. They have every right to distrust me. Do I not belong to that Hindu section, miscalled superior class or caste Hindus, who have ground down to powder the so-called untouchables? The marvel is that the latter have nevertheless remained in the Hindu fold. But whilst I can justify this opposition, I believe that they are in error. They will, if they can, separate depressed classes entirely from Hindu society and form them into a separate class—a standing and living reproach to Hinduism. I should not mind if thereby their interest could be really served. But my intimate acquaintance with every shade of untouchability convinces me that their lives, such as they are, are so intimately mixed with those of the caste Hindus in whose midst and for whom they live that it is impossible to separate them. They are part of an indivisible family. Their revolt against the Hindus with whom they live, and their apostacy from Hinduism, I should understand. But this, so far as I can see, they will not do. There is a subtle something quite indefinable in Hinduism which keeps them in it even in spite of themselves. And this fact makes it imperative for a man like me, with a living experience of it, to resist the contemplated separation even though the effort should cost life itself.

"The implications of this resistance are tremendous. No compromise which does not ensure fullest freedom for the depressed classes inside the Hindu fold can be an adequate substitute for the contemplated separation. Any betrayal of the trust can merely postpone the day of immolation for me and henceforth those who think with me The problem before responsible Hindus is to consider whether, in the event of social, civic or political persecution of the depressed classes, they are prepared to face the Satyagraha, in the shape of perpetual fast not of one reformer like me but an increasing army of reformers whom I believe to exist to-day in India, and who will count their lives of no cost to achieve the liberation of these classes, and there-through of Hinduism, from an age-long superstition.

"Let fellow reformers who have worked with me also appreciate the implications of the fast.

"It is either a hallucination of mine or an illumination. If it is the former, I must be allowed to do my penance in peace. It will be the lifting of the deadweight on Hinduism. If it is an illumination, may my agony purify Hinduism and even melt the hearts of those who are at present disposed to distrust me! Since there appears to be a misunderstanding as to the application of my fast. I may repeat that it is aimed at a statutory separate electorate, in any shape or form, for the depressed classes. Immediately that threat is removed once for all, my fast will end. I hold strong views about reservation of seats as also about the most proper method of dealing with the whole question. But I consider myself unfit, as a prisoner, to set forth my proposals. I should, however, abide by an agreement on the basis of joint electorates that may be arrived at between the responsible leaders of caste Hindus and depressed classes and which has been accepted by mass meetings of all Hindus.

"One thing I must make clear. The satisfactory ending of the depressed classes question, if it is to come, should in no way mean that I would be committed to the acceptance of His Majesty's Government's decision on the other parts of the communal question. I am personally opposed to many other parts of it which, to my mind, make the working of any free and democratic Constitution well-nigh impossible, nor would a satisfactory solution of this question in any way bind me to accept the Constitution that may be framed. These are political questions for the National Congress to consider and determine. They are utterly outside my province in my individual capacity. Nor may I, as a prisoner, air my individual views on these questions.

"My fast has a narrow application. The depressed classes question being predominantly a religious matter, I regard as specially my own by reason of life-long concentration on it. It is a sacred personal trust which I may not shirk.

"Fasting for light and penance is a hoary institution. I have observed it in Christianity and Islam. Hinduism is replete with instances of fasting for purification and penance. But if it is a privilege, it is also a duty. Moreover, to the best of my light, I have reduced it to a science. As an expert, therefore, I would warn friends and sympathisers against copying me blindly or out of false or hysterical sympathy. Let all such qualify themselves by hard work and selfless service of 'untouchables,' and they would have independent light if their time for fasting has come.

"Lastly, in so far as I know myself, this fast is being undertaken with the purest of motives and without malice or anger against any single soul. For me it is an expression of, and the last seal on, non-violence. Those, therefore, who would use violence in this controversy against those whom they may consider to be inimical to me, or the cause I represent, will simply hasten my end. Perfect courtesy and consideration towards opponents is an absolute essential of success in this case at least, if not in all cases."

'A Fight for Humanity'

On September 20, Press representatives were allowed to interview Gandhi in jail. The following account of the talk appeared in *The Times of India* of 21st September:—

For the first time in nine months, journalists were permitted to see Mahatma Gandhi in Yeravada

Jail this evening at 5-30, when they were treated to one of the most easily delivered and seriously thoughtful interviews to which it has ever been my fortune to listen. No journalist could see Mahatma Gandhi to-day and discuss the position with him five hours after he had commenced a 'fast unto death' without being immensely impressed.

We were ushered into a long narrow room surrounded by shelves in which were piled jail-made *durries*, blankets and other articles, the labour of a thousand convicts and Swadeshi to the last thread. There, sitting in a chair smiling a welcome, was the man upon whom the attention of all India, and of the entire Western world, as well as a very large proportion of the Orient, has been focussed for several days.

When asked if he was hopeful about a happy ending to the affair, he said, "I am an irrepressible optimist. Unless God has forsaken me, I hope that it will not be a fast unto death."

Mahatma Gandhi said that he had had many telegrams from people who had decided or wished to enter upon a fast in sympathy with him. "I urge everybody not to fast in sympathy. I have undertaken it at God's call, and therefore, unless there is a similar definite call to these people, they have no business to fast. For one day, for the sake of purification or identification with the cause, it is a good thing; but that is all. Such a fast is both a privilege and a duty, and the privilege accrues only to those who have disciplined themselves for it."

The interview then turned to the question of the day, the representation of the depressed classes, or as Mahatma Gandhi calls them, the suppressed classes. First of all he expressed surprise that the statement given to the Government of Bombay had not been released. That had been given five days ago. Had he to redraft it to-day, it would be rather different in the light of happenings since then, and he said at the end of the interview that his new statement was supplementary to the other, but not dependent on it.

"My cards are on the table," he said, "but, so far as the present instance is concerned, I could say tions are removed, I have answered the first call of the Press. My fast is only against separate electorates, and not against statutory reservation of seats. To say that I am damaging the cause by uncompromising opposition to statutory reservation of seats is only partly true. Opposed I was, and am even now, but there was never put before me for my acceptance or rejection a scheme for statutory reservation of seats. Therefore, there is no question of my having to decide upon that point. When I developed my own ideas about that point, I certainly expressed disappointment, and in my humble opinion, such statutory reservation, short of doing service, may do harm in the sense that it will stop natural evolution. Statutory reservation is like a support to a man. Relying on such support to any extent, he weakens himself."

"If people won't laugh at me, I would gently put forward a claim which I have always asserted, that I am a 'touchable' by birth, but an 'untouchable' by choice; and I have endeavoured to qualify myself to represent, not the upper ten even among the 'untouchables,' because be it said to their shame there are castes and classes among them, but my ambition is to represent and identify myself with, as far as possible, the lowest strata of 'untouchables,' namely, the 'invisibles' and the 'unapproachables,' whom I have always before my mind's eye wherever I go; for, they have indeed drunk deep of the poisoned cup. I have met them in Malabar and in Orissa, and am convinced that if they are ever to rise, it will not be by reservation of seats but will be by the strenuous work of Hindu reformers in their midst, and it is because I feel that this separation would have killed all prospect of reform that my whole soul has rebelled against it; and, let me make it plain, that the withdrawal of separate electorates will satisfy the letter of my vow but will never satisfy the spirit behind it, and in my capacity of being a self-chosen 'untouchable,' I am not going to nothing behind prison bars. Now that the restric-rest content with a patched-up pact between the 'touchables' and the 'untouchables.'

'THE DREAM OF MY LIFE'

"What I want, what I am living for, and what I should delight in dying for, is the eradication of untouchability, root and branch. I want, therefore, a living pact whose life-giving effect should be felt not in the distant to-morrow but to-day, and therefore, that pact should be sealed by an all-India demonstration of 'touchables' and 'untouchables' meeting together, not by way of a theatrical show, but in real brotherly embrace. It is in order to achieve this, the dream of my life for the past fifty years, that I have entered to-day the fiery gates. The British Government's decision was the last straw. It was a decisive symptom, and with the unerring eye of the physician that I claim to be in such matters, I detected the symptom. Therefore, for me, the abolition of separate electorates would be but the beginning of the end, and I would warn all those leaders assembled at Bombay and others against coming to any hasty decision.

'A CRY FOR JUSTICE'

"My life I count of no consequence. One hundred lives given for this noble cause, would, in my opinion, be poor penance done by Hindus for the atrocious wrongs they have heaped upon helpless men and women of their own faith. I, therefore, would urge them not to swerve an inch from the path of strictest justice. My fast I want to throw in the scales of justice. And if it wakes up caste Hindus from their slumber, and if they are roused to a sense of their duty, it will have served its purpose. Whereas, if out of blind affection for me, they would somehow or other come to a rough and ready agreement so as to secure the abrogation and then go off to sleep, they will commit a grievous blunder and will have made my life a misery. For, while the abrogation of separate electorates would result in my breaking the fast, it would be a living death for me if the vital pact for which I am striving is not arrived at. It would simply mean that, as soon as I call off the fast, I would have to give notice of another in order to achieve the spirit of the vow to the fullest extent.

"This may look childish to the onlooker but not so to me. If I had anything more to give, I would throw that in also to remove this curse but I have nothing more than my life.

'A FIGHT FOR HUMANITY'

"I believe that if untouchability is really rooted out, it will not only purge Hinduism of a terrible blot but its repercussion will be world-wide. My fight against untouchability is a fight against the impure in humanity, and, therefore, when I penned my letter to Sir Samuel Hoare I did so in the full faith that the very best in the human family will come to my assistance, if I have embarked on this thing with a heart, so far as it is possible for a human being to achieve, free of impurity, free of all malice and all anger. You will, therefore, see that my fast is based on faith first of all in the cause, faith in the Hindu community, faith in human nature itself, and faith even in the official world.

'ISSUE SURPASSING SWARAJ'

"In attacking untouchability I have gone to the very root of the matter, and, therefore, it is an issue of transcendental value, far surpassing Swaraj in terms of political constitutions, and I would say that such a Constitution would be a dead-weight if it was not backed by a moral basis, in the shape of the present hope engendered in the breasts of the downtrodden millions that that weight is going to be lifted from their shoulders. It is only because the English officials cannot possibly see this living side of the picture that, in their ignorance and self-satisfaction, they dare to sit as judges upon questions that affect the fundamental being of millions of people, and here I mean both caste Hindus and 'untouchables,' that is, suppressor and suppressed; and it was in order to wake up even officialdom from its gross ignorance, if I may make use of such an expression without being guilty of offence, that I felt impelled by a voice from within to offer resistance with the whole of my being."

He stated that he had made definite suggestions to the deputation from the Emergency Committee whom he received yesterday, and he presumed that these would have been communicated to the Press to-day in Bombay.

Referring to a possible photograph Mahatma Gandhi made a jocular remark concerning his funeral rites, whereupon I asked him if he had made any preparations for such rites when visited by his son Devadas yesterday, if the very worst happened; and I received a dramatic reply: "I have asked my son to say in my name at the Bombay Conference that he, as his father's son, was prepared to forfeit his father's life rather than see any injury being done to the suppressed classes in mad haste."

What did he really think about the possibilities of his fast lasting? He replied: "I am as anxious as anyone to live. Water has an infinite capacity for prolonging life, and I will take water whenever I feel I require it. You can depend upon me to make a supreme effort to hold myself together, so that the Hindu conscience may be quickened as also the British conscience and this agony may end. My cry will rise to the throne of the Almighty God."

THE YERAVADA PACT

The following is the text of the agreement which has been arrived at between the leaders acting on behalf of the depressed classes and of the rest of the Hindu community regarding the representation of the depressed classes in Legislatures and certain other matters affecting their welfare.

1. There shall be seats reserved for the depressed classes out of general electorates. Seats in Provincial Legislatures shall be as follows:

Madras	..	30
Bombay with Sindh	..	15
Punjab	..	8
Bihar and Orissa	..	18
Central Provinces	..	20
Assam	..	7
Bengal	..	30
United Provinces	..	20
Total	..	148

These figures are based on the total strength of the Provincial Councils announced in the Prime-Minister's decision.

2. Election to these seats shall be by joint electorates subject, however, to the following procedure:

All members of the depressed classes registered in the general electoral roll of a constituency, will form an electoral college which will elect a panel of four candidates belonging to the depressed classes, for each of such reserved seats, by the method of single vote and four persons getting the highest number of votes in such primary election shall be the candidates for election by the general electorate.

3. Representation of the depressed classes in the Central Legislature shall likewise be on the principle of joint electorates and reserved seats by the method of primary election in the manner provided for in clause 2 above for their representation in Provincial Legislatures.

4. In the Central Legislature eighteen per cent. of the seats allotted to the general electorate for British India in the said Legislature shall be reserved for the depressed classes.

5. The system of primary election to panel of candidates for election to the Central and Provincial Legislatures, as hereinbefore mentioned, shall come

to an end after the first ten years, unless terminated sooner by mutual agreement under the provision of clause 6 below.

6. The system of representation of the depressed classes by reserved seats in the Provincial and Central Legislatures, as provided for in clauses 1 and 4, shall continue until determined by mutual agreement between the communities concerned in this settlement.

7. The franchise for the Central and Provincial Legislatures for the depressed classes shall be as indicated in the Lothian Committee Report.

8. There shall be no disabilities attaching to anyone on the ground of his being a member of the depressed classes in regard to any elections to local bodies or appointment to public service.

Every endeavour shall be made to secure a fair representation of the depressed classes in these respects, subject to such educational qualifications as may be laid down for appointment to public service.

9. In every Province, out of the educational grant, an adequate sum shall be earmarked for providing educational facilities to members of the depressed classes.

Madan Mohan Malaviya
Tej Bahadur Sapru
M. R. Jayakar
B. R. Ambedkar
Srinivasan
M. C. Rajah
C. V. Mehta
C. Rajagopalachari
Rajendra Prasad
G. D. Birla
Rameswar Das Birla
Shankerlal Banker

B. S. Kamat
G. K. Devadhar
A. V. Thakkar
R. K. Bhakale
P. G. Solanki
P. Baloo
Govind Malaviya
Devadas Gandhi
Biswas
B. N. Rajbhoj
Gavai

The following signatures were added in Bombay at the final sitting of the Hindu Conference on September 25:—

Lallubhai Samaldas
Hansa Mehta
K. Natarajan
Kamakoti Natarajan
Purushottamdas Thakurdas
Mathuradas Vassanji
Walchand Hirachand
H. N. Kunzru
K. G. Limaye
P. Kodanda Rao
G. K. Gadgil
Manu Subedar
Avantikabai Gokhale
K. J. Chitalia
Radhakant Malaviya
A. R. Bhat
Colum
Pradhan

Before closing the subject of the first great fast, and the Poona Pact, we have to refer to another connected event which attracted wide attention. Mr. Kelappan, who had been doing public work in Malabar, particularly in the cause of Harijans, felt the force of a call from within and decided upon a fast to death almost simultaneously with Gandhi's epic fast.

His object was to persuade the Trustees to open the Guruvayoor temple to 'untouchables.' Gandhi studied the facts of the case and thought that sufficient notice was not given to the Trustees. It was borne in upon him that success was almost in sight, but Gandhi held that it was not the immediate prospect of success that should matter, but the pure ethics of the position. Here are the two relevant telegrams sent to Kelappan:

Yeravada, Sept. 29.

"The Zamorin wires asking me to appeal to you to suspend the fast for some months. He says the present entry of 'untouchables' would wound orthodox conscience and such wounding would amount to coercion. Ask yourself whether there is any room for you on this relevant ground to postpone the fast, and whether, in terms of the Zamorin's telegram, you had given sufficient notice of the extreme step."

Yeravada, Oct. 2.

"Your wire. Immediate prospective result must not affect decision. On pure ethics I must reiterate the opinion that you should suspend the fast, giving notice as per my telegram. God helping, I shall bear my share of the burden. Wire compliance."

Gandhi specifically promised to share the next fast with Kelappan if that became necessary and referred to it in his statements. When Gandhi discovered a flaw (namely, want of due notice) and intimated the same to Kelappan, the latter agreed to give up his fast.

At this stage, we may appropriately refer to a sympathetic fast by Gandhi on 2nd December, 1932, for S. P. Patwardhan of Ratnagiri. Syt. Patwardhan had asked for scavenger's work in jail but it was refused by the authorities. Gandhi wrote to the Bombay Government in the matter but to no effect. Consequently Syt. S. P. Patwardhan started a starvation fast by reducing his diet. Gandhi had agreed, in the truce period, to go on fast with Syt. Appasaheb Patwardhan if his demand was not granted, and so Gandhi in sympathy with him commenced this fast. But within two days the authorities gave an assurance to consider the demand and the fast was given up. Within about a week, the Secretary of State made the necessary amendments in jail rules and the bar against giving scavenging work to caste Hindus was removed and the Satyagraha thus became successful.

We have described the development of the Civil Disobedience movement in the year 1932, as well as the episode of the Poona Pact. The public response to Gandhi's call for the removal of untouchability did doubtless affect the progress of the Civil Disobedience movement.

In spite of that, the Congress programme was carried out. There was another reason for the slackening of the Civil Disobedience campaign. As things stood and as already stated, it could be conducted mainly by practising methods of secrecy which are not only abhorrent, but even opposed to and subversive of the fundamental principles of Satyagraha. The meeting of friends at Poona in connection with Gandhi's fast must have given an opportunity for exchange of thoughts on the subject amongst leading Congressmen who were then free, and accordingly two circulars were issued. The first pointed out the supreme claims on Congressmen of Civil Disobedience, work in connection with the removal of untouchability being primarily entrusted to nationalist non-Congressmen and such Congressmen as, for some reason or other, were unable to court imprisonment. The second insisted on the desirability of terminating secret methods which had crept in during the progress of the C.D. campaign.

The 4th January was the day on which the Government offensive had started in 1932, and the Acting President, Rajendra Prasad, who had succeeded Rajagopalachari, issued instructions to all Provincial offices that the anniversary should be observed on that day by reading a special statement which had been sent out and which gave in a short compass the progress of the movement and a survey of the problems holding the foremost place in the thoughts of the country at the time. Meetings were held at numerous places and the statement was read in the midst of arrests and *lathi*-charges followed by the arrest of the President himself on the 6th January, 1933. Thereafter, Mr. Aney became the Acting President.

When the fight commenced in January, 1932, Vallabhbhai Patel was the President of the Congress. The Working Committee had decided that, unlike in 1930, vacancies in the Working Committee should not be filled up and Vallabhbhai drew up a list of persons who were to succeed him and act as Presidents one after another during his absence. Rajendra Prasad, Dr. Ansari, Sirdar Sardul Singh Caveeshar, Gangadhararao Deshpande, Dr. Kitchlew, Rajagopalachari, Rajendra Prasad and Aney acted between January, 1932, and July, 1933, when the Congress organisation ceased to function. Amongst those who acted as Secretaries during this period and on whom fell the burden of carrying on the office work in the midst of indescribable difficulties may be mentioned the names of Jaya Prakash Narayan, Lalji Mehrotra, Girdhari Kripalani, Annada Choudhary and Jugul Kishor Agarwala.

The events of 1933 are briefly told. The Calcutta Session of the Congress was the most outstanding one. An account of this session and of the rest of the events up to the middle of September are succinctly given in the Report for 1933-34, presented by the General Secretaries of the Congress, and we have extracted the following paragraphs therefrom:—

THE CALCUTTA CONGRESS

The Calcutta Session of the Congress, like the preceding Delhi Session of April, 1932, was also held under a ban. Though it was organised when the Civil Disobedience movement was on the decline, the enthusiasm and spirit of resistance manifested were greater than at Delhi. Several Provinces sent their full quota of delegates. In all, about 2,200 delegates were elected from different parts of the country. The fact that Pandit Madan Mohan Malaviya had consented to preside at the session heightened the enthusiasm of the Nation. The decision of

Mrs. Motilal Nehru to attend the Congress despite age and infirmity was an inspiration to the coming delegates. The session met at Calcutta on March 31st, in an electric atmosphere. Dr. Prafulla Ghosh was the Chairman of the Reception Committee. The Government spared no effort to prevent the holding of the Congress. Pandit Madan Mohan Malaviya was not allowed to reach Calcutta. He was arrested at Asansol, an intermediate station. With him were arrested Mrs. Motilal Nehru, Dr. Syed Mahmud and others who formed the Presidential party. All were removed to Asansol Jail. Syt. M.S. Aney, the Acting President of the Congress, was also arrested and imprisoned while on his way to Calcutta. The office-bearers of the Reception Committee were put under arrest and several Congress leaders served with restraint orders at Calcutta. Chief among the latter were Mrs. Sen-Gupta and Dr. Mohammad Alam. Nearly a thousand delegates were arrested before their start or while on their way to Calcutta. The remaining delegates succeeded in reaching the city. In the face of the ban, about eleven hundred delegates met at the place selected for the session. The Police were soon upon the scene and *lathis* rained on the peaceful assembly of Congressmen. Many of the delegates were seriously injured and Mrs. Sen-Gupta and other leading Congressmen were arrested. The Police attempt to prevent the session by force, however, failed, for despite the continuance of the *lathi* blows the inner group of the delegates maintained their seats until all the seven resolutions which were to be submitted for adoption, were read out and passed. Most of those arrested in connection with the Calcutta Session of the Congress were, however, released as soon as the Congress was over. Others were tried and convicted. Mrs. Sen-Gupta also received a sentence of six months. On release from prison on 3rd April, Pandit Malaviya proceeded to Calcutta and soon placed before the country unimpeachable testimony as to the brutal manner in which the Police had tried to break up the Congress. He challenged the Government to hold an enquiry, but the challenge has never been taken up. We give below the resolutions of the Calcutta Session:

Resolutions passed at the 47th session of the Indian National Congress, Calcutta, March 31st, 1933.

"This Congress re-affirms the resolution passed at its 44th session at Lahore, in 1929, declaring Complete Independence as its goal."

"This Congress holds Civil Disobedience to be a perfectly legitimate means for the protection of the rights of the people, for the vindication of national self-respect, and for the attainment of the national goal."

"This Congress re-affirms the decision of the Working Committee arrived at on 1st January, 1932. On a careful survey of all that has happened during the past fifteen months, the Congress is firmly of opinion that, in the situation in which the country is placed, the Civil Disobedience movement should be strengthened and extended, and the Congress, therefore, calls upon the people to pursue the movement with greater vigour on the lines laid down by the Working Committee in its aforesaid resolution."

"This Congress calls upon all classes and sections of the people in the country to completely eschew foreign cloth, to give preference to khaddar and to boycott British goods."

"This Congress holds that no Constitution framed by the British Government, while it is engaged in conducting a campaign of ruthless repression, involving the imprisonment and internment of the most trusted leaders of the Nation and thousands of their followers, suppression of the fundamental rights of free speech and association, stringent restraint on the liberty of the Press and replacement of the normal Civil Law by virtual Martial Law, deliberately initiated by it on the eve of Mahatma Gandhi's return from England with a view to crush the national spirit, can be worthy of consideration by or acceptable to the people of India".

"The Congress is confident that the public will not be duped by the scheme outlined in the recently published White Paper which is inimical to the vital interests of India and is devised to perpetuate foreign domination in this country."

"This Congress offers its congratulations to the country on the successful termination of Mahatma Gandhi's fast of September, 1932, and hopes that untouchability will before long become a thing of the past."

"This Congress is of opinion that, to enable the masses to appreciate what 'Swaraj,' as conceived by the Congress, will mean to them, it is desirable to state the position of the Congress in a manner easily understood by them. With this object in view it reiterates resolution No. 14 of the Karachi Session of the Congress of 1931." (Resolution on Fundamental Rights).

GANDHIJI'S FAST

The Calcutta Congress was soon followed by an unexpected event in the country. With a view to help the increasing number of workers in the Harijan movement to fulfil their task with a purer and truer spirit of service, Mahatma Gandhi had started, on 8th May, 1933. a self-purificatory fast of 21 days. In his words, it was "a heart prayer for purification of myself and my associates for greater vigilance and watchfulness in connection with the Harijan cause."

"I therefore asked friends in India and all the world over to pray for me and with me that I may safely pass through the ordeal and that whether I live or die the cause for which the fast is to be taken may prosper. May I ask my Sanatanist friends to pray that, whatever be the result of the fast for me, the golden lid that hides truth may be removed?" He added in a Press interview: "A religious movement does not depend for its success on the intellectual or material resources of its sponsors; but it depends solely upon the spiritual resources, and fasting is a most known method of adding to these resources."

The Government issued a Communique on the same day stating that, in view of the nature of the object of the fast and the attitude of mind which it disclosed, the Government of India had decided that he (Gandhiji) should be set at liberty. Accordingly, Mahatma Gandhi was released on the evening of 8th May. Immediately on release, Gandhiji issued the following statement recommending the suspension of the C. D. campaign for six weeks.

Mr. Gandhi said:

"I cannot regard this release with any degree of pleasure, and as Sirdar Vallabhbhai rightly remarked to me yesterday, how can I take advantage of this release in order to prosecute the Civil Disobedience campaign or to guide it?

"This release, therefore, puts upon me, as a seeker after truth and a man of honour, a tremendous burden and a strain. This fast has to continue. I had hoped and I still hope not to excite myself over anything, nor to take part in any discussions of any nature whatsoever. The whole purpose of the fast will be frustrated if I allowed my brain to be occupied by any extraneous matter, that is, any matter outside the Harijan work.

"At the same time, having been released, I should be bound to give a little of my energies to a study of the Civil Disobedience movement.

"Of course, for the moment I can only say that my views about Civil Disobedience have undergone no change whatsoever. I have nothing but praise for the bravery and self-sacrifice of the numerous civil resisters. Having said that, I cannot help saying that the secrecy that has attended the movement is fatal to its success. If, therefore, the movement must be continued I would urge those who are guiding the movement in different parts of the country to discard all secrecy. I do not care if thereby it becomes difficult to secure a single civil resister.

"There can be no doubt that fear has seized the common mass. The Ordinances have cowed them down and I am inclined to think that the secret methods are largely responsible for the demoralisation.

"The movement of Civil Disobedience does not depend so much upon the quantity as on the quality of men and women taking part in it, and if I was leading the movement I should sacrifice quantity and insist on quality. If this could be done, it would immediately raise the level of the movement. Mass instructions on any other term is an impossibility. I can say nothing as to the actual campaign. The reflections I have given I had bottled up all these many months and I can say Sirdar Vallabhbhai is at one with me in what I have said.

"One word I would say whether I like it or not—during these three weeks all civil resisters will be in a state of terrible suspense. It would be better if the President of the Congress, Bapuji Madhavarao Aney, were to officially declare suspension for one full month or even six weeks.

"Now I would make an appeal to the Government. If they want real peace in the land and if they feel there is no real peace, if they feel that Ordinance rule is no rule, they should take advantage of this suspension and unconditionally discharge all the civil resisters.

"If I survive the ordeal, it will give me time to survey the situation and to tender advice both to the Congress leaders and, if I may venture to do so, to the Government. I would like to take up the thread at the point where I was interrupted on my return from England.

"If no understanding is arrived at between the Government and the Congress as a result of my effort and Civil Disobedience resumed, it will be open to the Government if they so choose to revive the Ordinance rule. If there is the will on the part of the Government I have no doubt that a *modus operandi* can be found. Of this, so far as I am concerned, I am absolutely certain.

"Civil Disobedience cannot be withdrawn so long as so many civil resisters are imprisoned and no settlement can be arrived at so long as Sirdar Vallabhbhai, Khan Saheb Abdul Gaffar Khan and

Pandit Jawaharlal Nehru and others are buried alive.

"Indeed to call off the civil resistance is not within the power of any of the men who are out of prison. It is possible for the then Working Committee to do so. I refer to the Working Committee that was in existence at the time I was arrested. I shall say no more on the Civil Disobedience movement. Perhaps I have already said too much, but if I was to say anything I could say so only whilst I have strength left in me.

"I would urge pressmen not to worry me any more. I would urge also would-be visitors once more to restrain themselves. Let them regard me as being still in prison. I shall be unfit for holding political discussions or any other discussions.

"I would like to be left in perfect peace and I would like to tell the Government that I shall not abuse the release, and if I come safely through the ordeal and I find the political atmosphere as murky as it is to-day, without taking a single step secretly or openly in furtherance of the Civil Disobedience, I shall invite them to take me back to Yeravada to join the companions whom I almost seem to have deserted.

"It was a great privilege for me to have been with Sirdar Vallabhbhai. I was well aware of his matchless bravery and his burning love of the country, but I have never lived with him as I have had the good fortune during the 16 months. The affection with which he covered me, recalls to me that of my own dear mother. I never knew him to possess motherly qualities. If the slightest thing happened to me, he would be out of his bed. He superintended every little detail in connection with my comforts. He and my other associates had conspired to let me do nothing, and I hope that Government will believe me when I say that he always showed a remarkable comprehension of the difficulties of the Government whenever we discussed any political problem. His solicitude for the farmers of Bardoli and Kaira I can never forget."

Close upon Gandhi's announcement, the Acting President of the Congress, Mr. M. S. Aney, made a like announcement suspending Civil Disobedience for six weeks. Government were not slow either in publishing their reply.

A Government Communique announced that mere suspension of the Civil Disobedience did not fulfil the conditions laid down for the release of prisoners. The Government were not prepared to negotiate with the Congress in the matter.

The official Communique of the Government of India dated Simla, May 9th, said:

"The release of Mr. Gandhi consequent on his undertaking a prolonged fast which, as he has stated, is wholly unconnected with the Government and solely connected with the Harijan movement, indicates no change whatever in the Government's general policy towards the release of the Civil Disobedience prisoners or towards those who openly or conditionally support the Civil Disobedience movement.

"The position of the Government in regard to the release of the Civil Disobedience prisoners was stated by the Home Member in the Legislative Assembly on April 1 last.

"In the course of his speech, he said: 'If, in fact, the Congress does not mean to revive the struggle, why should that not be made plain? Is there a mental reservation that, if the policy of the Government is not to their liking, they will hold over the head of the Government the threat of revival of the Civil Disobedience movement? There can be no co-operation under a menace of renewal of the Civil Disobedience.'

"We have no wish to keep these prisoners longer than the circumstances require but equally are we determined not to let them out when their release might lead to a renewal of the Civil Disobedience. We must not risk re-starting of trouble by premature action.

"Our position has been summed up in the words used by the Secretary of State in the Commons.

"He said:—'We must have convincing reasons to believe that their release would not be followed by a revival of the Civil Disobedience.'

"A mere temporary suspension of the Civil Disobedience movement intended to lead up to negotiations with the Congress leaders, in no way fulfils the conditions which would satisfy the Government of India that, in fact, the Civil Disobedience movement has been definitely abandoned. There is no intention of negotiating with the Congress for a withdrawal of the Civil Disobedience movement or of releasing prisoners with a view to arrive at any settlement with them in regard to these unlawful activities."

Simultaneously with this negative reply from Simla, there came a statement from Vienna signed by Syt. Vittalbhai J. Patel and Syt. Subash Chandra Bose. "The latest action of Mr. Gandhi in suspending Civil Disobedience is a confession of failure," declares the joint statement of Mr. V. J. Patel and Mr. Subash Bose given exclusively to Reuter from Vienna.[1]

The statement further states that "we are clearly of the opinion that Mr. Gandhi as a political leader has failed. The time has, therefore, come for a radical reorganisation of the Congress on a new principle with a new method, for which a new leader is essential, as it is unfair to expect Mr. Gandhi to work the programme not consistent with his life-long principles."

"If the Congress as a whole," the statement proceeds, "can undergo this transformation, it will be the best course. Failing that, a new party will have to be formed within the Congress, composed of radical elements."

In the meantime, opinion in Congress circles began to crystallize that the opportunity afforded by Gandhiji's release should be utilized for informal

---

[1] This is not, however, the first time that Gandhi met with adverse criticism from either of the distinguished signatories whose ill-health compelled their stay in a distant land during the campaign. Gandhi bore the world's criticisms, even as he bore his own sufferings, with patience faith and fortitude. His vow was fulfilled duly and he broke his fast on the 29th May, 1933.

consultation among Congressmen in regard to the situation in the country. In view of the necessity of holding such a Conference when Gandhiji should be physically fit to participate in it, the period of suspension of the campaign was extended by the Acting President for a further span of six weeks. The length of the fast, and the uncertainty in the minds of many as to its future course, caused the Nation's eyes to centre on 'Parnakuti,' the residence of Lady Thackersey in Poona where Gandhi abandoned his fast, and there was universal thanksgiving as the agony of the concluding days of the fast ended in the happy termination of the ordeal without any untoward incident.

THE POONA CONFERENCE:—The informal Conference of Congressmen summoned to review the political situation met in Poona on July 12th, 1933. Syt. Aney opened the proceedings with an introductory speech. Gandhiji placed his views on the situation in brief before the Conference. General discussion followed and at its conclusion the Conference adjourned to the next day. The second day's sitting opened with an exhaustive statement by Gandhiji dealing with the points raised by the members of the Conference and placing before them his suggestions. The Conference then proceeded to make its recommendations. It rejected a motion for the unconditional withdrawal of Civil Disobedience but also threw out a motion favouring individual Civil Disobedience. In the end, the Conference authorised Mahatma Gandhi to seek an interview with the Viceroy for arriving at a settlement with the Government. In accordance with that decision, Gandhiji wired to the Viceroy asking for an interview "with a view to explore the possibilities of peace." The Viceroy, in reply, however, referred in detail to misleading newspaper reports as to the trend of discussions at the Poona Conference, and, relying on such reports, he declined to grant the interview, unless the Congress first withdrew the Civil Disobedience movement. Gandhi sent a reply to the effect that Government had based its attitude on unauthorised publications of the confidential proceedings of the informal Conference and that, if an interview were granted, he could show that the proceedings taken as a whole were calculated to bring about an honourable peace. Gandhiji's efforts at peace failed to elicit response and forced the Nation, if it was to conserve national honour, to continue the struggle. Mass Civil Disobedience was, however, suspended and all who were able and willing were advised to offer individual Civil Disobedience. Under the orders of the Acting President, all Congress organisations and war councils ceased to function in view of the suspension of mass Satyagraha.

INDIVIDUAL CIVIL DISOBEDIENCE:—Gandhi inaugurated the campaign of individual Civil Disobedience by taking the drastic action of sacrificing what was his most precious possession and thus trying to share the sufferings endured by thousands of villagers in the course of the movement. He disbanded the Sabarmati Ashram and invited his fellow-workers in the Ashram to give up all the other activities and join the struggle. He vacated the whole Ashram, transferring the moveable property to certain bodies for public use, and not wishing to make others a party to paying revenue dues, he offered the land, building and crops to Government. All the response the Government made to his offer was a formal one-line acknowledgment of his letter.

When Government declined the offer, Gandhi made it over to the Harijan movement. In this connection we may recall a statement that Gandhi had made on the eve of his march to Dandi,—really it was a determination,—that he would never return to the Ashram until Swaraj was won. And true to his vow, he has not since the 12th of April, 1930, returned to the Ashram except on a casual visit to see an ailing friend. By this final act of transfer of the Ashram to the Harijan Sangh, he divested himself of any little germs of attachment to things mundane, which might possibly take root in his breast.

On 1st August, 1933, Gandhiji was to commence his march to the village of Ras, so famous throughout India ever since Sirdar Vallabhbhai's arrest there in February, 1930. But in the dead of the previous night Mahatma Gandhi and 34 other inmates of his Ashram were arrested and sent to prison. He was, however, released on the morning of the 4th, and served with an order to leave the limits of Yeravada village and reside in Poona. The order was, of course, not obeyed and, within half an hour of release, Gandhiji was arrested and sentenced to one year's imprisonment.

Following his arrest and imprisonment, the campaign of individual Civil Disobedience started in all Provinces, hundreds of workers courting imprisonment in the very first week. The Acting President, Syt. Aney, with thirteen companions, was arrested on August 14, while starting on a march from Akola. His successor as Acting President, Sirdar Sardul Singh Caveeshar, soon followed him to prison. Before imprisonment, however, he issued orders terminating the office of the Acting President and the line of Dictators in various Provinces and Districts, with a view to facilitate the campaign becoming truly one of individual Civil Disobedience. From all over the country, Congress workers followed the lead given by Gandhiji, and from August, 1933, to March, 1934, a regular stream of civil resisters maintained the campaign. It will not be possible without fuller material from provincial centres to report adequately on the campaign with due justice to all Provinces. The Provincial quotas of imprisoned civil resisters during this last stage of the movement have not all been recorded. It must here suffice to say that thousands responded to the call and every Province did the very best it could, under the circumstances, in serving the cause of freedom.

GANDHIJI'S RELEASE:—The Government's refusal to continue the facilities granted to him before his release in May, again forced Mahatma Gandhi to commence a fast, *i.e.*, within a few days of his re-arrest. The Government remained adamant. Gandhiji's condition, however, rapidly grew worse and on 20th August, the fifth day of the fast, he had to be removed to Sassoon

Hospital, Poona, still a prisoner. By 23rd August, however, it had become clear to Government that there was imminent danger to his life, and he was, therefore, released unconditionally on that date. This unexpected development placed him in a most embarrassing position. In view, however, of the circumstances of his discharge from jail, and as he did not wish to be a willing party to the undignified 'cat and mouse game' of arrest, fast, and release, he came to the conclusion that he must regard himself still not a free man, that he must impose on himself a limited self-restraint in regard to his activities up to the termination of the period of his sentence, that is, up to August 3rd, 1934, and that he must not court imprisonment by offering aggressive civil resistance. He made it clear, however, that while he would refrain from aggressive Civil Disobedience, he could not help guiding those who would ask his advice and preventing the national movement from running into wrong channels. He further decided to devote the intervening period largely to the furtherance of the Harijan movement.

JAWAHARLAL'S RELEASE:—Mrs. Motilal Nehru's health had been latterly worsening and about this time it had begun to cause widespread anxiety. The U.P. Government, therefore, decided to release Pandit Jawaharlal Nehru a few days before the expiry of his sentence so as to enable him to be with his mother in her serious illness. He was accordingly released on August 30th. As soon as Mrs. Motilal's health improved, Pandit Jawaharlal repaired to Poona where Mahatma Gandhi was recuperating and the two met for the first time since they separated on the occasion of Gandhiji's departure for the R.T.C. in 1931. There naturally followed friendly discussions as to the situation in the country and the programme before the people. The discussion eventually led to exchange of letters containing a statement of their views on the programme for the Nation. This correspondence was published for the information and guidance of Congressmen and the general public.

HARIJAN TOUR:—In accordance with his decision to devote to the Harijan cause the period of his forced inactivity in the purely political field, Gandhiji commenced a Harijan tour in the country in November, 1933. He covered, in about ten months, every Province of India and each day of those long months was a day of an intensive study of the problem of untouchability and the best methods of solving it. The tour had an extraordinary propagandist value. The response evoked at the gatherings in each Province and the attendance at the meetings organized were only less than those witnessed in the country in the days of 1930. The collections made by Gandhi in the course of the tour for the cause of the removal of untouchability totalled about eight lakhs of rupees which, in view of the trade depression and previously made calls on the public purse, was certainly an unexpectedly generous response to his appeal. The otherwise wholly successful tour was marred by two regrettable incidents. Gandhiji narrowly escaped at Poona, on 25th June, 1934, from what might have proved a great calamity for the Nation. An unknown and yet untraced person attempted to throw a bomb at him at a public function where he was to receive an address of welcome from the Poona Municipality. The perpetrator of the attempted crime, believed to be one who had been enraged at Gandhiji's campaign against untouchability, mistook for Gandhi's car another which reached the scene a few minutes earlier. His misaimed bomb, nevertheless, wounded seven innocent persons, none of whom, fortunately, received very serious injuries. The other incident took place at Ajmer only about a fortnight later, and this time it was an irate reformer who lost his balance and cut open with a *lathi* the head of Pandit Lalnath of Benares, a determined opponent of the Harijan movement. This latter happening led to a seven days' fast by Gandhiji as a penance against the intolerance shown by opponents towards each other in public controversies.

He had undertaken an all-India tour for Harijan work, but the month of December was the month of his test. Three months' notice being given by Mr. Kelappan to the Trustees in regard to the Guruvayoor temple, a final decision was to be reached on the 1st of January, 1934. And it might mean a fast unto death both for Kelappan and Gandhiji. So it was resolved to take a referendum at Guruvayoor amongst the temple worshippers, and the first experiment made in this behalf was a highly educative as well as successful experiment. In the meantime, Dr. Subbaroyan had given notice of a Temple Entry Bill for the Madras Presidency and Government's decision was being awaited. In the Guruvayoor referendum, 77 per cent. of the voters voted in favour of Temple Entry and the following report would be found interesting:—

"Out of 20,163 opinions actually given and recorded, excluding refusals to vote, the following is an analysis of the voting:—

In favour,	15,563 or 77 per cent.
Against,	2,579 or 13 per cent.
Neutral	2,016 or 10 per cent.

"A remarkable feature of the referendum was that more than 8,000 women recorded in favour of Temple-Entry by Harijans."

The new year opened auspiciously enough, as the apprehended fast of Gandhi over the Guruvayoor temple was averted. But the progress of events in the line of Civil Disobedience was none too satisfactory. The prisoners who were released were fagged. The provincial leaders who had promised to lead their Provinces at Poona, if mass Civil Disobedience were given up and individual Civil Disobedience continued, did not carry out their pledges except in a few cases. Those who were released from jails found themselves unable or unwilling to face another conviction. And those that were prepared to face it would not get it. Government had hit on the plan of *lathi*-charging or imprisoning and ill-treating in sub-jails, and releasing, re-arresting and releasing again, after an interval. The process was tiresome and the only rest that conviction would give was taken away. It was like a cat shaking the rat by the mouth and leaving it and then catching it again. It would neither kill nor release.

THE BIHAR EARTHQUAKE:—The whole of India staggered to its feet on 16th January, shocked at the news the morning papers brought to every home, of the unprecedented calamity that had overtaken Bihar on the previous afternoon. Within the space of a few minutes, the face of the Province was changed beyond recognition. Thousands of buildings fell into dust and buried within the bowels of the earth. From below ground, sand emerged to destroy extensive areas of rich crops. Water at a temperature of 110 degrees pushed its way to the surface from a depth of 1,500 feet. A sandy expanse stretched where, only a moment ago, river beds carried the life-endowing current which irrigated the land or where smiling fields bore the burden which fed and sustained the life of millions. Thousands of families were orphaned and widowed and their innocent babes crushed in death beneath falling debris within, almost literally, the twinkling of an eye. No cold figures can give a true picture of what Nature had miswrought in a few minutes in Bihar. Yet some may be quoted. The earthquake affected an area of 30,000 sq. miles and a population of about a crore and a half. Nearly 20,000 persons are recorded to have lost their lives. Houses numbering over 10 lakhs were damaged or destroyed. 65,000 wells and tanks were destroyed or damaged. Nearly 10 lakhs of bighas of crops were covered with sand and damaged.

To meet a catastrophe of this magnitude, both Bihar and India rose to the occasion. Over a crore of rupees were subscribed to the various funds, the amount received by the Bihar Central Relief Committee up to the end of June being over Rs. 27 lakhs. Most leaders and workers sped from many parts of India to come to the rescue of the afflicted and to help to organise systematic relief. The excellent report of that Committee, recently published, will give to all a realistic idea of the extent of damage and the measures of relief which over 2,000 workers have carried out at 258 centres.

Among the outside leaders who visited the devastated area was Pandit Jawaharlal Nehru. The visit was not only a token of sympathy. It was a personal example of service. On one occasion, when reports reached that living men lay buried under the debris of fallen houses, he put on a volunteer's badge, took a pick-axe on his shoulder, and, accompanied by a batch of volunteers with pick-axes, shovels and baskets, he marched to the place. He and others then plied their pick-axes and shovels, carrying the debris in baskets on their heads. The Bihar earthquake also intervened to change Gandhiji's programme. Bihar and its workers had at that time to face numerous complicated problems arising out of the situation created by the earthquake and the impending floods, and Gandhiji devoted a month to give them his guidance and advice. In the result, a conference was held of representatives from all parts of the country at which the Bihar Central Relief Committee was set up to control the relief operations, and the ground cleared for one of the biggest schemes of distress relief ever organised by Congress in recent years. During his stay in Bihar, Gandhiji visited the afflicted towns and villages, acquainted himself personally with the miserable plight of the victims of the great calamity and helped the newly formed Committee to chalk out its plans of work. He rushed some of his own trained workers to the scene and placed them at the service of Bihar. The Province has yet to confront problems of a complexity and a magnitude of which probably those outside the Province have no adequate conception. (An authoritative account of the relief operations is given in Appendix VIII).

On completion of his brief tour in Bihar, Pandit Jawaharlal found himself once again a prisoner of Government. During his visit to Calcutta, he had delivered two speeches on the situation in Bengal and the latest development in Midnapur District. The Bengal Government could brook no mention of the so-called terrorists of the Province except in terms of unqualified condemnation. Pandit Jawaharlal's frank speeches dealing with the psychology of terrorism, and the methods adopted by the authorities in meeting it, could not be tolerated by the Bengal bureaucracy. Decency prevented the Bengal Police from arresting him while he was on a mission of humanity in Bihar, but he had hardly reached his home in Allahabad when the prison gate again opened for him. He was tried for his two Calcutta speeches and given the heavy sentence of two years.

Ever since the Poona Conference of July, 1933, an increasing number of Congressmen were coming to form the view that, in the situation existing in the country as a result of Ordinance rule, a programme of entry into the Legislatures was necessary to find a way out of what was held to be a 'stalemate.' This view found an organised expression in a move to summon a Conference of Congress leaders sharing the above opinion for the purpose of giving concrete shape to the desire for a new line of action. This Conference met at Delhi on 31st March, 1933, under the Presidentship of Dr. Ansari. It resolved that the All-India Swaraj Party which had been in abeyance should be revived in order to enable Congressmen who were not offering Individual Civil Disobedience to undertake a thorough organisation of the electorate and carry out the constructive programme as contemplated in the Poona statement of Mahatma Gandhi (July 1933). The Conference also expressed the view that it was imperative for the Party to participate in the forthcoming elections to the Legislative Assembly. To that end it laid down that the elections should be fought on two main issues,—(1) to get all repressive laws repealed, and (2) to reject proposals contained in the White Paper and get them replaced by the National Demand on the lines indicated by Mahatma Gandhi at the R. T. C. The Conference, after coming to these tentative decisions, sent a deputation to Gandhiji consisting of Dr. Ansari, Syt. Bhulabhai Desai and Dr. Bidhan Roy with a view to discuss its resolutions with him and ascertain his opinion before acting upon the decisions.

Gandhi was at the time touring in the earthquake-affected area of Bihar and happened to spend his silence day (the 2nd April, 1934) at an out-of-the-way place called Saharsa where, without any knowledge of what had happened at Delhi, he independently drew up a statement which he wanted to issue to the Press. But just when it was to be so issued, a message was received from Dr. Ansari intimating to him that the deputation appointed by the Delhi Conference on the previous day was coming to meet him at Patna. He held over the statement pending consultation with them, and it was issued later on the 7th after full discussion with them. The publication of the statement was preceded by a letter to Dr. Ansari, and we give the letter and the statement below :—

Gandhiji's Letter to Dr. Ansari

Patna, April, 5, 1934.

"Dear Dr. Ansari,

It was good of you, Bhulabhai and Dr. Bidhan to come all the way to Patna to discuss the resolutions arrived at recently at an informal meeting of some Congressmen and to ascertain my opinion on them. I have no hesitation in welcoming the revival of the Swarajya Party and the decision of the meeting to take part in the forthcoming elections to the Assembly which you tell me is about to be dissolved.

"My views on the utility of the Legislatures in the present state are well known. They remain, on the whole, what they were in 1920. But I feel that it is not only the right but it is the duty of every Congressman who, for some reason or other, does not want to or cannot take part in civil resistance and who has faith in entry into the Legislatures, to seek entry and form combinations in order to prosecute the programme which he or they believe to be in the interest of the country. Consistently with my view above mentioned, I shall be at the disposal of the party at all times and render such assistance as it is in my power to give.

Yours sincerely
(Sd.) M. K. Gandhi."

Gandhi's Statement

(Dated, Patna, April 7, 1934)

"This statement was drafted by me on my day of silence at Saharsa, that is, Easter Monday, 2nd instant. I passed it on to Rajendra Babu and then it was circulated among the friends who were present. The original draft has undergone considerable revision. It is also abridged. But in essence it remains as it was on Monday. I regret that I have not been able to show it to all friends and colleagues with whom I would have been delighted to share it. But as I had no doubt whatsoever about the soundness of my decision and as I knew that the civil resistance of some friends was imminent, I was not prepared to take the risk of delaying publication by waiting for the opinion of friends. The decision and every word of the statement are in answer to intense introspection, searching of the heart, and waiting upon God. The decision carries with it reflection upon no single individual. It is a humble admission of my own limitations and a due sense of the tremendous responsibility that I have carried on my shoulders all these long years.

"This statement owes its inspiration to a personal chat with the inmates and associates of the Satyagraha Ashram who had just come out of prison and whom, at Rajendra Babu's instance, I had sent to Bihar. More especially is it due to a revealing information I got in the course of a conversation about a valued companion of long standing who was found reluctant to perform the full prison task and preferring his private studies to the allotted task. This was undoubtedly contrary to the rules of Satyagraha. More than the imperfection of the friend, whom I love more than ever, it brought home to me my own imperfection. The friend said he had thought that I was aware of his weakness. I was blind. Blindness in a leader is unpardonable. I saw at once that I must for the time being remain the sole representative of civil resistance in action.

"During the informal Conference week at Poona in July last, I had stated that, while many individual civil resisters would be welcome, even one was sufficient to keep alive the message of Satyagraha. Now, after much searching of the heart, I have arrived at the conclusion that in the present circumstances only one, and that myself, and no other should, for the time being, bear the responsibility of civil resistance, if it is to succeed as a means of achieving Purna Swaraj.

"I feel that the masses have not received the full message of Satyagraha owing to its adulteration in the process of transmission. It has become clear to me that spiritual instruments suffer in their potency when their use is taught through non-spiritual media. Spiritual messages are self-propagating. The reaction of the masses throughout the Harijan tour has been the latest forcible illustration of what I mean. The splendid response of the masses has been spontaneous. The workers themselves were amazed at the attendance and the fervour of vast masses whom they had never reached.

"Satyagraha is a purely spiritual weapon. It may be used for what appear to be mundane ends, and through men and women who do not understand it spiritually, provided the director knows that the weapon is spiritual. Every one cannot use surgical instruments. Many may use them if there is an expert behind them directing their use. I claim to be a Satyagraha expert in the making. I have need to be far more careful than the expert surgeon who is complete master of his science. I am still a humble searcher. The very nature of the science of Satyagraha precludes the student from seeing more than the step immediately in front of him.

"The introspection prompted by the conversation with the Ashram inmates has led me to the conclusion that I must advise all Congressmen to suspend civil resistance for Swaraj as distinguished from specific grievances. They should leave it to me alone. It should be resumed by others in my lifetime only under my direction, unless one arises claiming to know the science better than I do and inspires confidence. I give this opinion as the author and initiator of Satyagraha. Henceforth, therefore, all who have been impelled to civil resistance for Swaraj under my advice, directly given or indirectly inferred, will please desist from civil resistance. I am quite convinced that this is the best course in the interests of India's fight for freedom.

"I am in deadly earnest about this greatest of weapons at the disposal of mankind. It is claimed for Satyagraha that it is a complete substitute for violence or war. It is designed, therefore, to reach the hearts both of the so-called 'terrorists' and the rulers who seek to root out the 'terrorists' by emasculating the whole Nation. But the indifferent civil resistance of many, grand as it has been in its results, has not touched the hearts either of the 'terrorists' or the rulers as a class. Unadulterated Satyagraha must touch the hearts of both. To test the truth of the proposition, Satyagraha needs to be confined to one qualified person at a time. The trial has never been made. It must be made now.

"Let me caution the reader against mistaking Satyagraha for mere civil resistance. It covers much more than civil resistance. It means relentless search for Truth, and the power that such a search gives to the searcher can only be pursued by strictly non-violent means.

"What are the civil resisters, thus freed, to do? If they are to be ready for the call whenever it comes, they must learn the art and the beauty of self-denial and voluntary poverty. They must engage themselves in nation-building activities, the spread of khaddar through personal hand-spinning and hand-weaving, the spread of communal unity of hearts by irreproachable personal conduct towards one another in every walk of life, the banishing of untouchability in every shape or form in one's own person, the spread of total abstinence from intoxicating drinks and drugs by personal contact with individual addicts and, generally, by cultivating personal purity. These are services which provide maintenance on a poor man's scale. Those for whom the poor man's scale is not feasible should find place in small unorganised industries of national importance which give better wages. Let it be understood that civil resistance is for those who know and perform the duty of voluntary obedience to law and authority.

"It is hardly necessary to say that in issuing this statement I am in no way usurping the function of the Congress. Mine is mere advice to those who look to me for guidance in matters of Satyagraha."

Gandhi's statement was a result of "an intense introspection, searching of the heart, and waiting upon God." Adulteration of Satyagraha in the process of transmission, reaction of the masses manifested during Harijan tour,—all these impressed upon Gandhi the necessity of confining the movement to himself, an expert in Satyagraha, even as surgical instruments should be used only by expert surgeons. The result was the suspension of Civil Disobedience as a mass movement.

Dr. Ansari, in his statement issued at the same time, made it clear that the whole-hearted and spontaneous support of Mahatma Gandhi happily removed all chances of opposition and division in the Congress and that the dual programme, fight both within and without the Legislature, would remove political inertia and sullen discontent among the intelligentsia and the people.

A Conference was convened at Ranchi on 2nd and 3rd May, 1934, primarily to take necessary steps for making the Swaraj Party a pulsating and living organisation. One of the essential aims was to seek the approval and support of the All-India Congress Committee, vouchsafed to it by Gandhi. The first resolution was an approval of the Delhi Conference resolutions reviving the Swaraj Party and contesting of the Assembly elections on the issues of the rejection of the White Paper, the summoning of a Constituent Assembly for preparing the National Demand, and repealing the repressive laws. Then a revised Constitution of the Swaraj Party was adopted, according to which the Swaraj Party might not accept the Congress guidance in matters of internal administration and party finance. It was distinctly laid down that, on all broad policies, the Swaraj Party should be guided by the Congress organisation.

The programme of the Swaraj Party as laid down by the Ranchi Conference on 3rd May, 1934, provides for securing of the repeal of all acts and regulations that impede the healthy growth of the Nation and speedy attainment of Purna Swaraj, for securing the release of all political prisoners, for resisting all acts and proposals for legislative enactments which may be calculated to exploit the country, for organising villages, for effecting reform in matters such as labour, currency, exchange, agriculture, and finally for carrying out the constructive programme of the Congress.

All these subjects were finally discussed by the All-India Congress Committee at its meetings held in Patna on 18th and 19th May, 1934. It may be incidentally noted that the A.I.C.C. was the only body in the Congress organisation which had not come under the ban of Government. Civil Disobedience was suspended as per recommendation of Gandhi and the following resolution concerning the Swaraj Party was passed :—

"Inasmuch as there exists in the Congress a vast body of members who believe in the necessity of entry into the Legislatures as a step in the country's progress towards its goal, the All-India Congress Committee hereby appoints Pandit Madan Mohan Malaviya and Dr. M. A. Ansari to form a board, with Dr. Ansari, as President, called the Parliamentary Board, consisting of not more than 25 Congressmen.

"The Board shall run and control elections of, members to the Legislature on behalf of the Congress and shall have power to raise, possess and administer funds for carrying its duties.

"The Board shall be subject to the control of the All-India Congress Committee and shall have power to frame its Constitution and make rules and regulations from time to time for the management of its affairs. The Constitution as well as the rules and regulations shall be placed before the Working Committee for approval, but shall be in force pending the approval or otherwise of the Working Committee.

"The Board shall select only such candidates as will be pledged to carry out in the Legislatures the Congress Policy as it will be determined from time to time."

CHAPTER III

Marking Time

There being a general desire for an early session of the Indian National Congress, it was decided that the next ordinary session be held at Bombay in the first week of October, 1934, which date, owing to the uncertainty of the monsoon, was later changed to the last week of October.

The Working Committee of the Congress also held its sittings at Patna, just before and after the A.I.C.C., i.e., on 18th, 19th and 20th May, 1934. It made recommendations with regard to the suspension of civil resistance and the adoption of the Council-entry programme which were, as indicated above, accepted by the A.I.C.C. The Working Committee, in view of the decision of the A.I.C.C., suspending civil resistance, called upon all the Congressmen to abide by that decision. The Congressmen all over the country obeyed this direction and the civil resistance movement stood suspended on 20th May, 1934.

Simultaneously, the Working Committee, in modification of the instructions issued by the Acting President at Poona in July, 1933, called upon all Congressmen to reorganise all Congress Committees for the purpose of carrying on normal Congress activities. It appointed several leading Congressmen with full powers on behalf of the Working Committee, to help this reorganisation in different Provinces. In view of the suspension of civil resistance, the office of the Acting President naturally terminated and in the absence, in prison, of Sirdar

Vallabhbhai Patel, the President of the Congress, Syt. Jamnalal Bajaj was nominated by the Working Committee to act as President of that Committee and to exercise all the powers of the President till the ensuing session of the Congress.

It was not without some ado that the Patna decisions were arrived at. On the one hand there was a large body of opinion still extant which plumped for a no-change programme and which did not conceal its antipathy to Council work. On the other there was the steadily growing Socialist Party which, without sharing Gandhian ideals with the Congress, nevertheless stood four-square against Council-entry. All opposition, however, vanished into thin air when Gandhi stood up, rather sat down, and spoke. He had been touring in Orissa in the Harijan cause on foot. He had been making a new experiment in touring on foot. His visit to Patna was to him a wrench from work which was dearest to his heart. It was doubtless true that the new method considerably restricted the range of his travel and incidentally it meant a large curtailment of collections. But Gandhi began to feel that tour by rail and motor would mean that he was a machine for collecting funds. To make matters worse, it was contemplated that Gandhi should tour the U.P. in aeroplane as well. All this was repugnant to his taste. He had started the new experiment and must carry it on. But Patna disturbed him, nor did he resent it. He had invited the interruption by his famous statement of April 7th (1934). He must implement it. He must liquidate the Civil Disobedience movement, vesting all residual rights in himself. He had started it in a like fashion under a resolution of the Working Committee in February, 1930, authorising him to carry out Salt Satyagraha. The movement ended as it began, and Gandhi, in two remarkable speeches, poured out his whole soul before the A.I.C.C. once again in Patna.

The month of May, 1934, also saw the birth of the Socialist Party in India. It held its first All-India Conference at Patna on 17th May, 1934, under the Presidentship of Acharya Narendra Dev. Besides dealing with the question of Council-entry and the textile strike, it resolved that the time had come for the setting up of an All-India organisation of the Socialists in the Congress, and to that end it appointed a drafting committee to prepare a draft programme and constitution for such an organisation for submission to the Bombay Session of the All-India Socialist Conference. Since the Patna meeting, branches of the Socialist Party have been formed in several Provinces.

The Patna decisions were soon followed by a change in the centre of gravity of the Congress. The Civil Disobedience movement was switched off and the Council-entry programme was switched on. It was as if the belt in a workshop turning round the shaft was simply slipped off the fast on to the loose pulley. In the twinkling of an eye, faster than the fall of an object whose position is dislocated, quicker than the alternation of darkness with light when the current is off, more expeditiously than the stopping of a moving piece of machinery brought about by the pushing of a bar did the Civil Disobedience movement yield place to Council-entry. Gandhi alone remained free to practise the former, not that the country had none others to keep him company, but at Patna that was the position created by the resolutions passed by the A.I.C.C. Gandhi resumed his Harijan tour in Utkal and followed it up by a tour in U.P. The time-limit was about to expire which he had placed upon himself in respect of participation in a political programme. August 4th was the day on which he would have been released if his fast had not compelled Government to release him. Speculation was rife as to what he would do thereafter. Would he precipitate a crisis by going to the Frontier against the refusal of permission by the Government of India? Else why did he reserve to himself the right to practise individual Disobedience? But would he, having permitted the country to contest elections to the Assembly, plunge it into an abyss of sorrow and confusion, by seeking prison himself? That was unthinkable; that was not Gandhi-like. Whatever Gandhi might do or might not do, whosoever might contest or might not contest elections, there was enough to shape work for Congressmen throughout the country. Almost all the Congress and allied organisations had been declared unlawful bodies, with the exception of the All-India Congress Committee, early in 1932. Government took early steps to lift the ban on Congress organisations in the country and the ban was lifted on most of them on 12th June, 1934. Only those in the N.W.F. and in Bengal and some of the allied or affiliated organisations like the Hindustan Seva Dal in some Provinces continued to be under the ban. In some Provinces the Government still retained possession of the premises used by organisations which, according to it, were directly or indirectly connected with the Civil Disobedience movement and some were not restored even till the middle of 1935. The Government also announced a general policy of expediting the release of the Civil Disobedience prisoners, but many of them, specially from Gujarat, remained still behind the prison bars. Several Congressmen in Gujarat, though life-long residents in British India, were not allowed to enter it and are for all practical purposes under internment in Indian States. Persons in different parts of the country who were connected with the Civil Disobedience movement are not given passports to leave India on legitimate business.

Immediately after the Patna decisions, however, Congressmen all over the country had already started re-organising the Congress Committees and, by the month of June, most Congress Committees in the Provinces had resumed their normal functioning as before 1932. Accordingly, the Working Committee met at Wardha on June 12th and 13th, and again on June 17th and 18th at Bombay. It laid down for the newly organised Congress Committees a constructive programme, the main items of which were production of khaddar through self-spinning and spread thereof within the area of production, removal of untouchability, the promotion of inter-communal unity, the promotion of total abstinence from intoxicating drinks and drugs and advocacy of prohibition, promotion of education on national lines, promotion and development of useful small industries, organisation and reconstruction of village life in its economic, educational, social and hygienic aspects, spread of useful knowledge amongst the adult population in the villages, or organisation of industrial labour, and such other activities as are not inconsistent with the Congress objective or general policy and which will not involve any form of civil resistance. The Committee also decided to draw the attention of the Government to the discrepancy in the Communique withdrawing the ban on Congress organisations, which, through cancelling notifications against constituent parts of the Congress organisation, had retained the ban on the Khudai Khidmatgars, who were, since August, 1931, part of the Congress. The Government, however, while not denying the patent discrepancy, refused to withdraw their notification against the Khudai Khidmatgars as also the Afghan Jirga.

Another important question which came up before the Working Committee at its Bombay sitting was the one relating to the Congress policy in regard to the White Paper proposals and the Communal Award. The Congress Parliamentary Board having asked the Working Committee to enunciate this policy, the Committee passed its well-known resolution on the question. The resolution was preceded by discussions which disclosed a fundamental difference in the points of view of Pandit Malaviyaji and Syt. M. S. Aney on the one side, and the Working Committee on the other. The former felt that they could not, in view of this difference, retain their connection, respectively, with the Congress Parliamentary Board and the Working Committee and hence they tendered their resignations. As, however, it was felt that a fuller discussion might eventually prevent this development, they were persuaded by their colleagues to withdraw their resignations.

The Working Committee resolution dealing with the White Paper was as follows:—

"The White Paper in no way expresses the will of the people of India, has been more or less condemned by almost all the Indian political parties, and falls far short of the Congress goal, if it does not retard the progress towards it. The only satisfactory alternative to the White Paper is a Constitution drawn up by a Constituent Assembly elected on the basis of adult suffrage or as near it as possible, with the power, if necessary, to the important minorities to have their representatives elected exclusively by the electors belonging to such minorities.

"The White Paper lapsing, the Communal Award must lapse automatically. Among other things, it will be the duty of the Constituent Assembly to determine the method of representation of important minorities and make provision for otherwise safeguarding their interests.

"Since, however, the different communities in the country are sharply divided on the question of the Communal Award, it is necessary to define the Congress attitude on it. The Congress claims to represent equally all the communities composing the Indian Nation and, therefore, in view of the division of opinion, can neither accept nor reject the Communal Award as long as the division of opinion lasts. At the same time, it is necessary to re-declare the policy of the Congress on the communal question.

"No solution that is not purely national can be propounded by the Congress. But the Congress is pledged to accept any solution, falling short of the national, which is agreed to by all the parties concerned, and, conversely, to reject any solution which is not agreed to by any of the said parties.

"Judged by the national standard, the Communal Award is wholly unsatisfactory, besides being open to serious objections on other grounds.

"It is, however, obvious that the only way to prevent the untoward consequences of the Communal Award is to explore ways and means of arriving at an agreed solution and not by any appeal on this essentially domestic question to the British Government or any other outside authority."

While the suspension of the civil resistance campaign led to a grudgingly slow process of expediting the release of C.D. prisoners, it was clear that Government had made up their minds not to release Sirdar Vallabhbhai Patel, Pandit Jawaharlal or Khan Abdul Gaffar Khan. In the case of two of these, Sirdar Vallabhbhai and Khan Abdul Gaffar Khan, there was no fixed period of imprisonment. They were both imprisoned under the Regulations as early as 1932 and were State prisoners during the pleasure of the Government. Circumstances, however, soon developed which forced the hands of the Government. Sirdar Vallabhbhai had been suffering from serious nose trouble of a long standing nature, which grew worse and by the month of July had assumed a very serious aspect. The examination by a Medical Board appointed by Government disclosed the urgent necessity of an operation which could be properly done only if he was a free man. Accordingly, the Government released him on 14th July, 1934.

The discussions with Pandit Malaviya and Syt. Aney were renewed at the Benares meeting of the Working Committee held there from July 27th to 30th. Short of abandoning its fundamental attitude of non-acceptance and non-rejection of the Communal Award, the Working Committee explored all avenues for discovering a *via media* with a view to retain the co-operation of Pandit Malaviya and Syt. Aney. In view of the point made by them relating to the deep and long standing conviction of some leading Congressmen in regard to the question of electorates, Gandhiji offered a compromise providing for exception being made in the case of those among otherwise eligible candidates who had a conscientious objection to the Working Committee's resolution on the Communal Award. Gandhiji's formula was not found adequate by Pandit Malaviya and Syt. Aney. In view of this, the former resigned the Presidentship of the Congress Parliamentary Board and the latter the membership of the Working Committee and of the Congress Parliamentary Board. Bengal had a grievance too which related to the extra seats given to the Harijans, so that Bengal's opposition to the attitude of the Working Committee was based not merely on their hostility to the rest of the communal decision, but to the Poona Pact as well.

Doubts having arisen on the Congress policy in regard to Swadeshi, the Working Committee at this same meeting reaffirmed the Congress position on Swadeshi and laid down its policy, in unequivocal terms, as follows:—

> "Doubts having arisen on the Congress policy in regard to Swadeshi, it has become necessary to reaffirm the Congress position on it in unequivocal terms..
>
> "Notwithstanding what was done during the civil resistance struggle, no competition is permissible on Congress platform and in Congress exhibitions between mill-made cloth and hand-spun and hand-woven khadi. Congressmen are expected to use and encourage the use of only hand-spun and hand-woven khadi, to the exclusion of any other cloth.
>
> "In regard to articles other than cloth, the Working Committee adopts the following formula for the guidance of all Congress organisations:
>
> 'The Working Committee is of opinion that the activities of Congress organisations relating to Swadeshi shall be restricted to useful articles manufactured in India through cottage and other small industries which are in need of popular education for their support, and which will accept the guidance of the Congress organisations in regulating prices and in the matter of the wages and welfare of labour under their control.'
>
> "This formula must not be interpreted to mean any modification of the unbroken policy of the Congress to promote the Swadeshi spirit in the country and to encourage the personal use of only Swadeshi articles. The formula is a recognition of the fact that the large and organised industries which can or do command State aid are in no need of the services of Congress organisations or any Congress effort in their behalf."

On the question of discipline amongst the office-bearers, the Working Committee was of opinion that,

> "All Congressmen, whether they believe in the Congress programme and policies or not, are expected, and office-bearers and members of the Executive are

in honour bound, to carry them out, and that office-bearers and members of the Executive who carry on propaganda or act against the Congress programme and policies are, in accordance with the rules made by the A.I.C.C. dated May 24, 1929, under Art. XXXI. of the Constitution, clearly guilty of breach of discipline and liable to disciplinary action."

The Working Committee having considered the resignation of Syt. M. S. Aney, recognised the high-minded motive that had prompted the resignation and regretfully accepted it. The Working Committee placed on record its sense of the great assistance rendered by him to the Committee. Dr. Mohammad Alam also had sent in his resignation, but for a different reason.

Consequent upon their resignations, Pandit Malaviya and Syt. Aney summoned a Conference of Congressmen and others which met at Calcutta on the 18th and 19th August under the Presidentship of Pandit Malaviya. The Conference decided that a separate Party should be constituted with the object of carrying on agitation against the Communal Award and the White Paper, in the Legislatures and outside, and of setting up candidates for election to the Legislative Assembly for the promotion of that object. After laying down the principles which would govern its selection of Party candidates, and passing resolutions condemning the White Paper and the Communal Award, the Conference requested the Working Committee of the Congress to call a meeting of the A.I.C.C. with a view to revising its resolution on the Award.

In the concluding week of August took place an event which partly eased the political tension kept up in the country by the spirit of repression which Government was maintaining even after the suspension of civil resistance. The continued detention of Khan Abdul Gaffar Khan offended public opinion. The Frontier Province was one of those Provinces in the country which had borne the brunt of the fight, whether in 1930 or in 1932-34. The spirit of non-violence and patient suffering of the martial Pathans had been sorely tried, but—and that is the proud assertion of the Frontier's representatives—they never forsook the path of non-violence, despite provocations which only the medieval and autocratic tradition of the Province could make possible. There was, therefore, a widespread feeling that the detention in jail of the leader of the Province was unjust. Gandhi's mind was greatly exercised over the question of the Frontier and he was considering how to solve the problem of personally knowing the whole truth about that Province. The sudden release of Khan Abdul Gaffar Khan and his brother Dr. Khan Saheb in the last week of August was, therefore, a matter of general relief. But though free men, they were not free to visit their own Province and home. The Government, while releasing them, prohibited their entry into the Frontier Province, which had implicitly obeyed instructions in regard to the suspension of civil resistance.

In the month of September, the Working Committee met on the 25th at Wardha and reiterated the Congress goal and the means of its attainment, in view of the misgivings that rose in the minds of some Congressmen and others that the goal of Purna Swaraj was being watered down. It was virtually a repetition of the Karachi position. In respect of the 'coming elections,' the Working Committee urged that all provincial and other subordinate Congress organisations should regard it as their duty to help the Congress Parliamentary Board in its election activities, and that it was not open to them to support any Party or candidate opposed to the official policy of the Congress, and it expected every Congressman, save on grounds of conscience, to support the Congress candidates in the forthcoming elections. The Zanzibar Indians and their grievances over the contemplated forcible expropriation of their just rights in land was the subject of another resolution. A delicate situation arose over the new Party formed by Syt. M. S. Aney. A resolution was passed by this Party to the effect that a meeting of the A.I.C.C. should be convened so as to have the resolution of the Working Committee on the communal decision reviewed by the A.I.C.C. The President invited Pandit Malaviyaji and Syt. Aney to attend the meeting and present their view-point in person. The Working Committee duly met and gave several hours to the consideration of the question of calling a meeting of the A.I.C.C. and finally came to the conclusion that inasmuch as the Working Committee had no doubt about the propriety of its action, and in view of the fact that new elections for the A.I.C.C. were going on, the Working Committee could not take the responsibility of calling the meeting. It was mentioned at the meeting that, if members of the A.I.C.C. had any grievance against the Working Committee in respect of its resolution, it was open to any 30 members of the A.I.C.C. to send a requisition which would have compelled the Working Committee to convene such a meeting.

The Working Committee also discussed the question of releasing, on the grounds of conscience, candidates for election to the Assembly from the obligation to conform to the Working Committee resolution on the communal decision. The Working Committee came to the conclusion, in the absence of any such resolution on release by the Working Committee, that no exemption could be granted. Gandhi had made a proposal to Panditji, in answer to a message sent by the latter through Syt. Aney, that the way to avoid acrimony and conflict was to reach an agreement on the basis of examination of the prospects of success of rival candidates, the candidature of those who had less chance of success being withdrawn. But while on this no agreement could be reached, the Board decided not to contest seats where Pandit Malaviyaji and Syt. Aney stood as candidates. It was also decided not to enter into contest in Sindh and in the city of Calcutta.

About this time another important development took place in the history of the Congress. It was widely rumoured that Gandhi would leave the Congress. This was not a mere rumour, as Gandhi had been freely mentioning it to the friends who had gone to see him while he passed through his 7 days' fast in the middle of July, and to several other friends from Bengal, Andhra, and elsewhere, who went to Wardha to meet him for one reason or another. The wonder was that a matter so widely known was kept so private till a journalistic scoop brought it out with a gusto. On this subject, however, Gandhi made an elaborate statement which we publish below in full. Gandhi's procedure in deciding to leave the Congress was variously understood and interpreted. Few thought that he would cease to be a four-anna member. Some freely indulged in the criticism that his withdrawal from the Congress just as the elections were approaching (in November, 1934) was as unfortunate as it was indiscreet. A few thought that if his amendments to the Constitution were accepted, he might still remain in the Congress. But the Bombay Session of the Congress, which was to meet towards the last week of October, would clear all doubts. There were some that went to the length of asking why he should attend the Congress session if he was pre-determined to leave the Congress itself, and still others who asked why he should seek to amend the Congress Constitution on his own lines and then leave the body, much to the embarrassment of those in whose hands it would be left in an altered form. All these were not views expressed but aspects of 'thinking aloud.' No one comes to a conclusion, or accepts a conclusion reached by others, without subjecting it to a close and careful analysis. Some decide by instinct. They are great men and true. Some are content to accept others' decisions,—they are *Bhaktas* who believe, and are saved. Some want to reason and decide. They are wise men. Some are overborne by the logic of facts or situations,—to them law and logic are greater than life,—they are cynics. Some hug their own biases and would not change their minds. They are men of prejudices and predilections. Some are convinced against their will, but continue to be of their opinion still. All these classes of men were bestirred by Gandhi's statement, but all shared the common feature, that they were helpless against the masterful personality and his unalterable decisions arrived at by the play of instinct and not reason, by the urge of the *Zameer* or inner voice in him.

GANDHI'S STATEMENT

Wardhaganj, Sept. 17.

Mahatma Gandhi issued the following statement to the Press:—

"The rumour that I had contemplated severing all physical connection with the Congress was true. However, for the considerations urged by my friends who had come to Wardha during the meetings of the Working Committee and Parliamentary Board last week, I agreed with them that it might be safer for me to leave the Congress, if at all, after the forthcoming session. There was an intermediate course, suggested by Pandit Govind Ballabh Pant and

Mr. Rafi Ahmed Kidwai, of remaining in the Congress without participating in active administration of the organisation, but both Sirdar Vallabhbhai Patel and Moulana Abul Kalam Azad strongly disapproved of that course. Sirdar Vallabhbhai had agreed with me that the time had arrived for me to retire from the Congress, but many others would not endorse that view. After due consideration of all the pros and cons, I have adopted the safe and prudent course of postponing the final step at least till after the meeting of the Congress session in October. One attractive idea behind the insistence on postponement was that it would enable me to test the accuracy of my impression that a very large body of Congress intelligentsia were tired of my method and views, and programme based upon them, that I was a hindrance rather than a help to the natural growth of the Congress, that, instead of remaining the most democratic and representative organisation, it was dominated by my personality, that in it there was no free play of reason.

"If I am to test the truth or otherwise of my impression, naturally, I must put before the public the reasons on which my impression is based, and my own proposals based thereon. Congressmen might vote on them and thus clearly register their opinion.

"I must try to do this as briefly as I can. It has appeared to me that there is a growing and vital difference of outlook between many Congressmen and myself. I seem to be going in a direction just the opposite of what many of the most intellectual Congressmen would gladly and enthusiastically take if they were not hampered by their unexampled loyalty to me. No leader can expect greater loyalty and devotion than I have received from intellectually-minded Congressmen, even when they have protested and signified their disapproval of the policies I have laid before the Congress. For me any more to draw upon this loyalty and devotion is to put undue strain upon them. Their loyalty cannot blind my eyes to what appear to me to be fundamental differences between the Congress intelligentsia and me.

"Let me state them. I put the spinning-wheel and khadi in the forefront. Hand-spinning by Congress intelligentsia has all but disappeared. The general body of them have no faith in it and yet, if I could carry their reason with me, I would substitute the four-anna franchise by personal, daily hand-spinning. The khadi clause of the Congress Constitution has been almost a dead letter from the beginning and Congressmen have not been wanting who have reminded me that I am responsible for the hypocrisy and evasion about the working of the khadi clause. I ought to have realized that it was not passed out of deep conviction, but largely out of personal loyalty to me. I must own that there is considerable force in the argument. Nevertheless my conviction is growing that if India is to win Complete Independence in terms of the toiling millions and through unadulterated non-violence, the spinning-wheel and khadi have to be as natural to the educated few as to the partially unemployed and semi-starved millions who, for not using their hands for the purpose for which nature has endowed man with them, have become almost like beasts of burden. The spinning-wheel is thus an emblem of human dignity and equality in the truest sense of the term. It is the handmaid of agriculture. It is the Nation's second lung. We are perishing because we are using only one lung, yet only a few Congressmen have a living faith in the India-wide potency of the wheel. The removal of the khadi clause in the Constitution would mean removal of the living link between the Congress and millions whom it has from its inception sought to represent, and yet if it remains, it has to be rigidly enforced. But it cannot be, if a substantial majority of Congressmen have no living faith in it.

"Take again the Parliamentary Board. Though the author of Non-co-operation, I am convinced that in the present circumstances of the country and in the absence of any general scheme of civil resistance, a Parliamentary Party within the Congress is a necessary part of any programme that may be framed by the Congress, but there are sharp differences of opinion among us on that point. The force with which I urged the programme at the All-India Congress Committee meeting in Patna, I know, oppressed many of our best colleagues, but they hesitated to act according to their own conviction. Upto a point, suppression of one's views in favour of those of another, considered superior in wisdom or experience, is virtuous and desirable for healthy growth of organisation; it becomes a terrible oppression when one is called upon to repeat the performance from day to day. Though I have never wished any such untoward result, I cannot conceal from me or the public the tragic fact that such has been my own experience. Many have despaired of resisting me. This is a humiliating revelation to a born democrat,—I make that claim of complete identification with the poorest of mankind, an intense longing to live no better than they and a corresponding conscious effort to approach that level to the best one's ability can entitle one to make it.

"I have welcomed the formation of the Socialist group. Many of them are respected and self-sacrificing co-workers. With all this, I have fundamental differences with them on the programme published in their authorized pamphlets. But I would not, by reason of the moral pressure I may be able to exert, suppress the spread of ideas propounded in their literature. I may not interfere with the free expression of those ideas, however distasteful some of them may be to me. If they gain ascendancy in the Congress, as they well may, I cannot remain in the Congress. For, to be in active opposition should be unthinkable. Though identified with many organizations during a long period of public service, I have never accepted that position.

"Then there is the policy advocated by some in regard to the States which is wholly in difference from what I have advised. I have given many an anxious hour to the question but I have not been able to alter my view.

"Even on untouchability, my method of approach is perhaps different from that of many, if not of most Congressmen. For me, it is a deeply religious and moral issue. Many think that it was a profound error for me to have disturbed the course of the civil resistance struggle by taking up the question in the manner, and at the time, I did. I feel that I would have been untrue to myself if I had taken any other course.

"Last of all, take non-violence. After 14 years of trial, it still remains a policy with the majority of Congressmen, whereas it is a fundamental creed with me. That Congressmen do not still regard non-violence as a creed is no fault of theirs. It is undoubtedly my faulty presentation and, still more, the faulty execution that are responsible for this failure. I have no consciousness of faulty presentation or execution, but it is the only possible inference from the fact that it has not yet become an integral part of the lives of Congressmen.

"And if there is uncertainty about non-violence, there must be still more about civil resistance. In spite of my 27 years of study and practice of the doctrine, I cannot claim to know all about it. The field of research is necessarily limited, as occasions for civil resistance in a man's life must not be frequent. It can only come after voluntary obedience to authority, whether of parents, teachers or other elders, religious or secular. There need be no wonder that, as the only expert, however imperfect, among us, I should have come to the conclusion that it should, for some time to come, be limited only to me. This was necessary in order to minimise the errors and mischief proceeding from them, as also to explore its hidden possibilities, but again for no fault of the Congressmen. It has been increasingly difficult for me to carry the reason of fellow Congressmen with me in all the resolutions recently passed on the subject, whilst they have generously voted for them.

"Even the memory of the sense of oppression which they experienced at the time of voting, without an intelligent belief in these resolutions, oppresses me just as much as they were oppressed. They and I must be free from this oppression if we are at all to grow in pursuit of what we believe to be the common goal. Hence it is necessary for all concerned to act freely and boldly according to their convictions.

"I have, in my Patna statement recommending suspension of civil resistance, drawn attention to the failure of civil resistance to achieve two obvious results. If we had the full non-violent spirit in us, it should have been self-evident and should not have escaped the notice of the Government. Their Ordinances were certainly not warranted by any of the misdeeds done by or imputed to us. They were undoubtedly intended to break our spirit anyhow. But it would be wrong if we contended that civil resisters were above reproach. If we are non-violent through and through, our non-violence would have been self-evident. Nor were we able to show to the terrorists that we had greater faith in our non-violence than they in their violence. On the contrary, many of us made them feel that we had the same spirit of violence in our breasts that they had. Only, we did not believe in deeds of violence. The terrorists rightly argued that if the spirit of violence was common to both, the policy of doing or not doing violence was a matter of opinion. I need not repeat what I have said before, that the country has made great strides towards non-violence indeed and that many have exhibited great courage and self-sacrifice. All I want to say is that ours has not been unadulterated non-violence in thought, word and deed. It is now my paramount duty to devise ways and means of showing demonstrably to the Government and the terrorists the efficacy of non-violence as a means of achieving the right thing, including freedom in every sense of the term.

"For this experiment to which my life is dedicated, I need complete detachment and absolute freedom of action. Satyagraha, of which civil resistance is but a part, is to me the universal law of life. Satya, in truth, is my God. I can only search Him through non-violence and in no other way. And the freedom of my country, as of the world, is surely included in the search for Truth. I cannot suspend this search for anything in this world or another. I have entered the political life in pursuit of this search, and if it cannot carry the reason as well as the heart of educated Congressmen when I say that this search necessarily includes Complete Independence and many other things which may be part of Truth, it is plain I should work single-handed, in the implicit faith that what I fail to make clear to my countrymen to-day shall be clear to them some day of itself; or, if God wills it, through some apt word He may put in my mouth or some apt work which He may prompt me to do in matters of such tremendous importance. A mechanical vote or a grudging assent is wholly inadequate, if not injurious to the cause itself.

"I have referred to the common goal but I have begun to doubt if all Congressmen understand the same thing by the expression 'Complete Independence.' I want for India Complete Independence in the full English sense of that English expression. For me Purna Swaraj has an infinitely larger meaning than 'Complete Independence' but even Purna Swaraj is not self-explained. No one word or compound expression will give us a meaning which all can understand. Hence, on several occasions I have given several definitions of Swaraj. I hold that they are all hopelessly incomplete even when put together, but I do not wish to labour on it.

"My mention of the difficulty if not the impossibility of giving a complete definition leads me to another serious point of difference between many Congressmen and myself. I have always said, since 1903, that means and end are convertible terms and that, therefore, where the means are various and even contradictory the end must be different and even contradictory. We have always control over the means and never on the end. But we may not bother about its content if we all employ identical means with identical connotation for them. It will be admitted that many Congressmen do not admit this (to me) obvious truth. They believe that the end justifies the means, whatever they may be.

"It is the sum-total of these differences which has sterilised the existing Congress programme, because members who gave their lip-assent to it without believing in it, have naturally failed to reduce it to practice and yet I have no other programme save the Congress programme now before the country, that is, untouchability, Hindu-Muslim unity, total prohibition, hand-spinning with khadi cent. per cent. Swadeshi, in the sense of the revival of Village Industries and general re-organisation of the seven lakhs of villages, ought to give all satisfaction that one's love of one's country may demand. Personally I would like to bury myself in an Indian village, preferably in a Frontier village. If the Khudai Khidmatgars are truly non-violent, they will contribute the largest share to the promotion of the non-violent spirit and of Hindu-Muslim unity. For, if they are non-violent in thought, word and deed, and are lovers of Hindu-Muslim unity, surely through them we should see the accomplishment of the two things we need most in this land. The Afghan menace which we dread so much should then be a thing of the past. I am, therefore, yearning to test the truth for myself of the claim that they have imbibed the spirit of non-violence and are believers, in the heart, of unity of Hindus, Mussalmans and others. I should like also personally to deliver the message of the spinning-wheel to them in this and various such other ways. I would love to serve the Congress in my own humble manner, whether I am in or outside it.

"I have reserved to the last the reference to the growing corruption in our ranks. I have already said enough about it in public. In spite of all I have said, the Congress still remains in my estimation the most powerful and the most representative organisation in the country. It has a history of uninterrupted noble service and self-sacrifice, and from its inception it has weathered storms as no other institution has done. It has commanded a measure of self-sacrifice of which any country would be proud. It holds to-day the largest number of devoted men and women of unimpeachable character. If I must leave this organisation, I shall not do so without a wrench and I should do it only when I am convinced that being outside I would serve it, *i.e.*, the country, better than by being in it.

"I propose to test the feeling of the Congress on all the points I have touched by placing before the Subjects Committee certain resolutions giving effect to the views enunciated above. The first amendment I would propose is to replace the words 'legitimate and peaceful' by 'truthful and non-violent.' I should not have done so but for the furore of opposition which was raised against the utterly innocent use by me of the two adjectives in the place of 'legitimate and peaceful.' If Congressmen really believe in the necessity of truthfulness and non-violence for the attainment of our goal, they should have no hesitation about accepting the unequivocal adjectives.

"The second amendment would be to replace the four anna franchise by the delivery by every member to a Congress depot of 2,000 rounds (one round equal to four feet) per month of well-twisted even yarn of not less than 15 counts spun by himself or herself. The arguments for and against need not be repeated here. If we are to be a truly democratic body representing even the lowest paid labour, we cannot do it better than by devising a simple labour franchise. Hand-spinning is by common consent the lowest paid labour and yet the most dignified. It is the nearest approach to adult franchise within the means of almost every one who is willing to labour for the sake of the country for half an hour daily. Is it too much to expect the intelligentsia and the propertied classes to recognise the dignity of labour, irrespective of the material benefit it brings? Is not labour, like learning, its own reward? If we are true servants of the masses, we would take pride in spinning for their sakes. I recall what the late Maulana Mahomed Ali used to repeat from many a platform. As the sword was the symbol of brute force and might, he would say, the wheel or the *takli* was the symbol of non-violence, service and humility. When the wheel was accepted as part of the national flag, it was surely implied that the spinning-wheel would hum in every household. If

Congressmen do not believe in the message of the wheel, we must remove it from the national flag, and khaddar from the Constitution. It is intolerable that there should be unashamed fraud in the observance of the khaddar clause.

"The third amendment I should propose would be that no one shall be entitled to vote at any Congress election whose name has not been on the Congress register continuously for six months without default, and who has not been a habitual wearer wholly of khaddar for that period. A great difficulty has been experienced in the working of the khaddar clause. It can be easily avoided by giving powers, subject to appeal to the President of the Congress and to the chairmen of respective committees, to decide the question whether a particular voter is or is not a habitual wearer wholly of khaddar within the meaning of the Constitution. No one is to be considered such a wearer who, at the time of voting, is not manifestly wholly clad in khaddar. But no rule, however carefully and strictly worded, can produce satisfactory results if a large number do not voluntarily carry it out.

"Experience has shown that the Congress is an unwieldy organisation, even with 6,000 delegates. In practice, the full number has never attended the Congress, and when the Congress register nowhere contains a truly representative list, the delegation can hardly be claimed to be a reality. I would, therefore, have an amendment reducing the number to not more than 1,000 delegates nor more than one delegate per every thousand voters. To have the full number of delegates would mean one million voters, not an over-ambitious hope in a country having a population of 315 millions. The Congress would, by this amendment, gain in substance what it may lose in the show of numbers. The spectacular part of the session would be kept intact by making ample provision for visitors, but Reception Committees will be spared the wholly unnecessary anxiety of having to provide accommodation for an unwieldy number of delegates. Let us recognise the fact that the Congress enjoys a prestige, democratic in character and influence, not by the number of delegates and visitors it has drawn to its annual functions but by the ever-increasing amount of service it has rendered. Western democracy is on its trial. If it has already proved a failure, may it be reserved to India to evolve the true science of democracy by giving a visible demonstration of its buttress. Corruption and hypocrisy ought not to be the inevitable products of democracy, as they undoubtedly are to-day. Nor is bulk a true test of democracy. True democracy is not inconsistent with a few persons representing the spirit, the hope and the aspirations of those whom they claim to represent. I hold that democracy cannot be evolved by forcible methods. The spirit of democracy cannot be imposed from without. It has to come from within.

"I have mentioned here only the principal amendments I should propose in the Constitution. There would be other resolutions bringing out clearly the points I have touched upon in the foregoing paras. I do not need to burden this statement with them.

"My fear is that even the amendments I have named will hardly commend themselves to the large number of Congressmen who will attend the Congress. Nevertheless, if I am to guide the policy of the Congress, I hold them and the resolutions in keeping with the spirit of this statement to be essential for the earliest attainment of our goal. No voluntary organisation can succeed in its purpose without its resolutions and policies being carried out whole-heartedly by its members, and no leader can give a good account of himself if his lead is not faithfully, ungrudgingly and intelligently followed; and this is truest of a leader who has no resource at his disposal but what truth and non-violence can supply. It follows, therefore, that there is no room for compromise in the essentials of the programme I have endeavoured to adumbrate in these paras. Let the Congressmen, therefore, examine it dispassionately and on its merits. They must eliminate me from their consideration and give effect to the dictates of their reason."

The Bombay Session (October 26th to 28th, 1934) of the Indian National Congress would have been of the humdrum type and devoid of any exciting interest, but for the imminent exit of Gandhi from the arena of politics and the foreshadowed amendment of the Congress Constitution. The enthusiasm and interest awakened in the popular mind in respect of the very thought of a regular session of the Congress being held and people preparing to attend a session, after an interval of three and a half years, was itself a sufficient sustenance to the country at a time when a certain paralysis had overtaken it. Surely any kind of activity was better than the utter inactivity that prevailed. Ere long, the country's attention was rivetted on to this scheme. Parliamentary Board, Socialism, and Communal Award, —all receded into the background. In a moment every one began to discuss even before the Congress, and more so during the session, whether, after all, the Congress should cease to be a spectacular body thereafter, whether the All-India Congress Committee, which was to be composed of but a thousand delegates and to be brought into existence by the delegates assembled after its session, should on the one hand in its full strength function as the year's Congress and on the other, in its parts, play the role of the Provincial Congress Committee. It was argued that such an arrangement made for homogeneity of composition as well as continuity of policy through the creation of a handy, compact and close-knit body or bodies working throughout the year. Gandhiji's central idea was that the provincial representatives should sit together with their credentials and evolve, pooling their experience, a programme for the Congress in the All-India Congress Committee and break up once again to carry out that programme in their respective Provinces. This was the central theme. It was at the same time contemplated that the

Congress membership should be on a strict basis of manual labour, the fruits of which are tendered to the Congress, symbolising the ideal of service and sacrifice for which the Congress stands and the national duty which each Congressman had to observe in his daily life as a sacrament. Again no Congressman was to be entitled to vote unless his name had been in the Congress register for six months. This was designed to avoid corruption in Congress elections which flowed from an improvisation of membership by monied and influential people to advance their own ends. Then the President was to be a President in reality of a Cabinet formed exclusively by himself. The clause relating to the habitual wear of khaddar was of course to be there and Gandhi demanded that the Creed of the Congress which had lent itself to ambiguous interpretations should be made to imply indisputably the adherence of the Congress to 'truthful' and 'non-violent,' in place of 'peaceful' and 'legitimate' methods. There raged a storm in the country before the Congress session and during it. But no one is at his best so well and so readily as Gandhi in the midst of a *tufan*. He then summons all his calmness and resources to his aid and turns a seeming defeat into a substantial victory, not by any wiles and stratagems but by his only strategy in life, namely, the strategy of Truth and Non-violence. He had separated, early in the session, the constitutional section of his amendments from the Satyagrahic section and left the latter to be dealt with by the Working Committee as it chose, while the former was to be moved by him and made a test of confidence in the new President and his colleagues. Strangely enough, though not unexpectedly, the Working Committee accepted both the sections with suitable changes and the Congress itself has substantially accepted them all, much to the satisfaction of Gandhi himself. It is unnecessary to weary the reader with a repetition of the detailed changes introduced into Gandhi's draft by the Congress. Suffice it to say that the change of Creed was required to be circulated to the Provinces for opinion and is awaiting the decision of the Congress of 1936. The Labour franchise has been accepted as applicable to elective membership, and the habitual wear of khaddar is wholly endorsed. The Congress delegation has been reduced to a maximum of 2,000 apportioned between the rural and the urban areas in the proportion of 1,489 to 511. The A.I.C.C. is to be continued at half its strength and the delegates are to be elected at the rate of 1 to 500 members, instead of one to thousand as proposed by Gandhi. Thus the principle of modulating the strength of the delegates strictly to the membership of the Congress enunciated in Gandhi's draft is accepted, thereby making the delegates not visitors at a spectacular gathering but representatives of the Nation charged with the duty of electing an All-India Executive as well as the Provincial Congress Committees. The rest of Gandhi's draft has been virtually accepted by the Congress.

The issues before the Congress were, why it should change its Constitution, why it should change it now, and why it should be changed just as Gandhi was leaving the Congress. This naturally raises the question of Gandhi's exit from the Congress, which we shall deal with presently, but let it be remembered that it was Gandhi's bare duty to tell the Congress what, in his opinion, was wrong with it, as he was the General who had marshalled the forces these fourteen years, while it is equally the duty of the Congress to reconnoitre the situation during a period of respite so as to be able to set its house in order and prepare itself for future emergencies.

It was not, however, the new Constitution or the confirmation of the old resolutions on the Parliamentary Board, the constructive programme and the Communal Award, that should be reckoned as the events of the year. They are undoubtedly notable achievements. But really the more notable, though a trifle less noticed, achievement is the formation of an All-India Village Industries Association which is to work under the advice and guidance of Gandhi and apart from so-called politics. This is the logical fulfilment of the khaddar programme. Khaddar is but the forerunner of a series of village industries which make the village and the country self-sufficient. The arts and crafts of a Nation are the true index of its civilisation.

Scientific achievements are the common heritage of the world. Knowledge is universal property, but arts and artistic crafts speak out the soul of the Nation, and when they are dead, the Nation's individuality is dead. It may have an animal existence but its creative genius is gone,—gone no more to reappear. When, therefore, Gandhi has planned a revival of the dead and dying industries of Indian villages, he has really planned a revival of Indian civilisation, a rehabilitation of Indian economic prosperity and a re-aligning of Indian National Education. There is a universal demand for the formation of an All-India Board of National Education, but the public minds are not prepared for the revolutionary changes contemplated in that behalf by Gandhi. It is only when the Indian village is once again revivified and made self-sufficient that the true import of National Education will be understood. Gandhi's aim is not to build sky-scrapers of wealth or span the oceans for commerce and trade, but to add a little *makkhan* (butter) to the *rottee* (dry bread) of the starving millions of India. This he seeks to do through the A.I.S.A. and the A.I.V.I.A.

What comes last in this narration of achievements is perhaps the most outstanding event of the Bombay Session. Gandhi's exit from the Congress, notwithstanding his definite assertion in that behalf, was not taken literally by friends or foes. But it did not take them long to realise that Gandhi always means what he says and always does what he means. His anxiety is that his words should be taken at their face value.

This is not merely a formal declaration of an open mind but a trait of character which was noticed in 1929 when there was a strong feeling that he should preside over the Lahore Congress and not Jawaharlal. It was noticed again during the Bombay Session in 1934. But in both cases he was not convinced of the incorrectness of his earlier decisions. It was, therefore, stunning news alike to the Press and the public that Gandhi would not be even a primary member of the Congress. Albeit, it is true that Gandhi has left the Congress with a vote of confidence and a standing invitation to re-enter. Only, the Congress has to deserve what it desires. It must purge itself of all impurity, making Congress and khaddar equivalent to purity, sincerity and integrity. If that should be so, the Congress intelligentsia must lose no time in proving to the leaders that they stand for no selfish ends but for the ideal of service and sacrifice,—an ideal pursued through a programme of daily labour for at least 8 hours a month, the fruits of which are tendered to the Congress. Some people have misinterpreted this clause as a set-off or safeguard against the socialistic invasion of the Congress. It is not so. The Congress has been wedded to the cult of manual labour and the service of the poor, peasant and labourer alike, for the past fourteen years. The Congress is really socialistic in outlook. If only the Socialist would declare his faith in khaddar and village industries, in truth and non-violence, in a programme of daily duties to realise the high ideal set before the country, the Congressmen would be as much Socialists as the Socialists themselves should be Congressmen. And who is more socialistic not merely in name, but in fact, than Gandhi who has renounced his wealth and property and snapped his ties of blood relationship? The Labour franchise, therefore, is not a make-believe but an honest rendering of a socialistic ideal into the daily programme of Congressmen.

Another aspect of the so-called crisis in Bombay is involved in the oft-repeated questions as to what Gandhi would do and what the Congress should do hereafter. The simple query is raised on the one hand as to whether Gandhi has renounced politics, and or the other what political work the Congress would do if Gandhi should take away with him the Spinners' Association as well as the Village Industries Association. These questions betray a certain confusion in the public mind. If it is admitted that the constructive programme constitutes essentially political work, as Satyagrahis believe it does, then Gandhi has no more renounced politics after the Bombay Session than before it. Moreover, he has reserved to himself the right of Individual Civil Disobedience under the very Congress resolution which has withdrawn it for the Nation. Therefore, instead of renouncing politics he has taken away the whole of it,—constructive programme as well as destructive,— with himself. Then many people legitimately ask as to what is left to Congressmen. We may in turn ask, "what is not left to them?" The contructive programme is always there and has been really worked by Congressmen themselves in the past with the aid of outsiders. As for the destructive, it is always open to the Congress which has affirmed its faith once again in Civil Disobedience, to reorganise it at any time. In fact, the resolution congratulating the Nation and the workers on their sacrifices in the past, declared the faith of the Congress in Civil Disobedience and non-violence as a better means of achieving Swaraj than methods of violence which, as experience has abundantly shown, result in terrorism both by the oppressed and the oppressors. Gandhi had begun to feel that he is a big weight weighing down upon the Congress and the more he had suppressed himself, the more had he added to that weight. Civil Disobedience had to be inaugurated by him, withdrawn by him, and regulated by him. Peace and war were his concern. He is the one person to whom the Congress had been looking up for orders to halt or march, to advance or retreat. The withdrawal of such a mighty force could only make for the strength of the body on which it had been acting, even as the retirement of the father from the home would but strengthen the son, encourage him to take the initiative, fill him with a sense of responsibility and inspire him with hope and courage, the more so when the patriarch is prepared to make his advice and guidance available to the family or the Nation whenever necessary. Gandhi had given such an assurance. His object is to make the Indian National Congress a power in the land. It is not the numbers that give strength but the moral power behind them; and this power grows in proportion to the sense of responsibility entertained by the leaders. Instead of assuming such responsibility, the Congress has too long and too much relied on Gandhi and demands his co-operation on its own terms. That is impossible. Congressmen can get Gandhi's co-operation on his terms, and any day, on that basis, he is willing to return to the Congress and direct its work. Only, let the Congress set its house in order, create a genuine membership, though small in measure, bring into existence executives that are active throughout the year, which will purify and ennoble the Congress institutions, and then he will readily come and assume command. Gandhi is the founder of the New Congress wedded to the ideal of service as against power. He has taken public life to the villages and made them the foundation of Indian Nationalism. He has enlarged the scope and meaning of Politics so that it now embraces a programme of national reconstruction all round. He has given the Nation a cause, a flag and a leader. Gandhi may have retired, but Gandhi is always there as the first Servant of India to lead the Nation to its destiny in accordance with the high principles which he has all along applied to the Congress and its manifold activities.

The success of the Bombay Session was in no small measure due to the tact, energy and circumspection of its President, Babu Rajendra Prasad. His Address to the Congress is one of those model addresses which leave an abiding effect on the political situation. His criticism of the White Paper was detailed and scathing and his observations on the Congress programme were helpful.

The President concluded his short and telling Address thus:—

> "Independence is the natural outcome of all that the freedom movement in India has stood for. It cannot mean isolation, particularly when we remember that it has to be achieved by non-violence. It means the end of exploitation of one country by another, and of one part of the population of the same country by another part. It contemplates a free and friendly association with other nations for the mutual benefit of all. It forebodes evil to none,

not even to those exploiting us, except in so far as they rely upon exploitation rather than good-will. The sanction behind this Independence movement is non-violence which, in its positive and dynamic aspect, is good-will of and for all. We already see signs of how it has begun appealing to a certain extent to world opinion. This appeal has to become irresistible. It can do so according as the element of distrust and suspicion, which has its birth in fear, is eliminated and replaced by a sense of security born of confidence in the good-will of India. India having no designs on others, will not then need a large army either for its protection against foreigners or for internal peace which will stand guaranteed by the good-will of her inhabitants. Having no designs on others, she will be able to claim immunity from the evil designs of others, and her safety will be buttressed and protected by the good-will of the world at large. Conceived in this light, our Independence ought not to frighten even the Britishers, unless they aim at perpetuating the present unnatural conditions.

"The method too is crystal clear. It is active, dynamic, non-violent mass action. We may fail once; we may fail twice; but we are bound to succeed some day.

"Many have already lost their lives and all. Many more have sacrificed themselves in their struggle for freedom. Let us not be deterred by the difficulties which confront us nor diverted from our straight course by fear or favour. Our weapons are unique and the world is watching the progress of our great experiment with interest and high expectation. Let us be true to our creed, and firm in our determination. Satyagraha in its active application may meet with temporary set-backs, but it knows no defeat. It is itself a great victory, for, as James Lowell put it,

> 'Truth for ever on the scaffold,
> Wrong for ever on the throne,
> Yet that scaffold sways the future,
> And behind the dim unknown,
> Standeth God within the shadow,
> Keeping watch above His own.'"

Now we proceed to give a summary of the resolutions passed by the Bombay Session on October 26th to 28th, 1934, of which Syt. Rajendra Prasad was the President and Syt. K. F. Nariman was the Chairman of the Reception Committee.

The Congress opened with a resolution endorsing the resolutions passed by the Working Committee and the All-India Congress Committee at their meetings held in May, 1934, and thereafter, especially the resolutions regarding the Parliamentary Board and its policy and programme, the constructive programme, the status of Indian settlers overseas, condolence resolution, and the resolution on Swadeshi.

The Nation's sacrifices and faith in civil resistance were then dealt with.

The Congress congratulated the Nation on the heroic sacrifices made and the sufferings undergone by thousands of civil resisters,—men and women, young and old, drawn from cities as well as the villages in the different Provinces,—and placed on record its conviction that "without non-violent Non-co-operation and civil resistance there would never have been the phenomenal mass awakening that has taken place throughout the country." Whilst recognising the desirability and necessity of the suspension of the civil resistance campaign except with reference to Gandhiji, the Congress reiterated its undying faith in non-violent Non-co-operation and civil resistance "as a better means of achieving Swaraj than methods of violence which, as experience has abundantly shown, result in terrorism both by the oppressed and the oppressors."

A resolution was next passed expressing anxiety over the illness of Mrs. Jawaharlal Nehru, and hoping that the change to the hills would result in her restoration to health.

The All-India Village Industries Association was the topic on which interest was concentrated and a lengthy resolution was passed :—

> "Whereas organisations claiming to advance Swadeshi have sprung up all over the country, with and without the assistance of Congressmen, and whereas much confusion has arisen in the public mind as to the nature of Swadeshi, and whereas the aim of the Congress has been, from its inception, progressive identification with the masses, and whereas village re-organisation and re-construction is one of the items in the constructive programme of the Congress, and whereas such reconstruction necessarily implies revival and encouragement of dead or dying village industries besides the central industry of hand-spinning, and whereas this work, like the reorganisation of hand-spinning is possible only through concentrated and special effort, unaffected by and independent of the political activities of the Congress, Shri J. C. Kumarappa is hereby authorised to form, under the advice and guidance of Gandhiji, an association called the All-India Village Industries Association as part of the activities of the Congress. The said Association shall work for the revival and encouragement of the said industries and for the moral and physical advancement of the villages, and shall have power to frame its own Constitution, to raise funds, and to perform such acts as may be necessary for the fulfilment of its objects."

A consequential resolution was passed on the subject of exhibitions and demonstrations which ran thus :—

> "Inasmuch as it is desirable to free the Reception Committee from the distraction and expense

attendant upon the organisation of exhibitions and spectacular demonstrations that take place at the annual sessions of the Congress, and as these make it impossible for smaller places to invite the Congress, the Reception Committee shall henceforth be relieved of the task of organising exhibitions and spectacular demonstrations. But as exhibitions and spectacular demonstrations are a necessary part of the annual national gathering, the duty of organising these is hereby entrusted to the All-India Spinners' Association and the All-India Village Industries Association, which bodies shall organise these functions so as to combine instruction with entertainment of the general public, especially of the villagers, with the sole view to illustrate and popularise the activities of the two associations and, generally, to demonstrate the potentiality of village life."

The Congress Parliamentary Board claimed attention.

The Board itself was of opinion that, "inasmuch as this Board was constituted as an emergency measure, it is desirable that its life should be limited to one year and that thereafter it should be placed on an elective basis for the period and on the terms as might appear desirable." This resolution of the Board was forwarded to the Working Committee as a 'recommendation of the Board,' and the Congress accepted the said recommendation and resolved that the existing Parliamentary Board should be dissolved on 1st May, 1935, and a new Board of 25 should be elected by the A.I.C.C. on or before the aforesaid date. The elected Board should have the power to co-opt not more than five members. There should be a fresh election of the Parliamentary Board at every annual session of the Congress, with the same power of co-option. The elected Board should possess the same powers as are possessed by the existing Board.

The revised Constitution has been dwelt upon at length in these pages.

A separate resolution was passed prescribing a khaddar qualification which ran thus: "No member shall be eligible for election to any office or to any Congress Committee unless he is a habitual wearer wholly of hand-spun and hand-woven khaddar."

For the first time, a Labour qualification was introduced:—

> "No person shall be eligible to be a candidate for election to membership of any Congress Committee, unless he or she has performed some manual labour continuously for six months immediately before the date of nomination for election, on behalf of or for the Congress, equal in value to 500 yards per month of well-spun yarn of over ten counts, and in time to eight hours per month. The form of acceptable labour alternative to spinning shall be prescribed from time to time by the Working Committee, in consultation with the Provincial Congress Committees and the All-India Village Industries Association."

Gandhiji's retirement naturally demanded a resolution of confidence in him which was thus expressed ;—

> "This Congress reiterates its confidence in the leadership of Mahatma Gandhi and is emphatically of opinion that he should reconsider his decision to retire from the Congress. But inasmuch as all efforts to persuade him in that behalf have failed, this Congress, while reluctantly accepting his decision, places on record its deep sense of gratitude for the unique services rendered by him to the Nation and notes with satisfaction his assurance that his advice and guidance will be available to the Congress whenever necessary."

The next session of the Congress was invited to U.P. and the invitation was accepted.

Hardly had the Bombay Session concluded its sittings when the Nation was plunged into the elections to the Assembly. The change from the *lathi*-charges and the sufferings of the offensive movement to the lightning marches of an election campaign and its thundering orations was truly refreshing. People were restored for a while to their wonted tastes. They had a splendid case to present. Every District and every Tahsil was visited. An educative and propagandistic campaign was carried on throughout the country. Almost every general constituency seat was contested. The Nationalists under the lead of Pandit Malaviya and Mr. Aney chose to stand as Congress Nationalists, apart from the mere Congressmen. The seat that attracted general attention was that contested by Sir R. K. Shanmukham Chetti—the Commerce seat in South India. He had been sent to Ottawa by the Government of India to negotiate a scheme of trade relations based on Empire Preference and, on his return, had been elected President of the Assembly. He had the virtual support of the Madras Government and the Government of India. Sir Mohammad Osman, the ex-Home Member of the Madras Government, and the Raja of Bobbili, the Chief Minister, were amongst the first signatories to his manifesto. The English practice of not contesting the seat of the ex-President or Speaker of the Legislature was invoked. Government officers freely took part in the elections. The Congress worked for Sami Venkatachalam Chetti, the rival candidate, and it was no trite victory that the latter scored over the former. It was a victory really of the Congress over Government, of moral force over wealth and power; it was a victory of India over Britain and Ottawa put together. Government too wanted to make this election a test election, one intended to judge whether their man, who had espoused their cause at Ottawa and had the courage—some might say the hardihood—to act against informed commercial opinion in the country, had the support of a commercial constituency such as it was. In the end, the test proved to be not merely a test of support based on numerical strength which would have been true if the combatants had fought on a territorial electorate, but a test of support based on moral strength and intellectual conviction of a picked few competent to judge. This election was so timed as to lead almost every other election in India, and when the result was announced it had an effect just the opposite of what was anticipated and expected. South India swept the polls. Eleven territorial seats had a thumping majority for the Congress. In Bengal, Congress Nationalists got all the general seats. U.P., unlike in 1926, captured all the general seats and one Mussalman seat, Bihar and C. P., Maharashtra, Gujarat, Karnatak and Assam swept the polls for the Congress. Punjab alone lagged behind, with only one seat for the Congress. Altogether the Congress captured 44 clear Congress seats, apart from the seats of the Congress Nationalists, who were with the Congress on all points except on the question of the communal decision.

The Congress Party in the Assembly put up Mr. T.A.K. Sherwani as candidate for the Presidentship of the Assembly but he failed. Heavy tolls Congress had to pay to nature in the deaths of three successful candidates, *viz.*, Abhyankar and Sherwani and Sasmal, the last of whom was a Congress Nationalist, and all of whom passed away from our midst in the prime of their life, and after they had contributed their best to the country's cause.

The Congress Party soon set to work in the Assembly which began its session on January 21. An adjournment motion on the Government's Circular on the A.I.V.I.A. was talked out and that on the detention of Sarat Chandra Bose was passed by 58 to 54 votes. The refusal of permission to Syt. Sarat Chandra Bose who had been, while an internee, returned to the Assembly uncontested, to attend its sittings, attracted the earliest attention of the Congress Party which had marshalled its forces under the able leadership of Syt. Bhulabhai Desai. Syt. Desai brought to the Assembly the same prestige and glamour as Motilalji himself. He had been for some time Advocate-General of Bombay and did not care very much for the prize posts to which this recognised leadership of the Bar is the usual stepping stone. The Indo-British Trade Agreement was the object of the next attack and a resolution that it should be terminated was passed by 66 against 58 votes. The Pact was a scandalous piece of jobbery which was perpetrated as between the Secretary of State for India and the Secretary to the Board of Trade in the British Cabinet. Two members of the British Cabinet agreed to divide the spoils of trade in India and chose to call it by the dignified name of the Indo-British Trade Agreement. This Agreement is really a document intended to implement beforehand the forthcoming recommendations of the Joint Parliamentary Committee's Report on the commercial safeguards under the new Reforms. It was specifically laid down that the protection afforded to Indian industries "shall only be so much as, and no more than, will equate the prices of the imported goods to fair selling prices for similar goods produced in India and that, wherever possible, lower rates of duty will be imposed on goods of United Kingdom origin." Differential margins of duty as between English and foreign goods shall not be altered to the detriment of the United Kingdom goods.

Whenever the question of protection to any Indian industry is referred to the Tariff Board, the Government of India shall afford full opportunity to any industry concerned in the United Kingdom to state its case and answer cases presented by other interested parties. The privilege of duty-free entry of Indian pig-iron into the U. K. will be continued so long as the duties applicable to the article on iron and steel imported into India are not less favourable to the U. K. than hitherto. Now, this extraordinary Agreement was signed on the 10th January, 1935, and earned the unmitigated condemnation of the Assembly. The ban on Khudai Khidmatgars was asked to be removed by 74 to 46 votes. The Taxation policy of Government was the next subject of victory for the popular party and this was followed by that on Siamese rice and twenty-five or thirty other subjects big and small. We have reserved a reference to the victory on the J.P.C. Report to the last. The tadpole of the White Paper at the time of the elections had since developed into the frog of the Joint Parliamentary Committee Report. It has since passed both the Houses of Parliament and become Law. As these pages are nearing completion, we give a comprehensive survey of the recommendations of the J.P.C. and the case for their rejection in Appendix XIV, but the resolution passed by the Assembly is given below, as well as details of the procedure followed in this behalf.

The procedure followed by the Government in the Assembly in connection with the debate on the J.P.C. Report was different from that followed in the Provincial Councils. In the Provinces, the official bloc rightly refrained from taking part in the voting, so that only Indian opinion represented in Provincial Councils might register its vote on the Report. In the Assembly, however, the Government decided to intervene in the debate and cast all votes at their disposal against amendments to their proposition for the consideration of the Report. But for this intervention, the unambiguous resolution moved by the Congress Party recommending the Government, "not to proceed with any legislation based on the said scheme," would have been carried.

The Assembly, however, adopted the amendment moved by Mr. Jinnah. For the purpose of voting, the amendment was divided into two parts, the first part relating to the acceptance of the Communal Award. The Congress amendment of neutrality was first put to vote as an amendment to Mr. Jinnah's amendment, and was lost, there being 44 votes cast in its favour by the members of the Congress Party. After the Congress amendment was lost, the Congress group remained neutral and the first clause was carried with the votes of the Mussalmans and the Government.

The second and third clauses were put together as being an entire alternative and were adopted by the House by 74 against 58 votes. The Congress Party voted for the amendment; the Government and nominated members voted against it.

Mr. Jinnah's amendment was as follows :—

"1. That this Assembly accepts the Communal Award, so far as it goes, until a substitute is agreed upon by the various communities concerned.

"2. As regards the scheme of Provincial Governments, this House is of opinion that it is most unsatisfactory and disappointing inasmuch as it includes various objectionable features, particularly the establishment of Second Chambers, the Extraordinary and Special Powers of the Governors, provisions relating to Police rules, Secret Service and Intelligence Departments, which render the real control and responsibility of the Executive and

Legislature ineffective, and, therefore, unless these objectionable features are removed, it will not satisfy any section of Indian opinion.

"3. With respect to the scheme of the Central Government, called 'All-India Federation' this House is clearly of opinion that it is fundamentally bad and totally unacceptable to the people of British India, and, therefore, recommends to the Government of India to advise His Majesty's Government not to proceed with any legislation based on this scheme and urges that immediate efforts should be made to consider how best to establish in British India alone a real and complete Responsible Government, and with that view, take steps to review the whole position in consultation with Indian opinion without delay."

The amendment contained in clauses 2 and 3 which was put as an entire alternative scheme was treated by the Government, speaking through the Law Member, as being as much a rejection of the J.P.C. Report proposals as the more direct rejection of the same by the Congress. The Law Member, while describing the nature of Mr. Jinnah's amendment, said as follows:—

"Now, Sir, I was going to say that instead of the honest, direct and frontal attack which comes from my friend, Mr. Desai, we have this disingenuous and indirect attack from my hon. friend, Mr. Mahomed Ali Jinnah, although directed on the identical purpose. My hon. friend knows perfectly well that although, in form, it is an attack only on half, yet in substance, in effect, there is no difference in the amendment of my hon. friend, Mr. Jinnah, and the amendment of the Congress leaders."

The Government sustained a series of defeats in the Assembly when consideration of the Railway Budget came up for discussion. The Government policy in connection with the management of Indian Railways was exposed by the members from various points of view. Mr. Bhulabhai Desai, the Leader of the Opposition, moved a motion for the reduction of the Railway Board Grant to Re. 1.

In the course of his speech, Mr. Desai incidentally exposed the present policy of the Government which was, as he said, inspired by their Despatch in 1930. The reasons given there for such policy were, (a) rendering prompt and adequate service to Military authorities in times of political crisis, (b) safeguarding the enormous capital sunk in Indian Railways, (c) guaranteeing service of higher railway officers appointed by the Secretary of State, (d) to ensure future recruitment of Europeans on Military and other grounds, and (e) maintenance of the interests of the Anglo-Indian community in Railway Service. It was in pursuance of this policy that the proposed India Bill has made the Railways a subject of the Governor-General's special responsibilities.

Mr. Desai's motion was, as he pointed out in the course of the discussion, "not a token cut, but refusal of supplies." The motion was carried by 75 to 47 votes. In a free country, the adoption of the motion for refusal of supplies would have produced its inevitable effect on the Government. Other cut motions introduced in connection with the Railway Budget related to the Indianisation of the Railway services (passed by 81 votes against 44), greater facilities for 3rd class passengers, Railway policy, Wheatley Commission's recommendations on Labour, and reduction of freights for transport of agricultural produce.

The first meeting of the new Working Committee was held at Patna on the 5th, 6th and 7th of December, 1934. The Committee recorded its sorrow at the death of Syt. B. N. Sasmal who had passed away just on the day the result of his election to the Assembly was announced.

The Working Committee expressed itself on the Joint Parliamentary Committee Report and passed the following resolution :—

"Whereas the Congress has after full and earnest consideration resolved that the scheme of future Government of India adumbrated in the White Paper be rejected and that the only satisfactory alternative is a Constitution drawn up by a Constituent Assembly;

"And the said rejection and demand for a Constituent Assembly has been endorsed in a clear and unambiguous manner by the country at the recent general election to the Legislative Assembly;

"And whereas the proposals made in the Joint Parliamentary Committee Report are in several respects even worse than those contained in the White Paper and have been condemned by almost every shade of opinion in India as reactionary and unacceptable;

"And whereas the Joint Parliamentary Committee Scheme, designed as it is to facilitate and perpetuate the domination and exploitation of this country by alien people under a costly mask, is fraught with greater mischief and danger than even the present Constitution;

"This Committee is of opinion that the said Scheme should be rejected, well knowing that the rejection must involve the necessity of struggling under the present Constitution, humiliating and intolerable as it is, until it is replaced by one framed by a Constituent Assembly in accordance with the Congress resolution on the subject. This Committee requests the members of the Assembly to reject the Scheme of Government sought to be thrust upon India in the name of reform and appeals to the Nation to support the Congress in every step that it may decide upon to secure the national objective of Purna Swaraj."

The Working Committee after congratulating the country on the faith and confidence it had shown in the leadership of the Congress by its splendid response at the Assembly elections, asked Congress organisations and Congressmen to concentrate their attention for the next three months on (1) enrolment of Congress members and organisation of Congress Committees under the new Constitution, (2) collection of accurate and useful local data for village industries, and (3) education of the masses on the Fundamental Rights and duties and the economic programme as adopted by the Karachi Congress. The Committee deplored the action of the Government for the irritating and humiliating restrictions placed upon the liberty and movements of Syt. Subash Chandra Bose during his short sojourn in India at the time of his father's death. The Committee expressed its opinion that Congress members in the Legislatures should be habitual wearers of khaddar and requested them to adhere strictly to this rule. The Committee having been asked by the Nationalist Party of Bengal to reconsider the Congress attitude on the question of Communal Award, in view of the adverse verdict of the Hindu electorate in Bengal during the Assembly elections, the Committee recorded the opinion that the policy of the Congress being laid down by the resolution of the Bombay Congress, it could not alter it, particularly when it had been overwhelmingly endorsed by the country at large.

We may now profitably give a summary of the progress of events directly connected with the Congress in the year 1935—the fiftieth year of the Congress and the last year covered by this volume.

The Working Committee met again on 16th to 18th January, 1935, and it had to offer condolences to the families of Abhyankar of Nagpur and Acharya Gidwani. Both had suffered much and served the country nobly and long. The Purna Swaraj or Independence Day was observed this year as in previous years, and a particular resolution was prescribed for the whole of India. Here are the instructions and the resolution issued by the Working Committee:—

"As Civil Disobedience has been suspended by the Congress, the proceedings for the day should not be in breach of the Ordinances, or other laws or orders promulgated by local authority. Consistently with this precaution, silent processions should be taken to previously announced meeting places, and at the meetings the under-noted resolution worded in Hindustani or the local language should be read out by the Chairman and, without any speeches, passed by the audience standing. Where meetings are prohibited, every household should meet at the appointed time and pass the resolution and inform the nearest Congress Committee of having done so.

"At every meeting, or in every house, the passing of the resolution should be preceded by the unfurling of the National Flag.

"The resolution shall be as under:

'We remind ourselves on this, the solemn National Day, that Complete Independence is our birthright and we shall not rest till we have achieved it.

'To that end we shall strive to the utmost of our ability in thought, word and deed, to observe Truth and non-violence and shall consider no sacrifice or suffering too great to be undergone.

'As a token of the expression of the two essential qualities of Truth and non-violence, we shall seek to

(i) adopt and promote heart unity among different communities and to establish complete equality of status among all, irrespective of caste or creed or race;

(ii) to adopt and promote complete abstinence from intoxicating drink or drugs;

(iii) to promote hand-spinning and other village industries and to adopt for personal use khaddar and other products of village industries to the exclusion of other products;

(iv) to abolish untouchability;
(v) to serve the starving millions in every way we can; and,
(vi) to engage in all other national and constructive effort.'

"It is recommended that the National Day be devoted, in so far as it is possible, to some special constructive effort and a determination be made to develop greater dedication to the cause of Purna Swaraj.

"There should be no *hartal* observed."

The Jubilee celebrations connected with King George's reign naturally attracted special attention and was the subject of the following resolution :—

"Official announcement has been made that the Silver Jubilee of His Britannic Majesty's reign is to be celebrated in India. It is necessary for the Working Committee to guide the public as to the attitude to be adopted on the occasion.

"The Congress has and can have nothing but good wishes for the personal well-being of His Majesty, but the Congress cannot ignore the fact that the rule in India with which His Majesty is naturally identified has been a positive hindrance to the political, moral and material growth of the Nation. It now threatens to culminate in a Constitution which, if enforced, promises to exploit the Nation, to drain her of what she still possesses of wealth and to harden her political subjection as has perhaps never been attempted before.

"It is, therefore, impossible for the Working Committee to advise any participation in the forthcoming celebration. At the same time, the Working Committee has no desire, by hostile demonstrations, to wound the susceptibilities of Englishmen and others who will want to take part in the celebrations. The W. C., therefore, advises the general public, including Congressmen who may be members of elected bodies, to be satisfied with mere abstention from the events that may be arranged for celebration.

"The W. C. trusts that the authorities and responsible Englishmen will recognise and appreciate the honest and inevitable attitude of the W.C. and refrain from unnecessarily wounding national self-respect by compelling, directly or indirectly, participation in the forthcoming celebrations."

On the question of the Textile Mills the position was cleared:—

"As most of the textile mill-owners have broken their pledges given to the Congress, the W.C. is of opinion that it is no longer possible to continue the system of certification by the Congress or associated bodies, the old certificates issued should, therefore, be considered as cancelled.

"The W. C. is further of opinion that it is the duty of all Congressmen and those who sympathise with the Congress to confine their attention and give their support exclusively to the promotion of hand-spun and hand-woven cloth."

Under Article XII (d) (iii) of the amended Constitution, the W. C. framed disciplinary rules.

Doubts having been raised regarding the interpretation of 'Residential Qualifications' in the Congress Constitution, the same was made clear by a resolution of the Working Committee.

The Committee then discussed the problem of Burma under the Scheme of Reforms in the J.P.C. Report, and Burma as a Congress circle, and decided that the Burma Provincial Congress Committee should, for the time being, function as before.

With regard to the position of Indians in Burma under the new Scheme, the Committee was of opinion that as the whole Scheme was unacceptable and therefore no amendments could be suggested by the Congress, there was no bar to Burma Indians criticising parts of the Scheme which virtually affected their position and status.

The President was authorised to issue an appeal for funds for relieving the distress in the famine-stricken areas of Rayalaseema in Andhra.

Again the unity of command and action was demonstrated in the observance of an All-India Protest Day against the J.P.C. Report on the 7th February, 1935. In pursuance of an appeal in that behalf, meetings were held not merely in every town of any importance but also in distant nooks and corners of many Provinces, and the resolution suggested by the President was adopted at such meetings.

The demonstration held in Rangoon under the auspices of the Burma Provincial Congress Committee was also unique in the sense that Burmans and Indians came together on a common platform to press for the rejection of the Report.

We must now refer to the Unity Talks that took place in January and February, 1935.

Negotiations for an agreed settlement between the communities which could replace the so-called Communal Award, and which by minimising communal discord and bickerings could enable the country to present a united front, proceeded for more than a month between the Congress President, Babu Rajendra Prasad, and Mr. M. A. Jinnah, President of the All-India Muslim League. The talks started on January 23rd, and were continued with a short break upto 1st March, 1935, when they terminated without any tangible result, much to the disappointment of the country.

The policy of repression adopted by Government has received nothing but encouragement from the cessation of the Congress offensive. It is always a feature of despotic rule to take advantage of the enemy's passivity in order to wipe out traces of revolt. The universal condemnation of the J.P.C. Report and the Bill before Parliament which it gave birth to, only irritated the Government the more. In Calcutta, sedition prosecutions are being pursued. The Government of Bengal refused to allow the session of the All-India Trade Union Congress to be held in Calcutta. Police harassments of Congress workers in the peaceful pursuit of the Congress programme have become the subject of complaint from certain districts.

The year 1935 has not witnessed any change in the Government attitude or policy. The Congress has been looked upon with suspicion and as a potential enemy, and no opportunity has been lost of taking action against Congress workers even on the slightest pretext. Those suspected in connection with terrorist activities have continued to remain in detention either in jail or private residences, without trial, and their number in Bengal alone comes to 2,700. House searches have been held from time to time in various places and even offices of the A.I.C.C. and some of the P.C.C.'s like those of Bihar have not escaped attention. Khan Abdul Gaffar was sentenced to two years' imprisonment for a speech delivered in Bombay and Dr. Satyapal to a year's imprisonment for a speech in connection with the election campaign.

The detenus in Bengal are to be counted in thousands. Their families are left in a helpless condition. Government have detached from them the youngmen competent to maintain them. These youngmen have been interned or externed or detained for years without trial. The All-India Congress Committee, when it met at Jubbulpore on the 24th and 25 of April, passed a resolution expressing sympathy and decided to raise funds for the relief of the distress caused to the families and dependants of the detenus. The 19th of May was observed as a day of protest against the detention of large numbers of persons without trial by a court of law and for making collections, and the President sent a public appeal to the country in this behalf. The Bengal Government met this move on the part of the Congress by an order issued under Sec. 2-A. of the Indian Press (Emergency Powers) Act by which they prohibited absolutely the publication of any information connected with the observance of the Detenu Day throughout India in accordance with instructions issued by the President of the Congress. This evoked a protest from the journalists of Bengal who suspended the publication of their journals for a day on that account.

The All-India Congress Committee met at Jubbulpore on the 24th and 25th of April, passed a resolution Congress Parliamentary Board and an Election Dispute Panel, and appointed auditors. It expressed its condolence at the death of Mr. T. A. K. Sherwani. It expressed its satisfaction at the work of the Congress Party in the Assembly and drew the attention of the country to the continuance of the ban on Congress organisations in the N.W.F. Province and all Congress Committees in Midnapore district in Bengal, and on affiliated and allied bodies like the Khudai Khidmatgars, the Hindustan Seva Dal in Bengal, Gujarat and elsewhere, to the suppression of Labour and Youth League organisations in Bengal, the Bombay Presidency, the Punjab and elsewhere on the plea of alleged tendencies without reference to any overt acts and to organisation; and appealed to the people at large to increase the strength of the Congress organisation as a means of liberation.

The Committee noted the flagrant abuse of the ancient piece of legislation called the Foreigners' Act and the externment of Congressmen from British India under the said Act, thus depriving them of the opportunity of legitimate residence and carrying on their business in British India.

The Committee strongly condemned the continued repression in Bengal and the detention and internment of a large number of youths, depriving their families of their support and without themselves making any arrangement for the maintenance of these suffering families. It recorded its opinion that the Bengal Government should either discharge the detenus or give them a fair trial. It assured the people of Bengal and the detenus of its full sympathy in their affliction. It also called upon the Bengal Provincial Congress Committee to submit to the Working Committee a list of detenus with full particulars about the period of detention and financial condition of the families. It also resolved to start an All-India Fund for the relief of detenus' families, under the control of its Working Committee.

The Committee deplored the horrible acts of mob violence at Ferozabad culminating in the burning alive of the whole family of Doctor Jivaram, including children and patients, and drew the attention of leaders to the deplorable results to which frenzied communalism can go and appealed for effective steps to impress upon the public at large the need for living together in peace and friendship, with mutual good understanding and respect. The Committee laid down that the interests of the people of the Indian States are as much the concern of the Indian National Congress as those of the people of British India, and assured the States' people of its full support in the struggle for freedom.

The Working Committee, which met at the same time at Jubbulpore, fixed the maximum number of delegates returnable by each Province under the new Constitution and prepared a time-table for the various steps to be taken for the organisation of Congress Committees and election of delegates to the next Congress and members of the A.I.C.C. It dealt with certain election disputes in Provinces and provided for the representation of the N.W.F.P. and the District of Midnapore in Bengal in the Congress and the A.I.C.C., inasmuch as Congress organisations being under ban in those places no election could take place.

Hardly had 18 months elapsed since, on January 15th, 1934, the Bihar earthquake convulsed the country, when on the 31st of May, 1935, the earthquake at Quetta cast a shadow of gloom all over the land. That the initiative for relief should have been taken by Government is natural in view of the city being a Military centre, but that orders should be issued prohibiting outsiders from entering Quetta to give relief or organise aid, passes all understanding. Neither the Congress President nor Gandhi has been given permission to go to the place. Under the circumstances all organisation of help could be made only on the outskirts of the prohibited zone. The President of the Congress organised a Quetta Central Relief Committee which, with branches in Sindh, the Punjab and the N.W.F.P., has been giving relief to sufferers who have been sent to these Provinces from Quetta. June 30th was observed as a day for showing sympathy to sufferers and for prayers for the dead. The policy of Government in this regard is but the crowning piece of a policy of suspicion and distrust and has obliged the Working Committee to pass the following resolution on Quetta relief on 1-8-'35:—

> "The Working Committee records its sense of deep sorrow at the loss sustained in men and money by thousands of people during the recent earthquake in Quetta and other parts of Baluchistan and tenders its condolences and sympathy to the bereaved and the sufferers.
>
> "The Working Committee endorses the action taken by the President in forming a Central Relief Committee for collecting funds and administering relief. The Committee thanks all those who rendered valuable aid through personal care to thousands of the injured and distressed under very difficult circumstances and acknowledges the response of the public to appeals for funds.
>
> "The Working Committee, while recognising the efforts made by the authorities at Quetta to meet the situation with the resources at their disposal, is of opinion based on the published statements of eye-witnesses, official and non-official, that many persons under the debris could have been rescued if the digging operations had been undertaken on an adequate scale and not stopped after two days, and if the offered help from the public had not been rejected.
>
> "The Working Committee is of opinion that the Government should appoint a commission composed of officials and non-officials to enquire into the allegations made by the public and, in some respects, supported by published statements of officials, *viz.*,
>
> 1. that the statement made on behalf of the Government when assitance was offered, that they had ample resources to deal with the situation in Quetta, does not appear to be borne out by facts;

2. that they unjustifiably turned away such proffered assistance;
3. that they ought to have recruited available assistance from neighbouring areas to cope properly with the emergency;
4. that whilst every European resident of the affected area was accounted for, no adequate attempt was made in respect of the Indian residents and there was similar discrimination between Indians and Europeans in the matter of rescue, relief and salvage."

Another problem that agitated Congressmen, notably those in the Assembly and those who were keen on Council-entry, in the middle of 1935 relates to the question of acceptance of office under the new Constitution. It was somewhat unfortunate that this talk should have been started in the country while yet the Bill was before Parliament; nor can we ignore the fact that the attitude expressed in India by this wing of Congressmen was taken full advantage of by those in charge of the Bill, to assure Parliament that there were men who would work the new Reforms. The attitude of the Congress itself was definitely declared in the Congress resolution of Bombay (1934), and no one is competent to deal with this question before the next Congress sits. Accordingly, the Working Committee passed the following resolution at the end of July at Wardha, referring the question to the plenary session of the Congress:—

"Having read the resolution of several Congress Committees relating to the acceptance or non-acceptance of office under the new Constitution, this Committee is of opinion that any decision on the question would be premature at this stage and should be left over for the next session of the Congress. It declares that any expression of opinion on the question by individual Congressmen does not represent the view of the Congress."

The Indian States Peoples' Organisation was, in the course of the early part of the year, somewhat agitated over the opinion of Mr. Bhulabhai Desai, the leader of the Parliamentary Board, which he had tendered in his professional capacity to the Princes of India in relation to the question of Federation under the Government of India Bill, while yet the Bill was before the Commons, and a speech which he had delivered at Mysore. In the month of July, there was a demand for a meeting of the A.I.C.C. to consider the attitude of the Congress towards the rights of the people of the Indian States who base their demand on the following utterance of Gandhi at the second Round Table Conference:—

> "The Congress is not going to be satisfied with any Constitution which does not provide for the fundamental rights of citizenship for the States' people, with a right of representation on the Federal Legislature."

The Working Committee at its meeting held at Wardha on the 29th, 30th and 31st July, 1935, passed a resolution on the subject, embodying its considered opinion on the subject which was as follows:—

> "Although the policy of the Congress regarding the States in India has been defined in its resolutions, a persistent effort is being made by or on behalf of the people of the States to get a fuller declaration of the Congress policy. The Working Committee therefore issues the following statement concerning the policy of the Congress with regard to the Princes and the people of the States:
>
> "The Indian National Congress recognises that the people in the Indian States have an inherent right to Swaraj no less than the people of British India. It has accordingly declared itself in favour of the establishment of representative Responsible Government in the States and has in that behalf

not only appealed to the Princes to establish such Responsible Government in their States and to guarantee fundamental rights of citizenship, like freedom of person, speech, association and the Press to their people, but has also pledged to the States' people its sympathy and support in their legitimate and peaceful struggle for the attainment of full Responsible Government. By that declaration and by that pledge, the Congress stands. The Congress feels that even in their own interests the Princes will be well advised to establish at the earliest possible moment full Responsible Government within their States, carrying a guarantee of full rights of citizenship to their people.

"It should be understood, however, that the responsibility and the burden of carrying on that struggle within the States must necessarily fall on the States' people themselves. The Congress can exercise moral and friendly influence upon the States, and this it is bound to do wherever possible. The Congress has not other power under existing circumstances, although the people of India, whether under the British, the Princes or any other power, are geographically and historically one and indivisible.

"In the heat of controversy, the limitation of the Congress is often forgotten. Indeed, any other policy will defeat the common purpose.

"With regard to the impending constitutional changes, it has been suggested that the Congress should insist upon certain amendments of that portion of the Government of India Bill which deals with the relation of the Indian States to the Indian Federation. The Congress has more than once categorically rejected the entire Scheme of Constitutional Reforms on the broad ground of its not being an expression of the will of the people of India and has insisted on a Constitution to be framed by a Constituent Assembly. It may not now ask for an amendment of the Scheme in any particular part. To do so would amount to a reversal of the Congress policy.

"At the same time, it is hardly necessary to assure the people of the States that the Congress will never be guilty of sacrificing their interests in order to buy the support of the Princes. From its inception, the Congress has stood unequivocally for the rights of the masses of India as against the vested rights in conflict with their true interest."

Finally it was resolved that the fiftieth anniversary of the Congress be observed in a fitting manner on the day the Congress met for the first time in 1885, and for this purpose the Working Committee appointed a Sub-Committee to draw up a programme for the occasion.

The short interval between the Wardha meeting and the close of the year was more or less uneventful, except for the sudden release of Jawaharlal Nehru from the Almora Jail,—on account of the grave state of his wife's health on the 3rd September. He was straightway to leave for Europe and should he return to India before the term of his imprisonment expired, he would, as orders stood, have to return to prison.

The only other event of any importance or interest was the sitting of the A.I.C.C. in Madras on the 17th and 18th of October, 1935. There was a rich promise of a reinforced attack on the questions of 'office acceptance' and 'the Congress and the States' which was expected to be made at the meeting. The A.I.C.C., it may be said, met for the first time in the city of Madras, if we leave out of account the sittings of the body directly associated with a session of the Congress. It was, however, agreed in Madras that the statement of the Working Committee on the question of the States and the Congress be approved, and, on the question of acceptance of office, the A.I.C.C. thought that, considering the long interval that would elapse before the provincial elections under the new Constitution would take place, as well as the uncertain character of the political conditions in the interval, it would be not only premature, but inadvisable and impolitic to commit the Congress to any decision on the subject.

One minor but important point may be noted, in connection with the sitting of the A.I.C.C. in Madras. The Bengal members of the A.I.C.C. were informed that they would not be allowed to sit at the meeting as the Bengal P.C.C. had not paid in full its contribution of Rs. 500 to the A.I.C.C. A notice was also served by the Working Committee on the Executive of the B.P.C.C. to show cause why disciplinary action should not be taken against it for having deliberately defied the instructions of the Working Committee in the matter of the recognition of the Calcutta Central District Congress Committee.

In closing, we may just mention the fact that the Government of India Act was passed by Parliament and received the Royal assent on July 2nd, 1935. We have no wish to burden this volume with any criticism of the Act. Only, we feel tempted to quote a short extract from the speech of a member of the House of Commons with which the debates virtually terminated. On the 5th of June, 1935, Major Milner, speaking on the India Bill, compared Mr. Churchill and Sir Samuel Hoare to the villain and the hero of a play. The hero (Sir S. Hoare), said he, had beaten the villain. "He will doubtless finally dispose of him to-day (5-6-'35) without any loss of blood." "Then," declared Major Milner, "the two protagonists will be found to leave the stage-door arm in arm." Verily, this is the drama enacted in Parliament not only in 1935, but in 1920 as well. While it is broadly true that there is an ultra-conservative section in the English Parliament which in popular parlance is known as the 'die-hard' party, the fact remains that ultimately the object of all the parties is the same, namely, to evolve a picture which, as the *Manchester Guardian* once urged, looks like Swaraj to India and like British Raj to England. For this purpose, the different parties stage a quarrel on the floor of the Houses of Parliament, some appearing inclined to give, others appearing to resist, and the former prevailing upon the moderate elements in India to accept whatever is possible of being given under the circumstances, as the latter would not allow them to go even thus far. The party in power plays the part of the hero, and the party in opposition plays the part of the villain. The two stage a quarrel within the walls of Westminster, and once they leave the arena they congratulate each other on the magnificent, realistic turn given to their feigned differences. Between the two, India is befooled.

Before this chapter closes, let us say a word regarding the growing sense of responsibility that is being evinced by the Presidents of the Congress from year to year. Mrs. Besant had emphasised the conception of her being the President of the Congress throughout the year. Ever since, this high precedent has received full support at the hands of her numerous successors. Except for one or two Presidents who simply disappeared from public view soon after the spectacular sittings of the Congress were concluded, the rest have taken to their duties with a real zest and a high sense of responsibility. Following this noble precedent, Babu Rajendra Prasad, whose health is below par but whose energies and capacity for endurance, however, vary inversely as the square of his health, has had a whirlwind tour round the country, and in this respect has taken a new step altogether in order to keep himself in direct touch with the men and the movements in the country. His hands are already full with work relating to the Bihar Earthquake Relief. On the top of it, he has heavy duties as President of the Congress, duties of a routine character, and the earthquake in Quetta has further added to the weight of those duties. It is remarkable that in the midst of such pressing engagements he should have toured Maharashtra, Karnatak, Berar, the Punjab, part of C.P., Tamil Nadu, Andhra and Kerala. He is, in addition, connected with the A.I.S.A. and his 'no-change' proclivities have in no way lessened his interest or participation in the activities of the election campaign. The absence of Gandhi from the political arena has augmented the burdens on his shoulders, for, so long as Gandhi was there, it is an open secret that Congress was sitting lightly upon the shoulders of his colleagues. Not that they ever evaded their responsibilities, but that an overshadowing personality like Gandhi's would leave to his colleagues little share in the arduous tasks that public life demands. Thus has the Presidentship of the Congress become a throne of power burdened with heavy cares and responsibilities. Shall we not go one step further and say that the Congress has become a parallel organisation in the country to that of Government, with its own ideals which are repressed by Government, with its schemes of uplift for the villages which are sought to be outstripped by those of Government, with its own philosophy of Truth and non-violence which are discredited and reviled by a Government wedded to physical force? The Congress has worked for fifty years and been acclaimed a great success. Some say it has proved a failure. Success or failure, Satyagraha is a new force introduced into Congress politics. It is yet on its trial, but has been sufficiently long at work to be able to arrest public attention. This change of ideals, this alteration of methods and means, has been brought about by the initiative of one man who, though born and educated in

India, was in the formative period of his life an exile from the country, living in South Africa and making his strange 'Experiments with Truth' in a strange land. People ask whether the Congress is not a failure, whether Satyagraha is not weighed and found wanting, and finally whether Gandhi is not played out. We shall conclude this volume with an answer to each of these questions.

CHAPTER IV

CONCLUSION

I

We have rapidly reviewed the progress of events during the past fifty years and dealt with the latter half of the period in somewhat greater detail than the former half. During this long course of years, various eminent men have been called upon to lead the Nation. Dadabhai Naoroji presided over the Congress thrice and introduced the term *Swaraj* into Congress phraseology. W. C. Bonnerjee, the first President, presided a second time; Surendra Nath Banerjea—the 'Trumpet voice of India'—enjoyed the honour twice, and so did the white-robed Pandit Madan Mohan Malaviya as well as Pandit Motilal Nehru and Sir William Wedderburn. The Mussalmans contributed eight Presidents out of fifty-one—Tyabji, Sayani, Nawab Syed Mahomed Bahadur, Hasan Imam, Abul Kalam Azad, Hakim Ajmal Khan, Mahomed Ali and Dr. Ansari. Dadabhai Naoroji, Sir Pherozeshah Mehta and Wacha came as the representatives of that noble community—the Parsees—who have enriched India's Vedic and Islamic cultures by the confluence with them of their own culture,—the culture of Zend Avesta. Bengal stands foremost in having contributed men like W. C. Bonnerjee, Ananda Mohan Bose, Ramesh Chandra Dutt, Lal Mohan Ghose, Bhupendra Nath Basu, Sir S.P. Sinha, Ambika Charan Mazumdar, Rash Behari Ghosh and C.R. Das. To U.P. belong Bishan Narayan Dhar, Malaviya, Motilalji and his son Jawaharlal. The last of the Presidents, Rajendra Babu, comes from Bihar, which had earlier given Hasan Imam. The Punjab had the honor of giving Lala Lajpat Rai, and C. P.,

Mudholkar. From Gujarat came Gandhi and Vallabhbhai Patel. The crop from Bombay was abundant. Tyabji and Sayani have already been referred to, as also Mehta. Wacha, Gokhale and Chandavarkar complete the list from the western Province. From Madras came Ananda Charlu, an Andhra, then Sir C. Sankaran Nair, a Kerala-putra, and finally the Grand Old Man of the South—Mr. C. Vijiyaraghavachari who, along with Mr. S. Srinivasa Iyengar, hails from Tamil Nadu. Two ladies, Mrs. Besant and Mrs. Sarojini Naidu, have graced the Presidential throne. The European community had its own turn through Messrs. Yule, Webb, Wedderburn and Cotton. This varied list shows how the Congress is not merely a national but truly an international body.[1]

Let us now revert to the questions which we have set ourselves at the end of the last chapter—Is Congress a failure? Few will gainsay the fact that the past decade has witnessed the steady rise of new concepts controlling the time-honoured ideas of politics and culture. The domain of politics itself which is, broadly, the science of human well-being has been extended not only in India but all the world over so as to embrace a study and solution of the larger problems of a socio-economic character. And when to these we superadd ideas of culture and morality, we have elevated politics from the vulgar levels of the nineteenth century to the healthy and ethical standards to which India has been introduced during the past fifteen or sixteen years; and this has been done under the guidance of a world character, M. K. Gandhi, whose invulnerability is appropriately

[1] The Addresses of these distinguished Presidents fill over 2,000 printed pages and have been published by Messrs. G. A. Natesan & Co., Madras, in two volumes. The gratitude of the public is due to this enterprising and patriotic firm—forerunners in the field of national literature--for this act of additional service to Indian Nationalism, done in the 'Jubilee' year of the Congress.

and tersely described by Prof. Gilbert Murray in the following words:—

> "Be careful in dealing with a man who cares nothing for sensual pleasures, nothing for comfort or praise or promotion, but is simply determined to do what he believes to be right. He is a dangerous and uncomfortable enemy, because his body which you can always conquer, gives you so little purchase over his soul."

It is under the guidance of such a teacher that Congress has sought to impress politics with the ideal of service, emphasised the need for a wider culture and a higher patriotism amongst the classes and laboured for establishing village leadership. Congress has in fact founded a new religion—the religion of politics. We cannot, without being false to our creed, regard any great human issue as outside the sphere of religion. For religion stands not for any particular dogma or method of worship but for a higher life, a spirit of sacrifice, and a scheme of self-dedication. And when we speak of the Religion of Politics we merely make the sordid politics of the day sacred, the compartmental politics of the day comprehensive, the competitive politics of the day co-operative.

It is in this attitude and frame of mind that we have pleaded for Truth and Legitimacy as the cardinal factors in the upbuilding of Indian Nationalism. Untruth has always gained earlier and cheaper victories in life, dissimulation and duplicity have often triumphed easily over reason and rectitude. Yea, law and logic have scored over life itself in the past. But these victories and triumphs are as partial as they are fleeting, and have only betrayed the victors into unenviable positions. On a larger scale, the triumphs of the Great War have brought no success to the victors over the vanquished. On a smaller scale, the conquest, so-called, of England over India has brought no lasting happiness to the former as against the latter. The policy underlying the conduct of statesmen in organising the various Round Table Conferences has not ensured for ever India as the out-house of England. Every wave of repression has only reacted against the interests of the repressors and engendered a spirit of resistance, now manifesting itself as Civil Disobedience and now taking sterner and fiercer forms at the hands of the rising generation. To say that we have failed in our programme of Non-co-operation is but to read the wish for the thought, for in the long last, every failure is only seemingly such and is in reality but a step to success. Success itself is but the last phase of a series of failures.

It is thus that we judge the programme of the Congress. That programme is of a two-fold character. On the aggressive side, it has given battle to Government in a manner which no civilized Government dare condemn. Non-violence, in thought, word and deed, has been the key-note of that fight and Gandhi has been acknowledged the Chief Constable of India. Government may have affected to abominate his cult of Satyagraha but who can condemn the hold of Truth and of non-violence on the affections of the people? In an age when Royal families have been annihilated and monarchies have been upset and democratic constitutions have given way, in an age, too, when the bi-party or the tri-party system of old has disappeared from politics and the rise of opposition is subdued not by defeating the opponent at the polls but by annihilating the party literally, to speak of non-violence may sound a mockery. Our recent experiences have furnished a fit and timely warning to us that the victories won through bloodshed are only maintained through bloodshed and lost through more of it, and that, when once force has become installed as the arbiter between two nations, it tends to butt in between any two communities and, for the matter of that, between any two individuals on all possible occasions.

On the constructive side, the programme of the Congress has been simple,—incredibly so. We must admit it may not have appealed to the sophisticated classes of the country, who live in towns and cities, wear foreign cloth, speak a foreign tongue and serve a foreign master. A census of our towns would be a study in itself, revealing the surprising fact that almost every alternate man is dependent for his living, for his prosperity and for his fame, upon the good-will of the foreign rulers. These facts are not discerned readily, for we do not know who our masters really are. But we know that they range from the constable to the Excise Inspector, the Bank Agent and the English tailor. The P. W. D. lascar, the Revenue Collector, the Bench Magistrate and the Bill discounter are all the unpaid representatives of the British Empire Ltd., whose Local Board of Directors is the Government of India with sub-offices in the various Provinces. The British Government is entrenched behind the seven *prakarams* of the Army, the Police and the Services, the Courts, the Councils, the Colleges, the Local Bodies and the titled aristocracy. The eighty per cent. of rural population in the country lives in fear of the Revenue authorities and the balance of urban population in fear of the Municipalities, Local Boards, Income-tax officers, Excise authorities and the Police.

It has, therefore, become supremely important to cast off fear resulting from a recognition of force, and plant, in its stead, hope and courage that spring from a genuine love of non-violence. The constructive programme has, therefore, taken on hand activities typical of three respective classes which bring Congressmen engaged in them into close touch with the masses. When, therefore, we speak of khaddar, we not only help the poor to find a subsidiary occupation or even a living wage, but give them an opportunity of cultivating self-respect by throwing off the symbol of slavery that is on their backs. We conserve the sacredness of the home and give the craftsman that creative joy through the exercise of his craft which forms the true index of civilization. When people are asked to pay a bit more for khaddar, we teach them to give a voluntary bounty to a national industry which it is the legitimate duty of the State really to provide, but which it would not. Above all, we teach simplicity to our people and with simplicity of living come sublimity of thought, ideas of self-respect, self-sufficiency, self-reliance and self-realization. What we have sought to achieve on the economic plane through khaddar, we strive to attain on the moral plane through prohibition, and, on the social, through the removal of untouchability. There must be something unspeakably low, not to say worse, in a State objecting to the organisation of prohibition amongst its citizens. The problem is far too simple to need any discussion. The Nation is mainly composed of the two great communities —Hindu and Muslim—both of whom base their religious teachings on the prohibition of drink. The temperance movement in the country has worked on this basis; yet, when the Nation is serious and constructs this moral plank in its political platform and organizes it by picketing, Government comes down on the Congress like a wolf on the fold.

We have not fared better when we add a social plank to this platform in the removal of untouchability.

The Premier's decision had "rent asunder those whom God hath united" by carving out the Harijans into a separate electorate. Only the fast unto death of the great leader of India has made an amendment possible of that undesirable document and has established a broad unity in the Hindu community, though with some internal compartmentalism still lingering. And when we have sought to remove the prevailing bar to the entry of the Harijans into temples, even when a plebiscite has strengthened the hands of their trustees, Government have interposed their irresistible opposition to a progressive measure which is but permissive, and nipped it in the bud.

The problem that the country has to face is one of supreme complexity,—with a Government that would divide and rule, with towns and cities arrayed against villages, with the classes having interests conflicting with those of the masses, with an unholy opposition organised against elementary reforms, with an embargo upon khaddar, with obstruction to communal equality, and with resistance to the fostering of moral virtues. These have made it abundantly clear that Swaraj cannot be won, if at all, only through the votaries of English education, the followers of the learned professions and the captains of trade or industrial magnates. New values have had to be evolved. The power of the Nation has had to be developed through the development of a sense of national consciousness in the masses living in the villages, and their confidence secured not by a mere delivery of lectures or by contributions to the Press but by a day-to-day service rendered to the people at large. Once this confidence is secured, the programme set forth by the Congress for the emancipation of the Nation will be readily followed. Swaraj may not by this process readily fall into our hands like a ripe apple, but it will soon be evident that every act of service rendered to the people is a stone, well and truly laid, in the foundations of Swaraj, and every disability removed from society in its socio-economic structure is a storey raised in building the edifice of Swaraj. The process is doubtless slow, but the results are certain and abiding. Thus has the Congress taken its message to the villages and established what we have described as village leadership.

II

We must now say a word upon the new technique that has been brought into play in order to work out the programme of the Congress. We are as yet in the rudimentary stage of its evolution, and to study a movement while yet it is imperfect or even inchoate is perhaps as difficult and delicate a task as one may be called upon to discharge; the more so for ardent votaries thereof, who believe in its mighty potentialities and have become, therefore, the butt of ridicule by its opponents and the object of hatred by its enemies. All great movements have passed through similar stages. They are always interpreted—be it purposely or inadvertently—as the equivalent of their counterfeits, at best as but the variants of the cruder forms in which perhaps they had their beginnings. It is as if a diamond is studied as carbon with which it is chemically identical and of which it is the isomer; Satyagraha is likewise equated to mere Passive Resistance. But the two movements are substantially different, even as the scintillations of the gem in the jewel differ from the dark element of the chemist in the laboratory. Nay more, Passive Resistance and Satyagraha exhibit diametrically opposite qualities. Yet one need not be surprised that Satyagraha, though it was not initiated consciously by its founder as a kind of Passive Resistance, had been preceded earlier by some such manifestation a short time before Gandhi came into the movement, and people understood it as such. It was while Mrs. Besant was interned in 1917 that the Congress threatened Passive Resistance, but with her release, it aborted. And when Gandhi came on the scene and inaugurated a campaign of Satyagraha, first outside the Congress against the Rowlatt Acts, and next inside the Congress against the Khilaphat wrong and the Punjab tragedy, most of the Congressmen and the public understood it merely as a revival of the aborted movement contemplated earlier.

Recent political developments have ultimately evolved a movement which in its earlier manifestations had, from time to time, assumed different aspects under different names. As *Passive Resistance,* it was a movement of bitterness and pride which had perhaps even a tinge in it of hatred and violence. As *Non-co-operation,* it was an attitude of a sulky and sullen people, angry with their rulers and anxious to wound but unwilling to strike. When it was *Civil Disobedience,* it took time to emphasise the adjective equally with the noun. On the whole the idea of civility, little understood at first, gradually gained ground and paved the way for the next development of the idea to the level of *Satyagraha.* Ere long, we saw that the basis of Satyagraha was nothing short of love and non-violence. Non-violence was not merely to be a negative factor, but a positive force and was equivalent to "that love which does not burn others, but burns itself to death." When, on the basis of such a definition and demand, we discovered by the Bardoli resile in February, 1922, that one Chauri Chaura was enough to punish the whole country instead of isolating and penalizing the local District of Gorakhpur in U. P., we discovered too how Satyagraha was not merely a physical but a truly moral and spiritual force which is exacting in its demands, and which in its nature is active, aggressive and dynamic. It has taken long for people to see correctness of the position that, if the massacre of Jallianwala-bagh perpetrated by General Dyer could inaugurate a nation-wide movement like Satyagraha by the people, the massacre at Chauri Chaura perpetrated by the people must terminate that Satyagraha. Satyagraha is really a compendium of all the virtues known to man, for Truth is the main-spring of such virtues, and non-violence or love is its envelope. The country was thus plunged into a world of new values in which hatred and abhorrence, fear and cowardice, anger and vengeance were at once to yield place to love, courage, patience, self-suffering and chastity; in which, too, wealth is to yield place to service, and in which the enemy is not to be conquered but converted. We are taught that all fear revolves round ourselves as the centre, and when once we cast off fear and selfishness, we are able to welcome death itself. Every Satyagrahi is a seeker after Truth and must, therefore, give up the fear of man, of Government, of society, of poverty and of death. Non-co-operation as a discipline, as a *Sadhana* to achieve our ends, has, therefore, become a means of training in self-sacrifice pursued in that true spirit of humility which alone begets courage and not in that spirit of pride which generates fear. Thus, in a bound, has the author of the movement sublimated and spiritualised the sordid politics of the day.

Let us study the implications of the movement a little further. It furnishes a real key to an understanding of the basis of Indian society. That basis which is epitomised in the simple *Sutra, Ahimsa Paramodharmah* and in the simple prayer, *lokah samastah sukhino bhavantu,* is a positive force which is not only self-effacing but enjoins on every one to love those that hate us, in the true spirit of the Sermon on the Mount. To do good unto him that doth you good is at best a business proposition. To be non-violent to a person who is loving and kind-hearted is to claim virtue for not being brutal or diabolical. Satyagraha is not meant to overpower Vasishta or Janaka, and when people ask in despair how non-violence can fight the physical force of the British, we ask whether Satyagraha would not be superfluous and thrown out of fight if the opponents were saints. It is our old, old concepts and values that drive us to this kind of despair. The teaching of the West that life is a survival of the fittest in which the weaker must go to the wall, has made such deep impression upon us that it has only inflamed our passions and made us imbibe the vices of pride and its accompaniments which but engender cowardice and violence.

Indian society is based upon the cult of Satyagraha which does not ask us to abandon the world, but infuses in us the spirit of renunciation. Once we adhere to Truth and repress our passions and purify ourselves, a love of service and a spirit of humility will naturally follow. Once we subdue anger and practice forgiveness, non-violence will be enthroned as the only arbiter in human relations.

How shall we attain this end, by what disciplines shall we cultivate those qualities and virtues which are compendiously termed, 'Satyagraha'? The only means is *tapas*, by which is implied *Satya* and *sowcha, dana* and *dharma, dama* and *yama, kshama* and *daya*. To indulge the flesh is to give us over to our passions which, under the sway of pride and anger, commit us to the cult of violence and vengeance. It also promotes selfishness, with its love of wealth and pomp, and the untruthful way by which these are secured. What is wanted is a spirit of contentment, which does not mean that asceticism which abandons society, but that austerity which moderates one's wants and subdues one's passions. The new teaching liberates a volume of moral energy by which to revivify the land which has been enervated by vain philosophical teachings. It imposes on us the duty of seeking intercourse with our enemy, while withholding co-operation from him except on conditions that would ensure self-respect. It exhorts everybody to do his quota of labour as a daily sacrament and help the poor earn their food and raiment. To these ends, it is necessary for the mind to control the body, and the spirit to direct the body and the mind, so that the flesh craves for nothing which the intellect condemns and thought does not dwell upon aught that emotion forbids. What can be a better guide or means for the attainment of these ends than abstinence, which in relation to food and flesh is *fasting,* which in relation to thought and speech is *silence,* and which in relation to passions and emotions is *celibacy*?

When, therefore, people revile the tortures of the flesh that *fasting* to them means, when they jibe at that *mauna* (silence) which to them is a mere mockery, and when they talk with levity about that *Brahmacharya* which to them is simply impossible, they but indulge in that variety of criticism bordering on ridicule, which has been the inevitable lot of all progressive movements in the early period of their development. But all progressive movements have survived such cavil and abuse and regenerated the ideals of rising generations. Even so has public life in India been chastened and purified during the past 15 years.

When all is said, there is still an element of doubt in the potency or appropriateness of non-violence as a factor in the settlement of political disputes. The one argument against those to whom doubt occurs naturally is, that circumstanced as we are, non-violence, while it is unassailable as a principle in life, is unquestionable and unquestioned as a policy. The task of infusing life into a large mass of subject people like the Indians would be impossible, were it not for the avowal of, and adherence to, the principle of non-violence. People there are who would argue that non-violent Non-co-operation has failed, but no one has undertaken to bring success in one bound, notably when the mass of the population has been slow in taking to the new movement. Non-violence is the only abiding principle which can bring peace and contentment to two opposing parties, for, when once violence is installed on the throne of arbitrament, it is a weapon that can be used, as has already been pointed out, alike by the victor and the vanquished, leaving no end to *vendetta* and making life move eternally in a vicious circle.

III

What, then, is the secret of this abiding influence of Gandhi over millions of men, women and children? He was born into an age when there is not merely political commotion but political chaos. "It would seem to be the will of God," as Lowell puts it, "that from time to time the manhood of nations like that of individuals should be tried by great dangers or great opportunities. If the manhood be there, it makes the great opportunity out of the great danger; if it be not there, then the great danger out of the great opportunity." It was thus that Gandhi had made his great opportunity out of great danger and had inaugurated a new revolution, not indeed a sanguinary one, but one that invites suffering instead of inflicting it, and seeks to convert the enemy, not to conquer him. He has preached from housetops the right, yea, the duty of a civil rebellion, while recognizing equally the right of governments to hang men for it. He has set before himself not merely the immediate object of abolishing slavery in India, but the utter extirpation of all dogmas which seek to justify it in any shape,—physical, political, or economic,—in the wide world. He has shown that subjection and slavery are a moral wrong, a political blunder and a practical misfortune. To this end, he has all along addressed the intelligence of men, never their prejudice, or passion,—their sense of right, never their selfishness or ignorance. To him a moral wrong can never be local in its effects, and principles alien to Truth and non-violence can never result in peace or prosperity to a Nation.

Now let us see how the high-sounding principles elaborated in these pages have operated in their application to our day-to-day politics. For the first time we saw this principle brought into play at the Amritsar Congress in the year 1919, when Gandhi insisted upon the Congress condemning the violence of the people in killing four Englishmen and burning the National Bank and other buildings. The Subjects Committee of the Congress threw out the proposition late at night and Gandhi declared that he would have to leave the Congress. That was not really a threat, as the term is popularly understood, but an indication of an attitude which was inevitable according to his principles, and the proposition was accepted, though grudgingly, by the Subjects Committee the next day. It was then that Gandhi began to din into the ears of the Congress what non-violence really meant. The Congress, to which Swaraj meant the driving out of the English, was told that Englishmen were and would be welcome as fellow-citizens in India, and not a hair on the foreigner's head should be touched. Lo and behold! the test for the Nation came and the Nation was found wanting at Chauri Chaura. But the Congress did not despair. When the movement was withdrawn, loud protests came from influential quarters. But Gandhi was adamant. The Satyagrahi does not fear foes or friends or even colleagues. He fears Truth. Gandhi had, therefore, virtually suspended the movement for a period of six years. The later developments and happenings are well known and bear testimony to the potency of Satyagraha. Though they sound like the events of a fabled past, like the quick-moving scenes of a day-dream. yet they are but translation into practice of the sublime teachings of Satyagraha applied to life as a composite whole.

A graph of our progress during the past fifty years shows its own rises and falls. More correctly may the progress be described as a spiral. We are repeatedly coming upon the same programme,—of Swadeshi, Boycott, National Education and Swaraj of 1906. It was reiterated in 1917, but at a higher level—the level of Passive Resistance; the same was repeated in 1919-21,—on the still higher level of Civil Disobedience. Then we had the movement of 1930-34, on a yet higher level of Satyagraha. The course of ascent is like that of a hill railway where you clear the curves, and, as you pass higher and higher, you come upon the lower curves of the spiral until you attain your height. The course covered comprises a hard drive up-hill and an easy drive down-hill. Satyagraha representing a period of strenuous struggle, and Council entry, equally a struggle though less strenuous, adopted during the intervals of fight, have alternated with each other. The spiral is doubtless running its long-winded course and we have yet to attain to the height of our ascent—Swaraj.

But if Swaraj is a process, not a result, an attempt, not an attainment, a direction, not a destiny, to use language analogous to Lord Irwin's adopted by him before the truce of 1931 was concluded, then no one can ask the architect who is still ramming the concrete of foundations, why the edifice is not ready. The foundations and basement of even a brick-and-mortar building are built, and left to settle for a year or two. How much longer may the foundations of Swaraj not rest there to get consolidated, in order that they may bear the weight of the edifice to be raised on them!

We have described how all these years we have struggled on. But our remedy is clear. Let us make the home the centre of craft life, and the village the centre of Indian Nationalism, and let us make both as far as possible self-contained and self-contented. Let us carve out our Nation with equality as the base and liberty as the summit and fraternity as the cementing factor; not indeed that equality which is disrupting and fissiparous, nor indeed that other equality which is all vegetation on a level, a society of big spears of grass and small oaks, a neighbourhood of jealousies emasculating each other, but equality which is, civilly, all aptitudes having equal opportunities, politically, all votes having equal weight, and, religiously, all consciences having equal rights. Vast fields of public and popular activity are thus opened out and the collective power is employed so as to balance the 'ought' and the 'have,' to proportion enjoyment to effort, and gratification to need. In one word, let us evolve from the age-long social structure, for the benefit of those who suffer and those who are ignorant, more light to our homes and more comfort to their inmates. The Congress has recognised this to be the first of all natural obligations, yet the first of all political necessities, and therefore guarantees unto all, these two inalienable estates which every young man inherits in life,—namely, the labour which makes him free and the thought which makes him noble.

Thus has the stream of the Congress that had its humble origin in Bombay in 1885, flowed on for half a century,—now as a narrow channel and now as a wide river, here cutting across wood and forest and there eroding hill and dale, at one place, pooling its freshes into a bed of serene and even stagnant waters, and at another, presenting a mighty and roaring torrent,—all the while, swelling its volume and enriching its content by an unceasing flood of annual downpour of new ideas and new ideals and waiting, with pious faith, to realize its destiny by the final absorption of its national culture, integrated and purified, into the wider and vaster culture of inter-nationalism—or Cosmo-nationality.

Vallabhbhai Patel
1931 : Karachi

Lokamanya Tilak

Allan Octavian Hume

Appendix I

POST-WAR REFORMS

(Below we print the Memorandum submitted to H. E. the Viceroy by nineteen additional members of the Imperial Legislative Council with regard to post-war reforms. In all there are twenty seven non-official members, of whom two are Anglo-Indians, who were not consulted for obvious reasons, and three were away. Three Indians refused to sign: (1) Nawab Syed Nawab Ali Chowdhuri, (2) Mr. Abdur Rahim and (3) Sirdar Bahadur Sirdar Sunder Singh Majithia)

There is no doubt that the termination of the War will see a great advance in the ideals of Government all over the civilised world and especially in the British Empire, which entered into the struggle in defence of the liberties of weak and small Nationalities and is pouring forth its richest blood and treasure in upholding the cause of justice and humanity in the international relations of the world. India has borne her part in this struggle and cannot remain unaffected by the new spirit of change for a better state of things. Expectations have been raised in this country and hopes held out that, after the War, the problems of Indian administration will be looked at from a new angle of vision. The people of India have good reasons to be grateful to England for the great progress in her material resources and the widening of her intellectual and political outlook under British Rule, and for the steady, if slow, advance in her National life commencing with the Charter Act of India of 1833. Up to 1909, the Government of India was conducted by a bureaucracy almost entirely non-Indian in its composition and not responsible to the people of India. The reforms of 1909 for the first time introduced an Indian element in the direction of affairs in the administration of India. This element was of a very limited character. The Indian people accepted it as an indication on the part of the Government of a desire to admit the Indians into the inner counsels of the Indian Empire. So far as the Legislative Councils are concerned, the numbers of non-official members were merely enlarged with increased facilities for debate and interpellation. The Supreme Legislative Council retained an absolute official majority, and in the Provincial Legislative Councils, where a non-official majority was allowed, such majority included nominated members and the European representatives. In measures largely affecting the people, whether of legislation or taxation, by which Europeans were not directly affected the European members would naturally support the Government, and the nominated members, being nominees of Government, would be inclined to take the same side Past experience has shown that this has actually happened on various occasions. The non-official majorities, therefore, in the Provincial Councils have proved largely illusory and give no real power to the representatives of the people. The Legislative Councils, whether Supreme or Provincial, are at present nothing but advisory bodies without any power of effective control over the Government, Imperial or Provincial The people or their representatives are practically as little associated with the real government of the country as they were before the reforms, except for the introduction of the Indian element in the Executive Councils, where again the nomination rests entirely with the Government, the people having no voice in the selection of the Indian members.

The object which the Government had in view in introducing the reforms of 1909 was, as expressed by the Prime Minister in his speech in the House of Commons on the second reading of the Indian Councils Bill (1st April, 1909), that "it was most desirable in the circumstances to give to the people of India the feeling that these Legislative Councils are not mere automatons, the wires of which are pulled by the official hierarchy". This object, it is submitted, has not been attained. Apart from this question of the constitution of the Legislative and Executive Councils, the people labour under certain grave disabilities, which not only prevent the utilisation, but also lead to the wastage, of what is best in them, and are positively derogatory to their sense of National self-respect. The Arms Act which excludes from its operation Europeans and Anglo-Indians and applies only to the pure natives of the country, the disqualification of Indians for forming or joining Volunteer Corps and their exclusion from the commissioned ranks of the army, are disabilities which are looked upon with an irritating sense of racial differentiation. It would be bad enough if these were mere disabilities Restrictions and prohibitions regarding the possession and use of arms have tended to emasculate the civil population in India and expose them to serious danger. The position of Indians in India is practically this, that they have no real part or share in the direction of the Government of the country, and are placed under very great and galling disabilities from which the other members of the British Empire are exempt, and which have reduced them to a state of utter helplessness. The existence, moreover, of the system of indentured emigration gives to the British Colonies and the outside world the impression that Indians, as a whole, are no better than indentured coolies, who are looked upon as very little, if at all, above the slave. The present state of things makes the Indians feel that, though theoretically they are equal subjects of the King, they hold a ver inferior position in the British Empire. Other Asiatic races also hold the same, if not a worse, view about India and her status in the Empire. Humiliating as this position of inferiority is to the Indian mind, it is almost unbearable to the youth of India whose outlook is broadened by education and travel in foreign parts where they come in contact with other free races. In the face of these grievances and disabilities what has sustained the people is the hope and faith inspired by promises and assurances of fair and equal treatment which have been held out from time to time by our Sovereigns and British statesmen of high standing In the crisis we are now going through, the Indian people have sunk domestic differences between themselves and the Government, and have faithfully and loyally stood by the Empire. the Indian soldiers were eager to go to the battlefields of Europe, not as mercenary troops but as free citizens of the British Empire which required their services, and her civilian population was animated by one desire, namely, to stand by England in the hour of her need. Peace and tranquillity reigned throughout India when she was practically denuded of British and Indian troops The Prime Minister of England, while voicing the sentiments of the English people in regard to India's part in this great War, spoke of Indians as " the joint and equal custodians of one common interest and future. India does not claim any reward for her loyalty, but she has a right to expect that the want of confidence on the part of Government, to which she not unnaturally ascribes her present state, should now be a thing of the past, and that she should no longer occupy a position of subordination but one of comradeship. This would assure the Indian people that England is ready and willing to help them to attain Self-Government under the aegis of the British Crown, and thus discharge the noble mission which she has undertaken and to which she has so often given voluntary expression through her rulers and statesmen. What is wanted is not merely good Government or efficient administration, but Government that is acceptable to the people because it is responsible to them. This is what, India understands, would constitute the changed angle of vision.

If, after the termination of the War, the position of India practically remains what it was before, and there is no material change in it, it will undoubtedly cause bitter disappointment and great discontent in the country, and the beneficent effects of participation in common danger, overcome by common effort, will soon disappear, leaving no record behind save the painful memory of unrealised expectations. We feel sure that the Government is also alive to the situation and is contemplating measures of reform in the administration of the country. We feel that we should avail ourselves of this opportunity to respectfully offer to Government our humble suggestions as to the lines on which these reforms should proceed. They must, in our opinion, go to the root of the matter. They must give to the people real and effective participation in the Government of the country, and also remove those irritating disabilities as regards the possession of arms and a military career, which indicate want of confidence in the people and place them in a position of inferiority and helplessness. With this view, we would take the liberty to suggest the following measures for consideration and adoption :

1. In all the Executive Councils, Provincial and Imperial, half the number of members should be Indians; the European element in the Executive Councils should, as far as possible, be nominated from the ranks of men trained and educated in the public life of England, so that India may have the benefit of a wider outlook and larger experience of the outside world. It is not absolutely essential that the members of the Executive Councils, Indians or Europeans should have experience of actual administration, for, as in the case of ministers in England, the assistance of the permanent officials of the departments is always available to them. As regards Indians, we venture to say that a sufficient number of qualified Indians, who can worthily fill the office of members of the Executive Council and hold portfolios, is always available. Our short experience in this direction has shown how Indians like Sir S. P. Sinha, Sir Syed Ali Imam, the late Mr. Krishnaswami Aiyar, Sir Shams-ul-Huda and Sir Sankaran Nair have maintained a high level of administrative ability in the discharge of their duties. Moreover, it is well known that the Native States, where Indians have opportunities, have produced renowned administrators like Sir Salar Jang, Sir T. Madhava Rao, Sir Sheshadri Aiyar, Dewan Bahadur Raghunath Rao, not to mention the present administrators in the various Native States of India. The statutory obligation, now existing, that three of the members of the Supreme Executive Council shall be selected from the public services in India, and similar provisions with regard to Provincial Councils, should be removed. The elected representatives of the people should have a voice in the selection of the Indian members of the Executive Councils and for that purpose a principle of election should be adopted.

2. All the Legislative Councils in India should have a substantial majority of elected representatives. These representatives, we feel sure, will watch and safeguard the interests of the masses and the agricultural population with whom they are in closer touch than any European officer, however sympathetic, the latter can possibly be. The proceedings of the various Legislative Councils and the Indian National Congress and the Muslim League bear ample testimony to the solicitude of the educated Indians for the welfare of the masses and their acquaintance with their wants and wishes. The franchise should be broadened and extended directly to the people; Muslims or Hindus, whereas they are in a minority, being given proper and

adequate representation, having regard to their numerical strength and position.

3 The total number of the members of the Supreme Council should be not less than 150, and of the Provincial Councils not less than 100 for the major Provinces, and not less than 60 to 75 for the minor Provinces.

4. The Budget should be passed in the shape of money bills, fiscal autonomy being conceded to India.

5. The Imperial Legislative Council should have power to legislate on, and discuss and pass resolutions relating to, all matters of Indian administration, and the Provincial Councils should have similar powers with regard to Provincial administrations, save and except that the direction of military affairs, of foreign relations, declarations of war, the making of peace, and the entering into treaties, other than commercial, should not be vested in the Government of India As a safeguard, the Governor-General-in-Council or the Governor-in-Council, as the case may be, should have the right of veto, which, however, should be exercised subject to certain conditions and limitations.

6. The Council of the Secretary of State should be abolished. The Secretary of State should, as far as possible, hold in relation to the Government of India a position similar to that which the Secretary of State for the Colonies holds in relation to the Colonies The Secretary of State should be assisted by two permanent Under-Secretaries, one of whom should be an Indian. The salaries of the Secretary and the Under-Secretaries should be placed on the British estimates.

7. In any scheme of Imperial Federation, India should be given through her chosen representatives a place similar to that of the Self-Governing Dominions.

8 The Provincial Governments should be made autonomous, as stated in the Government of India's despatch dated 25th August, 1911.

9. The United Provinces, as well as the other major Provinces, should have a Governor brought from the United Kingdom and should have an Executive Council.

10 A full measure of Local Self-Government should be immediately granted.

11. The right to carry arms should be granted to Indians on the same conditions as to Europeans.

12. Indians should be allowed to enlist as volunteers and units of a territorial army established in India.

13. Commissions in the army should be given to Indian youths under conditions similar to those applicable to Europeans.

Manindra Chandra Nandy of Kasimbazar.
D. E Wacha
Bhupendranath Basu.
Bishan Dutt Shukul
Madan Mohan Malaviya.
K V Rangaswamiengar.
Mazharul Haque.
V S. Srinivasan
Tej Bahadur Sapru.
Ibrahim Rahimtoola.
B. Narasimheswara Sarma.
Mir Asad Ali
Kamini Kumar Chanda.
Krishna Sahay
R. N Bhanja Deo of Kanika.
M. B. Dadabhoy.
Sita Nath Roy
Mahomed Ali Mahomed.
M. A. Jinnah.

Appendix II

THE CONGRESS-LEAGUE SCHEME

(a) That having regard to the fact that the great communities of India are the inheritors of ancient civilisations and have shown great capacity for government and administration, and to the progress in education and public spirit made by them during a century of British Rule, and further having regard to the fact that the present system of Government does not satisfy the legitimate aspirations of the people and has become unsuited to existing conditions and requirements, the Congress is of opinion that the time has come when His Majesty the King-Emperor should be pleased to issue a Proclamation announcing that it is the aim and intention of British policy to confer Self-Government on India at an early date.

(b) That this Congress demands that a definite step should be taken towards Self-Government by granting the Reforms contained in the scheme prepared by the All-India Congress Committee in concert with the Reform Committee appointed by the All-India Muslim-League (detailed below).

(c) That in the reconstruction of the Empire, India shall be lifted from the position of a dependency to that of an equal partner in the Empire with the Self-Governing Dominions

REFORM SCHEME

I-Provincial Legislative Councils

1 Provincial Legislative Councils shall consist of four-fifths elected and of one-fifth nominated members.

2 Their strength shall be not less than 125 members in the major Provinces, and from 50 to 75 in the minor Provinces.

3 The members of Councils should be elected directly by the people on as broad a franchise as possible.

4. Adequate provision should be made for the representation of important minorities by election, and the *Muslims should be*

represented through special electorates on the Provincial Legislative Councils in the following proportions :—

Punjab-One-half of the elected Indian Members.		
United Provinces-30 p.c.	"	"
Bengal-40 p c.	"	"
Bihar-25 p c.	"	"
Central Provinces-15 p.c.	"	"
Madras 15 p.c.	"	"
Bombay-One-third	"	"

Provided that no Muslim shall participate in any of the other elections to the Imperial or Provincial Legislative Councils, save and except those by electorates representing special interests.

Provided further that no bill, nor any clause thereof, nor a resolution introduced by a non-official member affecting one or the other community, which question is to be determined by the members of that community in the Legislative Council concerned, shall be proceeded with, if three-fourths of the members of that community in the particular Council, Imperial or Provincial, oppose the bill or any clause thereof or the resolution.

5. The head of the Provincial Government should not be the President of the Legislative Council but the Council should have the right of electing its president.

6. The right of asking supplementary questions should not be restricted to the member putting the original question, but should be allowed to be exercised by any other member.

7. (*a*) Except customs, post, telegraph, mint, salt, opium, railways, army and navy, and tributes from Indian States, all other sources of revenue should be Provincial.

(*b*) There should be no divided heads of revenue. The Government of India should be provided with fixed contributions from the Provincial Governments, such fixed contributions being liable to revision when extraordinary and unforeseen contingencies render such revision necessary.

(*c*) The Provincial Council should have full authority to deal with all matters affecting the internal administration of the Province, including the power to raise loans, to impose and alter taxation and to vote on the Budget. All items of expenditure, and all proposals concerning ways and means for raising the necessary Revenue should be embodied in Bills and submitted to the Provincial Council for adoption.

(*d*) Resolution on all matters within the purview of the Provincial Government should be allowed for discussion in accordance with rules made in that behalf by the Council itself.

(*e*) A resolution passed by the Provincial Legislative Council shall be binding on the Executive Government, unless vetoed by the Governor-in-Council, provided however that if the resolution is again passed by the Council after an interval of not less than one year, it must be given effect to.

(*f*) A motion for adjournment may be brought forward for the discussion of a definite matter of urgent public importance, if supported by not less than one-eighth of the members present.

8. A special meeting of the Provincial Council may be summoned on a requisition by not less than one-eigth of the members.

9. A Bill, other than a Money Bill, may be introduced in Council in accordance with rules made in that behalf by the Council itself, and the consent of the Government should not be required therefor.

10. All Bills passed by Provincial Legislatures shall have to receive the assent of the Governor before they become Law, but may be vetoed by the Governor-General.

11. The term of office of the members shall be five years.

II-Provincial Governments

1. The head of every Provincial Government shall be a Governor who shall not ordinarily belong to the Indian Civil Service or any of the permanent services.

2. There shall be in every Province an Executive Council which, with the Governor, shall constitute the Executive Government of the Province

3. Members of the Indian Civil Service shall not ordinarily be appointed to the Executive Councils.

4 Not less than one-half of the members of the Executive Council shall consist of Indians to be elected by the elected members of the Provincial Legislative Council.

5. The term of office of the members shall be five years.

III-Imperial Legislative Council

1. The strength of the Imperial Legislative Council shall be 150.

2. Four-fifh of the members shall be elected.

3. The franchise for the Imperial Legislative Council should be widened as far as possible on the lines of the electorates for Muslims for the Provincial Legislative Councils, and the elected members of the Provincial Legislative Councils should also form an electorate for the return of members of the Imperial Legislative Council.

4. One-third of the Indian elected members should be Muslims elected by separate Muslim electorates in the several Provinces, in the proportion, as nearly as may be, in which they are represented on the Provincial Legislative Councils by separate Muslims electorates.

Vide provisos to section 1, clause 4.

5. The President of the Council shall be elected by the Council itself.

6. The right of asking supplementary questions shall not be restricted to the member putting the original question but should be allowed to be exercised by any other member.

7. A special meeting of the Council may be summoned on requisition by not less than one-eighth of the members

8. A Bill, other than a Money Bill, may be introduced in Council in accordance with rules made in that behalf by the Council itself, and the consent of the Executive Government should not be required therefor.

9. All Bills passed by the Council shall have to receive the assent of the Governor-General before they become law.

10. All financial proposals relating to sources of income and items of expenditure shall be embodied in Bills. Every such Bill and the Budget as a whole shall be submitted for the vote of the Imperial Legislative Council.

11. The term of office of members shall be five years.

12. The matters mentioned herein below shall be exclusively under the control of the Imperial Legislative Council.

(*a*) Matters in regard to which uniform legislation for the whole of India is desirable.

(*b*) Provincial legislation in so far as it may affect inter-Provincial fiscal relations.

(*c*) Questions affecting purely Imperial Revenue, excepting tributes from Indian States.

(*d*) Questions affecting purely Imperial expenditure, except that no resolution of the Imperial Legislative Council shall be binding on the Governor-General-in-Council in respect of military charges for the defence of the country.

(e) The right of revising Indian tariffs and customs duties, of imposing, altering, or removing any tax or cess, modifying the existing system of currency and banking, and granting any aids or bounties to any or all deserving and nascent industries of the country.

(f) Resolutions on all matters relating to the administration of the country as a whole.

13 A resolution passed by the Legislative Council should be binding on the Executive Government unless vetoed by the Governor-General in Council; provided however that if the resolution is again passed by the Council after an interval of not less than one year, it must be given effect to.

14. A motion for adjournment may be brought forward for the discussion of a definite matter of urgent public importance if supported by not less than one-eighth of the members present.

15. When the Crown chooses to exercise its power of veto in regard to a Bill passed by the Provincial Legislative Council or by the Imperial Legislative Council, it should be exercised within twelve months from the date on which it is passed, and the Bill shall cease to have effect as from the date on which the fact of such veto is made known to the Legislative Council concerned.

16. The Imperial Legislative Council shall have no power to interfere with the Government of India's direction of the military affairs and the foreign and political relations of India, including the declaration of war, the making of peace and the entering into treaties.

IV. The Government of India

1. The Governor-General of India will be the head of the Government of India.

2 He will have an Executive Council, half of whom shall be Indians.

3. The Indian members should be elected by the elected members of the Imperial Legislative Council.

4 Members of the Indian Civil Service shall not ordinarily be appointed to the Exective Council of the Governor-General.

5. The power of making all appointments in the Imperial Civil Services shall vest in the Government of India, as constituted under this scheme, due regard being paid to existing interests, subject to any laws that may be made by the Imperial Legislative Council.

6. The Goverment of India shall not ordinarily interfere in the local affairs of a Province, and powers not specifically given to a Provincial Government shall be deemed to be vested in the former. The authority of the Government of India will ordinarily be limited to general supervision and superintendence over the Provincial Governments.

7. In legislative and administrative matters the Government of India, as constituted under this scheme, shall, as far as possible, be independent of the Secretary of State.

8. A system of independent audit of the accounts of the Government of India should be instituted.

V. The Secretary of State in Council

1. The Council of the Secretary of State for India should be abolished.

2. The salary of the Secretary of State should be placed on the British Estimates.

3. The Secretary of State should, as far as possible, occupy the same position in relation to the Government of India, as the Secretary of State for the Colonies does in relation to the Governments of the Self-Governing Diminions.

4. The Secretary of State for India should be assisted by two Permanent Under-Secretaries, one of whom should always be an Indian.

VI. India and the Empire

1 In any Council or other body which may be constituted or convened for the settlement or control of Imperial affairs, India shall be adequately represented in like manner with the Dominions and with equal rights

2. Indians should be placed on a footing of equality in respect of status and rights of citizenship with other subjects of His Majesty the King throughout the Empire.

VII. Military and other Matters

1. The military and naval services of His Majesty, both in their commissioned and non-commissioned ranks, should be thrown open to Indians and adequate provision should be made for their selection, training and instruction in India.

2. Indians should be allowed to enlist as volunteers.

3. Executive Officers in India shall have no judicial powers entrusted to them, and the judiciary in every Province shall be placed under the highest Court of that Province.

Appendix II-A

MULSHIPETA SATYAGRAHA

Mulshipeta is about 30 miles from Poona. In 1920 The Tata Power Company launched a scheme of bunding the streams and water falls in that mountainous area for supplying electricity to G. I. P. Ry., B. B C. I Ry and the Bombay City. Mulshipeta was renowned for its excellent paddy crop and the Mavalas the inhabitants of that area—were the sturdy fighters in the army of Shivaji. When they (Mavalas) saw the army of labourers in their land they were confounded and consulted their friends in Poona as to the measures to be adopted for saving their land. The atmosphere was surcharged with Non-co-operation at that time. About 51 villages and 11,000 men, women and children were on the point of being rendered homeless and landless A meeting was held in the peta under the Presidentship of Syt. N. C. Kelkar and all the Mavalas gave out that they would either get back the land or die in the Satyagraha fight Noting this grim determination, the Poona leaders got ready to take the lead in the fight.

Consequently a draft pledge was prepared and it was agreed, that if 1,200 Mavalas would sign it, the fight was to be commenced. Mr. V. M. Bhuskute visited whole area and obtained about 1,300 signatures and in spite of Baramati, the leaders proceeded to launch the fight. The whole Maharashtra was agitated over the question Help in form of men and money was forthcoming. The Mavalas themselves contributed about 1,000 rupees worth of rice for the fight. The 16th of April 1921, the Rama Navami day, was chosen for the commencement of Satyagraha. It is claimed that Maharashtra undertook the fight as part of the programmes of Congress though not directly under its authority. If it succeeded the prestige of the Congress would be enhanced and Gandhiji's cult would be vindicated. If it failed, the responsibility would be theirs.

On Rama Navami day 1,200 Mavalas with women and children and all prominent leaders from Poona were present at the scene. They went and sat on the dam. Immediately 5,000 labourers of the Company stopped work. This Satyagraha went on for about a month strictly in accordance with the principles of Gandhi's Non-violence. It became successful, inasmuch as the Company discontinued the work. But the turning point came in the Monsoon. Like other peasants, the Mavalas were burdened with heavy debts and were at the mercy of the Sowkars. The latter were perturbed over the affair

They were afraid that if Satyagraha continued they would receive less compensation from the Company and they were backed by a section of leaders in this behalf. Negotiations went on with the Engineers and managers of the Company for getting adequate compensation The Mavalas were ignorant of these attempts. The Company depending on these assurances gave promises of liberal compensation The Managers of the Company entered into agreement with the Government and land was acquired under the Land Acquisition Act The Mavalas were out for land and wanted no such return however liberal it might be. It must be stated here that Maharashtra like other places was split up into "Pro-Changers and No-Changers". Most of the No-Changers were faithful followers of Gandhi and they determined to support the Mavalas in their fight for land They had two opponents now. Sowkars and the Company This struggle went on for two years and half. The second campaign was started in December 1921. Arrests, convictions, intimidations and oppression were in full swing S M. Paranjpe, Dr. Phatak, G. N. Kanitkar, S K. Damle. S. D Deo, Vasukaka Joshi, H. G Phatak, P. M. Bapat, V.M. Bhuskute Dastane, Dr. Palsule, J. S Karandikar and many others were, arrested and convicted In all 125 Mavalas, 500 volunteers and leaders including women suffered imprisonment. Rs 7,500 were spent for the fight. When all the local and outside leaders went behind the prison bars, Sowkars made their utmost to persuade the Mavalas to accept the compensation and in this attempt they were helped by those leaders who were not keen about the fight. Ultimately the Satyagraha had to be abandoned. Mr. P. M. Bapat and his colleagues made supreme sacrifices to the end for the cause. It must be stated that as a result of this Satyagraha the peasants were given rather fair compensation for the land. But the sum went into the coffers of Sowkars and thousands of peasants were rendered landless and homeless.

Appendix III

THE FARIDPUR PROPOSALS

1 That joint electorates with adult suffrage should form the basis of representation in the future constitution of India

2 (a) That with adult suffrage, reservation of seats only for minorities less than 25 per cent. in the Federal and Provincial Legislatures should be permitted, on the basis of population with the right to contest additional seats

(b) That in the provinces where Muslims are in a minority of less than 25 per cent seats shall be reserved for them on a population basis with the right to contest additional seats, but in case other communities are given weightage, Muslims shall be similarly treated and the present weightage enjoyed by them shall be maintained

(c) If adult franchise is not established, or franchise is not extended so as to reflect the proportion of the population on the electoral register, in the Punjab and Bengal seats shall be reserved for the Muslims, until adult suffrage is established or franchise is extended so as to reflect the proportion of population on the electoral register, in such position of minority or even of equality.

3 That the representation of Muslims in the Federal legislature shall be one-third of the respective houses.

4. That all appointments shall be made by a Public Service Commission, according to a minimum standard of efficiency, without at the same time depriving any community of its fair share in the services and that in the case of lower grades no monopoly shall be permitted.

5. That in the Federal and Provincial Cabinets, Muslim interests shall be adequately recognised by means of a convention agreed to by all the parties in the different legislatures.

6. That Sind shall be constituted into a separate Province.

7. That the N. W. F. Province and Beluchistan, shall have exactly the same form of Government and administration as other Provinces in British India.

8. That the future constitution of the country shall be federal and the residuary powers shall vest in the federating units.

9. (a) That there shall be a provision of fundamental rights in the constitution guaranteeing to all the citizens the protection of their cultures, language, script, education, profession and practice of religion, religious endowments and economic interests.

(b) That the fundamental rights and personal laws shall be effectively protected by specific provision to be embodied in the constitution.

(c) That there shall be no change in the Constitution so far as fundamental rights are concerned except with the concurrence of a three-fourth majority of each house of the federal legislature.

Strictly Confidential.

Appendix to Proceedings

ALTERNATIVE PROPOSALS & FORMULAE.
THE BHOPAL FORMULAE.

A.

ALL PARTIES FORMULA

(a) Joint Electorates to be introduced at the end of ten years with adult suffrage, provided that if the majority of the Muslim Members in any Legislature, Federal or Provincial, agree to accept Joint Electorates at any time before the expiry of ten years, separate electorates will be abolished *qua* such Legislature,

or

(b) First election under the new constitution to be on the basis of separate electorates and a referendum on the question of joint versus separate electorates at the beginning of the 5th year of the first Legislature

B

ALTERNATIVE SCHEME—NATIONALIST PARTY.

(a) Joint electorates to be adopted for the first ten years on the expiry of which period a referendum should be held on the question of electorates.

(b) In the first Legislature 50 per cent. of the Muslim Members to be elected by joint electorate and 50 per cent. by separate electorates. In the second legislature, 2/3 to be elected by joint and 1/3 by separate electorates. Thereafter joint electorates and adult suffrage.

C

AMENDMENT TO ABOVE :—

In the first legislature, 2/3 members to be elected by separate and 1/3 by joint electorates.

SOME FRIENDS' SUGGESTION.

50 : 50 for second legislature and joint thereafter and adult suffrage thereafter.

Separate electorate for first 5 years, Joint next five years, and a referendum at the beginning of the 9th year to obtain the community's verdict on the two,

or

2/3 representatives to be chosen by separate and 1/3 joint electorates, and referendum at the beginning of the 5th year.

B

D

A PROPOSAL—SHAUKAT ALI

When Joint electorates are introduced, whether in whole or in part, Maulana Mohammed Ali's formula should be accepted for the first 20 years.

* * * * *

F

PROPOSAL AT THE 2ND MEETING AT BHOPAL.

First five years Separate Electorates, after that Joint Electorates with Maulana Mohammed Ali's formula.
This formula, however, it will be open to the Muslim members of any Legislature to drop by a sixty per cent. majority.

G

FINAL FORMULA AT SIMLA.

First ten years Separate Electorates, after that Joint Electorates, unless the Muslim Members of any Legislature by a 2/3 majority vote against the introduction of Joint Electorates.

Appendix IV

THE G O. ON THE CLASSIFICATION OF PRISONERS.

Text of the Press Communique

Important decisions of the Government of India regarding the Jail Rules are announced in a Press Communique which runs :

The Government of India have for sometime had under consideration the amendment of jail rules in certain respects. The matter had been referred to Local Governments who have formulated their views after extensive consultation of unofficial opinion. A conference of the provincial representatives was thereupon held and the Government of India have also had discussions with some prominent members of the Legislative Assembly. The problems under examination have been found difficult and complex and have led to the expression of widely divergent opinions. The Government of India have endeavoured to give due weight to these even when they have not been able to accept in full the representations made. The conclusions at which they have arrived on the more important points and which are designed to secure on matters of principle substantial uniformity throughout India, are now announced.

Classification of Prisoners

Convicted prisoners will be divided into three divisions or classes, A, B and C. Prisoners will be eligible for class 'A' if (1) they are non-habitual prisoners of good character (2) they, by social status, education and habit of life, have been accustomed to a superior mode of living and (3) they have not been convicted of (a) offences involving elements of cruelty, moral degradation or personal greed, (b) seditious or premeditated violence, (c) seditious offences against property, (d) offences relating to possession of explosives, fire arms and other dangerous weapons with the object of committing an offence or of enabling an offence to be committed, (e) abetment or incitement of offences falling within these sub-clauses.

Prisoners will be eligible for class 'B' who, by social status, education or habit of life have been accustomed to a superior mode of living. Habitual prisoners will not be excluded automatically. The classifying authority will be allowed discretion to suggest their inclusion in this class, having regard to their character and antecedents, subject to confirmation or revision by the Local Government.

Class 'C' will consist of prisoner who are not classified in classes 'A' and 'B'.

The classifying authorities are High Courts, Session Judges, District Magistrates, Stipendiary Presidency Magistrates, Subdivisional Magistrates and Magistrates of the first class (the two latter through the District Magistrate) in cases tried by them originally or in any other case. The District Magistrate should make an initial recommendation for classification in classes A or B to the Local Government, by whom these recommendations will be confirmed or reviewed.

Privileges of prisoners.

Certain forecasts of their decisions which have been brought to the notice of the Government of India indicate considerable misapprehension in regard to this tripartite division and its effect upon the existing classes of prisoners. It should be clearly understood that all prisoners within the A Class are eligible for the privileges of that class. No class of prisoners will be eligible for any additional privileges on grounds of race All privileges now given to special class prisoners will be continued to 'A' class prisoners, such as separate accommodation, necessary articles of furniture, reasonable facilities for association and exercises, and suitable sanitary and bathing arrangements.

In other matters, the following decisions have been arrived at:

The diet for classes 'A' and 'B' will be superior to the ordinary prison diet given to prisoners in class C and will be based on a flat rate of cost per prisoner, within the limits of which the actual food may vary. The cost of the superior diet provided in the classes A and B should be borne by the Government, as special class prisoners are under the existing rules permitted to supplement prison diet at their own expense. This privilege will be retained as at present as regards 'A' class prisoners.

The existing rules regarding privileges of special class prisoners to wear their own clothes will continue. As regards 'A' class prisoners, if they desire to have clothing at Government expense, they will be provided with that prescribed for 'B' class prisoners. 'B' class prisoners will wear prison clothing modified in certain respects and of a better type than that worn by C class prisoners.

Accommodation

A separate jail in each Province for classes A and B is desirable, and its provision though it must depend on the available financial resources of the Local Governments, should be regarded as the goal to be aimed at. Meanwhile, the Government of India hope that Local Governments will carefully review the resources of the jails now existing in the Provinces and endeavour, by such measures as are within their power, to secure the end in view.

In addition to separate accommodation, the Government of India desire to emphasise the necessity of a special staff to deal with 'A' and 'B' class prisoners, and are of opinion that this matter should receive the earliest possible attention.

In accordance with the principle already applied, the importance of which is reaffirmed, the tasks allotted to prisoners in 'A' and 'B' classes should be assigned after due consideration on medical grounds, and with careful regard to the capacity, character, previous modes of life and antecedents of the prisoners.

PRISONERS' INTELLECTUAL REQUIREMENTS

The Government of India accept the principle that reasonable facilities, subject to safeguards, should be provided by the Government for the intellectual requirements of the educated and literate prisoners. Local Governments will be requested to examine the condition of jail libraries in the Provinces and in cases where those are non-existent or defective, to take early steps to establish or improve them. Literate prisoners may be allowed to read books and magazines from outside subject to the approval of the Jail Superintendent.

Newspapers will be allowed to 'A' class prisoners on the same conditions as under the existing rules, they are allowed to special class prisoners, that is, in special circumstances and with the approval of Local Government. As regards literate prisoners generally, where the Local Governments publish a jail newspaper or where they intend to publish it, this publication will be available once a week for literate prisoners. Where the Local Governments are unable to publish a weekly newspaper, the Government of India have decided that a few copies of a weekly paper approved by the Local Government should be provided at Government expense for 'A' and 'B' classes of prisoners.

"A" class prisoners will be allowed to write and receive one letter and have one interview a fortnight, instead of once a month as at present. "B" class prisoners will be allowed to write and receive one letter and have an interview once a month instead of at the considerably longer intervals now permitted under the various jail manuals. Publication of matters discussed at interviews or of the substance of the letters received from prisoners may entail the withdrawal or curtailment of the privilege.

TREATMENT OF UNDER-TRIAL PRISONERS.

The Government of India accept the principle that some differentiation of treatment is desirable in the case of under-trial prisoners who, by social status, education or habit of life, have been accustomed to a superior mode of living. There will therefore be two classes of under-trial prisoners based on the previous standard of living only. The classifying authority will be the trying court, subject to the approval of the District Magistrate. The diet provided for 'A' and 'B' class convicted prisoners will be given to the former and the diet of 'C' class prisoners to the latter Under-trial prisoners in either class, will be allowed to supplement this diet by private purchase through the jail authorities. Under the existing rules, they are allowed to wear their own clothing. The suggestion has been made that in cases where under-trial prisoners are inadequately clad or are unable to obtain clothing from outside, suitable clothing, which should not be prison clothing, should be provided by jail authorities. The Government of India commend this suggestion for adoption to the Local Governments.

The Government of India are of opinion that the interpretation of the existing rules in a liberal spirit, together with the modifications now proposed and the provision of better cellular accommodation, will effect improvements in the directions which enquiry has indicated as desirable. They, therefore, hope that Local Governments will make every effort to improve the existing accommodation and will at once utilize and adapt their existing resources to the best possible advantage In many of the opinions received by the Government of India, stress had been laid on the desirability of separating under-trial prisoners, who are habituals or charged with grave offences, from those who have not been previously convicted. On this subject, the Government of India consider that no further orders are necessary as they understand that this is the existing practice.

The Local Governments are now being invited to amend their jail manuals in the light of these principles, and to frame rules where necessary under Section 60 of the Prisoners Act. Pending such revision they are being requested as far as possible to give immediate practical effect to these changes.

Appendix IV-A

PEACE PROPOSALS IN JULY & AUGUST 1930

THE CORRESPONDENCE

Sir Tej Bahadur Sapru and Mr. Jayakar have made the following statement embodying the correspondence that passed between them and the Congress leaders in jail in the course of the last two months:

"The facts connected with the efforts which we have been making for over two months for the restoration of peaceful conditions in the country are as follows:

(1) On the 20th June 1930 Pandit Motilal Nehru gave an interview to Mr. George Slocombe, Special Correspondent of "The Daily Herald" (London) with regard to his views about attending the Round Table Conference. This interview has already appeared in India.

(2) Shortly thereafter Mr. Slocombe had a conversation with Pandit Motilal Nehru in Bombay as the result of which certain terms were drafted by Mr. Slocombe and submitted to Pandit Motilal Nehru and approved by him at a meeting in Bombay at which Pandit Motilal Nehru, Mr Jayakar and Mr. Slocombe alone were present. One copy of these terms was sent to Mr. Jayakar by Mr. Slocombe as agreed upon by Pandit Motilal Nehru as the basis of his (Mr. Jayakar's) or any third party's approach to the Viceroy.

(3) Mr. Slocombe likewise addressed a letter to Dr. Sapru at Simla forwarding a copy of these terms. In the course of this letter Mr. Slocombe said that Pandit Motilal Nehru had agreed to our acting as intermediaries for the purpose of approaching the Viceroy on the basis of these terms. We give below the full text of this document:

THE BASIS OF THE NEGOTIATIONS.

The statement submitted to Pandit Motilal Nehru in Bombay on June 25th, 1930, and approved as the basis of an informal approach to the Viceroy by a third party ran as follows:

If in certain circumstances the British Government and the Government of India, although unable to anticipate the recommendations that may in perfect freedom be made by the Round Table Conference or the attitude which British Parliament may reserve for such recommendations, would nevertheless be willing to give a private assurance that they would support the demand for full responsible Government for India, subject to such mutual adjustments and terms of transfer as are required by the special needs and conditions of India and by her long association with Great Britain and as may be decided by the Round Table Conference;

Pandit Motilal Nehru would undertake to take personally such an assurance—or the indication received from a responsible third party that such an assurance would be forthcoming—to Mr Gandhi and to Pandit Jawaharlal Nehru. If such an assurance were offered and accepted it would render possible a general measure of conciliation which should entail the simultaneous calling off of the civil disobedience movement, the cessation of Government's present repressive policy and a general measure of amnesty for political prisoners and would be followed by Congress participation in the Round Table Conference on terms to be mutually agreed upon.'

Letter to the Viceroy

On the basis of this document, we interviewed the Viceroy in Simla more than once in the early part of July last and explained to him the situation in the country and ultimately wrote to him the following letter.

Simla, July 13

Dear Lord Irwin,— We would beg leave to draw your Excellency's attention to the political situation in the country which in our opinion makes it imperative that some steps should be taken without any loss of time to restore normal conditions We are alive to the dangers of the civil disobedience movement with which neither of us have sympathised nor have been associated, but we feel in the contest between the people and the Government, which has involved the adoption of a policy of repression and consequent embitterment of popular feeling the true and abiding interests of the country are apt to be sacrificed. We think it is our duty to our country and to Government that we should make an endeavour to ameliorate the present situation by discussing the question with some of the leaders of the movement in the hope and belief that we may be able to persuade them to help in the restoration of normal conditions.

If we have read Your Excellency's speech aright, we think, while your Excellency and your Government feel compelled to resist the civil disobedience movement, you are not less anxious to explore every possibility in finding an agreed solution of the constitutional problem. We need scarcely say that we believe that with the cessation of the movement, there will be no occasion for the continuance on the part of Government of the present policy and those emergency measures which have been passed by Government to implement that policy.

We, therefore, approach Your Excellency with a request that you may be pleased to permit us to interview Mr. Gandhi, Pandit Motilal Nehru and Pandit Jawaharlal Nehru, so that we may put our points of view before them and urge them in the interest of the country to respond to our appeal to enable the big issue of consitutional advance being solved in a calm atmosphere. We desire to make it plain that in going to them we shall be going on our own behalf, and we do not profess to represent either the Government or any party in taking this step If we fail in our attempt the responsibility will be ours.

Should Your Excellency be pleased to grant us permission to see these gentlemen in jail, we shall request you to issue necessary orders to the local Governments concerned to allow us necessary facilities We further request that if the necessary permission is granted to us we may be allowed to talk to them privately without there being any officer of Government present at our interview. We further submit that in our opinion it is desirable we should see them at the earliest possible date.

The reply to this letter may be sent to Mr. Jayakar at Hotel Cecil.

Yours sincerely,
Tej Bahadur Sapru,
M R. Jayakar

THE VICEROY'S REPLY

To the above the Viceroy made the following reply: -

Dear Mr Jayakar,— I have received your letter ot 13th July You and Sir Tej Bahadur Sapru state your desire to do all in your power to bring about the return of peaceful conditions in the country and ask for permission to approach Mr. Gandhi, Pandit Motilal Nehru and Pandit Jawaharlal Nehru with this object. I had occasion in my address to the Legislature on the 9th July to define the at itude of myself and of my Government both to the civil disobedience movement and to the constitutional issues. We consider the civil disobedience movement is doing unmixed harm to the cause of India and many important communities, classes and parties hold the same view. With their help, therefore, Government must continue to oppose it by all means in their power, but you rightly recognise we are not less anxious to see the achievement of the solution of the constitutional problem by agreement among all interests concerned

It is evidently not possible for me to anticipate the proposals that will be made by the Government of India after they have had time to consider the Satatutory Commission's Report or by the Round Table Conference and still less the decision of Parliament, but I made it plain in my speech that it remains my earnest desire, as it is that of my Government, and I have no doubt also that of His Majesty's Government to do everything, that we can in our respective spheres to assist the people of India to obtain as large a degree of management of their own affairs as can be shown to be consistent with the making of provision for those matters in regard to which they are not at present in a position to assume responsibility. What those matters may be and what provisions may best be made for them will engage the attention of the conference, but I have never believed that with mutual confidence on both sides it should be impossible to reach an agreement. I, therefore, believe that by the action proposed, you may be able to assist in the restoration of normal conditions in the country, and it would not be right for me or my Government to interpose any obstacle to your efforts, nor do I think that those who have stood side by side with my Government in steadily opposing the civil disobedience movement and whose co-operation I so much value would wish me to do so. On hearing from you I will accordingly ask the Local Governments concerned to issue necessary instructions which will enable you to make your public spirited attempt in the cause of peace in India.

Yours sincerely,
Irwin."

GANDHIJI'S NOTE TO NEHRUS

With these two documents we interviewed Mr. Gandhi in Yeravada Jail, Poona, on the 23rd and 24th July 1930. During the interview, we explained to Mr. Gandhi the whole situation and gave him the substance of our conversation with the Viceroy. Mr Gandhi gave us the following note and letter to be handed over to Pandits Motilal Nehru and Jawaharlal Nehru at Naini Jail, Allahabad.

"(1) So far as this question is concerned my personal position is that if the Round Table Conference is restricted to a discussion of the safeguards that may be necessary in connection with full self-government during the period of transition, I should have no objection, it being understood that the question of Independence should not be ruled out if any body raised it. I should be satisfied before I could endorse the idea of the Cóngress attending the conference about its whole composition.

(2) If the Congress is satisfied as to the Round Table Conference, naturally civil disobedience would be called off. That is to say disobedience of certain laws for the sake of disobedience but peaceful picketing of foreign cloth and liquor will be continued unless Government themselves can enforce prohibition of liquor and foreign cloth. But the manufacture of salt by the populace will have to be continued and the penal clauses of the Salt Act should not be enforced. There will be no raids on Government salt depots or private depots. I

will agree even if this clause is not made a clause in these terms, but is accepted as an understanding in writing.

(3) (a) Simultaneously with the calling off of civil disobedience, all Satyagrahi prisoners and other political prisoners convicted or under trial who have not been guilty of violence or incitement to violence should be ordered to be released.

(b) Properties confiscated under the Salt Act, the Press Act and the Revenue Act and the like should be restored.

(c) Fines and securities taken from the convicted Satyagrahis or under the Press Act should be refunded.

(d) All officers including village officers who have resigned or who may have been dismissed during the civil disobedience movement and who may desire to rejoin Government service should be restored.

N.B. The foregoing should refer also to the Non-Co-operation periods.

(e) The Viceregal Ordinances should be repealed.

This opinion of mine is purely provisional because I consider a prisoner has no right to pronounce any opinion upon political activities of which he cannot possibly have full grasp while he is shut out of personal contact. I therefore feel my opinion is not entitled to the weight I should claim for it if I was in touch with the movement. Mr. Jayakar and Dr. Sapru may show this to Pandit Motilal Nehru, Pandit Jawaharlal Nehru, Mr. Vallabhbhai Patel and those who are in charge of the movement. Nothing is to appear in the press. This is not to be shown to the Viceroy at this stage. Even if the foregoing terms are accepted, I should not care to attend the conference unless in the event of going out of prison I gained self-confidence which I have not at present and unless among those Indians who would be invited there were preliminary conversations and agreement as to the minimum by which they should stand under all circumstances. I reserve to myself the liberty when occasion arises of testing every Swaraj scheme by its ability to satisfy the object underlying the eleven points mentioned in my letter to the Viceroy.

M. K. Gandhi,
23rd July,
Yeravada Central Prison"

GANDHI'S LETTER TO PT. MOTILAL

The following is Mr. Gandhi's covering letter to Pandit Motilal Nehru :—

"My position is essentially awkward. Being temperamentally so built, I cannot give a decisive opinion on matters happening outside the prison walls. What I have therefore given to our friends is the roughest draft of what is likely to satisfy me personally. You may not know I was disinclined to give anything to Mr. Slocombe and wanted him to discuss things with you, but I could not resist his appeal, and let him publish the interview before seeing you. At the same time, I do not want to stand in the way of an honourable settlement if the time for it is ripe. I have grave doubts about it but after all Pandit Jawaharlal's must be the final voice You and I can only give our advice to him. What I have said in my memorandum given to Sir Tej Bahadur Sapru and Mr. Jayakar is the utmost limit to which I can go, but Jawaharlal, for that matter also you may consider my position to be inconsistent with the intrinsic Congress policy or the present temper of the people. I should have no hesitation in supporting any stronger position upto the letter of the Lahore resolution. You need therefore attach no weight to my memorandum unless it finds an echo in the hearts of you both. I know that neither you or Jawahar were enamoured of the eleven points brought out in my first letter to the Viceroy, I do not know whether you still have the same opinion. My own mind is quite clear about them They are to me the substance of Independence. I should have nothing to do with anything that would not give the nation power to give immediate effect to them. In restricting myself to the *three* only in the memorandum, I have not waived the other *eight*, but *three* are now brought out to deal with the civil disobedience I would be no party to any truce which would undo the position at which we have arrived to-day.

Yours sincerely,
M. K GANDHI,
23rd July, 1930
Yerawada Mandir."

Accordingly on the 27th and 28th July we saw Pandits Motilal Nehru and Jawaharlal Nehru at Naini Jail, Allahabad and after a review of the entire position in the light of the Viceroy's letter and Mr. Gandhi's note and the letter referred to above. Pandits Motilal Nehru and Jawaharlal Nehru gave us the following two documents to be taken to Mr. Gandhi at Yeravada, Poona.

NEHRUS' NOTE TO GANDHIJI.

Memorandam dated 28th July, 1930 by Pandits Motilal Nehru and Jawaharlal Nehru, Central Prison, Naini, Allahabad.

"We have had a long conversation with Sir Tej Bahadur Sapru and Mr. Jayakar and they have informed us of the variation in events which led to their seeking interviews with Gandhiji and with us in our respective prisons in order, if possible to terminate or suspend the present hostilities between the people of India and the British Government. We appreciate their earnest desire for peace and would gladly explore all avenues which might lead to it provided such peace was an honourable one for the people of India who have already sacrificed so much in the national struggle and meant freedom for our country. As representatives of the Congress we have no authority to alter in any material particular its resolutions but we might be prepared under certain circumstances to recommend various details provided the fundamental position taken up by the Congress was accepted. We are, however, faced with initial difficulty. Both of us are in prison and for sometime past have been cut off from the outside world and the national movement. One of us for nearly three months was not allowed any daily newspaper Gandhiji has also been in prison for several months. Indeed almost all our colleagues, of the original Working Committee of the Congress, are in prison and the Committee itself has been declared an illegal organisation. Of the 360 members of the All-India Congress Committee which is the final authority in the National Congress organisation subject only to a full session of the Congress, probably 75 per cent. are in prison Cut off as we are from the national movement we cannot take upon ourselves the responsibility of taking a definite step without the fullest consultation with our colleagues and especially Gandhiji. As regards the Round Table Conference we feel untimely to achieve anything unless an agreement on all vital matters is previously arrived at. We attach great importance to such an agreement which must be definite and there must be no room for misunderstanding or misinterpretation. Sir Tej Bahadur Sapru and Mr. Jayakar have made very clear and Lord Irwin has also stated in his published letter to them that they are acting on their own behalf and cannot commit him or his Government. It is however possible they may succeed in paving way to such an agreement between the Congress and the British Government. As we are unable to suggest any definite terms for truce without consulting Gandhiji and other colleagues we refrain from discussing the suggestions made by Sir Tej Bahadur Sapru and Mr. Jayakar and by Gandhiji in the note of his dated 23rd July which has been shown to us. We might however agree generally with Gandhiji's 2nd and 3rd points, but we should like the details of these points and specially his point (1) to discuss with him and others before we can finally make our suggestions. We suggest this note of ours be treated confidential and be shown only to such persons as see Gandhiji's note dated 23-7-'30.

PT. JAWAHARLAL'S LETTER.

Letter dated 28-7-'30 from Pandit Jawaharlal Nehru, Central Prison, Naini, Allahabad to Mr. Gandhi, Yeravada Jail, Poona :—

CENTRAL PRISON, NAINI,
28—7—'30.

"My dear Bapuji,—It is a delight to write you again after a long interval even though it be from one prison to another. I would like to write at length, but I am afraid I cannot do so at present I shall, therefore, confine myself to the matter in issue. Dr. Sapru and Mr. Jayakar came yesterday and had a long interview with father and me. To-day they are coming again. As they have already put us in possession of all facts and shown us your note and letters and we felt we could discuss the matter between us two and arrive at some decision even without waiting for a second interview. Of course if anything new turns up at the second interview we are prepared to vary any previously formed opinion. Our conclusions for the time being are given in the note which we are giving to Sir Tej Bahadur Sapru and Mr. Jayakar. This is more or less brief but it will, I hope give you some idea of how our minds are working. I might add that father and I are in full agreement in regard to what our attitude should be. I might confess your point (1) regarding the constitutional issue has not won me over nor does father fancy it. I do not see how it fits in with our position or our pledges or,the realities of to-day. Father and I entirely agree with you that we can be "no parties to any truce which would undo the position at which we have arrived to-day." It is because of this that fullest consideration is essential before any final decision is arrived at. I must confess I do not see an appreciable advance yet from the other side and I greatly fear a false or weak move on our part. I am expressing myself moderately. For myself I delight in warfare. It makes me feel that I am alive. Events of the last four months in India have gladdened my heart and have made me prouder of Indian men, women and even children that I had ever been, but I realise that most people are not warlike and like peace and so I try hard to suppress myself and take a peaceful view. May I congratulate you on the new India you have created by your magic touch ! What the future will bring I know not but the past has made life worth living and our prosaic existence has developed something of epic greatness in it. Sitting here in Naini Jail, I have pondered on the wonderful efficacy of non-violence as a weapon and have become a greater convert with response of a convert to it than ever before. I hope you are not dissatisfied with the response of the country to the non-violence creed. Despite occasional lapses, the country has stuck to it wonderfully, certainly far more grimly than I had expected. I am afraid I am still somewhat of a protestant regarding your eleven points. Not that I disagree with any one of them Indeed they are important. Yet I do not think they take the place of Independence But I certainly agree with you that we should have "nothing to do with anything that would not give the nation power to give immediate effect to them. Father has been unwell the last eight days ever since he took an injection He has grown very weak. This long interview last evening tired him out.

(Sd.) Jawaharlal.

Please do not be anxious about me. It is only a passing trouble and I hope to get rid over it in two or three days. Love.

(Sd.) Motilal Nehru."

P. S.—"We have had another talk with Sir Tej Bahadur Sapru and Mr. Jayakar At their desire we have made some alterations in our note, but they do not make any vital difference. Our position is quite clear and I have no doubt whatever about it. I hope you will appreciate it."

Accordingly, Mr. Jayakar alone saw Mr. Gandhi on the 31st July, 1st August and 2nd August when Mr. Gandhi dictated to him the following notes:—

"(1) No constitutional scheme would be acceptable to Mr. Gandhi which did not contain a clause allowing India the right to secede from the Empire at her desire and another clause which gave the right and power to India to deal satisfactorily with his eleven points.

"(2) The Viceroy should be made aware of this position of Mr. Gandhi in order that the Viceroy should not consider later that these views of Mr. Gandhi had taken him by surprise when they were urged at the Round Table Conference. The Viceroy should also be made aware that Mr. Gandhi would insist at the Round Table Conference on a clause giving India the right to have examined by an independent tribunal all the British claims and concessions given to Britishers in the past."

CONGRESS LEADERS' DEMANDS.

After that a joint interview took place in Yeravada Jail, Poona, on the 14th and 15th August between us on the one hand and Mr. Gandhi, Pandits Motilal Nehru and Jawaharlal Nehru, Mr. Vallabhbhai Patel, Dr. Syed Mahomed, Mr. Jairamdas Daulat Ram and Mrs. Naidu on the other. As a result of our conversations with them on these occasions, the Congress leaders gave us a letter with permission to show it to the Viceroy. This letter is set out below.

Yerawada Central Prison,
15th August, 1930.

Dear Friends,

We are deeply grateful to you for having undertaken the duty of trying to effect a peaceful settlement between the British Government and the Congress. After having perused the correspondence between yourselves and His Excellency the Viceroy and having had the benefit of protracted talks with you and having discussed among ourselves, we have come to the conclusion that the time is not yet ripe for securing a settlement honourable for our country. Marvellous as has been the mass awakening during the past five months and great as has been the suffering of the people among all grades and classes representing the different creeds, we feel that the sufferings have been neither sustained enough nor large enough for the immediate attainment of the end. Needless to mention we do not in any way share your view or the Viceroy's that civil disobedience has harmed the country or that it is ill-timed or unconstitutional. English history teems with instances of bloody revolts whose praises Englishmen have sung unstintingly and taught us to do likewise. It therefore ill becomes the Viceroy or any intelligent Englishman to condemn a revolt that is in intention and that has overwhelmingly remained in execution peaceful, but we have no desire to quarrel with condemnation whether official or unofficial of the present civil disobedience campaign. The wonderful mass response to the movement is, we hold, its sufficient justification. What is, however, the point here is the fact that we gladly make common cause with you in wishing, if it is at all possible, to stop or suspend, civil disobedience. It can be no pleasure to us needlessly to expose the men, women and children of our country to imprisonment, lathi charges and worse. You will, therefore, believe us when we assure you and through you the Viceroy that we would leave no stone unturned to explore any and every channel for honourable peace, but we are free to confess as yet we see no such sign on the horizon. We notice no symptom of conversion of the English official world to the view that it is India's men and women who must decide what is best for India. We distrust the pious declarations of the good intentions, often well meant, of officials. The agelong exploitation by the English of the people of this ancient land has rendered them almost incapable of seeing the ruin, moral, economic and political of our country which this exploitation has brought about. They cannot persuade themselves to see, that one thing needful for them to do is to get off our backs and do some reparation for the past wrongs by helping us to grow out of the dwarfing process that has gone on for a century of British domination, but we know you and some of our learned countrymen think differently. You believe a conversion has taken place, at any rate, sufficient to warrant participation in the proposed Conference. In spite, therefore, of the limitation we are labouring under, we would gladly co-operate with you to the extent of our ability.

The following is the utmost response it is possible for us, circumstanced as we are, to make to your friendly endeavour.

We feel the language used by the Viceroy in the reply given to your letter about the proposed Conference is too vague to enable us to assess its value in terms of the National Demand framed last year in Lahore nor are we in a position to say anything authoritative without reference to a properly constituted meeting of the Working Committee of the Congress and if necessary to the A. I. C. C. but we can say that for us individually no solution will be satisfactory unless (a) it recognises in as many words the right of India to secede at will from the British Empire, (b) it gives to India complete national Government responsible to her people including the control of defence forces and economic control and covers all the eleven points raised in Gandhiji's letter to the Viceroy and (c) it gives to India the right to refer if necessary to an independent tribunal such British claims, concessions and the like including the so-called public debt of India as may seem to the National Government to be unjust or not in the interest of the people of India.

Note :—Such adjustments as may be necessitated in the interests of India during the transference of power to be determined by India's chosen representatives.

(2) If the foregoing appears to be feasible to the British Government and a satisfactory declaration is made to that effect, we should recommend to the Working Committee the advisability of calling off civil disobedience, that is to say disobedience of certain laws for the sake of disobedience, but peaceful picketing of foreign cloth and liquor will be continued unless Government themselves can enforce prohibition of liquor and foreign cloth. The manufacture of salt by the people will have to be continued and the penal clauses of the Salt Act should not be enforced. There will be no raids on Government or private salt depots.

(3) Simultaneously with the calling off of civil disobedience (a) all the satyagrahi prisoners and other political prisoners convicted or under trial who have not been guilty of violence or incitement to violence should be ordered to be released, (b) Properties confiscated under the Salt Act, the Press Act, the Revenue Act and the like should be restored, (c) Fines and securities taken from convicted satyagrahis or under the Press Act should be refunded, (d) all the officers including village officers

who have resigned or who may have been dismissed during the civil disobedience movement and who may desire to rejoin Government service should be reinstated.

Note :—The foregoing sub-clauses refer also the Non-Co-operation Period.

(e) All the Viceregal Ordinances should be repealed.

(4) The question of the composition of the proposed Conference and of the Congress being represented at it can only be decided after the foregoing preliminaries are satisfactorily settled."

Yours sincerely,

Motilal Nehru,
M. K. Gandhi,
Sarojini Naidu,
Vallabhbhai Patel.
Jairamdas Daulatram,
Syed Mahomed,
Jawaharlal Nehru.

PEACE-MAKERS' LETTER TO CONGRESSMEN

Copy of a letter dated Bombay 16th August 1930.

'We sent them the following reply from Winter Road Malabar Hill, Bombay, on 16-8-30.

Dear Friends-We desire to express our thanks to you all for the courteous and patient hearing which you have been good enough to give us on the several occasions on which we visited you either in Poona or in Allahabad We regret we should have caused you so much inconvenience by these prolonged conversations and we are particularly sorry that Pandit Motilal Nehru should have been put to the trouble of coming down to Poona at a time when his health was so bad.

We beg formally to acknowledge receipt of the letter which you have handed us and in which you state the terms on which you are prepared to recommend to the Congress the calling off of civil disobedience and participation in the Round Table Conference. As we have informed you, we took up this work of mediation on the basis of (1) the terms of the interview given by Pandit Motilal Nehru, then the Acting President of the Congress, to Mr. Slocombe in Bombay on 20th June 1930 and particularly (2) the terms of the statement submitted by Mr. Slocombe to Pandit Motilal Nehru in Bombay on the 25th June 1930 and approved by him (Pandit Motilal Nehru) as the basis of an informal approach to the Viceroy by us.

Mr. Slocombe forwarded both the documents to us and we thereupon approached His Excellency the Viceroy for a mission to interview Mahatma Gandhi, Pandits Motilal Nehru and Jawaharlal Nehru in order to explore the possibilities of a settlement A copy of the second document referred to above has been taken by you from us. We now find the terms embodied in the letter, you gave us on the 14th instant are such that, as agreed between us, it must be submitted to His Excellency the Viceroy for his consideration and we have to await his decision. We note your desire that material documents relating to these peace negotiations including your said letter to us should be published and we shall proceed to do this after His Excellency the Viceroy has considered your letter.

Before we conclude, you will permit us to say that we had reasons to believe, as we told you, that with the actual calling off of the civil disobedience movement the general situation would largely improve. Non-violent political prisoners would be released, all the Ordinances with the exception of those affecting the Chittagong and the Lahore Conspiracy Cases would be repealed and the Congress would get representation at the Round Table Conference larger than that of any other single political party. We need scarcely add that we emphasised also that in our opinion there was substantially no difference between the point of view adopted by Pandit Motilal Nehru in his interview and the statement sent to us by Mr. Slocombe with Pandit Motilal's approval and His Excellency the Viceroy's letter to us.

Yours sincerely,
T. B Sapru,
M. R. Jayakar.

VICEROY'S LETTER TO SIR T. B. SAPRU

Thereafter Mr. Jayakar alone took the letter of the Congress leaders to Simla on the 21st August and had conversations with the Viceroy. Sir Tej Bahadur Sapru joined him on the 25th. We then had several interviews with the Viceroy and some members of his Council between the 25th and 27th August. As a result of the same the Viceroy gave us a letter to show to the Congress leaders in Allahabad and Poona.

The following is the text of that letter :

Viceregal Lodge,
Simla, 28th August 1930.

Dear Sir Tej Bahadur,—I have to thank you for informing me of the results of the conversations held by Mr. Jayakar and yourself with the Congress leaders now in prison and for sending me copies of their joint letter of the 15th August and of your reply thereto. I should wish you and Mr. Jayakar both to know how great has been my appreciation of the spirit in which you have pursued your self-imposed public spirited task of endeavouring to assist in the restoration of normal conditions in India. It is worth recalling the conditions under which you entered upon your undertaking. In my letter of 16th July, I assured you that it was the earnest desire of myself, my Government and I had no doubt also of His Majesty's Government, to do everything we could to assist the people of India to obtain as large a degree of management of their own affairs as could be shown to be consistent with the making of provision for those matters in regard to which they were not at present in a position to assume responsibility. It would be among the functions of the Conference to examine in the light of all the material available what those matters might be and what provision might be made for them I had previously made two other points plain in my speech to the legislature on the 9th July. The first is that those attending the Conference would have the unfettered right of examining the whole constitutional problem in all its bearing. Secondly, that any agreement at which the Conference was able to arrive would form the basis of the proposals which His Majesty's Government would later submit to Parliament. I fear as you will no doubt recognise that the task you had voluntarily undertaken has not been assisted by the letter you have received from the Congress leaders. In view both of the General tone by which the letter is inspired and of its contents, as also of its blank refusal to recognise the grave injury to which the country has been subjected by the Congress policy, not the least in the economic field, I do not think any useful purpose would be served by my attempting to deal in detail with the suggestions there made and I must frankly say I regard discussion on the basis of the proposals contained in the letter as impossible. I hope if you desire to see the Congress Leaders again you will make this plain

" There is one further comment I must make upon the last paragraph of your reply to them dated 16th August. When we discussed these matters, I said if the civil disobedience movement was in fact abandoned, I should not desire to continue the Ordinances (apart from those connected with the Lahore Conspiracy Case and Chittagong) necessitated by the situation which *ex-hypothesi* would no longer exist. But I was careful to make it plain that I was unable to give any assurance, if and when the civil disobedience movement ceases, that Local Governments would find it possible to release all persons convicted or under trial for offences in connection with the movement not involving violence, and that while I should wish to see a generous policy pursued in this matter, the utmost that I could promise would be to move all the Local Governments to consider with sympathy all the cases individually on their merits.

"Upon the point of your reference to the representation of the Congress at the Conference in the event of their abandoning the civil disobedience movement and desiring to attend, my recollection is you explained that the demand of the Congess was not for predominant, in the sense of majority, representation at the conference and that I expressed the view that I should anticipate little difficulty in recommending to His Majesty's Government to secure that the Congress should be adequately represented. I added that if events so developed, I should be ready to receive a panel of names from the leaders of the Congress Party of those whom they would regard as suitable representatives. I feel that you and Mr. Jayakar would desire to be clearly informed of the position of myself and my Government as it may be desirable that the letters should be published at an early date in order that the public may be fully informed of the circumstances, in which your efforts have failed to produce the result you hoped and they so certainly deserved.

Yours sincerely,
(Sd.) Irwin.

NOTES OF CONVERSATIONS WITH VICEROY

His Excellency the Viceroy also permitted us to mention to the Congress leaders the result of our conversations with him on certain specific points raised by us in connection with the letter of the Congress leaders We left Simla on the 28th of August, and interviewed Pandit Motilal Nehru and Pandit Jawaharlal Nehru, and Dr. Syed Mahmood at Naini Jail, Allahabad, on August 30 and 31st. We showed them the said letter of the Viceroy, and placed before them the result of our conversations. We explained to them with reference to the several points raised in their letter to us of August 15 and not covered by the Viceroy's letter of 28th August, that we had reason to believe from the conversations we had with the Viceroy that a settlement was possible on the following basis:—

(*a*) On the constitutional question the position would be as stated in the four fundamental points in para 2 of the Viceroy's letter to us of 28th August.

(*b*) With reference to the question whether Mr. Gandhi would be allowed to raise at the Round Table Conference the question of India's right to secede from the Empire at will, the position was as follows: "As the Viceroy has stated in his said letter to us, the Conference was a free Conference. Therefore, anyone could raise any points he liked, but the Viceroy, thought it would be very unwise for Mr Gandhi to raise this question now. If, however, he faced the Government of India with such a question, the Viceroy would say the Government were not prepared to treat it as an open question. If, in spite of this, Mr. Gandhi desired to raise the question, the Government would inform the Secretary of State of his intention to do so at the Round Table Conference."

(c) As regards the right to raise the question at the Round Table Conference of India's liability to certain financial burdens and to get them examined by an independent Tribunal, the position was that the Viceroy could not entertain any proposition amounting to total repudiation of all debts, but it would be open to anyone to raise, at the Round Table Conference, any question as to any financial liability of India and to call for its examination.

(d) As regards the granting of relief against the Salt Act, the position of the Viceroy was that (1) the Salt Tax was going to be provincialised if the recommendation of the Simon Commission in that behalf was accepted, and (2) there has been already great loss of revenue and therefore the Government would not like to forego this source, but if the Legislature was persuaded to repeal the Salt Act and if any proposal was put forward to make good the loss of revenue occasioned by such repeal, the Viceroy and his Government would consider the question on its merits. It was not, however, possible for the Viceroy to condone open breaches of the Salt Act so long as it was Law. When goodwill and peace were restored and, if Indian leaders desired to discuss with H. E the Viceroy and his Government how best economic relief could be given to the poorer classes on his behalf, the Viceroy would be glad to call a small conference of Indian leaders.

(e) With reference to picketing, the position was that if picketing amounted to nuisance to any class of people or was coupled with molestation or intimidation or the use of force, the Viceroy reserved to the Government the right of taking such action as the law allowed or taking of such legal powers as might be necessary to meet any emergency that might arise. Subject to the above when peace was established, the Ordinance against picketing would be withdrawn.

(f) With regard to the re-employment of the officers who resigned or had been dismissed during the civil disobedience campaign, the position was that this matter was primarily a question for the discretion of Local Governments, subject however to there being vacancies and as long as it did not involve dismissing men who had proved loyal, the Local Government would be expected to re-employ men who had thrown up their appointments in a fit of excitement or who had been swept off their feet.

(g) As for the restoration of Printing Presses confiscated under the Press Ordinance, there would be no difficulty.

(h) As regards the restoration of fines and properties confiscated under the Revenue Law, that required closer definition. As to the properties confiscated or sold under such law, there might be the rights of third parties involved. As to refunding fines, there were difficulties. In short, all that the Viceroy could say was that the Local Governments would exercise their discretion with justice and take all the circumstances into consideration and try to be as accommodating as they could.

(i) As to the release of prisoners the Viceroy had already explained his views in his letter to us dated July 28th.

NEHRUS' FINAL NOTE TO GANDHIJI.

We made clear to Pandit Motilal Nehru and Pandit Jawaharlal Nehru and Dr. Syed Mahomed, during their said two interviews with us, that though the time before us was limited further progress with our negotiations was possible on the lines indicated above. They, however, expressed unwillingness to accept any settlement on this basis and gave us a note for Mr Gaudhi which is as follows :—

Naini Central Prison,
31st August, 1930.

" We have had further interviews with Mr. M. R Jayakar and Sir Tej Bahadur Sapru yesterday and to-day, and have had the advantage of long talks with them. They have given us a copy of the letter, dated August 28, addressed to them by His Excellency Lord Irwin. In this letter, it is stated clearly that Lord Irwin regards discussion on the basis of the proposals contained in our joint letter of August 15th to Sir Tej Bahadur Sapru and Mr. Jayakar as impossible, and under the circumstances, he rightly concludes their efforts have failed to produce any result. This joint letter, as you know was written after a full consideration by the signatories to it, and represented the utmost they were prepared to go in their individual capacities. We stated there that no solution would be satisfactory unless it fulfilled certain vital conditions, and that a satisfactory declaration to that effect was made by the British Government. If such a declaration was made, we would be prepared to recommend to the Working Committee the desirability of calling off of civil disobedience, provided simultaneously certain steps indicated in our letter were taken by the British Government in India.

" It was only after a satisfactory settlement of all these preliminaries that the question of the composition of the proposed London Conference and of the Congress being represented at it could be decided. Lord Irwin, in his letter, considers even a discussion on the basis of these proposals as impossible. Under the circumstances, there is or can be no common ground between us. Quite apart from the contents, the tone of the British Government in India clearly indicate that the Government has no desire for peace The proclamation of the Working Committee as an illegal body in the Delhi Province soon after a meeting of it was announced to be held there, and the subsequent arrest of most of its members can have that meaning and no other. We have no complaint against these or other arrests or other activities of the Government, "uncivilised" and "barbarous" as we consider some of those to be. We welcome them But, we feel, we are justified in pointing out that a desire for peace and an aggressive attack on the very body, which is capable of giving peace and with which it is sought to treat, do not go well together. The proscription of the Working Committee all over India and the attempt to prevent its meetings must necessarily mean that the National struggle must go on, whatever the consequences, and that there will be no possibility of peace, for those who may have some authority to represent the people of India will spread out in British prisons all over India.

"Lord Irwin's letter and the action taken by the British Government make it plain that the efforts of Sir Tej Bahadur Sapru and Mr. Jayakar have been in vain. Indeed, the letter and some of the explanations thad had been given to us take us back, in some respects, even from the position that was previously taken. In view of the great *hiatus* that exists between our position and Lord Irwin's, it is hardly necessary to go into details, but we should like to point out to you certain aspects of the letter. The first part of the letter is practically a repetition of his speech to the Legislative Assembly and of the phrases used in his letter dated July 16, addressed to Mr. Jayakar and Sir Tej Bahadur Sapru. As we pointed out in our joint letter, this phraseology is too vague for us to assess its value It may be made to mean anything or nothing In our joint letter we have made it clear that a complete National Government responsible to the people of India, including control over the Defence Forces and economic control, must be recognised as India's immediate demand. There is no question of what are usually called safeguards or any delay. Adjustments there necessarily must be for the transference of power and in regard to these we stated they were to be determined by India's chosen representatives.

As regards India's right of secession at will from the British Empire and her right to refer British claims and concessions to an independent tribunal all that we are told is that the Conference will be a free conference and any point can be raised there. This is no advance on the previous statement made. We are further told, however, that if the British Government in India were definitely faced with the possibility of the former question being raised, Lord Irwin would say they were not to treat it as an open question. All they could do was to inform the Secretary of State of our intention to raise the question at the Conference.

"As regards the other proposition, we are told that Lord Irwin could only entertain the idea of a few individual financial transactions being subjected for scrutiny. While such scrutiny may take place in individual cases, its scope will have to extend to the whole field of British claims including, as we have stated, the so-called Public Debt of India. We consider both these questions as of vital importance and previous agreement in our joint letter seems to us essential.

"Lord Irwin's reference to the release of prisoners is very restricted and unsatisfactory. He is unable to give an assurance that all of the non-violent civil disobedience prisoners even will be discharged. All he proposes to do is to leave the matter in the hands of the Local Governments. We are not prepared to trust in such a matter to the generosity or sympathy of Local Governments or local officials but apart from this, there is no reference in Lord Irwin's letter to other non-violent prisoners. There are a large number of Congressmen and others who were sent to prison for political offences prior to the civil disobedience movement We might mention in this connection the Meerut Case prisoners who have already spent an year and a half as undertrials. We have made it clear in our joint letter that all these persons should be released.

Regarding the Bengal and the Lahore Case Ordinances we feel no exception should be made in their favour as suggested by Lord Irwin. We have not claimed release for those political prisoners who may have been guilty of violence not because we would not welcome their release but because we felt that as our movement was strictly non-violent, we would not confuse the issue. But the least we can do is to press for ordinary trial for these fellow countrymen of ours and not by an extra-ordinary court constituted by an ordinance which denies them the right of appeal and the ordinary privileges of accused.

Amazing events including the brutal assaults that have occurred even in open court during the so called trial make it imperative that the ordinary procedure should be followed We understand that some of the accused in protest against the treatment accorded to them have been on hunger-strike for a long period and are now at death's door. The Bengal Ordinance, we understand, has been replaced by an Act based on it and most objectionable, and the fact that an unrepresentative body like the present Bengal Council has passed it, does not make it any the better.

"As regards the further picketing of foreign cloth and liquor shops, we are told, Lord Irwin is agreeable to the withdrawal of the Picketing Ordinance, but he states that if he thinks it necessary, he will take fresh legal powers to combat picketing. Thus he informs us that he might re-enact the Ordinance or do something in Simla to it whenever he considers it necessary. The reply regarding the Salt Act and certain other matters referred to in our joint letter is also wholly unsatisfactory. We need not deal with it at any length here as you are an acknowledged expert on salt-reason to modify our previous position as regards these matters.

"Thus Lord Irwin has declined to agree to all the major propositions and many of the minor ones laid down in our joint letter. The difference in his out-look and ours is very great, indeed fundamental. We hope you will show his note to Mrs. Sarojini Naidu, Mr. Vallabhbhai Patel, Mr. Jairamdas Daulaltram and in consultation with them give your reply to Mr. Jayakar and Sir Tej Bahadur Sapru. We feel that the publication of the correspondence must no longer be delayed, and we are not justified in keeping the public in the dark. Even apart from the question of publication, we are requesting Sir Tej Bahadur Sapru and Mr. Jayakar to send copies of all correspondence and relevant papers to Chaudhuri Khaliq Uzaman, the Acting President of the Indian National Congress We feel we ought to take no step without immediate information being sent to the Working Committee, which happens to be functioning."

(Sd) Motilal,
(Sd) Syed Mahmud.
(Sd.) Jawaharlal.

LEADERS' JOINT REPLY

We accordingly saw Mr. Gandhi and other Congress leaders in Yerawada Jail, Poona on the 3rd, 4th and 5th September, gave them the said letter, and discussed the whole question with them.

As a result of such conversations, they gave us the statement which is reproduced below :—

Yerawada Central Prison,
5-9-1930.

Dear Friends,—We have very carefully gone through the letter, written to you by H. E. the Viceroy dated 28-8-1930. You have kindly supplemented it with a record of your conversations with the Viceroy on points not covered by the letter. We have equally carefully gone through the Note signed by Pandit Motilal Nehru, Dr Syed Mahmud and Pandit Jawaharlal Nehru, and sent by them through you. The note embodies their considered opinion on the said letter and the conversation.

We gave two anxious nights to these papers and we had the benefit of a full and free discussion with you on all the points arising out of these papers. And as we have told you we have all arrived at the definite conclusion that we see no meeting ground between the Government and the Indian National Congress so far as we can speak for the latter, being out of touch with the outside world. We unreservedly associate ourselves with the opinion contained in the Note sent by the distinguished prisoners in the Naini Central Prison, but these friends expect us to give in our own words our view of the position finally reached in the negotiations for peace which you, with patriotic motives, have carried on during the past two months at considerable sacrifice of your own time and no less inconvenience to yourselves. We shall therefore allude as briefly as possible to the fundamental difficulties that have stood in the way of peace being achieved.

The Viceroy's letter dated 16-7-30 is, we have taken, intended to satisfy, so far as may be, the terms of the interview, Pandit Motilal Nehru gave to Mr. George Slocombe on June 20th, and the statement submitted by Mr. Slocombe to him, on June 25 and approved by him. We are unable to read in the Viceroy's language in his letter of July 16 anything like satisfaction of the terms of the interview of the said statement. Here are the relevant parts of the interview and the statement.

In the interview it was stated, "If the terms of the Round Table Conference are to be left open we are expected to go to London to argue the case for Dominion Status. I should decline. If it was made clear, however, that the Conference would meet to frame a constitution for a Free India subject to such adjustments of our mutual relations as are required by the special needs and conditions of India and our past agitation, I for one would be disposed to recommend to the Congressmen to accept the invitation to participate in the conference. We must be masters in our household, but we are ready to agree to reasonable terms for the period of transaction of power from a British administration in India to a responsible Indian Government. The Conference must be to meet British people discuss these terms as Nation to Nation and on an equal footing.

The statement contained the following. "The Government would give private assurance that they would support the demand for full responsible Government for India subject to such mutual adjustments and terms of transfer as are required by the special needs and conditions of India and by her long association with Great Britain and as may be decided by the Round Table Conference."

Here is the relevant part of the Viceroy's letter. "It remains my earnest desire, as it is, that of my Government and I have no doubt also that of His Majesty's Government to do everything we can in our respective spheres to assist the people of India to obtain as large a degree of management of their own affairs as can be shown to be consistent with making provision for those matters in regard to which they are not at present in a position to assume responsibilities. What those matters may be, and what provisions may best be made for them, will engage the attention of the conference, but I have never believed that, with mutual confidence on both the sides, it should be impossible to reach an agreement "

We feel that there is a vast difference between the two positions. Where Pandit Motilalji visualises a Free India enjoying a status different in kind from the present as a result of the deliberations of the proposed Round Table Conference, the Viceroy's letter merely commits him and his Government and the British Cabinet to an earnest desire to assist India to obtain as large a degree of the management of their own affairs as can be shown to be consistent with making provision for those matters in regard to which they are not at present in a positon to assume responsibility. In other words, the prospect held out by the Viceroy's letter is one of getting, at the most, something more along the lines of reforms commencing with those known to us as the Landsdowne Reforms As we had the fear that our interpretation was correct in our letter of 15-8-'30 signed also by Pandit Motilal Nehru, Dr Syed Mahmud and Pandit Jawahar Lal Nehru, we put our position negatively and said what would not in our opinion satisfy the Congress The letter you have now brought from H E the Viceroy reiterates the original position taken up by him in his first letter and we are grieved to say contemptuously dismisses our letter as unworthy of consideration and regards discussion on the basis of the proposals contained in the letter as impossible.

You have thrown further light on the question by telling us that if Mr. Gandhi definitely faced the Government of India with such a question (*i.e.*,) the right of secession from the Empire at India's will, the Viceroy would say, they were not prepared to treat it as an open question. We, on the other hand, regard the question as the central point in any constitution that India is to secure and one which ought not to need any argument. If India is now to attain full Responsible Government or full Self-Government or whatever other term it is to be known by, it can be only on an absolutely voluntary basis, leaving each party to sever the partnership or association at will. If

India is to remain no longer a part of the Emipire but is to become an equal and free partner in the Commonwealth, she must feel the want and warmth of that association and never otherwise. You will please observe this position is clearly brought out in the interview already alluded to by us. So long, therefore, as the British Government, or the British people regard this position as impossible or untenable, the Congress must, in our opinion, continue the fight for freedom.

The attitude taken up by the Viceroy over the very mild proposal made by us regarding the Salt Tax affords a further painful insight into the Government's mentality It is as plain as daylight to us that, from the dizzy heights of Simla, the Rulers of India are unable to understand or appreciate the difficulties of the starving millions living in the plains whose incessant toil makes Government from such a giddy height at all possible.

If the blood of innocent people that was split during the past five months to sustain the monopoly of a gift of nature next in importance to poor people only to air and water, has not brought home to the Government the conviction of its utter immorality, no Conference of Indian leaders as suggested by the Viceroy can possibly do so. The suggestion that those who ask for the repeal of the monopoly should show a source of equivalent revenue adds insult to injury. This attitude is an indication that if Government can help it the existing crushingly expensive system shall continue to the end of time. We venture further to point out that not only does the Government here, but Governments all the world over, openly condone breaches of measures which have become unpopular but which for technical or other reasons cannot straightaway be repealed. We need not now deal with many other important matters in which too there is no adequate advance from the Viceroy to the popular position set forth by us. We hope we have brought out sufficient weighty matters in which there appears at present to be an unbridged gulf between the British Government and the Congress.

There need, however, be no disappointment, for the apparent failure of the Peace negotiations The Congress is engaged in a grim struggle for Freedom The nation has resorted to a weapon which the Rulers being unused to it will take time to understand and appreciate. We are not surprised that a few months' suffering has not converted them The Congress desires to harm no single legitimate interest by whomsoever acquired It has no quarrel with Englishmen as such, but it resents and will resent with all the moral strength at its command, the intolerable British domination. Non-violence being assured to the end, we are certain of the early fulfilment of the national aspiration. This we say, in spite of the bitter and often insulting language used by the powers that be in regard to civil disobedience.

Lastly, we once more thank you for the great pains you have taken to bring about peace, but we suggest that the time has not arrived when any further peace negotiations should be carried on with those in charge of the Congress organisation. As prisoners, we labour under an obvious handicap. Our opinion is based, as it must be, on second-hand evidence and runs the risk of being faulty. It would be naturally open to those in charge of the Congress organisation to see any of us. In that case, and when the Government itself is equally desirous for peace, they should have no difficulty in having access to us.

(Sd.) M. K. Gandhi.
(Sd.) Sarojini Naidu.
(Sd.) Vallabhbhai Patel,
(Sd.) Jairamdas Doulatram.

We content ourselves with publishing for the information of the public material facts and documents and in strict conformity with our duties and obligations as intermediaries, we refrain in this statement from putting our own interpretation or offering our own comments on the facts and documents set out above. We may mention that we have obtained the consent of H. E. The Viceroy, and the Congress leaders to the publication of the documents above set out.

Appendix V

FORMS OF DECLARATION BY INDIAN MILLS.

We hereby declare :

1 That we have full sympathy with the national aspirations of the people.

2 That not less than 75 per cent. of the share capital of the Company is held by Indians. (The Special Committee nominated by the President of the Congress in this behalf may, however, permit exemptions in regard to this clause as special cases.)

3. That not less than 66 per cent. of the Directors of the Company apart from the ex-officio Directors are and will continue to be Indian. In the event of the ex-officio Directors being non-Indians, the Indian Directors should form a majority in the Board.

4. That there is no foreign interest in the Managing Agents' firm.

5. That the partners of the Agents' firm or the firm are not interested in any foreign insurance companies or in the import trade of foreign yarn or foreign piece-goods.

6. That we will assist in the propagation of Swadeshi, firstly by taking steps to eliminate the competition of mill cloth with khadi (*i.e.* handspun and handwoven cloth) and secondly by refraining from exploiting in our own interest the situation arising out of the movement in respect of the price or quality of cloth.

7 That the ownership as well as the management of the mills is Indian and the personnel of the management is Indian in outlook and spirit and is pledged to safeguard Indian interest.

In pursuance of the above declarations, we hereby undertake to do as follows:

1. No person connected with the management of the mills will engage himself in propaganda hostile to the national movement or participate in any activity organised voluntarily or at the instance or on behalf of the British Goverment in India in opposition to the movement.

2. Recruitment of staff will be restricted to Indians, except for special reasons.

3. We shall pass as early as possible the insurance business of our Company to Indian Insurance Companies.

4. As far as possible we shall pass our Banking and shipping business to Indian Banks and Indian Steamship Companies.

5. We shall henceforth employ as far as possible, Indians as our auditors, solicitors, shipping agents, buying or selling brokers, contractors or suppliers of goods required for our mills.

6. We shall purchase, as far as possible, store articles of Indian manufacture and will only buy such foreign articles as are indispensable and as cannot be replaced by Indian Swadeshi articles (List of such foreign articles as are indispensable is enclosed herewith).

7. We shall not make use of any kind of foreign yarn or foreign silk or artificial silk or thread or yarn made in mills on the boycott list.

8. We shall not bleach or dye any yarn or cloth that is foreign or produced in mills that are placed on the boycott list.

9. We shall put our stamps distinctly on both ends of each piece of cloth manufactured in our mills and will not send any cloth outside without the proper stamps.

10. We shall not name, stamp or style any of our cloth as khadi.

11. We shall not make cloth of the following specifications:

Any cloth, grey or bleached, warp, and weft counts each coarser than 18 plain weave, one up and down, single or double and weft including checks plain weave, also those made on drop box and circular box and carpets. (18 counts shall include either single or multifold yarn the count of which (multifold) comes to 18 or less).

The mills, however, shall be at liberty to make drills, satins, tussers, twills, cloth on jacquards and dobby patterns in the body, dyed cloth made from dyed cotton, blankets and malidas.

12. We shall, as far as possible, do all our selling or buying business with or through Indian concerns.

13. Persons connected with management of our mills will wear Swadeshi cloth.

Name of the Company.............

Address.........................

Names of the Agents or Proprietors.

FORM

Declaration by non-Indian Mills

We hereby declare:

1. That we have full sympathy with the national aspirations of the people.

2 That not less than 75 per cent. of the share capital of the company is held by Indians (The Special Committee nominated by the President of the Congress in this behalf may, however, permit exemption in regard to this clause as special cases).

3 That not less than 66 per cent of the Directors of the Company apart from the ex-officio directors are and will continue to be Indians. (In the event of the ex-officio Directors being non-Indians, Indian Directors should form a majority in the Board.

4. The partners of the Agents' firm are not in any way interested in the import trade of foreign yarn or foreign piecegoods.

5. That we will assist in the propagation of Swadeshi, firstly by taking steps to eliminate the competition of mill cloth with khadi (i.e. handspun and handwoven cloth) and secondly by refraining from exploiting in our own interest the situation arising out of the movement in respect of the price or quality of cloth.

6. That the personnel of the management is Indian in outlook and spirit and is pledged to safeguard Indian interest.

In pursuance of the above declaration we hereby undertake to do as follows:

1. No person connected with the management of the mills will engage himself in propaganda hostile to the national movement or participate in any activity organised voluntarily or at the instance or on behalf of the British Government in India in opoosition to the movement.

2. Recruitment of staff will be restricted to Indians except for special reasons.

3. As far as possible we shall pass our Insurance, Banking and Shipping business to Indian Insurance Companies, Indian Banks and Indian Steamship Companies.

4. We shall henceforth employ, as far as possible, only Indians as our auditors, solicitors, shipping agents, buying or selling brokers, contractors or suppliers of goods required for our mills.

5. We shall purchase, as far as possible, store articles of Indian manufacture and will only buy such foreign articles as are indispensable and as cannot be replaced by Indian Swadeshi articles (A list of such foreign articles is enclosed herewith.)

(To be supplied by the mills)

6. We shall not make use of any kind of foreign yarn or foreign silk or artificial silk or thread or yarn made in mills on the boycott list.

7. We shall not bleach or dye any yarn or cloth that is foreign or produced in mills that are placed on the boycott list.

8. We shall put our stamps distinctly at both ends on each piece of cloth manufactured in our mills and will not send any cloth outside without proper stamps.

9 We shall not name, stamp or style any of our cloth as khadi.

10 We shall not make cloth of the following specifications. Any cloth grey or bleached, warp and weft, counts each coarser than 18 plain weave, one up and down, single or double end weft including checks, plain weave, also those made on drop box and circular box and carpets (18 counts shall include either single or multifold yarn, the count of which (multifold) comes to 18 or less)

The mills, however, shall be at liberty to make drills, satins tussers, twills, cloth on jacquards and dobby patterns in the body dyed cloth, made from dyed cotton blankets and mallidas.

11. We shall hence forth do our selling or buying business as far as possible, with or through Indian concerns.

12. Persons connected with the management of our mills will wear Swadeshi cloth

Name of the Company............................

Address...

Managing Agents or Proprietors ....

FORM

DECLARATION ISSUED BY THE BOMBAY

PROVINCIAL CONGRESS COMMITTEE.

We declare that we have full sympathy with the national aspirations of the people and appreciate the impetus given to the cause of Swadeshi by the National Movement.

For the protection of Khadi we agree not to stamp or sell as Khadi any cloth manufactured at our mills and not to manufacture any cloth below average 10 counts except of certain sorts to be agreed upon by the mills and your Committee. (Bombay Provincial Congress Committee)

To preserve and promote Swadeshi character of our mill industry the following scheme was approved of and we agree to and accept the same, namely:

(a) That ownership and management of the mills is and will continue Indian and national in outlook and spirit, pledged to safeguard Indian interest.

(b) That no person connected with the management of the mills will engage in any anti-national activities.

(c) That not less than 75 per cent. of the share capital of the Company is and will continue to be held by Indians, except in cases and to the extent agreed to by the President of the Congress as special cases.

(d) That not less than 66 per cent of the Directors apart from the ex-officio Directors of every such Company are and will continue to be Indians

(e) That the management and control of the company will remain and continue Indian, except in the case of Mills (a list is settled by consent) which are now managed by non-Indian Mill agents and which have accepted these term saving this clause.

(f) That recruitment of the staff will be restricted to Indians excepting for special reasons.

(g) That the mills will confine their purchases to Indian Swadeshi products as far as possible and will place their business with Indian Banking, Insurance and Shipping Companies as far as possible.

(h) That the Mills will not dye or bleach any foreign yarn or cloth which has been declared non-Swadeshi by the Bombay Provincial Congress Committee.

(i) That the Mills will not use foreign yarn and will not use mercerised yarn and artificial silk after 31st December, 1930.

(j) That the Mills will stamp every piece of cloth with their name.

(k) That no Millowner, Mill Agent or other persons connected with the control and the management of the Mills will directly or indirectly import or deal in foreign yarn or piecegoods.

(I) That the Mills will not exploit in their own interest the spirit of Swadeshi generated and encouraged by the national movement and will guard against profiteering by middlemen and will make Swadeshi goods available to the consuming public at reasonable rates and in particular.

i. will sell during the period ending 31st December 1930 the current sorts produced at the Mills at current rates or rates prevailing on 12th March, 1930, whichever at the time be lower.

ii. will publish and circulate for the information of the general consuming public the selling prices of current sorts prevailing from time to time.

iii. will meet the representatives of the Bombay Provincial Congress Committee from time to time and adopt such further means as may be mutually agreed upon to prevent profiteering and to secure a constant supply of Swadeshi piecegoods to the consuming public at reasonable prices.

Appendix VI

The announcement by His Majesty's Government of the Communal Award has been made. The following is the full text :—

(1) In the statement made by the Prime Minister on December last, on behalf of His Majesty's Government, at the close of the second session of the Round Table Conference, which was immediately afterwards endorsed by both Houses of Parliament, it made plain that, if the communities in India were unable to reach a settlement acceptable to all parties on communal questions which the Conference had failed to solve, His Majesty's Government were determined that India's constitutional advance should not on that account be frustrated, and they would remove this obstacle by devising and applying themselves to a provisional scheme.

(2) On March 19 last, His Majesty's Government, having been informed that the continued failure of the communities to reach an agreement was blocking the progress of plans for the framing of the new constitution, stated that they were engaged upon a careful re-examination of the difficult and controversial questions which arise. They are now satisfied that, without the decision of at least some aspects of the problems connected with the position of the minorities under the new constitution no further progress can be made with the framing of the constitution.

SCOPE OF THE SCHEME.

(3) His Majesty's Government have accordingly decided that they will include provisions to give effect to the scheme set out below in the proposals relating to the Indian constitution to be laid in due course before Parliament. The scope of this scheme is purposely confined to the arrangements to be made for the representation of British Indian Communities in Provincial legislatures consideration of representation in the Legislature at the Centre being deferred for the reason given in paragraph 20 below The decision to limit the scope of the scheme does not imply a failure to realise that the framing of the constitution will necessitate the decision of a number of other problems of great importance to minorities, but has been taken in the hope that, once a pronouncement has been made upon the basic question of the method and proportions of representation, the communities themselves may find it possible to arrive at a '*modus vivendi*' on the other communal problems which have not as yet received the examination they require.

(4) His Majesty's Government wish it to be most clearly understood that they themselves can be no parties to any negotiations which may be initiated with a view to the revision of their decision, and will not be prepared to give consideration to any representation aimed at securing a modification of it, which is not supported by all the parties affected. But they are most desirous to close no door to an agreed settlement, should such happily be forthcoming. If, therefore, before the new Government of India Act is passed into law, they are satisfied that the communities who are concerned are mutually agreed upon a practicable alternative scheme, either in respect of any one or more of the Governor's Provinces, or in respect of the whole of British India, they will be prepared to recommend to Parliament that the alternative should be substituted for the provisions now outlined.

(5) Seats in the Legislative Councils in Governor's Provinces or in the Lower House, if there is an Upper Chamber, will be allocated as shown in para 24 below.

SEPARATE ELECTORATES

(6) Election to the seats alloted to Muslim, European and Sikh constituencies will be by voters voting in separate communal electorates, covering between them the whole area of the Province (apart from any portions which may, in special cases, be excluded from the electoral area as "backward".

Provision will be made in the constitution itself to empower revision of this electoral arrangement (and other similar arrangements mentioned below) after ten years, with the assent to the communities affected, for the ascertainment of which suitable means will be devised.

(7) All qualified electors, who are not voters either in a Muslim, Sikh, Indian Christian (see para. 10), Anglo Indian (see para. 11) of European constituency, will be entitled to vote in a general constituency.

(8) Seven seats will be reserved for Mahrattas in certain selected plural member general constituencies in Bombay.

DEPRESSED CLASSES

(9) Members of the "Depressed Classes" qualified to vote will vote in a general constituency. In view of the fact that, for a considerable period, these classes would be unlikely, by this means alone, to secure any adequate representation in a legislature, a number of special seats will be assigned to them as shown in para. 24 below. These seats will be filled by election from special

constituencies in which only members of the "Depressed Classes" electorally qualified will be entitled to vote. Any person voting in such special constituency will, as stated above, be also entitled to vote in a general constituency. It is intended that these constituencies should be formed in selected areas where the "Depressed Classes" are most numerous. and that, except in Madras they should not cover the whole area of the Province.

In Bengal, it seems possible that, in some general constituencies, the majority of voters will belong to the Depressed Classes. Accordingly, pending further investigation, no number has been fixed for members to be returned from special Depressed Classes constituencies in that Province It is intended to secure that the Depressed Classes should obtain not less than ten seats in the Bengal Legislature.

The precise definition in each Province of those who (if electorally qualified) will be entitled to vote in special Depressed Class constituencies has not yet been finally determined. It would be based as a rule on the general principles advocated in the Franchise Committee's Report. Modification may, however, be found necessary in some Provinces in Northern India where the application of the general criteria of untouchability might result in a definition unsuitable in some respects to the special conditions of the Province.

His Majesty's Government do not consider that these special Depressed Classes constituencies will be required for more than a limited time. They intend that the constitution shall provide that they shall come to an end after twenty years, if they have not previously been abolished under the general powers of electoral revision referred to in para. 6.

INDIAN CHRISTIANS.

(10) Election to the seats allotted to Indian Christians will be by voters voting in separate communal electorates. It seems almost certain that the formation of Indian Christian constituencies covering the whole area of a province will be impracticable and that, accordingly, special Indian Christian constituencies will have to be formed only in one or two selected areas in a Province Indian Christian voters in these areas will not vote in a general constituency Indian Christian voters outside these areas will vote in a general constituency, special arrangements may be needed in Bihar and Orissa, where a considerable proportion of the Indian Christian Community belongs to aboriginal tribes.

ANGLO-INDIANS

(11) Election to seats allotted to Anglo-Indians will be by voters voting in separate communal electorates. It is at present

intended, subject to investigation of any practical difficulties that may arise, that Anglo-Indian constituencies shall cover the whole area of each Province, postal ballot being employed; but no final decision has yet been reached.

(12) The method of filling seats assigned for representatives from backward areas is still under investigation, and the number of seats so assigned should be regarded as provisional, pending final decision as to the constitutional arrangements to be made in relation to such areas.

WOMEN

(13) His Majesty's Government attach great importance to securing that the new legislatures should contain at least a small number of women members. They feel that at the outset, this object could not be achieved without creating a certain number of seats specially allotted to women. They also feel it is essential that women members should not be drawn disproportionately from one community. They have been unable to find any system which would avoid this risk, and would be consistent with the rest of the scheme for representation which they have found it necessary to adopt, except that of limiting the electorate for each special woman's seat to voters from one community, subject to the exception explained in para. 24 below. Special women's seats have accordingly been specifically divided, as explained in para 24 below, between the various communities. The precise electoral machinery to be employed in these special constituencies is still under consideration.

SPECIAL INTEREST

(14) Seats allotted to "Labour" will be filled from non-communal constituencies. Electoral arrangements have still to be determined, but it is likely that, in most Provinces Labour constituencies will be partly Trade Union and partly special constituencies, as recommended by the Franchise Committee.

(15) Special seats allotted to Commerce and Industry, Mining and Planting will be filled by election through Chamber of Commerce and various Associations. Details of the electoral arrangements for these seats must await further investigation.

(16) Special seats allotted to Landholders will be filled by election by special Landholders' constituencies.

(17) The method to be employed for election to University seats is still under consideration.

(18) His Majesty's Government have found it impossible, in determining these questions of representation in provincial legislatures, to avoid entering into considerable detail. There

remains nevertheless the determination of the constituencies They intend that this task should be undertaken in India as early as possible.

It is possible, in some instances, delimitation of constituencies might be materially improved by a slight variation from the number of seats now given. His Majesty's Government reserve the right to make such slight variations for such purpose, provided they will not materially affect the essential balance between the communities. No such variations will, however, be made in the case of Bengal and the Punjab.

SECOND CHAMBERS

(19) The question of the composition of Second Chambers in the Provinces has so far received comparatively little attention in the constitutional discussions and requires further consideration before a decision is reached which Provinces shall have a Second Chamber or a scheme is drawn up for their composition.

His Majesty's Government consider that the composition of the Upper House in a Province should be such as not to disturb, in any essential, the balance between the communities resulting from the composition of the Lower House.

(20) His Majesty's Government do not propose at present to enter into the question of size and composition of the Legislature at the centre, since this involves, among other questions, that of representation of Indian States, which still needs further discussion They will, of course, when considering the composition, pay full regard to the claims of all communities for adequate representation therein.

SEPARATION OF SIND

(21) His Majesty's Government have already accepted the recommendation that Sind should be constituted a separate Province, if satisfactory means of financing it can be found As the financial problems involved still have to be reviewed in connection with other problems of federal finance, His Majesty's Government have thought it preferable to include, at this stage, figures for a legislature for the existing Province of Bombay, in addition to the schemes for separate legislatures for the Bombay Presidency proper and Sind

(22) The figures given for Bihar and Orissa relate to the existing Province. The question of constituting a separate Province of Orissa is still under investigation.

(23) The inclusion, in para 24 below, of figures relating to the legislature for the Central Provinces, including Berar, does not imply that any decision has yet been reached regarding the future constitutional position of Berar.

(24) The following will be the allocation of seats in provincial legislatures (Lower House only) :—

MADRAS

General seats (including six women)	...	134
Depressed Classes	..	18
Representative from Backward areas	...	1
Muslims (including one woman)	...	29
Indian Christians (including one woman)	..	9
Anglo-Indians	...	2
Europeans	...	3
Commerce and Industry, Mining and Planting.		6
Landholders	...	1
University	...	1
Labour	...	6
Total	...	210

BOMBAY

(INCLUDING SIND)

General seats (including five women)	...	97
Depressed Classes	...	10
Backward Areas	...	1
Muslims (including 1 woman)	..	63
Indian Christians	...	3
Anglo-Indians	..	2
Europeans	...	4
Commerce etc.	...	8
Landholders	...	3
University	...	1
Labour	...	8
		200

BENGAL

General seats (including 2 women)	...	80
Depressed Classes	..	—
Muslims (including 2 women)	...	119
Indian Christians	...	2
Anglo-Indians (including 1 woman)	...	4
Europeans	...	11
Commerce etc.	...	19
Landholders	...	5
University	...	2
Labour	...	8
Total	...	250

UNITED PROVINCES

General seats (including 4 women)	...	132
Depressed Classes	...	12
Muslims (including 2 women)	...	66
Indian Christians	...	2
Anglo-Indians	...	1
Europeans	...	2
Commerce etc.	...	3
Landholders	...	6
University	...	1
Labour	...	3
Total	...	228

PUNJAB

General seats (including one woman)	..	43
Sikhs (including 1 woman)	.	32
Muslims (including two women)	.	86
Indian Christians	.	2
Anglo-Indians	...	1
Europeans	...	1
Commerce etc.	...	1
Landholders	...	5
University	...	1
Labour	...	3
Total	..	175

BIHAR AND ORISSA

General seats (including 3 women)	..	99
Depressed Classes	...	7
Representatives from Backward Areas	...	8
Muslims (including 1 woman)	...	42
Indian Christians	...	2
Anglo-Indians	...	1
Europeans	...	2
Commerce etc.	...	4
Landholders	...	5
University	...	1
Labour	...	4
Total	...	175

CENTRAL PROVINCES

(INCLUDING BERAR)

General seats (including 3 women)	...	77
Depressed Classes	..	10
Representative from Backward Areas	...	1
Muslims	...	14
Anglo-Indians	...	1
Europeans	...	1
Commerce etc.	...	2
Landholders	...	3
University	...	1
Labour	...	2
Total	...	112

ASSAM

General seats (including one woman)	...	44
Depressed Classes	...	4
Representatives from Backward Areas	...	9
Muslims	...	34
Indian Christians	...	1
Europeans	..	1
Commerce etc.	...	11
Labour	..	4
Total	...	108

NORTH-WEST FRONTIER PROVINCE

General seats	...	9
Sikhs	...	3
Muslims	...	36
Landholderrs	...	2
Total	...	50

Seats are also allocated for Bombay without Sind and for Sind as follows:—

BOMBAY WITHOUT SIND

General seats (including five women)	...	109
Depressed Classes	...	10
Representative from Backward Areas	...	1
Muslims (including one woman)	...	30
Indian Christians	...	3
Anglo-Indians	...	2
Europeans	...	3
Commerce etc.	...	7
Landholders	...	2
University	...	1
Labour	...	7
Total	...	175

SIND

General seats (including one woman)	...	19
Muslims (including one weman)	...	34
Europeans	...	2
Commerce etc	...	2
Landholders	...	2
Labour	...	1
Total	...	60

SPECIAL CONSTITUENCIES

As regards seats for Commerce and Industry, Mining and Planting, it is stated that the composition of bodies through which election of these seats will be conducted, though in most cases either predominantly European or predominantly Indian, will not be statutorily fixed. It is accordingly not possible in each Province to state with certainty how many Europeans and Indians respectively will be returned.

It is, however, expected that, initially, the numbers will be approximately as follows:—

Madras: 4 Europeans and 2 Indians.
Bombay (including Sind) : 5 Europeans and 3 Indians.
Bengal : 14 Europeans and 5 Indians.
United Provinces: 2 Europeans and 1 Indian.
Punjab: 1 Indian.
Bihar and Orissa; 2 Europeans and 2 Indians.
Central Provinces (including Berar); 1 European and 1 Indian.

Assam: 8 Europeans and 3 Indians.
Bombay (without Sind) 4 Europeans and 3 Indians.
Sind: 1 European and 1 Indian.

As regards general seats allocated to Bombay, whether inclusive or exclusive of Sind, it is stated seven of them will be reserved for Mahrattas.

As regards allocation of seats for Depressed Classes in Bengal this number, which will not exceed ten, has not yet been fixed. The number of general seats will be thirty, less the number of special Depressed Class seats.

As regards Landholders' seats in the Punjab, it is stated one of these will be a 'Zamindars' seat Four Landholders' seats will be filled from special constituencies with joint electorates. It is probable from distribution of the electorate that the members returned will be one Hindu, one Sikh and two Muslims.

As regards allocation of one woman's seat among general seats in Assam, it is stated this will be filled from a non-communal constituency at Shillong.

PREMIER'S EXPLANATORY STATEMENT

The text of the decison of His Majesty's Government regarding certain Communal problems connected with the framing of the new Indian Constitution has now reached India and is being published simultaneously in both the countries.

On its publication, the Prime Minister has issued the following statements;—

"Not only as the Prime Minister, but as a friend of India who has for the last two years taken a special interest in the questions of minorities I feel that I ought to add a word or two of explanation to the extremely importart decision on communal representation that the Government are announcing to-day.

We never wished to intervene in the communal controversies of India. We made that abundantly clear during both the sessions of the R.T.C when we strove hard to get Indians to settle this matter between themselves. We have realised from the very first that any decision that we may make is likely, to begin with at any rate, to be criticised by every community purely from the point of view of its own complete demands, but we believe that in the end considerations of Indian needs will prevail and all communities will see that their duty is to co-operate in working the new constitution which is to give India a new place in the British Commonwealth of Nations.

SETTLEMENT SUBJECT TO REVISION BY AGREEMENT

Our duty was plain. As the failure of the communities to agree amongst themselves has placed an almost insurmountable obstacle in the way of any constitutional development, it was incumbent upon Government to take action in accordance, therefore, with the pledges that I gave on behalf of the Government at the Round Table Conference in response to repeated appeals from representative Indians and in accordance with the statement to British Parliament and approved by it Government are to-day publishing a scheme of representation in Provincial Assemblies that they intend in due course to lay before Parliament unless in the meanwhile the communities themselves agree upon a better plan.

We should be only too glad if, at any stage before the proposed Bill becomes law, the communities can reach an agreement amongst themselves. But guided by the past experience, Government are convinced that no further negotiations will be of any advantage, and they can be no party to them. They will, however, be ready and willing to substitute for their scheme any scheme whether in respect of any one or more of Governor's Provinces or in respect of the whole of British India that is generally agreed and accepted by all the parties affected.

THE CASE FOR SEPARATE ELECTORATES

In order to appreciate the Government's decision, it is necessary to remember the actual conditions in which it is being given. For many years past, separate electorates, namely, the grouping of particular categories of voters in territorial constituencies by themselves has been regarded by minority communities as an essential protection for their rights. In each of the recent stages of constitutional development, separate electorates have consequentially found a place. However much Government may have preferred a uniform system of joint electorates, they found it impossible to abolish the safeguards to which minorities still attach vital importance. It would serve no purpose to examine the cause which in the past have led to this state of affairs. I am rather thinking of the future. I want to see the greater and the smaller communities working together in peace and amity so that there will be no further need for a special form of protection. In the meantime, however, Government have to face facts as they are, and must maintain this exceptional form of representation.

THE POSITION OF THE DEPRESSED CLASSES

There are two features of the decision to which I must allude. One has to do with the Depressed Classes and the other with the representation of women. Government would be quite unable to ustify a scheme which omitted to provide what is really requisite for either.

Our main object in the case of the Depressed Classes has been while securing to them the spokesmen of their own choice in the legislatures of the Province where they are found in large numbers, at the same time to avoid electoral arrangements which would perpetuate their segregation. Consequently, Depressed Class voters will vote in general Hindu constituencies and an elected member in such a constituency will be influenced by his responsibility to this section of the electorate, but for the next 20 years there will also be a number of special seats filled from special Depressed Class electorates in the areas where these voters chiefly prevail. The anomaly of giving certain members of the Depressed Classes two votes is abundantly justified by the urgent need of securing that their claims should be effectively expressed and the prospects of improving their actual condition promoted.

WOMEN'S RIGHTS.

As regards women voters, it has been widely recognised in recent years that the women's movement in India holds one of the keys of progress. It is not too much to say that India cannot reach the position to which it aspires in the world until its women play their due part as educated and influential citizens. There are undoubtedly serious objections to extending to the representation of women the communal method, but if seats are to be reserved for women as such and woman members are to be fairly distributed among the communities, there is, in the existing circumstances, no alternative.

With this explanation, I commend the scheme to Indian Communities as a fair and honest attempt to hold the balance between the conflicting claims in relation to the existing position in India. Let them take it though it may not for the moment satisfy the full claims of any of them as a workable plan for dealing with the question of representation in the next period of India's constitutional development. Let them remember, when examining the scheme, that they themselves failed when pressed again and again to produce to us some plan which would give general satisfaction.

COMMUNAL CO-OPERATION AND CONDITION OF PROGRESS.

In the end, only Indians themselves can settle this question. The most that Government can hope for is that their decision will remove an obstacle from the path of constitutional advance and will thus enable Indians to concentrate their attention upon solving the many issues that still remain to be decided in the field of constitutional advance. Let leaders of all Indian Communities show, at this critical moment in India's constitutional development, their appreciation of fact that communal co-operation is a condition of progress and that is their special duty to put upon themselves the responsibility of making the new constitution work.

R. T. C. MINORITIES PACT AND COMMUNAL AWARD

A COMPARATIVE STUDY OF RECOMMENDATIONS

We publish below the recommendations of the Minorities Pact of the Round Table Conference and the decision of His Majesty's Government in parallel columns, which will illustrate how far His Majesty's Government's award differs from the claims put forward by the various minorities in London.

The Minorities Pact has given the total number of seats for each community, having taken into consideration the seats that may have to be given to various interests.

The Government's award deals with interests separately, and the numbers given in comparison should further be augmented by the seats which might be got by different communities through special interests.

Even without this addition to the communities through such special interests, a fair comparison may be made of the award and of the claims embodied in the Minorities Pact.

Province.		Strength of Chamber.	HINDUS Caste.	Depressed Classes.	Total.	Muslims.	Christians.	Anglo-Indians.	Europeans.	Tribal.	Sikhs.
Assam	M P. ...	100	38	13	51	35	3	1	10	...	
	Govt ...	108	44	4	48	34	1	...	7	9	
Bengal	M P. ...	200	38	35	73	102	2	3	20	...	
	Govt. ...	250	70	10	80	119	2	4	11	...	
Behar & Orissa	M P. ...	100	51	14	65	25	1	1	5	3	
	Govt. ...	175	99	7	106	42	2	1	2	8	
Bombay	M P. ...	200	88	28	116	66	2	3	13	...	
	Govt. ...	200	87	10	97	63	3	2	4	...	
Madras	M P. ...	200	102	40	142	30	14	4	8	2	
	Govt. ...	215	134	18	152	29	9	2	3	1	
Punjab	M.P ...	100	141	10	24	51	1·5	1 5	2	...	20
	Govt. ...	175	...		43	86	2	1	1	...	32
United-Provinces	M.P. ...	100	44	20	64	30	1	3	3	...	
	Govt. ..	228	132	12	144	66	2	1	2	...	
C P.	M-P. ...	100	58	20	78	15	1	2	2	2	
	Govt. ...	112	77	10	87	14	1	1	1	2	

Appendix VII

THE INDO-BRITISH TRADE AGREEMENT, 1935.

The text of the agreement signed yesterday, in London by Sir Walter Runciman, on behalf of His Majesty's Government, in the United Kingdom, and Sir B. N. Mitra, on behalf of the Government of India, provides *inter alia* that when the question of the grant of substantial protection to Indian Industry is referred for inquiry to the Tariff Board, the Government of India will afford full opportunity to any industry concerned in the United Kingdom to state its case and answer cases presented by other interested parties.

The Government of India further undertake that, in the event of any radical changes in the conditions affecting the protected industries during the currency of the period of protection, they will, on the request of His Majesty's Government, or on their own motion, cause an enquiry to be made as to the appropriateness of the existing duties from the point of view of the principles laid down in Article III and that, in the course of such an enquiry, full consideration will be given to any representations which may be put forward by any interested industry in the United Kingdom.

TEXT OF AGREEMENT.

New Delhi, Jan. 10, 1935.

The following is the Text of the Agreement signed yesterday in London by Sir Walter Runciman, on behalf of His Majesty's Government in the United Kingdom, and Sir B. N. Mitra, on behalf of the Government of India, as a supplement to the Ottawa Trade Agreement.

PREAMBLE.

His Majesty's Government in the United Kingdom and the Government of India hereby agree that, during the continuance of the Ottawa Trade Agreement, the following undertakings on the part of His Majesty's Government in the United Kingdom and of the Government of India shall be deemed to be supplementary to that Agreement namely :

Article 1 : It is recognised by His Majesty's Government in the United Kingdom and the Government of India that, while protection to Indian Industry against imports of whatever origin may be necessary in the interests of the economic well-being of India, conditions within the industries in India, in the United Kingdom and in the foreign countries may be such that Indian Industry requires a higher level of protection against foreign goods than against the imports of United Kingdom origin.

Article 2 : It is recognised by His Majesty's Government in the United Kingdom that, under the existing conditions, the import duties constitute an indispensable element in the revenues of the Government of India, and that revenue considerations must be given due weight in fixing the levels of the import duties

PRINCIPLES OF PROTECTION.

Article 3 : The Government of India undertake that protection be afforded to such industries only as, after due enquiries by the Tariff Board, have, in the opinion of the Government of India established claims thereto, in accordance with the policy of discriminating protection laid down in the resolution adopted by the Legislative Assembly on February 16, 1923, provided that this undertaking shall not apply to the safeguarding of the industries under the Safeguarding Act of 1933.

2. The Government of India further undertake that the measure of protection to be afforded shall only be so much as and no more than will equate the prices of the imported goods to fair selling price for similar goods produced in India and that, wherever possible, having regard to provisions of this Article, lower rates of duty will be imposed on goods of United Kingdom origin.

3 Differential margins of duty established in accordance with the principles laid down in the preceding clauses of this Article as between the United Kingdom goods on the one hand, foreign goods on the other, shall not be altered to the detriment of the United Kingdom goods.

4. Undertakings contained in this Article shall not prejudice the right of the Government of India in such cases in which they find is essential in the interests of revenue to impose an overriding revenue duty on the imported goods higher than the protective duty required.

INTERMEDIATE ENQUIRY.

Article 4 · When the question of the grant of substantive protection to the Indian Industry is referred for enquiry to the Tariff Board, the Government of India will afford full opportunity to any industry concerned in the United Kingdom to state its case and answer cases presented by other interested parties. The Government of India further undertake that in the event of any radical changes in the conditions affecting the protected industries during the currency of the period of protection, they will, on the request of His Majesty's Government or of their own motion, cause an enquiry to be made as to the appropriateness of the existing duties from the point of view of the principles laid down in Article 3, and that, in the course of such enquiry, full consideration will be given to any representation which may be put forward by any interested industry in the United Kingdom.

Article 5: His Majesty's Government in the United Kingdom will give consideration to the steps that might be taken in co-operation with the respective commercial interests to develop the import from India of raw or semi-manufactured materials used in the manufacture of the articles of such class on which importation into India are subject to the differential protective duties. In particular, they invite the Government of India to take note ot the steps that have already been taken in the United Kingdom in pursuance of Article 8, of the Ottawa Agreement, with a view to widening the area of the consumption of the Indian cotton, and they undertake to continue the use of all possible efforts in co-operation with the commercial interests to stimulate the consumption of Indian cotton in all possible ways, including technical research, commercial investigation, market liaison and industrial propaganda.

Article 6: His Majesty's Government in the United Kingdom undertake that, in accordance with the principles of the foregoing article, the privilege of duty-free entry of Indian pig iron into the United Kingdom will be continued so long as the duties applicable to the Article on Iron and Steel imported into India are not less favourable to the United Kingdom than those provided for in the Iron and Steel Protection Act of 1934, without prejudice, however, to the provisions in Sub-section 3 (4) and 3 (5) of the Indian Tariff Act 1894 as amended by Section 2 of the Iron and Steel Duties Act of 1934.

Article 7: His Majesty's Government in the United Kingdom and the Government of India undertake that, in all matters relating to this Agreement, they shall, at all times, receive and consider any conclusions, agreements or reports which may be framed as a result of the conferences between the accredited representatives of the industries concerned in the United Kindom and in India.

MODY-LEES AGREEMENT.

As an annexure to the supplement to the Ottawa Trade Agreement, the Notes that were exchanged between Sir Walter Runciman, President of the Board of Trade in England, and Sir B.N. Mitra, High Commissioner for India in London, are published.

The first Note from Sir Walter Runciman says:—

"Sir, I am authorised to undertake on behalf of H. M.'s Government in the United Kingdom, that, if at any time, any further or othe special steps are taken by the Colonies and Protectorates to facilitate the sale of United Kingdom cotton goods in competition with foreign cotton goods, they will invite the Governments of the Colonies and protectorates to accord as favourable a treatment to Indian cotton goods of any description, as may be proposed for similar United Kingdom cotton goods. The above undertaking shall remain in force so long as the Agreement of October 28, 1933, between the Lancashire Delegation and the Mill-owner's Association, Bombay, or any subsequent agreement which may be concluded between the cotton textile industries of the two countries remain in force".

Replying to Sir Walter Runciman's Note, Sir B. N. Mitra says:

"I have the honour to acknowledge receipt of your letter number 1 of to-day's date. I am authorised to undertake, on behalf of the Government of India, that, as soon as the second surcharge comes off as a general measure, the tariff rates on the United Kindom cotton piecegoods will be reduced to 20 per cent. *ad valorem* or three and a half annas per pound on plain grey goods, and 20 per cent. *ad valorem* on other goods, provided that, on the expiry of the period of the Agreement of October 28, 1933, between the Lancashire Delegation and Mill-owners' Association, Bombay, duties on United Kingdom goods for the remaining period of protection will be fixed on a review of the conditions then existing, and in the light of such experience as may have been gained. By reference to the second surcharge coming off as a general measure is meant the removal of the surcharge on a reasonably large proportion of, not necessarily all, items now subject to it. (Sd.) B. N. Mitra.

Acknowledging Sir B.N. Mitra's letter, Sir Walter Runciman says :—

"I have the honour to acknowledge receipt of your letter No. 2 of to-day's date.—(Sd.) Runciman."

Appendix VII-A

GUJRAT FLOODS

Before we closed the history of 1927, we owed it to Gujrat to give a short account of the remarkable work done by Congressmen in connection with the Gujrat floods that year. Towards the end of July 1927 the Province of Gujrat in the Western India was visited by a great natural catastrophe. Over fifty inches of rain fell in a sudden downpour over a large portion of Gujrat within four or five days. Whole villages were swept away,—cattle, cottages, belongings and all. Thousands of people were rendered destitute, rich lands with standing crops were covered with layers of sand several feet high, district towns were marooned, Railway and Telegraph communications cut off and the city of Ahmedabad itself was threatened. The outstanding feature of the catastrophe was the number of fallen houses all over the Districts of Gujrat including the territory in the Indian State of Baroda. At the lowest estimate no less than 4,000 villages were affected. The percentage of fallen houses varied between 50 and 60 to even 90.

The adversity made the people forget their social prejudices and their narrow domestic pettinesses, and they rose to the occasion in one grand effort at mutual help under the able leadership of Sirdar Vallabhbhai Patel who was then the Lord Mayor of Ahmedabad and the President of the Gujrat Provincial Congress Committee. An emergency relief organisation of nearly 2,000 workers sprang up as if in a night's time and before the Government official world would even realise the nature and extent of the disaster and take counsel at the high quarters as to their duty by way of relief activities, the Congress machine was working in full swing.

Though Gandhi was away in Mysore State at the time recouping his health after a sudden breakdown during one of his whirlwind tours round the country, he offered to go to Gujrat but the proposal was stoutly opposed by Sirdar Vallabhbhai who preferred his province to give an occular demonstration of how the Mahatma's teaching had leavened the social strata and had fired men with the spirit of service.

Through one vast expanse of water the Congress workers and volunteers carried provisions to the marooned villages as also to the Government officials who were in the same plight. In the service of the distressed they had no politics and no preferences. The District Magistrate of Kaira was cut off from the world for days and gratefully accepted the Congress help in the shape of provisions and other things sent by Sirdar Patel through special volunteers. The Government machinery had broken down completely for a week or so and while their officers at the head-quarters awaited reports from their subordinates in the Districts and regarded certain areas as unapproachable, the Congress organisation was busy distributing relief and giving succour to the distressed in the farthest villages affected. It was an unique demonstration of self-help and mutual help by an intelligent resourceful populace charged with the Spirit of Service.

But the extent of the disaster was beyond the power of any popular non-official agency to cope with. The immediate relief by way of distribution of food and other things being over the problem of resowing the entire crops, of reclaiming the valuable lands and rehabilitating the homeless families faced both the people and the Government. Valuable days were passing and the season for resowing would be lost. The Government hesitated and wavered. They raised technical objections It was again the intelligent public opinion all over the Province of Gujrat under the inestimable leadership of Sirdar Patel that compelled the unwilling Government of Sir Leslie Wilson to declare their policy in time and to set apart a sum of Rs. 1,54,00,000 (out of the Famine Insurance Fund set apart from the general revenue by the Government) for distributing relief to the cultivators and to the distressed by way of easy loans with which to purchase implements, bullocks, house building materials and so on. The Provincial Congress Committee in close co-operation with the Bombay Central Relief Committee (another non-official body set up by the leading citizens of Bombay in aid of distressed (Gujrat) distributed relief during the following months throughout Gujrat and so efficient was the Congress organisation that all other relief distributing agencies including Government themselves had to utilise it as their medium of operation. Government however made the best of it and bowing to the inevitiable, Sir C. V. Mehta, the then Finance Member of the Government of Bombay, made graceful gesture at the Relief Conference held at Anand as also at the Conference assembled at Nadiad by inviting Sirdar Patel and other Congress workers to the Conference and by accepting the Congress Agency for their distribution of relief. Besides Government amounts, nearly Rs. 3,00,000 were in all collected by the joint efforts of Congress and the non-official bodies and distributed. The Government, the Congress, the Baroda State and the various popular relief organisations sprung into existence for the time being were thus all blended into one vast organisation for making a huge effort of reconstruction under the Congress lead for nearly a year. It gave a splendid training to the Gujart youth and gave a new sense of self-confidence and a new hope to the people of Gujrat. So happy indeed was the new experience of all that the Finance Member while introducing the budget during the ensuing session of the Bombay Legislative Council ungrudgingly paid the following tribute, to the Congress and its great leader Mahatma Gandhi:

'The immediate work of relief required courage, promptness and resource. Bands of enthusiastic volunteers carried help to the distressed and the stranded and in some cases prevented possible loss of life, arranged for the conveyance of food and clothing with a cheerfulness and promptitude which excite admiration".

"Business absorbed Gujrat, till a few years ago, and it could scarcely boast of self-sacrificing social public work It must be an intense satisfaction to Mahatma Gandhi that his labours for the creation of a band of selfless workers to be poineers of missionary social activities, particularly in the rural areas, have met with an ample response and that the volunteers mostly drawn from the Vidyapith should have acquitted themselves so creditably in the absence of their beloved leader in the face of an unforseen calamity. How the mantle was at once taken up by Mr. Vallabhbhai Patel and with what energy he carried out his plan of work is now well known. These workers belong to the old school of no-changers and it is gratifying that they felt that this was no time to oppose or keep aloof from Government.

"It is my sincere hope that the atmosphere for missionary service created by Mahatma Gandhi will be permanent"

The flood disaster was thus rightly regarded by many as a blessing in disguise.

Appendix VIII

THE BIHAR EARTHQUAKE.

On the 15th of January 1934, large tracts of the Province of Bihar were devastated by a severe earthquake which has been regarded by reports as the greatest recorded in history both in the area affected and the damage caused. The area of greatest destruction covered not less than 30,000 Sqr. miles comprising large portions of the Districts of Champaran, Muzafferpur, Darbhanga, Sarai, Monghyr, Bhagalpur and Purnea. The population affected was no less than one crore and fifty lakhs. The number of deaths was estimated at about 20,000, the number of houses damaged and destroyed over 10 lakhs, number of wells and tanks damaged and destroyed nearly a lakh. More than 8 lakhs of acres of fertile land were covered with sand thrown out of fissures caused in the earth and vast tracts became covered with water similarly thrown out. Railways and roads were destroyed extensively and for months traffic became difficult in many parts

Apart from Government measures, relief on an extensive scale was organised by a non-official Committee, known as the Bihar Central Relief Committee on which Congressmen very largely preponderated. The brunt of the most arduous work of relief fell on Congressmen who had been in prison in connection with the Civil disobedience movement. The President of the Committee Babu Rajendra Prasad made an announcement offering co-operation to Government in the matter of relief work which was handsomely acknowledged by the Government. The response to the Committee's appeal for funds was most spontaneous and generous. The donations in cash amounted to nearly 29 lakhs of rupees besides large quantities of goods like blankets, wearing apparels, cloth, rice, flour, utensils, medicines, tea, invalid food, building materials, like bamboos, timber, corrugated iron sheets, tarpaulins, hessians, tents and other equipments valued at about three lakhs.

The distributions of relief was a most difficult affair in the absence of any pre-existing organisation. The Committee appointed agents in each District and centres were opened which ultimately came to more than 250 in number. Help came from all parts of the country not only in the form of money and goods but also in the form of volunteers headed by Mahatma Gandhi and Seth Jamnalal Bajaj and Pandit Jawaharlal Nehru, the last named being soon disabled from serving by imprisonment on a charge of sedition. The number of volunteers in the period of intensest activity was over 2,000 and it included Doctors, Engineers, expert accountants and auditors and public workers of note.

The forms that provision of immediate relief took were the removal of debris, disposal of dead bodies, supply of food, clothing, temporary shelter, water and medical help. One form of immediate relief was the supply of sugar cane crushers to enable agriculturists to save the vast sugar cane crop which would have been destroyed owing to more of the sugar factories having been put out of action by the earthquake. In this work of immediate relief the Committee distributed over seven thousand maunds of grain, Rs. 20,000-cash for food, 28,000 blankets, immense quantity of clothing, desilted more than two thousand wells, sank, 339 tubes and erected or helped in erecting over 72,000 shelters of huts. The total expenditure under these heads came to over a lakh and ninety thousands besides the value of the goods distributed.

The work of reconstruction was taken towards the end of March and the first item was the question of supply of water. The Committee succeeded in sinking nearly 7,000 wells and re-excavating nearly 700 tanks It had decided at an early stage not to encourage begging and had insisted on some sort of work being done for giving food and large numbers were employed in repairing village roads and re-excavating water channels and repairing embankments which had been damaged by the earthquake. and the Committee spent nearly a lakh of rupees in the form of unemployment relief. The number of persons who received doles in this form in Champaran alone which was the worst affected in this respect came to over a lakh.

In July and August the lands which had suffered severely from the earthquake and also large areas which has comparatively escaped much damage from the earthquake were subjected to heavy floods and the damage done was more or less of the same character as by the earthquake except that in some cases it was worse. The work of rescue and relief kept the organisation engaged till after October and a special form of relief which became even more urgent was the relief to cattle, all crops and fodder having been destroyed in vast tracts. The Committee had provided for nearly 150 boats for rescue work, 100 of which were placed at the disposal of the Government.

It was during and after the winter 1934—35 that the Committee took up the work of distributing relief on an extensive scale for building houses and has distributed nearly eight lakhs for this purpose besides a sum of nearly three lakhs spent on huts and semi permanent structures which included small grants to poorer people to set up small huts and structures. The amount spent on water supply comes to more than five lakhs, 35 thousands on flood relief over 2½ lakhs, cattle relief over 75 thousands including nearly Rs 49,000 earmarked by donors for the purpose, nearly 38,000 for medical relief, 36,000 on seeds. Another form of relief was the opening of cheap grain shops and cheap building materials shops which sold food grains and building materials to sufferers at reduced or cost prices and succeeded in keeping down the level of prices which showed a great tendency to rise.

An interesting item of work which is in hand is the rebuilding of a number of villages on new sites in the District of Muzafferpur. The work is being done from the funds contributed by the Viceroy's Relief Fund and the Bihar Central Relief Committee Funds and is being executed under the supervision of Dr. Pierre Ceresole who is the head of the international Voluntary Service for peace assisted by local workers.

One problem which at one time threatened to be most difficult and disastrous of all has been fortunately solved to a considerable extent by nature. The immense quantity of sand thrown out has not proved to be as destructive of crops as was feared and the greater portion of the area covered under it has borne crops. The work of the Committee is now drawing to a close, and its funds are nearly exhausted except what is allotted for particular purposes. Its accounts and reports have been published every quarter.

STATEMENT GIVING THE MAIN DATES, PLACE, OFFICE BEARERS, Etc., CONNECTED WITH THE INDIAN NATIONAL CONGRESS FROM 1915—1935.

STATEMENT GIVING DATES, Etc., DETAILS CONNECTED

Dates.	Place.	Total No. of Delegates.	Chairman of the Reception Committee.
27-12-1915	Bombay ..	2,259	D. E. Wacha ..
26-12-1916	Lucknow ..	2,301	Hon. Pt Jagatnarayan ..
26-12-1917	Calcutta ..	4,967	P. B. Baikuntha Nath Sen ..
Special Con. Sept. 1918.	Bombay ..	3,500	Vittalbhai J Patel ..
26-12-1918	Delhi ...	4,869	Hakim Ajmal Khan ..
26-12-1919	Amritsar ...	7,031	Swami Shraddhananda ...
Special Con. Sept 1920	Calcutta	—	B. Chakraverthi ..
26-12-1920	Nagpore	14,583	Seth Jamnalal Bajaj ..
27-12-1921	Ahmedabad	4,726	Sjt. V. J Patel ..
26-12-1922	Gaya	3,248	Brij Kishore Prasad ..
Special	Delhi ..	—	Dr. M. A. Ansari ..
28-12-1923	Cocanada ...	6,188	Desabhakta K. Venkatappaiah ...
26-12-1924	Belgaum ..	1,844	Gangadhar Rao Deshpande ...
26-12-1925	Cawnpore ..	2,688	Dr. Murali Lal ...
26-12-1926	Gauhati ...	3,000	Mr. T. R. Phookar ...
26-12-1927	Madras ...	2,694	Mr. C. Muthuranga Mudaliar ...
29-12-1928	Calcutta ...	5,221	J. M. Sen Gupta ...
25-12-1929	Lahore ...	—	Dr. Shafuddhin Kitchlew ...
March '31	Karachi ...	—	Dr. Choitram Gidwani ...
April '32	Delhi ..	—	Held while the Congress was under ban.
March '33	Calcutta ..	—	Dr. Prafulla Ghosh ..
24-10-1934	Bombay ...	—	K. F. Nariman ...

WITH THE INDIAN NATIONAL CONGRESS FROM 1915 to 1935.

Joint and General Secretaries.	Name of the President.
Nawab Syed Mahommed Bahadur and Mr. N. Subba Rao Pantulu.	Sir S. P. Sinha.
Do. ..	Hon. Babu Ambica Charan (Mazumdar)
Messers C. P Ramaswamy Iyer, Mr Bhurgri and Dewan Bahadur P Kesava Pillai.	Mrs Besant.
Do. ..	Mr Hassan Imam.
V. J. Patel, Fazalul Haq, and Pt Gokaran Nath Misra	Pt. M. M. Malavya.
V. J. Patel, Pt. Gokaran Nath Misra and Dr. M. A. Ansari.	Pt Motilal Nehru
Do.	Lala Lajapat Rai.
Motilal Nehru, Dr M A. Ansari, and C. Rajagopalachariar	Mr. C. Vijiaraghavachariar.
Motilal Nehru, C. Rajagopalachariar, V. J. Patel and A. Rangaswami Iyengar.	Acting President, Hakim Ajmal Khan for C. R Das (in Jail)
M Moazzam Ali, Vallabhbhai J. Patel and Babu Rajendra Prasad.	C. R. Das
Do.	Maulana Abul Kalam Azad
Jawaharlal Nehru, Shafuddin Kitchlew and Gangadhar Rao Deshpande and D. Gopalakrishnayya	Maulana Mohammad Ali.
Saheb Quireshi, B. F. Barucha and Jawaharlal Nehru.	Mahatma Gandhi.
M. A. Ansari, A. Rangaswami Iyengar and Pt. Santanam.	Mrs. Sarojini Naidu.
Do. and V J. Patel ...	Mr. S Srinivasa Iyengar.
Saheb Quireshi, Jawaharlal Nehru and Subash Chandra Bose.	Dr. M A Ansari.
M. A. Ansari and Jawaharlal Nehru.	Pt. Motilal Nehru.
Syed Mahommed, Sri Prakasa, Jairamdas Dowlatram.	Pt. Jawaharlal Nehru.
Syed Mahommed and Jawaharlal Nehru.	Sardar Vallabhbhai J. Patel.
Do. Do.	Seth Ranchod Lal Amrit Lal.
Do. Do.	Mrs. J. M. Sen Gupta.
J. B. Kripalni, Syed Mohammed and Jairamdas Dowlatram.	Sjt. Rajendra Prasad.

INDEX